CCNP®
Study Guide

CCNP®
Enterprise Certification
Study Guide

Ben Piper

A Wiley Brand

I dedicate this book to the Lord Jesus Christ through Whom all things were created and in Whom all things hold together

Acknowledgments

I'd like to thank the following people who helped create this *CCNP Enterprise Certification Study Guide: Exam 350-401*. A special thanks to Kenyon Brown, senior acquisitions editor, for the opportunity to write this book. Thanks to John Sleeva, project editor, for pushing me to meet my deadlines. His suggestions and edits helped make this book more user friendly. Thanks also go to Christine O'Connor, production editor; Pete Gaughan, content enablement manager; and Louise Watson at Word One, proofreader.

Jon Buhagiar reviewed the chapters and questions for technical accuracy. His comments guided by his expertise helped make this book more practical, accurate, and well rounded.

About the Author

 **Ben Piper** is a networking and cloud consultant who has authored multiple books including the *AWS Certified Solutions Architect Study Guide: Associate SAA-C01 Exam, Second Edition* (Sybex, 2019), *AWS Certified Cloud Practitioner Study Guide: Foundational CLF-C01 Exam* (Sybex, 2019), and *Learn Cisco Network Administration in a Month of Lunches* (Manning, 2017). You can contact Ben by visiting his website https://benpiper.com.

Contents at a Glance

Introduction   *xxi*

Assessment Test   *xxviii*

Chapter 1   Networking Fundamentals   1

Chapter 2   Spanning Tree Protocols   29

Chapter 3   Enterprise Network Design   67

Chapter 4   Wireless LAN (WLAN)   105

Chapter 5   Open Shortest Path First (OSPF)   135

Chapter 6   Enhanced Interior Gateway Routing Protocol
                (EIGRP)   171

Chapter 7   The Border Gateway Protocol (BGP)   197

Chapter 8   Network Address Translation and Multicast   233

Chapter 9   Quality of Service   275

Chapter 10 Network Virtualization   303

Chapter 11 Software-Defined Networking and Network
                Programmability   353

Chapter 12 Network Security and Monitoring   397

Appendix   Answers to Review Questions   443

Index   *463*

Contents

Introduction   *xxi*

Assessment Test   *xxviii*

Chapter	**1**	**Networking Fundamentals**	**1**

The OSI Model   2
    The Upper Layers: Application, Presentation, and Session   4
    Making Sense of Layers   4
    The Lower Layers: Physical, Data Link, Network,
        and Transport   6
Layer 1: The Physical Layer   7
Layer 2: The Data Link Layer   8
    A Brief History of Ethernet   8
    The MAC Address Table   10
    Maximum Transmission Unit   12
    Subnet Limits   12
Layer 3: The Network Layer   13
    Forwarding within a Subnet   14
    Forwarding between Subnets   14
    Address Resolution Protocol   16
    Fragmentation   17
    Routing vs. Forwarding   18
Layer 4: The Transport Layer   18
    Transmission Control Protocol   19
    Encapsulation and Decapsulation   21
Summary   22
Exam Essentials   22
Review Questions   24

Chapter	**2**	**Spanning Tree Protocols**	**29**

The Need for Spanning Tree   31
VLANs and Trunking   32
    Dynamic Trunking   34
    Unconditional Trunking   35
    Active and Allowed VLANs   36
Rapid Per-VLAN Spanning Tree   38
    Electing the Root Bridge   38
    Calculating the Root Ports   41
    Calculating the Root Ports of Indirectly
        Connected Switches   44

Modifying Port Cost   46
Modifying Port Priority   47
Calculating Blocked Ports   48
Port States   49
Port Roles   49
Link Types   49
Multiple Spanning Tree   50
Root Bridges and Port Priority   52
Internal Spanning Tree   53
Native VLAN   54
Topology Change Detection   55
Spanning Tree Extensions   55
Root Guard   55
BPDU Guard and BPDU Filter   57
Unidirectional Link Detection   58
Loop Guard   58
Summary   58
Exam Essentials   59
Exercises   60
Review Questions   62

Chapter   3   Enterprise Network Design   67

Physical Network Architectures   68
Comparing Campus and Data Center Networks   69
The Three-Tier Architecture   70
The Two-Tier Collapsed Core: A Cheaper Alternative   73
Layer 2 Design   74
Switched and Routed Interfaces   75
Switched Topologies   76
Routed Access Topology   81
EtherChannels   82
Load-Balancing Methods   83
Static EtherChannels   84
Port Aggregation Control Protocol   88
Link Aggregation Control Protocol   90
First-Hop Redundancy Protocols   91
Hot Standby Router Protocol   92
Virtual Router Redundancy Protocol   94
Gateway Load-Balancing Protocol   95
Summary   97
Exam Essentials   98
Review Questions   100

| **Chapter** | **4** | **Wireless LAN (WLAN)** | **105** |

Radio Frequency Fundamentals 106
    Frequency and Amplitude 107
    Carrier Frequency 109
    Power Levels 110
WLAN 802.11 Standards 115
    The Physical Layer: Frequencies and Channels 115
    Layer 2: 802.11 Media Access Control (MAC) 119
Access Point Modes 124
    Autonomous 124
    Lightweight 124
    Wireless LAN Controller Selection Process 125
Roaming and Location Services 126
    Roaming 126
    Location Services 128
Summary 128
Exam Essentials 129
Review Questions 130

Chapter   5   Open Shortest Path First (OSPF)   135

Link-State Advertisements 136
    OSPF Areas 137
    LSA Types 137
Neighbor Operations 141
Configuring OSPF 142
    Configuring Area 0 on a Broadcast Network 142
    Viewing Neighbor Adjacencies 143
    Rigging the Designated Router Election 144
    Viewing and Understanding LSAs 146
    Authentication 154
    Passive Interfaces 158
    Injecting a Default Route 159
    Inter-Area Summarization 161
    Route Filtering 162
    Distribute Lists 162
Summary 163
Exam Essentials 164
Exercises 164
Review Questions 166

Chapter	**6**	**Enhanced Interior Gateway Routing Protocol (EIGRP)**	**171**
		EIGRP Fundamentals	172
		EIGRP Packet Types	172
		The Diffusing Update Algorithm (DUAL)	173
		Weighted Metrics	176
		Configuring EIGRP	178
		Equal Cost Multipathing	181
		Modifying Metrics	182
		Switching Types	186
		Unequal Cost Multipathing	187
		Summary	190
		Exam Essentials	190
		Exercises	191
		Review Questions	192
Chapter	**7**	**The Border Gateway Protocol (BGP)**	**197**
		BGP Fundamentals	198
		BGP AS Numbers	199
		BGP Session States	201
		Configuring BGP	202
		Advertising Prefixes	204
		Path Selection	205
		Route Redistribution among BGP, OSPF, and EIGRP	210
		Testing IP Reachability Using Tcl Scripts	214
		Troubleshooting	215
		Modifying Weight	218
		Advertising Summary Routes Using Route Aggregation	220
		Route Filtering Using Route Maps and Prefix Lists	222
		Summary	225
		Exam Essentials	226
		Exercises	226
		Review Questions	228
Chapter	**8**	**Network Address Translation and Multicast**	**233**
		Network Address Translation	234
		Address Types	234
		Static NAT	236
		Dynamic NAT	241
		NAT Overload with Port Address Translation	247
		Outside Static NAT	250
		Removing NAT Configurations	251

Multicast	252
IP Multicast	253
LAN Multicast	253
Multicast Routing	257
Configuring PIM	258
Configuring a Multicast Receiver	262
IP Multicast and Ethernet	264
Summary	265
Exam Essentials	267
Exercises	268
Review Questions	270

Chapter	**9**	**Quality of Service**	**275**

Understanding Quality of Service	276
Classification and Marking	277
Differentiated Services	277
Layer 2 Marking	280
Class Maps and Policy Maps	280
Wireless QoS	281
Policing	284
Single-Rate, Two-Color Policing	284
Single-Rate, Three-Color Policing	285
Two-Rate Policing	287
Queuing	288
Class-Based Weighted Fair Queuing	288
Low-Latency Queuing	293
Explicit Congestion Notification	295
Shaping	295
Summary	297
Exam Essentials	297
Exercises	298
Review Questions	299

Chapter	**10**	**Network Virtualization**	**303**

Virtual Machines, Hypervisors, and Network Virtualization	304
Virtual Machines and Server Virtualization	305
Network Virtualization	307
Generic Routing Encapsulation Tunnels	312
Configuring a GRE Tunnel to Tunnel IPv4 and IPv6 over IPv4	312
Recursive Routing	318
IP Security	319
Internet Key Exchange	320
Encapsulating Security Payload	320

Configuring IPsec in Transport Mode with a GRE Tunnel   321
Configuring IPsec in Tunnel Mode   324
Location/ID Separation Protocol   326
LISP Terminology   328
Configuring LISP   328
Simulating IP Mobility   332
Is LISP a Routing Protocol?   334
Virtual Extensible Local Area Network   334
MAC Address Learning   335
Forwarding   335
Configuring VXLAN   336
VXLAN Control Planes   336
Configuring the Underlay   337
Configuring the Overlay   338
Configuring R1 and R2   339
Virtual Routing and Forwarding   340
Configuring a VRF   340
Configuring Multi-VRF EIGRP   342
Summary   345
Exam Essentials   345
Exercises   346
Review Questions   347

Chapter   11   **Software-Defined Networking and Network
Programmability**   **353**

What Is Software-Defined Networking?   355
Software-Defined Access   356
SD-Access Layers   357
Physical Layer   357
Network Underlay   358
Fabric Overlay   359
Controller Layer   363
Management Layer   364
Software-Defined WAN   369
vManage Network Management System   370
vSmart Controller   370
vBond Orchestrator   371
vEdge Routers   371
Network Programmability and Automation   372
The Cisco DNA Center Intent API   372
vManage REST API   379
NETCONF   383
Embedded Event Manager   386
Configuration Management Platforms   388

Summary	391
Exam Essentials	391
Exercises	392
Review Questions	393

Chapter   12   Network Security and Monitoring   397

Infrastructure Security	398
Device Access	399
Authentication, Authorization, and Accounting	402
Access Control Lists	407
Control Plane Policing	412
Cisco Security Products	414
AnyConnect Secure Mobility Client	414
Umbrella	414
Advanced Malware Protection ThreatGrid	414
Advanced Malware Protection for Endpoints	415
Firepower Next-Generation Firewall	415
TrustSec	416
MAC Security	418
Wireless Security	418
WebAuth	418
Configuring WPA2 with 802.1X	422
Configuring 802.1X on the Client	422
Configure Preshared Keys	424
Monitoring	425
Conditional Debugs	425
Simple Network Management Protocol (SNMP)	425
Syslog	426
Network Time Protocol	428
NetFlow and Flexible NetFlow	429
Switched Port Analyzer	432
IP Service Level Agreement	434
Summary	436
Exam Essentials	437
Exercises	438
Review Questions	439

Appendix   Answers to Review Questions   443

Chapter 1: Networking Fundamentals	444
Chapter 2: Spanning Tree Protocols	445
Chapter 3: Enterprise Network Design	447
Chapter 4: Wireless LAN (WLAN)	448
Chapter 5: Open Shortest Path First (OSPF)	450

Chapter 6: Enhanced Interior Gateway Routing Protocol
   (EIGRP)   451
Chapter 7: The Border Gateway Protocol (BGP)   453
Chapter 8: Network Address Translation and Multicast   454
Chapter 9: Quality of Service   456
Chapter 10: Network Virtualization   457
Chapter 11: Software-Defined Networking and Network
   Programmability   459
Chapter 12: Network Security and Monitoring   460

Index   *463*

Introduction

Networking is uniquely challenging in that it's not a single technology, but a collection of interdependent technologies that every other aspect of IT depends on. Without networking, there are no connected applications and that means there are no IT employees. Even if you're not sure that you want networking to become your permanent career, becoming an expert at networking will open the doors for other in-demand areas of IT, including security, software development, and cloud computing.

Cisco's Professional Network Certifications

In 2019, Cisco announced updates to its Cisco Certified Network Professional (CCNP) certification program. There are six professional level certifications to choose from:

- CCNP Enterprise
- CCNP Data Center
- CCNP Security
- CCNP Service Provider
- CCNP Collaboration
- Cisco Certified DevNet Professional

Each certification requires passing one core exam and one concentration exam. The core exam for the CCNP Enterprise certification is 350-401 ENCOR, "Implementing Cisco Enterprise Network Core Technologies." The concentration exams let you focus on a specific specialty, such as routing, wireless, network design, automation, or software-defined networking (SDN). Regardless of the concentration exam you choose, you must pass the ENCOR exam to attain your CCNP Enterprise certification.

Is CCNP Certification Right for You?

Many who attain the Cisco Certified Network Associate (CCNA) don't go on to pursue more advanced Cisco certifications. So why should you consider the CCNP Enterprise certification, and is it right for you? It may be right for you if

- You have a passion for networking.
- You want to set yourself apart as someone who has a passion for technology and isn't just in it for the money (although there is plenty of that!).
- You want to specialize in security, wireless, network automation, cloud, or software-defined networking.
- You enjoy tweaking the "nerd knobs" on individual technologies just to see what will happen.
- You love facing and overcoming the challenges of troubleshooting.

Study Tips

Before taking the CCNP ENCOR exam, there are a few things to keep in mind. There's no reason that you can't pass the exam the first time. To help you do that, I want to share with you some study tips that have helped me pass several Cisco certification exams on the first try. One of the neglected skills required on any Cisco exam is speed. Being able to troubleshoot a 10-router Open Shortest Path First (OSPF) topology is good. Taking 15 minutes to do it is not so good. I can't stress enough the importance of spending quality time with the command-line interface (CLI). You should spend at least 50 percent of your study time on configuring and troubleshooting a variety of topologies and technologies.

There's an old Latin proverb that repetition is the mother of learning. Repetition—in terms of both study and practice—is going to be your best friend. Understanding networking requires making connections that aren't always obvious, and the more you practice and study, the more opportunities your mind has to make those connections. For years I've used SuperMemo (https://super-memory.com), a flashcard-like program that lets you create your own question-and-answer pairs, quizzes you, and shows you how well you're retaining the information. What makes SuperMemo superior to flashcards is that it identifies the information you've already retained, and it doesn't waste time continuing to quiz you on it. That means you can safely load your collection with hundreds of items while still using your time efficiently.

One last tip: As you read this study guide cover to cover, keep a running list of questions and things you're not sure about. Chances are if you find something confusing, a lot of other people did too, and that makes it good fodder for the exam. Be sure to visit https://benpiper.com/encor for book resources, updates, and errata.

Prerequisites and Lab Requirements

The CCNA certification isn't required to attain the CCNP Enterprise certification. Nevertheless, I strongly recommend that you obtain your CCNA certification or the equivalent experience before embarking on your CCNP Enterprise journey. Refer to the CCNA exam blueprint (www.cisco.com/c/en/us/training-events/training-certifications/certifications/associate/ccna.html) for a full list of topics you should already be familiar with. Because the CCNP Enterprise is a professional-level certification, I don't review some of the basics covered by the CCNA such as subnetting, IPv4, and IPv6 addressing.

You'll need a virtual or physical lab, which you should already have from your previous networking studies. Your lab should be able to support at least eight routers and two layer 3 switches running IOS version 15.2 or later. You should be able to configure your lab on your own by looking at layer 2 and layer 3 diagrams. Topology diagrams will be included in each chapter.

If your existing lab doesn't meet the requirement, Cisco Virtual Internet Routing Lab (http://virl.cisco.com) includes virtual machine images for a variety of switches and routers. These images are virtual machines that run using QEMU and are light on CPU and memory, so you don't need a beast of a server to run simulations, although more resources always help. Other options, although not blessed by Cisco, are GNS3 (`https://gns3.com`) and EVE-NG (`www.eve-ng.net`).

How to Use This Book

Hands-on experience is crucial for exam success. Each chapter in this study guide contains hands-on exercises that you should strive to complete during or immediately after your reading of the chapter. The exercises are there to test your understanding, and not to cover every possible permutation of configurations. The exercises are your foundation, and you should build on them by experimenting with them, breaking things, and then figuring out how to fix them.

Each chapter contains review questions to thoroughly test your understanding of the services and concepts covered in that chapter. They also test your ability to integrate the concepts with information from preceding chapters. I've designed the questions to help you realistically gauge your understanding and identify your blind spots. Once you complete the assessment in each chapter, referring to the answer key will give you not only the correct answers but a detailed explanation as to why they're correct. Even if you feel comfortable on a certain topic, resist the urge to skip over the pertinent chapter. I strongly encourage you to carefully read this book from cover to cover so that you can discover your strengths and weaknesses—particularly the ones you may not be aware of. Remember, even though you can't learn networking just by reading a book, it's equally true that you can't learn *without* reading a book.

The book also contains a self-assessment exam with 36 questions, two practice exams with 50 questions each to help you gauge your readiness to take the exam, and flashcards to help you learn and retain key facts needed to prepare for the exam.

What Does This Book Cover?

This book covers topics you need to know to prepare for the CCNP ENCOR exam:

Chapter 1: Networking Fundamentals   This chapter overviews the fundamentals of networking theory and network design.

Chapter 2: Spanning Tree Protocols   This chapter covers Spanning Tree protocols, including Rapid Spanning Tree and Multiple Instance Spanning Tree. We also cover VLANs, trunking, and pruning.

Chapter 3: Enterprise Network Design   In this chapter, you'll learn the advantages and disadvantages of different physical and layer 2 network designs. We also dive into EtherChannels and first-hop redundancy protocols.

Chapter 4: Wireless LAN (WLAN)   This chapter explains the fundamentals of radio frequency, WLAN 802.11 standards, wireless security, and WLAN controller (WLC) design and deployment considerations.

Chapter 5: Open Shortest Path First (OSPF)   In this chapter, you'll learn how to configure and troubleshoot OSPF adjacencies, authentication, route filtering, summarization, and more.

Chapter 6: Enhanced Interior Gateway Routing Protocol (EIGRP)   This chapter covers advanced EIGRP concepts, including redistribution, multipathing, and path control.

Chapter 7: The Border Gateway Protocol (BGP)   In this chapter, you'll learn all about BGP, including path selection, redistribution, summarization, and filtering.

Chapter 8: Network Address Translation and Multicast   This two-for-the-price-of-one chapter gives you complete coverage of network address translation and multicast.

Chapter 9: Quality of Service   This chapter covers QoS concepts, including queuing, policing, shaping, and classification.

Chapter 10: Network Virtualization   This chapter dives deep into virtualization concepts such as server virtualization, network virtualization, generic routing encapsulation, IPsec, LISP, and VXLAN.

Chapter 11: Software-Defined Networking and Network Programmability   In this chapter, you'll learn about Cisco's software-defined networking (SDN) solutions, SD-Access, Cisco DNA Center, and SD-WAN. You'll also learn about network automation tools such as Python, RESTCONF, NETCONF, Ansible, Chef, Puppet, and SaltStack.

Chapter 12: Network Security and Monitoring   This chapter will show you how to implement infrastructure security best practices and wireless security configurations. You'll also learn about Cisco security products and how to monitor your network using NetFlow, IPSLA, debugs, Syslog, SNMP, and more.

Interactive Online Learning Environment and Test Bank

The interactive online learning environment that accompanies this *CCNP Enterprise Certification Study Guide: Exam 350-401* provides a test bank with study tools to help you prepare for the certification exam—and increase your chances of passing it the first time! The test bank includes the following:

Sample Tests   All the questions in this book are provided, including the assessment test at the end of this introduction and the chapter tests that include the review questions at the end of each chapter. In addition, there are two practice exams with 50 questions each. Use these questions to test your knowledge of the study guide material. The online test bank runs on multiple devices.

Flashcards The online text banks include 100 flashcards specifically written to hit you hard, so don't get discouraged if you don't ace your way through them at first. They're there to ensure that you're really ready for the exam. And no worries—armed with the review questions, practice exams, and flashcards, you'll be more than prepared when exam day comes. Questions are provided in digital flashcard format (a question followed by a single correct answer). You can use the flashcards to reinforce your learning and provide last-minute test prep before the exam.

Other Study Tools A glossary of key terms from this book is available as a fully searchable PDF.

 Go to www.wiley.com/go/sybextestprep to register and gain access to this interactive online learning environment and test bank with study tools.

Exam Objectives

The CCNP ENCOR exam is intended for people who have experience implementing enterprise network technologies including IPv4 and IPv6 architecture, virtualization, monitoring, security, and automation. In general, you should have the following before taking the exam:

- A minimum of two years of hands-on experience configuring and troubleshooting routers and switches
- Ability to design and configure a network based on customer requirements
- Ability to provide implementation guidance
- A mastery of IPv4 and IPv6

The exam covers six different domains, with each domain broken down into objectives.

Objective Map

The following table lists each domain and its weighting in the exam, along with the chapters in the book where that domain's objectives are covered.

Domain	Percentage of exam	Chapter
Domain 1: Architecture	**15%**	
1.1 Explain the different design principles used in an enterprise network		1, 3
1.2 Analyze design principles of a WLAN deployment		4
1.3 Differentiate between on-premises and cloud infrastructure deployments		11
1.4 Explain the working principles of the Cisco SD-WAN solution		11
1.5 Explain the working principles of the Cisco SD-Access solution		11
1.6 Describe concepts of wired and wireless QoS		9
1.7 Differentiate hardware and software switching mechanisms		1
Domain 2: Virtualization	**10%**	
2.1 Describe device virtualization technologies		10
2.2 Configure and verify data path virtualization technologies		10
2.3 Describe network virtualization concepts		10
Domain 3: Infrastructure	**30%**	
3.1 Layer 2		1, 2, 3
3.2 Layer 3		1, 5, 6, 7
3.3 Wireless		4
3.4 IP Services		3, 8, 12
Domain 4: Network Assurance	**10%**	
4.1 Diagnose network problems using tools such as debugs, conditional debugs, trace route, ping, SNMP, and syslog		12
4.2 Configure and verify device monitoring using syslog for remote logging		12

Domain	Percentage of exam	Chapter
4.3 Configure and verify NetFlow and Flexible NetFlow		12
4.4 Configure and verify SPAN/RSPAN/ERSPAN		12
4.5 Configure and verify IPSLA		12
4.6 Describe Cisco DNA Center workflows to apply network configuration, monitoring, and management		11
4.7 Configure and verify NETCONF and RESTCONF		11
Domain 5: Security	**20%**	
5.1 Configure and verify device access control		12
5.2 Configure and verify infrastructure security features		12
5.3 Describe REST API security		11
5.4 Configure and verify wireless security features		4, 12
5.5 Describe the components of network security design		4, 12
Domain 6: Automation	**15%**	
6.1 Interpret basic Python components and scripts		11
6.2 Construct valid JSON encoded file		11
6.3 Describe the high-level principles and benefits of a data modeling language, such as YANG		11
6.4 Describe APIs for Cisco DNA Center and vManage		11
6.5 Interpret REST API response codes and results in payload using Cisco DNA Center and RESTCONF		11
6.6 Construct EEM applet to automate configuration, troubleshooting, or data collection		11
6.7 Compare agent vs. agentless orchestration tools, such as Chef, Puppet, Ansible, and SaltStack		11

Assessment Test

1. IP depends on which of the following?

   A. Address Resolution Protocol

   B. Data link layer

   C. Network layer

   D. Transport layer

2. Which is *not* a function of a bridge?

   A. Simulating some properties of a shared physical Ethernet cable

   B. MAC-based routing

   C. Reducing the size of a broadcast domain

   D. Frame check sequence validation

3. What are the purposes of TCP sequence numbers? (Choose two.)

   A. Error control

   B. Ordering

   C. Flow control

   D. Reliable delivery

4. Three switches are connected via 802.1Q trunk links. You need to prevent VLAN 25 traffic from reaching two of the switches. Which of the following can accomplish this? (Choose two.)

   A. Prune VLAN 25 on the trunk links.

   B. Use routed interfaces instead of trunks.

   C. Configure Spanning Tree to block the ports to the switches.

   D. Delete VLAN 25 on the switches.

5. Switch SW1 is running RPVST+ and is connected via a routed interface to SW2, which is running Multiple Spanning Tree. If you add VLAN 2 to both switches and map VLAN 2 to MST1 on SW2, which switch will necessarily be the root for VLAN 2?

   A. SW1

   B. SW2

   C. The switch with the lowest bridge priority

   D. Both SW1 and SW2

6. Which of the following can effectively prune a VLAN from a trunk?

   A. BPDU Guard

   B. BPDU Filter

   C. Loop Guard

   D. UDLD

7. Which of the following is the most scalable physical architecture for East-West traffic patterns?

   A. Two-tier collapsed core

   B. Leaf-and-spine architecture

   C. Routed

   D. Three-tier

8. What are two reasons to choose a routed topology over a switched topology?

   A. Better scalability

   B. Better use of IP address space

   C. The ability to stretch subnets

   D. Faster convergence

9. Which protocol does not use multicast?

   A. LACP

   B. EtherChannel

   C. VRRP

   D. HSRP

10. An access point running in lightweight mode has clients connected to two SSIDs. The total number of connected clients is 25. How many CAPWAP tunnels are there between the AP and its WLAN controller (WLC)?

   A. 1

   B. 2

   C. 25

   D. Lightweight mode doesn't use a WLC.

11. A client performs an intra-controller roam, keeping its IP address. Which of the following is true of this roam?

   A. The SSID changes.

   B. The VLAN changes.

   C. It's a layer 2 roam.

   D. It's a layer 3 roam.

12. What are two disadvantages of 5 GHz Wi-Fi versus 2.4 GHz Wi-Fi?

   A. Incompatibility with 802.11g

   B. Incompatibility with 802.11n

   C. Increased free space path loss

   D. Lower throughput

13. There are three OSPF routers connected to the same subnet. Which is the designated router?

   A. The one with the lowest router ID

   B. The first one that became active

   C. The one with the highest router ID

   D. The one with the highest priority

14. Two OSPF routers are connected to each other. One router's interface is configured as a broadcast network type, whereas the other router's interface is configured as a point-to-point network type. Which of the following is true of this configuration? (Choose two.)

   A. They won't form an adjacency.

   B. They will form an adjacency.

   C. They won't exchange routes.

   D. They will exchange routes.

15. You have a router with an interface that's connected to a subnet dedicated to servers. You want to advertise this subnet into OSPF but don't want any servers running OSPF software to form an adjacency with the router. How can you accomplish this?

   A. Configure null authentication.

   B. Use a distribute list.

   C. Advertise a default route.

   D. Configure the interface as a passive interface.

16. An OSPF autonomous system boundary router (ASBR) is redistributing the prefix 192.168.0.0/16 into EIGRP AS 1. What is the administrative distance of the route?

   A. 20

   B. 110

   C. 170

   D. 200

17. Which of the following are considered in calculating an EIGRP metric? (Choose all that apply.)

   A. Bandwidth

   B. Delay

   C. MTU

   D. Reliability

   E. Latency

   F. Weight

18. Consider the following EIGRP output.

```
P 10.0.36.0/29, 1 successors, FD is 3328
via 10.0.45.4 (3328/3072), GigabitEthernet0/3.
via 10.0.56.6 (5632/2816), GigabitEthernet0/0.
```

Which of the following is the feasible successor?

A. 10.0.36.1

B. 10.0.56.6

C. 10.0.45.4

D. 10.0.36.2

19. What occurs when an eBGP router receives a route that already has its own AS number in the path?

A. Removes the AS and advertises the route

B. Advertises the route as is

C. Discards the route

D. Installs the route in its BGP RIB

E. Discards all routes from the router it received the route from

20. R1 has the prefix 172.16.0.0/16 in its IP routing table, learned from EIGRP AS 16. There are no other BGP, IGP, or static routes in the routing table. You execute the following BGP router configuration commands on R1:

```
network 172.16.0.0 mask 255.255.255.0
redistribute eigrp 16
```

Which of the following will be true regarding the route R1 advertises for the 172.16.0.0/16 prefix?

A. 172.16.0.0/16 will have an incomplete origin type.

B. 172.16.0.0/24 will have an incomplete origin type.

C. R1 will not advertise the 172.16.0.0/16 prefix.

D. 172.16.0.0/16 will have an IGP origin type.

21. Consider the following prefix list and route map on router R1:

```
ip prefix-list all-private: 3 entries
   seq 5 permit 10.0.0.0/8 le 32
   seq 10 deny 0.0.0.0/0 le 32
route-map allow-public, deny, sequence 10
  Match clauses:
    ip address prefix-lists: all-private
```

```
Set clauses:
  Policy routing matches: 0 packets, 0 bytes
route-map R4, permit, sequence 20
  Match clauses:
  Set clauses:
  Policy routing matches: 0 packets, 0 bytes
```

Which prefix will this route map allow?

- **A.** 10.255.255.0/24
- **B.** 10.0.0.0/32
- **C.** 10.0.0.0/8
- **D.** 0.0.0.0/0

22. Consider the following output from a NAT router:

```
R2#debug ip nat
IP NAT debugging is on
R2#
NAT*: s=7.0.0.12->2.0.0.2, d=10.0.12.1 [155]
```

Which of the following is the inside global address?

- **A.** 2.0.0.2
- **B.** 10.0.12.1
- **C.** 7.0.0.12
- **D.** 10.0.12.155

23. A router running PIM has a single multicast RIB entry marked (223.3.2.1, 239.8.7.6). What does this indicate?

- **A.** The router has received an IGMP Membership Report from 223.3.2.1.
- **B.** 239.8.7.6 has sent unicast traffic to 223.3.2.1.
- **C.** 223.3.2.1 has sent multicast traffic to 239.8.7.6.
- **D.** The router has received a PIM Join/Graft from 223.3.2.1.

24. Which of the following commands individually configures port address translation?

- **A.** ip nat inside source list 1 pool natpool
- **B.** ip nat inside destination list 1 pool natpool overload
- **C.** ip nat outside source list 1 pool natpool overload
- **D.** ip nat inside source list 1 interface gi0/2 overload

25. Which QoS Class Selector has the lowest priority?

    A. CS0

    B. CS1

    C. CS7

    D. EF

26. Which of the following prevent TCP global synchronization? (Choose two.)

    A. Explicit congestion notification

    B. Policing

    C. Weighted random early detection

    D. Fair queuing

27. Which of the following queues can never exceed its bandwidth allocation during times of congestion?

    A. Low-latency queue

    B. Class-based weighted fair queue

    C. Policing queue

    D. Priority queue

28. What is another term for reflective relay?

    A. Virtual network function

    B. Virtual Ethernet bridge

    C. Virtual switching

    D. External edge virtual bridging

29. Which of the following might you need to allow in order to use IPsec in transport mode? (Choose two.)

    A. TCP port 50

    B. IP protocol 50

    C. UDP port 500

    D. IP protocol 51

    E. IP protocol 41

30. By default, what does VXLAN use for MAC address learning? (Choose two.)

    A. Multicast

    B. EVPN

    C. Data plane learning

    D. Control plane learning

31. What type of encapsulation does SD-Access use?

    A. LISP

    B. IPsec

    C. VXLAN

    D. GRE

32. Which of the following is *not* a component of SD-WAN?

    A. DTLS

    B. BGP

    C. OMP

    D. IPsec

33. Which of the following HTTP response codes indicates successful authentication using a GET or PUT request?

    A. 200

    B. 201

    C. 204

    D. 401

    E. 500

34. You want to control which commands administrators can run on a router. Which of the following should you configure?

    A. TACACS+ authorization

    B. RADIUS authorization

    C. Local authentication

    D. TACACS+ accounting

35. Which of the following can authenticate only a machine but not a user?

    A. PEAP

    B. 802.1X

    C. MAC authentication bypass

    D. WebAuth

36. Which of the following can't be used to block ARP packets or Spanning Tree BPDUs? (Choose two.)

    A. Port ACL

    B. VLAN access map

    C. MAC ACL

    D. Extended IP ACL

Answers to Assessment Test

1. **B.** The Data Link layer facilitates data transfer between two nodes. IP addresses are logical addresses based on an abstraction of the Data Link layer. See Chapter 1 for more information.

2. **C.** A bridge maintains a Media Access Control (MAC) address table that it uses to perform a crude form of routing. This reduces the need for flooding but doesn't reduce the size of the broadcast domain. Bridges forward received frames, thus simulating some of the properties of a shared physical Ethernet cable. Bridges discard frames that fail frame check sequence validation. See Chapter 1 for more information.

3. **B, D.** Transmission Control Protocol (TCP) uses sequence numbers for ordering and ensuring reliable delivery by detecting lost packets. See Chapter 1 for more information.

4. **A, B.** You can block VLAN 25 from reaching the switches in two ways. First, you can prune the virtual LAN (VLAN) from the trunk. Second, instead of running a trunk between switches, you can use routed links. See Chapter 2 for more information.

5. **D.** Because SW1 and SW2 are connected via routed interfaces, they are in separate broadcast domains and hence form separate Spanning Trees. See Chapter 2 for more information.

6. **C.** Loop Guard will block a VLAN on a port if it doesn't receive Bridge Protocol Data Units (BPDUs) for that VLAN. Unidirectional Link Detection (UDLD) and BPDU Guard can shut down an entire port. BPDU Filter doesn't block traffic. See Chapter 2 for more information.

7. **B.** Leaf-and-spine architecture is the most scalable choice for networks with predominantly East-West traffic patterns such as data center networks. Routed is not a physical architecture, but rather a layer 2 architecture. See Chapter 3 for more information.

8. **A, D.** Routed topologies scale better and converge faster than switched topologies, but they require consuming more IP address space. See Chapter 3 for more information.

9. **B.** EtherChannel doesn't use multicast. Link Aggregation Control Protocol (LACP), which negotiates EtherChannels, and Virtual Router Redundancy Protocol (VRRP) and Hot Standby Router Protocol (HSRP), which are first-hop redundancy protocols (FHRPs), do use multicast. See Chapter 3 for more information.

10. **A.** An access point (AP) forms a single Control and Provisioning of Wireless Access Points (CAPWAP) tunnel with a wireless LAN controller (WLC). See Chapter 4 for more information.

11. **C.** In an intracontroller roam, the client associates with a different AP that's connected to the same WLAN controller. Neither the VLAN nor the Service Set Identifier (SSID) changes. Because the client's IP address didn't change, you can conclude this is a layer 2 roam. See Chapter 4 for more information.

12. A, C. 5.4 GHz Wi-Fi standards include 802.11n and 802.11ac, but not 802.11g. 5.4 GHz offers higher throughput, but at the price of increased free space path loss. See Chapter 4 for more information.

13. B. The first Open Shortest Path First (OSPF) router to become active on a subnet becomes the designated router (DR) for the subnet. It's commonly taught that the DR is chosen based on the highest router ID, but the first OSPF router to become active always becomes the DR. A DR election occurs only when the existing DR and backup DR fail. See Chapter 5 for more information.

14. B, C. Network types don't have to match in order to form an adjacency, but they do need to match in order for the routers to exchange routes. See Chapter 5 for more information.

15. D. When an interface is configured as a passive interface, OSPF will advertise the prefix for that interface, but will not form an adjacency with other routers on the subnet. See Chapter 5 for more information.

16. C. The route is an external Enhanced Interior Gateway Routing Protocol (EIGRP) route, so it has an administrative distance of 170. See Chapter 6 for more information.

17. A, B. By default, only bandwidth and delay are used in calculating the metric. See Chapter 6 for more information.

18. B. 10.0.56.6 is the feasible successor. See Chapter 6 for more information.

19. C. Border Gateway Protocol (BGP) uses the autonomous system (AS) path for loop prevention. Upon receiving a route with its own AS in the AS path, an exterior Border Gateway Protocol (eBGP) router will discard the route, meaning it won't install it in its BGP Routing Information Base (RIB) or IP routing table, nor will it advertise the route. See Chapter 7 for more information.

20. A. 172.16.0.0/24 doesn't exist in R1's routing table, so the network command will have no effect. Instead, the redistribute eigrp 16 command will redistribute the 172.16.0.0/16 prefix into BGP with an incomplete origin type. See Chapter 7 for more information.

21. C. The prefix list matches any prefix with a subnet falling into the 10.0.0.0/8 range with a prefix length from 8 to 32. This includes 10.0.0.0/8, 10.0.0.0/32, and 10.255.255.0/24. The first sequence in the route map is a deny sequence that matches the IP prefix list. Hence, these prefixes will match the sequence and will be denied. The second sequence in the route map is a permit sequence that matches all prefixes that don't match the first sequence. See Chapter 7 for more information.

22. A. R2 is translating the source address 7.0.0.12 to 2.0.0.2; therefore 7.0.0.12 is the inside local address and 2.0.0.2 is the inside global address. See Chapter 8 for more information.

23. C. Multicast RIB entries take the form (source, group). The entry indicates that the source—223.3.2.1—has sent multicast traffic to the multicast group address 239.8.7.6. See Chapter 8 for more information.

24. D. Port address translation—also known as network address translation (NAT) overload—translates multiple inside local source addresses to a single global address. The global address can come from an outside interface or from a pool. See Chapter 8 for more information.

25. B. CS1 gets a lower priority than CS0. CS0 is the default class and is for best-effort traffic. CS1 is the bottom-of-the-barrel traffic that you may not even want on your network, such as torrents, gaming, or cat videos. See Chapter 9 for more information.

26. A, C. TCP global synchronization occurs when multiple TCP flows back off, then ramp up simultaneously. This can happen when a queue fills and excess packets are tail-dropped. Weighted random early detection (WRED) randomly drops packets as the queue fills. Explicit congestion notification (ECN) works by getting a TCP sender to slow down the rate at which it sends by reducing its congestion window. See Chapter 9 for more information.

27. A. The low-latency queuing (LLQ) is serviced before any other queues, so packets in the LLQ won't wait any longer than necessary. The LLQ has a limited bandwidth. See Chapter 9 for more information.

28. D. The term edge virtual bridging (EVB) describes using a physical switch to pass layer 2 traffic between VMs running on the same host. The IEEE 802.1Qbg standard calls this reflective relay. See Chapter 10 for more information.

29. B, C. Internet Key Exchange (IKE) uses User Datagram Protocol (UDP) port 500, whereas Encapsulating Security Payload (ESP) uses IP protocol 50. See Chapter 10 for more information.

30. A, C. By default, Virtual Extensible LAN (VXLAN) uses multicast to flood unknown unicasts, allowing it to perform data plane learning. See Chapter 10 for more information.

31. C. SD-Access uses VXLAN encapsulation because it can carry Ethernet frames. The others can't. See Chapter 11 for more information.

32. B. Software-defined networking in a wide area network (SD-WAN) doesn't use BGP. See Chapter 11 for more information.

33. A. When authenticating using a GET or PUT request, you should get a 200 response code if authentication succeeds. See Chapter 11 for more information.

34. A. Terminal Access Controller Access-Control System Plus (TACACS+) supports authorization, authentication, and accounting. Remote Authentication Dial-In User Service (RADIUS) doesn't support command authorization. See Chapter 12 for more information.

35. C. MAC authentication bypass is the only option that can authenticate a machine but not a user. See Chapter 12 for more information.

36. A, D. You can't use a port access control list (ACL) to block certain control plane traffic, including ARP and Spanning Tree BPDUs. You also can't use an extended IP ACL because ARP and Spanning Tree Protocol (STP) don't use IP. See Chapter 12 for more information.

Chapter

1

Networking Fundamentals

THE CCNP ENCOR EXAM OBJECTIVES COVERED IN THIS CHAPTER INCLUDE THE FOLLOWING:

Domain 1.0: Architecture

✓ **1.1 Explain the different design principles used in an enterprise network**

✓ **1.7 Differentiate hardware and software switching mechanisms**

Domain 3.0: Infrastructure

✓ **3.1 Layer 2**

✓ **3.2 Layer 3**

Forgetting the fundamentals is by far the biggest cause of failures—both network failures and failing Cisco exams. Just visit any networking forum and look at the posts from people who failed an exam by a narrow margin. Almost without exception, they can trace back their failure to misunderstanding or simply failing to learn fundamental networking concepts.

Networking fundamentals can at times seem abstract and even impractical. It's important to remember that networks are both logical and physical, so you need to keep a tight grip on both. If you neglect theory and just focus on typing in commands, you'll end up with a jalopy network. It might work, but not very well, and probably not for long. On the other hand, learning theory that you fail to put into practice leads to being educated but unemployed.

This chapter will give you a solid theoretical foundation on which to build practical skills. Much of the theory should already be familiar to you, and you'll likely have some "I already know this stuff" moments. But more often than not you'll gain new insights on something you already understood.

There's a lot of networking information out there, much of which is poorly explained, if not just plain wrong. Networking myths abound on forums, blogs, and even Wikipedia. Even official Cisco documentation has been known to contain the occasional errata. It's not intentional, of course. Learning networking is no different than learning any other complex topic. Some concepts are easy, whereas others just never quite click. Those harder concepts are fertile breeding ground for misconceptions that eventually get passed around until they become common knowledge, or worse, "best practices." Almost every network professional I've encountered holds at least one glaring misconception about networking that eventually ends up stumping them (sometimes on an exam!). Chances are you, too, have been the unfortunate recipient of such information. The sooner we identify and dispel those myths, the better. That's what this chapter is all about.

The OSI Model

The origin of many networking myths can be traced back to the Open Systems Interconnection (OSI) reference model developed by Charles Bachman of Honeywell and formalized by the International Organization for Standardization (ISO). The ISO intended the OSI model to be a standard framework for data networks. It describes a set of "activities necessary for systems to interwork using communication media" (ISO/IEC 7498-4). The model organizes these activities or functions into the following seven layers:

7. Application
6. Presentation

5. Session

4. Transport

3. Network

2. Data Link

1. Physical

The seven layers are taught zealously in most introductory networking courses. You may have had them permanently drilled into your head with the help of one or two fun little mnemonics! (My favorite is "All people seem to need data processing.") As we discuss the functions of the different layers, keep in mind that the layers of the OSI model are arbitrary. They're not written on stone tablets, nor are they the result of a rigorous scientific process that conclusively proved that the perfect network has these seven layers. The ISO arrived at each layer by attempting to group similar network functions together in a layer and then organizing the layers in a hierarchical fashion so that each layer of functions is dependent on the one below it. This led to impressive results in layers 1–4 (the lower layers) and utter confusion in layers 5–7 (the upper layers).

Table 1.1 shows what common protocols fall into each of the lower layers.

TABLE 1.1   The lower layers and their associated protocols

Layer	Name	Example protocols
1	Physical	Thicknet (10BASE5)
		Thinnet (10BASE2)
		1000BASE-T
		T1/E1
2	Data Link	IEEE 802.3/Ethernet II (DIX)
		Point-to-Point Protocol (PPP)
		High-Level Data Link Control (HDLC)
3	Network	IPv4
		IPv6
4	Transport	TCP
		UDP

The Upper Layers: Application, Presentation, and Session

One thing that has always been clear about the OSI model is that the Application layer includes application data and application protocols. The Hypertext Transfer Protocol (HTTP) is an application protocol that a web browser uses for communicating with web servers. Application data would be an HTTP GET request that the browser sends to a web server. Likewise, the web page that the server sends in response would also be application data. In short, application data is whatever the application sends or receives over the network.

Incidentally, an application can use more than one protocol. For example, when a web browser uses the Hypertext Transfer Protocol Secure (HTTPS) protocol to send a request to a web server, it's making use of two protocols: HTTP and Transport Layer Security (TLS). Despite the latter's confusing name, both are application protocols.

For all practical purposes, the upper layers (Session, Presentation, and Application) are one layer: the Application layer. The actual functions of the Session and Presentation layers—things like authentication and negotiating an application protocol—occur in the application anyway. They don't include any network functions and are concerned only with application data and application protocols.

Making Sense of Layers

The ISO never clearly defined what a layer is. The closest they came was a circular definition. But we can infer from the OSI reference model what they had in mind.

 For the curious, the ISO defined a layer as a "subdivision of the OSI architecture, constituted by subsystems of the same rank" (ISO/IEC 7498-1). While it's tautological that "subsystems of the same rank" are conceptually in the same layer, it still doesn't tell us what a layer *is*.

The concept of layering comes straight from software development (many of the OSI folks were operating system developers). The idea was that applications would treat the network as a software abstraction, somewhat like a filesystem. A filesystem acts as a layer that sits between the application and physical storage (e.g., disks). When the application needs to store some data, it just sends that data to the filesystem layer, which in turn takes care of the specifics of writing it to disk.

The OSI folks thought that in the same way that an application can store data on a filesystem without having to know anything about the underlying disks, so could it also send data over a network without requiring any network-specific coding or knowing anything about the network's infrastructure. Each layer would consist of a set of network-related functions implemented by the operating system or some middleware that would sit between the application and the host's physical network interface. Collectively, these layers would handle all the mechanisms of getting the application data onto the network and giving the network enough information to make sure the data got to its destination.

With the exception of the Physical layer, the layers of the OSI model are purely imaginary. Just as a filesystem is a software abstraction that hides the details of physical storage, the layers of the OSI model are just collections of software functions that hide the details of the network from applications and users. You can't see a filesystem with your eyes in the same way that you can see a hard drive, and you can't see the Data Link layer in the same way that you can see a switch. Layers are software abstractions and nothing more.

Figure 1.1 illustrates the concept of how layering might work using the Transmission Control Protocol (TCP) and Internet Protocol (IP), which are both included in the kernels of modern operating systems (Linux, Unix, and Windows). Keep in mind that the only real objects in this figure are the host and the physical network interface.

FIGURE 1.1   How layers abstract the network from an application

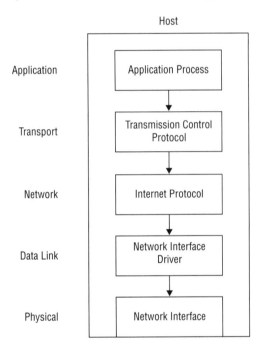

> **NOTE**   You may see some striking similarities between the layers in Figure 1.1 and the so-called TCP/IP or Internet protocol suite model. It and the OSI model are often juxtaposed as competing models. The fact is that the TCP/IP model is just a specific implementation of the OSI model based on the TCP/IP protocol suite.

In this high-level example, when an application needs to send data it places the data in what the OSI model generically calls an application protocol data unit (PDU). The specifics of the application PDU aren't important and, with the exception of firewalls that do deep packet inspection, are opaque to the network. The application passes its PDU to a protocol in the layer directly below, as shown in Figure 1.2. The protocol generates a new PDU and tacks the application PDU onto the end of it—a process called *encapsulation*. It then passes this new PDU down to a protocol at the next lower layer, and so on. What ends up on the wire is a giant PDU that contains several smaller PDUs from the protocols operating at the higher layers. Later in the chapter we'll walk through a detailed example of how encapsulation works, but first, we need to talk about what happens at each of these lower layers.

FIGURE 1.2   At each layer, data is encapsulated in a PDU and passed down to the next lower layer.

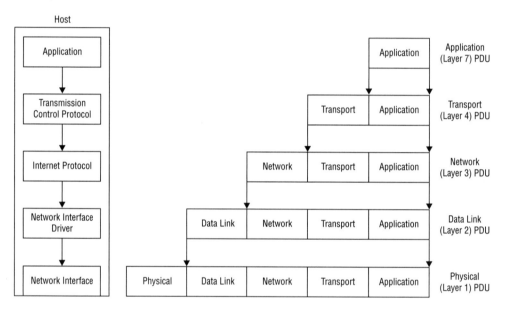

The Lower Layers: Physical, Data Link, Network, and Transport

The purpose of a network is to allow applications running on different hosts to communicate with one another. Robert Metcalfe, one of the inventors of the original Ethernet, said it succinctly in 1972: "Networking is interprocess communication." Thus, at a minimum, a network needs to perform three basic functions:

Layer 1: Physical Connectivity between Nodes   A node can be a workstation, server, router, switch, firewall, or any network-connected device that has a processor and memory.

Layer 2: Node-to-Node Data Transfer   Data transfer between two nodes physically connected to a shared medium.

Layer 3: Forwarding/Routing   Data transfer between any two nodes, regardless of whether they're physically connected to the same medium.

The OSI model sorts these three functions along with many others into the first four layers of the OSI model, as shown in Table 1.2. Not all protocols that operate in a given layer implement all the functions listed for that layer.

TABLE 1.2   Networking functions provided by each layer

Function	1 Physical	2 Data Link	3 Network	4 Transport
Transmission of bitstreams over physical media	X			
Enabling/disabling physical network interface	X			
Node-to-node data transfer over a shared medium		X		
Forwarding/routing		X	X	
Error control		X	X	X
Flow control		X	X	X
Multiplexing/splitting		X	X	X
Ordering		X	X	X
Fragmentation/reassembly			X	X

The OSI replicates some functions in most layers, blurring the distinction among them. It becomes apparent that what distinguishes the layers isn't what they do but what they *don't* do. Higher layers lack functionality provided by lower layers, something you'd expect given the hierarchical structure of layers. One layer whose functions differ starkly from the others is the Physical layer.

Layer 1: The Physical Layer

The main function of the Physical layer is to convert bits to electromagnetic energy such as light, electrical current, or radio waves, and transmit them over some medium such as fiber-optic or copper cables or the airwaves. Whereas the functions of the other layers are performed in software, this particular function is performed by a node's physical network interface.

A challenge of using electromagnetic energy to send bits is that the physical media can carry only one bitstream at a time. In the early days of networking, two nodes would be connected via a pair of wires. If both simultaneously sent a signal, their signals would interfere with each other and create a collision. Hence, both nodes were in the same collision domain. To avoid this, the nodes had to use half-duplex communication wherein only one node could transmit at a time. Half-duplex wired communication may seem an irrelevant relic from the past, but as you'll learn in a moment, during its heyday half-duplex communication had an unfortunate impact on the Ethernet standards that still haunts us to this day. Broadcast storms and the infamous Spanning Tree Protocols (STPs) can be traced back to the early use of half-duplex communication.

Today, full-duplex communication is the norm in wired networks and something we take for granted. All that's needed for full-duplex communication is for the physical interface to separate the transmit and receive functions. Twisted-pair copper cabling, for example, does this by using two pairs of wires: one pair for transmitting and another pair for receiving. Likewise, fiber-optic cables have separate strands for transmitting and receiving. Wavelength-division multiplexing achieves full-duplex communication on a single fiber strand by using one light frequency for transmitting and another for receiving.

Layer 2: The Data Link Layer

The primary function of the Data Link layer is to facilitate data transfer between two (and only two) nodes that are connected to a shared medium. Some physical media can support only two nodes, as is the case with a crossover cable or point-to-point serial link. Other media, such as wireless, can support more than two nodes.

When only two nodes share the same media, data transfer is easy. As long as both nodes are aware of the point-to-point nature of the link, one node can send the data, and the other node receives it, knowing that it's the intended recipient. The Point-to-Point Protocol (PPP) and High-level Data Link Control (HDLC) are two common layer 2 protocols used on T1 serial links.

But when multiple nodes can share a medium, as they did with early Ethernet, things get tricky. At this point you're rightly thinking that with the exception of wireless, nobody connects nodes to a shared medium anymore. Hubs went out of fashion long ago. Now we connect devices to switches (the marketing term for bridges). However, switches actually *simulate* the behavior of a shared medium. Time for a quick history lesson.

A Brief History of Ethernet

The original Ethernet standards from the 1970s were designed for nodes all connected to a shared electrical bus that often took the form of a thick yellow cable (you may have heard the term Thicknet). Whenever one node would transmit a signal, all other nodes connected to the cable would receive it. Communication was half-duplex, and all nodes were in the same collision domain. As a way of detecting errors introduced by collisions, the original Ethernet II (DIX) specification got a frame check sequence (FCS, sometimes called a cyclic redundancy check, or CRC) to detect errors. Even today as back then, nodes discard frames that fail the FCS check.

The multi-access nature of Ethernet made it necessary to assign each node's network interface a unique, 48-bit Media Access Control (MAC) address. The sending node would construct a frame that included the destination node's MAC address and the data to send. All nodes would receive the frame, but only the destination node would process it.

Now let's fast-forward to today. We still use MAC addresses, even though the original rationale for using them is long gone. To maintain backward compatibility over the years, we never got rid of them. Figure 1.3 shows the original DIX frame format that we still use today. We're still using a technology designed specifically for devices that were all sharing a thick yellow cable. Today, however, instead of nodes sharing this thick yellow cable, they're connected to a switch.

FIGURE 1.3 Layer 2 frame and layer 1 packet, structurally identical to the revised (1997) IEEE 802.3 format that we use today

	6 Bytes	6 Bytes	2 Bytes	Variable	4 Bytes
Layer 2 Frame	Destination MAC Address	Source MAC Address	Type/ Length	Data	Frame Check Sequence

	8 Bytes	6 Bytes	6 Bytes	2 Bytes	Variable	4 Bytes
Layer 1 Packet	Preamble	Destination MAC Address	Source MAC Address	Type/ Length	Data	Frame Check Sequence

You may have seen diagrams that show the Ethernet frame with an 8-byte preamble at the beginning. The preamble is not actually part of the frame but is a series of bits that provide clock synchronization for the Physical layer and signal the start of the frame. The entire collection of bits—including the preamble and frame—compose a layer 1 Ethernet packet. Although most of the time when you hear "packet" it refers to an IP packet (layer 3), "packet" is a generic term for any PDU. To avoid confusion, you can think of the raw bits as a layer 1 Ethernet PDU.

Switches replace the shared cable of the early Ethernet with multiple cables, breaking the inherent broadcast nature of the thick yellow cable. Switches thus have to perform some interesting hackery to maintain backward compatibility with the early Ethernet standards. When a switch receives an Ethernet frame, by default it forwards that frame to all other devices connected to the switch—a process called flooding or broadcasting. This creates the illusion that all nodes are connected to the same thick yellow cable. (In networking parlance, they're all in the same broadcast domain or segment.) This illusion is called transparent bridging (aka switching) because to the nodes, the switch is invisible. Incidentally, you'll recognize this simulated yellow cable by its common name: a local area network (LAN).

The MAC Address Table

Although switches eliminate collision domains by offering full-duplex communication, they still waste bandwidth by flooding traffic to nodes that don't need it. To mitigate flooding, switches implement a form of routing. When a switch receives a frame on an interface, it records the ingress interface and source MAC address in its MAC address table. Subsequently, when a switch receives a frame destined for that same MAC address, it queries the MAC address table, which returns the interface number. The switch then forwards the frame only out of that interface, rather than flooding it.

The MAC address table is stored in a type of memory called content-addressable memory (CAM). CAM is often used as a synonym for the MAC address table. The CAM takes a MAC address and VLAN as input and returns an interface name and number as the output. CAM provides faster read times than RAM.

```
SW3#show mac address-table dynamic
          Mac Address Table
-------------------------------------------

Vlan    Mac Address       Type        Ports
----    -----------       --------    -----
   1    0c3c.8a00.5e02    DYNAMIC     Gi0/2
   1    0c3c.8ad7.9101    DYNAMIC     Gi0/2
   1    0c3c.8afd.c101    DYNAMIC     Gi0/1
   1    0c3c.8afd.c102    DYNAMIC     Gi0/2
  10    0c3c.8ad7.800a    DYNAMIC     Gi0/0
  20    0c3c.8ad7.8014    DYNAMIC     Gi0/0
Total Mac Addresses for this criterion: 6
```

The use of the MAC address table changes the fundamental nature of MAC addresses. They no longer function as just names for identification, but also as addresses for location.

On the other hand, if a switch receives a frame for a MAC address that doesn't have a mapping in the MAC address table—called an unknown unicast—it reverts to its default behavior and floods the frame out of all other interfaces.

Unknown unicasts are more common than you might think. Entries in the MAC address table don't last forever. By default, a MAC address entry is deleted or ages out 300 seconds (5 minutes) after the switch last sees the traffic from the MAC address. Note that aging time is not based on when the entry was created.

```
SW3#show mac address-table aging-time vlan 1
Global Aging Time:  300
Vlan    Aging Time
----    ----------
   1    300
```

You can adjust the global aging time to between 10 and 1,000,000 seconds or disable aging by setting the aging time to 0.

```
SW3(config)#mac address-table aging-time ?
  <0-0>       Enter 0 to disable aging
  <10-1000000>  Aging time in seconds
```

You can also adjust the aging time on a per-VLAN basis.

```
SW3(config)#mac address-table aging-time 300 vlan ?
  <1-4094>  VLAN id
```

Disabling aging might sound like a good idea, as it would prevent flooding, right? Not necessarily. The CAM has a finite amount of space, and once the MAC address table is full, the switch will flood traffic to every destination MAC not in the table.

The MAC address table mitigates flooding but doesn't eliminate it. The fundamental flooding behavior of Ethernet remains. To make matters worse, Ethernet implements a special MAC address called a broadcast address (FFFF.FFFF.FFFF). Frames sent to this address are flooded out of all ports. You can imagine the number of major outages that arose from this unwise decision!

The end result is that any node in a broadcast domain can send a frame to another node and the destination node will receive it. We may have added more cables and more devices, but the fundamental behavior of Ethernet hasn't changed in 50 years, as shown in Figure 1.4. When it comes to networking, history has a way of repeating itself.

FIGURE 1.4   Early Ethernet over a shared medium compared to Ethernet using a switch

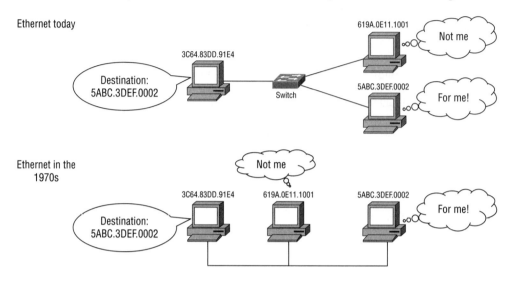

Maximum Transmission Unit

Another interesting side effect we inherited from the use of the legendary thick yellow cable is that Ethernet had to impose a limit on the maximum frame size to keep a single node from hogging the medium with colossal frames. The Ethernet maximum transmission unit (MTU) defines the maximum size of the Data field in bytes. DIX and IEEE 802.3 support a maximum MTU of 1,500 bytes. Higher-layer protocols trying to send packets larger than the MTU must break apart their packets into fragments that will fit into the frame's Data field. To avoid fragmentation, some interfaces support jumbo frames with an interface MTU of 9,000 bytes to 9,216 bytes.

Subnet Limits

When you think of the term subnet, you probably think of an IP subnet address and mask, such as 192.168.1.0/24. The IP subnet address and mask collectively form a CIDR block, or just CIDR for short. But a subnetwork (subnet) is actually a collection of connected nodes that all use the same Data Link layer protocol. For example, a collection of nodes in the same VLAN is an example of a subnetwork. To avoid confusion, I'll refer to the combination of IP subnet address and mask as either a CIDR or an IP subnet.

The moral of the convoluted story behind Ethernet and bridges is that no matter how many tricks and kluges you invent, you can't extend a subnet beyond a few hundred nodes. Regardless of the protocols used, the number of nodes in a subnet is limited by the underlying physical media. To create large networks that include thousands or millions of nodes, we need to join multiple subnets together. This brings us to the Network layer.

Layer 3: The Network Layer

Recalling that a subnet consists of connected nodes running the same Data Link layer protocol, the Network layer's primary function is to enable data transfer between nodes that may or may not be in the same subnet. Hence, Network layer protocols must ensure that two things happen:

- Nodes in different subnets will communicate using a gateway/router.

- Nodes in the same subnet will communicate with one another using the Data Link layer protocol.

It may seem redundant for the Network layer to enable connectivity between nodes in the same subnet, since the Data Link layer already provides this functionality. But the purpose of the Network layer is to abstract the physical and data link characteristics of the network away so that applications don't need to be concerned with them. Instead, the application just deals with Network layer addresses—usually IP addresses.

To see how IP abstracts away the Data Link layer, compare the layer 2 and layer 3 topologies shown in Figure 1.5.

FIGURE 1.5   Simple layer 2 and layer 3 topologies

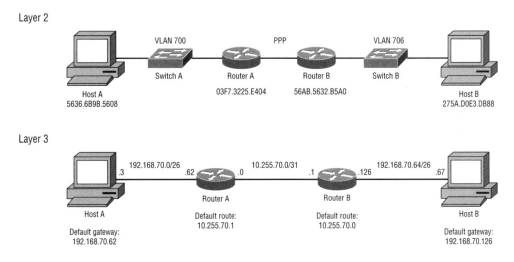

IP creates an addressing scheme on top of the Data Link layer, giving each subnet a different CIDR—a combination of an IP subnet address and subnet mask:

VLAN 700—192.168.70.0/26

PPP—10.255.70.0/31

VLAN 706—192.168.70.64/26

A CIDR is the name that IP uses to address a subnet. Hence, a CIDR and subnet should always be tightly coupled, but they're not the same thing. The purpose of a CIDR (IP subnet address and mask) is to help a node determine based on the destination's IP address whether it's in the same subnet or a different subnet. If the destination's IP is in the same CIDR, the node assumes it's in the same subnet and will address the frame to the node's MAC address. Otherwise, the node will assume the destination is in another subnet and will address the frame to the MAC address of the default gateway for the subnet.

 The OSI's dream of turning the network into a software abstraction begins to show cracks in the Network layer. Applications do indeed need to have some knowledge of the network, even if it's just IP addresses.

Forwarding within a Subnet

If the destination is in the same subnet, the node will simply communicate with the destination at the Data Link layer. For example, if Host A (192.168.70.3) attempts to ping Router A (192.168.70.62), the following will happen:

1. Host A will note that Router A's IP is in the same subnet.

2. Host A will send an Address Resolution Protocol (ARP) request to the broadcast destination address, asking who has 192.168.70.62.

3. Switch A will flood the ARP request and Router A will receive it.

4. Router A will send an ARP reply to Host A's MAC address. The reply will contain Router A's IP address (192.168.70.62) and MAC address.

5. Switch A will forward the ARP reply to Host A.

6. Host A will encapsulate the IP packet inside an Ethernet frame addressed to Router A's MAC address. Host A will set the Type field in the frame to 0x0800, indicating that the frame contains an IP packet.

 A ping is an Internet Control Message Protocol (ICMP) echo request. ICMP is an integral part of IP.

Forwarding between Subnets

On the other hand, if Host A (192.168.70.3) attempts to ping Host B (192.168.70.67), the following happens:

1. Host A compares its IP address with Router B's IP and determines that they are in different subnets.

2. Host A consults its IP routing table for a closest-match route to 10.255.70.1. Not finding an exact match, the closest match is the default route (0.0.0.0/0). Host A's default gateway is 192.168.70.62, the IP belonging to Router A's Ethernet interface.

3. Because Router A's and Host A's IP addresses are in the same subnet, Host A sends an ARP request asking for Router A's MAC address.

4. Switch A floods the ARP request to Router A.

5. Router A sends an ARP reply to Host A's MAC address. The reply contains Router A's IP address and MAC address.

6. Host A encapsulates the IP packet inside an Ethernet frame addressed to Router A's MAC address. The Type field will contain the value `0x0800` to indicate that the Data field contains an IP packet.

7. Router A receives the Ethernet frame and, based on the Type field in the Ethernet frame, knows it contains an IP packet.

8. Router A looks at the destination IP address in the IP packet and checks its forwarding information base (FIB) for an exact match. Cisco Express Forwarding (CEF) uses the FIB to make forwarding decisions. The FIB is fed by the IP routing table (also known as the Routing Information Base, or RIB). Not finding an exact match for the destination IP address in the FIB, it will use the default route, which has Router B (10.255.70.1) as its next hop.

9. Router A will encapsulate the IP packet in a PPP frame and send it to Router B.

10. Router B will decapsulate the IP packet, look at the destination IP address, and check its FIB for a match. Because the destination IP (192.168.70.67) is in the same subnet as Router B's Ethernet interface, Router B will send an ARP request.

11. Switch B will flood the ARP request to Host B, which will send an ARP reply to Router B's MAC address. The ARP reply will contain Host B's MAC address and IP address.

12. Router B will encapsulate the IP packet in an Ethernet frame addressed to Host B's MAC address.

The reason that the process takes so many steps is that the ICMP data is zigzagging up and down the different layers at each node. Figure 1.6 puts everything in context with a layered view of the topology.

FIGURE 1.6   Layered representation of the network

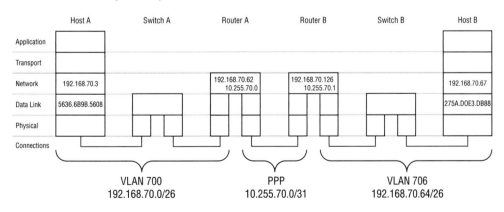

It's worth noting that when you create multiple VLANs on a switch, you're simply creating separate broadcast domains. Nodes in one VLAN can't communicate with nodes in the other using MAC addresses because they're in different subnets. Even if those nodes are connected to the same switch, they must use IP and go through a router to communicate with nodes in the other VLAN.

> It's crucial that a CIDR block belong to only one subnet—that is, one section of the network where all the connected nodes use the same Data Link layer protocol. A common mistake is to try to split a CIDR across different subnets that are usually in geographically separated areas, like different data centers. The rationale for subnet splitting is to achieve some sort of resiliency with minimal inconvenience, particularly by being able to migrate virtual machines from one site to another without changing any IP addresses. This requires using some network virtualization technology like Virtual Extensible LAN (VXLAN) to create the illusion of extending the subnet, when in fact it's stuffing Ethernet frames inside of IP packets and sending them across multiple subnets, in essence creating a virtual subnet! Remember that a subnet can't scale beyond a few hundred nodes—not even a virtual subnet.

Address Resolution Protocol

Most devices with an IP address—including workstations, servers, routers, and switches—maintain an ARP cache to store ARP replies. The purpose of the ARP cache is to avoid having to send an ARP request every time the node needs to resolve an IP address to a MAC address.

When a node needs to resolve the MAC address of an IP address not in its ARP cache, it sends an ARP request to the broadcast address (FFFF.FFFF.FFFF). Upon receiving a reply, it stores the mapping in its ARP cache. The following example illustrates the process using two switches:

- SW3 has a switched virtual interface (SVI) in VLAN 20 with an IP address of 10.10.20.3.
- SW4 has an SVI also in VLAN 20 with an IP address of 10.10.20.4.

SW3:

```
! Show the ARP cache on SW3
SW3#show arp dynamic
Protocol  Address          Age (min)  Hardware Addr   Type   Interface
Internet  10.10.10.4               0  0c3c.8ad7.800a  ARPA   Vlan10
! Trigger an ARP request for 10.10.20.4 by sending a ping to it
SW3#ping 10.10.20.4
Type escape sequence to abort.
Sending 5, 100-byte ICMP Echos to 10.10.20.4, timeout is 2 seconds:
.!!!!
```

```
Success rate is 80 percent (4/5), round-trip min/avg/max = 10/10/10 ms
! The ping succeeded, implying an ARP reply was received. Show the ARP cache
again.
SW3#show arp dynamic
Protocol  Address          Age (min)  Hardware Addr   Type   Interface
Internet  10.10.10.4              0  0c3c.8ad7.800a  ARPA   Vlan10
Internet  10.10.20.4              0  0c3c.8ad7.8014  ARPA   Vlan20
```

SW4:

```
! ARP Snooping debugging has been enabled on SW4. Note the destination broadcast
! address.
SW4#
ARP Packet (Gi1/0/20) Src: 0c3c.8aab.8014, Dst: ffff.ffff.ffff, SM:
0c3c.8aab.8014, SI: 10.10.20.3, TM: ffff.ffff.ffff, TI: 10.10.20.3
Packet bridged by platform.
ARP Packet (Gi1/1/20) Src: 0c3c.8aab.8014, Dst: ffff.ffff.ffff, SM:
0c3c.8aab.8014, SI: 10.10.20.3, TM: ffff.ffff.ffff, TI: 10.10.20.3
Packet bridged by platform.
! Although not shown in the output, SW4's ARP reply is addressed to SW3's
! SVI MAC address.
```

The default timeout for an ARP entry is 4 hours. You can modify this on a per-interface basis, as shown on SW3:

```
SW3#show interfaces vlan 20 | i ARP
  Encapsulation ARPA, loopback not set
  ARP type: ARPA, ARP Timeout 04:00:00
SW3#configure terminal
Enter configuration commands, one per line.  End with CNTL/Z.
SW3(config)#interface vlan 20
SW3(config-if)#arp timeout ?
  <0-2147483>  Seconds
```

You'll hear disagreement as to whether ARP is a layer 2 or layer 3 protocol, some even going so far as to call it a layer 2.5 protocol! ARP packets fit the definition of what the OSI model calls protocol control information. In addition to just providing a mapping between MAC and IP addresses, the fact that a node sends ARP packets indicates its willingness to use IP. In that respect, ARP is decidedly a layer 2 protocol.

Fragmentation

If an IP packet exceeds the MTU of any interfaces it has to traverse (the path MTU), then any intermediate router may fragment the packet into multiple datagrams. Each datagram must be no greater than the path MTU. The sender can optionally set the don't fragment (DF) bit in the IP header to prevent intermediate routers from fragmenting the packet.

IPv6 differs from IPv4 when it comes to fragmentation. IPv4 packets can be fragmented by any router along the path unless the DF bit is set. IPv6 can be fragmented only by the sender. If an IPv6 packet will exceed an intermediate router's interface MTU, the router will respond to the sender with an ICMPv6 "packet too big" message and discard the packet.

Routing vs. Forwarding

What's the difference between routing and forwarding? Not much, really. Forwarding is about sending the data one step closer to its destination. Routing is about figuring out what that next step is.

The routing versus forwarding distinction has nothing to do with layers. Recall that switches perform a crude version of routing by snooping the data plane to find out which port a MAC address is connected to. They compile this into a MAC address table, which they use to make forwarding decisions.

When it comes to IP, route calculation and route advertisements are performed by interior gateway routing protocols such as Enhanced Interior Gateway Routing Protocol (EIGRP) and Open Shortest Path First (OSPF). Although we don't normally think of them in this way, routing protocols are actually applications that run on routers. They just populate the IP routing table that feeds into the FIB, but CEF does the forwarding.

Layer 4: The Transport Layer

So far, we've seen how protocols at the first three layers enable communication between two host interfaces. The primary purpose of the Transport layer is to facilitate application-to-application (end-to-end) data transfer. Whereas Network layer protocols (e.g., IPv4, IPv6) provide a way to move data from one host's interface to another host's interface, the Transport layer protocols—TCP and UDP—provide a means for applications to distinguish different communication streams. They both do this using 16-bit port numbers, as shown in Table 1.3.

TABLE 1.3   Common applications and their TCP and UDP port numbers

Application protocol	Transport protocol	Source IP	Source port	Destination IP	Destination port
HTTP	TCP	192.168.88.10	5230	18.213.128.4	80
HTTP	TCP	192.168.88.10	5231	18.213.128.4	81
DNS	UDP	192.168.88.10	56801	192.168.88.1	53

For example, when a web browser retrieves a web page it may open multiple TCP connections to the same web server. Each TCP connection originates from a different ephemeral (short-lived) source port chosen by the operating system, allowing the web browser and web server to keep track of which requests go with which connection.

The protocol data unit for TCP is called a *segment*, and for UDP it's called a *datagram*.

When a host receives an IP packet, the host's networking stack looks at the Protocol field to determine to which upper-layer protocol to send the data. If the Protocol field in the IP header is 6, the data contains a TCP segment. If it's 17, then it contains a UDP datagram. Consequently, a single host can use the same UDP and TCP port numbers simultaneously.

Transport layer protocols aren't always necessary. The interior gateway protocols EIGRP and OSPF ride directly over IP, using the IP protocol numbers 88 and 89, respectively.

Transmission Control Protocol

RFC 793 somewhat redundantly describes TCP as a "connection-oriented, end-to-end reliable protocol." TCP provides the following features:

- Reliable delivery
- Ordering
- Error control
- Flow control
- Congestion avoidance

The phrase "connection oriented" refers to TCP's attempt to simulate the properties of a physical connection. Sound familiar? An ideal connection provides reliability and order. The data the sender sends is exactly what the receiver receives and in the same order.

TCP guarantees both order and reliability through the use of sequence numbers and acknowledgments. The sender marks each TCP segment with a sequence number that increments in a predictable fashion. This allows the receiver to reassemble the segments in the correct order should they arrive out of order. The receiver sends an acknowledgment (ACK) in response to each segment, indicating the sequence number of the segment it received. If the sender fails to receive an ACK after a period of time, it will retransmit the segment.

Connection Establishment

You should be familiar with TCP's famous three-way handshake. Its purpose is to allow both sides to establish initial sequence numbers. Here's how it works:

1. Node A sends Node B a segment with the synchronize (SYN) flag set, along with its initial sequence number (ISN), which is usually random.

2. Node B responds with a SYN and its own ISN, which is different from Node A's ISN. Node B also sends an ACK to acknowledge Node A's initial SYN.

3. Node A acknowledges Node B's SYN by sending an ACK.

Connection Termination

When the client is ready to terminate the connection, it sends a segment with the finish (FIN) flag set. The server responds with an ACK; however, it can continue to send data. This is called a half-close state. When the server is ready to terminate the connection, it too sends a segment with the FIN flag set. The client ACKs this segment, and the connection is fully closed.

Connection Reset

The TCP Reset (RST) flag is useful for cleaning up old and duplicate connections. Generally, when a TCP receives a segment for a port that it's not listening on, it will respond with a RST, letting the sender know that the connection was refused. This can happen if the sender tries to send data over an old connection that it believes is still open.

In another case, if a TCP doesn't receive any ACKs from a host, it will abort the connection by sending a RST. This may happen if there's a unidirectional link or someone abruptly shuts down the host, precluding it from gracefully terminating the connection. On the off chance that the host receives the RST, it will abandon the connection and may attempt to open a new one.

Error Control

Error control detects whether application data was lost or corrupted during transit. Aside from port numbers, this is the only feature both TCP and UDP have in common. Both TCP and UDP provide error control by calculating a checksum over the entire packet and including it in the header. The recipient calculates its own checksum over the entire packet and compares it to what's in the header. If they don't match, the recipient discards the packet.

Flow Control

Flow control prevents a sender from sending data faster than the receiver can receive it. TCP provides flow control through the use of windows and acknowledgments. The receiver specifies a window—the number of bytes that the sender may send before stopping to wait for an acknowledgment from the receiver.

Congestion Avoidance

Congestion avoidance can be described as TCP's politeness algorithm. If a sender fails to receive an ACK or receives duplicate ACKs, TCP assumes that there's congestion somewhere in the network and slows down the rate at which it sends.

Encapsulation and Decapsulation

The entire process of moving data from one application to another over the network rests on two processes: encapsulation and decapsulation. Without encapsulation and decapsulation, there is no network. In short, each time a higher-layer protocol passes data down to a lower-layer protocol, it's encapsulated. Whenever a lower-layer protocol passes data up to a higher-layer protocol, it's decapsulated.

Encapsulation and Multiplexing

Although they're technically different, in networking parlance multiplexing and encapsulation are used interchangeably. Multiplexing is the act of sending multiple streams of data over a single connection. Nodes achieve multiplexing by using encapsulation, as shown in Figure 1.7.

FIGURE 1.7   Encapsulation of a TCP segment and IP packet inside an Ethernet frame

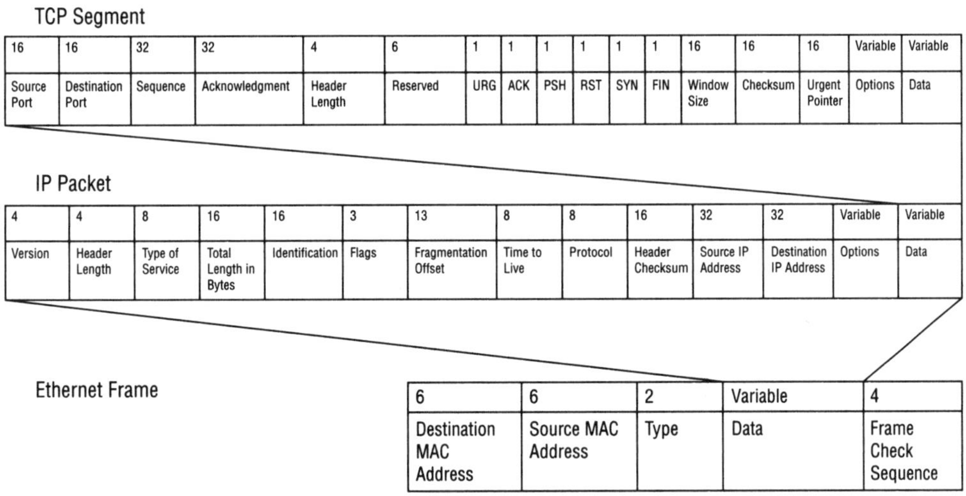

TCP Segment

16	16	32	32	4	6	1	1	1	1	1	1	16	16	16	Variable	Variable
Source Port	Destination Port	Sequence	Acknowledgment	Header Length	Reserved	URG	ACK	PSH	RST	SYN	FIN	Window Size	Checksum	Urgent Pointer	Options	Data

IP Packet

4	4	8	16	16	3	13	8	8	16	32	32	Variable	Variable
Version	Header Length	Type of Service	Total Length in Bytes	Identification	Flags	Fragmentation Offset	Time to Live	Protocol	Header Checksum	Source IP Address	Destination IP Address	Options	Data

Ethernet Frame

6	6	2	Variable	4
Destination MAC Address	Source MAC Address	Type	Data	Frame Check Sequence

As an example, suppose a TCP-based client application needs to send some data to a server. The application instructs the host operating system to open a TCP connection to the server. Once the connection is open, the application uses it to send some data to the server. Here's what happens: The host's operating system creates a TCP segment, places the application data in the Data field, and populates the rest of the fields in the TCP header appropriately. The OS encapsulates the TCP packet inside an IP packet, with the Protocol field set to 6 (TCP). It then sends the IP packet to the Ethernet driver, which encapsulates the IP packet in an Ethernet frame, which has the Type field set to 0x0800 (IP). The Ethernet driver passes the frame to the network interface, which converts the data to bits and puts it out on the wire.

Decapsulation and Splitting

Splitting or demultiplexing is the multiplexing process played backward. Continuing with the preceding example, when the server receives the Ethernet frame containing the IP packet from the client, the Ethernet driver looks at the Type field in the Ethernet header and sees that it's 0x0800, indicating an IP packet. The Ethernet driver decapsulates the IP packet from the frame and passes it to the operating system's IP stack. The IP stack looks at the Protocol field and sees that it's 6, indicating that the Data field contains a TCP segment.

Summary

The backstory of the OSI model and Ethernet seems to have little relevance to "modern" networking. But upon closer inspection, many of the fundamentals of networking haven't changed in 50 years. Essentially, the goal of networking is and always has been to enable applications to transfer data. The challenge of networking is to make that happen without having to hard-code gritty networking details into each application. That's where the layering concept of the OSI model comes in. Each layer is an abstraction that conceals some part of the network from the application. Although the OSI model is abstract, the protocols that networks implement today in a mostly consistent manner are very real.

Data Link layer protocols such as Ethernet, PPP, and WLAN conceal the details of network interfaces and provide a common frame format that can be used across different media types. Network layer protocols such as IPv4 and IPv6 hide the different Data Link layer protocols in use across different networks. This is why the Network layer is sometimes called the *Inter*network layer. Applications can use Transport layer protocols such as TCP and UDP to distinguish different communication streams.

The upper layers—Application, Session, and Presentation—have always posed a challenge for the OSI model. It's clear that these are all one layer: the Application layer. What makes Application layer protocols unique is that they are "the end of the line." That is, there is no higher-layer protocol for an application to pass data up to. Hence, many things that we previously thought of as simply networking protocols are actually applications: ARP, BGP, EIGRP, and OSPF, just to name a few. PDUs generated by these aren't passed up to any higher-layer protocol. When you look at the Application layer in this way, the network suddenly looks a lot simpler.

Exam Essentials

Understand why IP addresses and MAC addresses name interfaces, not nodes.   An interface is bound to a subnet, and a node can have multiple interfaces. Other nodes in the same subnet can't determine whether any two MAC or IP addresses belong to the same node.

Know how switches extend a subnet across different physical media.   Switches use flooding to forward broadcasts and unknown unicasts to all connected nodes in a given VLAN.

Understand how routers enable IP connectivity between subnets.   When a router receives a layer 2 frame containing an IP packet, it decapsulates the packet and looks at the destination IP address. It checks its FIB to determine the next hop's IP address. If the next hop is reachable via Ethernet, it re-encapsulates the packet in an Ethernet frame addressed to the next-hop node's MAC address and forwards it. If the next hop is reachable via a PPP or HDLC connection, it encapsulates the IP packet in a PPP or HDLC frame and forwards it.

Know the encapsulation and decapsulation process for the protocols at each layer.   With the exception of the Application layer, the PDU at each layer contains a reference to a protocol in the layer above. For example, an Ethernet frame contains a Type field that indicates a Network layer protocol, such as IPv4 (0x0800) or IPv6 (0x86DD). An IP packet contains a Protocol field indicating a Transport layer protocol, such as TCP (6) or UDP (17).

Understand the primary purpose of each layer.   The Data Link layer facilitates data transfer between two nodes connected to a shared medium. The Network layer enables data transfer between nodes that may or may not be in the same subnet. The Transport layer facilitates application-to-application data transfer and provides error detection.

Review Questions

You can find the answers in the appendix.

1. Which of the following protocols operate at the Physical layer?
   - **A.** HDLC
   - **B.** IEEE 802.3
   - **C.** PPP
   - **D.** Twisted pair

2. What protocol operates at the Data Link layer?
   - **A.** IPv4
   - **B.** OSPF
   - **C.** PPP
   - **D.** UDP

3. What layer does ARP operate at?
   - **A.** 2
   - **B.** 3
   - **C.** 4
   - **D.** 7

4. Protocols at what layer provide for node-to-node data transfer over a shared medium?
   - **A.** Physical
   - **B.** Data Link
   - **C.** Network
   - **D.** Transport

5. What are two examples a single collision domain?
   - **A.** A single fiber strand that carries separate light frequencies for sending and receiving
   - **B.** Wireless
   - **C.** Two fiber strands, one for sending and another for receiving
   - **D.** A twisted-pair cable with a single pair of wires for sending and receiving

6. What can be done to achieve full-duplex communication?
   - **A.** Use fiber-optic cables
   - **B.** Use TCP
   - **C.** Use different pairs of wires for transmitting and receiving
   - **D.** Set the interface speeds to something greater than 10 Mbps

7. Workstation A is connected to a switch port that's in VLAN 10. Workstations B and C are connected switch ports in VLAN 20 on the same switch. Both workstations are configured with IP addresses in the 172.16.7.0/24 range. How many broadcast domains are there?

   A. 0

   B. 1

   C. 2

   D. 20

8. A server is connected to a switch. Both the server's network interface card (NIC) and the switch port are configured for full-duplex communication. How many collision domains are there?

   A. 0

   B. 1

   C. 2

   D. 3

9. What's the default global aging time for the MAC address table?

   A. 30 seconds

   B. 5 minutes

   C. 1 hour

   D. 4 hours

10. What occurs when the MAC address table is full?

    A. All entries in the table are deleted.

    B. The oldest entries are aged out.

    C. Frames addressed to a MAC address that's not in the table are flooded.

    D. Frames addressed to a MAC address that's not in the table are dropped.

11. What is an Ethernet interface MTU?

    A. The minimum size of an Ethernet frame

    B. The maximum size of an Ethernet frame

    C. The speed of an Ethernet interface

    D. The maximum size of the Data field in an Ethernet frame

12. Which of the following is a function of a bridge?

    A. MAC-based routing

    B. IP-based routing

    C. Connecting two VLANs together

    D. Reducing the size of a broadcast domain

13. What information does the MAC address table store? (Choose two.)

   A. IP address

   B. VLAN

   C. ARP entries

   D. Interface

14. What does ARP do?

   A. Maps MAC addresses to IP addresses

   B. Maps MAC addresses to interfaces

   C. Maps IP addresses to MAC addresses

   D. Maps IP addresses to interfaces

   E. Maps MAC addresses to VLANs

15. Client A in VLAN 3 has the IP address 172.16.3.3/24. Server A in VLAN 4 has the IP address 172.16.3.10/24. What will occur if client A attempts to ping Server A? (Choose two.)

   A. The ping will succeed.

   B. Client A will send an ARP request for 172.16.3.10.

   C. The ping will fail.

   D. Server A will send an ARP reply.

16. What destination address is an ARP request sent to?

   A. The MAC address 0000.0000.0000

   B. The MAC address FFFF.FFFF.FFFF

   C. The MAC address 0100.5E01.0001

   D. The IP address 255.255.255.255

17. What destination address is an ARP reply sent to?

   A. The IP address that sourced the ARP request

   B. 255.255.255.255

   C. FFFF.FFFF.FFFF

   D. The MAC address that sourced the ARP request

18. What's the default ARP entry timeout on Cisco routers and switches?

   A. 5 minutes

   B. 1 hour

   C. 4 hours

   D. 6 hours

19. What's the purpose of TCP connection establishment?

   A. Error control

   B. Synchronization of sequence numbers

   C. Reservation of bandwidth

   D. Synchronization of polling intervals

20. What is the IP protocol number for TCP?

   A. 1

   B. 6

   C. 17

   D. 89

Spanning Tree Protocols

THE CCNP ENCOR EXAM OBJECTIVES COVERED IN THIS CHAPTER INCLUDE THE FOLLOWING:

Domain 3.0: Infrastructure

✓ 3.1 Layer 2

Unlike IP packets, Ethernet frames don't have a time-to-live (TTL) to prevent routing loops. That means if a LAN is configured in a physical loop, it may blindly forward the same frame over and over again. Switches don't keep track of frames they've already seen, so in a looped topology, a switch actually ends up multiplying the same frame in the network each time it forwards it! Eventually, this consumes all available bandwidth and pegs the CPU on each switch, causing a network meltdown.

The goal of STP is to impose a loop-free logical topology by strategically dropping certain Ethernet frames on specific interfaces (what STP calls ports) to prevent them from endlessly looping through the network. Radia Perlman began work on the original STP (802.1D) in 1984. Because this was prior to the widespread use of VLANs, 802.1D worked by simply blocking interfaces, a logical choice since the physical topology and the logical topology were the same. An interface could be a member of only a single LAN.

The advent of VLANs required a different approach. Each VLAN represented a different logical topology such that one VLAN might be configured in a loop while another VLAN would be loop-free. No longer could STP prevent loops by blocking interfaces. Instead, it had to determine the logical topology of each VLAN, and then selectively drop any Ethernet frames that might cause a loop—an approach called Per-VLAN Spanning Tree (PVST). Much of Spanning Tree's reputation for being complicated is due to this decoupling of the physical and logical topologies. It's not that Spanning Tree itself is hard to understand but that it behaves differently depending on the VLAN.

The first step to understanding and configuring Spanning Tree is to get a handle on the logical topology of each VLAN, so we'll start by looking at VLANs and trunking. After that, you'll learn about Rapid Per-VLAN Spanning Tree (RPVST+ or RSTP), which is the most common Spanning Tree protocol in use today. We'll then cover Multiple Spanning Tree Protocol (MSTP) and finally some Cisco-proprietary Spanning Tree extensions. You can classify each STP type by the approach it uses to prevent loops. There are three approaches:

- **802.1D**—Avoids a loop in the LAN.

- **PVST**—Prevents loops in a VLAN. Most of the time this is what people mean when they say "Spanning Tree."

- **MST**—Prevents loops in an arbitrary group of VLANs.

Keep these differences in mind as you read through this chapter.

The Need for Spanning Tree

There's nothing inherently problematic about having physical loops. The physical loops become problematic only when they create layer 2 loops. In Figure 2.1, all links are in VLAN 1, creating a loop between each pair of switches as well as among them. We could easily eliminate these layer 2 loops in two ways:

- By removing the physical loops
- By doing away with a stretched VLAN and turning each link into a routed (layer 3) link, where each link represents a separate broadcast domain

FIGURE 2.1   Physical looped topology

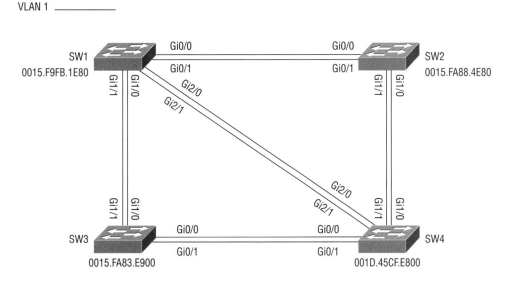

The latter option would eliminate any chance of a broadcast storm and, from a scalability and stability perspective, would be ideal. We'll cover routed topologies in Chapter 3, "Enterprise Network Design." Although a routed topology is ideal, implementing it requires planning and effort that the organization may not be willing or able to spend. Many therefore extend VLANs across several switches connected together, often in a loop for redundancy.

The goal of STP is to impose a loop-free logical topology by strategically dropping certain Ethernet frames on specific interfaces (what STP calls ports) to prevent them from endlessly looping through the network. You should already have at least a passing familiarity with Spanning Tree. Before continuing, take a moment to test your understanding by trying to calculate the root bridge and root ports for the topology in Figure 2.1.

To refresh your memory, the STP process is as follows:

1. All switches elect a root bridge. The root bridge doesn't block any traffic but forwards frames normally.

2. Each non-root switch determines its root port. The root port is the port that provides the lowest-cost path back to the root bridge. Any other ports leading back to the root block frames to prevent a loop from forming between the root and the non-root bridge.

3. Each connected pair of non-root switches elects a designated bridge for that link or segment. The designated bridge forwards frames over that link normally, whereas the other bridge doesn't forward any frames. The result is a logical loop-free topology, as shown in Figure 2.2.

FIGURE 2.2   Converged STP topology with SW1 as the root

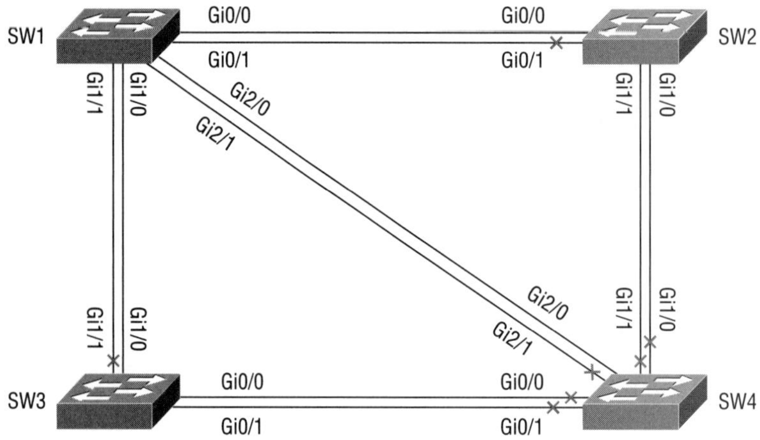

VLANs and Trunking

The first step in configuring or troubleshooting Spanning Tree is to ensure your VLANs and trunks are configured properly. Although we naturally think of Spanning Tree as an answer to loops caused by redundant physical connections, bridging loops actually only occur when a layer 2 loop exists in a VLAN. It's possible—indeed, preferable—to configure your trunks in such a way that they don't form a loop to begin with. We'll cover design considerations around VLANs and trunks in Chapter 3. But for Spanning Tree, recognize that the first step is to figure out what VLANs you should have on each switch and what trunks those VLANs should traverse.

Most networks have multiple VLANs stretching across 802.1Q trunks. Ideally, you'll selectively prune VLANs from trunks where you don't need those VLANs. Because any given trunk may carry some VLANs and not others, it's possible for there to be layer 2 loops in one VLAN but not in another. Consider the two VLANs in Figure 2.3. All trunks carry VLAN 3, creating a loop. But only the trunks between SW1 and SW2, SW3, and SW4 carry VLAN 2.

FIGURE 2.3   Multiple VLANs over 802.1Q trunks

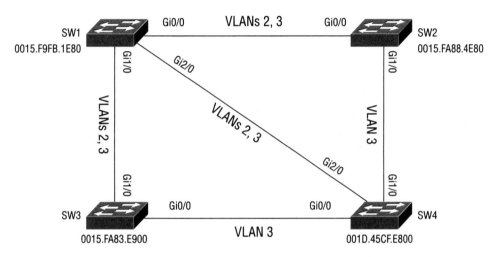

To eliminate the bridging loops in VLAN 3, Spanning Tree must block VLAN 3 traffic from traversing two links. (As a fun exercise, see if you can figure out which two.) VLAN 2 has no loops, so there's no need to block anything. Although we typically say that STP "blocks a port," this isn't quite accurate. If Spanning Tree were to truly block a port, it would block traffic for all VLANs, not just the one with the loop. This isn't what happens. What it does to break the loop is drop Ethernet frames ingressing a particular port on a particular VLAN. Hence, in order for Spanning Tree to be useful in a multi-VLAN environment, it must treat each VLAN independently.

Per-VLAN Spanning Tree+ (PVST+) is Cisco's implementation of the original Spanning Tree specification, IEEE 802.1D. PVST+ creates a separate Spanning Tree instance for each VLAN. You can configure each Spanning Tree instance differently so that a port blocked for one VLAN will be forwarding for another. This way, you can simultaneously use all available physical links. PVST+ is also sometimes called Shared Spanning Tree Protocol (SSTP).

RPVST+ performs the same basic function as PVST+ but has a faster convergence time—the speed at which each switch settles on which ports to block. As of IOS 15.2(4)E, RPVST+ is the default mode.

MST (802.1s) is similar to RPVST+, except instead of having one Spanning Tree instance per VLAN, MST lets you choose the specific VLANs that belong to each Spanning Tree instance. It's useful for when you have a large number of VLANs and want to minimize the number of Spanning Tree instances to conserve switch resources. In order for a pair of switches to run a PVST+, RPVST+, or MST instance for a VLAN, you need a confluence of several things:

All switches in the topology must have the VLAN configured.   It sounds obvious, but a Spanning Tree instance can't participate on a VLAN that doesn't exist. The VLAN must be configured locally on the switch before Spanning Tree can become active for that VLAN.

All switches must have trunks between them.   A trunk is always between only two switches. For both switches to establish a trunk, two things must occur:

Both switches must be configured to form a trunk.

Both must agree on the trunk encapsulation type to use 802.1Q or Cisco Inter-Switch Link **(ISL).**

The VLANs must be allowed on the trunk.   Simply establishing a trunk isn't sufficient to carry traffic for a VLAN. Both switches must have the VLAN allowed on the trunk. By default, all VLANs are allowed on a trunk, but it's possible to remove or prune a VLAN from a trunk. We'll look at an example of this in a moment.

Dynamic Trunking

Connected switches can form a trunk between themselves automatically using the Dynamic Trunking Protocol (DTP). DTP can operate in one of two modes:

- **Desirable**—DTP actively attempts to negotiate a trunk with the switch on the other end. An easy way to remember this is that the switch desires to form a trunk.

- **Auto**—DTP will not attempt to form a trunk but will respond to the other switch's request to form a trunk. This is the default mode.

You can configure the DTP mode using the `switchport mode dynamic` interface command:

```
SW4(config-if)#switchport mode dynamic ?
  auto       Set trunking mode dynamic negotiation parameter to AUTO
  desirable  Set trunking mode dynamic negotiation parameter to DESIRABLE
```

If the dynamic option is set to auto on both ends, the switches won't form a trunk. Instead, each switch's interface will fall back to static access mode for VLAN 1, unless you explicitly configure a different VLAN using the `switchport access vlan` interface command.

Cisco switches support two encapsulation protocols: 802.1Q and the Cisco-proprietary ISL. You should be using 802.1Q whenever possible, since it's standard and interoperates with pretty much every other piece of networking equipment out there. But be aware that Cisco switches still support ISL (for compatibility reasons, of course), so you may still encounter it.

You can explicitly set the encapsulation type or have the switches negotiate it. If both sides have the negotiate option set, they'll negotiate ISL. To ensure that they settle on 802.1Q, be sure to specify the dot1q option:

```
SW4(config-if)#switchport trunk encapsulation ?
  dot1q     Interface uses only 802.1q trunking encapsulation when trunking
  isl       Interface uses only ISL trunking encapsulation when trunking
  negotiate Device will negotiate trunking encapsulation with peer on
            Interface
```

Let's look at a quick example of an interface that's configured as dynamic desirable and has the encapsulation type set to 802.1Q:

```
SW4#show interfaces gi0/0 switchport
Name: Gi0/0
Switchport: Enabled
Administrative Mode: dynamic desirable
Operational Mode: trunk
Administrative Trunking Encapsulation: dot1q
Operational Trunking Encapsulation: dot1q
Negotiation of Trunking: On
! Output truncated
```

Administrative Mode and Administrative Trunking Encapsulation refer to the interface configuration. Operational Mode and Operational Trunking Encapsulation refer to what the switch has negotiated with its peer. In this case, both switches have negotiated an 802.1Q trunk. The operational parameters of the trunk can also be viewed using the following command:

```
SW4#show interfaces gigabitEthernet 0/0 trunk
```

Port	Mode	Encapsulation	Status	Native vlan
Gi0/0	desirable	802.1q	trunking	1

Unconditional Trunking

If you don't want to depend on DTP to negotiate a trunk on a specific interface, you can create a manual or unconditional 802.1Q trunk. To do this, you must first explicitly set the encapsulation type:

```
! Set the encapsulation type to 802.1Q
SW4(config-if)#switchport trunk encapsulation dot1q
```

Thereafter, you can create the unconditional trunk:

```
SW4(config-if)#switchport mode trunk
```

NOTE   If one interface is configured as dynamic auto or dynamic desirable and the other end is configured as an unconditional trunk, both switches will form a trunk.

In order for the trunk to be truly unconditional, both switches must have this configuration. To verify, use the show interfaces command:

```
SW4#show interfaces gi0/0 switchport
Name: Gi0/0
Switchport: Enabled
Administrative Mode: trunk
Operational Mode: trunk
Administrative Trunking Encapsulation: dot1q
Operational Trunking Encapsulation: dot1q
Negotiation of Trunking: On
```

Administrative Mode is now trunk. What may surprise you is that Negotiation of Trunking is set to On. Creating an unconditional trunk doesn't disable DTP. If the switch on the other end of the link attempts to negotiate a trunk—that is, if its interface is in dynamic desirable mode—both switches will still negotiate a trunk. If you're concerned about trunks forming unexpectedly, you can disable DTP as follows:

```
SW4(config-if)#switchport nonegotiate
SW4(config-if)#do show interface gi0/0 switchport | i Negotiation
Negotiation of Trunking: Off
```

It's perfectly safe to disable DTP on all interfaces and explicitly create your unconditional trunks instead. Also, it's a wise idea to disable DTP on interfaces that will connect to end-user devices. If a malicious attacker is able to connect a device and form a trunk, they can potentially sniff traffic traversing all VLANs active on that trunk.

Active and Allowed VLANs

In order for two switches to participate in a Spanning Tree instance for a VLAN, they must each have the VLAN configured and the VLAN must be allowed on the trunk. For example, to have a Spanning Tree instance for VLAN 100 between SW1 and SW2, both need VLAN 100 configured:

```
SW1#conf t
Enter configuration commands, one per line.  End with CNTL/Z.
SW1(config)#vlan 100
SW1(config-vlan)#no shut
%VLAN 100 is not shutdown.
SW1(config-vlan)#end
```

```
SW1#show vlan id 100

VLAN Name                             Status    Ports
---- -------------------------------- --------- -------------------------------
100  VLAN0100                         active    Gi0/0, Gi0/1, Gi1/0, Gi1/1
                                                Gi2/0, Gi2/1
```

VLAN 100 is active on the switch, meaning it's not shut down. Notice that it's active on six ports, all of which are terminating 802.1Q trunks. Using Gi0/0 as an example, we can see that VLAN 100 is allowed and active on the trunk:

```
SW1#show interfaces gi0/0 trunk

Port       Mode             Encapsulation  Status       Native vlan
Gi0/0      on               802.1q         trunking     1

Port       Vlans allowed on trunk
Gi0/0      1-4094

Port       Vlans allowed and active in management domain
Gi0/0      1-10,100

Port       Vlans in spanning tree forwarding state and not pruned
Gi0/0      1-10,100
```

A VLAN must be configured on the switch before it can be allowed or active on a trunk. All VLANs are allowed on an 802.1Q trunk by default, but it is possible to remove or prune a VLAN, like so:

```
SW1(config)#int gi0/0
SW1(config-if)#switchport trunk allowed vlan remove 100
SW1(config-if)#do show interfaces gi0/0 trunk

Port       Mode             Encapsulation  Status       Native vlan
Gi0/0      on               802.1q         trunking     1

Port       Vlans allowed on trunk
Gi0/0      1-99,101-4094

Port       Vlans allowed and active in management domain
Gi0/0      1-10

Port       Vlans in spanning tree forwarding state and not pruned
Gi0/0      1-10
```

To allow a VLAN on a trunk, replace remove in the preceding command with add:

```
SW1(config-if)#switchport trunk allowed vlan add 100
```

Be careful with this command. If you leave out add, then the trunk will allow *only* VLAN 100 and prune all other VLANs.

Rapid Per-VLAN Spanning Tree

RPVST+ is Cisco's implementation of the IEEE 802.1w specification titled "Rapid Reconfiguration of Spanning Tree." Beginning with IOS 15.2(4)E, RPVST+ replaces PVST+ as the default Spanning Tree mode. There are some significant differences between the two that we'll cover in a moment. But the configuration commands for RPVST+ and PVST+ are almost identical. PVST+ still exists only for backward compatibility with older equipment, but whenever possible, you should use RPVST+. If you encounter an older IOS version that has PVST+ enabled, you can enable RPVST+ by issuing the global configuration command spanning-tree mode rapid-pvst.

Electing the Root Bridge

The first step in the Spanning Tree process is to elect the root bridge. Each switch has a base MAC address, also known as a burned-in address (BIA). Unlike an interface MAC address, the BIA is tied to the switch itself, not a particular interface. A bridge is elected as the root if

- **It has the lowest priority**—You must configure the priority per VLAN in multiples of 4,096. The reason is that the VLAN ID is appended to the configured priority. The default configured bridge priority is 32,768, so for VLAN 1, the priority would be 32,769 (32,768 + 1), the priority for VLAN 2 would be 32,770, and so on. The priority value can range from 0 to 61,440. All bridges have equal priority by default.

- **It has the lowest base MAC address**—Assuming the priorities of all the bridges are equal, the bridge with the lowest BIA becomes root.

Here's how the election process works. Initially, each switch assumes it is the root. It places all of its ports into a listening state, and every two seconds, sends a configuration/ Hello Bridge Protocol Data Unit (BPDU) out of every nonblocking port. The BPDU is addressed to the multicast MAC address 0100.0ccc.cccd and sourced from the interface MAC. The BPDU itself contains a transmitting bridge identifier (ID) that uniquely identifies the sending switch. The transmitting bridge identifier includes

- Transmitting bridge priority
- Transmitting bridge BIA
- VLAN ID

The BPDU also contains a root identifier that includes the following:

- Root priority
- Root BIA
- VLAN ID

Because each switch considers itself the root, the root identifier and transmitting bridge ID information is initially identical. The following is a BPDU from a switch advertising itself as the root bridge:

```
Spanning Tree Protocol
    Protocol Identifier: Spanning Tree Protocol (0x0000)
    Protocol Version Identifier: Rapid Spanning Tree (2)
    BPDU Type: Rapid/Multiple Spanning Tree (0x02)
    BPDU flags: 0x3c, Forwarding, Learning, Port Role: Designated
    Root Identifier: 32768 / 1 / 00:15:f9:fb:1e:80
        Root Bridge Priority: 32768
        Root Bridge System ID Extension: 1
        Root Bridge System ID: Cisco_fb:1e:80 (00:15:f9:fb:1e:80)
    Root Path Cost: 0
    Bridge Identifier: 32768 / 1 / 00:15:f9:fb:1e:80
        Bridge Priority: 32768
        Bridge System ID Extension: 1
        Bridge System ID: Cisco_fb:1e:80 (00:15:f9:fb:1e:80)
    Port identifier: 0x8001
    Message Age: 0
    Max Age: 20
    Hello Time: 2
    Forward Delay: 15
    Version 1 Length: 0
```

Notice that the root ID and the transmitting bridge ID are the same, indicating that the switch believes it's the root. However, if a switch receives a BPDU with a superior root ID, it stops advertising itself as the root. Instead, it begins advertising the bridge with the superior bridge ID as the root. In the end, all switches in the topology will advertise the same switch—the one with the lowest bridge ID—as the root. That bridge wins the election and becomes the root.

> An interesting implication of the election process is that older switches tend to be elected as the root. It's not unheard of for someone to purchase a used replacement switch and plug it into an existing network of newer switches, only to have the used switch take over as root and cause a temporary network outage.

Imagining this process is difficult, so let's look at an example. Consider the switches shown in Figure 2.2. Assuming all switches have equal priority, SW1 would be elected root because it has the lowest base MAC address.

```
SW1#show spanning-tree vlan 1


VLAN0001
  Spanning tree enabled protocol rstp
  Root ID    Priority    32769
             Address     0015.f9fb.1e80
             This bridge is the root
             Hello Time   2 sec  Max Age 20 sec  Forward Delay 15 sec

  Bridge ID  Priority    32769  (priority 32768 sys-id-ext 1)
             Address     0015.f9fb.1e80
             Hello Time   2 sec  Max Age 20 sec  Forward Delay 15 sec
             Aging Time  300 sec
```

Because this spanning tree instance is for VLAN 1, the priority for this bridge is 32,769—the default of 32,768 plus the VLAN ID. If you don't want SW1 to be the root, you can increase its priority in increments of 4,096, like so:

```
SW1#configure t
Enter configuration commands, one per line.  End with CNTL/Z.
SW1(config)#spanning-tree vlan 1 priority ?
  <0-61440>  bridge priority in increments of 4096

SW1(config)#spanning-tree vlan 1 priority 36864
```

Notice that 32,768 + 4,096 = 36,864. IOS won't allow priorities that aren't in increments of 4,096. In short order, SW3 (bridge ID 0015.fa83.e900) takes over as the root:

```
SW1#show spanning-tree vlan 1


VLAN0001
  Spanning tree enabled protocol rstp
  Root ID    Priority    32769
             Address     0015.fa83.e900
             Cost        4
             Port        5 (GigabitEthernet1/0)
             Hello Time   2 sec  Max Age 20 sec  Forward Delay 15 sec
```

```
Bridge ID  Priority    36865  (priority 36864 sys-id-ext 1)
           Address     0015.f9fb.1e80
           Hello Time   2 sec  Max Age 20 sec  Forward Delay 15 sec
           Aging Time  300 sec
```

Refer to Figure 2.4. Even though SW3's base MAC address is higher—0015.fa83.e900 is greater than 0015.f9fb.1e80—it's elected because it has a lower priority than SW1, and a lower base MAC address than SW2 and SW4.

FIGURE 2.4   Converged STP topology with SW3 as the new root

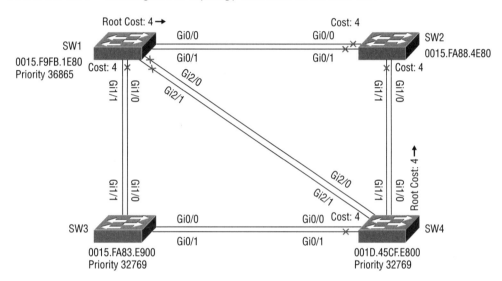

Alternatively, you could select the root bridge you want by decreasing its priority to less than that of the other bridges. For example, if you wanted to specifically choose SW3 as the root bridge, you could decrease its priority to 28,672 (32,768 − 4,096).

> The bridge with the next lowest bridge ID to the root gets the status of the designated bridge and is also called the *secondary root bridge*. The designated bridge stands by, waiting to take over in case the primary root bridge fails or ceases to have the best bridge ID, for example, if you were to increase its priority.

Calculating the Root Ports

The root bridge always has all of its ports in a forwarding state, so it's up to the non-root bridges to prevent bridging loops. Each non-root bridge must determine its root port—the port that has the lowest-cost path to the root bridge. For switches connected directly to the root, this is easy. If a non-root bridge has only one interface to the root, that interface becomes the root port. On the other hand, if a bridge has multiple connections to the root, only the one with the lowest cost to the root will become the root port. All other ports leading back to the root bridge are blocked, thus preventing a loop.

For a switch connected directly to the root, the root port will be the port with the lowest cost. If the costs are equal, the root port will be the one with the lowest designated port ID. To see how this works, refer to Figure 2.5. SW3 is the root for VLAN 1. SW1 has two direct links to the root: Gi1/0 and Gi1/1. The port with the lowest cost to the root will become the root port. The port cost is based on interface bandwidth, as shown in Table 2.1.

TABLE 2.1 STP port costs by speed

Speed	Cost
10 Mbps	100
100 Mbps	19
1 Gbps	4
10 Gbps	2

FIGURE 2.5 VLAN 1 topology with SW3 as root

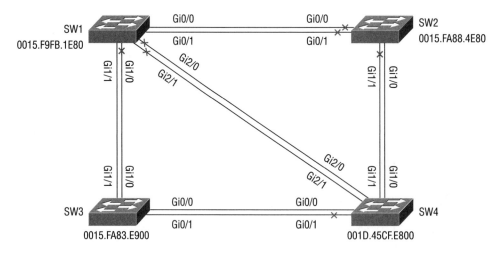

Because Both of SW1's interfaces facing SW3 are 1 Gbps interfaces, they each have a cost of 4, as shown in the following output from SW1:

```
SW1#show spanning-tree vlan 1

VLAN0001
  Spanning tree enabled protocol rstp
  Root ID    Priority    32769
             Address     0015.fa83.e900
             Cost        4
             Port        5 (GigabitEthernet1/0)
             Hello Time   2 sec  Max Age 20 sec  Forward Delay 15 sec

  Bridge ID  Priority    36865  (priority 36864 sys-id-ext 1)
             Address     0015.f9fb.1e80
             Hello Time   2 sec  Max Age 20 sec  Forward Delay 15 sec
             Aging Time  300 sec

Interface           Role Sts Cost      Prio.Nbr Type
------------------- ---- --- --------- -------- --------------------------------
Gi0/0               Desg FWD 4         128.1    P2p
Gi0/1               Desg FWD 4         128.2    P2p
Gi0/2               Desg FWD 4         128.3    P2p
Gi0/3               Desg FWD 4         128.4    P2p
Gi1/0               Root FWD 4         128.5    P2p
Gi1/1               Altn BLK 4         128.6    P2p
! Output truncated
```

STP must block one port, and the output shows that Gi1/0 is the root port. Why was Gi1/0 selected instead of Gi1/1? Here's where confusion sets in for a lot of people. You might assume that Gi1/0 was selected because the port ID—listed in the Prio.Nbr column—is lower for Gi1/0 than Gi1/1. But this is *not* the reason. Observe the following output from SW1:

```
SW1#show spanning-tree interface gigabitEthernet 1/0 detail
 Port 5 (GigabitEthernet1/0) of VLAN0001 is root forwarding
   Port path cost 4, Port priority 128, Port Identifier 128.5.
   Designated root has priority 32769, address 0015.fa83.e900
   Designated bridge has priority 32769, address 0015.fa83.e900
   Designated port id is 128.5, designated path cost 0
   Timers: message age 16, forward delay 0, hold 0
   Number of transitions to forwarding state: 1
   Link type is shared by default
```

```
    BPDU: sent 38, received 293
SW1#show spanning-tree interface gigabitEthernet 1/1 detail
 Port 6 (GigabitEthernet1/1) of VLAN0001 is alternate blocking
   Port path cost 4, Port priority 128, Port Identifier 128.6.
   Designated root has priority 32769, address 0015.fa83.e900
   Designated bridge has priority 32769, address 0015.fa83.e900
   Designated port id is 128.6, designated path cost 0
   Timers: message age 16, forward delay 0, hold 0
   Number of transitions to forwarding state: 0
   Link type is shared by default
   BPDU: sent 4, received 295
```

Notice that for each port there are two slightly different references to a port ID:

- Gi1/0
  - Port ID: 128.5
  - Designated port ID: 128.5
- Gi1/1
  - Port ID: 128.6
  - Designated port ID: 128.6

The port ID is what SW1 has configured on its interface, whereas the designated port ID is what SW3 has configured on its facing interface. SW1's STP instance uses the designated port ID to select the root port. How does SW1 know SW3's port ID? It's transmitted in the BPDU from SW3. In other words, the root port is determined by the port ID on the opposite end of the link.

Calculating the Root Ports of Indirectly Connected Switches

It's fairly easy to determine the root port for a bridge that's directly connected to the root. But what about the root port of a bridge that's indirectly connected, perhaps separated by one or two switches? Looking at Figure 2.4, you can see that SW2 has four possible paths back to the root:

- SW1—BIA 0015.f9fb.1e80, bridge priority 36865
  - Gi0/0
  - Gi0/1
- SW4—BIA 001d.45cf.e800, bridge priority 32769
  - Gi1/0
  - Gi1/1

SW2 will first consider which port offers the lowest cost to the root, which is the sum of all interface costs between SW2 and the root. Let's first look at the path through SW1.

1. SW2 Gi0/0 or Gi0/1 has an interface cost of 4.

2. SW1 Gi1/0 (root port) has an interface cost of 4.

SW2's path through SW1 to the root has a total cost of 8. Now let's consider the path through SW4.

1. SW2 Gi1/0 or Gi1/1 has an interface cost of 4.

2. SW4 Gi0/0 has an interface cost of 4.

SW2's path through SW4 to the root also has a cost of 8. Because both path costs are equal, SW2 will choose the bridge with the lowest bridge ID, which in this case is SW4. Although SW4 has a higher BIA than SW1, it has a lower priority. Because the costs are equal, SW2 will select the port with the lowest port priority as the root port, as shown in the following output:

```
SW2#show spanning-tree vlan 1 interface gigabitEthernet 1/0 detail
 Port 5 (GigabitEthernet1/0) of VLAN0001 is root forwarding
   Port path cost 4, Port priority 128, Port Identifier 128.5.
   Designated root has priority 32769, address 0015.fa83.e900
   Designated bridge has priority 32769, address 001d.45cf.e800
   Designated port id is 128.5, designated path cost 4
   Timers: message age 15, forward delay 0, hold 0
   Number of transitions to forwarding state: 1
   Link type is shared by default
   BPDU: sent 37, received 823
SW2#show spanning-tree vlan 1 interface gigabitEthernet 1/1 detail
 Port 6 (GigabitEthernet1/1) of VLAN0001 is alternate blocking
   Port path cost 4, Port priority 128, Port Identifier 128.6.
   Designated root has priority 32769, address 0015.fa83.e900
   Designated bridge has priority 32769, address 001d.45cf.e800
   Designated port id is 128.6, designated path cost 4
   Timers: message age 15, forward delay 0, hold 0
   Number of transitions to forwarding state: 0
   Link type is shared by default
   BPDU: sent 3, received 822
```

SW4 is advertising a port priority of 128.5 on Gi1/0, which is lower than the port priority of 128.6 that it's advertising on Gi1/1. SW2 will thus select Gi1/0 as the root port. But suppose that you wanted Gi1/1 to be the root port instead. Although there are a few ways to do this, I recommend one of the following:

- Decrease the port cost of Gi1/1 on SW2

- Decrease the port priority of Gi1/1 on SW4

Alternatively, you could increase the port cost or priority, but it's best not to. If you were to add another connection between the switches later—say using a lower port number like Gi0/3—it would then become the root port. By decreasing the port cost or priority, you can ensure that your desired port always remains the root port.

Modifying Port Cost

To get SW2 to use Gi1/1 as the root port, you can decrease the port cost from 4 to 2:

```
SW2(config)#int gigabitEthernet 1/1
SW2(config-if)#spanning-tree vlan 1 cost ?
  <1-200000000>  Change an interface's per VLAN spanning tree path cost

SW2(config-if)#spanning-tree vlan 1 cost 2
SW2(config-if)#do show spanning-tree vlan 1


VLAN0001
  Spanning tree enabled protocol rstp
  Root ID    Priority    32769
             Address     0015.fa83.e900
             Cost        6
             Port        6 (GigabitEthernet1/1)
             Hello Time   2 sec  Max Age 20 sec  Forward Delay 15 sec

  Bridge ID  Priority    32769  (priority 32768 sys-id-ext 1)
             Address     0015.fa88.4e80
             Hello Time   2 sec  Max Age 20 sec  Forward Delay 15 sec
             Aging Time  300 sec

Interface           Role Sts Cost      Prio.Nbr Type
------------------- ---- --- --------- -------- --------------------------------
Gi0/0               Altn BLK 4         128.1    P2p
Gi0/1               Altn BLK 4         128.2    P2p
Gi0/2               Desg BLK 4         128.3    P2p
Gi0/3               Desg BLK 4         128.4    P2p
Gi1/0               Altn BLK 4         128.5    P2p
Gi1/1               Root FWD 2         128.6    P2p
! Output truncated
```

Gi1/1 is now the root port. Let's change it back to 4:

```
SW2(config-if)#spanning-tree vlan 1 cost 4
SW2(config-if)#do show spanning-tree vlan 1
```

```
VLAN0001
  Spanning tree enabled protocol rstp
  Root ID    Priority    32769
             Address     0015.fa83.e900
             Cost        8
             Port        5 (GigabitEthernet1/0)
             Hello Time   2 sec  Max Age 20 sec   Forward Delay 15 sec

  Bridge ID  Priority    32769  (priority 32768 sys-id-ext 1)
             Address     0015.fa88.4e80
             Hello Time   2 sec  Max Age 20 sec   Forward Delay 15 sec
             Aging Time  300 sec

Interface           Role Sts Cost      Prio.Nbr Type
------------------- ---- --- --------- -------- --------------------------------
Gi0/0               Altn BLK 4          128.1    P2p
Gi0/1               Altn BLK 4          128.2    P2p
Gi0/2               Desg BLK 4          128.3    P2p
Gi0/3               Desg BLK 4          128.4    P2p
Gi1/0               Root FWD 4          128.5    P2p
Gi1/1               Altn BLK 4          128.6    P2p
! Output truncated
```

Gi1/0 is once again the root port.

Modifying Port Priority

You can change the port priority for Gi1/1 on SW4 as follows:

```
SW4(config)#int gigabitEthernet 1/1
SW4(config-if)#spanning-tree vlan 1 port-priority ?
  <0-224>   port priority in increments of 32

SW4(config-if)#spanning-tree vlan 1 port-priority 64
```

On SW2, you can see the designated port ID for Gi1/1 is now 64.6, and it's the root port:

```
SW2#show spanning-tree vlan 1 interface gi1/1 detail
 Port 6 (GigabitEthernet1/1) of VLAN0001 is root forwarding
   Port path cost 4, Port priority 128, Port Identifier 128.6.
   Designated root has priority 32769, address 0015.fa83.e900
   Designated bridge has priority 32769, address 001d.45cf.e800
   Designated port id is 64.6, designated path cost 4
```

```
Timers: message age 15, forward delay 0, hold 0
Number of transitions to forwarding state: 3
Link type is shared by default
BPDU: sent 43, received 1851
```

The converged topology is shown in Figure 2.6.

FIGURE 2.6 Converged VLAN 1 topology with SW2 Gi1/0 blocking

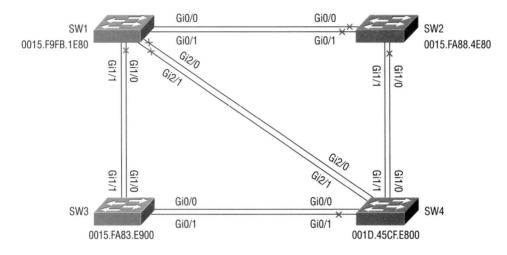

Calculating Blocked Ports

Now we come to perhaps the easiest part of Spanning Tree: determining which remaining ports to block. Consider the connections between SW1 and SW4. Both are directly connected to the root, SW3, and have no need of a link to each other. Because SW1 has the higher bridge priority, it will block both its ports, like so:

```
SW1#show spanning-tree vlan 1 | i Gi2/0|Gi2/1
Gi2/0              Altn BLK 4          128.9      P2p
Gi2/1              Altn BLK 4          128.10     P2p
```

Blocked ports don't forward traffic, but they still receive and process BPDUs. This ensures that every bridge can learn about changes to the Spanning Tree topology. SW4 has a lower bridge priority and has both its ports forwarding:

```
SW4#show spanning-tree vlan 1 | i Gi2/0|Gi2/1
Gi2/0              Desg FWD 4          128.9      P2p
Gi2/1              Desg FWD 4          128.10     P2p
```

Any non-root ports that aren't blocking are called designated ports. The job of designated ports is to forward BPDUs from the root bridge so that Spanning Tree can reconverge in the event of a topology change.

Port States

In RSTP, a port can have one of three states: learning, forwarding, or discarding. A port eventually settles into either a forwarding or discarding state. The learning state is transitory and only occurs when RSTP is in the process of determining which ports to block.

- **Discarding**—The port processes incoming BPDUs but doesn't send them. IOS lists a port in the discarding state as BLK or blocking. This is the initial state for all ports.

- **Learning**—The port sends and receives BPDUs but doesn't forward data traffic. The switch looks at ingressing Ethernet frames and adds the source MAC addresses to its MAC address table.

- **Forwarding**—Sends and receives BPDUs, and it also passes normal user and control plane traffic.

Port Roles

In addition to the root and designated port roles, RSTP has two additional port roles you need to know: alternate and backup.

- **Alternate**—An alternate port provides an alternate path to the root. If a root port fails, the switch will place the best (lowest cost) alternate port into a forwarding state. This lets the topology reconverge in a matter of milliseconds.

- **Backup**—You're unlikely to ever see a backup port role, except on an exam. Imagine that two ports are connected to a hub and hence are on the same segment. The port with the lowest cost—or if the costs are equal, the port with the lowest designated port priority— will be the designated port. The other port connected to the segment will be the backup.

Link Types

One way that RSTP achieves a fast convergence time is by avoiding putting some ports through the three-step process of discarding, learning, and forwarding. The idea is that by predefining ports that are directly connected to another switch or to an edge device, RSTP can more quickly figure out which ports to block and which to transition to the forwarding state. RSTP defines three link types:

- Point-to-point (P2P)
- P2P Edge
- Shared

Point-to-Point (P2P)

The P2P link type indicates that the link is a link between only two switches. Thus, each switch knows that it needs to negotiate with only one switch on the other end of the link. RSTP will automatically set the P2P link type on any full-duplex link. You can manually set the P2P link type using the interface command `spanning-tree link-type point-to-point`.

P2P Edge

This type is reserved for edge devices that don't run Spanning Tree, such as computers, servers, and phones. An edge port skips over the learning state and transitions instantly to a forwarding state. RSTP still sends BPDUs on edge ports just in case there's a switch on the other end. But if it receives a BPDU, it will change the port type to a normal Spanning Tree port. If you're familiar with PortFast, this is essentially the same thing. In fact, IOS uses the portfast keyword to configure an edge port, as follows:

```
SW2(config)#int gi1/3
SW2(config-if)#spanning-tree portfast edge ?
  trunk  Enable portfast edge on the interface even in trunk mode
  <cr>
SW2(config-if)#spanning-tree portfast edge trunk
%Warning: portfast should only be enabled on ports connected to a single
 host. Connecting hubs, concentrators, switches, bridges, etc... to this
 interface  when portfast is enabled, can cause temporary bridging loops.
 Use with CAUTION
```

Keep in mind that an edge port can be an access port or a trunk port that's connected to multiple devices. If the port is a single-VLAN access port, you should use the spanning-tree portfast edge interface command. But if it's a trunked interface—such as one connected to a server running virtual machines or a computer plugged in behind an IP phone on a separate voice VLAN—you must use the spanning-tree portfast edge trunk interface command.

Shared

The Shared port type is one you shouldn't expect to see very often. It's for a port that may be connected to multiple devices, usually via a hub. RSTP considers any half-duplex link to be shared. In this case, RSTP falls back to timer-based 802.1D behavior and may take up to 50 seconds to converge.

Multiple Spanning Tree

MST is designed as an alternative to PVST+. MST allows you to reduce the number of Spanning Tree instances required when you have a large number of VLANs. In per-VLAN Spanning Tree, you must have one Spanning Tree instance per VLAN. For example, if you have 500 VLANs, you must have 500 instances of Spanning Tree.

MST, on the other hand, lets you map multiple VLANs to a single Spanning Tree instance. To keep track of instances, MST uses instance numbers. Because VLAN-to-instance mappings are arbitrary, all switches in the topology must agree on the mappings.

To deal with this, MST uses regions. An MST region is a collection of MST instances that share three common values:

- Region name
- Revision number
- List of VLAN-to-instance mappings

   As long as all three parameters match on each switch in the topology, they're considered to be in the same region and will form a stable Spanning Tree topology. When you enable MST, it spawns a default Spanning Tree instance called MST0. By default, MST0 maps to all VLANs (1-4094). MST0 is also known as the Internal Spanning Tree (IST). The following example on SW1 illustrates how you could map VLANs 1, 3, and 5 to instance MST1, and VLANs 2, 4, and 6 to MST2:

```
! Enable MST
SW1(config)#spanning-tree mode mst
! Enter MST configuration mode
SW1(config)#spanning-tree mst configuration
! Set the region name to myRegion
SW1(config-mst)#name myRegion
! Map VLANs 1, 3, and 5 to instance 1
SW1(config-mst)#instance 1 vlan 1,3,5
! Map VLANs 2,4 and 6 to instance 2
SW1(config-mst)#instance 2 vlan 2,4,6
! Configure the revision number
SW1(config-mst)#revision 1
! Display the pending configuration
SW1(config-mst)#show
Pending MST configuration
Name      [myRegion]
Revision  1    Instances configured 3

Instance  Vlans mapped
--------  -----------------------------------------------------------------------
0         7-4094
1         1,3,5
2         2,4,6
          -----------------------------------------------------------------------
! Remember to issue the exit command to save the MST configuration to the
running config
SW1(config-mst)#exit
! Exit global configuration mode, then save the running configuration
SW1(config)#exit
SW1#write memory
```

When you map multiple VLANs to an instance, at least one of those VLANs must be active and allowed on the trunk between the switches in the topology. This implies that at least one of the VLANs mapped to an instance must also be configured in the switch's local VLAN database. In the preceding example, VLAN 2, 4, or 6 must be allowed and active in order for MST2 to be active.

Behind the scenes, each MST instance uses RSTP.

Root Bridges and Port Priority

Each MST instance has its own root bridge. By having multiple instances with different root bridges, you can distribute the traffic load across all the links. Using Figure 2.7 as an example, you could make SW1 the root for MST1 and SW4 the root for MST2.

FIGURE 2.7   Multiple Spanning Tree

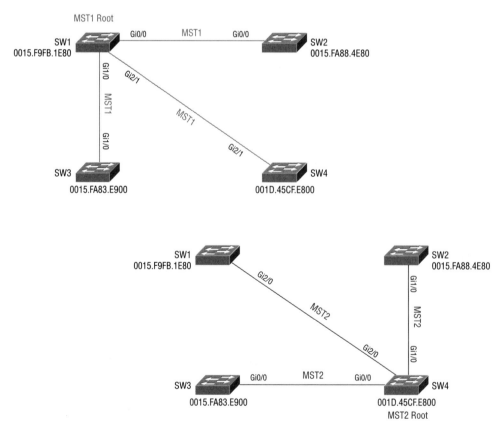

The command for adjusting the MST bridge priority is almost identical for (R)PVST+. The difference is that instead of specifying a VLAN, you specify the MST instance. For example, to make SW1 the root for MST1, you would do the following:

```
Enter configuration commands, one per line.  End with CNTL/Z.
SW1(config)#spanning-tree mst 1 priority 0
SW1(config)#exit
SW1#show spanning-tree mst 1


##### MST1    vlans mapped:   1,3,5
Bridge        address 0015.f9fb.1e80  priority     1     (0 sysid 1)
Root          this switch for MST1
! Output truncated
```

In Figure 2.7, SW1 and SW4 are directly connected via two links. To ensure that both links are used, we'll lower the MST1 port priority for Gi2/1 on SW1. This will cause SW4 to use the link for MST1 instead of blocking it. The command for adjusting the port priority is also much the same as in (R)PVST+:

```
SW1(config)#interface gi2/1
SW1(config-if)#spanning-tree mst 1 port-priority 32
```

Internal Spanning Tree

MST can interoperate with other Spanning Tree protocols and even other MST regions. When an MST region is connected to switches in another MST region, or simply not running MST at all, it will make the MST region appear as a single RPVST+ or PVST+ topology, depending on what the peer switch is running. This is called *PVST simulation*. To illustrate, let's change SW2 back to RPVST+ mode:

```
SW2(config)#spanning-tree mode rapid-pvst
SW2(config)#do show spanning-tree vlan 1-10 summary
Switch is in rapid-pvst mode
Root bridge for VLAN0001 is 32768.0015.f9fb.1e80.
Root bridge for VLAN0002 is 32768.0015.f9fb.1e80.
Root bridge for VLAN0003 is 32768.0015.f9fb.1e80.
Root bridge for VLAN0004 is 32768.0015.f9fb.1e80.
Root bridge for VLAN0005 is 32768.0015.f9fb.1e80.
Root bridge for VLAN0006 is 32768.0015.f9fb.1e80.
Root bridge for VLAN0007 is 32768.0015.f9fb.1e80.
Root bridge for VLAN0008 is 32768.0015.f9fb.1e80.
Root bridge for VLAN0009 is 32768.0015.f9fb.1e80.
Root bridge for VLAN0010 is 32768.0015.f9fb.1e80.
! Output truncated
```

SW1 advertises itself as the root for all VLANs, even though in the MST topology it's only the root for the MST1 instance. If a switch outside of the MST topology attempts to become root, the MST switches will block the ports, placing them into a PVST Simulation Inconsistent state. For example, let's try to make SW2 the root for VLAN 1:

```
SW2(config)#spanning-tree vlan 1 priority 0
! SW1 will block the port that's connected to SW2 and place it into a broken
state, resulting in no traffic traversing the link:
*Sep 15 01:01:21.412: %SPANTREE-2-PVSTSIM_FAIL: Blocking root port Gi0/0:
Inconsistent inferior PVST BPDU received on VLAN 7, claiming root 32775:0015.
fa88.4e80


SW1#show spanning-tree int gi0/0

Mst Instance           Role Sts Cost      Prio.Nbr Type
-------------------    ---- --- ---------  -------- --------------------------------

MST0                   Root BKN*20000      128.1    P2p Bound(PVST) *PVST_Inc

MST1                   Mstr BKN*20000      128.1    P2p Bound(PVST) *PVST_Inc

MST2                   Mstr BKN*20000      128.1    P2p Bound(PVST) *PVST_Inc


SW1#show spanning-tree inconsistentports

Name                   Interface                 Inconsistency
-------------------    -----------------------   -----------------

MST0                   GigabitEthernet0/0        PVST Sim. Inconsistent

MST1                   GigabitEthernet0/0        PVST Sim. Inconsistent

MST2                   GigabitEthernet0/0        PVST Sim. Inconsistent


Number of inconsistent ports (segments) in the system : 3
```

Native VLAN

On any 802.1Q trunk, the native VLAN is the VLAN whose traffic isn't tagged. By default, this is VLAN 1. VLAN 1 is a special VLAN that plays a crucial role in many protocols, including Spanning Tree. If you're using an 802.1Q trunk, by default VLAN 1 traffic is sent untagged. You can force a switch to tag native VLAN traffic using the global configuration command vlan dot1q tag native. This is useful to prevent untagged traffic from inadvertently slipping into VLAN 1, as well as to prevent VLAN hopping attacks.

VLAN 1 always exists on all switches, and you can't disable it. But you can prune it from a trunk. If you prune VLAN 1 from a trunk on a switch running (R)PVST+, the switch won't forward any BPDUs for VLAN 1. However, if the switch is running MST, it will continue to forward BPDUs for VLAN 1—untagged—to maintain compatibility with switches that don't support 802.1Q trunks.

Topology Change Detection

When a non-edge port on a bridge transitions to the forwarding state—something that can happen if a new switch is added, for example—it notifies other bridges in the topology in order to trigger a reconvergence. The bridge flushes any MAC addresses associated with the port and begins sending BPDUs with the topology change (TC) bit set. It also begins a timer called the TC While timer that's twice the value of its Hello time (by default, the Hello time is 2 seconds, so the TC While timer would be 4 seconds). It continues sending BPDUs with the TC bit set until the TC While timer expires.

When another bridge receives a BPDU with the TC bit set, it clears its MAC address table for all ports except the port on which it received the BPDU. It begins its own TC While timer and sends BPDUs with the TC bit set out of all of its designated ports and its root port. Eventually, all bridges become aware of the topology change.

Spanning Tree Extensions

Cisco has added a few extra features to IOS that let you customize Spanning Tree behavior and prevent loops in certain edge cases:

- Root Guard
- BPDU Guard
- BPDU Filter
- Unidirectional Link Detection and Loop Guard

Root Guard

Root Guard is a Spanning Tree extension that prevents another switch from becoming root. This can happen if someone adds a new switch with a lower bridge priority. You configure Root Guard on a per-interface basis. If the switch receives a superior BPDU on the port, it will place the port into a Root Inconsistent state and stop forwarding traffic to or from that port. Enable Root Guard by executing the interface command `spanning-tree guard root` on any ports that you do not want to become root ports.

For an example of how Root Guard works, refer to Figure 2.5 from our discussion on RSTP. SW3 is the current root. To prevent SW2 from becoming the root, we can configure Root Guard on the following ports:

- SW1:
    - Gi0/0
    - Gi0/1
- SW4:
    - Gi1/0
    - Gi1/1

Let's configure Root Guard on SW1:

```
SW1(config)#int range gi0/0-1
! Enable root guard on the interfaces
SW1(config-if-range)#spanning-tree guard root
! Enable Spanning Tree events debugging
SW1(config-if)#do debug spanning-tree events
```

And on SW4:

```
SW4(config)#int range gi1/0-1
! Enable root guard on the interfaces
SW4(config-if-range)#spanning-tree guard root
SW4(config-if-range)#
*Sep 13 21:40:28.908: %SPANTREE-2-ROOTGUARD_CONFIG_CHANGE: Root guard enabled on
port GigabitEthernet1/0.
*Sep 13 21:40:28.921: %SPANTREE-2-ROOTGUARD_CONFIG_CHANGE: Root guard enabled on
port GigabitEthernet1/1.do
SW4(config-if-range)#do debug spanning-tree events
Spanning Tree event debugging is on
```

SW3 is the current root. Let's attempt to make SW2 the root:

```
SW2(config)#spanning-tree vlan 1 priority 0
```

SW1 marks its ports facing SW2—Gi0/0 and Gi0/1—as Root Inconsistent:

```
SW1(config-if)#
*Sep 13 21:46:17.848: %SPANTREE-2-ROOTGUARD_BLOCK: Root guard blocking port
GigabitEthernet0/0 on VLAN0001.
SW1(config-if)#do show spanning-tree inconsistentports

Name                    Interface               Inconsistency
--------------------    --------------------    ------------------
VLAN0001                GigabitEthernet0/0      Root Inconsistent
VLAN0001                GigabitEthernet0/1      Root Inconsistent
```

```
Number of inconsistent ports (segments) in the system : 2
```

Likewise, SW4 blocks its SW2-facing ports, placing them into a Broken (BKN) status:

```
SW4(config-if-range)#do show spanning-tree inconsistentports

Name                   Interface                Inconsistency
-------------------    ----------------------   ------------------
VLAN0001               GigabitEthernet1/0       Root Inconsistent
VLAN0001               GigabitEthernet1/1       Root Inconsistent

Number of inconsistent ports (segments) in the system : 2

SW4(config-if-range)#do show span vl 1 | i Gi1/0|Gi1/1
Gi1/0                  Desg BKN*4        128.5    P2p *ROOT_Inc
Gi1/1                  Desg BKN*4        128.6    P2p *ROOT_Inc
```

BPDU Guard and BPDU Filter

Although BPDU Guard and BPDU Filter have confusingly similar names, they have opposite effects. BPDU Guard error-disables a port if it receives a BPDU. This is useful if someone accidentally connects a cheap workgroup switch to a port that's meant for an end user. The interface command to enable it is `spanning-tree bpduguard enable`.

Rather than issuing this command on every interface, you can issue the global command `spanning-tree portfast edge bpduguard default`. This will automatically enable BPDU Guard for any interface that has PortFast enabled.

When an interface is error-disabled, you must reenable it manually by shutting and unshutting the port. Alternatively, you can have IOS automatically reenable the port after a period of time using the following global configuration commands:

```
errdisable recovery cause bpduguard
errdisable recovery interval 30
```

BPDU Filter prevents a switch from sending or processing received BPDUs. This effectively ensures that the port is always in a forwarding state, even if it creates a loop. The interface command to unconditionally enable BPDU Filter is spanning-tree bpdufilter enable.

If you want to enable BPDU Filter only on access ports in PortFast mode, you can instead use the global configuration command `spanning-tree portfast edge bpdufilter default`. This will not enable BPDU Filter if the port is trunked, even if it's in PortFast trunk mode.

Unidirectional Link Detection

The Unidirectional Link Detection (UDLD) protocol detects and shuts down unidirectional links. A unidirectional link is usually caused by one strand of a fiber cable being damaged. When this occurs, a switch may be able to send BPDUs but not receive them. This can destabilize a Spanning Tree topology and cause lost traffic or bridging loops.

UDLD periodically tests for bidirectional communication between switches. It sends Hello packets to its neighbor by default every 15 seconds. The neighbor echoes the packets back. If the sender does not receive the echo, it assumes a unidirectional link and responds according to its configured UDLD mode.

There are two UDLD modes: normal and aggressive. In aggressive mode, UDLD will try eight times to reestablish a bidirectional connection with a neighbor. After that, it will place the entire interface into an error-disabled state. It's important to note that when UDLD disables the interface, it will stop all traffic on that interface.

You can enable UDLD on a per-interface basis, or you can have IOS automatically enable it on fiber-optic ports. The interface command to enable aggressive mode is udld port aggressive. In normal mode, UDLD will only detect a unidirectional link but won't disable the port. To enable normal mode, use the interface command udld port. To have IOS automatically enable UDLD normal or aggressive mode on all fiber-optic ports, use the global configuration command udld enable or udld aggressive, respectively.

Similar to BPDU Guard, if UDLD error-disables a port, you must either recover the port manually or configure error-disable recovery using the following global configuration commands:

```
errdisable recovery interval 30
errdisable recovery cause udld
```

Loop Guard

Loop Guard is a Spanning Tree extension that places a Spanning Tree port into a loop-inconsistent state if it fails to receive BPDUs for a VLAN. Unlike UDLD aggressive mode, which disables an interface, Loop Guard blocks ports on a per-VLAN basis. You can enable Loop Guard using the interface command spanning-tree guard loop.

Summary

As with any networking technology, practice and experience are going to do more to solidify your conceptual understanding of Spanning Tree than simply studying it. Be sure to work through the exercises at the end of this chapter until you feel comfortable completing them on your own without referencing anything else.

Having your VLANs and trunks set up properly is a prerequisite for configuring or troubleshooting Spanning Tree. A VLAN must be configured on a switch before a Spanning Tree instance can exist for it. And for multiple switches to participate in Spanning Tree for a VLAN, they need to have trunks with the VLAN allowed and active.

The most common Spanning Tree mode you'll encounter is RPVST+. It goes by a variety of names, including RSTP and 802.1w. Two things that make for a rapid convergence time are what set it apart from the original PVST+: the absence of timer-based port states and the introduction of link types.

MST is useful when you have a large number of VLANs. Rather than using RPVST+, which creates a separate Spanning Tree instance for each VLAN, MST lets you map multiple VLANs to a single instance.

Exam Essentials

Be able to determine the root bridge, root ports, and designated ports for any Spanning Tree topology.   Because a layer 2 loop can bring down a network, you must be able to understand what Spanning Tree will do *before* you configure it or add a new switch to an existing network. Experimenting is a recipe for disaster!

Understand the differences among PVST+, RPVST+, and MST.   PVST+ is the original Cisco implementation of the timer-based 802.1D Spanning Tree specification. RPVST+ doesn't use timers, introduces link types, and has a faster convergence time. (R)PVST+ creates a separate Spanning Tree instance for each VLAN. MST lets you map multiple VLANs to a single MST instance, which is useful if you have a large number of VLANs.

Know how to manipulate active and allowed VLANs on a trunk.   By default, all VLANs (1-4094) are allowed on a trunk. In order for a VLAN to be allowed and active on one end of a trunk, the VLAN must exist on the switch and not be shut down. If a VLAN is shut down, it will show as allowed but not active. If a VLAN is pruned or blocked, it will show as neither allowed nor active.

Be able to configure all Spanning Tree modes.   Although PVST+ is deprecated, its configuration commands are similar to RPVST+, and you may still encounter PVST+ on older gear. Be able to configure (R)PVST+ and MST to customize the root bridge, root ports, and designated ports.

Understand the interactions between RPVST+ and MST.   Although this is something that you're more likely to see on an exam than in real life, practicing running RPVST+ and MST concurrently in your lab will solidify your understanding of both. In particular, understand how MST simulates RPVST+.

Exercises

EXERCISE 2.1

Configure the full-mesh topology in the following figure. Set up 802.1Q trunks among the switches. Configure VLANs 100 and 200 on each switch. Configure one switch to be the primary root for VLAN 100 and another switch to be the primary root for VLAN 200.

FIGURE 2.8   Physical topology for Exercise 2.1

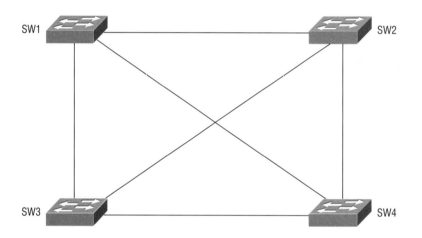

EXERCISE 2.2

Configure the primary root for VLAN 100 to be the secondary root for VLAN 200.

EXERCISE 2.3

Configure the primary root for VLAN 200 to be the secondary root for VLAN 100.

EXERCISE 2.4

On the switch that's the root for VLAN 100, prune VLAN 100 from all trunks. What happens?

EXERCISE 2.5

Locate a blocked port in the VLAN 200 topology. Unblock this port using whatever means you wish. (Hint: Try modifying port priority).

EXERCISE 2.6

Configure MST on the switches. Place VLANs 100 and 200 in MST1.

EXERCISE 2.7

Take note of the root bridge for MST1. Pick a different switch and make it the root bridge.

Review Questions

You can find the answers in the appendix.

1. Which of the following can reduce the size of a broadcast domain? (Choose two.)

    A. Prune VLANs

    B. Use 802.1Q trunks

    C. Use routed instead of switched interfaces

    D. Tag the native VLAN

2. You have three switches connected to VLAN 50. They're all running Spanning Tree and have the following base MAC addresses:

    SW1 0010.84b0.ee30

    SW2 007c.5d8a.e100

    SW3 0084.8ede.fdd0

    Which of the following will be the root for VLAN 50?

    A. SW1

    B. SW2

    C. SW3

    D. None of these

3. You have three switches connected to VLAN 10. They have the following base MAC addresses and are set to the default priority:

    SW1 0010.84b0.ee30

    SW2 007c.5d8a.e100

    SW3 0084.8ede.fdd0

    You plan to add another switch, SW4, to the topology but don't want it to become root. SW4 has a base MAC address of 000c.0f43.01a3. How can you accomplish this?

    A. Set SW4's bridge priority to 0

    B. Set SW4's bridge priority to 32768

    C. Set SW4's bridge priority to 61440

    D. Connect SW4 without making any other changes

4. When you enable Spanning Tree on a switch, what does it advertise as the root bridge?

    A. The 0000.0000.0000 address

    B. The highest root bridge ID it receives

    C. The first root ID it receives

    D. Its own bridge ID

5. How does a switch calculate the lowest cost to the root bridge?

   A. Adding its own bridge priority to the bridge priority it receives in a BPDU

   B. Adding its own interface cost to the cost it receives in a BPDU

   C. Adding its own port priority to the port priority it receives in a BPDU

   D. Using the path via the bridge with the lowest bridge ID

6. You have a switch running IOS 12.4. Which global configuration command will ensure Rapid Spanning Tree is enabled for VLAN 1?

   A. `spanning-tree rapid-pvst`

   B. `spanning-tree mode pvst`

   C. `spanning-tree mode rapid-pvst`

   D. `spanning-tree vlan 1 mode rapid-pvst`

7. How frequently does a switch running Rapid Spanning Tree send configuration BPDUs?

   A. Every 1 second

   B. Every 2 seconds

   C. Every 5 seconds

   D. Every 15 seconds

8. What's the difference between the transmitting bridge ID and the root bridge ID? (Choose two.)

   A. The transmitting bridge ID contains information about the switch that sent the BPDU.

   B. The transmitting bridge ID doesn't contain any information about the root.

   C. The root bridge ID contains the base MAC address of the root bridge.

   D. The root bridge ID contains a MAC address based on one of the root bridge's interfaces.

9. You have three connected switches with the following bridge priorities:

   SW1: 32788

   SW2: 32770

   SW3: 36885

   There are no other switches in this topology. Which of the following can you conclude from this information? (Choose two.)

   A. SW2 is the root for VLAN 20.

   B. SW1 is the root for VLAN 20.

   C. SW2 is in VLAN 2.

   D. SW3 will never be the root.

10. Consider the following two switches: SW1 has a base MAC address of 0000.1234.ABC9 with a bridge priority of 0. SW2 has a base MAC of 0000.1234.ABCA with a priority of 0. If both switches are placed in the same VLAN, which will become the Spanning Tree root?

    A. SW1

    B. SW2

    C. Neither

    D. Both

11. Switch SW1 is running RPVST+ on VLAN 1 and is the root. It's connected to SW2, which has VLAN 1 mapped to the MST1 instance. You want to add VLAN 2 to both switches and make SW2 the root for VLAN 2 without impacting VLAN 1. How can you accomplish this?

    A. Make SW2 the root for MST0

    B. Map VLAN 2 to MST1

    C. Map VLAN 2 to MST0

    D. Make SW1 the root for MST1

12. Which of the following must be the same on all switches in order for them to be in the same MST region? (Choose two.)

    A. Trunk encapsulation

    B. Region name

    C. Allowed VLANs

    D. VLAN-to-instance mappings

13. Which of the following MST configuration commands will map VLANs 100, 400, and 900 to MST3?

    A. `instance 100,400,900 vlan 3`

    B. `instance 3 vlan 100,400,900`

    C. `spanning-tree mst 1 vlan 100,400,900`

    D. `vlan 100,400,900 instance 3`

14. You attempted to configure MST to map VLAN 2 to MST2. However, running `show spanning-tree mst 2` gives the error `No mst information available for instance(s) 3`. What are two possible explanations?

    A. You used the wrong show command. Try `show spanning-tree vlan 2` instead.

    B. VLAN 2 isn't configured on the switch.

    C. You failed to type `exit` in MST configuration mode to save your changes.

    D. You failed to issue a `write memory` command after making the changes.

15. SW1 is running MST and has VLANs 2 through 10 mapped to MST10. SW1 is connected to SW2, which is running RPVST+. There are no physical loops in the topology. All of SW1's ports are forwarding in all VLANs. Which of the following is true? (Choose two.)

    A. SW1 is the root for VLAN 1.

    B. SW1 is the root for VLAN 2.

    C. SW2 is the root for VLAN 1.

    D. SW2 is the root for VLAN 2.

16. You want to ensure that a switch always remains root. Which of the following Spanning Tree extensions should you configure?

    A. BPDU Guard

    B. BPDU Filter

    C. Root Filter

17. Which of the following Spanning Tree extensions can prevent loops caused by a user plugging a hub into a network jack in their cubicle?

    A. Loop Guard

    B. BPDU Filter

    C. BPDU Guard

    D. Root Guard

18. What command provides the simplest way to enable BPDU Guard on all interfaces that are connected to user workstations?

    A. The global configuration command `errdisable recovery cause bpduguard`

    B. The global configuration command `spanning-tree bpduguard enable`

    C. The interface command `spanning-tree bpduguard enable`

    D. The global configuration command `spanning-tree portfast edge bpduguard default`

19. You want to configure UDLD on a pair of switches connected by fiber-optic cable. In the event of a unidirectional link, you want to ensure that no switches block any ports. Which UDLD mode should you configure, and which command should you use? (Choose two.)

    A. `udld port`

    B. `udld port aggressive`

    C. Normal mode

    D. Aggressive mode

20. Which are true regarding UDLD and Loop Guard? (Choose three.)

    A. Loop Guard disables ports on a per-VLAN basis.

    B. Loop Guard can be configured to take no action in response to a loop.

    C. UDLD can be configured to take no action in response to a loop.

    D. UDLD can stop all traffic on an interface.

21. You need to configure an 802.1Q trunk between two switches, SW1 and SW2. Which of the following interface commands, if configured on each switch, will result in a working 802.1Q trunk? (Choose two.)

A. `switchport mode trunk on`

B. `switchport trunk encapsulation dot1q`

C. `switchport mode dynamic auto`

D. `switchport mode dynamic desirable`

E. `switchport trunk encapsulation negotiate`

22. You've inherited a large network with several hundred switches. You're not using VLAN 1, but it's active on all trunks as the native VLAN. How can you remove it from all trunks? (Choose two.)

A. Enable native VLAN tagging

B. Disable native VLAN tagging

C. Remove VLAN 1 from all switches

D. Prune VLAN 1 from all trunks

E. Shut down VLAN 1 on all switches

Enterprise Network Design

THE CCNP ENCOR EXAM OBJECTIVES COVERED IN THIS CHAPTER INCLUDE THE FOLLOWING:

Domain 1.0: Architecture

✓ **1.1** Explain the different design principles used in an enterprise network

Domain 3.0: Infrastructure

✓ **3.1** Layer 2

✓ **3.4** IP Services

Ultimately, the performance and flexibility of any network hinges on the physical topology—that is, the physical connectivity between devices. After that, every subsequent decision is a logical configuration decision that depends in some way on the physical topology. In other words, the physical topology determines the path traffic *can* take, but the logical layer 2 topology determines what path the traffic *will* take. In this chapter, we'll look at how different layer 2 designs influence traffic patterns, which in turn influence bandwidth and reliability. We'll then turn to EtherChannels, which can help you make efficient use of your physical links as well as make your network resilient to link failures. Finally, we'll cover three first-hop redundancy protocols that let you create a highly available default gateway for hosts in a subnet.

Physical Network Architectures

The physical design is the first important decision you'll make when designing or revising a network. Recall from Chapter 1, "Networking Fundamentals," that everything else rests on the physical design: the Data Link protocols you can use, the number of subnets you can support, and the size of those subnets. It also goes without saying that the physical design influences bandwidth and reliability. More physical connections can give you more bandwidth and redundancy. However, there's another consideration that's often overlooked: traffic patterns. The path traffic takes in a network has a profound influence on throughput and reliability. Every network design should take into account, first and foremost, the expected traffic patterns.

The physical topology of a network is its least flexible and most unforgiving aspect. If you botch a configuration, you can fix it with a few keystrokes. If you botch the physical design, it can lead to poor performance and even downtime. A poor physical design can't be fixed with configuration commands. The physical design also determines the network's scalability in terms of the number of devices that can use it and how much data they can push through it.

Good physical network design isn't hard, but the physical design of a network strongly influences its cost, and not everyone can afford to build a dream network right out of the gate. So, in this section you'll learn about two physical architectures: the three-tier architecture, whose strength is scalability, and its more cost-effective but less-scalable relative, the two-tier collapsed core architecture.

Comparing Campus and Data Center Networks

As with many technology buzzwords, the term "enterprise network" gets thrown around a lot without any clear definition. Although there isn't a unanimously accepted definition of the term, we can loosely define an enterprise network as a private network that's under the control of a single organization and that consists of at least one of two type of networks: campus networks and data center networks.

Campus Networks

Enterprise networks include campus locations, a fancy term for where users sit with their end-user devices, such as computers and phones, as well as shared devices such as printers, copy machines, and wireless access points. Typically, a campus location is an office but could be any place where multiple users work, such as a warehouse.

The key feature of a campus network is that it connects users to the network resources that are not on campus—be they applications running in a company data center or web applications on the Internet. The majority of traffic traversing a campus network is *not* between devices on the campus. Instead, it's mostly client-to-server traffic, also known as *North-South* traffic.

Data Center Networks

An enterprise network may also include a data center consisting of servers and mass storage devices. Typically, a data center resides in a dedicated facility. The company may own the facility, or they may lease rack space from someone else. Consequently, a key feature of data center networks is that they *don't* include end-user devices. Instead, users connect to a data center network over a wide area network (WAN) connection such as a private line, Multiprotocol Label Switching (MPLS) layer 3 virtual private network (VPN), or the Internet.

Naturally, data centers have substantial client-server traffic flows. But in a data center network, the bulk of traffic is server-to-server traffic, also known as *East-West* traffic. East-West traffic includes countless activities, such as

- An application server pulling data from a database server

- Migration of a virtual machine (VM) from one VM host to another

- Data replication from a server to a backup storage device

East-West traffic includes a lot of sustained or bandwidth-intensive traffic. Figure 3.1 illustrates the East-West traffic flow typical of data center networks.

The design shown in Figure 3.1 is known as the *leaf-and-spine architecture*. It's a popular design in data center networks because it provides a predictable number of hops between any two servers. Equal-cost multipath routing (ECMP) can simultaneously use multiple equal paths between servers to increase available bandwidth.

FIGURE 3.1   East-West traffic flow in a data center network using the leaf-spine design

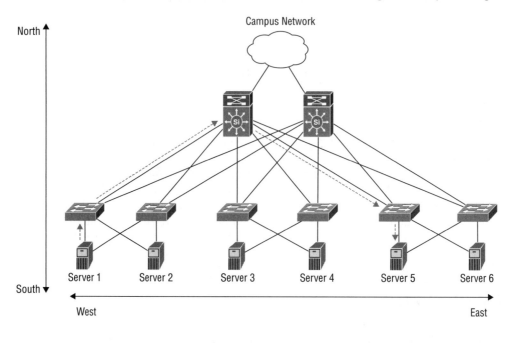

> It's not unusual for a company to have a data center (or in a small company, a data closet) in a campus location, particularly if that location is the company headquarters. Even in this situation, a clear line of delineation must exist between the data center network and the rest of the campus. To put a finer point on it, there shouldn't be a server sitting in someone's office!

The Three-Tier Architecture

The three-tier architecture has been the standard for enterprise networks for years. It's a modular design that has the advantage of easily scaling to accommodate growth. The three-tier architecture is shown in Figure 3.2 and consists of three layers: core, distribution or aggregation, and access.

Scalability is an area in which the three-tier architecture really shines. The modular approach means costs and configurations are predictable and consistent. The biggest drawback to this architecture is the cost. Unless you need maximum scalability, it's not very cost-effective.

FIGURE 3.2   Core, distribution, and access tiers

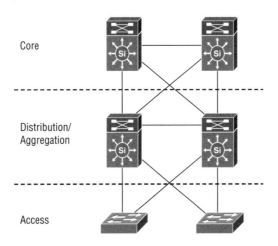

Core

Distribution/
Aggregation

Access

Core Layer

From a physical design perspective, the core layer is the center of the campus or data center network. As such, core switches tend to have a high port density and carry a hefty price tag. Configuration in the core should be minimal to reduce the need for changes and the chance of a misbehaving protocol taking down the entire network. Hence, connections within the core should always be routed. Routed (layer 3) connections provide several key advantages, including load balancing, rapid convergence, and scalability—all necessary features given that the core is the heart of the network. Recalling that large broadcast domains don't scale and provide poor isolation from failures, there shouldn't be a single VLAN that all of your core switches share. Rather, each interswitch link should be a separate broadcast domain, which of course necessitates point-to-point IP routing on each and every link.

Another defining feature of the core is that servers and end-user devices such as computers and phones don't connect directly to core switches. The only devices that connect directly to the core are routers and other switches. But these devices aren't connected willy-nilly. Rather, they're connected in a modular fashion via an access-distribution block.

Access-Distribution Block

The next two layers, the distribution or aggregation and access layers, together form what's called an *access-distribution block*, or just distribution block for short. The term "block" isn't accidental. Think of an access-distribution block as a building block that can be plugged into the core, allowing the network to be expanded in a modular fashion. Figure 3.3 illustrates two access-distribution blocks connected to the core.

FIGURE 3.3   Two access-distribution blocks connected to the core

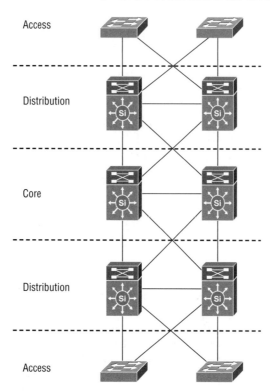

Ideally, each module contains devices that share a similar function. For example, desktops and phones may be in one block, routers in another block, and on-premises servers in yet another block. Notice that if devices in a distribution block need to talk to each other (such as two servers), this architecture makes it possible for them to do so without going through the core. This makes scaling the network by adding more devices straightforward. For example, if you have a block with hundreds of web servers, adding more may simply entail adding more access switches without having to make any connectivity changes to the core. The modular approach also provides isolation within the network. Changes in one block are less likely to affect changes in another block. For example, a switch failure in the desktop block shouldn't affect resources in any other blocks, which also aids in troubleshooting.

Distribution or Aggregation Layer

The distribution layer (sometimes called the aggregation layer) serves two important purposes. First, it provides a reliable and consistent connection to the core while conserving valuable switch port space on the core switches. Notice that in Figure 3.3, the distribution switches have redundant connections to each other and the core switches.

Second, the distribution layer can keep the access-distribution block scalable to accommodate device sprawl. You should take into account the number of additional devices you'll need to connect in the future so that you can avoid having to install and connect additional distribution switches to the core. You therefore want to avoid filling up the ports on your distribution switches with a bunch of end-user devices. Instead, you'll connect those devices to switches in the access layer, which we'll get to in a moment. However, this doesn't mean that you can't connect *any* other devices to the distribution layer. It's perfectly fine to connect things like servers or storage area network (SAN) devices directly to distribution layer switches. In this case, these devices will generally have redundant connections to the distribution layer.

Depending on the devices you're connecting, you may not even need distribution switches in every block. In its simplest incarnation, the distribution layer may consist of nothing but routers connected directly to the core to provide private WAN or Internet access. In this scenario, the layer is called the WAN aggregation layer.

Because client-server traffic passes through the distribution layer, distribution switches and routers are sometimes used to apply policies such as traffic filtering and access control. Just keep in mind that applying policy at the distribution layer is a matter of preference and not a technical requirement.

Access Layer

In a campus network, the purpose of the access layer is to provide physical connectivity to end-user and shared devices such as printers. Access switches may also offer power-over-Ethernet (PoE) to power phones and wireless access points. Switches in the access layer usually have redundant connections to the distribution layer (although this isn't always the case, as you'll see later).

Ideally, you want to keep complexity as close to the access layer (or edge) as possible. For instance, security features such as port security, dynamic ARP inspection, and DHCP snooping should be implemented close to edge devices. Quality of service (QoS) markings also should be applied at the access layer.

The Two-Tier Collapsed Core: A Cheaper Alternative

The two-tier collapsed core architecture is a simplified (and cheaper) version of the three-tier architecture. It flattens or collapses the distribution layer into the core, leaving a collapsed core. As a result, it sacrifices the modularity and scalability of the three-tier architecture. See Figure 3.4 for an example.

FIGURE 3.4   Collapsed core

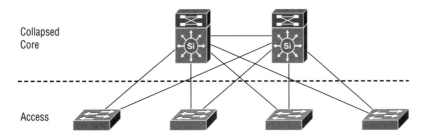

The two-tier collapsed core architecture is more cost effective for networks that will remain at a relatively fixed size. But it does come with some drawbacks. Expanding the network is possible but becomes more complex the more it grows. Adding additional access switches is easy enough. But if the core switches reach capacity so that they can no longer accommodate additional access switches, you'll need to either add additional core switches or redesign a portion of your network using the three-tier architecture.

The lack of modularity also makes change control harder. For example, suppose that you need to add some additional VLANs and trunk ports for servers. Making a change to a collapsed core could bring down the entire network, so that change must be coordinated with everyone who might be affected by it. Contrast this with the three-tier architecture, where the change could be isolated to the distribution switches and thus wouldn't require any coordination with other parts of the network.

Layer 2 Design

There are really only two types of interswitch connections: switched and routed. As I noted earlier, connections within and to the core should always be routed. But when it comes to the access-distribution block, the choice to use routed or switched interswitch connections is up to you. Essentially, the routed versus switched decision comes down to whether a subnet needs to span multiple access and distribution switches. Referring to Figure 3.5, notice that the main difference between switched and routed is where the layer 2/layer 3 line of demarcation sits. Ultimately, you need to answer the question "Where should IP routing take place?"

FIGURE 3.5   Switched vs. routed topology

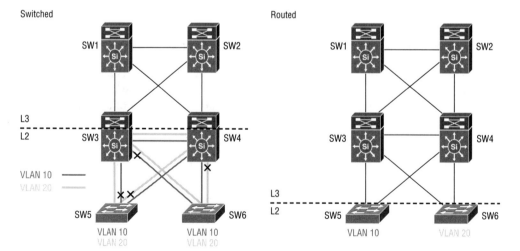

Switched and Routed Interfaces

Let's start by clarifying the difference between a switched (layer 2) interface and a routed (layer 3) interface. Fundamentally, the difference is in how each handles an incoming Ethernet frame. A switched interface is just what you normally think of as a switchport. Although it doesn't show in the configuration, the interface command to turn an interface into a switched interface is simply `switchport`. You can verify the switchport status of an interface as follows:

```
SW3#show interfaces gigabitEthernet 0/0 switchport
Name: Gi0/0
Switchport: Enabled
Administrative Mode: trunk
Operational Mode: trunk (member of bundle Po1)
Administrative Trunking Encapsulation: dot1q
Operational Trunking Encapsulation: dot1q
Negotiation of Trunking: On
Access Mode VLAN: 1 (default)
Trunking Native Mode VLAN: 1 (default)
! Output truncated
```

A switchport can be an access port with membership in a single VLAN, or it can be a trunk port that carries traffic for multiple VLANs, as in the preceding example. If a switched interface receives an Ethernet frame, it will either flood the frame or forward it according to its MAC address table. A switched interface cannot have an IP address assigned to it. However, you can create an SVI with membership in a VLAN, and that SVI can have an IP address. When using a switch as a default gateway for a VLAN, you create an SVI and assign it an IP address. You then configure the hosts in that VLAN to use that IP as their default gateway.

A routed interface, on the other hand, effectively terminates a layer 2 connection. Put another way, a routed link is a point-to-point link in its own broadcast domain. If a routed interface receives an Ethernet frame, it checks to see whether the destination MAC address is the same as its interface MAC address. If it's not (as would be the case with, for example, a broadcast frame), the switch will discard the frame. A routed interface is useful when you need a point-to-point link between a switch and only one other device, such as a firewall or an Internet router. Although you could just as well create a dedicated VLAN and SVI for such a purpose, doing so requires more steps, adds complexity to the configuration, and consumes more switch resources. To configure a routed interface, just use the `no switchport` interface command and configure an IP address using the `ip address` command, as follows:

```
SW3(config)#int gi0/3
SW3(config-if)#no switchport
SW3(config-if)#
```

```
%LINK-3-UPDOWN: Interface GigabitEthernet0/3, changed state to up
SW3(config-if)#ip address 3.3.3.1 255.255.255.252
SW3#show interfaces gigabitEthernet 0/3 switchport
Name: Gi0/3
Switchport: Disabled
SW3(config)#exit
SW3#show ip interface brief gi0/3
Interface            IP-Address      OK? Method Status           Protocol
GigabitEthernet0/3   3.3.3.1         YES manual up               up
```

Table 3.1 lists the differences between switched and routed interfaces.

TABLE 3.1   Switched vs. routed interfaces

Switched	Routed
Access or trunk port	Not a member of a VLAN
Participates in Spanning Tree	Doesn't participate in Spanning Tree
IP address can't be assigned to the interface; must use an SVI instead	Can be assigned a primary and a secondary IP address

Switched Topologies

We've already established that routed links offer superior scalability and convergence times as well as load balancing—that's why the core uses them. So why even consider a switched topology in the access-distribution block? In a word: convenience.

You may use a switched topology if you need a VLAN to span multiple access layer switches. For example, a switched topology is useful for VM clusters where a VM needs to move from one host to another but retain the same IP address. In order for this to happen, both VM hosts need to have interfaces in the same VLAN. This clearly is something that you're more likely to see in a data center, but it certainly does exist in office server rooms around the world. To use another example, in a branch office you may have a collection of networked printers connected to different switches. It's much more convenient for the help-desk personnel at a remote office to be able to move a printer from one location to another without having to reconfigure the printer.

A switched topology is a low-maintenance, plug-and-play solution. But it comes with significant disadvantages. Because it uses transparent bridging, it doesn't scale. A broadcast storm can lead to a catastrophic failure spanning multiple switches. One faulty network interface on a workstation can bring down the entire VLAN, which could impact dozens of devices. Inasmuch as it's up to you, avoid stretching VLANs across switches. Consider yourself warned! However, if convenience or the status quo necessitates using a switched topology, you might as well make the most of it. There are two types of switched topologies to consider: looped and loop-free.

Looped Topologies

Looped and loop-free topologies differ from each other in terms of resiliency. In the looped topology, you deliberately configure physical loops, and Spanning Tree prevents bridging loops from occurring by blocking some of those redundant logical connections. The looped triangle, shown in Figure 3.6, is the most common example of a looped topology.

FIGURE 3.6   A looped triangle topology

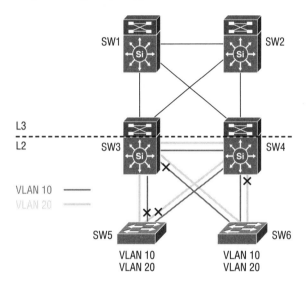

Notice that in the looped triangle, each access switch is connected to both distribution switches. If you were to add another access switch, it would consume at least two additional ports on the distribution switches. When a logical link failure occurs, Spanning Tree reconverges, unblocking those previously blocked links to allow traffic to flow freely. To put it simply, you're relying on Spanning Tree to provide resiliency. Again, this is convenient, but the price you pay is that reconvergence in the face of a logical link failure can take several seconds. Another downside is that you waste some port space due to blocking. However, if you have multiple VLANs, you can overcome this somewhat by load-balancing VLANs across different links.

The looped square, shown in Figure 3.7, consumes fewer switchports on the distribution switches. In this case, each access switch connects to only one distribution switch and one access switch. Adding another access switch would thus consume at least one additional port on just one distribution switch. Hence, if you need a VLAN to span multiple access switches but your distribution switch port space is at a premium, you may want to consider this setup. But keep in mind that the looped square carries with it the additional disadvantage that a logical link failure or misconfiguration could cause traffic to start flowing horizontally through an access switch, leading to an inefficient use of bandwidth.

FIGURE 3.7 A looped square topology

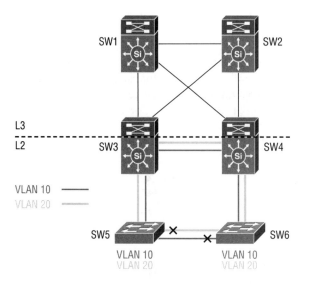

Loop-Free Topologies

In the loop-free topologies, you avoid configuring physical loops in the access and distribution layers so that bridging loops aren't possible. You'll still run Spanning Tree just in case, but you won't depend on it. One aspect of the loop-free topologies is that they don't consume much port space on the distribution switches. There are a few ways to configure a loop-free topology, but the one shown in Figure 3.8 stands out above the rest and is the one Cisco recommends.

FIGURE 3.8 Recommended loop-free topology

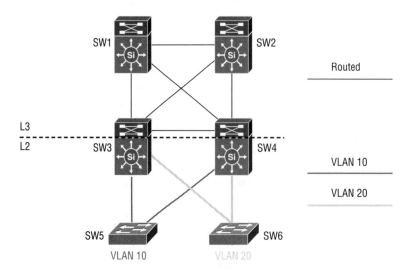

This particular topology allows simultaneous use of all links and provides some resiliency in case of a distribution switch failure. The only consideration is that no VLAN can span more than two access switches, but as you already know, limiting the size of a broadcast domain isn't a bad thing. Note that the connections in the core layer *are* looped, which isn't a problem because those connections are all routed.

Loop-Free U-Topologies

If you think you'll ever need to extend a VLAN to more than one access switch, consider one of the loop-free U-topologies, named for the distinctive U shape of the layer 2 domain. The loop-free U-topology, as shown in Figure 3.9, lets you span a VLAN between two access switches. The failure of a distribution switch will send all traffic through another access switch, but you won't lose connectivity. Notice that the connections between the distribution switches are layer 3.

FIGURE 3.9   Loop-free U-topology

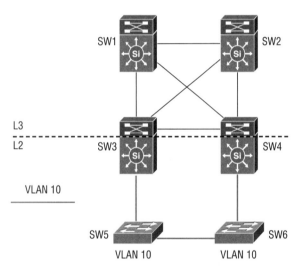

If you want to extend a VLAN to more than two switches, the loop-free inverted-U topology in Figure 3.10 lets you do so at the cost of sacrificing resiliency. If a distribution switch fails, its connected access switches will lose all upstream connectivity. To achieve the upside-down U shape, the connections between the distribution switches are layer 2, whereas connections between access switches are absent.

FIGURE 3.10   Loop-free inverted-U topology

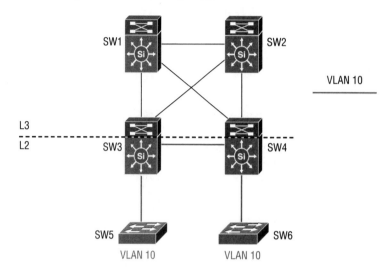

Virtual Switching System

The virtual switching system (VSS) allows two switches to operate as a single logical switch. By implementing VSS and EtherChannels in a virtual switched topology, you can remove layer 2 loops while still using all available links. (EtherChannels let you combine physical interfaces into a single logical interface. We'll cover EtherChannels in a moment). This essentially gives you the advantages of a loop-free topology while making efficient use of bandwidth. The only disadvantage is that it requires switches that support the VSS. Figure 3.11 illustrates the logical and physical layout of a virtual switch topology.

FIGURE 3.11   Virtual switch topology

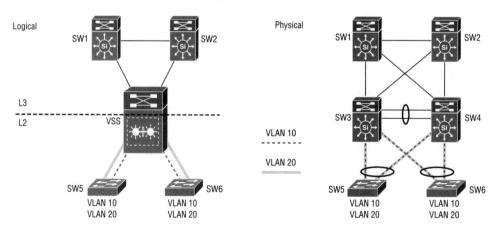

You'll notice that the physical topology looks just like the looped triangle from Figure 3.6. Although the underlying physical topologies are the same, the VSS topology is logically quite different in that it's loop-free and doesn't have any blocked links.

In the VSS topology, both distribution switches are physically connected together using a set of links bundled into a single logical EtherChannel. This logical connection is called the *virtual switch link (VSL)*. When you configure VSS, one switch becomes the active switch and the other is the standby. The active switch handles all configured layer 2 and layer 3 protocols, such as Spanning Tree and dynamic routing protocols. The active switch replicates configuration information to the standby so that it's ready to take over control in the event the active switch fails.

Notice that each access switch is physically connected to both the active and standby switches. Each pair of ports is configured as an EtherChannel, allowing the access switch to utilize both physical connections, treating them as a single logical port. On the VSS side, these connections are configured as multichassis EtherChannels (MECs). This allows all links to be forwarding and precludes the need for Spanning Tree to block any links. Also, in the event of a switch failover, this configuration will allow traffic to keep flowing with minimal interruption.

Keep in mind that VSS doesn't require you to connect access switches to the distribution switches using EtherChannels. You can still implement a looped topology between the access and distribution switches and depend on Spanning Tree to block one of the redundant links. But during a switch failover, you'll be waiting on Spanning Tree to reconverge, which can take much longer.

Stateful switchover is a feature that synchronizes state information such as the FIB and CEF adjacencies between the active and standby switches. Virtual switching thus eliminates the need to run a first-hop redundancy protocol, since both switches function as a single switch. You configure endpoints with the virtual switch's IP as the default gateway. In the event one switch fails, stateful switchover occurs seamlessly, allowing IP forwarding to continue without interruption in a process called *non-stop forwarding (NSF)*. The switchover typically takes anywhere from less than one second to three seconds.

Routed Access Topology

The routed access topology, shown in Figure 3.12, is the best choice all-around. You get rapid convergence times, load balancing, efficient use of all links, stability, and scalability. In a routed topology, a VLAN can't span more than a single access switch, thus each access switch must serve as the default gateway for its respective VLAN. This means there's no need for a first-hop redundancy protocol (FHRP) and no risky bridging loops. Unlike a switched topology, the routed access topology is not very susceptible to a catastrophic meltdown. The only downside is that it's a bit more complex to configure up front, considering you have to allocate two private IP addresses for each point-to-point routed link. Additionally, you'll need to configure a dynamic routing protocol, such as OSPF or EIGRP. We'll cover those in Chapter 5, "Open Shortest Path First (OSPF)," and Chapter 6, "Enhanced Interior Gateway Routing Protocol (EIGRP)."

FIGURE 3.12   Routed access topology

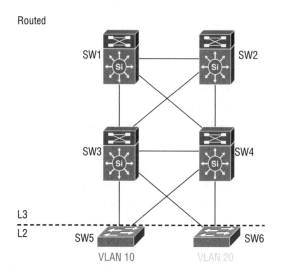

To help you better understand the differences among the different layer 2 topologies, take a look at Table 3.2.

TABLE 3.2   Comparing layer 2 topologies

Topology	Resilient to distribution switch failure?	All links forwarding?	Maximum number of access switches a VLAN can span
Looped	Yes	No	Unlimited
Loop-free U	Yes	Yes	2
Loop-free inverted U	No	Yes	Unlimited
Routed	Yes	Yes	1
Virtual switching	Yes	Yes	Unlimited

EtherChannels

EtherChannels provide redundancy and increased bandwidth by letting you combine up to eight physical interfaces into a single logical interface called a port channel. You can also have eight backup links that can take over if one of the active links fails. This means that, for example, with four 1 Gbps interfaces, you can push up to 4 Gbps through a single port channel. It also lets you hide the physical ports from Spanning Tree and instead present a single logical interface, avoiding the nasty problem of blocking and slow reconvergence times.

Consider the physical topology in Figure 3.13. There are two links between the distribution switches, SW3 and SW4. Without EtherChannel configured, Spanning Tree will block one of these ports. However, by configuring EtherChannel, each switch and any protocols running on it—including Spanning Tree—will view the port pair as a single logical interface.

FIGURE 3.13   EtherChannel between SW3 and SW4

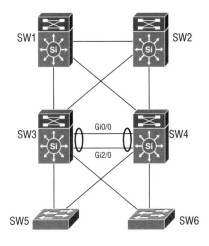

Load-Balancing Methods

Rather than splitting up an Ethernet frame, sending pieces across all four links, and having the opposite end reassemble them, EtherChannel takes a much simpler approach. It uses a hash algorithm—the load-balancing method—to determine which frames to forward over a particular link. The load-balancing method can create a hash based on the source MAC, source IP, destination MAC, or destination IP in a frame. There are six load-balancing methods that you can configure on a per-switch basis, as follows:

```
SW3(config)#port-channel load-balance ?
  dst-ip       Dst IP Addr
  dst-mac      Dst Mac Addr
  src-dst-ip   Src XOR Dst IP Addr
  src-dst-mac  Src XOR Dst Mac Addr
  src-ip       Src IP Addr
  src-mac      Src Mac Addr
```

By default, the switch determines which link to use based only on the source MAC. This is called the source MAC load-balancing mode. To understand how it works, suppose that SW3 receives a frame with the source MAC address 0123.4567.0002, and the frame is addressed to a device that's reachable via SW4, which is on the other end of a port channel. SW3 will hash the source MAC address, and based on the output, will send the frame out of either Gi0/0 or Gi2/0.

In addition to source MAC, there are five other load-balancing methods you can choose from: destination MAC, source IP, destination IP, source IP XOR with the destination IP, and source MAC XOR with the destination MAC. The XOR, or eXclusive OR, methods hash the source and destination addresses together. To understand how to decide which one to choose, consider the port channel between SW4 and SW5. Suppose you have a workstation connected to SW4 and two servers connected to SW5. All are in the same VLAN. The workstation needs to download data from both servers. Because the workstation will be sending frames addressed to different servers, the best load-balancing methods for SW4 would be destination MAC or destination IP. The best load-balancing method for SW5, on the other hand, would be source MAC or source IP, since traffic from the servers is coming from two different MAC and IP addresses.

Configuring a working EtherChannel is not a one-sided operation. You have to perform the appropriate configuration on both ends of the link. To configure an EtherChannel, you select a group of ports you want to combine into a single port channel interface. This group of ports is called the *port channel group*, and each individual port within the group is a *member port*. After you decide the ports you want to join together in an EtherChannel, you must configure the EtherChannel mode. There are three different modes:

- Static (on)
- Port Aggregation Protocol (PAgP)
- Link Aggregation Control Protocol (LACP)

Static EtherChannels

Static, or "on," mode unconditionally places the selected ports into a port channel group, no questions asked. As long as you configure both sides with the same parameters, everything should work fine.

Whenever you are configuring a port channel, it's crucial that all member ports be configured with the same parameters, such as trunk status, trunk encapsulation, speed, and duplex. The port channel will inherit its configuration from the physical interfaces. It's easy to inadvertently create bridging loops by configuring a port channel on one side but not on the other. In that case, Spanning Tree will block one of the links. Thus, it's also a good idea to shut down the ports before creating a port channel to avoid bridging loops.

Each port channel group is identified by a channel group number. Channel group numbers are locally significant and must be unique per switch, but they don't have to match on both ends. However, to avoid confusion, it's a good idea to use the same number on both ends for identification. Let's start by configuring SW3. First, we'll set Gi0/0 and Gi2/0 to their defaults.

```
SW3(config)#default interface range gigabitEthernet 0/0, gigabitEthernet 2/0
SW3(config)#int range gigabitEthernet 0/0, gigabitEthernet 2/0
! Shutdown the ports
SW3(config-if-range)#shutdown
```

We'll configure both ports as 802.1Q trunks.

```
SW3(config-if-range)#switchport trunk encapsulation dot1q
```

Next, let's add both ports to the EtherChannel.

```
SW3(config-if-range)#channel-group 1 mode on
! Verify the configuration
SW3(config-if-range)#do show etherchannel 1 summary
Flags:  D - down        P - bundled in port-channel
        I - stand-alone s - suspended
        H - Hot-standby (LACP only)
        R - Layer3      S - Layer2
        U - in use      N - not in use, no aggregation
        f - failed to allocate aggregator

        M - not in use, minimum links not met
        m - not in use, port not aggregated due to minimum links not met
        u - unsuitable for bundling
        w - waiting to be aggregated
        d - default port

        A - formed by Auto LAG


Number of channel-groups in use: 1
Number of aggregators:           1

Group  Port-channel  Protocol    Ports
------+-------------+-----------+-----------------------------------------------
1      Po1(SD)          -        Gi0/0(D)    Gi2/0(D)
```

The "D" in parentheses means "down" because the ports are shut down. Hence, the port-channel interface is down also. Now let's perform the same configuration on SW4:

```
SW4(config)#default interface range gigabitEthernet 0/0, gigabitEthernet 2/0
SW4(config)#int range gi0/0, gi2/0
SW4(config-if-range)#shutdown
SW4(config-if-range)#switchport trunk encapsulation dot1q
SW4(config-if-range)#switchport mode trunk
SW4(config-if-range)#channel-group 1 mode on
Creating a port-channel interface Port-channel 1
```

Now, we'll bring the interfaces back up.

```
SW4(config-if-range)#no shutdown
SW4(config-if-range)#
%LINK-3-UPDOWN: Interface GigabitEthernet0/0, changed state to up
%LINK-3-UPDOWN: Interface GigabitEthernet2/0, changed state to up
%LINEPROTO-5-UPDOWN: Line protocol on Interface GigabitEthernet2/0, changed
state to up
%LINEPROTO-5-UPDOWN: Line protocol on Interface GigabitEthernet0/0, changed
state to up
%LINK-3-UPDOWN: Interface Port-channel1, changed state to up
%LINEPROTO-5-UPDOWN: Line protocol on Interface Port-channel1, changed state to up
```

Notice that after bringing the member interfaces back up, the port channel interface Port-channel1 comes up as well. The interfaces on the opposite end at SW3 are shut down, but because we've configured a static EtherChannel, SW4 doesn't do any checking to determine whether SW3's port channel is active. Let's jump back to SW3 and reenable the ports there:

```
SW3(config-if-range)#no shut
SW3(config-if-range)#
%LINK-3-UPDOWN: Interface GigabitEthernet0/0, changed state to up
%LINK-3-UPDOWN: Interface GigabitEthernet2/0, changed state to up
%LINEPROTO-5-UPDOWN: Line protocol on Interface GigabitEthernet0/0, changed
state to up
%LINEPROTO-5-UPDOWN: Line protocol on Interface GigabitEthernet2/0, changed
state to up
%LINK-3-UPDOWN: Interface Port-channel1, changed state to up
%LINEPROTO-5-UPDOWN: Line protocol on Interface Port-channel1, changed state to up
! Verify the configuration
SW3(config-if-range)#do show etherchannel 1 summary
Flags:  D - down        P - bundled in port-channel
```

```
      I - stand-alone s - suspended
      H - Hot-standby (LACP only)
      R - Layer3      S - Layer2
      U - in use      N - not in use, no aggregation
      f - failed to allocate aggregator


      M - not in use, minimum links not met
      m - not in use, port not aggregated due to minimum links not met
      u - unsuitable for bundling
      w - waiting to be aggregated
      d - default port


      A - formed by Auto LAG



Number of channel-groups in use: 1
Number of aggregators:           1

Group  Port-channel  Protocol    Ports
------+-------------+-----------+---------------------------------------------
1      Po1(SU)         -         Gi0/0(P)   Gi2/0(P)
```

The "SU" in parentheses next to Po1 indicates that this is a layer 2 (switched) interface rather than a layer 3 (routed) interface. The port channel will inherit the characteristics of the parent interfaces. For example, if Gi0/0 and Gi2/0 were routed interfaces, Po1 would be a routed (layer 3) interface as well.

```
SW3(config-if-range)#do show interfaces port-channel1 trunk

Port        Mode         Encapsulation  Status        Native vlan
Po1         on           802.1q         trunking      1


Port        Vlans allowed on trunk
Po1         1-4094


Port        Vlans allowed and active in management domain
Po1         1,10,20


Port        Vlans in spanning tree forwarding state and not pruned
Po1         1,10,20
```

To remove a static port channel configuration, just delete the interface as follows:

```
SW3(config)#no interface po1
SW3(config)#
! To avoid creating bridging loops, IOS will shut down the member interfaces.
%LINK-5-CHANGED: Interface GigabitEthernet0/0, changed state to administratively
down
%LINK-5-CHANGED: Interface GigabitEthernet2/0, changed state to administratively
down
%LINEPROTO-5-UPDOWN: Line protocol on Interface GigabitEthernet0/0, changed
state to down
%LINEPROTO-5-UPDOWN: Line protocol on Interface GigabitEthernet2/0, changed
state to down
```

Port Aggregation Control Protocol

PAgP is a Cisco-proprietary protocol that attempts to negotiate a port channel with a connected switch. PAgP first performs some sanity checks to make sure both ends are compatible before creating the EtherChannel. If any pair of ports aren't compatible due to a mismatched speed, duplex, native VLAN, or trunk encapsulation, PAgP will still attempt to form an EtherChannel with the remaining ports that are compatible.

PAgP has two modes: Auto and Desirable. In Desirable mode, the switch will actively attempt to form an EtherChannel. In Auto mode, it will not actively try to negotiate a port channel. However, if the other side is set to Desirable mode, then the switch set to Auto will negotiate the port channel. Table 3.3 lists how the combination of configuration modes determines whether a port channel will form.

TABLE 3.3 PAgP configuration modes

Switch A mode	Switch B mode	Will form EtherChannel?
Desirable	Desirable	Yes
Auto	Desirable	Yes
Auto	Auto	No
Desirable	ON	No
Auto	ON	No

You may find it helpful to remember the Auto and Desirable modes by remembering that Ag (as in PAgP) is the chemical symbol for silver, and silver is *auto*matically *desirable*. It's cheesy, but it works for me! The configuration commands for PAgP are similar to those of a static EtherChannel, as follows:

```
! SW4 has already been configured in Desirable mode. Now we'll configure SW3 to use
! Desirable mode.
SW3(config)#int range gi0/0,gi2/0
SW3(config-if-range)#channel-group 1 mode ?
  active    Enable LACP unconditionally
  auto      Enable PAgP only if a PAgP device is detected
  desirable Enable PAgP unconditionally
  on        Enable Etherchannel only
  passive   Enable LACP only if a LACP device is detected
```

We'll choose Desirable mode. We could also choose Auto mode and it would establish a port channel since the other side is set to Desirable.

```
SW3(config-if-range)#channel-group 1 mode desirable
Creating a port-channel interface Port-channel 1
```

The member interfaces are shut down, so we'll bring them up.

```
SW3(config-if-range)#no shut
%LINK-3-UPDOWN: Interface GigabitEthernet0/0, changed state to up
%LINK-3-UPDOWN: Interface GigabitEthernet2/0, changed state to up
%LINEPROTO-5-UPDOWN: Line protocol on Interface GigabitEthernet0/0, changed
state to up
%LINEPROTO-5-UPDOWN: Line protocol on Interface GigabitEthernet2/0, changed
state to up
%LINEPROTO-5-UPDOWN: Line protocol on Interface Port-channel1, changed state to up
! Verify the configuration
SW3(config-if-range)#do show etherchannel 1 summary
Flags:  D - down        P - bundled in port-channel
        I - stand-alone s - suspended
        H - Hot-standby (LACP only)
        R - Layer3      S - Layer2
        U - in use      N - not in use, no aggregation
        f - failed to allocate aggregator

        M - not in use, minimum links not met
        m - not in use, port not aggregated due to minimum links not met
        u - unsuitable for bundling
```

```
      w - waiting to be aggregated
      d - default port

      A - formed by Auto LAG


Number of channel-groups in use: 1
Number of aggregators:           1

Group  Port-channel  Protocol    Ports
------+-------------+-----------+------------------------------------------------
1      Po1(SU)         PAgP       Gi0/0(P)   Gi2/0(P)
```

Link Aggregation Control Protocol

LACP is an open standard protocol that performs essentially the same function as PAgP. Note that LACP and PAgP are not compatible with each other, so you must use the same protocol on both ends.

You can configure LACP to operate in two modes: Active or Passive. In Active mode, the switch will actively try to negotiate a port channel. In Passive mode, it won't actively try to negotiate a port channel, but if the other end is set to Active, then both switches will form a port channel. Table 3.4 lists the outcomes of the different mode combinations.

TABLE 3.4   LACP configuration modes

Switch A mode	Switch B mode	Will form EtherChannel?
Active	Active	Yes
Active	Passive	Yes
Passive	Passive	No
Active	ON	No
Passive	ON	No

Configuring LACP is almost identical to configuring PAgP. In the following example, we configure SW4 to use LACP in Active mode:

```
! SW3 is already configured for LACP Active mode.
SW4(config)#int range gi0/0,gi2/0
```

```
SW4(config-if-range)#channel-group 1 mode active
Creating a port-channel interface Port-channel 1
%LINEPROTO-5-UPDOWN: Line protocol on Interface Port-channel1, changed state to up
SW4(config-if-range)#do show etherchannel 1 summary
Flags:  D - down        P - bundled in port-channel
        I - stand-alone s - suspended
        H - Hot-standby (LACP only)
        R - Layer3      S - Layer2
        U - in use      N - not in use, no aggregation
        f - failed to allocate aggregator

        M - not in use, minimum links not met
        m - not in use, port not aggregated due to minimum links not met
        u - unsuitable for bundling
        w - waiting to be aggregated
        d - default port


        A - formed by Auto LAG


Number of channel-groups in use: 1
Number of aggregators:           1

Group  Port-channel  Protocol    Ports
------+-------------+-----------+-----------------------------------------------
1      Po1(SU)         LACP       Gi0/0(P)   Gi2/0(P)
```

First-Hop Redundancy Protocols

Recall that in a switched topology, the default gateway for a VLAN typically will run on one of the two distribution switches. But ideally, you'd run a FHRP so that either one can serve as the default gateway. That way, if one switch fails, the other can take over without requiring any reconfiguration, and hosts can still reach their configured default gateway. FHRPs include

- Hot Standby Router Protocol (HSRP)
- Virtual Router Redundancy Protocol (VRRP)
- Gateway Load Balancing Protocol (GLBP)

When a host needs to reach a different IP subnet, it has to traverse a gateway or router. In most cases a host will have only one default gateway IP configured. Suppose the default gateway for a server is 1.1.1.1. If that server needs to send an IP packet to 2.2.2.2, it takes the IP packet, encapsulates it inside an Ethernet frame, and then addresses the frame to the default gateway's MAC address. If the default gateway goes down, the server won't be able to reach any other subnets.

This is where FHRPs come in. When you use VRRP, HSRP, or GLBP, you can have multiple gateways that share a single virtual IP address that you configure on hosts as the default gateway. If one of the gateways goes down, one of the others will take over, allowing hosts to continue to communicate outside the subnet.

 In a switched topology, you configure IP routing protocols and FHRPs on layer 3 switches. But you can configure them on routers, too.

Hot Standby Router Protocol

HSRP is a Cisco-proprietary protocol that currently comes in two versions: version 1 and version 2. Version 1, described in RFC 2281 (www.ietf.org/rfc/rfc2281), is the default. The biggest practical difference between the two versions is that only version 2 supports IPv6. From a configuration and operation perspective, however, they're pretty much the same. If you consider using version 2, keep in mind that the versions aren't cross-compatible.

Here's how it works. Suppose that SW3 and SW4 both have SVIs in VLAN 30. SW3 is 3.3.3.3/24, and SW4 is 3.3.3.4/24. To configure HSRP to provide a highly available default gateway for the 3.3.3.0/24 subnet, you'd configure both SVIs to be part of the same HSRP group. You identify the HSRP group by a number between 0 and 255. When you configure an HSRP group, you must specify a virtual IP address, which is the IP that hosts in the subnet will use for their default gateway. The virtual IP resolves to a virtual MAC address in the format 0000.0c07.acxx, xx being the group number in hexadecimal. For example, if you use group number 3, the last part of the MAC address is ac03. HSRP peers communicate with one another using the "all routers" multicast address 224.0.0.2.

HSRP uses an active-passive configuration. The active router listens on the virtual IP address, and the other router is the standby. With HSRP, the router with the highest priority will become active. If the priorities of all routers in the group are equal, then the router with the highest IP will be the active router. All other routers in the group are standby.

In the following example, we'll configure SW3 and SW4 with SVIs for the 3.0.0.0/24 subnet in VLAN 30 and place them both in HSRP group 3. The virtual IP address will be 3.3.3.254, which is what hosts should use as their default gateway. We'll then configure the priority on SW3 to be higher, so it becomes the active router. Lastly, we'll configure MD5 authentication. Let's begin on SW3.

```
! Configure the SVI
SW3(config)#int vlan 30
SW3(config-if)#ip address 3.3.3.3 255.255.255.0
```

We'll create HSRP group 3 with the virtual IP address 3.3.3.254.

```
SW3(config-if)#standby 3 ip 3.3.3.254
```

Let's set the priority to the highest possible value to ensure SW3 is the active router.

```
SW3(config-if)#standby 3 priority 255
```

Next, let's configure MD5 authentication.

```
SW3(config-if)#standby 3 authentication md5 key-string 1337$ecr37
! Verify the configuration
SW3(config-if)#do show standby
Vlan30 - Group 3
  State is Active
  Virtual IP address is 3.3.3.254
  Active virtual MAC address is 0000.0c07.ac03 (MAC In Use)
    Local virtual MAC address is 0000.0c07.ac03 (v1 default)
  Hello time 3 sec, hold time 10 sec
    Next hello sent in 2.304 secs
  Authentication MD5, key-string
  Preemption disabled
  Active router is local
  Standby router is unknown
  Priority 255 (configured 255)
  Group name is "hsrp-Vl30-3" (default)
```

Now let's create the corresponding configuration on SW4:

```
SW4(config)#int vlan 30
SW4(config-if)#ip address 3.3.3.4 255.255.255.0
SW4(config-if)#standby 3 ip 3.3.3.254
SW4(config-if)#standby 3 authentication md5 key-string 1337$ecr37
SW4(config-if)#do show standby
Vlan30 - Group 3
  State is Standby
  Virtual IP address is 3.3.3.254
  Active virtual MAC address is 0000.0c07.ac03 (MAC Not In Use)
    Local virtual MAC address is 0000.0c07.ac03 (v1 default)
  Hello time 3 sec, hold time 10 sec
    Next hello sent in 0.272 secs
  Authentication MD5, key-string
  Preemption disabled
  Active router is 3.3.3.3, priority 255 (expires in 8.752 sec)
```

```
Standby router is local
Priority 100 (default 100)
Group name is "hsrp-Vl30-3" (default)
```

A quick and dirty way to verify the configuration is working is to ping the virtual IP address from anywhere other than the active router.

```
SW4(config-if)#do ping 3.3.3.254
Type escape sequence to abort.
Sending 5, 100-byte ICMP Echos to 3.3.3.254, timeout is 2 seconds:
.!!!!
Success rate is 80 percent (4/5), round-trip min/avg/max = 4/9/17 ms
```

Virtual Router Redundancy Protocol

The VRRP, defined in RFC 3768 (https://tools.ietf.org/html/rfc3768) is an open-standard FHRP that operates much the same as HSRP. Also like it, VRRP uses a group number, a virtual IP address, and a virtual MAC address. But in this case, the MAC address is 0000.5e00.01xx, with xx being the group number in hexadecimal. VRRP routers communicate with one another using the reserved multicast address 224.0.0.18.

In VRRP, the master router listens on the virtual IP address and virtual MAC address. The other routers are called the backups. One significant difference between VRRP and HSRP is that with VRRP the virtual IP address can be the same as one of the interface IPs. This makes it easier to implement VRRP in an existing topology without having to modify the hosts' currently configured default gateway. For example, if hosts are using the default gateway 192.168.7.1, you can continue to use that IP without readdressing any interfaces. The following example shows how this is done on SW3:

```
SW3(config)#int vlan 30
SW3(config-if)#ip address 3.3.3.3 255.255.255.0
SW3(config-if)#vrrp 30 ip 3.3.3.3
SW3(config-if)#
%VRRP-6-STATECHANGE: Vl30 Grp 30 state Init -> Master
%VRRP-6-STATECHANGE: Vl30 Grp 30 state Init -> Master
SW3(config-if)#do show vrrp
Vlan30 - Group 30
  State is Master
  Virtual IP address is 3.3.3.3
  Virtual MAC address is 0000.5e00.011e
  Advertisement interval is 1.000 sec
  Preemption enabled
```

```
Priority is 255
Master Router is 3.3.3.3 (local), priority is 255
Master Advertisement interval is 1.000 sec
Master Down interval is 3.003 sec
```

SW3 is the master. Notice that the priority is set to 255. As with HSRP, in VRRP, the router with the highest priority wins. Note that in this case, SW3's SVI address is the same as the virtual IP address. This means SW3 is the address owner. In this situation, SW3 sets its own priority to 255, the highest possible value, thus ensuring that it's the master as long as the interface is up. Now let's configure SW4:

```
SW4(config)#int vlan 30
SW4(config-if)#ip address 3.3.3.4 255.255.255.0
SW4(config-if)#vrrp 30 ip 3.3.3.3
SW4(config-if)#
%VRRP-6-STATECHANGE: Vl30 Grp 30 state Init -> Backup
%VRRP-6-STATECHANGE: Vl30 Grp 30 state Init -> Backup
SW4(config-if)#do show vrrp
Vlan30 - Group 30
  State is Backup
  Virtual IP address is 3.3.3.3
  Virtual MAC address is 0000.5e00.011e
  Advertisement interval is 1.000 sec
  Preemption enabled
  Priority is 100
  Master Router is 3.3.3.3, priority is 255
  Master Advertisement interval is 1.000 sec
  Master Down interval is 3.609 sec (expires in 2.730 sec)
```

SW4 is the backup. Because SW4 isn't the IP address owner, it assumes the default priority of 100.

Gateway Load-Balancing Protocol

GLBP is another Cisco-proprietary protocol that provides first-hop redundancy by load-balancing traffic across multiple gateways. You may want to use GLBP if you have a lot of traffic and want to spread the load among multiple smaller routers. Just place them together in a GLBP group and they can function as a single virtual router. Routers in a GLBP group use the multicast address 224.0.0.102.

Just as with HSRP and VRRP, a GLBP group has a virtual IP address that hosts use as their configured default gateway. In a GLBP group, one router serves as the active virtual gateway (AVG), whereas all routers in the group function as the active virtual forwarder (AVF), or just forwarder for short. Every router in the group listens on a virtual MAC address in the format 0007.B400.xxyy, where xx is the group number and yy is the forwarder number. You can have up to four virtual MAC addresses in a group. If there are more than four routers in a GLBP group, the additional routers will function as secondary AVFs, ready to take over in case a primary AVF fails.

The AVG listens for ARP requests for the virtual IP address. Here's where the load balancing part comes in and how GLBP differs from HSRP and VRRP. Instead of responding to the ARP request with a single virtual MAC address that all routers share, the AVG responds with the virtual MAC address of one of the forwarders in the group. Using the default round-robin load-balancing method, each time the AVG receives an ARP request for the virtual IP address, it replies with a different virtual MAC address. The actual router a host uses as its default gateway can change based on the MAC address that it receives in the ARP reply from the AVG.

To understand this better, consider a simple example. Suppose you configure a GLBP group on two switches, Switch A and Switch B, configured in that order. Both switches are in GLBP group 5 and have a virtual IP address of 192.168.5.254.

- Switch A's virtual MAC address would be 0007.B400.0501, indicating a group number of 5 and a forwarder number of 1.

- Switch B's virtual MAC address would be 0007.B400.0502, indicating group 5 and forwarder 2.

Both routers are AVFs. But which one is the AVG? The AVG is elected based on the highest priority, the default priority being 100. Valid priorities range from 1 to 255. If the priorities of all routers are tied, then the one with the highest IP address wins. In the preceding example, Switch A would be the AVG since it was configured first. Since Switch A is the AVG, it will listen for ARP requests for the virtual IP address 192.168.5.254. It will respond with one of the virtual MAC addresses of an AVF, 0007.B400.0501 or 0007.B400.0502.

 By default, once a router becomes the AVG, it will remain the AVG as long as it's up. Even if you later configure another router with a higher priority, the first configured router will remain the AVG. You can overcome this behavior by enabling preemption. With preemption enabled, the router with the highest priority will always take over as the AVG.

There are three load-balancing methods you can configure with GLBP:

- **Round-robin**—The AVG will cycle through the group, replying with the virtual MAC address of each AVF in order. This is the default method.

- **Weighted**—You configure a weight (1–254) on each AVF, indicating the ratio of traffic you want each gateway to handle. For example, if you want Switch A to handle 80 percent of the traffic and Switch B to handle 20 percent, you'd configure Switch A with a weight of 80 and Switch B with a weight of 20.

- **Host-dependent**—Each host MAC address is mapped to a specific AVF so that the host will always use that AVF as its default gateway.

If you don't want to use the default round-robin method, you should configure the load-balancing method on any switch that might become the AVG. Not surprisingly, the commands to configure GLBP mirror those of VRRP and HSLP. The following example shows how to configure GLBP group 3 with a virtual IP address of 3.3.3.254. We'll give SW4 a weighting of 80 and enable preemption so it's always the AVG:

```
SW4(config)#int gi0/0
! Configure GLBP group 3 with the virtual IP address 3.3.3.254.
SW4(config-if)#glbp 3 ip 3.3.3.254
! Set the priority to 255 so that SW4 is always the AVG
SW4(config-if)#glbp 3 priority 255
! Set the load-balancing method to weighted
SW4(config-if)#glbp load-balancing weighted
! Set the weight to 80
SW4(config-if)#glbp 3 weighting 80
! Enable preemption so SW4 is always the AVG
SW4(config-if)#glbp 3 preempt
```

We'll then configure SW3 and give it a weighting of 20:

```
SW3(config)#int gi0/0
SW3(config-if)#glbp 3 ip 3.3.3.254
SW3(config-if)#glbp load-balancing weighted
! Set the weight to 20
SW3(config-if)#glbp 3 weighting 20
```

Summary

The physical network layout determines what path traffic *can* take, so it's tempting to assume that creating a full mesh of connections between switches would be the perfect framework for maximizing bandwidth and resiliency. But this approach leaves out an important consideration: scalability. A network is by definition a distributed system, and its whole purpose is to move data between applications, wherever they may happen to live. As a rule, the number of applications and hence the number of devices will inevitably grow. Therefore, scalability is *the* most important consideration when it comes to designing your physical network. That's why a modular approach using a three-tier architecture is always going to be your best bet. However, in a smaller network that's not expected to grow much, a two-tier collapsed core is a good lower-cost alternative.

Regardless of the physical topology, the layer 2 topology you choose will make all the difference when it comes to actual traffic patterns. As with the physical topology, you're concerned with performance, reliability, and scalability. And you can certainly achieve all three. But because the layer 2 topology is just determined by device configuration, you also need to consider configuration complexity.

Switched topologies that make heavy use of transparent bridging are naturally easier to manage. But with the exception of the virtual switch topology, all switched topologies make inefficient use of bandwidth. They also carry the potential for asymmetric routing, which can result in suboptimal use of bandwidth and can make troubleshooting issues a bit more complicated. Switched topologies are divided into three classes: looped, loop-free, and virtual switching. Looped topologies let you extend a VLAN to a practically unlimited number of switches while still maintaining some resiliency. They also waste bandwidth thanks to Spanning Tree blocking redundant links, and they consume more ports on your distribution switches. Loop-free topologies make use of all available links but are less resilient.

Routed and VSS topologies are comparable in that they give you maximum bandwidth, resiliency, and scalability. The big difference between the two is that in a routed topology, a VLAN can exist on only one access switch. This actually makes the routed topology more stable and easier to troubleshoot.

EtherChannels provide a silver lining for switched topologies in particular, allowing you to use redundant physical links without worrying about Spanning Tree blocking them. It's important to note that using EtherChannels in a looped topology will still result in some links being blocked. But EtherChannels aren't good only for switched topologies. You can also use EtherChannels in a routed topology by placing routed interfaces into a port channel group.

If you go with a switched topology other than VSS, the FHRPs VRRP, HSRP, and GLBP are a necessary hack to ensure that your hosts can maintain reachability to other subnets if one of your distribution switches fails. This isn't an issue in a VSS topology because both distribution switches function as a single logical switch, so the failure of one switch is essentially transparent to the hosts. In a similar vein, a routed topology doesn't need an FHRP because the dynamic routing protocols running on the switches will detect and route around link failures.

Exam Essentials

Know the functions of the layers in the two-tier and three-tier architectures.   The three-tier architecture consists of a core layer, distribution/aggregation layer, and access layer. The two-tier architecture collapses the core and distribution layer into a single layer called a collapsed core.

Know the difference between switched (layer 2) and routed (layer 3) interfaces.   A switched interface is a VLAN access or trunk port and can't have an IP address assigned. A routed interface has no VLAN and can have an IP address assigned to it.

Understand the common layer 2 topologies.   Switched topologies include looped, loop-free, and VSS. The routed topology eliminates spanned VLANs and instead places each interswitch link into a separate broadcast domain.

Be able to configure layer 2 and layer 3 EtherChannels.   An EtherChannel can consist of 1–8 active links. You can create a static port channel or let LACP or PAgP negotiate one for you. The difference between a layer 2 and a layer 3 EtherChannel is determined by whether the member interfaces are switched or routed.

Be able to configure the first-hop redundancy protocols.   The configuration semantics of VRRP, HSRP, and GLBP are strikingly similar, often differing by only one word. I suggest mastering VRRP first. You'll then be able to transfer much of that knowledge to HSRP and GLBP.

Review Questions

You can find the answers in the appendix.

1. Which of the following best describes traffic between a database server and a web server?
   A. North-South
   B. East-West
   C. Client-server
   D. Intra-VLAN

2. Which of the following best describes traffic between an IP phone and a DNS server?
   A. North-South
   B. East-West
   C. Point-to-point
   D. Inter-VLAN

3. Which of the following is the most scalable physical architecture for North-South traffic patterns?
   A. Leaf-and-spine architecture
   B. Two-tier collapsed core
   C. Three-tier
   D. Routed

4. Which of the following layers should always be routed?
   A. Access
   B. Aggregation
   C. Distribution
   D. Core

5. Which of the following should be in the same distribution block? (Choose two.)
   A. Web application load balancer
   B. An IP phone
   C. A web server
   D. An Internet router

6. Which of the following is true regarding a routed interface on a switch?
   A. It must be assigned an IP address.
   B. It consumes one VLAN.
   C. It can be configured as a trunk port.
   D. It can be assigned two IP addresses.

7. Which of the following layer 2 topologies let you span a VLAN across more than two switches? (Choose two.)

   A. Looped

   B. Loop-free U

   C. Loop-free inverted-U

   D. Routed

8. Which of the following is true of using a VSS topology?

   A. You should disable Spanning Tree when using VSS.

   B. There's no need to run a FHRP.

   C. Access switches must connect to the virtual switch using multichassis EtherChannels.

   D. The active and standby both perform IP routing to avoid asymmetric routing.

9. Given two distribution switches and one VLAN that spans four access switches, which layer 2 topology will consume the fewest number of ports on the distribution switches?

   A. Looped triangle

   B. Looped square

   C. Routed

   D. Loop-free U

10. What are two differences between the VSS topology and the looped triangle? (Choose two.)

   A. The looped triangle can't use EtherChannels.

   B. The looped triangle has blocked links.

   C. The VSS requires access switches to be directly connected to one another.

   D. The VSS has no links blocking.

11. On Switch A, you issue the `channel-group 7 mode on` command on a range of interfaces. Which command, if configured on the facing switch's links, will result in a working EtherChannel?

   A. `channel-group 7 mode active`

   B. `channel-group 1 mode on`

   C. `channel-group 7 mode desirable`

   D. `port-group 7 mode on`

12. You've configured a pair of links to use LACP Active mode. Configuring which of the following configuration commands on the facing switch will form an EtherChannel?

   A. `channel-group 2 mode passive`

   B. `channel-group 3 mode on`

   C. `channel-group 4 mode auto`

   D. `channel-group 3 mode desirable`

13. Up to how many active ports can you have in an EtherChannel?

    A. 1

    B. 4

    C. 8

    D. 16

14. How many backup ports can you have in an EtherChannel?

    A. 1

    B. 4

    C. 8

    D. 16

15. Which of the following modes is PAgP compatible with?

    A. On

    B. Active

    C. Passive

    D. Auto

16. Which of the following can result in a VRRP router having a priority of 255?

    A. Preemption is enabled.

    B. The default priority is 255.

    C. It's the first router configured in the group.

    D. The router is the group's IP address owner.

17. What is the default priority for HSRP?

    A. 0

    B. 100

    C. 254

    D. 255

18. Which protocol uses the multicast address 224.0.0.2?

    A. HSRP

    B. VRRP

    C. GLBP

    D. LACP

19. What's the virtual MAC address format for VRRP?

    A. 0000.5e00.01xx, with xx being the group number in hexadecimal

    B. 0000.5e00.01xx, with xx being the group number in decimal

    C. 0007.B400.01xx, with xx being the group number in hexadecimal

    D. 0007.0c07.acxx, with xx being the forwarder number in hexadecimal

20. Which of the following is true of GLBP? (Choose two.)

   A. There can be multiple active AVGs at a time.

   B. An AVG can be an AVF.

   C. There can be multiple active AVFs at a time.

   D. You configure the load-balancing method on each AVF.

21. Which of the following modes is LACP compatible with? (Choose two.)

   A. Desirable

   B. Passive

   C. Auto

   D. Active

Chapter

4

Wireless LAN (WLAN)

THE CCNP ENCOR EXAM OBJECTIVES COVERED IN THIS CHAPTER INCLUDE THE FOLLOWING:

Domain 1: Architecture

✓ 1.2 Analyze design principles of a WLAN deployment

Domain 3: Infrastructure

✓ 3.3 Wireless

Domain 5: Security

✓ 5.4 Configure and verify wireless security features

✓ 5.5 Describe the components of network security design

There was a time when being a network engineer meant having to understand how data is converted into pulses of electrical current and carried along a wire. But thanks to the ubiquity of Ethernet standards, you don't need to think much about the physical medium of wired networks or how layer 1 interfaces with it. In wired networking, you can direct the signal where you need it. It's easy to imagine the mechanics of wired networks because you can see the medium connecting nodes together. You can easily explain twisted-pair cabling to a networking novice because they can touch it, manipulate it, and see where the signals are going simply by following the medium. This is because almost everyone's familiar with how electrical current behaves. You take it for granted that in order to charge your smartphone, you have to plug it into a charger. Likewise, you don't expect the remote control to work if it doesn't have batteries. Aside from these mundane examples, you may have even had some unpleasant close encounters with current, such as accidentally touching a conductor carrying alternating current and feeling an unpleasant buzz. All of these instances reinforce your understanding that electrical current—and hence data—follows the path of a conductor that you can see and touch.

Wireless doesn't require a physical medium that you can see or touch. Although we say radio signals travel over the "airwaves," the fact is that they don't need air to propagate. Radio signals don't need any medium at all. Radio waves are made up of electromagnetic energy—essentially light—which can move through empty space. This means everyone running a wireless network is using the same shared medium—not unlike early Ethernet! This has some interesting implications for layers 1 and 2 that we'll look at in this chapter. But first, let's get a better understanding of what radio waves are made of and how they propagate.

Radio Frequency Fundamentals

When it comes to radio, visualizing the physical medium and direction of signals becomes more difficult because it's invisible energy traveling through empty space. Because of this significant difference, you need to take a moment to understand the mysterious properties of radio waves. Don't worry—the math is easy, and you don't need a physics background. Just as you don't need to have a degree in electrical engineering to use twisted-pair Ethernet, you don't need to understand the physics behind radio theory to manage a wireless network. The underlying theory behind radio is complex, so it will be necessary for you to simply accept and memorize some information even if you don't completely understand it. What's most important is that you can apply what you learn.

When I was 16, I began studying to get my amateur radio license. During my studies, one thing that stood out to me was the different ways people would conceptualize radio waves. One person would compare them to waves on the water, whereas another would liken them to sound waves traveling through the air. These comparisons always left me with the obvious nagging question: what's a radio wave made of? After all, every other sort of wave is made of something. A sound wave is made of vibrating air molecules, and a water wave is made of water molecules. In these cases, a wave is a bunch of particles bumping into one another in such a way as to create a wave pattern and motion. Even a visible light wave is made up of subatomic particles called photons that vibrate at a certain frequency. But a radio wave turns out to be fundamentally different.

Frequency and Amplitude

Photons are what actually carry all forms of electromagnetic energy, from microwaves to visible light to X-rays. Radio waves *use* electromagnetic energy, but a radio wave is fundamentally different than a wave on the ocean or a light wave. A radio wave has two components: frequency or wavelength and amplitude, often represented in a graph as shown in Figure 4.1. Frequency or wavelength is the measured change in electromagnetic energy within a specific time period called a cycle. In the following section I will explain that concept further.

FIGURE 4.1   Representation of radio wave at 10 Hz with an amplitude of 1

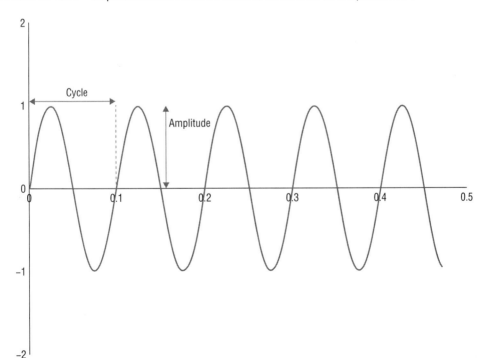

Without any context, you're likely to look at the diagram in Figure 4.1 and assume that this is what a radio wave looks like. It's too easy to walk away with the idea that a radio wave is like a rope jutting out from an antenna and bobbing about in a wavelike motion, slapping some distant receiver. Although this makes for a funny visual, the reality is a bit more sensible.

Frequency

Frequency is measured in Hertz (Hz), what used to be called *cycles-per-second (cps)*. To simplify things, visualize a radio wave as a burst of a cloud of photons emanating from an antenna and moving outward at roughly the speed of light (the exact direction depends on the design of the antenna). Photons are carriers of electromagnetic energy, so you may also think of photons as simply energy if you prefer. Each burst of photons is a single wave. The number of waves that are emitted per second is called the frequency. The number of photons emitted in each burst is the amplitude.

Amplitude

The amplitude of a signal measures the power of a radio wave at a given point in space. The strength of a radio signal is proportional to the photon density. As the waves move farther from the transmitter, the amplitude decreases. A receiver standing right next to the transmitter will get hit with a lot more photons—and hence a lot more energy—than a receiver 10 miles away. The farther away you are, the fewer photons you can receive, and the weaker the signal will be. Signal strength decreases with distance.

You can visualize a radio wave as a flashing beacon light sitting atop a high tower. If the beacon flashes once every second, its frequency is 1 Hz. The brightness of the beacon is the amplitude. You could say that the beacon is a radio station transmitting at a certain frequency. If this sounds simple, it's because it really is. The complexity of radio waves comes into play when you use them to transmit data. More on that in a moment, but first, let's get a clearer handle on the significance of frequency.

Imagine you're viewing the beacon through dense fog at night. The brightness is such that you can barely make out the flashes, and you can't see the bulb or tower at all. Suddenly, the flashes start coming at a different frequency: twice every second. What happened? Here are a few possibilities:

- The beacon increased its frequency to 2 Hz.
- A pirate beacon appeared next to the first one and began operating at 1 Hz.
- A pirate beacon appeared next to the first one and began operating at 2 Hz.

Or it could be a combination of these, such as both beacons flashing at 2 Hz in perfect sync. The same dilemma occurs with radio frequencies, and it's why in many cases laws forbid different radio stations from operating on the same or similar frequencies unless they're separated by a sufficient distance.

If it were the case that a pirate were operating a second beacon at the same 1 Hz frequency, we'd have a case of interference, and it would be impossible to distinguish the pirate beacon from the legitimate one. On the other hand, if you could reasonably assume that no pirate beacon was operating on the same frequency, then we'd know that our beacon simply increased its frequency to 2 Hz.

Radio waves don't come in different "colors" the way visible light does, so for the purposes of the analogy, the color of the beacon is irrelevant. But if you want to consider it, think of the color (let's say it's red) as the medium—that is, radio. A different color such as blue would be a different medium, such as a copper wire carrying an electrical current.

Carrier Frequency

Now that you understand how radio waves function, let's turn to how you use them to send information. The concept of carrier frequency is the foundation of all radio transmissions. Essentially, the carrier frequency is what carries data. Both the sender and the receiver must be tuned into the same carrier frequency to be able to communicate. To view it another way, the carrier frequency is a clocking mechanism that allows a receiver to stay in sync with the sender so that it's able to properly decode what the sender's sending. To illustrate how it works, we'll construct a scenario using the beacon analogy.

Imagine that you need to use a flashing beacon to transmit digital data. To keep things simple, let's assume the only symbols you need to transmit are 0 and 1. The first thing you must do is decide on a carrier frequency. Suppose you choose a carrier frequency of 2 Hz so that the beacon flashes twice every second when no data is being sent. To encode data using your beacon, you have two options; you can encode signals by modifying the frequency of the beacon or by modifying the brightness of it. These correspond to frequency modulation (FM) and amplitude modulation (AM), respectively.

Frequency Modulation (FM)

To encode data using FM, you could lower the frequency by 1 Hz to encode a 0, while increasing it by 1 Hz to encode a 1. Hence, a frequency of 3 Hz indicates a 1, and a frequency of 1 Hz indicates a 0.

Using this scheme, imagine that a receiver sees three flashes in a second (3 Hz), followed by a single flash a second later (1 Hz), and then two flashes every second thereafter (2 Hz). Because the receiver knows the carrier is 2 Hz, it simply compares the frequencies of the received signals to the carrier frequency and decodes the information accordingly. The received bits are 1 and 0, followed by no more data.

Notice that the throughput potential of this approach is quite limited. We can't transmit more than one bit per second. When used with digital data, frequency modulation is called *frequency-shift keying (FSK)*.

There is another scheme called *phase-shift keying (PSK)*. Both PSK and FSK modify the frequency of the carrier signal. You don't need to understand the subtle differences between PSK and FSK—just know that both are limited in terms of the amount of throughput they can achieve. In Wi-Fi networks, quadrature PSK (QPSK) is used as a fallback mechanism in environments with radio interference, but it can't support throughput rates much above 18 Mbps.

Amplitude Modulation (AM)

To encode data using AM, you can make use of different amplitudes. The amplitude is analogous to the beacon's brightness level. Suppose the beacon has three different brightness levels: low, medium, and high. We'll use a low brightness to encode a 0 and a high brightness to encode a 1. A flash of medium brightness indicates no data.

Suppose a receiver sees the beacon very bright for 1 second, dim the next second, and then bright the third second. The carrier frequency is 2 Hz, and the frequency of the beacon flashes doesn't change, so the receiver must interpret the amplitude at each cycle. Hence, the data received is 110011.

Something profound about amplitude modulation is that the achievable throughput is proportional to the carrier frequency. For instance, by raising the frequency to 100 MHz, it's possible to encode 100,000,000 bits per second (100 Mbps)!

It's also possible to combine modulation methods. Quadrature amplitude modulation (QAM) uses AM and PSK to achieve unbelievably high throughput. In fact, in Wi-Fi networks QAM is exclusively used to achieve speeds of 24 Mbps and up.

To see a beacon light through dense fog, it may be necessary to increase the amplitude or brightness. In the same way, in order for a radio signal to get where it needs to go, the transmitter must send it out with sufficient power to overcome distance, obstacles, and even radio interference. I briefly mentioned amplitude as a measurement of power. At a transmitter, amplitude is proportional to the number of photons (i.e., the amount of energy) emitted in a given cycle. But when it comes to radio, what really matters is the power of the signal *at the receiver*.

Power Levels

When we are dealing with large broadcast transmitters, radio transmission power is measured in watts (W). But the output power of Wi-Fi radios typically doesn't reach even 1 watt, so their power is measured in milliwatts (mW), or 1/1000 of a watt.

A typical Wi-Fi access point (AP) may have an output power of 100 mW. As the signal from the AP travels and encounters obstacles, its power will decrease. By the time it reaches a client, the signal strength may be 0.00001 mW! However, suppose the client moves a bit closer to the AP and now is receiving a signal strength of 0.0001 mW. That's better, but how much better? Is it worth moving the client permanently to a different location for an improvement of a fraction of a mW?

This leads us to an interesting discovery about radio waves (and all electromagnetic energy). You know the power of a signal decreases with distance, but it doesn't decrease linearly. If you consider that a radio wave is a cloud of photons radiating outward, like an expanding sphere, it's intuitive that as the sphere grows, the density of the photons—the amplitude—will decrease exponentially. To use another illustration, think of a balloon. As you inflate a balloon, the skin becomes thinner and thinner. In the same way, the amplitude or power density of a signal decreases with the square of the distance, as shown in Figure 4.2.

FIGURE 4.2 Amplitude decreases with the square of the distance.

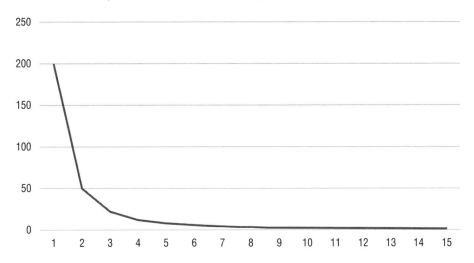

This shape is called a *power law distribution*. If a station is close to the AP, any move closer or farther is going to make a dramatic difference in received signal strength. On the other hand, if a station is far from the AP, moving the client slightly closer is going to make only an infinitesimal difference.

Decibel (dB)

The decibel compares two different power levels and yields an absolute number that indicates the ratio between them. Decibels are useful for representing ratios that range from extremely large to very small, such as you might have when comparing power levels that vary by orders of magnitude. In radio, dB is often used to represent signal gain or loss. Let's use the earlier example with the tiny mW levels, plugging them into the following decibel formula:

$$A2 = 0.0001 \text{ mW}$$
$$A1 = 0.00001 \text{ mW}$$
$$dB = 10*\log (A2/A1)$$

You want to compare the new and improved signal value (A2) against the original or reference value (A1). Plugging the values into the formula yields a value of 10 dB. Hence, you can say that moving the station resulted in an increase of 10 dB. See how this corresponds with the fact that A2 is 10 times the value of A1. This exemplifies one of the well-known decibel laws called the *law of 10s*, which states that every 10 dB indicates a tenfold difference between the numbers being compared. Suppose now you move the receiver closer to the AP and get a received mW power of 0.1 mW. This would yield a result of 40 dB, indicating that the new signal is 10,000 times as much as the reference signal!

The *law of 3s* states that every 3 dB difference indicates a twofold difference in the numbers being compared. This time we'll use a different example. Suppose a station has a received signal strength of 2 mW from an AP. The station moves closer and now has a received signal strength of 4 mW—a twofold increase. There isn't even a need to perform the dB calculation. Using the law of 3s, you can determine that the received signal strength increased by about 3 dB.

It's worth noting that dB values will be negative when the reference value is less than the given value. Using the last example, if the station with a 4 mW received signal strength moves away from the AP and winds up with a received signal strength of 0.8 mW, the difference is about −7 dB.

The closer the dB value gets to 0, the less of a difference there is between the compared signals. In cases of very tiny differences, it's possible to have fractional dB. And 0 dB indicates that the signals are the same, a fact aptly named the *law of zeros*.

Decibel-Milliwatt (DBm)

In most Wi-Fi networks you're not going to run into power levels much above a few watts, and even then only in environments like warehouses or large outdoor venues where an AP needs to crank out a lot of power to overcome dense obstacles or cover long distances. For the most part, you'll be dealing with milliwatts. The dBm measures power relative to a single milliwatt and simplifies dB calculations by assuming a 1 mW reference power. To see how to use dBm, consider a scenario where you want to find the signal loss between a 300 mW transmitter and a receiver. You'd start by calculating the dBm at the transmitter:

$$dBm = 10*\log(300mW/1mW)$$

The power of the signal being transmitted is about 25 dBm. Now suppose that the signal strength at the receiver is 0.0000001 mW. Measured in dBm, the received signal level would be −70 dBm. With a little simple math, you can determine the net signal loss by subtracting the received signal level from the transmitted level:

$$25\ dBm - -70\ dBm = 95\ dBm$$

The total signal loss is 95 dBm.

Antenna Types

Thus far we've focused on power from two perspectives: the power of a signal generated by a transmitter, and the power of a signal received by a receiver. But this is an oversimplification. There's another factor you now need to consider: antennas.

Antennas are the unsung heroes of radio. They're what radiate energy out into space and make radio transmission possible. You're not likely going to be designing your own antennas, so you don't need to understand the theory behind how they work, but you do need to know the different types of antennas used in Wi-Fi networks.

The isotropic antenna is a theoretical antenna that radiates energy in all directions equally. Even though it doesn't exist, it's used as a reference example of a perfect antenna against which we can measure our real antennas. Because it radiates equally in all directions, changing its orientation in space relative to the receiver won't provide any signal gain. Hence, we say that is has zero gain. Gain is a measurement of how much an antenna's radiation pattern favors a particular direction. With an isotropic antenna, a receiver can hover over the antenna, stand next to it, or sit below it, and as long as the distance from the antenna remains the same, the receiver will receive the same amount of power from the antenna. You measure antenna gain in terms of dB-isotropic (dBi), indicating the comparison to the perfect isotropic antenna. The higher the dBi, the more directional the radiation pattern. Gain can vary widely among antennas, even of the same type.

Omnidirectional antennas are what you think of when you hear the word "antenna." Long, flimsy omnidirectional antennas are typically called whip antennas. Antennas like the ones you find on Wi-Fi radios are shorter, just a few inches in length, and are straight and rigid. Omnidirectional antennas radiate outward in a donut-like pattern. Just imagine placing a donut over the shaft of an antenna, and you have a good visual of the radiation pattern. The gain of omnidirectional antennas varies greatly. Antennas integrated into Wi-Fi radios typically have a gain of about 2 dBi, whereas external antennas may go up to 15 dBi.

Directional antennas concentrate the radiation pattern in a certain direction. The Yagi antenna, for example, is a type of directional antenna that forms an approximately 90-degree beam. This works nicely if you want to cover just one spot, such as an outdoor field. The parabolic dish antenna creates a tighter beam of about 10 degrees. Yagis have a typical gain of 10 to 15 dBi. Parabolic dishes are usually used on dedicated point-to-point wireless links such as those between two buildings or between a building and a tower. Parabolic antennas can have a gain of up to 30 dBi or higher.

Effective Isotropic Radiated Power (EIRP)

Although you typically don't see it, there's usually a cable connecting the transmitter and antenna. In the case of an external antenna, the cable can be quite long. The longer the cable, the more signal loss will occur, and such loss is measured in dB. The EIRP is the power measured in dBm radiated from an antenna after taking into account the transmitter power, cable loss, and antenna gain. For regulatory purposes, EIRP is the gold standard for measuring power output. In the United States, the maximum allowed EIRP for the 2.4 GHz band is 36 dBm, or 4 watts.

Suppose you have a transmitter generating a 12 dBm output. Its antenna cable has a cable loss of 3 dB, and its antenna has a gain of 5 dBi. For our scenario, the EIRP is calculated as follows:

$$EIRP = 12 \text{ dBm} - 3 \text{ dB} + 5 \text{ dBi}$$

The EIRP would be 14 dBm.

Free Space Path Loss and Wavelength

As we've established, as a radio wave travels, it experiences a decrease in amplitude proportional to the square of the distance. I briefly mentioned that one reason for this is that the energy density of the wave spreads out thinner and thinner as it radiates outward, much like a puff of smoke becoming thinner as it dissipates. The distance affects what the amplitude of the signal is when it reaches a receiver's antenna.

The decrease with distance happens regardless of frequency. But as you move up into higher frequencies, the rate of amplitude decrease actually grows. This might seem surprising, since there's no intuitive reason a signal would weaken faster just because it's at a higher frequency. In fact, the reason for this latter phenomenon has to do with antenna lengths which are influenced by frequency!

To understand the significance of antenna lengths, you need to understand wavelengths. The wavelength (λ) of a signal is related to its frequency. Recall that frequency measures cycles per second. The formula for wavelength is given as

$$\text{Wavelength} = \text{speed of light} / \text{frequency}$$

You may see it written as $\lambda = c/f$, where λ is wavelength, c is the speed of light (m/s), and f is frequency (Hz). Wavelength is simply the distance a single radio wave travels during one cycle. For example, if an FM radio station is transmitting at 88.3 MHz, its transmitter is sending out a burst of energy 88,300,000 times every second! To calculate the wavelength, we'd do the following:

$$\lambda = (299{,}792{,}458 \text{ m/s}) / 88{,}300{,}000 \text{ Hz}$$

The wavelength is about 3.4 meters. That means when the transmitter sends a burst of energy, that energy will travel only about 3.4 meters before the next burst comes. Without getting into the physics, if an antenna is too long or too short relative to the wavelength, it won't radiate the signal as well. To maximize radiation, the length of the antenna should be the same as the wavelength. This isn't always practical, so half-wavelength or quarter-length wavelength antennas are often used.

The higher you get up into the frequencies, the shorter the antennas have to be. The wavelength for the 2.4 GHz frequency is about 5 inches. If you've got a 2.4 GHz AP nearby, measure the length of its antenna, and you'll find it to be pretty close to that. The 5 GHz frequency has a wavelength of about 2.36 inches, allowing for some rather short antennas! Higher frequencies mean shorter antennas.

Free space path loss measures the total signal loss as a function of increasing distance and frequency. The formula for calculating it is complex and you don't need to know it, but an example is instructive. Consider an AP and client 100 feet apart, transmitting at 2.4 GHz. The free space path loss between them is about 67 dB.

Now suppose you replace these devices with their 5 GHz counterparts. The free space path loss increases to 74 dB! The reason for the difference is that the increased frequency means decreased wavelength, which necessitates smaller antennas at the sender and receiver. Thankfully, you can easily overcome such losses by increasing the amplitude of the transmitting signal or using a higher gain antenna.

  Free space path loss doesn't include amplitude loss due to encounters with obstacles or interference.

Received Signal Strength

The power of a particular signal received by a station, after making deductions for cable loss and antenna gain, is given by the received signal strength indicator (RSSI), which is measured in dBm. The RSSI ranges from –100 dBm to 0 dBm. A receiver can detect a signal down to its sensitivity level, which varies according to the way the radio is designed. Generally it's going to be closer to the –100 dBm end of the range.

All radio frequencies interfere with one another constantly. Ever present in any environment is a collection of random intertwined signals called *noise*. Noise consists of radio frequency (RF) energy from other stations, electrical wires, lightning, and even the sun. The sum of all these signals is called the *noise floor*. In order for a receiver to make out a signal, the RSSI must be greater than the noise floor. Both the signal amplitude and the noise floor can shift. For instance, if the noise floor is –80 dBm and the RSSI of a signal is –50 dBm, then the receiver can make out the signal just fine. A moment later, however, the signal may drop to –75 dBm, and the noise floor may increase to –70 dBm. Now the receiver can no longer pick out the signal among all the noise, even though it has actually received it.

Signal-to-Noise Ratio (SNR)

The difference between the RSSI and the noise floor is called the *signal-to-noise ratio (SNR)*. Supposing the noise floor is –85 dBm and the RSSI is –50 dBm, the SNR would be

$$-50 dBm - -85\ dBm = 35\ dBm$$

In order for the signal to be intelligible, the SNR must be greater than 0. A higher SNR is better. Another way of looking at it is that the greater the SNR, the more variation in signal loss and noise floor increase the receiver can tolerate and still be able to use the signal.

To hearken back to the beacon analogy one last time, imagine that you're looking at a flashing beacon in the dark of night. The SNR is extremely high since no other light is competing with the light from the beacon. Later, the sun rises just behind the beacon, overpowering its flashing strobe. The SNR in that situation is exceptionally low, possibly even zero, because the beacon is competing with the noise of too much ambient light.

WLAN 802.11 Standards

Now that you have a good understanding of radio theory, it's time to turn to using the airwaves to transport data. Just as IEEE 802.3 Ethernet defines the rules for wired networks of various flavors, the IEEE 802.11 family of standards defines the physical (layer 1) and data link (layer 2) standards for operation of WLANs.

The Physical Layer: Frequencies and Channels

You're no doubt aware of the various physical standards that the IEEE has put out over the years, dating from about 1999 to the present (2020). As of this writing, in order of earliest to latest they are

- 802.11a
- 802.11b
- 802.11g

- 802.11n
- 802.11ac
- 802.11ax

802.11n and 802.11ac are the most common today. Although the earlier standards are obsolete, you may still run into the occasional 802.11g network. You may wonder why there have been so many changes to 802.11 when Ethernet seems to have undergone relatively few. Both Ethernet and 802.11 have undergone layer 1 changes to take advantage of new technology in order to achieve faster speeds and longer range. In fact, 802.3 Ethernet has actually undergone *more* physical layer changes than 802.11.

The biggest difference between wired and wireless networks is the physical medium. It's obvious that wireless networks need different layer 1 standards to encode data as radio signals, rather than bits on a wire. Sounds simple enough. But compared to wired networking, wireless introduces two new distinct but related problems.

First, you can't change the physical medium. When you want to go from Gigabit Ethernet to 10 Gigabit Ethernet, you have to use a different physical medium that can support the new speed. In other words, you need new cables. But when it comes to wireless, you can't change the medium. Therefore, any improvements you make to wireless at layer 1 will have to be improvements in how you *use* the medium.

Second, with wireless, you're sharing the same airwaves with everyone else! Remember from Chapter 1, "Networking Fundamentals," that the problem early Ethernet ran into was having too many devices sharing a single electrical bus. The solution was to break the medium up into separate collision domains. Clearly, you need a way to break up the wireless medium into separate collision domains. But unlike with an electrical bus, you can't just "disconnect" a portion of space from another, creating an impenetrable wall through which radio signals can't pass. You need a different approach.

The IEEE 802.11 layer 1 standards break up the airwaves into separate frequency ranges called channels. Devices that communicate on the same channel share a set of frequencies and are in the same collision domain. Ideally, devices in one channel should form a single collision domain and be isolated at layer 1 from devices on another channel. To use a crude analogy, devices in one channel are like workstations connected to an Ethernet hub.

Channels

A channel is a range of consecutive frequencies. The frequency range of each channel is its channel bandwidth (or just channel width). Bandwidth directly affects attainable data throughput because 802.11 simultaneously transmits on multiple frequencies at once. This approach is called *spread spectrum* because it multiplexes a single data stream over multiple frequencies. The more bandwidth is allocated to a channel, the more parallel data streams you can send. (Incidentally, this is precisely why the terms *bandwidth* and *throughput* are often used interchangeably.)

Different layer 1 802.11 standards allocate channels from different RF bands. The 802.11b/g/n standards all operate in the 2.4 GHz frequency band, whereas 802.11ac uses the 5 GHz band. These bands differ not only in their frequencies, but also in the way they allocate channel bandwidth.

The 2.4 GHz Band

The 2.4 GHz band is divided into 14 channels, each with a 20 MHz bandwidth, as listed in Table 4.1. If you look at the frequency ranges, you'll see that each channel has 22 MHz allocated but that only 20 MHz is actually used for each channel.

TABLE 4.1   The 2.4 GHz band

Channel	Center frequency (MHz)	Frequency range (MHz)
1	2412	2401–2423
2	2417	2406–2428
3	2422	2411–2433
4	2427	2416–2438
5	2432	2421–2443
6	2437	2426–2448
7	2442	2431–2453
8	2447	2436–2458
9	2452	2441–2463
10	2457	2446–2468
11	2462	2451–2473
12	2467	2456–2478
13	2472	2461–2483
14	2484	2473–2495

Notice that the frequencies of the channels overlap considerably. Each frequency represents a separate collision domain, so only one station at a time can talk on a given frequency. For example, channel 1 shares frequencies with channels 2, 3, 4, and 5. This means that adjacent channels can easily bleed into one another, defeating the whole purpose of channels to begin with. So why design it this way? The reasons were purely practical. When wireless networks were being dreamed up, there were other devices in the 2.4 GHz spectrum, and they didn't require more than 5 MHz of bandwidth. There's an old saying (usually falsely attributed to Bill Gates) that goes something like "640 KB of memory ought to be enough for anyone." Well, the folks who came up with the 2.4 GHz band plan figured 5 MHz of bandwidth ought to be good enough for anyone. It was a reasonable assumption at the time.

Even in its early days, there wasn't a lot of room to work with. Today, not much has changed. Radio frequencies near the 2.4 GHz spectrum are used for mobile phones and industrial and scientific equipment. The 2.4 GHz band is crowded, and that's not going to change any time soon. The good news is that you can carefully select channels that don't have overlap. For example, if you're setting up three WLAN APs in an office, you can assign channels 1, 6, and 11 to avoid overlap. Of course, this works only if there aren't already any other wireless networks in the vicinity using nearby channels. The 2.4 GHz band is generally not a great place to be unless you're in a rural area.

The 5 GHz Band

IEEE 802.11n/ac makes use of the less crowded 5 GHz band. The exact frequencies of the 5 GHz band vary by country but range from 4910 to 5875 MHz. Unlike the straightforward numbering of the 2.4 GHz channels, the 5 GHz band is pretty convoluted. IEEE 802.11ac supports bandwidths of 20 MHz, 40 MHz, 80 MHz, and 160 MHz. But there are some strict limits for channel/bandwidth combinations, as shown in Table 4.2.

TABLE 4.2   Channel bandwidths for the 5 GHz band

Channel bandwidth	Usable channel numbers
20 MHz	36, 40, 44, 48, 52, 56, 60, 64, 100, 104, 108, 112, 116, 120, 124, 128, 132, 136, 140, 144, 149, 153, 161, 165, 169
40 MHz	38, 46, 54, 62, 102, 110, 118, 126, 134, 142, 151, 159
80 MHz	42, 58, 106, 122, 138, 155
160 MHz	50, 114

For bandwidths above 20 MHz, each channel consumes channels above and below it. For example, if you use channel 46 with a 40 MHz bandwidth, you'll be borrowing bandwidth from channels 44 and 48. To avoid using overlapping frequencies, your best bet is to use the same bandwidth for all your APs. That means if you want to make use of an 80 MHz bandwidth per channel, you have only six channels to choose from. Hence, if you need 25 APs at a site, you should stick with a 20 MHz bandwidth so as not to have any two APs competing on the same frequencies.

Dealing with Signal Degradation

If the signal degrades due to distance or interference, it's naturally going to introduce errors that will affect throughput and reliability. When an AP and client have a good connection, they'll use QAM to achieve high throughput. As the client moves away and the signal degrades, QAM doesn't work as well, and some packets may get dropped and have to be retransmitted, resulting in lower throughput. To compensate for this, they'll switch over to QPSK, which offers lower throughput but greater reliability.

Comparing 802.11 Physical Standards

You don't need to know the details of every 802.11 standard ever made, but you do need to understand the capabilities of the more modern standards. It goes without saying that an AP and client must use the same standard in order to interoperate. For example, a client that supports only 802.11g can't connect to an AP that supports only 802.11ac. Table 4.3 highlights key capabilities of each standard.

TABLE 4.3   Comparing bandwidths and data rates of 802.11 standards

Standard	Supported band	Supported bandwidth (MHz)	Maximum data rate
802.11g	2.4	20	54 Mbps
802.11n	2.4, 5	20, 40	600 Mbps
802.11ac	5	20, 40, 80, 160	3.464 Gbps
802.11ax	2.4, 5	20, 40, 80, 160	9.6 Gbps

Layer 2: 802.11 Media Access Control (MAC)

Remember that OSI layer 2 sets up the rules for node-to-node communication within a subnet. You might guess that because both Ethernet and WLANs are standardized under the 802 family of standards, they provide a way for wired and wireless clients to interoperate with one another in the same subnet. And you'd be right! However, achieving that interoperability isn't as easy as you might expect.

Ethernet was originally designed for a shared medium—the thick yellow cable—so it would seem natural to just take the existing Ethernet standards and tweak them to apply to wireless networking. But surprisingly, this approach doesn't work. Ethernet uses MAC addresses to uniquely identify each node, and communication simply requires one node to address an Ethernet frame to another node. Notice that Ethernet takes it for granted that the two nodes are already physically connected to each other in some way. If you have devices connected at layer 1, the thinking goes, then they obviously should be able to communicate at layer 2. Devices that aren't physically connected just aren't part of the network. It's as simple as that.

But when it comes to wireless, these assumptions don't hold true. A wireless client isn't "connected at layer 1" in the same sense that a wired client is connected to a switch. Wireless clients can move in and out of range of an AP and each other. Furthermore, because the physical medium is everywhere and unrestricted, you have no control over whether someone blasts signals into your office or home. And radio is lossy and prone to interference, so data can get lost or corrupted easily. Let's look at how 802.11 overcomes these and other problems caused by using the lossy shared medium of radio.

Media Access

In a WLAN, accessing the medium really just means transmitting a radio signal. The distributed coordination function (DCF) is similar to Ethernet's CSMA/CD, except instead of sensing collisions, DCF attempts to avoid them. Thus, it takes what's called a CSMA/collision avoidance (CA) approach. DCF requires a station to wait for radio silence before transmitting. If the airwaves are busy, the station waits a random amount of time before trying again. There are other MAC methods, but DCF is the one that all 802.11 networks must support.

Authentication

Authentication mechanisms control which stations may establish an association with an AP, whereas encryption prevents data from being sniffed or modified in transit. Technically authentication and encryption are separate processes, but authentication and encryption often are used together. We'll cover encryption in a moment. The 802.11 family of standards offers the following authentication mechanisms:

Open System or Open Authentication   This is practically the same as no authentication, and any station that requests it will be authenticated. Open systems don't provide any in-transit encryption. Public Wi-Fi hotspots almost always use this.

WebAuth   WebAuth is a variant of open authentication that redirects users to a captive portal to complete some action before they're allowed to access network resources. See if this scenario sounds familiar: You go to a public hotspot and connect. You open your web browser and get redirected to a captive portal page that requires some action. It may prompt you to agree to some terms or it may ask you for a password or other credentials. After you enter the requested information and are authenticated, the system lets you browse the Internet. Since it's really just an open system, WebAuth doesn't include in-transit encryption.

Shared Key or Preshared Key   A station must provide a password to associate with the AP. Shared-key authentication is almost exclusively used in conjunction with WPA personal mode encryption, which we'll cover in a moment.

802.1X   This requires the connecting station (called the supplicant) to authenticate to an authentication server before it can join the WLAN. The authentication server can be the same one you use for other IT resources, such as a Kerberos or RADIUS server. IEEE 802.1X uses the Extensible Authentication Protocol (EAP) to integrate with a variety of authentication providers.

Association

The association process is how a station and AP negotiate the rules for communicating with one another. Association establishes layer 2 connectivity with the WLAN, and it can occur only after authentication is successful. When a station wants to associate with an access point, it sends an association request with the service set identifier (SSID) of the

WLAN it wants to connect to as well as its supported data rates. The AP sends an association response with its own supported data rates. The station and AP can use the association frames to negotiate other options such as those related to flow control and encryption. Other options include performance and compatibility enhancements for the older 802.11 physical standards.

Encryption

In theory, radio signals can be picked up by anyone, so encrypting data sent over the air is the most significant thing you can do to secure a WLAN. Many open systems rely on encryption as a substitute for authentication. IEEE 802.11 offers three encryption mechanisms:

Wired Equivalent Privacy (WEP)   Part of the original 802.11 specification, WEP was intended to mimic the privacy characteristics of a wired LAN. WEP uses the insecure RC4 cipher to encrypt data, but because it was incorrectly implemented, it's vulnerable to reverse-engineering the encryption key. It's been easily crackable for well over a decade. Never use it!

Wi-Fi Protected Access (WPA) with Temporal Key Integrity Protocol (TKIP)   WPA-TKIP, also known as WPA1, was the answer to WEP's weaknesses. It also uses RC4 but implements it in a slightly more secure way than WEP. However, because it uses RC4, it's still vulnerable to exploits, so I recommend you don't use it. One reason WPA uses the computationally light RC4 cipher is so that older devices that support only WEP can be given WPA capability with a simple firmware upgrade.

WPA2 with CCMP   WPA2 uses the AES cipher implemented using an encryption mechanism called CCMP (an acronym that has four different meanings depending on who you ask). The AES cipher is much more secure than RC4, and the CCMP implementation of cryptography is superior to TKIP. WPA2 much more computationally intensive than WEP and WPA1, but modern hardware is more than capable of handling it.

WPA3 with CCMP   This is the latest iteration of WPA, and like WPA2, it uses AES and CCMP. But it adds some additional security for personal (preshared key) implementations. It also implements forward secrecy, which prevents an attacker from decrypting captured traffic even if they know the shared key.

Encryption isn't the same as authentication, but it does provide a way to control access to the WLAN. For example, if you enable WPA2 with a preshared key, users must type the key into their device to be able to connect. WPA used with a preshared key is called *WPA personal mode*. But this isn't the only option. Encryption can be used in conjunction with 802.1X authentication. When 802.1X and EAP are used in conjunction with WPA, it's called *WPA enterprise mode*. Once the user authenticates using whatever method you've allowed (user credentials, smartcard, certificate, one-time-password, etc.), their client and the AP will automatically negotiate WPA2 encryption without any further action on the user's part. This makes for a robust and seamless solution that provides authentication and encryption.

Error Control and Flow Control

The contention-based nature of wireless requires some coordination among transmitting stations. Unlike in a full-duplex Ethernet, Wi-Fi stations just blindly transmitting whenever they have data to send would result in radio interference and data errors. However, since there are few physical restrictions to the airwaves, radio interference is unavoidable. IEEE 802.11 provides flow control mechanisms to coordinate transmission and avoid errors, as well as error control features to detect and recover from data errors caused by interference.

Acknowledgments

In a way similar to TCP, 802.11 uses acknowledgments to indicate when a unicast frame is received. The sender marks each frame with a sequence number, and the receiving station responds with an ACK. If the sender doesn't receive an ACK to a frame, it will retransmit it. Retransmissions are usually the result of interference, obstacles, or insufficient signal strength. With the exception of a software bug or hardware error, retransmissions occur in only two cases:

- The intended recipient never receives the frame, resulting in the sender retransmitting it.
- The recipient receives the frame and sends an ACK, but the ACK doesn't make it back to the sender intact.

As you might expect, waiting for an ACK to a frame before transmitting the next frame slows things down quite a bit. To improve throughput, 802.11 offers the option of using block acknowledgments. Rather than waiting for an ACK to each frame, the sender sends a block of frames, and then waits for a single acknowledgment frame that indicates all the frames were received. You can think of this process as a two-way handshake. Unlike TCP's three-way handshake, there's no acknowledgment of the ACK itself.

    Acknowledgments aren't sent for multicast frames.

Frame Check Sequence (FCS)

Radio interference has the propensity to corrupt data in transit, so all frames include a 32-bit checksum to aid in detecting corrupted frames. If a frame doesn't pass the FCS, it's silently discarded. If a sender receives a corrupted frame, it will not send an ACK in response. Likewise, if the sender receives a corrupted ACK frame, it will ignore it. Interference can cause data throughput to drop like a lead balloon!

Request-to-Send/Clear-to-Send (RTS/CTS)

RTS/CTS is an optional feature of 802.11 that helps avoid interference in cases where stations can't hear one another but can hear the AP. Therefore, these stations are more likely to transmit simultaneously, causing interference. Enabling RTS/CTS on these stations will cause them to defer to the AP before transmitting. When a station wants to transmit, it sends an RTS frame to the AP. The AP responds with a CTS that grants the station the privilege of transmitting for a short period of time. All other stations also receive the CTS and take note of the duration, so they know not to transmit during this window. This process dramatically reduces the potential for interference, although it's still possible for two stations to send RTS frames simultaneously. Note that enabling RTS/CTS in an environment where all stations can hear one another is unnecessary and will decrease throughput.

802.2 Logical Link Control (LLC)

In WLANs, layer 2 is actually divided into two sublayers: 802.11 MAC and 802.2 logical link control (LLC). This division is arbitrary and trivial but highlights another difference between 802.11 and Ethernet. The Type field of the 802.2 LLC frame serves the same function as the EtherType field in an Ethernet frame. The reason for using a separate LLC frame for this instead of just placing a Type field in the 802.11 frame is simply that IEEE has dictated that all 802 networks except Ethernet must use LLC.

Achieving High Throughput with Multiple-Input and Multiple-Output

Increasing transmit power and using complex modulation schemes can take us only so far when it comes to increasing data throughput rates. To get much over 100 Mbps, it's necessary to use multiple radios to create multiple simultaneous data streams. This method is called multiple-input and multiple-output (MIMO). There are two forms of MIMO:

Spatial Multiplexing   The theory behind spatial multiplexing is simple: if you can push 50 Mbps using a single radio, you can push 100 Mbps by transmitting simultaneously using two radios on different frequencies. Spatial multiplexing takes the data to be sent, splits it up, and simultaneously transmits it using multiple radios. The receiver, of course, has to have multiple receiving radios and the capability to reassemble the separate signals into a single data stream. If a device has four radios for transmitting and two for receiving, then it's a 4×2 MIMO device. If a device has two radios for transmitting and two for receiving, it's a 2×2 MIMO device. 802.11n/ac/ax uses spatial multiplexing to achieve hundreds-of-megabits-per-second throughput.

Diversity   The theory behind diversity is similar to that of spatial multiplexing, but with one small difference. One of the enemies of throughput is signal degradation. Diversity works by sending the *same* data simultaneously on different frequencies using antennas positioned differently. Because the signals are on different frequencies and take slightly different paths, there's a chance that one of them will encounter less interference or arrive at the receiver with greater strength. The receiver selects the best signal at any given moment, resulting in more consistent throughput.

Access Point Modes

An access point is a bridge between wireless clients and the wired LAN. Just as the area a switch can cover is limited by cable length restrictions, the area an AP can cover is limited by the RF environment and the AP's and clients' capabilities. This leads to the need to deploy multiple APs to ensure coverage.

Cisco access points can operate in one of two modes: autonomous or lightweight. As the name suggests, in autonomous mode you configure each AP independently and it functions independently. This isn't so bad if you need to cover a small area, but if you have to cover a large campus, it becomes a management nightmare. To wrangle dozens or even hundreds of APs, you need a centralized management infrastructure. Thankfully, Cisco APs provide a lightweight mode, wherein the AP gives up its autonomy and relies on a wireless LAN controller (WLC) for its configuration and some of its functionality.

Autonomous

Autonomous APs are much like what you'd have at home, just a stand-alone AP that serves a small area. For the most part, autonomous mode APs work out of the box, acting as a bridge between a wireless client and a VLAN. Each AP functions as a self-contained unit, performing authentication, encryption, IP address assignment, traffic filtering, and 802.1Q tagging. If you need to cover just a small area with just a few APs, then autonomous mode might be right for you.

Autonomous mode is also ideal if you have wireless clients in the same area that need to communicate with one another. For example, wireless workstations may need to print to a wireless printer. By connecting all of them to the same AP and having them in the same VLAN, you ensure that traffic will flow through the AP without having to ever touch the wired network. This approach is particularly useful for small offices where there isn't a wired infrastructure.

But if you need to set up a larger collection of APs, autonomous mode can be cumbersome. You have to independently configure each AP and its connections to the wired LAN. If you want users to be able to seamlessly roam between autonomous APs, you'll have to trunk the same data VLAN to each AP. Extend a VLAN to a large number of APs and you'll wind up with a large, unwieldy broadcast domain, the potential for ugly bridging loops, and complex Spanning Tree topologies that may end up blocking ports you don't want blocked.

Lightweight

If you need more than 10 access points, you should consider the lightweight approach. In lightweight mode, an AP surrenders its autonomy and some of its functionality to a centralized WLC. The AP performs the physical layer functions of 802.11 and encryption, whereas the WLC controls the configuration of the AP and handles association and 802.1X authentication. This split-brain architecture is officially called the *split-MAC architecture*.

The WLC also terminates connections to the wired LAN, effectively acting as the LAN bridge for the AP. This lightweight approach greatly simplifies management and deployment of APs. Rather than trunking needed VLANs to each AP, you just trunk them to the WLC that APs use.

Each AP transports control and data traffic to and from the WLC via a dedicated Control and Provisioning of Wireless Access Points (CAPWAP) tunnel. Each AP needs only an IP address, which it can use to build a tunnel to a WLC. For the curious, the details of CAPWAP are codified in RFC 5415 (`https://tools.ietf.org/rfc/rfc5415.txt`).

A WLC can handle multiple APs, and because the CAPWAP tunnels terminate at layer 3, there's no need for the WLC and APs to be in the same VLAN. This tremendously improves scalability and makes it easy to centrally locate the WLC in a data center or wherever the network core happens to be. A disadvantage of the centralized approach is that if the WLC goes down or the AP loses connectivity to it, the AP ceases to function properly.

As an alternative to the centralized WLC, you can maintain a WLC in the same access layer as your APs. A simple way to do this is to use the Embedded Wireless Controller (EWC) functionality built into some Cisco switches and access points. This option represents a compromise between the autonomous and centralized topologies.

Wireless LAN Controller Selection Process

When you plug in a lightweight AP, it will attempt to automatically discover and set up a CAPWAP tunnel with a suitable WLC. Naturally, each AP needs a management IP address that you can configure manually. Otherwise, it will use DHCP to get one. After that, the discovery process begins.

WLC Discovery

Because APs in lightweight mode require a WLC to function, they have to pull out all the stops to make sure they're able to join a WLC. There are several methods they can use to locate a WLC.

To speed the discovery process, you can preconfigure an AP with the IP addresses of up to three controllers in order of priority—primary, secondary, and tertiary. You can alternatively configure DHCP option 43 on a DHCP server, populating the value with candidate WLC IP addresses.

Barring these two approaches, if the AP has never connected to a WLC before, it will broadcast a CAPWAP discovery request on UDP port 5246. Any WLCs that receive the broadcast will respond with a CAPWAP discovery response. On the other hand, if the AP has previously connected to one or more WLCs, it will have stored their IP addresses, and it will send the discovery request as a unicast to all of them.

Finally, just before giving up and starting over, the AP will try to resolve the domain name CISCO-CAPWAP-CONTROLLER.*domain.local*, where *domain.local* is the domain suffix learned from DHCP option 15. If it resolves to an IP address, the AP will assume it's for a WLC and will proceed to the selection stage.

The WLCs that respond with a discovery response compose the WLC candidate list that the AP will choose from in the selection process. When a WLC responds with a discovery response, it includes a metric indicating its current load. The load is a metric indicating the number of APs connected to it and how many total APs it can support. The AP will use the load information to determine which WLC to join.

Selection and Join

The AP sends a CAPWAP join request to the candidate WLC with the lowest load. This helps to ensure an even load distribution in environments with multiple WLCs. Once the WLC returns a join response, both the AP and WLC build an encrypted CAPWAP tunnel that they'll use for control and data traffic.

After joining, if the AP is running a software release that is different than the WLC, it will download the appropriate image from the WLC and reboot. After that, the AP will rejoin the WLC and download its configuration, which includes channel and authenticating settings and SSIDs.

If a WLC becomes unavailable or unresponsive after the AP joins, the AP can fall back to another one of the controllers in its candidate list. To improve availability, you can configure WLCs in a high-availability (HA) active-standby pair. If the active controller fails, by using stateful switchover (SSO) the standby controller can instantly take over.

Roaming and Location Services

By their nature, wireless clients don't tend to stay in one place. They roam around, often switching their association from one access point to another. In this section, we'll look at the different types of roaming, how they work, and how you can use data collected from APs to pinpoint the physical location of clients using location services.

Roaming

When a client senses that the signal from its associated AP is weak, it begins to look for another AP to associate with. It's up to the client to decide when to roam and which AP to associate with. Essentially, when a client roams, it disassociates from one AP and associates with a different one, so there is necessarily a temporary loss of connectivity. As long as 802.1X authentication isn't being used, roaming can occur quickly, in a matter of a few milliseconds. With 802.1X authentication, it takes closer to a second. The primary concern with roaming is not so much how quickly the client roams, but whether the APs and WLCs are configured to provide seamless WLAN connectivity to clients as they roam about.

Roaming between Autonomous APs

When using autonomous APs, you'll likely have them connected to a dedicated wireless VLAN. Using the power of transparent bridging, extending a subnet across all APs facilitates almost seamless roaming. When a client connected to one AP roams to another, it simply has to associate with the closer AP. It maintains its IP address, and as soon as it sends a frame, the switches update their MAC address tables accordingly to reflect the client's new location. Roaming just works, and it works even if there are several APs.

Roaming between Lightweight APs

In a lightweight topology, the functionality of each AP is shared between the AP and its connected WLC. As long as both APs are connected to the same controller, the roaming process works smoothly. This is called an *intracontroller roam.*

When a client roams between APs that are connected to different WLCs, it's called an *intercontroller roam.* This may occur when a client moves between buildings and associates with an AP on another controller. How clients roam between WLCs boils down to whether the WLCs share the same VLAN.

Layer 2 roaming—WLCs share a VLAN In layer 2 roaming, if both WLCs are connected to the same VLAN, the roam occurs similarly to how it does with autonomous APs. The client roams to a different AP, maintains its IP address, and the wired switching infrastructure updates its MAC address tables.

You'll notice that this scenario is not ideal from a design perspective. A single WLC can handle hundreds of APs, so you wouldn't likely have multiple WLCs except in a large environment. Extending a VLAN across such a huge network just isn't a good idea. Layer 2 roaming—like autonomous roaming—depends on the magic of transparent bridging. It works flawlessly until it doesn't.

Layer 3 roaming—WLCs don't share a VLAN The term "layer-3 roaming" is a bit misleading. It more accurately could be called "layer-2-over-layer-3 roaming." If the WLCs are in different VLANs, they have to do a little behind-the-scenes magic. First, some terminology: The controller the client is roaming from is called the *anchor controller.* The one it's roaming to is the *foreign controller.* During a roam the foreign controller forms a CAPWAP tunnel with the anchor controller. All client traffic passes over the tunnel to the anchor controller, and the client keeps its original IP address. All that's really happening is that the foreign and anchor controllers are forwarding layer 2 traffic over layer 3. Using this process, the client can roam from controller to controller while maintaining layer 2 connectivity to its anchor controller.

Auto-Anchor Mobility

You may want to force certain clients to always go through a particular WLC regardless of the AP they're connected to. To use a common scenario, you may have an SSID for guest Internet access. You want this to be available everywhere, but you want all traffic to get routed through a firewall at your data center. You can achieve this by using auto-anchor mobility to force all guest clients to go through a WLC at your data center. Whenever a client connects to the guest SSID, regardless of what AP they hit, they will be automatically anchored to the WLC at the data center. This is also called *guest tunneling.*

Location Services

It may be desirable to know the location of wireless clients, be it for asset tracking, emergency services, just-in-time directions, or location-based advertising. The Location Services feature collects signal information from three or more APs and uses it to create a real-time map of Wi-Fi devices. You provide the physical location of your APs by placing them on a map, and Location Services uses a propagation model based on received signal strength to estimate the location of detected Wi-Fi devices. Location Services even works with devices that aren't associated with an AP. All Wi-Fi devices periodically send out probe requests to discover nearby APs, and all APs in earshot will receive these beacons.

Optionally, you can provide your own custom floor layout, making it easier to visually pinpoint a device's location. For greater accuracy, you can calibrate the model by placing a client in a specific location and picking out the location on the map. Location Services adjusts its model accordingly.

 Cisco DNA Spaces provides cloud-based location services, and Cisco Connected Mobile Experiences (CMX) can be deployed on premises or in the cloud.

Summary

Wireless comes with more layer 1 and layer 2 scalability challenges than wired networks do. Today, 802.11 wireless standards and technology have matured to the point that with proper planning, wireless networks can be fast and reliable.

The 2.4 GHz band has been the standby for WLANs since the early 2000s. It's crowded, and that isn't likely to change soon. The 5 GHz band offers some breathing room, and especially if you're thinking of deploying wireless in a populated area, it's your best option for getting fast data speeds and avoiding interference.

Otherwise, when it comes to speed and reliability, the distance between your APs and clients is the most significant factor. Free space path loss and noise can be overcome by shrinking the distance between the transmitter and receiver. Hence, generally speaking, the larger your Wi-Fi environment, the more APs you'll need.

You may have noticed the conspicuous absence of any mention of wireless site surveys. These used to be popular tools in planning deployments when APs were so expensive that companies tried to achieve wireless coverage using as few of them as possible. But today site surveys are rarely necessary. APs are so inexpensive that there's no excuse not to have full coverage.

With a plethora of APs comes the problem of management. Wireless LAN controllers can push configuration to hundreds of APs, collect client location information, and facilitate rapid roaming between APs. WLCs can be integrated into switches or APs, so even when there's no robust wired infrastructure (such as in a small branch office), you can still enjoy the benefits of a centrally managed WLAN.

Exam Essentials

Understand when retransmissions occur.   Retransmissions are usually the result of interference, obstacles, or insufficient signal strength. They have a profound impact on throughput and can result in the AP and client switching to a slower but more reliable modulation scheme. Reducing interference and increasing RSSI can keep you out of the woods.

Know the major differences between 802.11 standards.   You don't need to know all the details, but knowing which standards use the 2.4 GHz and 5 GHz bands, as well as the top data throughput speeds of each standard, is important. Remember that 2.4 GHz and 5 GHz radios aren't compatible.

Understand the various authentication and encryption types.   Authentication and encryption are different but are often used together. An open system has no encryption and may or may not use WebAuth for authentication. This is what you'll typically find in coffee shops. WPA Personal mode uses a preshared key for both authentication and encryption. WPA Enterprise mode uses 802.1X and EAP.

Be able to describe how roaming works in autonomous and lightweight deployments.   Roaming is what sets wireless networks apart from wired networks. Clients are free to move about and expect the network to follow them, in a sense. Roaming is the client disassociating from one AP and associating with another using the same SSID. What matters is how the backend WLAN infrastructure handles this MAC move.

Understand the various antenna types.   Omnidirectional antennas are the most common and have a relatively low gain. Directional or high-gain antennas are used to direct a signal toward a specific area. Directional antennas are most often used to connect two backhaul radios in a point-to-point fashion.

Review Questions

You can find the answers in the appendix.

1. What's the dB difference between 100 mW and 200 mW?

    A. 0 dB

    B. 3 dB

    C. 6 dB

    D. 10 dB

2. You have a station indicating a received signal strength of 80 mW. After moving away from the AP, the receiver indicates a loss of 6 dB. What is the new received strength in mW?

    A. 20 mW

    B. 40 mW

    C. 60 mW

    D. 74 mW

3. The power of a signal decreased by 10×. What is the dB of this change?

    A. –100 dB

    B. –10 dB

    C. 0 dB

    D. 10 dB

    E. 100 dB

4. A 100 mW signal increases by about 13 dB. What is the new approximate power level?

    A. 113 mW

    B. 1300 mW

    C. 2000 mW

    D. 2600 mW

5. A transmitter is emitting a signal with a power of 40 dBm. It's connected to an external antenna using a cable with a loss of 4 dB. The connected antenna has a gain of 12 dBi. What's the EIRP?

    A. 52 dBm

    B. 36 dBm

    C. 40 dB

    D. 48 dBm

6. Which of the following standards has the highest data rate?

    A. 802.11a

    B. 802.11g

    C. 802.11n

    D. 802.11ac

7. How might an access point respond when an 802.11 client's signal strength decreases?

    A. Switch to a different channel

    B. Reduce data throughput

    C. Increase antenna gain

    D. Initiate a roam

8. How many antennas does a 3×2 MIMO device have?

    A. 2

    B. 3

    C. 5

    D. 6

9. Which of the following is Open Authentication compatible with?

    A. WPA

    B. 802.1X

    C. Shared key

    D. WebAuth

10. WPA2 enterprise mode uses which of the following? (Choose two.)

    A. Preshared key

    B. 802.1X

    C. WebAuth

    D. EAP

11. A wireless client and a wireless printer are both connected to the same AP, which is operating in autonomous mode. The client and printer are in the same subnet. The AP is connected to a layer 3 switch. When the client prints to the printer, what path will traffic take?

    A. Client → printer

    B. Client → AP → printer

    C. Client → AP → switch → AP → printer

    D. None of these. Traffic can't flow between clients connected to the same AP.

12. How many CAPWAP tunnels are there between an AP and a WLC?

A. 0

B. 1

C. 2

D. One per VLAN

13. What are two ways an AP can discover a WLC? (Choose two.)

A. Subnet broadcast on TCP port 5246

B. DHCP option 43

C. DNS query

D. Over-the-air broadcast

14. You want an AP to always use the WLC with the IP address 192.168.99.99. How can you achieve this?

A. Add 192.168.99.99 as a value for DHCP option 43.

B. Configure 192.168.99.99 as the primary WLC.

C. Create a DNS A record for the hostname CISCO-CAPWAP-CONTROLLER that resolves to 192.168.99.99.

D. Use a crossover cable to connect the AP to the WLC and boot the AP.

15. Using a subnet broadcast, an AP has discovered two WLCs: one embedded in a switch and another embedded in another AP. Which one will it attempt to build a CAPWAP tunnel with?

A. Both

B. It will select one at random.

C. The least loaded WLC

D. The one embedded in a switch

E. The one embedded in an AP

16. Which of the following always occurs when a client roams from one autonomous AP to another?

A. It associates with a different SSID.

B. It associates with a different AP.

C. It changes VLANs.

D. It disassociates from a WLC.

17. A client connected to a lightweight AP leaves a building and roams to another AP on a different WLC. Each building has its own subnet. The client keeps its IP address. Which of the following two things are true of this roam?

A. It's an intercontroller roam.

B. It's an intracontroller roam.

C. It's a layer 2 roam.

D. It's a layer 3 roam.

18. Which of the following does Location Services use to determine a wireless station's location?

A. RSSI

B. Cell tower triangulation

C. Gyrometers

D. WLC location

E. Noise floor level

19. Which of the following *doesn't* use a CAPWAP tunnel?

A. Layer 2 roaming

B. Intracontroller roaming

C. Autonomous mode

D. Lightweight mode

20. How can you force a client to always use a particular WLC regardless of what AP they connect to?

A. 802.1X authentication

B. Intercontroller roaming

C. Guest trunking

D. Auto-anchor mobility

Open Shortest Path First (OSPF)

THE CCNP ENCOR EXAM OBJECTIVES COVERED IN THIS CHAPTER INCLUDE THE FOLLOWING:

Domain 3.0 Infrastructure

✓ 3.2 Layer 3

OSPF is one of the most popular interior gateway protocols (IGPs) in use today. It was originally designed as a replacement for the simple Router Information Protocol (RIP), but it scales better and converges faster. OSPF is without a doubt the most complex IGP you'll use. In this chapter, we'll start by covering the basics of OSPF, including

- Areas
- Link-state advertisements (LSAs)
- Neighbor operations
- Network types

Most importantly, you'll learn how to configure OSPF and several key features, including authentication, passive interfaces, default route injection, inter-area summarization, and route filtering.

The exercises at the conclusion of the chapter align with the examples in the chapter. I recommend reading the chapter first, and then performing the exercises on your own, falling back on the chapter text as your guide in case you get stuck. Regardless of how you approach the exercises, be sure to complete them in your own Cisco lab. When it comes to understanding routing protocols, there's no substitute for hands-on configuring and troubleshooting.

Link-State Advertisements

OSPF is a link-state protocol, meaning that all routers in an autonomous system (AS) share the states of their local network links—their link-state information—with one another using *link-state advertisements (LSAs)*. An LSA includes but isn't limited to the following key pieces of information:

- **Link state ID**—Often contains an IP address or prefix.
- **Advertising router ID (RID)**—The RID uniquely describes a router in an OSPF topology, so it must be unique. If you don't explicitly configure it, the RID will be the highest numbered loopback IP address on the router when the OSPF process starts. If no loopbacks are configured, the RID will be the highest numbered IPv4 address configured on a physical interface.

Using the LSAs it receives, each router builds its own *link-state database (LSDB)*, which it uses to form a map of the entire network. Using this network map, the router uses the Dijkstra Shortest Path First (SPF) algorithm to calculate the best path to each IP prefix.

OSPF Areas

Assuming all OSPF routers receive the same LSAs, they'll all end up with identical copies of the LSDB, and the end result is that all routers arrive at the same routing decisions. But that's a big assumption. And in a large network with potentially thousands of routers, this doesn't sound very scalable in terms of bandwidth and memory. For example, if you had just 100 routers, and a single interface on one of those routers went down, it would require flooding link-state updates to the other 99 routers. The size of the LSDB grows exponentially with the number of interfaces, and that just doesn't scale.

To deal with this, OSPF lets you create a two-level routing hierarchy by breaking the AS up into areas. Within an area, or intra-area, routers exchange full link-state information with one another, giving each router the flexibility to choose the truly shortest path to any prefix in the area. However, between areas, or inter-area, the link-state information that's shared is limited, in terms of both size and frequency.

OSPF area numbers can be written in 32-bit dotted decimal notation like an IP address, but they usually are just integers to avoid confusion with RIDs and IP addresses. Area 0 (or Area 0.0.0.0), also known as the backbone area, always exists in every AS. It sits at the top of the routing hierarchy and connects to all other non-backbone areas. Routers in non-backbone areas can't route directly to one another but must always go through Area 0. Also, Area 0 can't be split—that is, links in Area 0 must follow a continuous path with no other areas in between.

Nonzero areas must border Area 0. For example, a router may have an interface in Area 1 (or Area 0.0.0.1), another interface in Area 20 (or Area 0.0.0.20), and yet another interface in Area 0. As long as the router borders Area 0, it can have multiple interfaces in nonzero areas.

An OSPF area is a collection of links, not a collection of routers. Instead of having an entire router in one area, a single router may have interfaces in different areas.

LSA Types

OSPFv2 (RFC 2328) is the version of OSPF for IPv4. To control the frequency of LSAs and to keep each router's LSDB manageable, OSPFv2 includes six LSA types:

- Type 1—Router LSA
- Type 2—Network LSA
- Type 3—Summary LSA

- Type 4—AS Boundary Router (ASBR) Summary LSA
- Type 5—AS External LSA
- Type 7—Not-So-Stubby-Area (NSSA) External LSA

You need to know only types 1 through 3 for the ENCOR exam. Types 4, 5, and 7 are beyond the scope of this book; however, I'm going to briefly cover types 4 and 5 because you're likely to see them in other exams or on a lab.

Type 1—Router LSA

Router LSAs contain the IP prefix of each connected interface. Each OSPF router always generates type 1 Router LSAs and floods them to all OSPF routers in the area. When you have more than two routers connected to a broadcast network, Router LSAs become redundant, if not problematic. For example, suppose the following three routers are connected to one another:

- R1: 192.168.1.1/24
- R2: 192.168.1.2/24
- R3: 192.168.1.3/24

R1 would send three LSAs each to R2 and R3—one LSA for each router. R2 would likewise send three LSAs each to R1 and R3, and so on. This is ridiculously wasteful because they're all connected to the same broadcast segment! And you can imagine how much worse the problem would become if you were to add a few more routers. To deal with this, OSPF includes another LSA type: the type 2 Network LSA.

Type 2—Network LSA

OSPF avoids the aforementioned absurd problem by using type 2 Network LSAs. These come into play when routers are connected to a broadcast (or multiaccess) network. Simply put, the type 2 Network LSA describes the subnet they're connected to.

A *designated router (DR)* collects type 1 LSAs from other OSPF routers on the broadcast segment and combines them into a type 2 Network LSA that describes all the routers on the segment. It then sends the type 2 Network LSA to its OSPF neighbors. Suppose that R1 from the preceding example is the DR. Instead of every router flooding a type 1 LSA to every other router, R2 and R3 instead send their type 1 LSAs only to R1, the DR. R1 generates a type 2 network LSA that advertises the 192.168.1.0/24 subnet, and it sends this LSA to R2 and R3.

When OSPF routers in a broadcast domain form an adjacency, they elect a DR. Each router interface has a configurable priority value, which is 1 by default. The router with the highest interface priority on the segment becomes the DR. If there's a tie, the router with the highest RID wins. We'll cover the election process in more detail—and how you can manipulate it—a bit later in this chapter.

Network Types

Whether routers attempt to elect a DR depends on the configured interface network type. The network type describes the nature of the interface and can be one of the following:

- **Point-to-point**—Routers will not attempt to elect a DR. Instead, because they assume there are only two routers on the segment, both will flood their type 1 Router LSAs. This type is used for point-to-point serial interfaces and loopbacks.

- **Broadcast or transit network**—Because of the possibility of more than two routers on the segment, the routers will attempt to elect a DR. This type is the most common on Ethernet networks.

OSPF intelligently chooses the network type based on the interface type. An Ethernet interface by default will be broadcast, whereas a serial link will be point-to-point. However, you can manually configure an interface as point-to-point or broadcast. Make sure both ends are configured with the same network type. Network types don't have to match in order to form an adjacency, but they do need to match in order for the routers to exchange routes.

If you enable OSPF on a loopback interface, OSPF considers it a loopback network type, and always advertises the loopback IPv4 address with a /32 subnet mask. If you want to advertise the loopback interface with its configured subnet mask, change the network type to point-to-point.

There are two other network types: stub network and virtual link. These types are for OSPF extensions (sometimes affectionately called *kluges*) and are beyond the scope of this book. Translation: you should never have to use them.

Type 3—Summary LSA

A type 3 Summary LSA includes inter-area prefixes—prefixes from other areas. The purpose of the summary LSA is to summarize the type 1 and type 2 LSAs from an area and repackage them in a single summary LSA to share with other areas. This reduces the amount of inter-area flooding.

A router that's connected to two or more areas is called an *area border router (ABR)*. ABRs are responsible for generating type 3 summary LSAs. When traffic moves inter-area—that is, from one OSPF area to another—it must pass through an ABR. This is the two-tier hierarchical design in action. It does create suboptimal routing in which inter-area routing isn't necessarily going to take the shortest path, but the benefit is that OSPF becomes more scalable.

Despite the name, the term *Summary LSA* doesn't imply a route summary in the sense of supernetting or collapsing many smaller IP subnets into a single large subnet. Rather, it refers to summarizing the type 1 and type 2 LSAs from an area.

For example, take a look at the layer 3 topology in Figure 5.1. R2 connects Areas 0 and 23, making it an ABR. R2 takes the type 1 and 2 LSAs from Area 0 and creates a type 3 network summary LSA that it floods into Areas 23 and 27.

FIGURE 5.1   An OSPF topology

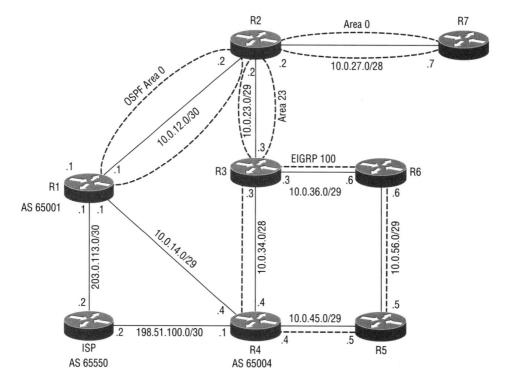

Type 4—Autonomous System Boundary Router (ASBR) Summary LSA and Type 5—AS External LSA

An ASBR redistributes routes between OSPF and another routing protocol, such as EIGRP or Border Gateway Protocol (BGP). An ASBR may also redistribute static or connected routes. The routes the ASBR redistributes into OSPF are called external routes, and the ASBR advertises them using type 5 AS External LSAs. The type 5 LSA describes the external prefix and the address of the next hop to reach it. The type 4 ASBR Summary LSA is generated by an ABR and tells routers in other areas how to reach the next hop listed in the type 5 AS External LSA. Unlike type 1, 2, and 3 LSAs that remain within an area, type 5 AS External LSAs get flooded across all normal OSPF areas.

Neighbor Operations

A Cisco router or layer 3 switch can have multiple OSPF processes, each with its own link-state database and routing topology. Each OSPF process has a process number that's locally significant to the router. One router can use OSPF process number 1, whereas its adjacent neighbor can use process number 2. Internal to the router, OSPF processes are separate. Different OSPF processes on a router don't share an LSDB, but it is possible to configure redistribution between them.

Before two OSPF routers can exchange LSAs, they need to form an adjacency. Each OSPF router has an RID, which is formatted like an IPv4 address, even though it's not. You can configure the RID to be any 32-bit dotted-decimal number between 0.0.0.1 and 255.255.255.255.

OSPF routers communicate using IP protocol number 89, so they don't use TCP or UDP. When you enable OSPF on an interface, the router sends Hello messages to the multicast address 224.0.0.5, which is the All OSPF Routers multicast address. These Hello messages are how OSPF routers discover each other, and they also function as keepalives to detect a down OSPF neighbor.

On broadcast and point-to-point interfaces, routers send Hello packets every 10 seconds by default. The Hello timer determines the frequency at which the Hellos are sent. If an OSPF router doesn't receive a Hello from a neighbor, it will wait four times the Hello timer before it considers the neighbor down and drops the adjacency. This is determined by the dead time, which by default is 40 seconds (four times the Hello interval of 10 seconds). Hello and Dead timers must match in order for routers to form and maintain an adjacency. The MTUs on both routers' interfaces must match as well.

When two OSPF routers establish an adjacency over a point-to-point interface, they exchange LSAs with each other by sending them to the multicast address 224.0.0.5. However, if the routers are connected to a broadcast network, they elect a DR and send their LSAs to the DR by sending them to the DR multicast address 224.0.0.6. The DR will then get the LSAs to the other routers by sending them to the 224.0.0.5 address. Again, this limits flooding of redundant LSAs.

An OSPF adjacency can take one of seven states:

- **Down**—In this state the router sends Hello packets out of its OSPF configured interfaces. All OSPF interfaces begin in a down state.

- **Init**—Once an OSPF router receives a Hello from a neighbor, it replies with an acknowledgment.

- **Two-way**—Once the routers receive and acknowledge each other's Hello messages, they enter the two-way state, referring to having achieved bidirectional or two-way communication. During this state, the routers elect a DR. We'll cover the election process shortly.

- **Exstart**—The routers negotiate sequence numbers that they use to ensure reliable delivery of packets in case some are lost. Although not a particularly exciting step, it's necessary because OSPF doesn't use TCP for transport.

- **Exchange**—Routers begin to exchange LSA headers, but not the full LSAs. These LSA headers are sent in database description packets (you may also see these called database descriptors).

- **Loading**—Routers exchange full link-state information.

- **Full**—Once the router's link-state databases are synchronized, the routers become fully adjacent. Note that non-DR routers in a broadcast network will never enter into full adjacency with one another, remaining instead in a two-way state since they don't exchange LSAs.

Configuring OSPF

In the following example, we'll configure OSPF on routers R1, R2, and R3, shown in Figure 5.1. Area 0 includes the interfaces in the 10.0.12.0/30 subnet on both R1 and R2. Area 23 includes the link between R2 and R3 in the 10.0.23.0/29 subnet. In order for a pair of routers to form an OSPF adjacency, their interfaces need to be in the same subnet.

Configuring Area 0 on a Broadcast Network

Let's start with R1:

We'll turn on debugging so we can see Hello messages.

```
R1#debug ip ospf hello
OSPF hello debugging is on
R1#conf t
Enter configuration commands, one per line.  End with CNTL/Z.
```

Let's enable the OSPF process using process number 1.

```
R1(config)#router ospf 1
```

We'll set the RID to 1.1.1.1. The RID doesn't have to be an IP address, but it must be between 0.0.0.1 and 255.255.255.255.

```
R1(config-router)#router-id 1.1.1.1
```

Next, let's enable OSPF on the GigabitEtherneti0/0 interface which has the address 10.0.12.1, placing it in area 0. The 0.0.0.0 wildcard mask is like an inverse subnet mask, matching only the given IP. address. This ensures OSPF isn't enabled on any other interfaces.

```
R1(config-router)#network 10.0.12.1 0.0.0.0 area 0
R1(config-router)#
```

```
! OSPF begins sending Hellos out looking for another router to form an adjacency
! with.
OSPF-1 HELLO Gi0/0: Send hello to 224.0.0.5 area 0 from 10.0.12.1
```

Moving on to R2:

```
R2#debug ip ospf hello
OSPF hello debugging is on
R2#conf t
Enter configuration commands, one per line.  End with CNTL/Z.
R2(config)#router ospf 1
R2(config-router)#router-id 2.2.2.2
R2(config-router)#network 10.0.12.2 0.0.0.0 area 0
R2(config-router)#
OSPF-1 HELLO Gi0/0: Send hello to 224.0.0.5 area 0 from 10.0.12.2
! R2 receives a Hello from R1 and responds
OSPF-1 HELLO Gi0/0: Rcv hello from 1.1.1.1 area 0 10.0.12.1
OSPF-1 HELLO Gi0/0: Send immediate hello to nbr 1.1.1.1, src address 10.0.12.1
OSPF-1 HELLO Gi0/0: Send hello to 10.0.12.1 area 0 from 10.0.12.2
R2(config-router)#
! R1 and R2 exchange LSAs and form a full adjacency
%OSPF-5-ADJCHG: Process 1, Nbr 1.1.1.1 on GigabitEthernet0/0 from LOADING to
FULL, Loading Done
```

Viewing Neighbor Adjacencies

You can manually view all OSPF neighbor adjacencies using the show ip ospf neighbor command, which will show you the DR status for each neighbor.

```
R2#show ip ospf neighbor
! R1 and R2 have a full adjacency, and R2 is the DR
Neighbor ID     Pri   State          Dead Time   Address        Interface
1.1.1.1           1   FULL/BDR        00:00:35   10.0.12.1      GigabitEthernet0/0
```

Because both routers have Ethernet interfaces, they participate in a DR election, even though they're the only two routers on the subnet. This adds a negligible amount of time to the time it takes to form an adjacency. In this case, R1 is listed as the backup DR (BDR). By process of elimination, we can infer that R2 is the DR.

Notice that the remaining Dead Time is listed as 35 seconds, which just happens to be where the timer was when the show command was run. Recall that the Dead Time interval is 40 seconds (four times the Hello interval). This is how long R2 will wait for a Hello from

R1 before considering the adjacency down. Because the Hello timer is 10 seconds, the Dead Time value should never drop below 30 seconds.

Rigging the Designated Router Election

It would be more appropriate to call the DR election process a game of musical chairs. The first OSPF router to become active on a subnet becomes the DR for the subnet. The second OSPF router on the subnet becomes the BDR.

The election process comes into play when the DR disappears. When that happens, the router with the highest OSPF interface priority will be elected the new DR. By default, all routers have an interface priority of 1, with an allowable range of 0 to 255. If the priorities are tied, the router with the highest RID will be elected the new DR, with the next lowest RID becoming the BDR.

The interface priority is configurable per interface, letting you control which router on a subnet is elected as the DR. For example, in the 10.0.12.0/30 subnet you have R1 and R2. If you prefer R2 as the DR for the subnet, you can configure it with the highest priority of 255, as shown here:

```
R2#conf t
Enter configuration commands, one per line.  End with CNTL/Z.
R2(config)#int gi0/0
R2(config-if)#ip ospf priority 255
```

You can verify the priority as follows:

```
R2#show ip ospf interface gigabitEthernet 0/0
GigabitEthernet0/0 is up, line protocol is up
  Internet Address 10.0.12.2/30, Area 0, Attached via Network Statement
  Process ID 1, Router ID 2.2.2.2, Network Type BROADCAST, Cost: 1
  Topology-MTID    Cost    Disabled    Shutdown      Topology Name
        0           1        no          no            Base
  Transmit Delay is 1 sec, State DR, Priority 255
! Output truncated
```

Keep in mind that this doesn't ensure that R2 will always be the DR. If R1 comes up first, it will elect itself as the DR (musical chairs, remember?). However, there is a way to make sure R2 always becomes the DR.

If a router has an interface priority of 0, it will never be elected as a DR. Hence, we can configure R1 with an interface priority of 0, ensuring that R2 is always the DR.

```
R1#conf t
Enter configuration commands, one per line.  End with CNTL/Z.
R1(config)#int gi0/0
R1(config-if)#ip ospf priority 0
```

If you set the priority of a DR or BDR to 0, it will immediately relinquish its role, triggering a new election.

To test this, we'll clear the OSPF process on R2, forcing it to momentarily drop its adjacency with R1:

```
R2#clear ip ospf process
Reset ALL OSPF processes? [no]: y
R2#
%OSPF-5-ADJCHG: Process 1, Nbr 1.1.1.1 on GigabitEthernet0/0 from FULL to DOWN,
Neighbor Down: Interface down or detached
R2#show ip ospf interface gi0/0
GigabitEthernet0/0 is up, line protocol is up
  Internet Address 10.0.12.2/30, Area 0, Attached via Network Statement
  Process ID 1, Router ID 2.2.2.2, Network Type BROADCAST, Cost: 1
  Topology-MTID   Cost    Disabled   Shutdown    Topology Name
       0           1        no         no           Base
  Transmit Delay is 1 sec, State WAITING, Priority 255
```

R2 advertises itself as the DR, but it waits 40 seconds (the Dead Time interval) for another router to advertise itself as the BDR. Because R1 doesn't advertise itself as a DR or a BDR, it will take 40 seconds for R1 and R2 to form a full adjacency.

```
%OSPF-5-ADJCHG: Process 1, Nbr 1.1.1.1 on GigabitEthernet0/0 from LOADING to
FULL, Loading Done
```

Let's verify that R2 is the DR:

```
R2#show ip ospf interface
GigabitEthernet0/0 is up, line protocol is up
  Internet Address 10.0.12.2/30, Area 0, Attached via Network Statement
  Process ID 1, Router ID 2.2.2.2, Network Type BROADCAST, Cost: 1
  Topology-MTID   Cost    Disabled   Shutdown    Topology Name
       0           1        no         no           Base
  Transmit Delay is 1 sec, State DR, Priority 255
  Designated Router (ID) 2.2.2.2, Interface address 10.0.12.2
  No backup designated router on this network
! Output truncated
```

The last line of the output indicates that there's no BDR. That's because R1 has a priority of 0, so it will never advertise itself as a DR or BDR.

```
R2#show ip ospf neighbor

Neighbor ID    Pri   State           Dead Time   Address         Interface
! R1 has a priority of 0 and is neither a DR nor a BDR
1.1.1.1         0    FULL/DROTHER    00:00:31    10.0.12.1       GigabitEthernet0/0
3.3.3.3         0    FULL/  -        00:00:39    10.0.23.3       GigabitEthernet0/1
```

R2 is the DR, and R1 is listed as DROTHER, indicating it's neither a DR nor a BDR, but just an OSPF router that has an adjacency with the DR. Remember that non-DRs don't exchange LSAs with one another.

Viewing and Understanding LSAs

LSAs carry a lot of redundant information, so before we dig into the individual LSA details, let's first get a bird's-eye view of R2's entire LSDB. Refer to Figure 5.1 as you read through the output.

R2 is connected to Area 0 and Area 23, making it an ABR, so it's going to have quite a few LSAs. The output is broken down into LSA types by area. The link ID uniquely identifies each LSA, and ADV Router indicates the RID of the router that generated the LSA.

```
R2#show ip ospf database

            OSPF Router with ID (2.2.2.2) (Process ID 1)
! Type 1 Router LSAs for Area 0 are listed first.
            Router Link States (Area 0)

Link ID        ADV Router      Age       Seq#       Checksum Link count
1.1.1.1        1.1.1.1         381       0x80000006 0x007581 1
2.2.2.2        2.2.2.2         304       0x80000006 0x003AB2 1
! Next we have Type 2 Network LSAs for Area 0. These are generated by the DR (R2) and
! describe the IP subnet for the segment (in this case, the link between R1 and R2).
            Net Link States (Area 0)

Link ID        ADV Router      Age       Seq#       Checksum
10.0.12.2      2.2.2.2         304       0x80000005 0x00A468

! Here we have Type 3 Summary LSAs advertised into Area 0. The 10.0.23.0 subnet is in
! Area 23, and R2 is the ABR, so it generates this LSA and advertises it into Area 0
! to tell routers in Area 0 how to reach the subnet.
            Summary Net Link States (Area 0)

Link ID        ADV Router      Age       Seq#       Checksum
10.0.23.0      2.2.2.2         304       0x80000005 0x00A471
```

```
! Remember that Type 1 Router LSAs never leave an area, so these LSAs in Area 23 are
! different than the ones in Area 0.
                 Router Link States (Area 23)

Link ID          ADV Router      Age        Seq#        Checksum Link count
2.2.2.2          2.2.2.2         304        0x80000006 0x00D4EE 2
3.3.3.3          3.3.3.3         317        0x80000031 0x001B79 2

! R2 generates a complementary Type 3 Summary LSA for Area 23, telling those routers
! how to reach the 10.0.12.0 subnet in Area 0.
                 Summary Net Link States (Area 23)

Link ID          ADV Router      Age        Seq#        Checksum
10.0.12.0        2.2.2.2         304        0x8000002E 0x00E310
```

Viewing Type 1 Router LSAs

Let's view the type 1 Router LSAs for area 0. Remember that at this point, we have only two routers, each with a single connected interface, so we should expect to see only two Router LSAs, one from R1 and another from R2.

```
R2#show ip ospf database router

            OSPF Router with ID (2.2.2.2) (Process ID 1)


            Router Link States (Area 0)

  LS age: 493
  Options: (No TOS-capability, DC)
  LS Type: Router Links
! The Link state ID uniquely describes the Router LSA, and it's always identified by
! the router RID. This is a good reason to deliberately configure the RID to be
! something that helps you easily identify the router.
  Link State ID: 1.1.1.1
! The following LSA was generated by R1
  Advertising Router: 1.1.1.1
  LS Seq Number: 80000002
  Checksum: 0x7D7D
  Length: 36
! As expected, R1 has only one configured link (to R2).
  Number of Links: 1
```

```
! This LSA describes this link as connected to a transit network, OSPF parlance for a
! multi-access network. Notice that it has no IP subnet information, but it does
! reference the interface address (10.0.12.1). The subnet information is contained in
! a separate Network LSA that we'll look at in a moment.
    Link connected to: a Transit Network
! Notice that this LSA lists the DR for the segment, which is R2.
      (Link ID) Designated Router address: 10.0.12.2
      (Link Data) Router Interface address: 10.0.12.1
      Number of MTID metrics: 0
       TOS 0 Metrics: 1


! The second Router LSA describing R2 begins here.
  LS age: 492
  Options: (No TOS-capability, DC)
  LS Type: Router Links
  Link State ID: 2.2.2.2
! This LSA was generated by R2. It's almost a mirror image of the preceding LSA
! generated by R1.
  Advertising Router: 2.2.2.2
  LS Seq Number: 80000002
  Checksum: 0x42AE
  Length: 36
  Number of Links: 1
    Link connected to: a Transit Network
    (Link ID) Designated Router address: 10.0.12.2
    (Link Data) Router Interface address: 10.0.12.2
     Number of MTID metrics: 0
       TOS 0 Metrics: 1
```

Viewing Type 2 Network LSAs

On a broadcast network, the DR generates and sends a type 2 Network LSA describing the IP subnet as well as the routers attached to it.

```
R2#show ip ospf database network

        OSPF Router with ID (2.2.2.2) (Process ID 1)

          Net Link States (Area 0)

  LS age: 1762
  Options: (No TOS-capability, DC)
```

```
  LS Type: Network Links
! R2 is the DR, so it generates and sends the Network LSA
  Link State ID: 10.0.12.2 (address of Designated Router)
  Advertising Router: 2.2.2.2
  LS Seq Number: 80000029
  Checksum: 0x5C8C
  Length: 32
! The Network LSA describes the subnet (10.0.12.0/30) and the routers attached to it:
! R2 and R1.
  Network Mask: /30
      Attached Router: 2.2.2.2
      Attached Router: 1.1.1.1
```

A transit network can't span multiple OSPF areas. All OSPF interfaces connected to the same subnet must be in the same area.

Configuring Area 23 on a Point-to-Point Network

Now let's configure the adjacency between R2 and R3 in Area 23. To illustrate what a point-to-point adjacency looks like, we'll configure the interfaces connecting R2 and R3 as the OSPF point-to-point network type. This will prevent R2 and R3 from attempting to elect a DR.

```
R2(config)#interface gi0/1
R2(config-if)#ip ospf network ?
  broadcast            Specify OSPF broadcast multi-access network
  non-broadcast        Specify OSPF NBMA network
  point-to-multipoint  Specify OSPF point-to-multipoint network
  point-to-point       Specify OSPF point-to-point network

R2(config-if)#ip ospf network point-to-point
R2(config-if)#router ospf 1
R2(config-router)#network 10.0.23.2 0.0.0.0 area 23
```

Now let's configure R3.

```
R3(config)#interface gi0/1
R3(config-if)#ip ospf network
R3(config-if)#ip ospf network point-to-point
R3(config-if)#router ospf 1
R3(config-router)#router-id 3.3.3.3
```

```
R3(config-router)#network 10.0.23.3 0.0.0.0 area 23
R3(config-router)#
%OSPF-5-ADJCHG: Process 1, Nbr 2.2.2.2 on GigabitEthernet0/1 from LOADING to FULL,
Loading Done
R3(config-router)#exit
R3(config)#exit
%SYS-5-CONFIG_I: Configured from console by console


R3#show ip ospf neighbor
```
! There's no DR because this is a point-to-point link.
```
Neighbor ID    Pri   State       Dead Time   Address       Interface
```
2.2.2.2   0   FULL/ -   00:00:35   10.0.23.2   GigabitEthernet0/1

Let's view the type 1 Router LSAs in R3's LSDB. Keep in mind that it contains type 1 Router LSAs only from R2 and R3 since they're the only routers in Area 23.

In a bizarre twist, you'll notice that each router actually generates and sends two Router LSAs into Area 23. The reason for this is convoluted and well beyond the scope of the ENCOR exam, but I'll touch on it in a moment.

```
R3#show ip ospf database router


            OSPF Router with ID (3.3.3.3) (Process ID 1)


            Router Link States (Area 23)


  LS age: 40
  Options: (No TOS-capability, DC)
  LS Type: Router Links
  Link State ID: 2.2.2.2
  Advertising Router: 2.2.2.2
  LS Seq Number: 80000004
  Checksum: 0xD8EC
  Length: 48
```
  ! R2 is an ABR because it's connected to area 0 and area 23.
  Area Border Router
```
  Number of Links: 2
```
! This first LSA describes the link connected to R3.
```
    Link connected to: another Router (point-to-point)
    (Link ID) Neighboring Router ID: 3.3.3.3
    (Link Data) Router Interface address: 10.0.23.2
```

```
      Number of MTID metrics: 0
       TOS 0 Metrics: 1
! This next LSA describes the 10.0.23.0/29 subnet.
    Link connected to: a Stub Network
     (Link ID) Network/subnet number: 10.0.23.0
     (Link Data) Network Mask: 255.255.255.248
      Number of MTID metrics: 0
       TOS 0 Metrics: 1

! Following are the Router LSAs generated by R3. Notice that R3 is not listed as
! an ABR because it has interfaces only in Area 23.
    LS age: 39
    Options: (No TOS-capability, DC)
    LS Type: Router Links
    Link State ID: 3.3.3.3
    Advertising Router: 3.3.3.3
    LS Seq Number: 80000002
    Checksum: 0x794A
    Length: 48
    Number of Links: 2

      Link connected to: another Router (point-to-point)
       (Link ID) Neighboring Router ID: 2.2.2.2
       (Link Data) Router Interface address: 10.0.23.3
        Number of MTID metrics: 0
         TOS 0 Metrics: 1

      Link connected to: a Stub Network
       (Link ID) Network/subnet number: 10.0.23.0
       (Link Data) Network Mask: 255.255.255.248
        Number of MTID metrics: 0
         TOS 0 Metrics: 1
```

Historically, point-to-point links were serial links that used HDLC or PPP. An interface connected to such a link didn't even need an address. One router would just drop data onto the wire, and it would come out the other end. However, most connections today are Ethernet, which requires using MAC addresses, even if only between two directly connected routers. So, we have to assign an IP subnet to every Ethernet link, even if it's physically point-to-point. OSPF calls this subnet a *stub network*, and it advertises it using a type 2 Network LSA.

Intriguingly, the subnet masks on point-to-point interfaces don't have
to match in order for OSPF neighbors to form an adjacency or exchange
routes.

Viewing Type 3 Summary LSAs

Summary LSAs are generated by an ABR, in this case R2. Therefore, from R2 we can view
the Summary LSAs it advertises into Area 0 and Area 23.

```
R2#show ip ospf database summary

              OSPF Router with ID (2.2.2.2) (Process ID 1)
! This Summary LSA is advertised into Area 0 and describes the 10.0.23.0/29 subnet
! in Area 23
              Summary Net Link States (Area 0)

  LS age: 1253
  Options: (No TOS-capability, DC, Upward)
  LS Type: Summary Links(Network)
  Link State ID: 10.0.23.0 (summary Network Number)
  Advertising Router: 2.2.2.2
  LS Seq Number: 80000005
  Checksum: 0xA471
  Length: 28
  Network Mask: /29
        MTID: 0       Metric: 1


! This one is advertised into Area 23 and describes the 10.0.12.0/30 subnet in area 0.
              Summary Net Link States (Area 23)

  LS age: 1253
  Options: (No TOS-capability, DC, Upward)
  LS Type: Summary Links(Network)
  Link State ID: 10.0.12.0 (summary Network Number)
  Advertising Router: 2.2.2.2
  LS Seq Number: 8000002E
  Checksum: 0xE310
  Length: 28
  Network Mask: /30
        MTID: 0       Metric: 1
```

To put it all together, let's take a look at R3's LSDB. It has only one Summary LSA.

```
R3#show ip ospf database summary

          OSPF Router with ID (3.3.3.3) (Process ID 1)

            Summary Net Link States (Area 23)

  LS age: 1130
  Options: (No TOS-capability, DC, Upward)
  LS Type: Summary Links(Network)
! The IP subnet is 10.0.12.0/30
  Link State ID: 10.0.12.0 (summary Network Number)
! R2 advertised this Summary LSA, so it's logically the next hop to reach the
! 10.0.12.0/30 subnet
  Advertising Router: 2.2.2.2
  LS Seq Number: 80000001
  Checksum: 0x3EE2
  Length: 28
  Network Mask: /30
      MTID: 0        Metric: 1
```

R3 funnels this information to the IP routing table to generate the router's RIB. Without seeing the IP routing table, you can figure out from the Summary LSA what the route will look like. The destination subnet is `10.0.12.0/30` and the next hop will be R2's interface address.

```
R3#show ip route ospf
! Output truncated
Gateway of last resort is not set

      10.0.0.0/8 is variably subnetted, 7 subnets, 4 masks
! This is an OSPF inter-area (IA) route. The next hop is R2's interface address.
O IA     10.0.12.0/30 [110/2] via 10.0.23.2, 00:08:28, GigabitEthernet0/1
```

Notice that the route has an administrative distance (AD) of 110. All OSPF-learned routes, whether inter-area, intra-area, or external, have the same AD. Let's run a traceroute to R1's interface address (`10.0.12.1`).

```
R3#traceroute 10.0.12.1 source 10.0.23.3
Type escape sequence to abort.
Tracing the route to 10.0.12.1
```

```
VRF info: (vrf in name/id, vrf out name/id)
  1 10.0.23.2 8 msec 4 msec 4 msec        ! R2
  2 10.0.12.1 9 msec 7 msec 10 msec       ! R1
```

As we expected, the path goes through R2 to R1. Because the traceroute worked, we can also conclude that R1 has learned a Summary LSA for R3's interface subnet (10.0.23.0/29). However, it's always a good idea to verify your configurations. Let's check R1:

```
R1#show ip ospf database summary

            OSPF Router with ID (1.1.1.1) (Process ID 1)

            Summary Net Link States (Area 0)

  LS age: 1761
  Options: (No TOS-capability, DC, Upward)
  LS Type: Summary Links(Network)
  Link State ID: 10.0.23.0 (summary Network Number)
  Advertising Router: 2.2.2.2
  LS Seq Number: 80000005
  Checksum: 0xA471
  Length: 28
  Network Mask: /29
      MTID: 0        Metric: 1
```

R1 has a Summary LSA for the 10.0.23.0/29 subnet that it learned from R2. It uses this to build its router RIB, as shown:

```
R1#show ip route ospf
! Output truncated

Gateway of last resort is not set

      10.0.0.0/8 is variably subnetted, 5 subnets, 3 masks
O IA     10.0.23.0/29 [110/2] via 10.0.12.2, 02:45:05, GigabitEthernet0/0
```

Authentication

OSPF offers two ways to control which routers become part of an OSPF topology:

- **Interface authentication**—Each router must authenticate to its neighbor before forming an adjacency.

- **Area authentication**—Enables interface authentication on all interfaces in a particular area.

These two methods aren't mutually exclusive. You can use either or both. The primary goal of authentication is to prevent OSPF routers from being accidentally or maliciously added to a network.

Authentication Types

OSPF offers three types of authentication:

- **Null**—This is the same as no authentication, which is still for some reason considered an authentication type.

- **Clear text**—The authentication password is sent unencrypted between routers.

- **Cryptographic or message-digest**—This uses the MD5 hashing algorithm to hash the authentication password, and then sends the hash instead of sending the password in the clear.

Configuring Interface Authentication

Configuring interface authentication requires configuring a shared key on both routers. If both routers don't have the same authentication type and password, they won't form an adjacency. In this example, we'll configure R2 and R7 to use interface authentication using the MD5 authentication type, starting with R2:

```
R2(config)#int gi0/2
! We'll assign the key an ID of 1. The key ID must match on both ends.
R2(config-if)#ip ospf message-digest-key 1 md5 secretpassword
! Here are the options for configuring the different authentication types
R2(config-if)#ip ospf authentication ?
  key-chain      Use a key-chain for cryptographic authentication keys
! MD5 authentication. This is the one we want.
  message-digest Use message-digest authentication
! Null authentication
  null           Use no authentication
! Simply hitting enter without further keywords will give you
! clear text authentication
  <cr>
R2(config-if)#ip ospf authentication message-digest
R2(config-if)#router ospf 1
R2(config-router)#network 10.0.27.2 0.0.0.0 area 0
! Verify that the interface is configured to use authentication
R2(config-router)#do show ip ospf interface gi0/2 | b Crypto
  Cryptographic authentication enabled
    Youngest key id is 1
```

`Cryptographic authentication` is a cryptic reference to MD5 authentication. Now let's configure R7:

```
R7(config)#int gi0/2
! Configure the same key ID and shared secret
R7(config-if)#ip ospf message-digest-key 1 md5 secretpassword
R7(config-if)#ip ospf authentication message-digest
R7(config-if)#router ospf 1
R7(config-router)#network 10.0.27.7 0.0.0.0 area 0
R7(config-router)#
! Because the keys match, R2 and R7 immediately form a full adjacency
%OSPF-5-ADJCHG: Process 1, Nbr 2.2.2.2 on GigabitEthernet0/2 from LOADING to
FULL, Loading Done
```

Don't confuse the `ip ospf message-digest-key` interface command with the `ip ospf authentication-key` command. The latter is for clear-text authentication only.

Finally, let's verify that R7 is receiving Router and Network LSAs from R2:

```
R7#show ip route ospf
! Output truncated
Gateway of last resort is not set

      10.0.0.0/8 is variably subnetted, 4 subnets, 4 masks
! The route to the 10.0.12.0/30 prefix (between R1 and R2) is an inter-area
! route, designated by an "O".
O       10.0.12.0/30 [110/2] via 10.0.27.2, 00:02:43, GigabitEthernet0/2
! The prefix from the 10.0.23.0/29 subnet between R2 and R3 is an inter-area (IA) route.
O IA    10.0.23.0/29 [110/2] via 10.0.27.2, 00:02:43, GigabitEthernet0/2
```

Configuring Area Authentication

Area authentication is just a shortcut way to enable authentication on all interfaces in an area. However, it doesn't save you much typing because you still have to specify a shared secret on each interface.

Configuring area authentication is a lot like configuring interface authentication. To illustrate, let's configure area 0 authentication on R1 and R2 using MD5, beginning with R1:

```
! Gi0/0 is the interface facing R2. We'll configure the shared secret
! "oursecret" using MD5
R1(config-router)#int gi0/0
```

```
R1(config-if)#ip ospf message-digest-key 1 md5 oursecret
```
! Enable area 0 authentication using MD5
```
R1(config-router)#area 0 authentication message-digest
R1(config-router)#
```
! Because R2's interface facing R1 isn't yet configured for authentication,
! the Dead Timer
! expires and the adjacency drops
```
%OSPF-5-ADJCHG: Process 1, Nbr 2.2.2.2 on GigabitEthernet0/0 from FULL to DOWN,
Neighbor Down: Dead timer expired
```

And R2:

```
R2(config)#int gi0/0
R2(config-if)#ip ospf message-digest-key 1 md5 oursecret
R2(config-if)#router ospf 1
R2(config-router)#area 0 authentication message-digest
R2(config-router)#
%OSPF-5-ADJCHG: Process 1, Nbr 1.1.1.1 on GigabitEthernet0/0 from LOADING to
FULL, Loading Done
```

The adjacency comes up immediately. To verify that area authentication is enabled, do the following:

```
R2#show ip ospf | s Area
   Area BACKBONE(0)
       Number of interfaces in this area is 2
```
! Area 0 has MD5 authentication enabled. Incidentally, the incomplete sentence
! "Area ranges are" is strange looking, but normal.
```
       Area has message digest authentication
       Area ranges are
   Area 23
       Number of interfaces in this area is 1
```
! Area 23 isn't configured to use authentication
```
       Area has no authentication
       Area ranges are
```

It's always a good idea to make sure the new configurations didn't break anything, so let's verify that R2 still has all the adjacencies it's supposed to have:

```
R2#show ip ospf interface brief
Interface   PID   Area              IP Address/Mask     Cost  State  Nbrs F/C
Gi0/2       1     0                 10.0.27.2/28        1     DR     1/1
Gi0/0       1     0                 10.0.12.2/30        1     DR     1/1
Gi0/1       1     23                10.0.23.2/29        1     P2P    1/1
```

Passive Interfaces

There are instances where you want an OSPF router to advertise a prefix for a subnet but don't want the router to form an OSPF adjacency on that subnet. A common example of this is if you have a subnet that's dedicated to servers or clients. None of these host devices should be running OSPF, but someone accidentally launching some open source OSPF software or putting a router in the wrong VLAN could cause an undesired adjacency to form.

To avoid this dilemma, you can configure an OSPF interface to be passive. As a passive interface, OSPF will advertise the prefix for that interface but will not form an adjacency with other routers on the subnet. Let's configure R1's Gi0/1 interface facing R4 as a passive interface. This is done not under the interface configuration itself but under the OSPF router configuration.

```
R1(config)#router ospf 1
R1(config-router)#passive-interface gi0/1
! Now let's advertise the subnet 10.0.14.0/29 into area 0.
R1(config-router)#network 10.0.14.1 0.0.0.0 area 0
! Verify
R1(config-router)#do show ip ospf int gi0/1
GigabitEthernet0/1 is up, line protocol is up
  Internet Address 10.0.14.1/29, Area 0, Attached via Network Statement
  Process ID 1, Router ID 1.1.1.1, Network Type BROADCAST, Cost: 1
  Topology-MTID    Cost    Disabled    Shutdown       Topology Name
        0            1         no         no              Base
  Transmit Delay is 1 sec, State DR, Priority 1
  Designated Router (ID) 1.1.1.1, Interface address 10.0.14.1
  No backup designated router on this network
  Timer intervals configured, Hello 10, Dead 40, Wait 40, Retransmit 5
    oob-resync timeout 40
! R1 doesn't send Hellos out of this interface because it's passive
  No Hellos (Passive interface)
```

R1 does generate a Router LSA containing the 10.0.14.0/29 network as a stub network.

```
R1#show ip ospf database router 1.1.1.1

            OSPF Router with ID (1.1.1.1) (Process ID 1)


            Router Link States (Area 0)


  LS age: 301
  Options: (No TOS-capability, DC)
  LS Type: Router Links
```

```
Link State ID: 1.1.1.1
Advertising Router: 1.1.1.1
LS Seq Number: 80000021
Checksum: 0x5960
Length: 48
Number of Links: 2

  Link connected to: a Stub Network
   (Link ID) Network/subnet number: 10.0.14.0
   (Link Data) Network Mask: 255.255.255.248
    Number of MTID metrics: 0
      TOS 0 Metrics: 1
! Output truncated
```

Other routers in Area 0 will thus learn about the subnet. To illustrate, let's look at R2's routing table:

```
R2#show ip route 10.0.14.0
Routing entry for 10.0.14.0/29
  Known via "ospf 1", distance 110, metric 2, type intra area
  Last update from 10.0.12.1 on GigabitEthernet0/0, 00:08:44 ago
  Routing Descriptor Blocks:
  * 10.0.12.1, from 1.1.1.1, 00:08:44 ago, via GigabitEthernet0/0
      Route metric is 2, traffic share count is 1
```

Injecting a Default Route

You're already familiar with default routes. Often, they're manually configured as static routes. But in a large, dynamic routing topology, manually configuring static routes can be a nightmare, not just because it's a lot of work, but because it can bring about all sorts of unintended consequences, including routing loops.

Having OSPF advertise a default route into a normal area is simple. The first step is to create a static default route. As a rule, a router must have a route in its IP routing table to advertise it. We'll configure a static default route on R1 pointing to 203.0.113.2 as the next hop:

```
R1(config)#ip route 0.0.0.0 0.0.0.0 203.0.113.2
R1(config)#do show ip route static
! Output truncated

S*    0.0.0.0/0 [1/0] via 203.0.113.2
```

Next, we instruct OSPF to inject this static default route:

```
R1(config-router)#default-information originate
```

Notice that there's no indication of an area. In fact, it's not possible to specify an area because an injected default route is advertised as a type 5 External LSA, which is flooded to all normal areas. A brief view of the LSDB confirms this:

```
R1#show ip ospf database external

        OSPF Router with ID (1.1.1.1) (Process ID 1)

          Type-5 AS External Link States

  LS age: 139
  Options: (No TOS-capability, DC, Upward)
  LS Type: AS External Link
  Link State ID: 0.0.0.0 (External Network Number )
  Advertising Router: 1.1.1.1
  LS Seq Number: 80000001
  Checksum: 0x1D91
  Length: 36
  Network Mask: /0
        Metric Type: 2 (Larger than any link state path)
        MTID: 0
        Metric: 1
        Forward Address: 0.0.0.0
        External Route Tag: 1
```

To further confirm, let's check R3's routing table:

```
R3#show ip route ospf
! Output truncated
! The default route is an external (E2) route, indicating that it was learned from a
! type 5 External LSA
O*E2  0.0.0.0/0 [110/1] via 10.0.23.2, 00:02:49, GigabitEthernet0/1
      10.0.0.0/8 is variably subnetted, 9 subnets, 4 masks
O IA     10.0.12.0/30 [110/2] via 10.0.23.2, 02:34:19, GigabitEthernet0/1
O IA     10.0.14.0/29 [110/3] via 10.0.23.2, 00:20:37, GigabitEthernet0/1
O IA     10.0.27.0/28 [110/2] via 10.0.23.2, 03:37:51, GigabitEthernet0/1
```

Once again, R1 must have the static default route configured in order to advertise it. If we were to remove the route, it would cease advertising the type 5 External LSAs, and the other OSPF routers in the topology would likewise lose the injected default route.

Inter-Area Summarization

Earlier I mentioned that type 3 Summary LSAs don't refer to summarizing multiple IP prefixes into a larger prefix. However, you can configure an ABR to summarize inter-area routes. R2 is an ABR bordering Area 0 and Area 23. It's advertising three type 3 Summary LSAs into Area 23:

```
R2#show ip ospf database
! Output truncated
            Summary Net Link States (Area 23)

Link ID        ADV Router      Age        Seq#        Checksum
10.0.12.0      2.2.2.2         1998       0x8000000D 0x0026EE
10.0.14.0      2.2.2.2         1998       0x80000004 0x00140B
10.0.27.0      2.2.2.2         1998       0x8000000A 0x003ED6
```

These three subnets are generated from Router LSAs in Area 0. R2 packages them as type 3 Summary LSAs and advertises them into Area 23. We'll configure R2 to summarize these three subnets as 10.0.0.0/19 and advertise only the summary route.

```
R2#conf t
R2(config)#router ospf 1
R2(config-router)#area 0 range 10.0.0.0 255.255.224.0
```

Notice that the command specifies Area 0 rather than Area 23. That's because the command specifies the source of the routes to summarize rather than the destination. This means that R2 will summarize the routes from Area 0 into Area 23, but it will not summarize the routes from Area 23 into Area 23. Let's verify that R2 is now advertising only the summary into Area 23:

```
R2#show ip ospf database
! Output truncated
            Summary Net Link States (Area 23)

Link ID        ADV Router      Age        Seq#        Checksum
10.0.0.0       2.2.2.2         15         0x80000001 0x003910
```

Consequently, R3 in Area 23 should have the summarized route but none of the component routes:

```
R3#show ip route ospf
! Output truncated

O*E2  0.0.0.0/0 [110/1] via 10.0.23.2, 01:46:58, GigabitEthernet0/1
      10.0.0.0/8 is variably subnetted, 7 subnets, 4 masks
O IA     10.0.0.0/19 [110/2] via 10.0.23.2, 00:01:18, GigabitEthernet0/1
```

Route Filtering

Let's configure R2 not to advertise any prefixes that fall in the 10.0.0.0/19 range:

```
R2(config-router)#area 0 range 10.0.0.0 255.255.224.0 not-advertise
```

R2 should cease sending any type 3 Summary LSAs into Area 23. The best way to verify this is from R3:

```
R3#show ip ospf database summary

        OSPF Router with ID (3.3.3.3) (Process ID 1)
```

R3 has no Summary LSAs. Consequently, it doesn't have a route for any of the prefixes in the 10.0.0.0/19 range:

```
R3#show ip route ospf
! Output truncated
O*E2  0.0.0.0/0 [110/1] via 10.0.23.2, 02:22:35, GigabitEthernet0/1
```

If you want more granular control over what prefixes are advertised inter-area, you can use a prefix list. Let's configure R2 not to advertise into Area 0 a Summary LSA for the 10.0.23.0/29 prefix.

```
! Create the prefix list to deny only the 10.0.23.0/29 prefix, while allowing
! all others.
R2(config)#ip prefix-list no-23 deny 10.0.23.0/29
R2(config)#ip prefix-list no-23 permit 0.0.0.0/0 le 32
R2(config)#router ospf 1
! Any prefixes that match the no-23 prefix list will not be advertised into area 0
R2(config-router)#area 0 filter-list prefix no-23 in
```

At this point, R2 shouldn't be advertising any Summary LSAs into Area 0 or Area 23. Hence, there should be no Summary LSAs in its LSDB.

```
R2#show ip ospf database summary

        OSPF Router with ID (2.2.2.2) (Process ID 1)
```

Distribute Lists

You've learned how to perform inter-area filtering at an ABR, but there are times when you may want to filter prefixes within an area. OSPF is a link-state protocol, so every router in an area must have an identical copy of the LSDB. However, there's no requirement that every router must install every LSA in its routing table! You can use distribute lists to prevent a router from installing an OSPF-learned route. R3 is learning a default route via a type 5 External LSA. We'll use a distribute list to prevent it from installing a default route.

! **Create a prefix list to match only the default route**
R3(config)#ip prefix-list nodefault deny 0.0.0.0/0
R3(config)#ip prefix-list nodefault permit 0.0.0.0/0 le 32
R3(config)#router ospf 1
! **R3 will refuse to install in its routing table any prefix denied by the**
! **nodefault prefix list**
R3(config-router)#distribute-list prefix nodefault in
R3(config-router)#do show ip route 0.0.0.0
% Network not in table

R3 is still learning the prefix from R2, and it still exists in the LSDB, but it's not installed in the IP routing table:

R3(config-router)#do show ip ospf database external

            OSPF Router with ID (3.3.3.3) (Process ID 1)

            Type-5 AS External Link States

  LS age: 1916
  Options: (No TOS-capability, DC, Upward)
  LS Type: AS External Link
  Link State ID: 0.0.0.0 (External Network Number)
  Advertising Router: 1.1.1.1
  LS Seq Number: 80000005
  Checksum: 0x1595
  Length: 36
  Network Mask: /0
        Metric Type: 2 (Larger than any link state path)
        MTID: 0
        Metric: 1
        Forward Address: 0.0.0.0
        External Route Tag: 1

Not only that, if we were to later add another router to Area 23, R3 would continue to share this External LSA.

Summary

Link-state advertisements are the currency of OSPF. Not only do they carry router and prefix information, but also each OSPF router uses them to independently form a map of the network. OSPF routers form adjacencies at layer 2 and exchange LSAs. LSA types 1–4 remain in an area, whereas LSA type 5 is flooded to all normal areas. On a broadcast network, one router is elected as the DR and is responsible for receiving type 1 Router LSAs and using them to generate type 2 Network LSAs. On a point-to-point network, routers exchange type 1 Router LSAs directly.

Configuring OSPF requires placing an interface into an area using the network statement. Rather than specifying the interface directly, you specify the subnet that the link resides in. This makes it easy to enable OSPF on a single interface or all interfaces. You can enable OSPF Area 0 on all interfaces using the `network 0.0.0.0 0.0.0.0 area 0` command.

Exam Essentials

Know how OSPF adjacencies form.   How adjacencies form depends on the network type, which can be broadcast or point-to-point. Know how to configure the network type and understand how it impacts LSA exchanges and neighbor states.

Understand the purposes of the various LSA types.   The variety of OSPF LSA types isn't to make your life difficult, but to make OSPF more scalable. Understand what information each LSA type carries and why it exists.

Be able to configure OSPF.   You should be able to configure OSPF and its key features from scratch. A crucial part of configuration is verification, so be able to confirm that your configuration works as expected.

Know how to read the LSDB.   Each router uses its LSDB to build the IP routing table. Being able to read and understand the link-state database on a router is an important troubleshooting skill.

Exercises

EXERCISE 5.1

Configure the layer 2 topology shown in Figure 5.2. Address the interfaces according to the layer 3 topology in Figure 5.1.

FIGURE 5.2   Layer 2 topology

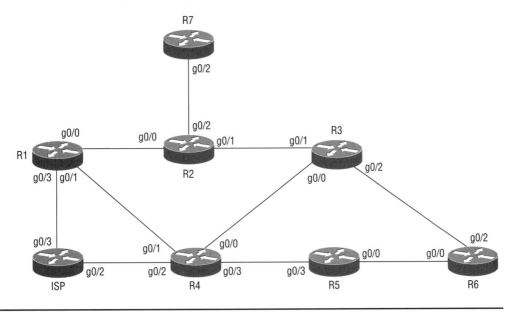

EXERCISE 5.2

Configure OSPF Area 0 between R1 and R2 and Area 23 according to the IPv4 topology diagram in Figure 5.1. Don't enable OSPF on any other interfaces. Use the following RIDs:

- R1—1.1.1.1

- R2—2.2.2.2

- R3—3.3.3.3

EXERCISE 5.3

Configure OSPF Area 0 between R2 and R7 according to the IPv4 topology diagram in Figure 5.1. Assign R7 the RID 7.7.7.7. Configure interface authentication between R2 and R7.

EXERCISE 5.4

Configure area authentication for OSPF Area 0. Remember to configure it on all interfaces in Area 0.

Review Questions

You can find the answers in the appendix.

1. How can you ensure that a router becomes a DR for a specific subnet?

   A. Set the OSPF interface priority to 0.

   B. Enable OSPF on the router before enabling it on any other routers.

   C. Configure the OSPF RID to be the highest in the subnet.

   D. Set the OSPF interface priority to 255.

2. Which command will ensure a router never becomes a DR or a BDR?

   A. `ip ospf dr disable`

   B. `ip ospf priority 255`

   C. `ip ospf priority 0`

   D. `router-id 0.0.0.0`

3. What's the administrative distance of OSPF inter-area routes?

   A. 20

   B. 90

   C. 110

   D. 120

4. What IP address and protocol number does OSPF use to send Hello packets?

   A. `224.0.0.10` over IP protocol 89

   B. `224.0.0.6` over IP protocol 89

   C. `224.0.0.5` over IP protocol 88

   D. `224.0.0.5` over IP protocol 89

5. Which of the following must match for OSPF routers to form an adjacency?

   A. OSPF process number

   B. MTU

   C. network statement

   D. Router IDs

6. What LSA type is advertised to all normal areas?

   A. Type 5 External

   B. Type 3 Summary

   C. Type 1 Router

   D. Type 2 Network

7. An OSPF router has one interface in Area 51 and no interfaces in any other areas. Which of the following areas can it not have another interface in?

    A. Area 0.0.0.0

    B. Area 1

    C. Area 51

    D. Area 0

8. Which of the following LSAs reduces flooding in a broadcast domain?

    A. Type 5 External LSA

    B. Type 3 Summary LSA

    C. Type 1 Router LSA

    D. Type 2 Network LSA

9. Which of the following suggests the absence of a type 2 Network LSA?

    A. Backup designated router

    B. Transit network type

    C. Broadcast network type

    D. Point-to-point network type

10. Which of the following is true of a type 3 Summary LSA?

    A. It advertises an IP network summary into an area.

    B. It summarizes the information in type 1 LSAs from one area.

    C. It summarizes the information in type 2 LSAs from multiple areas.

    D. It is generated by an ASBR.

11. An OSPF router bordering areas 0 and 1 redistributes EIGRP routes into OSPF. Which two of the following describe this router?

    A. ASBR

    B. DR

    C. BDR

    D. ABR

12. OSPF router R1 has a single interface with the IP address 1.0.0.1/24. It has two full adjacencies: one with a DR with a RID of 1.0.0.2 and another with a BDR with a RID of 1.0.0.3. Which of the following values can you configure for the OSPF RID on R1?

    A. 1.0.0.2

    B. 2.0.0.1

    C. 1

    D. 0.0.0.0

13. Which of following must match for two routers to form a full OSPF adjacency?

   A. Network type

   B. Subnet

   C. Area number

   D. RID

14. Router R1 has interfaces in Area 0, Area 7, and Area 12. Router R2 is connected to Area 7, and router R3 is connected to Area 12. The routers have no other connected interfaces. Which of the following is true of this topology?

   A. R2 and R3 can't have interfaces in the same area.

   B. R2 and R3 can connect via Area 0.

   C. R2 and R3 can connect via a nonzero area.

   D. R1 can't have another interface in Area 7 or Area 12.

15. Assuming everything is properly configured for a broadcast network, which state do OSPF neighbors stay in if neither is a DR or a BDR?

   A. Init

   B. Full

   C. Two-way

   D. Exstart

16. In which OSPF state do routers first exchange full link-state information?

   A. Two-way

   B. Full

   C. Exchange

   D. Loading

17. What hashing algorithm does OSPF cryptographic authentication use?

   A. MD5

   B. SHA1

   C. SHA256

   D. CRC32

18. Which of the following OSPF router commands enables MD5 authentication for all router interfaces in Area 2?

   A. `area 2 authentication`

   B. `ip ospf authentication message-digest`

   C. `area 2 authentication message-digest`

   D. `ip ospf message-digest-key 1 md5 mypassword`

19. Which of the following is *not* a valid OSPF authentication type?

  A. Null

  B. Secret

  C. Clear text

  D. Message digest

20. Which two commands make Gi0/3 an OSPF passive interface?

  A. `router ospf 1`

  B. `interface gi0/3`

  C. `passive-interface gi0/3`

  D. `ip ospf passive-interface`

Enhanced Interior Gateway Routing Protocol (EIGRP)

THE CCNP ENCOR EXAM OBJECTIVES COVERED IN THIS CHAPTER INCLUDE THE FOLLOWING:

Domain 3.0 Infrastructure

✓ 3.2 Layer 3

EIGRP (RFC 7868) is a distance vector protocol. Instead of keeping link-state information for every router in the topology the way OSPF does, an EIGRP router only knows each neighbor's cost to a given prefix. The concept of distance vector protocols is fairly easy to grasp. The most complex thing about EIGRP is the way it calculates the cost of each route.

In this chapter, you'll learn about the following:

- EIGRP packet types

- The Diffusing Update Algorithm (DUAL)

- EIGRP's weighted metric formula

- Equal and unequal cost multipathing

- Modifying cost metrics

As in the last chapter, the exercises align with the examples, so feel free to follow along. If you've completed the exercises from the previous chapter, leave what you have intact and continue with the same topology.

EIGRP Fundamentals

EIGRP neighbors communicate using IP protocol 88 by sending Hello packets to the multicast address 224.0.0.10, which is the EIGRP multicast group address. Like OSPF, EIGRP has a concept of internal and external routes. However, unlike OSPF, internal and external routes have a different AD. Internal routes, ones that originate from within an EIGRP AS, have an AD of 90. External routes—those routes redistributed from outside of the EIGRP AS—have an AD of 170. External routes include redistributed connected and static routes.

EIGRP Packet Types

EIGRP routers use five packet types to establish adjacencies and share routing information with one another:

- Hellos

- Updates

- Acknowledgments

- Queries
- Replies

EIGRP uses a mechanism called the Reliable Transport Protocol (RTP) to deliver EIGRP packets. Depending on the type, a packet may be sent reliably or unreliably. When sent reliably, the router includes a sequence number for ordering and expects an ACK from the recipient. When sent unreliably, the router doesn't use a sequence number and doesn't expect an ACK.

Hellos

Hellos are used in the EIGRP neighbor discovery and recovery process. After you enable EIGRP on an interface, the EIGRP process begins sending out Hello messages. On a broadcast network type, EIGRP sends multicast Hellos every 5 seconds. It does so unreliably, meaning it doesn't expect an ACK.

Each Hello packet includes a hold time value that tells the neighbor how long it should wait before expecting to receive a subsequent Hello message. The hold time is three times the Hello interval, which on broadcast networks would be 15 seconds. If the hold timer expires, the router declares its neighbor unreachable.

Updates

Updates carry route prefix and metric information. EIGRP sends updates only when necessary, such as when a new destination prefix becomes reachable or the cost to an already reachable destination prefix changes. Hence, updates are called nonperiodic, meaning they're not sent out at scheduled intervals. Additionally, EIGRP sends updates only to the neighbors that need them. Updates are thus said to be bounded, as opposed to flooded. When a router receives an update, it sends an ACK to confirm that it received the update.

Acknowledgments

ACK packets are unicast Hello packets that carry no data, just a sequence number.

The Diffusing Update Algorithm (DUAL)

To understand the next two packet types—queries and replies—you need to understand the algorithm EIGRP uses to make routing decisions. DUAL is a highfalutin-sounding name for the algorithm EIGRP uses to find the shortest loop-free path to a destination.

The first iteration of DUAL was created by Edsger Dijkstra, who also created the Dijkstra shortest path first algorithm used by OSPF. Same guy, different algorithm. The main difference between DUAL and the Dijkstra algorithm in OSPF is that the DUAL algorithm considers only the networks advertised by its adjacent neighbors. Typically, distance vector protocols calculate only the next hop for a prefix, leaving the potential for routing loops. DUAL was designed to achieve the shortest path while avoiding loops.

Consider the four routers in Figure 6.1: West, North, South, and East. The East router is advertising the 172.13.37.0/24 prefix using EIGRP. West therefore learns this prefix from its three adjacent neighbors: North, South, and East.

FIGURE 6.1 Simple EIGRP topology

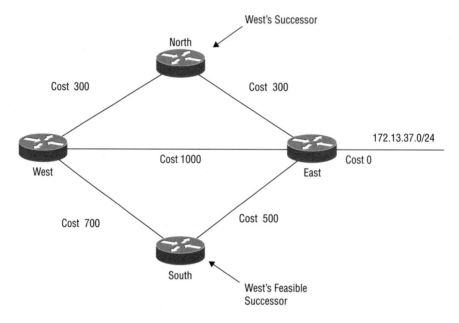

South's Cost < West's Feasibility Condition => Feasibility Condition Met

- The path through North has a cost of 600 (300 + 300).
- The path directly to East has a cost of 1000.
- The path through South has a cost of 1200 (700 + 500).

These metrics are just illustrative. We'll get to EIGRP metric formulations later. The path with the lowest cost is called the *feasible distance (FD)*, and the next-hop router along that path is the successor. Hence, North becomes West's successor, which is just another way of saying "next hop."

Feasible Successors

To provide fast convergence, EIGRP attempts to precompute backup next hops in case the successor goes down. These secondary next hops are called feasible successors. An EIGRP router determines whether a neighbor can be a feasible successor based on whether routing through it might create a routing loop. To ensure a loop-free topology, EIGRP requires that a feasible successor meet what's called the *feasibility condition*. To understand how the feasibility condition calculation works, let's take the West router as an example.

In addition to its successor route (via North), West has two other possible routes to the 172.13.37.0/24 prefix: one via South and another via East. The route via East has the lowest cost (1000), and it's obvious that routing directly to it would not cause a loop, since East is directly connected to the 172.13.37.0/24 prefix. But what about routing via South?

South's cost to East is 500. South advertises this cost to West, and this is called the *advertised distance* or *reported distance*. South's advertised distance of 500 is less than West's feasible distance of 600 (via North). The feasibility condition is said to be met if the advertised distance is less than the feasible distance. In this case, the route through South meets the feasibility condition, so South becomes a feasible successor.

The primary purpose of the feasibility condition is to ensure that the feasible successor offers a loop-free path to the destination in case the best path becomes unavailable. This is how EIGRP achieves fast convergence, because it doesn't have to figure out the next hop on the fly. A router can choose multiple feasible successors. In this case, West will choose both East and South as feasible successors, since they both meet the feasibility condition.

It's worth taking a moment to think through the successor and feasible successors each router will choose. Take the South router for our next example. South will already have chosen East as its successor to the prefix. But what about its feasible successor? West's advertised distance to the 172.13.37.0/24 prefix is 600 (via North). Of course, this is not less than South's feasible distance (500 via East). Therefore, South has no feasible successor. This raises the obvious dilemma about what South will do if its direct adjacency with East goes down. If that happens, South will need to recalculate a route to the 172.13.37.0/24 subnet.

Queries and Replies

When a router loses its successor route for a prefix and has no feasible successors, it must recalculate a new route to the prefix. For this example, we'll continue to assume that the link between West and North is down. Assuming South's adjacency with East then goes down, South will place the 172.13.37.0/24 route into an active state. Confusingly, "active" refers to the DUAL algorithm actively recomputing the cost to the prefix. In reality, it's not the route that's active, but the DUAL algorithm working to figure out a new path to the prefix. To put it succinctly, an active route is a route in flux.

South will set the feasible distance of the prefix to infinity, removing the route from its own IP routing table. It will then send a query packet to West asking West's cost to the prefix. West sends a reply packet to South containing its cost to the prefix, a cost of 600, via North. Since a cost of 600 is clearly better than a cost of infinity, South installs West as its successor for the prefix. South's new cost to the prefix is 1300 (700 + 600). Once South reconverges and settles on a new successor for the route, it places the route into a passive state, meaning the DUAL algorithm has converged on a final cost metric and is no longer computing a new cost to the prefix.

When a router sends a query message for a route to its neighbor, it gives the neighbor 3 minutes to reply. This is called the *active timer*. If the active timer expires before the router receives a reply, the route is said to be *stuck-in-active* (SIA). If this happens, the router resets its adjacency with its neighbor. SIA usually occurs when there's packet loss, which can happen in the face of congestion or a unidirectional link. Also, keep in mind that when a router sends a query to a neighbor, the neighbor may have to send out its own queries, and so on, potentially creating a cascade of queries. Thus, if there are slow links or slow routers, the entire reconvergence process can take some time.

Let's suppose now that the adjacency between West and North goes down. West has already calculated East as its feasible successor. Hence, West will immediately install East as its successor, and send an update packet to South with a new advertised cost of 1000.

Now suppose the link between South and East comes back up. South installs East as its new successor and sends an update to West telling it about its new advertised cost (500, via East). West sees that South's advertised cost (500, via East) is less than its current feasible distance (1000, via East), so it considers South a feasible successor again.

Weighted Metrics

Unlike ancient IGPs such as the RIP, EIGRP considers more than just hop count in calculating distance. EIGRP uses the weighted metric formula shown in Figure 6.2 to calculate its cost metrics.

FIGURE 6.2   EIGRP weighted metric formula

$$256 \times \left(\left(K_1 \times bandwidth + \frac{K_2 \times bandwidth}{256 - load} + K_3 \times delay \right) \times \frac{K_5}{K_4 + reliability} \right)$$

This rather obtuse formula might look familiar to you. You don't need to memorize it, but you should at least understand what it means. EIGRP uses this formula to calculate the weighted metric for a route, taking into account attributes such as bandwidth, delay, reliability, and load. Each of these attributes is given different weight, specified by a different K value. As shown here, K1 and K2 relate to bandwidth, K3 relates to the interface delay, and K4 and K5 relate to the reliability of the link:

Bandwidth	Delay	Reliability
K1, K2	K3	K4, K5

By default, not all of these K values are used. In fact, K1 and K3 have a default value of 1, and the other K values are 0. Few people ever adjust these values. EIGRP ignores reliability when using the default K values. By using the default K values, we can greatly simplify the weighted metric formula to this:

$$256 \times (bandwidth + delay)$$

Bandwidth

Unless you change the default K values, the preceding is the formula EIGRP will use to calculate its metrics. You may notice something a bit strange about the formula. You'd expect that a higher bandwidth would yield a lower cost metric, but the way the formula is written suggests that it would yield a higher cost metric. In the EIGRP weighted metric formula, the bandwidth variable is actually the *inverse* of the constrained bandwidth, which is the smallest bandwidth along a path. Specifically, the bandwidth variable in the formula is 10^7 divided by the actual constrained bandwidth in kilobits per second (kbps). Confusing? Yes. Let's clarify this with an example.

Suppose the route to a particular prefix requires traversing 100 Mbps link and a 1 Gbps link. The constrained bandwidth would be 100 Mbps because that's the smallest bandwidth along the path. EIGRP converts the constrained bandwidth to kbps and inverts it. The bandwidth used in the formula would be

$$10^7 \div 100,000 \text{ kbps} = 100$$

What you really need to know is that the bandwidth and metric are inversely proportional. The higher the constrained bandwidth, the lower the metric. The lower the constrained bandwidth, the higher the metric.

Delay

Delay is the sum of the interface delays along the path. In keeping with the quirky complexity of the way EIGRP does things, delay is measured in *tens* of microseconds (μsec). Suppose the path to a prefix traverses a link with a 20 μsec delay and another with delay of 10 μsec. The cumulative delay along the path is 30 μsec. As shown in the following calculation, dividing this by 10 gives a value of 3, which is the delay value that EIGRP uses in its formula.

$$30\mu\text{sec} \div 10 = 3$$

You can view the delay of an interface as follows:

```
R5#show interfaces gi0/0 | i DLY
  MTU 1500 bytes, BW 1000000 Kbit/sec, DLY 10 usec,
```

Load

Load refers to how saturated all the interfaces are along a given path. The load value can be between 1 and 255 inclusive, with 255 being the most loaded. Using the default K2 value of 0, load isn't a part of the metric calculation. You can view the actual load of an interface using the following command:

```
R4#show interfaces gi0/0 | i load
     reliability 255/255, txload 1/255, rxload 1/255
```

Interface load statistics are updated every 5 minutes, but you can reduce this to as little as 30 seconds as follows:

```
R4#conf t
Enter configuration commands, one per line.  End with CNTL/Z.
R4(config)#int gi0/0
R4(config-if)#load-interval ?
  <30-600>  Load interval delay in seconds
R4(config-if)#load-interval 30
```

Reliability

Reliability measures the error rates of all the interfaces along a given path. Although it's not used with the default K values, you should know that the allowable range is 0 to 255, with 255 being the most reliable.

Configuring EIGRP

In this example, we'll configure EIGRP AS 100 as shown in Figure 6.3. Keep in mind that to exchange EIGRP routes, routers must use the same EIGRP AS number. Let's move clockwise, starting with R3.

FIGURE 6.3   EIGRP layer 3 topology

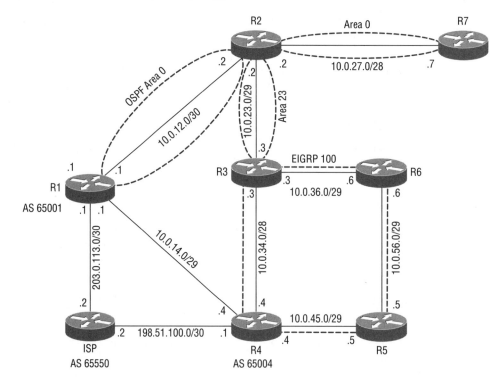

```
R3(config)#router eigrp 100
! Set the router ID to 3.3.3.3
R3(config-router)#eigrp router-id 3.3.3.3
! Enable EIGRP on the link facing R4
R3(config-router)#network 10.0.34.3 0.0.0.0
! And on the link facing R6
R3(config-router)#network 10.0.36.3 0.0.0.0
```

We want R3 to advertise the 10.0.23.0/29 prefix into EIGRP. To avoid accidentally establishing an adjacency with R2, we'll make Gi0/1 a passive interface.

```
R3(config-router)#passive-interface gi0/1
```

To advertise the prefix, we'll use the network command. Even though it specifies the interface IP address, it will advertise the prefix that the interface is in. This will cause EIGRP to advertise the 10.0.23.0/29 route without trying to form an adjacency on the interface.

```
R3(config-router)#network 10.0.23.3 0.0.0.0
Now onto R6:
R6(config)#router eigrp 100
! Set the router ID
R6(config-router)#eigrp router-id 6.6.6.6
```

Enable EIGRP on all interfaces with addresses in the 10.0.0.0/8 network. If you don't specify a subnet mask, EIGRP will use the classful mask.

```
R6(config-router)#network 10.0.0.0
R6(config-router)#
! The adjacency with R3 immediately comes up
%DUAL-5-NBRCHANGE: EIGRP-IPv4 100: Neighbor 10.0.36.3 (GigabitEthernet0/2) is
up: new adjacency
```

While we're here, let's look at the default K values and ADs for EIGRP routes:

```
R6(config)#do show ip protocols | s eigrp
Routing Protocol is "eigrp 100"
  Outgoing update filter list for all interfaces is not set
  Incoming update filter list for all interfaces is not set
  Default networks flagged in outgoing updates
  Default networks accepted from incoming updates
  EIGRP-IPv4 Protocol for AS(100)
! Notice the default metric weights
    Metric weight K1=1, K2=0, K3=1, K4=0, K5=0
    Soft SIA disabled
    NSF-aware route hold timer is 240
    Router-ID: 10.0.56.6
    Topology : 0 (base)
      Active Timer: 3 min
! The administrative distance for internal EIGRP routes is 90.
! For external routes, it's 170.
    Distance: internal 90 external 170
    Maximum path: 4
    Maximum hopcount 100
    Maximum metric variance 1
```

Let's now assign R5 a router ID and configure it to establish an adjacency with R6 and R4:

```
R5(config)#router eigrp 100
R5(config-router)#eigrp router-id 5.5.5.5
R5(config-router)#network 10.0.56.5 0.0.0.0
R5(config-router)#
%DUAL-5-NBRCHANGE: EIGRP-IPv4 100: Neighbor 10.0.56.6 (GigabitEthernet0/0) is
up: new adjacency
R5(config-router)#network 10.0.45.5 0.0.0.0
```

Finally, we'll configure R4 to exchange routes with R5 and R3:

```
R4(config)#router eigrp 100
R4(config-router)#eigrp router-id 4.4.4.4
R4(config-router)#network 10.0.45.4 0.0.0.0
R4(config-router)#
%DUAL-5-NBRCHANGE: EIGRP-IPv4 100: Neighbor 10.0.45.5 (GigabitEthernet0/3) is
up: new adjacency
R4(config-router)#network 10.0.34.4 0.0.0.0
R4(config-router)#
%DUAL-5-NBRCHANGE: EIGRP-IPv4 100: Neighbor 10.0.34.3 (GigabitEthernet0/0) is
up: new adjacency
R4(config-router)#exit
R4(config)#exit
```

Now that all adjacencies are up, let's go back to R5 and view its EIGRP neighbor table:

```
R5#show ip eigrp neighbors
EIGRP-IPv4 Neighbors for AS(100)
H   Address            Interface          Hold Uptime    SRTT   RTO  Q   Seq
                                          (sec)          (ms)        Cnt Num
1   10.0.45.4          Gi0/3              12  00:00:07   23     138  0   47
0   10.0.56.6          Gi0/0              12  00:00:07   13     100  0   100
```

R5 shows two adjacencies, one with R4 and another with R6. The H column indicates the order in which the adjacencies were formed. The Q Cnt column is the number of outstanding queries. Normally, this should be zero. If it's consistently above zero, then it indicates that a route is SIA. R5 should now have received update packets from its neighbors. We can view these received routes by viewing the EIGRP topology table:

```
R5#show ip eigrp topology
EIGRP-IPv4 Topology Table for AS(100)/ID(10.0.56.5)
Codes: P - Passive, A - Active, U - Update, Q - Query, R - Reply,
       r - reply Status, s - sia Status
```

```
! Each next hop has two values in parentheses. The first value is the
! feasible distance, and the second value is the next-hop's advertised distance.
! For the first entry for the 10.0.34.0/28 prefix, the feasible distance
! to R4 is 3072, while R4's feasible distance to the prefix is 2816.
P 10.0.34.0/28, 1 successors, FD is 3072
        via 10.0.45.4 (3072/2816), GigabitEthernet0/3
P 10.0.56.0/29, 1 successors, FD is 2816
        via Connected, GigabitEthernet0/0
P 10.0.36.0/29, 1 successors, FD is 3072
        via 10.0.56.6 (3072/2816), GigabitEthernet0/0
P 10.0.45.0/29, 1 successors, FD is 2816
        via Connected, GigabitEthernet0/3
P 10.0.23.0/29, 2 successors, FD is 3328
        via 10.0.45.4 (3328/3072), GigabitEthernet0/3
        via 10.0.56.6 (3328/3072), GigabitEthernet0/0
```

Pay special attention to the 10.0.23.0/29 route. Notice that it has two successors. In parentheses, the first value (3328) is the feasible distance. Here, there are two equal cost paths, one via R6 and another via R4.

```
R5#show ip route eigrp
! Output truncated

Gateway of last resort is not set

     10.0.0.0/8 is variably subnetted, 7 subnets, 3 masks
! EIGRP routes are flagged with a D for DUAL
! The 10.0.23.0/29 prefix has two equal cost paths, one via R6 and another via R4. In
! brackets, 90 is the administrative distance, and 3328 is the feasible distance.
D        10.0.23.0/29 [90/3328] via 10.0.56.6, 00:02:22, GigabitEthernet0/0
                      [90/3328] via 10.0.45.4, 00:02:22, GigabitEthernet0/3
D        10.0.34.0/28 [90/3072] via 10.0.45.4, 00:05:39, GigabitEthernet0/3
D        10.0.36.0/29 [90/3072] via 10.0.56.6, 00:05:37, GigabitEthernet0/0
```

Equal Cost Multipathing

When EIGRP has two equal cost routes to a prefix, it will install both of them in the IP routing table. Because the feasible distance to the 10.0.23.0/29 prefix is 3328—via both R4 and R6—EIGRP considers both routers successors. When R5 sends a packet to the prefix, it will perform *equal cost multipathing (ECMP)* between the two routes. A look at the Cisco Express Forwarding (CEF) FIB confirms this:

```
R5#show ip cef 10.0.23.0 detail
10.0.23.0/29, epoch 0, per-destination sharing
  nexthop 10.0.56.6 GigabitEthernet0/0
  nexthop 10.0.45.4 GigabitEthernet0/3
```

Note per-destination sharing, which indicates the default algorithm CEF uses to do load sharing. Per-destination sharing is actually based on the source and destination IP addresses of the traffic. For example, if R5 receives a packet with a source address of 1.2.3.4 and a destination of 10.0.23.1, CEF will switch the packet out of the Gi0/3 interface every time. You can test this and other source-destination pairs using the show ip cef exact-route command:

```
R5#show ip cef exact-route 1.2.3.4 10.0.23.2
1.2.3.4 -> 10.0.23.2 =>IP adj out of GigabitEthernet0/3, addr 10.0.45.4
```

In contrast, a packet sourced from a different IP but to the same destination egresses a different interface:

```
R5#show ip cef exact-route 5.6.7.8 10.0.23.2
5.6.7.8 -> 10.0.23.2 =>IP adj out of GigabitEthernet0/0, addr 10.0.56.6
```

A traceroute illustrates the load sharing more starkly:

```
R5#traceroute 10.0.23.3
Type escape sequence to abort.
Tracing the route to 10.0.23.3
VRF info: (vrf in name/id, vrf out name/id)
  1 10.0.45.4 6 msec. ! Hop 1, probe 1 via R4
    10.0.56.6 10 msec ! Hop 1, probe 2 via R6
    10.0.45.4 8 msec
  2 10.0.36.3 9 msec
    10.0.34.3 10 msec
    10.0.36.3 7 msec
```

 By default, EIGRP will install up to four successor routes in the IP routing table. You can decrease this to 1 or increase it to 32 using the EIGRP router maximum-paths command.

Modifying Metrics

Notice that in the preceding traceroute the next hop alternates between R4 and R6. This makes for an efficient use of bandwidth but can also lead to asymmetric routing. So perhaps you don't want to use ECMP. The simplest way to avoid ECMP is to adjust the bandwidth or delay along one of the possible paths so that their costs are no longer equal. Let's look at the current bandwidth and delay values on the Gi0/0 interface facing R6:

```
R5#show int gi0/0
GigabitEthernet0/0 is up, line protocol is up
  Hardware is iGbE, address is 0cdb.ae03.8600 (bia 0cdb.ae03.8600)
  Internet address is 10.0.56.5/29
! Note the bandwidth (BW) and delay (DLY) values the EIGRP weighted metric
! formula uses
  MTU 1500 bytes, BW 1000000 Kbit/sec, DLY 10 usec,
     reliability 255/255, txload 1/255, rxload 1/255
! Output truncated
```

We'll reduce the configured bandwidth from 1,000,000 kbps to 500,000 kbps. Note that this will not actually reduce the speed of the interface, but only the bandwidth value that the interface reports to EIGRP.

```
R5#conf t
Enter configuration commands, one per line.  End with CNTL/Z.
R5(config)#int gi0/0
R5(config-if)#bandwidth 500000
```

This command won't actually slow anything down. Only the speed command would change the interface speed. (You could also modify the interface delay value using the delay command without affecting the speed of the interface.) Now compare the new EIGRP topology table with the previous one:

```
R5(config-if)#do show ip eigrp topology
EIGRP-IPv4 Topology Table for AS(100)/ID(10.0.56.5)
Codes: P - Passive, A - Active, U - Update, Q - Query, R - Reply,
       r - reply Status, s - sia Status


P 10.0.34.0/28, 1 successors, FD is 3072
        via 10.0.45.4 (3072/2816), GigabitEthernet0/3
P 10.0.56.0/29, 1 successors, FD is 5376
        via Connected, GigabitEthernet0/0
        via 10.0.45.4 (3584/3328), GigabitEthernet0/3
! The 10.0.36.0/29 prefix has R4 as its successor and R6 as its feasible successor
P 10.0.36.0/29, 1 successors, FD is 3328
       via 10.0.45.4 (3328/3072), GigabitEthernet0/3.    ! R4 is successor
       via 10.0.56.6 (5632/2816), GigabitEthernet0/0.    ! R6 is feasible successor
P 10.0.45.0/29, 1 successors, FD is 2816
        via Connected, GigabitEthernet0/3
```

```
! The 10.0.23.0/29 prefix has R4 as its sole successor and R6 as a feasible successor
P 10.0.23.0/29, 1 successors, FD is 3328
       via 10.0.45.4 (3328/3072), GigabitEthernet0/3.    ! R4 is successor
       via 10.0.56.6 (5888/3072), GigabitEthernet0/0.    ! R6 is feasible successor
```

For the 10.0.23.0/29 prefix, R4 is now the only successor with a feasible distance of 3328. R6's advertised distance of 3072 is less than the feasible distance of 3328. Hence, R6 meets the feasibility condition, meaning R6 is a feasible successor!

Contrast this with the 10.0.34.0/28 prefix, which also has R4 as its successor. But for this route, there's no feasible successor, so if R5's link to R4 were to fail, R5 would place this route into the active state and have to recalculate the cost via a new path. Let's see this in action! We'll enable query and reply packet debugging on R5:

```
R5#debug eigrp packet query detail reply detail
    (QUERY Detail, REPLY Detail)
EIGRP Packet debugging is on
```

Now shut down the interface facing R4:

```
R5(config)#int gi0/3
R5(config-if)#shutdown
R5(config-if)#
%DUAL-5-NBRCHANGE: EIGRP-IPv4 100: Neighbor 10.0.45.4 (GigabitEthernet0/3) is
down: interface down
EIGRP: Enqueueing QUERY on Gi0/0 - paklen 0 tid 0 iidbQ un/rely 0/1 serno 64-65
! R5 sends a Query packet to R6
EIGRP: Sending QUERY on Gi0/0 - paklen 90 tid 0
  AS 100, Flags 0x0:(NULL), Seq 60/0 interfaceQ 0/0 iidbQ un/rely 0/0 serno 64-65
  {type = 602, length = 45}
  {vector = {afi = 1, tid = 0}
          {routerid = 5.5.5.5
          {offset = 0, priority = 0, reliability = 220, load = 0,
! The hop count of 255 indicates that the prefix is unreachable
          mtu = {0:[00, 00, 00]}), hopcount = 255,
! The delay value is extremely large. This is the biggest number EIGRP can
! handle, effectively yielding a cost metric of infinity.
          delay = 281474976710655, bw = 4294967295,
          reserved = 00, opaque_flags = 04}
  {nh:00000000}
  {1D0A002D 00}
  }
```

```
! Output truncated
! R6 doesn't generate any Reply packets, but simply passes the following
! Reply packet from R3.
EIGRP: Received REPLY on Gi0/0 - paklen 45 nbr 10.0.56.6.
  AS 100, Flags 0x0:(NULL), Seq 51/60 interfaceQ 0/0 iidbQ un/rely 0/1 peerQ un/
rely 0/0
  {type = 602, length = 45}
  {vector = {afi = 1, tid = 0}
! Reply from R3 for the 10.0.34.0/28 prefix. Notice the MTU, reliability, and
load are
! advertised, but they're not considered in the metric calculation.
          {routerid = 3.3.3.3
          {offset = 0, priority = 0, reliability = 255, load = 1,
           mtu = {1500:[00, 05, DC]), hopcount = 1,
           delay = 20000000, bw = 1000000,
           reserved = 00, opaque_flags = 00}
          {nh:00000000}
          {1C0A0022 00}
  } route: 10.0.34.0/28
! Output truncated
```

You can infer from the output that R6 is the new successor for the 10.0.34.0/28 prefix. Let's verify this:

```
R5#show ip eigrp topology 10.0.23.0/29
EIGRP-IPv4 Topology Entry for AS(100)/ID(5.5.5.5) for 10.0.23.0/29
! The route in in the Passive state, meaning DUAL isn't actively
! recomputing a new route. There's only one successor with a
! feasible distance of 3328.
  State is Passive, Query origin flag is 1, 1 Successor(s), FD is 3328
  Descriptor Blocks:
  10.0.56.6 (GigabitEthernet0/0), from 10.0.56.6, Send flag is 0x0
      Composite metric is (5888/3072), route is Internal
      Vector metric:
        Minimum bandwidth is 500000 Kbit
        Total delay is 30 microseconds
        Reliability is 255/255
        Load is 1/255
        Minimum MTU is 1500
        Hop count is 2
        Originating router is 3.3.3.3
```

Switching Types

The switching type is responsible for forwarding packets. Although it gleans information from the IP routing table, the switching type is what ultimately chooses the next-hop address and outbound interface. There are two switching types.

Cisco Express Forwarding (CEF)

As you know, CEF is the default switching type. The IP routing table feeds into CEF to create two different data structures:

The Forwarding Information Base (FIB)   Each entry contains an IP network prefix, the next hop address, and the outgoing interface. You can view the FIB using the show ip cef command.

```
R5#show ip cef
Prefix                 Next Hop           Interface
0.0.0.0/0              no route
0.0.0.0/8              drop
0.0.0.0/32             receive
10.0.0.0/16            10.0.45.4          GigabitEthernet0/3
10.0.14.0/29           10.0.45.4          GigabitEthernet0/3
10.0.23.0/29           10.0.45.4          GigabitEthernet0/3
10.0.32.0/19           10.0.45.4          GigabitEthernet0/3
10.0.34.0/28           10.0.45.4          GigabitEthernet0/3
10.0.36.0/29           10.0.45.4          GigabitEthernet0/3
10.0.45.0/29           attached           GigabitEthernet0/3
10.0.45.0/32           receive            GigabitEthernet0/3
10.0.45.4/32           attached           GigabitEthernet0/3
10.0.45.5/32           receive            GigabitEthernet0/3
10.0.45.7/32           receive            GigabitEthernet0/3
10.0.56.0/29           attached           GigabitEthernet0/0
10.0.56.0/32           receive            GigabitEthernet0/0
10.0.56.5/32           receive            GigabitEthernet0/0
10.0.56.6/32           attached           GigabitEthernet0/0
10.0.56.7/32           receive            GigabitEthernet0/0
127.0.0.0/8            drop
198.51.100.0/30        10.0.45.4          GigabitEthernet0/3
203.0.113.0/30         10.0.45.4          GigabitEthernet0/3
224.0.0.0/4            drop
224.0.0.0/24           receive
240.0.0.0/4            drop
255.255.255.255/32     receive
```

The Adjacency Table   Contains the layer 3 protocol (e.g., IP or IPv6), the outgoing interface, and a precomputed layer 2 header. View the details of the adjacency table using the `show adjacency detail` command.

```
R5#show adjacency detail
Protocol Interface              Address
IP       GigabitEthernet0/0     10.0.56.6(7)
                                0 packets, 0 bytes
                                epoch 0
                                sourced in sev-epoch 0
                                Encap length 14
                                0CDBAE67EE000CDBAE0386000800
                                ARP
IP       GigabitEthernet0/3     10.0.45.4(18)
                                0 packets, 0 bytes
                                epoch 0
                                sourced in sev-epoch 0
                                Encap length 14
                                0CDBAE9F42030CDBAE0386030800
                                ARP
```

Process Switching

Process switching performs an IP routing table lookup for each packet that needs to be switched. This is the most CPU-intensive switching type. You can enable process switching globally by disabling CEF by using the `no ip cef` global configuration command. Or you can disable it per interface by using the `no ip route-cache` interface configuration command.

Unequal Cost Multipathing

Earlier you saw that EIGRP will perform equal-cost multipathing when it has multiple successors. However, you may want to take advantage of load sharing even if there are unequal cost paths to a prefix. You can do so by enabling unequal cost load balancing. Let's bring up the `Gi0/3` interface on R5:

```
R5(config)#int gi0/3
R5(config-if)#no shut
R5(config-if)#
%LINK-3-UPDOWN: Interface GigabitEthernet0/3, changed state to up
%LINEPROTO-5-UPDOWN: Line protocol on Interface GigabitEthernet0/3, changed
state to up
R5(config-if)#
%DUAL-5-NBRCHANGE: EIGRP-IPv4 100: Neighbor 10.0.45.4 (GigabitEthernet0/3) is
up: new adjacency
```

We can see that R5 has one successor and one feasible successor for the `10.0.36.0/29` prefix:

```
R5#show ip eigrp topology 10.0.36.0/29
EIGRP-IPv4 Topology Entry for AS(100)/ID(5.5.5.5) for 10.0.36.0/29
  State is Passive, Query origin flag is 1, 1 Successor(s), FD is 3328
  Descriptor Blocks:
! Successor
10.0.45.4 (GigabitEthernet0/3), from 10.0.45.4, Send flag is 0x0
      Composite metric is (3328/3072), route is Internal
      Vector metric:
        Minimum bandwidth is 1000000 Kbit
        Total delay is 30 microseconds
        Reliability is 255/255
        Load is 1/255
        Minimum MTU is 1500
        Hop count is 2
        Originating router is 3.3.3.3
! Feasible successor
  10.0.56.6 (GigabitEthernet0/0), from 10.0.56.6, Send flag is 0x0
      Composite metric is (5632/2816), route is Internal
      Vector metric:
        Minimum bandwidth is 500000 Kbit
        Total delay is 20 microseconds
        Reliability is 255/255
        Load is 1/255
        Minimum MTU is 1500
        Hop count is 1
        Originating router is 6.6.6.6
```

The feasible distance via R4 is 3,328, and the distance via R6 is 5,632. Because the costs are unequal, EIGRP will not perform ECMP. However, we can force EIGRP to install both routes in the IP routing table by adjusting the metric variance multiplier. Let's first calculate the ratio of R6's distance to R4's distance:

$$5,632 \div 3,328 \approx 1.7$$

If we configure the variance metric multiplier to be greater than this ratio, EIGRP will perform unequal cost load balancing. Let's view the current value:

```
R5#show ip protocols | s eigrp
Routing Protocol is "eigrp 100"
  Outgoing update filter list for all interfaces is not set
  Incoming update filter list for all interfaces is not set
```

Default networks flagged in outgoing updates
Default networks accepted from incoming updates
EIGRP-IPv4 Protocol for AS(100)
  Metric weight K1=1, K2=0, K3=1, K4=0, K5=0
  Soft SIA disabled
  NSF-aware route hold timer is 240
  Router-ID: 5.5.5.5
  Topology : 0 (base)
    Active Timer: 3 min
    Distance: internal 90 external 170
! EIGRP will install up to 4 routes for a prefix in the IP routing table
    Maximum path: 4
    Maximum hopcount 100
! We need to configure the metric variance value to 2 so that it's greater than 1.7
    Maximum metric variance 1

The variance value must be an integer between 1 and 128, so we'll set it to 2:

```
R5#conf t
Enter configuration commands, one per line.  End with CNTL/Z.
R5(config)#router eigrp 100
R5(config-router)#variance 2
R5(config-router)#do show ip eigrp topology | s 10.0.36.0
P 10.0.36.0/29, 2 successors, FD is 3328
        via 10.0.56.6 (5632/2816), GigabitEthernet0/0
        via 10.0.45.4 (3328/3072), GigabitEthernet0/3
```

Now R5 has two successors, each with a different cost, and installs them both in the IP routing table:

```
R5(config-router)#do show ip route eigrp | s 10.0.36.0
D        10.0.36.0/29 [90/5632] via 10.0.56.6, 00:01:53, GigabitEthernet0/0
                      [90/3328] via 10.0.45.4, 00:01:53, GigabitEthernet0/3
```

When it comes to unequal cost multipathing, the name is misleading. Cost isn't the only thing that's unequal; the distribution of traffic is as well. R5 will not evenly distribute the traffic between R4 and R6. Rather, it will distribute the traffic according to each route's cost metric. Pay attention to traffic share count listed in the following output:

```
R5#show ip route 10.0.36.0
Routing entry for 10.0.36.0/29
  Known via "eigrp 100", distance 90, metric 3328, type internal
  Redistributing via eigrp 100
  Last update from 10.0.56.6 on GigabitEthernet0/0, 00:21:10 ago
```

```
Routing Descriptor Blocks:
   10.0.56.6, from 10.0.56.6, 00:21:10 ago, via GigabitEthernet0/0
     Route metric is 5632, traffic share count is 71
     Total delay is 20 microseconds, minimum bandwidth is 500000 Kbit
     Reliability 255/255, minimum MTU 1500 bytes
     Loading 1/255, Hops 1
 * 10.0.45.4, from 10.0.45.4, 00:21:10 ago, via GigabitEthernet0/3
     Route metric is 3328, traffic share count is 120
     Total delay is 30 microseconds, minimum bandwidth is 1000000 Kbit
     Reliability 255/255, minimum MTU 1500 bytes
     Loading 1/255, Hops 2
```

The traffic share count values are weights that determine how R5 distributes traffic among each next hop. They're derived from the cost metrics of each route. Adding up the weights (120 + 71) gives you a total of 191; 120 ÷ 191 is about 0.63, and 71 ÷ 191 is about 0.37. So roughly 63 percent of traffic for the 10.0.36.0/29 subnet will go through R4 and 37 percent through R6.

  EIGRP generates the traffic share counts and passes them to CEF, which decides the interface and next-hop address.

Summary

When it comes down to OSPF versus EIGRP, OSPF is far more common. However, if you need a simple routing protocol for a relatively small topology, EIGRP is quick and easy to set up. The DUAL algorithm makes use of feasible successors that provide loop-free backup routes in case the best path or successor route fails. This makes EIGRP a good choice for networks where you need submillisecond convergence time.

The EIGRP weighted metric formula can take into account bandwidth, delay, load, and reliability. By default, only the first three are considered, but you can adjust this, as well as the weighting of each, by adjusting the associated K values. Most of the time people just stick with the default K values. Influencing successor and feasible successor calculations can be done easily by changing the bandwidth or delay value of an interface. If you change either one of these on one end of a link, remember to change it on the opposite end as well to avoid asymmetric routing.

Exam Essentials

Understand how the DUAL algorithm chooses successors and feasible successors. You should be able to determine the successors and feasible successors just by looking at a layer 3 network diagram.

Be able to configure EIGRP and adjust metrics.   As with all IGPs, be able to configure EIGRP and modify metrics to control the successor and feasible successor selections.

Know the differences between equal cost multipathing and unequal cost multipathing. ECMP is used when there are multiple successors—that is, when multiple routes have an equal cost. Unequal cost multipathing can be enabled by adjusting the variance. By default, EIGRP will install up to four routes to the same prefix.

Exercises

EXERCISE 6.1

Configure the EIGRP AS 100 topology in Figure 6.3. For the underlying layer 2 topology, refer to Figure 6.4. Make sure R3 advertises the `10.0.23.0/29` prefix as an EIGRP internal route.

FIGURE 6.4   Layer 2 topology

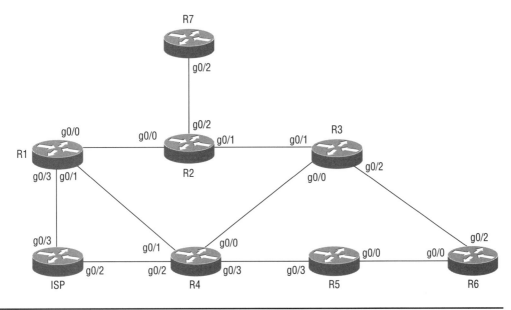

EXERCISE 6.2

For the `10.0.23.0/29` prefix, ensure R5 chooses R4 as its successor and R6 as its feasible successor.

Review Questions

You can find the answers in the appendix.

1. What multicast address does EIGRP use for Hello packets?
    A. 255.255.255.255
    B. 224.0.0.5
    C. 224.0.0.10
    D. 224.0.0.9

2. What IP protocol does EIGRP use?
    A. 87
    B. 88
    C. 89
    D. 1

3. What is the default AD of an external EIGRP route?
    A. 20
    B. 90
    C. 110
    D. 170

4. What is the default AD of an internal EIGRP route?
    A. 20
    B. 90
    C. 110
    D. 200

5. What is CEF per-destination load sharing based on?
    A. Source port-destination port pair
    B. Source IP-destination IP pair
    C. Destination IP
    D. Source IP

6. The show eigrp topology command shows the following two possible next hops for the 10.0.36.0/29 prefix:

    ```
    via 10.0.56.6 (5632/2816), GigabitEthernet0/0
    via 10.0.45.4 (3328/3072), GigabitEthernet0/3
    ```

Assuming a variance of 1, which of the following is true?

A. `10.0.45.4` and `10.0.56.6` are both successors.

B. `10.0.56.6` is a successor.

C. `10.0.45.4` is a feasible successor.

D. `10.0.56.6` is a feasible successor.

7. What is the primary purpose of EIGRP's feasibility condition?

A. Rapid convergence

B. Shortest path selection

C. Loop prevention

D. Route filtering

8. When a successor route goes down and there is no feasible successor, which of the following things occur? (Choose all that apply.)

A. The route becomes SIA.

B. The router advertises the route with an infinite metric.

C. The route becomes active.

D. The router sends a query to its neighbors.

E. The active timer stops.

9. What happens when a router's EIGRP active timer for a neighbor expires?

A. The adjacency with the neighbor is reset.

B. The active route is removed from the IP routing table.

C. The router sends an update to the neighbor.

D. The router sends a query to the neighbor.

10. Which of the following EIGRP K values are associated with bandwidth in the weighted metric formula? (Choose all that apply.)

A. K1

B. K2

C. K3

D. K4

E. K5

11. Which of the following EIGRP K values is associated with delay in the weighted metric formula?

A. K1

B. K2

C. K3

D. K4

E. K5

12. Assuming the default K values, what is the EIGRP weighted metric formula?

A. 256 × (bandwidth × delay)

B. 256 × (bandwidth + delay)

C. 256 + (bandwidth + delay)

D. 256 × (bandwidth + reliability)

13. Consider the following EIGRP output:

```
P 203.0.113.0/30, 1 successors, FD is 26368, tag is 65550
via 10.0.56.5 (26368/26112), GigabitEthernet0/0
via 10.0.36.3 (282112/26112), GigabitEthernet0/2
```

How can you enable unequal cost multipathing?

A. Increase the maximum paths to 2.

B. Disable CEF.

C. Adjust the metrics to make both routes equal.

D. Set the variance multiplier to 11.

14. What is the default SIA timer?

A. 10 seconds

B. 30 seconds

C. 3 minutes

D. 5 minutes

15. What value does EIGRP use for bandwidth in the weighted metric formula?

A. Constrained bandwidth

B. Constrained bandwidth ÷ 256 − load

C. 10^7 ÷ cumulative bandwidth

D. 10^7 ÷ constrained bandwidth

16. EIGRP routers R1 and R2 have an adjacency over a 1 Gbps link, whereas routers R2 and R3 have an adjacency over a 10 Gbps link. For the path traversing R1, R2, and R3, what is the constrained bandwidth?

A. 10,000,000 kbps

B. 1 Gbps

C. 10 Gbps

D. 11 Gbps

E. 9 Gbps

17. EIGRP routers R1 and R2 have an adjacency over a link with a 100 μsec delay, whereas routers R2 and R3 have an adjacency over a link with a 30 μsec delay. For the path traversing R1, R2, and R3, what is the delay value EIGRP considers in calculating a metric?

    A. 30 μsec

    B. 70 μsec

    C. 100 μsec

    D. 130 μsec

18. A router has two EIGRP paths: one via R1 with a distance of 3,328 and another via R2 with a distance of 5,632. Using unequal cost multipathing, approximately what percentage of traffic will go through R1?

    A. 26%

    B. 37%

    C. 50%

    D. 64%

    E. 71%

19. Which of the following is *not* included in the EIGRP weighted metric formula?

    A. Load

    B. Delay

    C. Reliability

    D. MTU

20. Which of the following can cause a route to get SIA?

    A. MTU mismatch

    B. Redistribution

    C. A cut fiber

    D. A routing loop

The Border Gateway Protocol (BGP)

THE CCNP ENCOR EXAM OBJECTIVES COVERED IN THIS CHAPTER INCLUDE THE FOLLOWING:

Domain 3 Infrastructure

✓ 3.2   Layer 3

In this chapter you'll learn about Border Gateway Protocol (BGP), defined in RFC 4271. BGP was designed as the successor to the Internet's early distance-vector routing protocols, the Exterior Gateway Protocol (EGP). BGP has held the Internet together for over 30 years, a testament to its scalability and flexibility. In addition to its ubiquity on the Internet, many organizations use BGP internally. BGP is a huge topic, so we're going to focus on the aspects of it that you're most likely to encounter on the job and those most relevant to the ENCOR exam, including the following:

Differences between BGP and IGPs

BGP AS numbers

BGP session establishment

Prefix advertisement

Path selection algorithm

Route redistribution between BGP and IGPs

Route summarization and filtering

BGP Fundamentals

You're familiar with how IGPs make routing decisions. The limitation of IGPs is that they don't scale in very large networks, such as the Internet. Recall from Chapter 5, Open Shortest Path First (OSPF), and Chapter 6, Enhanced Interior Gateway Routing Protocol (EIGRP), that both of these protocols require propagating updates throughout the network, one hop at a time. And if a link goes down, the routers may have to perform new route computations, potentially causing packet loss. Another potential problem with trying to use an IGP in a large network is that if you ever need to merge two networks running different IGPs—such as in the case of an acquisition—you'll have the additional administrative burden of configuring mutual route redistribution, not to mention the potential for redistribution loops and routing loops.

BGP was designed to allow different ASs to connect to one another over the Internet or through private networks without the risk and hassle inherent in using IGPs. According to RFC 1930, a BGP autonomous system is "a connected group of one or more IP prefixes run by one or more network operators which has a single and clearly defined routing policy." In contrast to IGPs, BGP errs on the side of route stability and scalability, with the tradeoff being that new routes and routing updates take longer to propagate. BGP doesn't periodically send route updates at least every 30 minutes the way OSPF does.

Distance vector protocols such as EIGRP try to find the shortest path to a destination. BGP, on the other hand, is a path vector protocol—sometimes called a reachability protocol. Rather than trying to find the shortest distance to a given prefix, it attempts to find the path through the fewest ASs. What's the difference? A distance vector protocol considers the number of hops—or distance—it takes to get to a destination prefix. BGP doesn't care about individual hops. Instead, it's concerned with the number of ASs a packet must traverse to get to a destination prefix.

BGP AS Numbers

BGP identifies an AS using an AS number. Originally, BGP as numbers were limited to 16 bits (2 bytes) in length, so the range of possible BGP AS numbers was 0 to 65535. RFC 4893 opened up 32-bit (4-byte) AS numbers, expanding the range from 0 to 4,294,967,295. Keep in mind that these are the AS numbers BGP itself allows. In practice, the specific AS numbers you can use are much more limited. The Internet Assigned Numbers Authority (IANA) assigns BGP AS numbers for use on the public Internet. The range of public AS numbers is from

- 1 to 64,495
- 131,072 to 4,199,999,999

Mercifully, you don't need to memorize those numbers. Just know that allowable AS numbers on the public Internet can be quite large. If you want to use an AS number on your private network, you can use one of the reserved private AS number ranges:

- 64512 to 65,534
- 4,200,000,000 to 4,294,967,294

It's likely that, unless you have a love of typing large numbers, you would stick with one of the 16-bit private AS numbers.

AS Path Length

BGP uses AS numbers for two main purposes:

- To determine the best path to a prefix
- To prevent routing loops between ASs

Consider the BGP routers in Figure 7.1. Suppose that AS 65111 needs to send a packet to AS 65116. The packet will take the shortest path—hence the term path vector—going from AS 65111, to AS 65112, to AS 65116. This list of AS numbers is called the AS path. BGP doesn't know how many hops the packet traverses within each AS; it only knows the AS path. Within each AS, a packet may traverse any number of routers running an IGP, but those IGP hops aren't counted in the AS path length. In other words, IGPs are responsible for routing within each AS, but BGP is responsible for routing between the ASs.

FIGURE 7.1   BGP peers in different autonomous systems

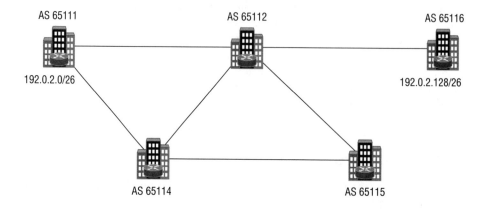

Now let's see how BGP route advertisements work, using the 192.0.2.128/26 prefix in AS 65116 as an example. AS 65116 advertises the prefix to AS 65112, which advertises the prefix to its neighbors:

- AS 65111
- AS 65114
- AS 65115

Each of these advertises the prefix to its neighbors, and so on. Each time a route advertisement passes through an AS, the BGP router prepends its own AS number to the beginning of the AS path list.

AS 65111 will receive two routes—one from AS 65112 and another from AS 65114—but it will choose only the route with the shortest AS path as the best path. For the route that AS 65111 receives from AS 65112, the AS path will look like this:

```
65111 65112 65116
```

This AS path contains three AS numbers, giving it an AS path length of 3. Because of AS prepending, the AS numbers are listed in reverse order. The route originated from the rightmost AS 65116, then went to AS 65112, and finally to AS 65111.

For the route that AS 65111 receives from AS 65114, the AS path will look like this:

```
65111 65114 65112 65116
```

This AS path length is 4, so AS 65111 will discard this longer path in favor of the shorter path. AS 65111's best path to the 192.0.2.128/26 prefix is therefore via AS 65112. And if this were the whole story, BGP would be pretty simple. But when making a best path selection, BGP does consider other factors, which we'll cover shortly.

Loop Prevention

Now let's look at Figure 7.2 to see how BGP routers use the AS path to prevent routing loops. If a BGP router sees its own AS in the AS path of a route it receives from another AS, it will simply discard the route. Consider this scenario: AS 65111 has received a route for the 192.0.2.128/26 prefix from AS 65112. AS 65111 then advertises the

`192.0.2.128/26` prefix to AS 65114, which in turn advertises it to AS 65112. The AS path that AS 65112 sees will look like this:

`65114 65111 65112 65116`

AS 65112 will see its own AS number in the AS path and discard the route because it knows that installing the route would create a loop. Also, because AS 65112 discards the route, it won't advertise it to any of its neighbors.

FIGURE 7.2   Route propagation and loop prevention among BGP neighbors in different autonomous systems

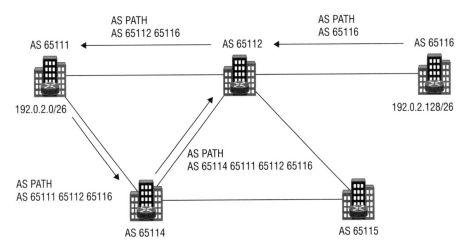

BGP Session States

Before BGP routers can exchange routes, they have to set up a peering session, sometimes called a neighborship. When BGP routers with different AS numbers peer, it's called external BGP (eBGP) peering. On the other hand, if two BGP routers with the same AS number peer, it's called internal BGP (iBGP) peering. Typically, IGPs advertise routes within an AS, whereas BGP advertises routes to peers outside the AS. Outside of a lab environment, most of your encounters will be with eBGP, so in this chapter, we're going to cover only eBGP peerings. Regardless of the peering type, all BGP peers communicate over TCP port 179 and go through the following states to establish a peering session:

Idle   In the Idle state, a BGP router tries to initiate a TCP connection with its peer. At the same time, it begins to listen for an incoming connection from that peer.

Connect   BGP waits for the TCP connection with the peer to complete. Once the connection is complete, the router with the higher IP address manages the connection state.

Active   In the Active state, the router with the higher IP—the active router—initiates another TCP connection (also on port 179) with its peer—the passive router. The passive router naturally listens for this new connection. This new connection will actually be used for exchanging routes.

OpenSent   In this state, the peers begin performing some BGP-specific sanity checks. They check that their BGP versions match, that the source IP address and AS number of the peer match what's configured, and that the BGP RIDs are unique. If anything is amiss, the peers reset to the Idle state and try again.

OpenConfirm   The peers wait to receive a keepalive message from one another. By default, each peer sends one every 60 seconds. Incidentally, the hold time is 180 seconds, which is three times the keepalive interval.

Established   After each peer receives a keepalive, the BGP session is established and the peers exchange routes.

Configuring BGP

Working from Figure 7.3, we'll configure a full mesh of BGP peerings among R1, R4, and the Internet service provider (ISP) router. We'll begin by configuring the ISP router to use AS 65550 and to peer with the following neighbors:

- R1 (203.0.113.1) in AS 65001
- R4 (198.51.100.1) in AS 65004

FIGURE 7.3   Layer 3 topology using BGP, OSPF, and EIGRP

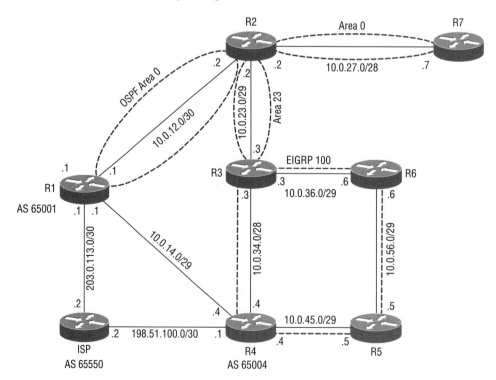

First, we'll specify the AS number to use:

```
ISP#conf t
Enter configuration commands, one per line.  End with CNTL/Z.
ISP(config)#router bgp 65550
```

Next, specify the IP addresses and AS numbers of the neighbors to peer with:

```
ISP(config-router)#neighbor 203.0.113.1 remote-as 65001
ISP(config-router)#neighbor 198.51.100.1 remote-as 65004
```

Now let's configure R1:

```
R1#conf t
Enter configuration commands, one per line.  End with CNTL/Z.
R1(config)#router bgp 65001
```

Configure the peering with ISP:

```
R1(config-router)#neighbor 203.0.113.2 remote-as 65550
R1(config-router)#
```

The neighborship with ISP comes up:

```
%BGP-5-ADJCHANGE: neighbor 203.0.113.2 Up
```

Configure the peering with R4:

```
R1(config-router)#neighbor 10.0.14.4 remote-as 65004
```

And finally let's configure R4:

```
R4#conf t
Enter configuration commands, one per line.  End with CNTL/Z.
R4(config)#router bgp 65004
R4(config-router)#neighbor 198.51.100.2 remote-as 65550
R4(config-router)#
%BGP-5-ADJCHANGE: neighbor 198.51.100.2 Up
R4(config-router)#neighbor 10.0.14.1 remote-as 65001
R4(config-router)#
%BGP-5-ADJCHANGE: neighbor 10.0.14.1 Up
```

Let's view R4's neighborships with R1 and ISP:

```
R4(config-router)#do show ip bgp summary
BGP router identifier 198.51.100.1, local AS number 65004
BGP table version is 5, main routing table version 5
Neighbor        V         AS MsgRcvd MsgSent   TblVer  InQ OutQ Up/Down  State/PfxRcd
10.0.14.1       4      65001      16      17        5    0    0 00:10:49        0
198.51.100.2    4      65550      52      55        5    0    0 00:44:38        0
```

Advertising Prefixes

For a BGP router to advertise a prefix, the route must first exist in the router's IP routing table. By default, a BGP router won't originate any routes, but it will advertise received routes to other eBGP peers. If you want to originate a route for a prefix, you must explicitly instruct BGP to do so. For example, if we want R4 to advertise the 10.0.23.0/29 prefix, we'll first check to make sure it exists in the IP routing table.

```
R4(config-router)#do show ip route | i 10.0.23.0/29
! The route exists in the IP routing table as an EIGRP-learned route
D        10.0.23.0/29 [90/3072] via 10.0.34.3, 1d05h, GigabitEthernet0/0
```

The route exists as an EIGRP-learned route, so to advertise it via BGP, we need to use the network statement, specifying the prefix with its exact subnet mask.

```
R4(config-router)#network 10.0.23.0 mask 255.255.255.248
```

It's crucial to specify the subnet mask for any non-classful prefixes; otherwise, BGP would try to advertise the classful network—in this case 10.0.0.0/8. Both the subnet *and* mask must match exactly what's in the IP routing table, or BGP won't advertise the prefix. For example, if you were to use the mask 255.255.255.0 instead of the correct mask of 255.255.255.248, the network statement would have no effect at all.

This will install the route in the BGP RIB, which we can verify as follows:

```
BGP table version is 6, local router ID is 198.51.100.1
Status codes: s suppressed, d damped, h history, * valid, > best, i - internal,
              r RIB-failure, S Stale, m multipath, b backup-path, f RT-Filter,
              x best-external, a additional-path, c RIB-compressed,
Origin codes: i - IGP, e - EGP, ? - incomplete
RPKI validation codes: V valid, I invalid, N Not found
     Network          Next Hop          Metric LocPrf Weight Path
 *>  10.0.23.0/29     10.0.34.3           3072          32768 i
```

The route is essentially a copy of what's in the IP routing table. The asterisk (*) indicates the next hop address—R3's 10.0.34.3—is reachable. More pointedly, the asterisk means that the IP routing table has a route to reach the next hop. In a moment, we'll cover the metric and weight attributes. For now, note that BGP adopts the EIGRP metric of 3,072, and that because the route is locally originated, it assigns a weight of 32,768.

If the next hop isn't reachable, the route isn't valid, and BGP will never select it as the best path. Therefore, BGP also won't install the route in the IP routing table.

The greater-than symbol (>) indicates this is the best path. Although this is obviously the only path, this fact is significant because BGP advertises only the best path to its peers. Let's jump to R1 to verify that it's receiving this route:

```
R1#show ip bgp
BGP table version is 6, local router ID is 203.0.113.1
Status codes: s suppressed, d damped, h history, * valid, > best, i - internal,
              r RIB-failure, S Stale, m multipath, b backup-path, f RT-Filter,
              x best-external, a additional-path, c RIB-compressed,
Origin codes: i - IGP, e - EGP, ? - incomplete
RPKI validation codes: V valid, I invalid, N Not found
     Network          Next Hop            Metric LocPrf Weight Path
! This route is via ISP. Notice the AS path contains the ASes of ISP (65550)
! and R4 (65004)
 *   10.0.23.0/29     203.0.113.2                         0 65550 65004 i
! The path directly via R4 is the best
 *>                   10.0.14.4             3072          0 65004 i
```

R1 is learning two BGP routes for the 10.0.23.0/29 prefix, one via ISP (203.0.113.2) and the other via R4 (10.0.14.4). The route via R4 is tagged as the best path because it has the shortest AS path length. BGP installs the best path in the IP routing table.

```
R1#show ip route bgp
! Output truncated
Gateway of last resort is 203.0.113.2 to network 0.0.0.0
      10.0.0.0/8 is variably subnetted, 6 subnets, 4 masks
B        10.0.23.0/29 [20/3072] via 10.0.14.4, 00:14:16
```

Path Selection

AS path length is not the only attribute BGP uses to determine the best path to a prefix. In Cisco routers, BGP determines the best path for a prefix by considering each of the following attributes in order:

- Weight
- Local preference
- Shortest AS path
- Origin type
- Multi-exit discriminator
- eBGP over iBGP
- Lowest IGP cost to the BGP next hop
- Oldest route
- Lowest RID

The rules for BGP best path selection aren't set in stone. BGP is designed so that each AS can have its own routing policies, so you can modify these attributes as needed to influence best path selection to your liking. That's one of the reasons the Internet has been using it for over 30 years!

Weight

You can use weight to control which route is chosen as the best path. It's a Cisco-proprietary attribute that's only locally significant, so it's not advertised to other routers. Because it's considered first, weight overrides all other attributes. The default weight value for learned routes is 0, and for self-generated routes it's 32,768. A higher weight is more preferred.

Local Preference

Local preference influences the path traffic takes to prefixes outside of an AS. For example, if you have two BGP routers in the same AS and both are learning the 5.0.0.0/8 prefix from an external AS, you can use local preference to control which of the routers will be used as the next hop to reach the prefix. The local preference attribute can be advertised only among BGP routers within an AS. The default value for local preference is 100.

Shortest AS Path

The path with the shortest number of AS hops is preferred. You can manually tweak the AS path attribute by adding or removing AS numbers in order to influence best path selection. But just because you can doesn't mean you should. Remember that the AS path is also used for loop prevention, so removing AS numbers willy-nilly can inadvertently create a routing loop.

The Origin Type

The origin type indicates how BGP learned the route. It can be incomplete (designated by a question mark), which means the source prefix was redistributed, or it can be IGP, meaning the route was originated using the BGP network statement. This seems counterintuitive, so be careful not to get confused. A route redistributed from an IGP does *not* have an origin type of IGP, but of incomplete. BGP prefers the IGP origin type over the incomplete type.

The Multi-Exit Discriminator

The multi-exit discriminator (MED) is in a sense the reverse of local preference. Whereas local preference influences the direction of traffic leaving an AS, the MED—also called the metric—influences how traffic ingresses an AS. A lower MED is more preferred. Suppose you have two BGP routers in your AS that are peered to routers in AS 64999. If you want traffic from AS 64999 to ingress a particular router, you can configure that router to advertise a lower MED.

eBGP over iBGP

eBGP-learned routes take precedence over iBGP routes. Also, remember that eBGP routes have an AD of 20, whereas iBGP routes have an AD of 200. This will naturally lead to the eBGP routes supplanting the iBGP routes in the IP routing table.

Lowest IGP Cost to the BGP Next Hop

Because BGP uses IP unicasts, BGP neighbors don't have to establish their neighborship over a shared subnet. In this scenario—called multi-hop BGP—it's possible that a BGP router has to learn an IGP route to reach its BGP neighbor. In that case, the next hop for a BGP route would be learned via an IGP. If there are multiple BGP routes that are otherwise equal, the lowest IGP cost to the next hop becomes the tiebreaker.

Oldest Route

Because BGP places more importance on stability, it prefers the oldest installed route. If a router already has a best path route to a prefix and receives another route that is otherwise equal, BGP will hold onto the existing installed route as the best path.

Lowest RID

If the best path goes down and BGP has two backup paths that are otherwise equal, it will choose the path from the router with the lowest RID. The RID is the highest-numbered loopback IP, if configured. Otherwise, it's the highest-numbered IP address of all the physical interfaces.

These aren't the only attributes BGP considers, but they are the most common ones that you need to know for the ENCOR exam. Again, it's possible to configure the rules around how BGP uses these attributes or whether it even considers them at all.

To understand how best path selection works, we'll configure the ISP router to advertise both its connected routes:

```
ISP#show ip route connected | i C
Codes: L - local, C - connected, S - static, R - RIP, M - mobile, B - BGP
C        198.51.100.0/30 is directly connected, GigabitEthernet0/2
C        203.0.113.0/30 is directly connected, GigabitEthernet0/3
```

There are actually two ways to go about this. We'll use the network statement to advertise the 198.51.100.0/30 prefix with the IGP origin type. We'll then redistribute the connected routes into BGP to advertise the 203.0.113.0/30 prefix with the incomplete origin type.

```
ISP#conf t
Enter configuration commands, one per line.  End with CNTL/Z.
ISP(config)#router bgp 65550
```

We'll explicitly advertise the 198.51.100.0/30 prefix.

```
ISP(config-router)#network 198.51.100.0 mask 255.255.255.252
```

Now let's redistribute connected routes, which include 203.0.113.0/30 and 198.51.100.0/30:

```
ISP(config-router)#redistribute connected
```

You'll notice that there seems to be some overlap between the two commands. The network command advertises 198.51.100.0/30, but so does the redistribute connected command. However, remember that redistributed routes are given an origin type of incomplete, whereas prefixes advertised using the network statement are given an origin type of IGP, BGP preferring the latter. Hence, 198.51.100.0/30 will be advertised with the IGP origin type, and 203.0.113.0/30 will be advertised with an incomplete origin type. ISP will advertise these routes to both R1 and R4, which will in turn advertise them to each other. Let's view the BGP RIB on R1:

```
R1#show ip bgp
BGP table version is 14, local router ID is 203.0.113.1
Status codes: s suppressed, d damped, h history, * valid, > best, i - internal,
              r RIB-failure, S Stale, m multipath, b backup-path, f RT-Filter,
              x best-external, a additional-path, c RIB-compressed,
Origin codes: i - IGP, e - EGP, ? - incomplete
RPKI validation codes: V valid, I invalid, N Not found
     Network          Next Hop            Metric LocPrf Weight Path
 *   10.0.23.0/29     203.0.113.2                          0 65550 65004 i
 *>                   10.0.14.4           3072             0 65004 i
 ! The routes advertised using the network statement. Notice they have an
 ! origin code of IGP.
 *   198.51.100.0/30  10.0.14.4                            0 65004 65550 (i)
 *>                   203.0.113.2              0           0 65550 (i)
 ! The routes advertised using the redistribute connected command have an
 ! incomplete origin.
 r   203.0.113.0/30   10.0.14.4                            0 65004 65550 (?)
 r>                   203.0.113.2              0           0 65550 (?)
```

The BGP RIB can be tricky to read when there are multiple paths to a prefix. Consider the 198.51.00.0/30 prefix. There are two paths:

- The best path via ISP (next hop 203.0.113.2)

- Followed by the route via R4 (next hop 10.0.14.4)

Let's get a closer look at the RIB to see exactly why R1 prefers the route via ISP:

```
BGP routing table entry for 198.51.100.0/30, version 13
! Even though the actual paths aren't numbered, BGP indicates that the
! second path is the best.
```

```
Paths: (2 available, best #2, table default)
  Advertised to update-groups:
      1
  Refresh Epoch 2
  65004 65550
     10.0.14.4 from 10.0.14.4 (198.51.100.1)
       Origin IGP, localpref 100, valid, external
       rx pathid: 0, tx pathid: 0
  Refresh Epoch 1
! The route via ISP is the best path.
65550
  203.0.113.2 from 203.0.113.2 (203.0.113.2)
     Origin IGP, metric 0, localpref 100, valid, external, best
     rx pathid: 0, tx pathid: 0x0
```

The local preference and weight values are equal, so BGP will use the AS path length as the tiebreaker. The route via ISP has the shortest AS path, since R1 and ISP are directly connected, so BGP selects it as the best path and installs it in the IP routing table:

```
R4#show ip route | i B
Codes: L - local, C - connected, S - static, R - RIP, M - mobile, B - BGP
B       203.0.113.0 [20/0] via 198.51.100.2, 13:28:30
```

Note that the administrative distance for the route is 20. For eBGP routes, the default AD is 20, whereas for iBGP routes it's 200. Now let's look at the routes for 203.0.113.0/30, which is one of R1's directly connected networks:

```
R1#show ip route | i 203.0.113.0/30
C       203.0.113.0/30 is directly connected, GigabitEthernet0/3
```

This is a connected route, and BGP can't install its own route over a connected route because connected routes have an AD of 0. However, routes for the prefix still appear in the BGP RIB.

```
R1#show ip bgp
BGP table version is 14, local router ID is 203.0.113.1
Status codes: s suppressed, d damped, h history, * valid, > best, i - internal,
              r RIB-failure, S Stale, m multipath, b backup-path, f RT-Filter,
              x best-external, a additional-path, c RIB-compressed,
Origin codes: i - IGP, e - EGP, ? - incomplete
RPKI validation codes: V valid, I invalid, N Not found
     Network          Next Hop            Metric LocPrf Weight Path
 *   10.0.23.0/29     203.0.113.2                         0 65550 65004 i
 *>                   10.0.14.4             3072          0 65004 i
 *   198.51.100.0/30  10.0.14.4                           0 65004 65550 i
 *>                   203.0.113.2              0           0 65550 i
 r   203.0.113.0/30   10.0.14.4                           0 65004 65550 ?
 r>                   203.0.113.2              0           0 65550 ?
```

Both routes are listed with an r for RIB failure, indicating that BGP wasn't able to install the route in the IP routing table. A RIB failure can occur when a route with a lower administrative distance has already been installed in the IP routing table. In this case, the route already exists in the IP routing table as a connected route with an AD of 0. EBGP routes have an AD of 20, so the connected route will take precedence.

Route Redistribution among BGP, OSPF, and EIGRP

When you connect networks running different IGP instances, mutual redistribution is often required to advertise routes and ensure IP reachability. An advantage of redistributing between IGPs and BGP is that new IGP routes automatically get advertised into BGP, and vice versa. This is less of a management headache than manually reconfiguring each routing protocol every time you need to advertise a new route. We'll configure mutual redistribution between the following routers shown in Figure 7.3:

▪ BGP and OSPF on R1

▪ BGP and EIGRP 100 on R4

Our goals are to advertise all prefixes in the topology to the ISP router, and to make sure all the other routers have a route back to it. Whenever you configure mutual redistribution, expect to have to do a fair bit of troubleshooting.

Mutual Redistribution between BGP and OSPF

Let's start by redistributing BGP AS 65001 routes into OSPF:

```
R1(config)#router ospf 1
R1(config-router)#redistribute bgp 65001 subnets
```

We can verify the redistribution is taking place by viewing type 5 External LSAs in the OSPF LSDB.

```
R1(config-router)#do show ip ospf database | b Type-5
            Type-5 AS External Link States
Link ID        ADV Router      Age       Seq#        Checksum Tag
0.0.0.0        1.1.1.1         92        0x800000CE 0x00815F 1
10.0.23.0      1.1.1.1         38        0x80000005 0x00DEC7 65004
198.51.100.0   1.1.1.1         38        0x80000005 0x002F12 65550
```

Each redistributed route is tagged with the AS number that originated it. The route for the 198.51.100.0/30 prefix has a route tag of 65550 (ISP). This tagging occurs automatically when redistributing from BGP, making it easy to tell where a route originated. Now let's redistribute OSPF routes into BGP 65001.

```
R1(config-router)#router bgp 65001
R1(config-router)#redistribute ospf 1
R1(config-router)#do show ip bgp
BGP table version is 17, local router ID is 203.0.113.1
```

```
Status codes: s suppressed, d damped, h history, * valid, > best, i - internal,
              r RIB-failure, S Stale, m multipath, b backup-path, f RT-Filter,
              x best-external, a additional-path, c RIB-compressed,
Origin codes: i - IGP, e - EGP, ? - incomplete
RPKI validation codes: V valid, I invalid, N Not found
     Network          Next Hop         Metric LocPrf Weight Path
 *>  10.0.12.0/30     0.0.0.0               0        32768 ?
 *>  10.0.14.0/29     0.0.0.0               0        32768 ?
 *   10.0.23.0/29     203.0.113.2                        0 65550 65004 i
 *>                   10.0.14.4          3072             0 65004 i
 *>  10.0.27.0/28     10.0.12.2             2        32768 ?
 *   198.51.100.0/30  10.0.14.4                         0 65004 65550 i
 *>                   203.0.113.2           0            0 65550 i
 r   203.0.113.0/30   10.0.14.4                         0 65004 65550 ?
 r>                   203.0.113.2           0            0 65550 ?
```

The three routes redistributed from OSPF show as having the incomplete origin type, as indicated by a question mark. Something interesting here is that `10.0.12.0/30` and `10.0.14.0/29` are both connected networks but R1 isn't redistributing connected routes directly into BGP, nor have we configured a network statement to advertise these. Rather, R1 is advertising these routes into OSPF and then redistributing OSPF into BGP. As an alternative to redistributing OSPF routes into BGP, you could use the network statement to advertise the same connected prefixes with the IGP origin type.

Mutual Redistribution between BGP and EIGRP

Next, let's configure mutual EIGRP and BGP redistribution on R4. When redistributing into EIGRP, you must specify values for the variables that the EIGRP weighted metric formula uses: bandwidth, delay, reliability, and load. Additionally, you must specify MTU. If you don't specify these values, redistribution won't occur.

```
R4(config)#router eigrp 100
R4(config-router)#redistribute bgp 65004 metric 100000 1 255 1 1500
! There are three routes redistributed from BGP into EIGRP
R4(config-router)#do show ip eigrp topology | i tag
P 203.0.113.0/30, 1 successors, FD is 25856, tag is 65550
P 10.0.12.0/30, 1 successors, FD is 25856, tag is 65001
P 10.0.27.0/28, 1 successors, FD is 25856, tag is 65001
```

As before, the redistributed routes are tagged with the AS number that originated them. Even though we didn't explicitly configure tags, it happened automatically when we redistributed BGP into EIGRP. Let's finish the job by redistributing EIGRP into BGP.

```
R4(config-router)#router bgp 65004
R4(config-router)#redistribute eigrp 100 ?
  metric     Metric for redistributed routes
  route-map  Route map reference
  <cr>
```

```
R4(config-router)#redistribute eigrp 100
R4(config-router)#do show ip bgp
BGP table version is 24, local router ID is 198.51.100.1
Status codes: s suppressed, d damped, h history, * valid, > best, i - internal,
              r RIB-failure, S Stale, m multipath, b backup-path, f RT-Filter,
              x best-external, a additional-path, c RIB-compressed,
Origin codes: i - IGP, e - EGP, ? - incomplete
RPKI validation codes: V valid, I invalid, N Not found
     Network          Next Hop         Metric LocPrf Weight Path
 *   10.0.12.0/30     198.51.100.2                       0 65550 65001 ?
 *>                   10.0.14.1             0             0 65001 ?
 r   10.0.14.0/29     198.51.100.2                       0 65550 65001 ?
 r>                   10.0.14.1             0             0 65001 ?
 *>  10.0.23.0/29     10.0.34.3         3072         32768 i
 *   10.0.27.0/28     198.51.100.2                       0 65550 65001 ?
 *>                   10.0.14.1             2             0 65001 ?
 *>  10.0.34.0/28     0.0.0.0              0         32768 ?
 *>  10.0.36.0/29     10.0.34.3         3072         32768 ?
 *>  10.0.45.0/29     0.0.0.0              0         32768 ?
 *>  10.0.56.0/29     10.0.34.3         3328         32768 ?
 r   198.51.100.0/30  10.0.14.1                           0 65001 65550 i
 r>                   198.51.100.2         0             0 65550 i
 *   203.0.113.0/30   10.0.14.1                           0 65001 65550 ?
 *>                   198.51.100.2         0             0 65550 ?
```

R4 redistributes four EIGRP routes into BGP, as indicated by the incomplete origin type and the fact that there are no numbers in the AS path column. Also, note from the Metric column that BGP adopts the EIGRP metric as its own. Between R1 and R4, all routes in the topology are being advertised to ISP via BGP. Now let's verify this by viewing the BGP RIB on the ISP router:

```
ISP#show ip bgp
BGP table version is 24, local router ID is 203.0.113.2
Status codes: s suppressed, d damped, h history, * valid, > best, i - internal,
              r RIB-failure, S Stale, m multipath, b backup-path, f RT-Filter,
              x best-external, a additional-path, c RIB-compressed,
Origin codes: i - IGP, e - EGP, ? - incomplete
RPKI validation codes: V valid, I invalid, N Not found
     Network          Next Hop         Metric LocPrf Weight Path
 *   10.0.12.0/30     198.51.100.1                       0 65004 65001 ?
 *>                   203.0.113.1          0             0 65001 ?
 *   10.0.14.0/29     198.51.100.1                       0 65004 65001 ?
```

```
*>                      203.0.113.1           0          0 65001 ?
*    10.0.23.0/29       203.0.113.1                      0 65001 65004 i
*>                      198.51.100.1       3072          0 65004 i
*    10.0.27.0/28       198.51.100.1                     0 65004 65001 ?
*>                      203.0.113.1           2          0 65001 ?
*    10.0.34.0/28       203.0.113.1                      0 65001 65004 ?
*>                      198.51.100.1          0          0 65004 ?
*    10.0.36.0/29       203.0.113.1                      0 65001 65004 ?
*>                      198.51.100.1       3072          0 65004 ?
*    10.0.45.0/29       203.0.113.1                      0 65001 65004 ?
*>                      198.51.100.1          0          0 65004 ?
*    10.0.56.0/29       203.0.113.1                      0 65001 65004 ?
*>                      198.51.100.1       3328          0 65004 ?
*>   198.51.100.0/30    0.0.0.0               0      32768 i
*>   203.0.113.0/30     0.0.0.0               0      32768 ?
```

All prefixes are accounted for. With a careful reading of the BGP RIB, you can see that some prefixes have R1 (203.0.113.1) as the next hop, whereas others have R4 (198.51.100.1). This is more obvious with a quick look at the IP routing table:

```
ISP#show ip route bgp
Codes: L - local, C - connected, S - static, R - RIP, M - mobile, B - BGP
       D - EIGRP, EX - EIGRP external, O - OSPF, IA - OSPF inter area
       N1 - OSPF NSSA external type 1, N2 - OSPF NSSA external type 2
       E1 - OSPF external type 1, E2 - OSPF external type 2
       i - IS-IS, su - IS-IS summary, L1 - IS-IS level-1, L2 - IS-IS level-2
       ia - IS-IS inter area, * - candidate default, U - per-user static route
       o - ODR, P - periodic downloaded static route, H - NHRP, l - LISP
       a - application route
       + - replicated route, % - next hop override, p - overrides from PfR
Gateway of last resort is not set
      10.0.0.0/8 is variably subnetted, 8 subnets, 3 masks
B        10.0.12.0/30 [20/0] via 203.0.113.1, 02:49:53
B        10.0.14.0/29 [20/0] via 203.0.113.1, 02:49:53
B        10.0.23.0/29 [20/3072] via 198.51.100.1, 20:41:50
B        10.0.27.0/28 [20/2] via 203.0.113.1, 02:49:53
B        10.0.34.0/28 [20/0] via 198.51.100.1, 00:49:29
B        10.0.36.0/29 [20/3072] via 198.51.100.1, 00:49:29
B        10.0.45.0/29 [20/0] via 198.51.100.1, 00:49:29
B        10.0.56.0/29 [20/3328] via 198.51.100.1, 00:49:29
```

Testing IP Reachability Using Tcl Scripts

The real test of whether mutual redistribution succeeded is whether we have full IP reachability between the ISP router and all the other routers. To ping all of the router interfaces from ISP, we'll use a Tool Command Language (Tcl) script. IOS allows you to run Tcl scripts from the command line. To run the script, enter the Tcl shell on ISP:

```
ISP#tclsh
ISP(tcl)#
```

At the shell, enter and execute the following script:

```
foreach address {
10.0.12.1
10.0.12.2
10.0.14.1
10.0.14.4
10.0.23.2
10.0.23.3
10.0.27.2
10.0.27.7
10.0.34.3
10.0.34.4
10.0.36.3
10.0.36.6
10.0.45.4
10.0.45.5
10.0.56.5
10.0.56.6} { ping $address repeat 2 timeout 1
}
```

It will take a few moments for the router to ping all the addresses. For brevity, I'm leaving out the output except for the following failed pings:

```
Sending 2, 100-byte ICMP Echos to 10.0.36.6, timeout is 1 seconds:
..
Success rate is 0 percent (0/2)
Sending 2, 100-byte ICMP Echos to 10.0.45.5, timeout is 1 seconds:
..
Success rate is 0 percent (0/2)
Type escape sequence to abort.
Sending 2, 100-byte ICMP Echos to 10.0.56.5, timeout is 1 seconds:
..
Success rate is 0 percent (0/2)
Type escape sequence to abort.
```

```
Sending 2, 100-byte ICMP Echos to 10.0.56.6, timeout is 1 seconds:
..
Success rate is 0 percent (0/2)
```

These failed pings are to R5's and R6's interface addresses. The fact that the pings to their neighboring routers succeed (R3 and R4, respectively) indicates that the problem is most likely that R5 and R6 don't have a route back to the ISP router. Let's begin troubleshooting.

Troubleshooting

When troubleshooting IP reachability, the first two questions you should always ask are "What's the destination address?" and "What's the source address?" The latter question is most significant here. ISP has two interfaces. When pinging the failed addresses, we need to determine which source address ISP was using.

```
ISP#show ip route bgp | i 36|45|56
B        10.0.36.0/29 [20/3072] via 198.51.100.1, 01:14:54
B        10.0.45.0/29 [20/0] via 198.51.100.1, 01:14:54
B        10.0.56.0/29 [20/3328] via 198.51.100.1, 01:14:54
```

ISP is learning all of these routes from R4, which it's connected to on the 198.51.100.0/30 subnet. Hence, ISP sourced the pings from its 198.51.100.2 interface address. Therefore, we need to verify that R5 and R6 have routes back to this subnet. Our troubleshooting adventure will begin on R6.

```
R6#show ip route 198.51.100.0
% Network not in table
R6#show ip eigrp topology 198.51.100.0/30
EIGRP-IPv4 Topology Entry for AS(100)/ID(6.6.6.6)
%Entry 198.51.100.0/30 not in topology table
```

 NOTE   When viewing the EIGRP topology table, be careful to specify the correct subnet mask. If you don't, EIGRP will assume the classful mask and might not show you the prefix you're looking for!

R5 doesn't have a route to the subnet, which suggests that neither of its EIGRP neighbors (R3 and R5) is advertising it. Let's jump over to R3 and see whether it has a route:

```
R3#show ip route 198.51.100.0
Routing entry for 198.51.100.0/30, 1 known subnets
O E2     198.51.100.0 [110/1] via 10.0.23.2, 01:48:39, GigabitEthernet0/1
```

R3 has a route, but it's learned via OSPF. Recall that R3 is running both OSPF and EIGRP but it's not performing redistribution, so it's not advertising the prefix into EIGRP. We can verify this by looking at the EIGRP topology table:

```
R3#show ip eigrp topology 198.51.100.0/30
EIGRP-IPv4 Topology Entry for AS(100)/ID(3.3.3.3)
%Entry 198.51.100.0/30 not in topology table
```

It's tempting to go for the quick fix by redistributing OSPF into EIGRP. But that's not necessary, and doing so could have undesirable consequences. When doing mutual redistribution between routing protocols on a single router, the router takes care not to circularly redistribute the same route over and over. However, if you configure redistribution on multiple routers, you must be careful not to create a redistribution loop. If we were to enable redistribution between OSPF and EIGRP on R3, we'd end up with mutual redistribution occurring on three routers:

- BGP ⟷ OSPF
- OSPF ⟷ EIGRP
- EIGRP ⟷ BGP

This wouldn't necessarily cause a problem, but it would needlessly complicate an already complex topology. Instead, let's turn our attention to the other router ISP wasn't able to ping: R5.

```
R5#show ip route 198.51.100.0
% Network not in table
R5#show ip eigrp topology 198.51.100.0/30
EIGRP-IPv4 Topology Entry for AS(100)/ID(5.5.5.5)
%Entry 198.51.100.0/30 not in topology table
```

R5 doesn't have the route either, indicating that R4 is not advertising it. Let's pay R4 a visit:

```
R4#show ip route 198.51.100.0
Routing entry for 198.51.100.0/24, 2 known subnets
  Attached (2 connections)
  Variably subnetted with 2 masks
C       198.51.100.0/30 is directly connected, GigabitEthernet0/2
L       198.51.100.1/32 is directly connected, GigabitEthernet0/2
```

Not surprisingly, R4 has the route because it's actually connected to the subnet. But it's not advertising the prefix into EIGRP:

```
R4#show ip eigrp topology 198.51.100.0/30
EIGRP-IPv4 Topology Entry for AS(100)/ID(4.4.4.4)
%Entry 198.51.100.0/30 not in topology table
```

Even though it's redistributing BGP into EIGRP, it isn't redistributing this particular route because it's not a BGP route but rather a connected route! The solution is to instruct

EIGRP to redistribute connected routes. A quick view of the EIGRP router configuration reveals that it's not currently doing this:

```
R4#show run | s router eigrp
router eigrp 100
 network 10.0.34.4 0.0.0.0
 network 10.0.45.4 0.0.0.0
 redistribute bgp 65004 metric 100000 1 255 1 1500
 eigrp router-id 4.4.4.4
```

Let's remedy this:

```
R4(config)#router eigrp 100
R4(config-router)#redistribute connected
R4(config-router)#do show ip eigrp topology 198.51.100.0/30
EIGRP-IPv4 Topology Entry for AS(100)/ID(4.4.4.4) for 198.51.100.0/30
  State is Passive, Query origin flag is 1, 1 Successor(s), FD is 2816
  Descriptor Blocks:
  0.0.0.0, from Rconnected, Send flag is 0x0
      Composite metric is (2816/0), route is External
      Vector metric:
        Minimum bandwidth is 1000000 Kbit
        Total delay is 10 microseconds
        Reliability is 255/255
        Load is 1/255
        Minimum MTU is 1500
        Hop count is 0
        Originating router is 4.4.4.4
      External data:
        AS number of route is 0
        External protocol is Connected, external metric is 0
        Administrator tag is 0 (0x00000000)
```

Now R5 and R6 should have routes to the prefix:

```
R5#show ip route 198.51.100.0
Routing entry for 198.51.100.0/30, 1 known subnets
  Redistributing via eigrp 100
D EX    198.51.100.0 [170/3072] via 10.0.45.4, 00:01:28, GigabitEthernet0/3
R6#show ip route 198.51.100.0
Routing entry for 198.51.100.0/30, 1 known subnets
  Redistributing via eigrp 100
D EX    198.51.100.0 [170/3328] via 10.0.56.5, 00:01:37, GigabitEthernet0/0
```

Let's move back to the ISP router and try those pings to R5 and R6 again:

```
ISP#ping 10.0.56.5
Type escape sequence to abort.
Sending 5, 100-byte ICMP Echos to 10.0.56.5, timeout is 2 seconds:
!!!!!
Success rate is 100 percent (5/5), round-trip min/avg/max = 10/10/11 ms
ISP#ping 10.0.56.6
Type escape sequence to abort.
Sending 5, 100-byte ICMP Echos to 10.0.56.6, timeout is 2 seconds:
!!!!!
Success rate is 100 percent (5/5), round-trip min/avg/max = 9/10/16 ms
ISP#ping 10.0.45.5
Type escape sequence to abort.
Sending 5, 100-byte ICMP Echos to 10.0.45.5, timeout is 2 seconds:
!!!!!
Success rate is 100 percent (5/5), round-trip min/avg/max = 8/11/20 ms
ISP#ping 10.0.36.6
Type escape sequence to abort.
Sending 5, 100-byte ICMP Echos to 10.0.36.6, timeout is 2 seconds:
!!!!!
Success rate is 100 percent (5/5), round-trip min/avg/max = 9/10/12 ms
```

All pings succeed and running the Tcl script again proves that we now have full IP reachability between ISP and the rest of the topology.

Modifying Weight

Let's toy around a bit with BGP to force ISP to always route out of its Gi0/3 interface facing R1. This is the kind of thing you may do if you want to have one connection as active and another functioning as a standby. To achieve this, we'll increase the weight of the BGP routes ISP receives from R1.

```
ISP(config)#router bgp 65550
ISP(config-router)#neighbor 203.0.113.1 weight ?
  <0-65535>  default weight
ISP(config-router)#neighbor 203.0.113.1 weight 100
```

The default weight is 0, so we'll increase it to 100 for any routes learned from R1. To force BGP to reconverge quickly, we'll perform a soft reconfiguration:

```
ISP(config-router)#do clear ip bgp * soft
ISP(config-router)#do show ip route bgp | i B
Codes: L - local, C - connected, S - static, R - RIP, M - mobile, B - BGP
B       10.0.12.0/30 [20/0] via 203.0.113.1, 00:00:50
B       10.0.14.0/29 [20/0] via 203.0.113.1, 00:00:50
```

```
B        10.0.23.0/29 [20/0] via 203.0.113.1, 00:00:50
B        10.0.27.0/28 [20/2] via 203.0.113.1, 00:00:50
B        10.0.34.0/28 [20/0] via 203.0.113.1, 00:00:50
B        10.0.36.0/29 [20/0] via 203.0.113.1, 00:00:50
B        10.0.45.0/29 [20/0] via 203.0.113.1, 00:00:50
B        10.0.56.0/29 [20/0] via 203.0.113.1, 00:00:50
```

All eBGP routes now have R1 as the next hop. To simulate a failure, we'll shut down the neighborship with R1:

```
ISP(config-router)#neighbor 203.0.113.1 shutdown
ISP(config-router)#
%BGP-3-NOTIFICATION: sent to neighbor 203.0.113.1 6/2 (Administrative Shutdown)
0 bytes
ISP(config-router)#
%BGP-5-NBR_RESET: Neighbor 203.0.113.1 reset (Admin. shutdown)
%BGP-5-ADJCHANGE: neighbor 203.0.113.1 Down Admin. shutdown
%BGP_SESSION-5-ADJCHANGE: neighbor 203.0.113.1 IPv4 Unicast topology base
removed from session  Admin. shutdown
```

BGP immediately reconverges and fails over to the routes with R4 as the next hop:

```
ISP(config-router)#do show ip route bgp | i B
Codes: L - local, C - connected, S - static, R - RIP, M - mobile, B - BGP
B        10.0.12.0/30 [20/0] via 198.51.100.1, 00:00:16
B        10.0.14.0/29 [20/0] via 198.51.100.1, 00:00:16
B        10.0.23.0/29 [20/3072] via 198.51.100.1, 00:00:16
B        10.0.27.0/28 [20/0] via 198.51.100.1, 00:00:16
B        10.0.34.0/28 [20/0] via 198.51.100.1, 00:00:16
B        10.0.36.0/29 [20/3072] via 198.51.100.1, 00:00:16
B        10.0.45.0/29 [20/0] via 198.51.100.1, 00:00:16
B        10.0.56.0/29 [20/3328] via 198.51.100.1, 00:00:16
```

To simulate a recovery, we'll remove the previous statement used to shut the neighborship down:

```
ISP(config-router)#no neighbor 203.0.113.1 shutdown
ISP(config-router)#
%BGP-5-ADJCHANGE: neighbor 203.0.113.1 Up
ISP(config-router)#do show ip route bgp | i B
Codes: L - local, C - connected, S - static, R - RIP, M - mobile, B - BGP
B        10.0.12.0/30 [20/0] via 203.0.113.1, 00:00:25
B        10.0.14.0/29 [20/0] via 203.0.113.1, 00:00:25
B        10.0.23.0/29 [20/0] via 203.0.113.1, 00:00:25
B        10.0.27.0/28 [20/2] via 203.0.113.1, 00:00:25
B        10.0.34.0/28 [20/0] via 203.0.113.1, 00:00:25
```

```
B          10.0.36.0/29 [20/0] via 203.0.113.1, 00:00:25
B          10.0.45.0/29 [20/0] via 203.0.113.1, 00:00:25
B          10.0.56.0/29 [20/0] via 203.0.113.1, 00:00:25
```

Advertising Summary Routes Using Route Aggregation

BGP advertises the specific prefixes you specify using the network statement as well as those that it redistributes from an IGP. But it's possible to have BGP advertise a summary route that aggregates multiple component prefixes into a single larger prefix. For example, all the private subnets in our topology could be summarized into the 10.0.0.0/16 prefix. You may want to do this to keep the routing table small or to ensure reachability to new prefixes that aren't explicitly advertised.

As with most things BGP, you have a lot of options when it comes to advertising a summary. You can advertise the summary while continuing to advertise the component routes. Or you can advertise only the summary and suppress the component routes so that they're not advertised. Let's configure R1 to advertise a summary for the 10.0.0.0/16 prefix and suppress the component routes.

```
R1(config-router)#aggregate-address 10.0.0.0 255.255.0.0 summary-only
R1(config-router)#do show ip bgp | b Network
        Network          Next Hop          Metric LocPrf Weight Path
! R1 advertises the summary route with itself as the next hop
 *>   10.0.0.0/16       0.0.0.0                            32768 i
! But it suppresses the component routes
 s>   10.0.12.0/30      0.0.0.0                0           32768 ?
 s>   10.0.14.0/29      0.0.0.0                0           32768 ?
 s    10.0.23.0/29      203.0.113.2                           0 65550 65004 i
 s>                     10.0.14.4              3072            0 65004 i
 s>   10.0.27.0/28      10.0.12.2              2           32768 ?
 s    10.0.34.0/28      203.0.113.2                           0 65550 65004 ?
 s>                     10.0.14.4              0               0 65004 ?
 s    10.0.36.0/29      203.0.113.2                           0 65550 65004 ?
 s>                     10.0.14.4              3072            0 65004 ?
 s    10.0.45.0/29      203.0.113.2                           0 65550 65004 ?
 s>                     10.0.14.4              0               0 65004 ?
 s    10.0.56.0/29      203.0.113.2                           0 65550 65004 ?
 s>                     10.0.14.4              3328            0 65004 ?
 *>   198.51.100.0/30   203.0.113.2            0               0 65550 i
 *                      10.0.14.4                              0 65004 65550 i
 r>   203.0.113.0/30    203.0.113.2            0               0 65550 ?
 r                      10.0.14.4                              0 65004 65550 ?
```

The summary route is the first in the list, and the component routes are now marked with an s for suppressed. They still exist in R1's RIB and IP routing table, but R1 isn't advertising these component prefixes to its neighbors R4 and ISP. Let's visit ISP to see what routes it has:

```
ISP#show ip route bgp | i B
Codes: L - local, C - connected, S - static, R - RIP, M - mobile, B - BGP
! Summary route with R1 as the next hop
B        10.0.0.0/16 [20/0] via 203.0.113.1, 00:04:40
! The component routes have R4 as the next hop
B        10.0.23.0/29 [20/3072] via 198.51.100.1, 00:03:43
B        10.0.34.0/28 [20/0] via 198.51.100.1, 00:03:43
B        10.0.36.0/29 [20/3072] via 198.51.100.1, 00:03:43
B        10.0.45.0/29 [20/0] via 198.51.100.1, 00:03:43
B        10.0.56.0/29 [20/3328] via 198.51.100.1, 00:03:43
```

ISP has the summary route with R1 as the next hop. However, it also has five component routes from R4. Remember that ISP is configured to place a higher weight of 100 on prefixes learned from R1. However, R1 is no longer advertising the component prefixes, while R4 is still advertising them. Hence, ISP will learn the component prefixes from R4. This has some interesting and counterintuitive results. For instance, the route to 10.0.23.0/29 has a higher metric than 10.0.0.0/16, but ISP still chooses the more specific route—sometimes called the longest-match route.

```
ISP#show ip cef 10.0.23.0/29
10.0.23.0/29
  nexthop 198.51.100.1 GigabitEthernet0/2
```

Also notice that R4 isn't advertising all the same component prefixes R1 was. Specifically, 10.0.12.0/30, 10.0.14.0/29, and 10.0.27.0/28. This means ISP will use R1's summary route to reach these prefixes. Let's verify this:

```
ISP#show ip cef 10.0.12.0
10.0.0.0/16
  nexthop 203.0.113.1 GigabitEthernet0/3
ISP#show ip cef 10.0.14.0
10.0.0.0/16
  nexthop 203.0.113.1 GigabitEthernet0/3
ISP#show ip cef 10.0.27.0
10.0.0.0/16
  nexthop 203.0.113.1 GigabitEthernet0/3
```

Let's now configure R4 to advertise a different summary route—10.0.32.0/19—suppressing the component prefixes. This summary will cover all the prefixes in the EIGRP topology.

```
R4(config-router)#aggregate-address 10.0.32.0 255.255.224.0 summary-only
ISP(config-router)#do show ip bgp | b Network
     Network          Next Hop         Metric LocPrf Weight Path
 *>  10.0.0.0/16      203.0.113.1          0         100 65001 i
 *                    198.51.100.1                     0 65004 65001 i
```

```
*>  10.0.23.0/29     198.51.100.1        3072            0 65004 i
*>  10.0.32.0/19     198.51.100.1           0            0 65004 i
*>  198.51.100.0/30  0.0.0.0                0        32768 i
*>  203.0.113.0/30   0.0.0.0                0        32768 ?
```

The outcome of all this is that traffic for the following prefixes will take the 10.0.0.0/16 summary route via R1:

- 10.0.12.0/30
- 10.0.14.0/29
- 10.0.27.0/28

while the following prefixes will take the 10.0.32.0/19 summary route via R4:

- 10.0.34.0/28
- 10.0.36.0/29
- 10.0.45.0/29
- 10.0.56.0/29

Notice there's one prefix that's still advertised—10.0.23.0/29. This outlier is there because only R4 has a route to it, but it falls outside of the summary prefix R4 is advertising. R4 does advertise it to R1, but R1 doesn't advertise it because it falls under R1's wider summary route of 10.0.0.0/16.

Route Filtering Using Route Maps and Prefix Lists

Finally, we're going to clean up this split-brain routing scenario by forcing all traffic from ISP to route through R1. To achieve this, we need to reconfigure ISP to filter out the 10.0.32.0/19 and 10.0.23.0/29 route from R4 so that it doesn't install them in its IP routing table and is thus forced to use R1's summary.

The first step is to create a prefix list to match the two prefixes we want to filter. We'll use this prefix list in a moment in conjunction with a route map. The following two commands will cause the prefix list to match the two prefixes:

```
ISP(config)#ip prefix-list R4-summary permit 10.0.32.0/19
ISP(config)#ip prefix-list R4-summary permit 10.0.23.0/29
```

The next command will ensure that the prefix list does not match any other prefixes. The le 32 at the end indicates "less than or equal to 32" and specifies the prefix length that will match. This will cover all IP subnets from 0.0.0.0 to 255.255.255.255 and all prefix lengths from 0 to 32—in other words, all possible prefixes.

```
ISP(config)#ip prefix-list R4-summary deny 0.0.0.0/0 le 32
ISP(config)#do show ip prefix-list
ip prefix-list R4-summary: 3 entries
   seq 5 permit 10.0.32.0/19
   seq 10 permit 10.0.23.0/29
   seq 15 deny 0.0.0.0/0 le 32
```

An IP prefix list is processed in the order of its sequence numbers. You can specify sequence numbers if you want, but if you don't, the router will order the prefixes in the order you enter them. The permit keywords in the IP prefix list means that the entry matches the particular prefix. Conversely, a deny means the entry won't match. By itself, an IP prefix list does nothing. It's only used as a way to match or not match a prefix. This is similar to the way access control lists (ACLs) work. An ACL by itself doesn't do anything—only when it's applied to an interface does it permit or deny traffic.

The second step is to create a route map that will make use of this access list. A route map is structured differently than an IP prefix list, but one thing they both have in common is they have sequence numbers. We'll configure a route map to deny any prefixes that match the IP prefix list we just created:

```
! Create sequence 10 to deny the prefixes that match the prefix list
ISP(config)#route-map R4 deny 10
ISP(config-route-map)#match ip address prefix-list R4-summary
```

In this case, we specify a deny sequence number of 10 and then specify the prefix list. Any prefixes that are permitted in the prefix list are denied by the route map. The logic here is confusing to many, so take your time to understand this if it doesn't immediately click. Viewing the route map to verify can also help:

```
ISP(config-route-map)#do show route-map
route-map R4, deny, sequence 10
  Match clauses:
    ip address prefix-lists: R4-summary
  Set clauses:
  Policy routing matches: 0 packets, 0 bytes
```

Again, the first sequence 10 matches any prefixes that are matched (to a permit statement) in the IP prefix list, namely 10.0.32.0/19 and 10.0.23.0/29. Right now, neither the route map nor the prefix list is doing anything. To use the route map to filter or deny those specific prefixes from R4, we need to jump to the BGP router configuration:

```
! Prior to making any changes, make a note of the routes in the BGP RIB
ISP(config-router)#do show ip bgp | b Network
     Network          Next Hop          Metric LocPrf Weight Path
 *>  10.0.0.0/16      203.0.113.1            0         100 65001 i
 *                    198.51.100.1                       0 65004 65001 i
 *>  10.0.23.0/29     198.51.100.1        3072           0 65004 i
 *>  10.0.32.0/19     198.51.100.1           0           0 65004 i
 *>  198.51.100.0/30  0.0.0.0                0       32768 i
 *>  203.0.113.0/30   0.0.0.0                0       32768 ?
ISP(config-route-map)#router bgp 65550
! Apply the route map to incoming routes from R4
ISP(config-router)#neighbor 198.51.100.1 route-map R4 in
! Perform a BGP soft reconfiguration to force reconvergence. This is faster
```

```
! than a hard reset that tears down and reestablishes the neighbor
! relationships.
ISP(config-router)#do clear ip bgp * soft
ISP(config-router)#do show ip bgp | b Network
    Network         Next Hop         Metric LocPrf Weight Path
 *>  10.0.0.0/16     203.0.113.1          0         100 65001 i
 *>  198.51.100.0/30 0.0.0.0              0       32768 i
 *>  203.0.113.0/30  0.0.0.0              0       32768 ?
```

Surprisingly, *all* routes from R4 are missing! This illustrates something route maps have in common with ACLs: the default-deny behavior. Any prefixes that aren't explicitly permitted in the route map are denied. To remedy this, we need to create a permit sequence that matches any prefixes not matched by the preceding deny sequence:

```
ISP(config-router)#route-map R4 permit 20
ISP(config-route-map)#do show route-map R4
route-map R4, deny, sequence 10
  Match clauses:
    ip address prefix-lists: R4-summary
  Set clauses:
  Policy routing matches: 0 packets, 0 bytes
route-map R4, permit, sequence 20
  Match clauses:
  Set clauses:
  Policy routing matches: 0 packets, 0 bytes
```

Even though we don't specify a match clause, any prefixes not matched in sequence 10 will be matched to sequence 20 and thus permitted.

```
ISP(config-route-map)#do show ip bgp | b Network
    Network         Next Hop         Metric LocPrf Weight Path
 *   10.0.0.0/16     198.51.100.1                      0 65004 65001 i
 *>                  203.0.113.1          0         100 65001 i
 *>  198.51.100.0/30 0.0.0.0              0       32768 i
 *>  203.0.113.0/30  0.0.0.0              0       32768 ?
```

Now ISP learns the summary route from both R4 (198.51.100.1) and R1 (203.0.113.1) and installs the route via R1 as the best path. However, suppose that you later change your mind and decide you want to use R4 as the best path instead. There's quite a simple way to do this using the route map. In addition to permitting or denying routes, you can use a route map to influence best path selection by modifying BGP attributes. For instance, say you want to give the R4 summary route a higher weight than the summary from R1. You can do this with a quick modification to sequence 20 of the route map:

```
ISP(config-router)#route-map R4 permit 20
ISP(config-route-map)#set weight ?
  <0-65535>  Weight value
```

```
ISP(config-route-map)#set weight 101
ISP(config-route-map)#do show route-map R4
route-map R4, deny, sequence 10
  Match clauses:
    ip address prefix-lists: R4-summary
  Set clauses:
  Policy routing matches: 0 packets, 0 bytes
route-map R4, permit, sequence 20
  Match clauses:
  Set clauses:
    weight 101
  Policy routing matches: 0 packets, 0 bytes
```

All allowed prefixes from R4—which in this case is just 10.0.0.0/16—will be given a weight of 101.

```
ISP(config-route-map)#do show ip bgp | b Network
     Network          Next Hop         Metric LocPrf Weight Path
  *  10.0.0.0/16      203.0.113.1           0         100 65001 i
  *>                  198.51.100.1                    101 65004 65001 i
  *> 198.51.100.0/30  0.0.0.0               0       32768 i
  *> 203.0.113.0/30   0.0.0.0               0       32768 ?
```

Now the route via R4 is the best path because it has a higher weight than the route via R1. You can use route maps to modify other BGP attributes, such as weight, local preference, and even the origin type, giving you granular control over specific routes. Also keep in mind that you can use route maps to modify BGP attributes such as the MED and AS path for outbound routes, allowing you to influence the best path selection of other BGP routers.

Summary

In contrast to IGPs, BGP focuses on stability at the expense of rapid convergence. One of the things to watch out for, particularly when troubleshooting, is the slow nature of BGP. When you make a change, such as advertising a new prefix or modifying a BGP attribute, it can take some time, perhaps even minutes, for the change to propagate. To speed things along, get into the habit of using the clear ip bgp * soft command to trigger a soft reconfiguration. Many folks have wasted valuable time troubleshooting a problem that didn't exist because they simply didn't wait long enough. Use the soft reconfiguration command to save yourself from this error.

When dealing with IGPs, it's less common—although not unheard of—to redistribute routes between IGPs. However, it's extremely commonplace to perform mutual redistribution between BGP and IGPs. It's also just as common to explicitly advertise routes into BGP using the network command. You therefore want to be comfortable doing it both ways.

As always, practice, practice, practice! Interpreting the BGP RIB, IGP RIBs, the IP routing table, and the CEF FIB are fundamental skills that come only from hands-on experience. Complete the exercises for this chapter, using the chapter examples as a guide. After performing the exercises, don't hesitate to experiment and try your hand at breaking and troubleshooting things.

Exam Essentials

Know the attributes BGP uses for path selection.   It's not always practical to configure every scenario, so you should be able to determine which route BGP will select as the best path just by looking at the route's attributes.

Understand the difference between redistributed routes and routes advertised using the network command.   BGP can originate routes by redistributing them from an IGP, connected routes, or static routes. You can also have BGP originate a route from any entry in the IP routing table by using the network command.

Be able to configure eBGP peerings, advertise and filter routes, and modify attributes. Naturally, you should be able to configure eBGP peerings and originate routes. You'll also need to be comfortable with using IP prefix lists and route maps to modify and filter routes, not just for BGP but for IGPs as well.

Exercises

EXERCISE 7.1

Referring to Figure 7.3, configure BGP peering among ISP, R1, and R4. Use the network statement to make sure each router advertises its connected routes.

EXERCISE 7.2

Referring to Figure 7.3, configure mutual redistribution between OSPF and BGP on R1. Then, configure mutual redistribution between EIGRP and BGP on R4. Verify that ISP receives routes for all prefixes in the topology. Don't worry about full IP connectivity.

EXERCISE 7.3

Configure R1 to advertise a summary route of 10.0.0.0/16, suppressing all component prefixes. Shut down the link between R4 and ISP, force a BGP soft reconfiguration, and verify IP reachability to all private prefixes (10.0.0.0/8) in the topology.

EXERCISE 7.4

Configure ISP to block routes from R4 for the 10.0.32.0/19 and 10.0.23.0/29 prefixes.

Review Questions

You can find the answers in the appendix.

1. What type of protocol best describes BGP?
    A. Hybrid
    B. Distance vector
    C. Path vector
    D. Link state

2. Which of the following does BGP consider first to determine the best path?
    A. Oldest route
    B. AS path length
    C. Origin of the route
    D. Remote preference

3. Which of the following is true of BGP?
    A. It identifies an AS using a 4-byte process number.
    B. It converges faster than OSPF.
    C. It periodically sends route updates.
    D. It can consider IGP metrics in best path decisions.

4. Which of the following BGP AS numbers can be used on the public Internet?
    A. 777
    B. 64555
    C. 65535
    D. 65536
    E. 101101

5. An eBGP router in AS 67677 receives a route for the `192.0.9.0/24` prefix that has AS 67677 already in the path. Which of the following will it do?
    A. Discard all routes with the `192.0.9.0/24` prefix
    B. Remove the AS number and advertise the route
    C. Discard only the received route
    D. Advertise the received route as is

6. How do BGP neighbors communicate?
    A. TCP port 179
    B. TCP port 8179
    C. IP protocol 179
    D. IP protocol 88

7. How frequently do BGP peers send keepalive messages?

   A. 30 seconds

   B. 60 seconds

   C. 80 seconds

   D. 180 seconds

8. What is the default BGP hold timer?

   A. 30 seconds

   B. 60 seconds

   C. 80 seconds

   D. 180 seconds

9. In which of the following session states do BGP peers exchange routes?

   A. Open

   B. OpenConfirm

   C. Active

   D. Established

10. Which of the following two configuration commands will configure a BGP router in AS 65001 to form a neighborship with BGP router 203.0.113.2 in AS 65550? (Choose two.)

   A. `router bgp 65550`

   B. `router bgp 65001`

   C. `neighbor 203.0.113.2 remote-as 65550`

   D. `neighbor 203.0.113.2 remote-as 65001`

   E. `neighbor 203.0.113.2 local-as 65001`

11. You've configured routers R1 and R2 to form an eBGP session. Which of the following commands will conclusively tell you whether they have established a BGP session?

   A. `show ip route`

   B. `show bgp`

   C. `show ip bgp`

   D. `show ip bgp neighbors`

12. Router R1 has the prefix 10.0.24.0/24 installed in its IP routing table as an OSPF-learned route. Which of the following BGP router configuration commands cause R1 to advertise the prefix 10.0.24.0/24 to its BGP peers?

   A. `network 10.0.24.0`

   B. `network 10.0.24.0 mask 0.0.0.255`

   C. `network 10.0.24.0 mask 255.255.255.0`

   D. `redistribute connected`

13. A BGP router receives two routes with equal AS path length. What will the router analyze next to determine the best path?

A. Weight

B. Local preference

C. Origin type

D. MED

E. Lowest AS number

14. Which of the following BGP origin types is most preferred?

A. Incomplete

B. IGP

C. EGP

D. Oldest

15. R1 has the prefix `10.9.0.0/16` in its IP routing table, learned from EIGRP AS 50. There are no other BGP, IGP, or static routes in the routing table. You execute the following BGP router configuration commands on R1:

```
network 10.9.0.0 mask 255.255.255.0
redistribute eigrp 50
redistribute connected
```

Which of the following will be true regarding the route R1 advertises for the `10.9.0.0/16` prefix?

A. `10.9.0.0/24` will have an incomplete origin type.

B. `10.9.0.0/16` will have an incomplete origin type.

C. `10.9.0.0/16` will have an IGP origin type.

D. `10.9.0.0/24` will have an IGP origin type.

16. Which of the following BGP attributes is *not* advertised outside of an AS?

A. AS path

B. Local preference

C. MED

D. Origin type

17. What are two possible outcomes of modifying the AS path attribute?

A. The origin type changes

B. Creates a routing loop

C. Makes two routes equally preferred

D. Prefers one route over another

18. A BGP router has a connected route to the prefix 12.7.3.0/24. The prefix is being advertised via OSPF process 1. Which of the following BGP router configuration commands will advertise a route to this prefix with an IGP origin type?

A. redistribute connected

B. redistribute ospf 1

C. redistribute connected metric igp

D. network 12.7.3.0 mask 255.255.255.0

19. Which of the following commands will perform a soft BGP reconfiguration with neighbor 1.3.3.7?

A. neighbor 1.3.3.7 reset

B. neighbor 1.3.3.7 shutdown

C. clear ip bgp * soft

D. clear bgp * soft

20. Consider the following prefix list and route map on router R1:

```
ip prefix-list all-private: 3 entries
 seq 5 permit 10.0.0.0/8 le 32
 seq 10 deny 0.0.0.0/0 le 32
route-map allow-public, deny, sequence 10
Match clauses:
  ip address prefix-lists: all-private
Set clauses:
Policy routing matches: 0 packets, 0 bytes
route-map R4, permit, sequence 20
Match clauses:
Set clauses:
Policy routing matches: 0 packets, 0 bytes
```

What is the effect of applying this route map to inbound routes from an eBGP neighbor?

A. R1 won't install any BGP routes for the 10.0.0.0/16 prefix.

B. R1 will install BGP routes for the 10.0.0.0/8 prefix.

C. R1 won't advertise any BGP routes for the prefix 10.0.0.0/24.

D. R1 won't install any BGP routes.

Network Address Translation and Multicast

THE CCNP ENCOR EXAM OBJECTIVES COVERED IN THIS CHAPTER INCLUDE THE FOLLOWING:

Domain 3 Infrastructure

✓ **3.4 IP Services**

In this chapter, you'll learn about network address translation (NAT) and multicast. NAT was originally designed to conserve public IPv4 addresses by allowing multiple hosts inside a private network to share a single public IP address. But NAT's usefulness extends beyond that, allowing a router to change the source or destination IP address of any IP packet it receives—something that can come in handy when you're trying to merge two networks with duplicate IP subnets.

Multicast allows a sender to efficiently distribute content to multiple receivers simultaneously. Imagine that you need to stream audio to 500 hosts in real time. Using multicast, you just send the audio packets to a single multicast group IP address, and the network does the heavy lifting of distributing the packets to all the hosts that need it.

Network Address Translation

You're already familiar with NAT as a mechanism to hide multiple private IP addresses behind one or a few public IP addresses. As originally conceived in RFC 1631 way back in 1994, the purpose of NAT was to conserve public IP addresses. And so far, it has done a fantastic job. One of the biggest reasons we don't see more IPv6 deployments is that despite the "sky is falling" alarmism that started almost a decade ago, the Internet still hasn't run out of IPv4 addresses, thanks to the effectiveness of NAT. NAT isn't going away any time soon.

Address Types

NAT isn't restricted to any particular range of IP addresses. You can use NAT to translate to or from any source or destination IP address. A lot of networking students assume that NAT always involves translating between a public and a private (RFC 1918) IP address. In fact, NAT makes no distinction based on the numeric value of an IP address. Rather, NAT classifies IP addresses into four categories:

- Inside local
- Inside global
- Outside local
- Outside global

Inside and outside are relative, but they commonly distinguish network ownership. Although we tend to talk of inside and outside networks, when configuring NAT, you actually specify at least one inside and outside interface. To avoid confusion, I recommend always thinking of *your* network as the *inside network*—the one under your control. The *outside network* is one outside your control, where you have no power to change IP addresses or anything like that. Just remember that in the end, inside and outside are just names, and you're free to make the inside or outside interfaces whatever you wish.

Local and global refer to the routing scope of the addresses. A *local address* is reachable only from the inside network, whereas a *global address* is reachable from both the inside and outside networks.

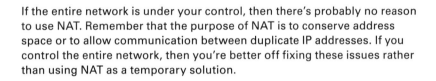

> If the entire network is under your control, then there's probably no reason to use NAT. Remember that the purpose of NAT is to conserve address space or to allow communication between duplicate IP addresses. If you control the entire network, then you're better off fixing these issues rather than using NAT as a temporary solution.

Consider the inside and outside networks in Figure 8.1. Which is which depends on your perspective, but we'll assume your private network is the one on the left, so it would be the inside network. The network on the right is an external network outside of your control, so you'd consider it an outside network. Again, the designation is relative and has nothing to do with whether you're translating between globally routable and RFC 1918 private addresses.

FIGURE 8.1   Inside versus outside networks

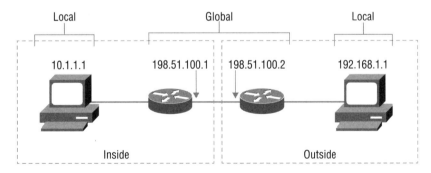

Inside Local

An inside local address is one on the internal network. Referring to Figure 8.1, suppose you have a host with an internal IP address of 10.1.1.1 and you want NAT to translate its source IP to a public IP address of 198.51.100.1. Because 10.1.1.1 is inside your network and has an IP address from your local address space, it's an inside local address.

Inside Global

The address 198.51.100.1 is an inside global address. It's inside because it's configured on your local router, and it's global in that the address is reachable from the outside network.

Outside Global

The address 198.51.100.2 is an outside global address because it's configured on a router in the outside network, but it's a globally reachable address. In practice, the outside global address is really the only outside address you'll ever see.

Outside Local

We don't know whether the router in the outside network is performing NAT, but let's suppose it is. We'll assume the outside router translates the 198.51.100.2 global address to the 192.168.1.1 address of the host. From the perspective of your inside network, 192.168.1.1 is the outside local address. In practice, you'll almost never see an outside local address because it's hidden by NAT. The only exception is if you control both the inside and outside networks and are performing NAT between hosts because of some edge case, such as having to enable communication between hosts with duplicate IP addresses.

 What if the outside router isn't doing NAT? In that case, the outside host would likely have its own global address. And your inside host would not connect to the 198.51.100.2 address of the router but would instead connect to the global address of the outside host. So, the concepts of outside local versus outside global would be moot. There would simply be one outside global address.

Static NAT

The original purpose of NAT was to conserve public IP addresses, but as you're about to see, it has another interesting use that's not related to IP address conservation. *Static NAT* translates between one inside local address and one inside global address. It's nearly the polar opposite of address conservation, since instead of hiding multiple local IP addresses behind a single global address, static NAT consumes both a private *and* a public address.

In Figure 8.2, on the left once again is the inside network, and on the right is the outside network—the Internet—with a web server having the outside global IP address of 18.213.128.4. The inside router is configured to perform static NAT between the inside local IP (10.1.1.1) and the inside global IP address of 198.51.100.1.

FIGURE 8.2   Static NAT

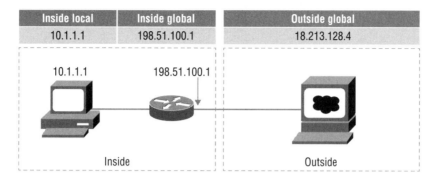

When the host 10.1.1.1 sends a packet to the outside global IP address of 18.213.128.4, the web server at that address sees 198.51.100.1 as the source IP address of the packet. The process is fairly simple, but it's still easy to get confused, so let's look at a quick example.

Host 10.1.1.1 sends a packet to 18.213.128.4. The original packet looks like this:

Source IP	Destination IP
10.1.1.1	18.213.128.4

The inside router performing NAT—or the NAT router—translates this packet as follows:

Source IP	Destination IP
198.51.100.1	18.213.128.4

The translated packet is what the web server actually receives. Now let's reverse the process. When the web server sends a packet back, it will send it to our inside global IP address, 198.51.100.1, so the original packet will look like this:

Source IP	Destination IP
18.213.128.4	198.51.100.1

This is the packet our NAT router will receive, and it will translate it as follows before sending it to 10.1.1.1:

Source IP	Destination IP
18.213.128.4	10.1.1.1

This is the packet that the inside host 10.1.1.1 will receive. Notice that the outside global IP address (18.213.128.4) is the only one that never changes. It's especially important to understand why this is. Both the inside host and the NAT router need to be able to reach the outside global address. This naturally implies that routing is properly configured on our inside network. The inside host and the NAT router both need to know a next hop to reach the outside global address. In most cases, the inside local hosts will have a default gateway set to a NAT router. The NAT router will likewise have a default gateway set to an Internet router. But whatever routing looks like, the point is that the devices on the inside local network need to know how to reach outside global addresses. This is true not just for static NAT, but for any form of NAT.

Configuring Static NAT

In this example, we'll configure a static NAT mapping between R2's 10.0.12.2 address and R7's 10.0.27.7 address, as shown in Figure 8.3.

FIGURE 8.3   Layer 3 topology

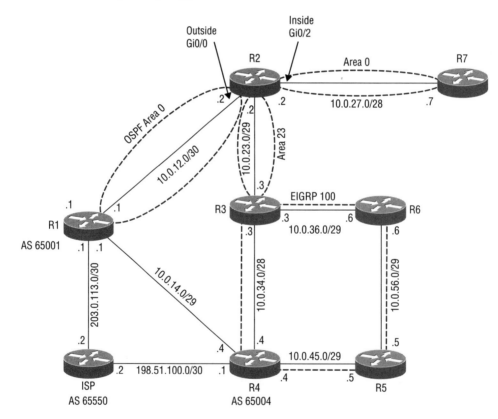

The first step in configuring NAT on a router is to specify the inside and outside interfaces. In this case, the entire network is under our control, so which we choose as the inside and outside interfaces is arbitrary. What's important is that we remain consistent in our choice and don't get confused. We'll choose R2's Gi0/0 interface (facing R1) as the outside interface, and its Gi0/2 interface (facing R7) as the inside interface. For context, the entire layer 2 topology is shown in Figure 8.4.

FIGURE 8.4 Layer 2 topology

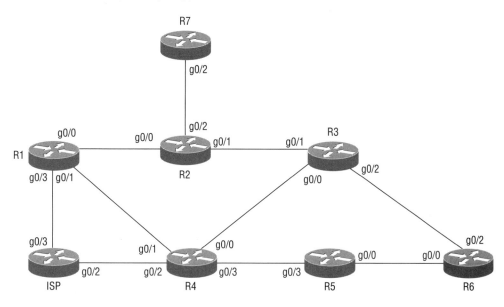

The entirety of the configuration will be done on R4. We'll begin by specifying the inside and outside interfaces:

```
R2#conf t
Enter configuration commands, one per line.  End with CNTL/Z.
R2(config)#int gi0/2
R2(config-if)#ip nat inside
! You may experience a few seconds delay while the router enables NAT
%LINEPROTO-5-UPDOWN: Line protocol on Interface NVI0, changed state to up
R2(config-if)#int gi0/0
R2(config-if)#ip nat outside
```

Next, we'll configure a static NAT translation between the inside global address 10.0.12.2 and the inside local address 10.0.27.7.

```
R2(config)#ip nat inside source static 10.0.27.7 10.0.12.2
R2(config)#do show ip nat translation
! The inside global address is the source address that the outside network sees.
! The inside local address is the source address R4 is translating, and as such
! is hidden from the outside network.
Pro Inside global      Inside local      Outside local      Outside global
--- 10.0.12.2          10.0.27.7         ---                ---
```

When a packet arrives at R2's inside interface with a source IP address of 10.0.27.7, R2 will translate that inside local address to the inside global address 10.0.12.2. In other words, R7 (10.0.27.7) is going to borrow R2's Gi0/0 interface address (10.0.12.2).

Take a moment to see how this lines up with the last command. The inside source keywords indicate that we're translating the source address of a packet that hits the inside interface. The static keyword means that we're doing a one-to-one mapping between a local and global address.

Conditional Debugging

Now let's go to R1 and turn on some IP packet debugging so we can see the source address:

```
R1(config)#access-list 101 permit ip 10.0.12.2 0.0.0.0 10.0.12.1 0.0.0.0
R1(config)#exit
R1#debug ip
%SYS-5-CONFIG_I: Configured from console by console
R1#debug ip packet 101 detail
IP packet debugging is on for access list 101
```

We'll just ping R1's 10.0.12.1 address, sourcing it from 10.0.27.7:

```
R7#ping 10.0.12.1 source 10.0.27.7 repeat 1
Type escape sequence to abort.
Sending 1, 100-byte ICMP Echos to 10.0.12.1, timeout is 2 seconds:
Packet sent with a source address of 10.0.27.7
!
Success rate is 100 percent (1/1), round-trip min/avg/max = 23/23/23 ms
```

The ping succeeds, indicating that NAT translation is working. The IP packet debug on R1 shows the source address of the packet at 10.0.12.1, R1's inside global address.

```
R1#
IP: s=10.0.12.2 (GigabitEthernet0/0), d=10.0.12.1, len 100, input feature, MCI
Check(109), rtype 0, forus FALSE, sendself FALSE, mtu 0, fwdchk FALSE
IP: tableid=0, s=10.0.12.2 (GigabitEthernet0/0), d=10.0.12.1 (GigabitEthernet0/0),
routed via RIB
IP: s=10.0.12.2 (GigabitEthernet0/0), d=10.0.12.1 (GigabitEthernet0/0), len 100, rcvd 3
IP: s=10.0.12.2 (GigabitEthernet0/0), d=10.0.12.1, len 100, stop process pak for forus
packet
R1#undebug all
All possible debugging has been turned off
```

On R2, the NAT translation table will show an additional entry:

```
R2(config)#do show ip nat translation
Pro Inside global      Inside local      Outside local      Outside global
icmp 10.0.12.2:3       10.0.27.7:3       10.0.12.1:3        10.0.12.1:3
--- 10.0.12.2          10.0.27.7         ---                ---
```

Here we see the outside global address 10.0.12.1, which is R1's interface address facing R2. Interestingly, the outside local address is also 10.0.12.1. The reason is that R2 is not translating the 10.0.12.1 source address. From R2's perspective, 10.0.12.1 is both an outside global and an outside local address. Also note that the protocol field is ICMP along with an ICMP identifier of 3, which is generated by the sender.

In the initial ICMP echo request to R1, the source IP address is 10.0.27.7. R2 changes the source address to 10.0.12.2 before sending the packet along to R1. Once R1 receives the ICMP echo request, it sends an echo reply. This packet has a source address of 10.0.12.1 and a destination of 10.0.12.2 (R2). When R2 receives this packet (on its outside interface), it changes the destination IP address to 10.0.27.7 before sending the packet along to R7.

Dynamic NAT

Dynamic NAT is an interesting application of NAT that you're unlikely to see in a real network. But that makes it good fodder for an exam! Like static NAT, dynamic NAT performs one-to-one mapping of an inside local to an inside global address. However, the mapping is only temporary, and the inside global address is dynamically allocated from a pool of global addresses. For this reason, dynamic NAT is sometimes called *pooled NAT*.

Consider the following example. Suppose the global address pool is 198.51.200.0/29. That covers 198.51.200.1 through 198.51.200.6 for usable addresses. On the inside network, we have six different hosts in the 10.1.1.0/24 range. In sequence, six different hosts on the inside network send a packet to a host that's reachable on the outside network. 10.1.1.5 is the first host to send a packet, so it gets assigned a global translation of 198.51.200.1. The next host, 10.1.1.44, gets translated to the inside global address 198.51.200.2, and so on. The dynamic allocation process continues until the global address pool is exhausted, resulting in a NAT translation table that looks like Table 8.1.

TABLE 8.1   NAT translation table

Inside local	Inside global
10.1.1.5	198.51.200.1
10.1.1.44	198.51.200.2
10.1.1.29	198.51.200.3
10.1.1.193	198.51.200.4
10.1.1.150	198.51.200.5
10.1.1.85	198.51.200.6

Once that happens, the NAT router will drop packets from subsequent hosts that send traffic to the outside network. It won't allocate any of them an address from the global pool.

The dynamic translations remain until they time out after a period of inactivity. By default, this is 24 hours, but you can configure it to be anywhere from 0 seconds to roughly 6 days.

Configuring Dynamic NAT

To illustrate dynamic NAT, we'll need to add a few more IP addresses to the mix. We'll reconfigure R2 to dynamically translate any 7.0.0.0/24 addresses on the inside network (facing R7) to the following inside global addresses:

- 2.0.0.1/32

- 2.0.0.2/32

- 2.0.0.3/32

We'll configure these addresses on loopback interfaces on R2. To ensure reachability, we'll need to advertise them to R1. To simulate host traffic from the 7.0.0.0/24 subnet, we'll configure some loopback addresses on R7 that it will source traffic from. We'll also advertise the 7.0.0.0/24 addresses to R2.

Let's begin on R2. Before configuring dynamic NAT, we need to remove the static NAT translation we configured earlier.

```
R2(config-router)#no ip nat inside source static 10.0.27.7 10.0.12.2
```

Configuring and Advertising Loopback Interfaces

Now we'll configure the loopback interfaces. These will be the inside global addresses that we'll use in the dynamic NAT pool.

```
R2(config)#int loopback1
%LINEPROTO-5-UPDOWN: Line protocol on Interface Loopback1, changed state to up
R2(config-if)#ip address 2.0.0.1 255.255.255.255
R2(config-if)#int lo2
%LINEPROTO-5-UPDOWN: Line protocol on Interface Loopback2, changed state to up
R2(config-if)#ip address 2.0.0.2 255.255.255.255
R2(config-if)#int lo3
%LINEPROTO-5-UPDOWN: Line protocol on Interface Loopback3, changed state to up
R2(config-if)#ip address 2.0.0.3 255.255.255.255
R2(config)#do show ip int br | i Lo
Loopback1                 2.0.0.1          YES manual up                 up
Loopback2                 2.0.0.2          YES manual up                 up
Loopback3                 2.0.0.3          YES manual up                 up
```

And then we'll advertise the loopbacks into OSPF area 0 (facing R1):

```
R2(config-if)#router ospf 1
R2(config-router)#network 2.0.0.0 0.0.0.255 area 0
```

Now we go to R7 to configure the loopbacks that we'll use to source traffic. To more closely simulate a real host environment, we'll use three arbitrary addresses:

- 7.0.0.12/32
- 7.0.0.77/32
- 7.0.0.144/32

```
R7#conf t
Enter configuration commands, one per line.  End with CNTL/Z.
R7(config)#int lo1
R7(config-if)#ip address 7.0.0.12 255.255.255.255
R7(config-if)#int lo2
R7(config-if)#ip address 7.0.0.77 255.255.255.255
R7(config-if)#int lo3
R7(config-if)#ip address 7.0.0.144 255.255.255.255
! Advertise the routes for the loopbacks into OSPF area 0
R7(config-if)#router ospf 1
R7(config-router)#network 7.0.0.0 0.0.0.255 area 0
```

Configuring the Global Address Pool

To configure dynamic NAT on R2, we'll specify an inclusive range of addresses, starting with 2.0.0.1 and ending with 2.0.0.3:

```
R2(config-router)#ip nat pool R2dynamicNAT 2.0.0.1 2.0.0.3 netmask
255.255.255.248
```

Even though the loopback addresses have a 32-bit netmask, we'll configure a different netmask here to cover the entire range. The reason for the netmask is that the range must be from a contiguous IP block.

Configuring the Source NAT Access List

NAT (not just dynamic NAT) lets you specify which specific source addresses will be translated. We need to NAT only source addresses in the 7.0.0.0/24 subnet, so we'll create an access list to match.

```
R2(config)#access-list 1 permit 7.0.0.0 0.0.0.255
R2(config)#do sh access-l 1
Standard IP access list 1
    10 permit 7.0.0.0, wildcard bits 0.0.0.255
```

For the final configuration piece, we'll configure dynamic NAT, specifying ACL 1 and the inside global address pool:

```
R2(config)#ip nat inside source list 1 pool R2dynamicNAT
```

The inside source keywords specify the ACL to match inside local source addresses to. The pool keyword followed by the IP pool name specifies the global addresses that R2 will use as the translated source addresses. Before testing, let's enable NAT debugging so we can see the exact translations as they occur:

```
R2#debug ip nat
IP NAT debugging is on
```

To test, we'll move to R7 and ping 10.0.12.1, sourcing each ping from a different loop-back address:

```
R7#ping 10.0.12.1 so 7.0.0.12 repeat 1
Type escape sequence to abort.
Sending 1, 100-byte ICMP Echos to 10.0.12.1, timeout is 2 seconds:
Packet sent with a source address of 7.0.0.12
!
Success rate is 100 percent (1/1), round-trip min/avg/max = 25/25/25 ms
```

The ping succeeds, indicating that NAT's working correctly. The debug output on R2 confirms this:

```
R2#
! The packet from R7 to R2's inside interface
NAT*: s=7.0.0.12->2.0.0.2, d=10.0.12.1 [155]
! The packet from R1 to R2's outside interface
NAT*: s=10.0.12.1, d=2.0.0.2->7.0.0.12 [155]
```

The packet hitting R2's inside interface has a source address of 7.0.0.12. R2 changes the source address to 2.0.0.2 before sending it out of the outside interface.

The next packet is the ICMP reply from 10.0.12.1. The destination address in the reply packet is 2.0.0.2, which R2 translates to a destination address of 7.0.0.12. This is essentially the reverse of the initial source translation. R2's NAT translation table shows the same information in tabular form:

```
R2#show ip nat translations
Pro Inside global      Inside local      Outside local       Outside global
icmp 2.0.0.2:16        7.0.0.12:16       10.0.12.1:16        10.0.12.1:16
--- 2.0.0.2            7.0.0.12          ---                 --
```

Now let's jump back to R7 and source pings from its remaining loopback addresses:

```
R7#ping 10.0.12.1 so 7.0.0.77 repeat 1
Type escape sequence to abort.
Sending 1, 100-byte ICMP Echos to 10.0.12.1, timeout is 2 seconds:
Packet sent with a source address of 7.0.0.77
!
Success rate is 100 percent (1/1), round-trip min/avg/max = 12/12/12 ms
R7#ping 10.0.12.1 so 7.0.0.144 repeat 1
Type escape sequence to abort.
Sending 1, 100-byte ICMP Echos to 10.0.12.1, timeout is 2 seconds:
Packet sent with a source address of 7.0.0.144
!
Success rate is 100 percent (1/1), round-trip min/avg/max = 16/16/16 ms
```

These pings also succeed. Let's check the NAT translation table on R2 once again:

```
R2#show ip nat translations
Pro Inside global     Inside local      Outside local      Outside global
icmp 2.0.0.2:16       7.0.0.12:16       10.0.12.1:16       10.0.12.1:16
--- 2.0.0.2           7.0.0.12          ---                ---
icmp 2.0.0.3:17       7.0.0.77:17       10.0.12.1:17       10.0.12.1:17
--- 2.0.0.3           7.0.0.77          ---                ---
icmp 2.0.0.1:18       7.0.0.144:18      10.0.12.1:18       10.0.12.1:18
--- 2.0.0.1           7.0.0.144         ---                ---
```

Note that each inside local (7.0.0.0/24) source address is translated to a different inside global (2.0.0.0/24) address. Recall that the global address pool consists of only three addresses (2.0.0.1 through 2.0.0.3), all of which are consumed. Hence, any packets sourced from a different 7.0.0.0/24 address won't be translated. But don't take my word for it! Let's test it out by adding another loopback interface on R7:

```
R7(config)#int lo4
R7(config-if)#ip address 7.0.0.99 255.255.255.255
R7(config-if)#do ping 10.0.12.1 so 7.0.0.99 repeat 1
Type escape sequence to abort.
Sending 1, 100-byte ICMP Echos to 10.0.12.1, timeout is 2 seconds:
Packet sent with a source address of 7.0.0.99
U
Success rate is 0 percent (0/1)
```

The ping elicits a host unreachable response from R2. The NAT debug output on R2 tells us why:

```
R2#
NAT: translation failed (A), dropping packet s=7.0.0.99 d=10.0.12.1
```

Without any fanfare, R2 fails to translate the source address because it has no more global addresses to pull from. Thus, it drops the packet and returns an ICMP host unreachable response to R7. However, if we clear the NAT translations on R2 and try the ping again, we'll get a different result:

```
R2#clear ip nat translation *
```

We'll source the ping from the same address as last time:

```
R7#ping 10.0.12.1 so 7.0.0.99 re 1
Type escape sequence to abort.
Sending 1, 100-byte ICMP Echos to 10.0.12.1, timeout is 2 seconds:
Packet sent with a source address of 7.0.0.99
!
Success rate is 100 percent (1/1), round-trip min/avg/max = 19/19/19 ms
```

This time the ping succeeds. The debug output on R2 shows a successful translation:

```
R2#
NAT*: s=7.0.0.99->2.0.0.2, d=10.0.12.1 [185]
NAT*: s=10.0.12.1, d=2.0.0.2->7.0.0.99 [185]
R2#show ip nat translation
Pro Inside global     Inside local      Outside local     Outside global
icmp 2.0.0.2:26       7.0.0.99:26       10.0.12.1:26      10.0.12.1:26
--- 2.0.0.2           7.0.0.99          ---               ---
```

Dynamic NAT operates on a "first come, first served" basis. Hence, if you choose to use it, make sure you have enough addresses in the global pool to cover all inside source addresses.

 It's important to realize that the addresses NAT translates don't have to be physical interface addresses. NAT simply changes the source or destination IP address in a packet, without regard to where the address exists. What matters is that the routers receiving the packet have a route to the destination IP address. This is why we had to advertise R7's loopback addresses to R2, and R2's loopback addresses to R1. Without full IP reachability, that NAT process would have still occurred, but our pings would've failed.

NAT Overload with Port Address Translation

Last but not least, NAT overload or *port address translation* (PAT) fulfills the original purpose of NAT—to conserve public IP addresses. As late as the early 2000s, almost every device on the Internet had its own public IP address. Nowadays, thanks to NAT overload, multiple network devices can access the Internet using a single shared global IP address. This is how NAT saved the Internet from public IP address exhaustion.

The biggest difference between dynamic NAT and PAT is that with PAT, multiple inside source addresses can be translated to the same inside global address. PAT—also known as *NAT overload*—translates multiple inside local source addresses to a single global address. The global address can come from an outside interface or from a pool. In other words, the inside global address can be overloaded, which is where we get the term NAT overload. Why is it called port address translation? PAT translates not only the inside local source IP address to an inside global IP address, but it also translates the original source port to a different source port. Because multiple hosts share a single inside global IP address, the NAT router keeps track of individual connections by changing the source port and maintaining the mapping in the NAT translation table.

Configuring Port Address Translation with a Single Global Address

From a configuration perspective, PAT will seem very similar to dynamic NAT. We'll reconfigure R2 to overload its 10.0.12.2 inside global address. Any source addresses in the 7.0.0.0/24 range hitting R2's inside interface will be translated. We begin by removing the existing dynamic NAT configuration from R2:

```
R2(config)#no ip nat inside source list 1 pool R2dynamicNAT forced
! Earlier we created access list 1 to match addresses in the 7.0.0.0/24 range.
R2#show access-list 1
Standard IP access list 1
    10 permit 7.0.0.0, wildcard bits 0.0.0.255 (34 matches)
! We'll make use of this same ACL to configure PAT
R2#conf t
Enter configuration commands, one per line.  End with CNTL/Z.
R2(config)#ip nat inside source list 1 ?
  interface  Specify interface for global address
  pool       Name pool of global addresses
R2(config)#ip nat inside source list 1 interface gi0/0 overload
```

Most of the commands should look familiar by now. The interface keyword specifies the outside interface from which to borrow the inside global IP address. To test, R7 will once again simulate a few hosts, pinging 10.0.12.1 from different IP addresses:

```
R7#ping 10.0.12.1 source 7.0.0.12 repeat 1
Type escape sequence to abort.
Sending 1, 100-byte ICMP Echos to 10.0.12.1, timeout is 2 seconds:
```

```
Packet sent with a source address of 7.0.0.12
!
Success rate is 100 percent (1/1), round-trip min/avg/max = 14/14/14 ms
R7#ping 10.0.12.1 source 7.0.0.77 repeat 1
Type escape sequence to abort.
Sending 1, 100-byte ICMP Echos to 10.0.12.1, timeout is 2 seconds:
Packet sent with a source address of 7.0.0.77
!
Success rate is 100 percent (1/1), round-trip min/avg/max = 16/16/16 ms
R7#ping 10.0.12.1 source 7.0.0.144 repeat 1
Type escape sequence to abort.
Sending 1, 100-byte ICMP Echos to 10.0.12.1, timeout is 2 seconds:
Packet sent with a source address of 7.0.0.144
!
Success rate is 100 percent (1/1), round-trip min/avg/max = 12/12/12 ms
```

Back on R2, the NAT translation table shows multiple inside local addresses being translated to a single inside global address—R2's Gi0/0 interface IP:

```
R2(config)#do show ip nat translation
Pro Inside global       Inside local        Outside local        Outside global
icmp 10.0.12.2:27       7.0.0.12:27         10.0.12.1:27         10.0.12.1:27
icmp 10.0.12.2:28       7.0.0.77:28         10.0.12.1:28         10.0.12.1:28
icmp 10.0.12.2:29       7.0.0.144:29        10.0.12.1:29         10.0.12.1:29
```

However, using pings doesn't fully demonstrate what's going on behind the scenes with PAT. ICMP uses sequence numbers but not port numbers. To see how PAT translates source port numbers, we need to send a UDP or TCP packet. The traceroute command on Cisco devices uses UDP, so on R7 we'll send a traceroute to 10.0.12.1, sourced from 7.0.0.12:

```
R7#traceroute 10.0.12.1 so 7.0.0.12
Type escape sequence to abort.
Tracing the route to 10.0.12.1
VRF info: (vrf in name/id, vrf out name/id)
  1 10.0.27.2 9 msec 8 msec 9 msec
  2 10.0.12.1 24 msec 22 msec 16 msec
```

The NAT translation table on R2 clearly shows the port translations:

```
R2(config)#do show ip nat translation
Pro Inside global       Inside local        Outside local        Outside global
udp 10.0.12.2:49171     7.0.0.12:49171      10.0.12.1:33437      10.0.12.1:33437
udp 10.0.12.2:49172     7.0.0.12:49172      10.0.12.1:33438      10.0.12.1:33438
udp 10.0.12.2:49173     7.0.0.12:49173      10.0.12.1:33439      10.0.12.1:33439
```

Take a look at the first entry. The inside global and local addresses both have the same source port (49171). PAT will strive to preserve the source port number when possible. However, if multiple inside hosts use the same source port, PAT will perform source port translation so that the packets egressing the outside interface have unique source port numbers. Before moving on, let's remove the existing PAT configuration:

```
R2(config)#no ip nat inside source list 1 interface gi0/0
```

Configuring PAT with a Global Address Pool

You're not limited to doing NAT overload with a single global address. You can use PAT to translate inside source addresses to multiple inside global addresses. The way you do this is nearly identical to dynamic NAT, but with the addition of the overload keyword. We'll use the existing NAT pool from earlier:

```
R2(config)#do show run | i nat pool
R2(config)#ip nat inside source list 1 pool R2dynamicNAT overload
```

The overload keyword refers to overloading the global addresses by mapping multiple inside local addresses to a smaller number of inside global addresses. PAT will initially select a single inside global IP address and utilize all available source ports under that address before pulling a different global IP from the pool. To illustrate, look at the NAT translation table after sourcing traceroutes from a few different loopback addresses on R7:

```
R2#show ip nat translations
Pro Inside global      Inside local        Outside local        Outside global
udp 2.0.0.2:53930      7.0.0.12:53930      10.0.12.1:33435      10.0.12.1:33435
udp 2.0.0.2:53924      7.0.0.77:53924      10.0.12.1:33435      10.0.12.1:33435
udp 2.0.0.2:53927      7.0.0.144:53927     10.0.12.1:33435      10.0.12.1:33435
```

R2 doesn't pull more addresses from the NAT pool than it needs. There are three addresses in the pool, but R2 needs only one, so it allocates only one:

```
R2#show ip nat statistics | b Dynamic
Dynamic mappings:
-- Inside Source
[Id: 3] access-list 1 pool R2dynamicNAT refcount 3
 pool R2dynamicNAT: netmask 255.255.255.248
        start 2.0.0.1 end 2.0.0.3
        type generic, total addresses 3, allocated 1 (33%), misses 24
```

Let's remove the configuration before continuing:

```
R2(config)#no ip nat inside source list 1 pool R2dynamicNAT overload
```

Outside Static NAT

So far, we've looked at NAT in the context of translating source IP addresses. However, it's possible to have NAT translate an inside local destination IP address of a packet to an outside global address. This is called *outside static NAT*. It's one of those configurations you're unlikely to see in a professionally managed network, but it can come in handy as a temporary solution for dealing with duplicate IP addresses on a network. In this scenario, when R2 receives a packet destined for 1.1.1.1, we want it to change the destination IP to 10.0.12.1 and send it out of its outside interface.

```
R2(config)#ip nat outside source static 10.0.12.1 1.1.1.1 add-route
```

Note the use of the outside keyword instead of inside. Instead of translating source addresses on packets that hit the inside interface, R2 will translate destination addresses on packets that egress the outside interface. Where did the 1.1.1.1 address come from? We created it out of thin air. The add-route keyword creates a static route for the 1.1.1.1/32 prefix with 10.0.12.1 (R1) as the next hop.

```
R2(config)#do show ip route | i 1.1.1.1
S        1.1.1.1 [1/0] via 10.0.12.1
```

Again, we'll use R7 as our simulated host, so we must advertise this static route to R7 so that it knows how to forward packets to 1.1.1.1.

```
R2(config)#router ospf 1
R2(config-router)#redistribute static subnets
```

This will give R7 a route to the 1.1.1.1/32 prefix, with R2 as the next hop. We should then be able to ping 1.1.1.1 from any of R7's addresses.

```
R7#show ip route 1.1.1.1
Routing entry for 1.1.1.1/32
  Known via "ospf 1", distance 110, metric 20, type extern 2, forward metric 2
  Last update from 10.0.27.2 on GigabitEthernet0/2, 00:01:13 ago
  Routing Descriptor Blocks:
  * 10.0.27.2, from 2.2.2.2, 00:01:13 ago, via GigabitEthernet0/2
      Route metric is 20, traffic share count is 1
R7#ping 1.1.1.1
Type escape sequence to abort.
Sending 5, 100-byte ICMP Echos to 1.1.1.1, timeout is 2 seconds:
!!!!!
Success rate is 100 percent (5/5), round-trip min/avg/max = 8/9/12 ms
```

A look at R2's NAT translation table shows two entries:

```
R2(config-router)#do show ip nat translation
Pro Inside global      Inside local      Outside local      Outside global
--- ---                ---               1.1.1.1            10.0.12.1
icmp 10.0.27.7:45      10.0.27.7:45      1.1.1.1:45         10.0.12.1:45
```

The first entry shows the static mapping of the outside local address (1.1.1.1) to the outside global address (10.0.12.1). Recall that in NAT parlance, a local address is one whose scope is the inside network. The 1.1.1.1 address doesn't necessarily have to be reachable on the outside network (although in this case it is because we're advertising it into OSPF area 0).

The second entry is a specific mapping for the ping sourced from R7's physical interface address. The inside local and inside global addresses are the same. Recall also that global addresses are reachable from both the inside and outside networks. The ICMP echo request that R1 receives has the source address of 10.0.27.7, R7's physical interface IP. To appreciate this, let's turn on conditional debugs on R1:

```
R1(config)#access-list 102 permit ip host 10.0.27.7 host 10.0.12.1
R1(config)#exit
R1#debug
R1#debug ip packet 102
IP packet debugging is on for access list 102
! Behind the scenes, R7 sends a single ping to 1.1.1.1
R1#
IP: s=10.0.27.7 (GigabitEthernet0/0), d=10.0.12.1, len 100, input feature, MCI
Check(109), rtype 0, forus FALSE, sendself FALSE, mtu 0, fwdchk FALSE
IP: tableid=0, s=10.0.27.7 (GigabitEthernet0/0), d=10.0.12.1
(GigabitEthernet0/0), routed via RIB
IP: s=10.0.27.7 (GigabitEthernet0/0), d=10.0.12.1 (GigabitEthernet0/0), len 100,
rcvd 3
IP: s=10.0.27.7 (GigabitEthernet0/0), d=10.0.12.1, len 100, stop process pak for
forus packet
```

The source address is 10.0.27.7, and the destination is 10.0.12.1. But remember that R7 sent the ping to 1.1.1.1. R2, our friendly NAT router, which translated the destination IP address. On the return trip, the ICMP reply from R1 has a source IP of 10.0.12.1. R2 translates that source IP to 1.1.1.1 before sending it along to R7.

Removing NAT Configurations

To clean things up, and to prepare for the next section on multicast, we'll remove the NAT configurations from R2 and R4:

```
R2(config)#no ip nat outside source static 10.0.12.1 1.1.1.1 add-route
R4(config)#no ip nat inside source static 10.0.45.5 198.51.100.1
```

Multicast

Generically, the term *multicast* refers to any form of one-to-many communication. The operating principle behind multicast is simple: a sender or source sends data addressed to a special multicast group address and the network distributes that data to all the hosts that have requested to receive traffic for that multicast group. Everyone in the group receives the exact same data at roughly the same time.

To appreciate the practical usefulness of multicast, imagine trying to use unicast to stream real-time audio to 500 hosts. Supposing the audio stream requires sending one packet per second, the source would have to send 500 packets every second—one packet for each host. The reason is that because it's using unicast, each packet must have a different destination IP address. Every second, the sender dumps 500 unicast packets onto the network. Depending on where the receivers sit on the network, this could saturate some links. It's a grossly inefficient use of network bandwidth, not to mention it puts quite a strain on the source.

Now consider implementing this using multicast. Each second, the source would have to send only one packet to a single multicast IP address. The routers on the network would replicate the packet and distribute it to the hosts that want it. Even if the routers were to blindly flood the packet everywhere, the network would still have to transport only one packet per second instead of 500.

Multicast doesn't offer any mechanism for retransmitting dropped packets. This is somewhat analogous to tuning into a radio station to hear a particular program. If you're listening at the time of the broadcast, you'll receive it. But if you're not tuned in, or if some interference momentarily interrupts your listening, you're out of luck. This critical limitation of multicast makes it less useful for interactive content such as video on demand. To be blunt, multicast is a one-way street, and it's only useful for distributing non-interactive content. Naturally, the first such non-interactive application that comes to many people's minds is something like video or audio streaming, or more generically, live data feeds, such as from stock market tickers and real-time video. These are all valid and common uses of multicast.

That's the gist of multicast. The implementation, however, is a bit more nuanced. Ethernet networks can actually implement two different forms of multicasting:

- IP Multicast

- LAN Multicast

Think back to when you were first learning about the difference between layer 2 and layer 3, or more specifically, the differences between IP addresses and MAC addresses. Almost everything you've learned about IP and MAC is based on a unicast paradigm: one host sends one frame or packet to one destination. The theme of unicast is "one-to-one."

Multicast is slightly different in that one host sends one packet, but the network floods the packet to multiple destinations. Hence, the theme of multicast is "one-to-many." It may help to think of multicast as a sort of parallel universe, where we still have Ethernet, MAC addresses, and IP addresses, but the rules for forwarding frames and packets are slightly different. I'll therefore be drawing a lot of comparisons between unicast and multicast.

IP Multicast

An IP multicast packet is just an IP packet destined to a special multicast IP address. Multicast IP addresses fall into the 224.0.0.0/4 range, which covers 224.0.0.0 through 239.255.255.255. RFC 5771 further divides multicast addresses into different categories, the most common of which are the following three.

Local Network Control Block (*224.0.0.0/24*)

Traffic sent to addresses in this block don't leave the broadcast domain. In this respect, addresses in this block function similarly to Ethernet broadcasts. Most of your experience with multicast probably centers around reserved multicast IP addresses taken from this block, such as those that OSPF (224.0.0.5, 224.0.0.6) and EIGRP (224.0.0.10) use.

Internetwork Control Block (*224.0.1.0/24*)

Packets sent to addresses in this block may be routed over the public Internet. These addresses are similar to public unicast IP addresses, and they're also assigned by the IANA. If you look at the assignments (www.iana.org/assignments/multicast-addresses/multicast-addresses.xhtml#multicast-addresses-2), you'll see that these addresses are commonly used for stock ticker feeds and streaming video.

Administratively Scoped Block (*239.0.0.0/8*)

Addresses in this block are for use on non-publicly routable networks. Think of them as the RFC 1918 addresses for multicast.

These are the multicast addresses you're most likely to see, and I bring them up because they're the three that most closely parallel unicast IP address ranges. Just remember that any address in the 224.0.0.0/4 range is a multicast IP address.

LAN Multicast

Before covering routing IP multicast, we need to cover *LAN multicast*. The reason is simple: IP multicast always implies LAN multicast. Whenever a source sends a multicast IP packet, it tucks it inside an Ethernet frame addressed to a multicast MAC address. We'll start by covering what those multicast MAC addresses look like, and then we'll look at the mechanism that translates multicast IP addresses to multicast MAC addresses.

A multicast frame is just an Ethernet frame sent to a special multicast address. There's an easy way to tell the difference between unicast and multicast MAC addresses. The second-to-left hexadecimal digit of a multicast address is always odd, whereas the same digit of a unicast address is always either even or zero. Consider the following addresses:

- Unicast
  - 0000.0000.0000
  - 0200.0000.0000
  - 0A00.0000.0000

- Multicast:
  - 0100.0000.0000
  - 0500.0000.0000
  - 0B00.0000.0000

The difference between unicast and multicast addresses may not jump out at you, but Ethernet devices treat them differently. In LAN multicast, a multicast frame is forwarded to many, but not necessarily all, hosts in a subnet. This is one-to-many communication within a subnet. Ethernet interfaces never use multicast addresses as a source address. This means that you'll never find a dynamic entry for a multicast address in a switch's content addressable memory (CAM) table. Generally, when a switch receives a frame destined for a multicast MAC, it will flood the frame, but there are exceptions, which we'll cover in a moment.

Hearkening back to our discussion of Ethernet and broadcast domains in Chapter 1, "Networking Fundamentals," a broadcast frame has a destination of FFFF.FFFF.FFFF and is flooded to all hosts in a subnet. Incidentally, the broadcast address qualifies as a multicast address. Not only that, but it's never used as a source address. Broadcast is just a form of multicast!

Just as there are some reserved multicast IP addresses, so there are some reserved multicast MAC addresses. One you've seen before is 0100.0CCC.CCCC, reserved for Cisco Discovery Protocol (CDP), VLAN Trunking Protocol (VTP), and UDLD. Two others are 0180.C200.0000 used by 802.1D Spanning Tree and 0100.0CCC.CCCD used by RSTP. Traffic sent to these addresses is link-local—that is, it isn't forwarded.

Converting between Multicast MAC and IP Addresses

The relationship between LAN multicast and IP multicast is almost the same as the relationship between LAN unicast and IP unicast. In practice with unicast, we use IP for addressing and largely forget about the MAC addresses, so we depend on ARP to translate unicast IP addresses to unicast MAC addresses. Multicast, however, doesn't use ARP. Instead, it uses a rather convoluted layer 2–to–layer 3 mechanism to translate a multicast IP address to a multicast MAC address. Two multicast MAC address ranges are reserved for IPv4 and IPv6 multicast:

- IPv4—0100.5E00.0000 through 0100.5E7F.FFFF
- IPv6—3333.0000.0000 through 3333.FFFF.FFFF

IPv6 multicast is beyond the scope of the ENCOR exam. In this chapter, we'll stick to covering IPv4 multicast.

As you already know, each IP subnet has its own broadcast address, the last address in the subnet range. To give some examples, the broadcast address for 10.3.7.0/24 is

10.3.7.255; for 192.168.0.0/28 it's 192.168.0.15, and so on. When it comes to resolving these layer 3 broadcast addresses to MAC addresses, ARP isn't necessary. A broadcast IP address always translates to the broadcast MAC address (FFFF.FFFF.FFFF). Similarly, we can translate multicast IP special reserved multicast MAC addresses—without the need for ARP.

Converting an IPv4 multicast address to a MAC address is complicated. Don't feel the need to memorize it, but make sure you at least understand it. For your reference, the whole convoluted process is defined in RFC 1112 (https://tools.ietf.org/html/rfc1112). When you're translating an IP multicast address to a MAC address, the latter always follows the format 0100.5exx.xxxx, and each x is 4 bits. Now consider the multicast IP address 239.9.8.7. Translating this multicast IP address to a MAC address requires some binary gymnastics that are best broken down into steps:

1. Write out hexadecimal 0100.5e in binary, padding to eight places:

01	00	5e
00000001	00000000	01011110

2. Tack on a single zero immediately to the right of the binary you just wrote out. Fill in the remaining seven places (to the right) with x's.

01	00	5e	xx
00000001	00000000	01011110	0xxxxxxx

3. Convert the multicast IP address to binary, once again padding to eight places. 239.9.8.7 would be

239	9	8	7
11101111	00001001	00001000	00000111

4. Take the rightmost (low order) 23 bits of the multicast IP address and fill them in where the x's are in the MAC address. Convert the binary back to hexadecimal:

01	00	5e	09	08	07
00000001	00000000	01011110	00001001	00001000	00000111

The MAC address for 224.9.8.7 would be 0100.5e09.0807. This seems simple enough, but don't let that fool you. When the second IP octet from the left is 128 or greater, some strange things start to happen. Consider the multicast addresses 224.192.1.1 and 224.64.1.1. Both convert to the exact same MAC address: 0100.5e40.0101. (I can't say why this is so, but perhaps it's a strange play on the theme of "one-to-many.") This means we can't reverse the process; it's not possible to convert a multicast MAC address to a multicast IP address. Thankfully, for the rest of the chapter, we'll be dealing mostly with multicast IP addresses.

Internet Group Management Protocol

A receiver that wants to receive multicast traffic from a source may be in a different subnet than the source. A receiver therefore must have a way to indicate that it wants to receive multicast traffic for a particular group. Multicast routers and receivers use the Internet Group Management Protocol (IGMP) to coordinate with each other to ensure that routers forward multicast packets only to those hosts that need them.

IGMP is the protocol a receiver uses to tell its next-hop router which multicast groups it wants to receive traffic for. When a receiver has requested traffic for a group, we say it *joins* the group. When a receiver joins a multicast group, it sends an IGMP Membership Report to the multicast group address it wants to receive traffic for. When it no longer wants to receive traffic for the group, it sends a Leave Group message to its next-hop router.

Every 60 seconds, the next-hop router sends an IGMP Membership Query to determine whether any connected hosts want to receive multicast traffic. (The Membership Query is addressed to 224.0.0.1 and has a TTL of 1). Any host that does want to receive multicast traffic will reply with an IGMP Membership Report.

IGMPv2 (RFC 2236) is the most common version and what IOS uses by default. When a receiver joins a group, it will receive all traffic destined to that group, regardless of the source. IGMPv3 (RFC 3376) adds the ability to request multicast traffic from a specific source—a feature called *source filtering*. All versions of IGMP use IP protocol number 2.

IGMP Snooping

There may be a switch or two between a receiver and a router. Switches by default will flood multicast packets the same way they flood broadcasts and unknown unicasts, so the presence of switches generally won't be a problem. However, some switches support a feature called *IGMP snooping*, wherein the switch will sniff IGMP Membership Reports to determine which ports multicast group traffic should be forwarded out of. Cisco switches have IGMP snooping enabled by default.

When IGMP snooping is enabled and the switch sees an IGMP Membership Report on an interface, the switch adds the multicast source MAC address and interface to an entry in its MAC address table. From then on, when the switch receives multicast traffic for the group, it will forward that traffic only out of the interfaces listed in the entry. This way, IGMP snooping can reduce unnecessary flooding in larger broadcast domains. There is, however, an exception. Traffic sent to local network control block addresses (224.0.0.0/24) is always forwarded to all ports.

IGMP snooping represents a striking similarity between unicast and multicast. A switch sniffs unicast source MAC addresses to build its CAM table and avoid flooding. Likewise, the difference is that, unlike unicast entries, which map one MAC address to one interface, there may be multiple interfaces for a single multicast group address. Also, when a switch receives an IGMP Leave Group message on an interface, it will remove that interface from the MAC address table entry for the group.

Multicast Routing

Multicast senders and receivers may not be in the same subnet. In fact, they're usually separated by multiple subnets and hence multiple routers. Any multicast router that sits between the source and the receiver is upstream from the receiver and downstream from the source.

Imagine that the receiver has sent its next-hop router a Membership Report indicating it wants to join the multicast group 239.1.3.3. That next-hop router must tell its upstream routers to forward multicast traffic for 239.1.3.3. Likewise, that upstream router must tell its upstream routers it wishes to receive multicast traffic for the group, and so on. Essentially, each router must build a multicast IP routing table that links incoming interfaces (facing the source) with outgoing interfaces (facing the receivers).

Here's where we come to a significant difference between unicast and multicast. If a router receives a unicast packet to a destination, it will always forward that packet according to information in its IP routing table. It doesn't matter whether the destination exists or wants to receive the traffic. The router will forward it regardless. In multicast, however, a router may or may not forward a multicast packet to its neighbors. Each router must decide whether to drop or forward a multicast packet, and if the latter, where to forward it. To make a long story short, building a multicast RIB is far more complicated than building a simple unicast IP routing table based solely on destination prefixes.

Protocol Independent Multicast

Protocol-Independent Multicast (PIM) is a multicast routing protocol that performs the heavy work of building each router's multicast IP routing table. PIM can operate in two modes:

Dense Mode Dense mode is like a broadcast on steroids. The router initially floods every multicast packet out of every interface except the interface it was received on. This is somewhat akin to "push" behavior, with one small difference: If a router and its downstream routers have no connected group members, it will send a Prune message to its upstream routers (toward the multicast source), telling them to stop sending traffic for the group. If a downstream receiver needs to receive group traffic after the router has pruned it, the router will send a Graft message upstream to request that group traffic be sent. PIM dense mode (PIM-DM) is specified in RFC 3973 (https://tools.ietf.org/html/rfc3973).

Sparse Mode In sparse mode, a router doesn't forward any multicast packets unless they are explicitly requested. When a router receives an IGMP Membership Report for a group, it will send a PIM Join message to its upstream routers indicating that it wants to receive multicast traffic for that group. The upstream routers will begin to forward group traffic from the source toward the receiver. This is "pull" behavior. When a router no longer needs to receive traffic for a group, it will send a Prune message upstream (just like in dense mode). PIM sparse mode (PIM-SM) is specified in RFC 7761 (https://tools.ietf.org/html/rfc7761).

Sparse mode uses a rendezvous point (RP) that acts as a hub linking multicast sources and receivers. Rendezvous points are beyond the scope of the ENCOR exam, and they add complexity to a multicast configuration. But it's helpful to understand the RP's purpose and why sparse mode requires one. The efficiency is that only the RP has to know the sources of multicast traffic. The rest of the routers only have to know how to reach the RP. Multicast sources send their multicast traffic to the RP, whereas receivers send Join/Prune requests toward the RP. Essentially, the RP becomes the hub or rendezvous point for all multicast traffic in the network. As we continue with our multicast discussion and begin configuring multicast routing, this concept will become clearer.

Configuring PIM

PIM operates similar to IGPs in that neighboring routers have to form an adjacency to exchange information on the multicast sources they want to receive. With PIMv2, routers form adjacencies by sending Hello messages every 30 seconds. PIM Hello messages are sent to the destination address 224.0.0.13 over IP protocol 103. PIM takes a page from the book of OSPF by electing a DR that's responsible for forwarding multicast traffic into a subnet when there are multiple connected routers. Without a DR, multiple routers could end up needlessly sending the same multicast traffic into a subnet. As with most things networking, the best way to understand it is to configure it. We'll configure an IP multicast routing setup using the topology shown in Figure 8.5.

FIGURE 8.5   Multicast topology

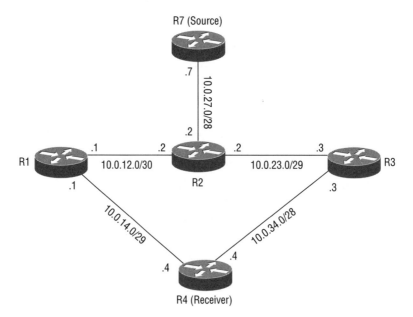

R7 will be the multicast source for group 239.7.7.7. R4 will simulate a multicast receiver. R1, R2, and R3 will be PIM routers operating in dense mode. Technically, we will configure them using what Cisco calls sparse-dense mode. In sparse-dense mode, the routers will operate in dense mode unless they detect an RP, which they won't since we won't be configuring one. Let's begin by configuring PIM sparse-dense mode on R2:

```
! Enable IP multicast routing
R2(config)#ip multicast-routing
! Enable PIM on interfaces facing R1, R3, and R7
R2(config-if)#int range gi0/0,gi0/1,gi0/2
R2(config-if-range)#ip pim sparse-dense-mode
R2(config-if-range)#
%PIM-5-DRCHG: DR change from neighbor 0.0.0.0 to 10.0.12.2 on interface
GigabitEthernet0/0
%PIM-5-DRCHG: DR change from neighbor 0.0.0.0 to 10.0.23.2 on interface
GigabitEthernet0/1
%PIM-5-DRCHG: DR change from neighbor 0.0.0.0 to 10.0.27.2 on interface
GigabitEthernet0/2
```

Now we'll configure R1:

```
R1(config)#ip multicast-routing
! Enable PIM on Gi0/0 (facing R2) and Gi0/1 (facing R4, which we'll use later)
R1(config)#int range gi0/0,gi0/1
R1(config-if-range)#ip pim sparse-dense-mode
R1(config-if-range)#
%PIM-5-NBRCHG: neighbor 10.0.12.2 UP on interface GigabitEthernet0/0
%PIM-5-DRCHG: DR change from neighbor 0.0.0.0 to 10.0.12.2 on interface
GigabitEthernet0/0
R1(config-if-range)#
%PIM-5-DRCHG: DR change from neighbor 0.0.0.0 to 10.0.14.1 on interface
GigabitEthernet0/1
```

And finally, R3:

```
R3(config)#ip multicast-routing
! Enable PIM on Gi0/1 (facing R2) and Gi0/0 (facing R4, which we'll use later)
R3(config-if)#int range gi0/0,gi0/1
R3(config-if-range)#ip pim sparse-dense-mode
R3(config-if-range)#
%PIM-5-NBRCHG: neighbor 10.0.23.2 UP on interface GigabitEthernet0/1
%PIM-5-DRCHG: DR change from neighbor 0.0.0.0 to 10.0.23.3 on interface
GigabitEthernet0/1
%PIM-5-DRCHG: DR change from neighbor 0.0.0.0 to 10.0.34.3 on interface
GigabitEthernet0/0
```

Simulating a Multicast Source

R7 acting as a multicast source will send IP traffic to the multicast group 239.7.7.7. We'll do this using a ping, which will fail, but the goal is to send traffic to the multicast group. Remember that multicast is one-way.

```
R7#ping 239.7.7.7
Type escape sequence to abort.
Sending 1, 100-byte ICMP Echos to 239.7.7.7, timeout is 2 seconds:
.
R7 floods these ping packets out of all its up interfaces, including Gi0/2 facing R2.
```

Viewing the Multicast IP Routing Table

Once R2 receives the multicast from R7, it adds a couple of entries to its multicast routing table.

```
R2#show ip mroute 239.7.7.7 | b Timers
 Timers: Uptime/Expires
 Interface state: Interface, Next-Hop or VCD, State/Mode
(*, 239.7.7.7), 00:01:38/stopped, RP 0.0.0.0, flags: D
  Incoming interface: Null, RPF nbr 0.0.0.0
  Outgoing interface list:
    GigabitEthernet0/1, Forward/Sparse-Dense, 00:01:38/stopped
    GigabitEthernet0/0, Forward/Sparse-Dense, 00:01:38/stopped
(10.0.27.7, 239.7.7.7), 00:01:38/00:01:21, flags: PT
  Incoming interface: GigabitEthernet0/2, RPF nbr 0.0.0.0
  Outgoing interface list:
    GigabitEthernet0/0, Prune/Sparse-Dense, 00:01:38/00:01:21
    GigabitEthernet0/1, Prune/Sparse-Dense, 00:01:38/00:01:21
```

Entries in the multicast routing table follow the format (source, group). The top entry marked (*, 239.7.7.7) is a placeholder entry that just indicates that R2 is aware of the multicast group 239.7.7.7. This type of entry is usually abbreviated as an (*,G) entry. There are three ways a router can become aware of a group, resulting in an (*,G) entry:

▪ It receives group traffic from a source.

▪ It receives an IGMP Membership Report from a receiver.

▪ It receives a PIM Join/Graft for the group.

The bottom entry is marked (10.0.27.7, 239.7.7.7). This type of entry is abbreviated as an (S,G) entry, indicating 10.0.27.7 is the source and 239.7.7.7 is the destination. Such entries are created when the router receives multicast traffic from a source. In this (S,G) entry, the incoming interface shows Gi0/2, the interface facing R7, which is our multicast source. In the outgoing interface list, both Gi0/0 and Gi0/1 are showing pruned, indicating

R2 isn't forwarding group multicast traffic out of those interfaces. The reason is that no hosts have joined the multicast group; therefore, R2's neighbors (R1 and R3) sent Prune messages indicating they don't want to receive traffic for the group. In a moment we'll have R4 simulate a host that joins the group. The multicast routing table on R1 shows the same (S,G) entry for the 239.7.7.7 group:

```
R1#show ip mroute 239.7.7.7 | b Timers
 Timers: Uptime/Expires
 Interface state: Interface, Next-Hop or VCD, State/Mode
(*, 239.7.7.7), 00:01:38/stopped, RP 0.0.0.0, flags: D
  Incoming interface: Null, RPF nbr 0.0.0.0
  Outgoing interface list:
    GigabitEthernet0/0, Forward/Sparse-Dense, 00:01:38/stopped
(10.0.27.7, 239.7.7.7), 00:01:38/00:01:21, flags: PT
  Incoming interface: GigabitEthernet0/0, RPF nbr 10.0.12.2
  Outgoing interface list: Null
```

R1 learns this entry from R3 via PIM. Although R1 isn't actually receiving traffic for the 239.7.7.7 group, it could receive it on its Gi0/0 interface from R2 (10.0.12.2). When multicast routing is properly configured, the interface that a multicast packet ingresses should be the same interface that unicast traffic to the multicast source would take. This is best understood by example, so let's look at the CEF FIB to see the egress interface for traffic sent to the multicast source address 10.0.27.7:

```
R1#show ip cef 10.0.27.7
10.0.27.0/28
  nexthop 10.0.12.2 GigabitEthernet0/0
```

Reverse Path Forwarding Check

Notice that the outgoing interface (Gi0/0) and next hop in the CEF FIB entry are the same as the incoming interface and reverse path forwarding (RPF) neighbor (RPF nbr) entries in the multicast RIB (S,G) entry. The path that the multicast takes from 10.0.27.7 to R1 is the reverse of the path that a unicast packet from R1 to 10.0.27.7 would take. This is an example of RPF. Hence, Gi0/0 is said to be the RPF interface. The router performs an RPF check to avoid loops by ensuring that the multicast path will overlap/align with the unicast path, which is assumed to be loop-free. Remember that multicast IP packets have a TTL, so they won't loop endlessly in a network. Nevertheless, the RPF check avoids wasting bandwidth and putting undue strain on the network. On R3, we see an entry for the same source and group combination:

```
R3#show ip mroute 239.7.7.7 | b Timers
 Timers: Uptime/Expires
 Interface state: Interface, Next-Hop or VCD, State/Mode
```

```
(*, 239.7.7.7), 00:01:38/stopped, RP 0.0.0.0, flags: D
  Incoming interface: Null, RPF nbr 0.0.0.0
  Outgoing interface list:
    GigabitEthernet0/1, Forward/Sparse-Dense, 00:01:38/stopped
(10.0.27.7, 239.7.7.7), 00:01:38/00:01:21, flags: PT
  Incoming interface: GigabitEthernet0/1, RPF nbr 10.0.23.2
  Outgoing interface list: Null
```

Again, because there are no members to receive traffic, the outgoing interface list is empty. But if R3 were to receive any multicast traffic for this (S,G) combination, it would be on Gi0/1. The RPF check passes here as well:

```
R3#show ip cef 10.0.27.7
10.0.0.0/16
  nexthop 10.0.23.2 GigabitEthernet0/1
```

A quick and easy way to find the full reverse path back to a multicast source is to use the mtrace command. Just specify the multicast source address as follows:

```
R3#mtrace 10.0.27.7
Type escape sequence to abort.
Mtrace from 10.0.27.7 to 10.0.23.3 via RPF
From source (?) to destination (?)
Querying full reverse path...
 0  10.0.23.3
-1  10.0.23.3 ==> 10.0.23.3 PIM  [10.0.0.0/16]
-2  10.0.23.2 ==> 10.0.27.2 PIM_MT  [10.0.27.0/28]
-3  10.0.27.7
```

Configuring a Multicast Receiver

Now we'll configure R4 as a multicast client. Remember that we've configured PIM on R1's and R3's interfaces facing R4. However, normally, a multicast client will have just one interface, so we'll have R4 send an IGMP Membership Report to join the multicast group using only its Gi0/0 interface (facing R3):

 Configuring a router to send an IGMP Membership Report isn't something you normally do. But using a router to simulate a client is a convenient way to test your multicast routing setup.

```
R4(config)#int gi0/0
R4(config-if)#ip igmp join-group 239.7.7.7
```

On R7, we'll send some packets to 239.7.7.7. The multicast routing table on R3 shows the following (S,G) entry:

```
R3#show ip mroute 239.7.7.7 10.0.27.7 | b Timers
 Timers: Uptime/Expires
 Interface state: Interface, Next-Hop or VCD, State/Mode
(10.0.27.7, 239.7.7.7), 00:02:47/00:00:12, flags: T
  Incoming interface: GigabitEthernet0/1, RPF nbr 10.0.23.2
  Outgoing interface list:
    GigabitEthernet0/0, Forward/Sparse-Dense, 00:02:47/stopped
```

R3 forwards the multicast traffic out of the Gi0/0 interface facing R4. Moving one hop closer to the source, the multicast routing table on R2 shows the following:

```
R2#show ip mroute 239.7.7.7 10.0.27.7 | b Timers
 Timers: Uptime/Expires
 Interface state: Interface, Next-Hop or VCD, State/Mode
(10.0.27.7, 239.7.7.7), 00:01:11/00:01:47, flags: T
  Incoming interface: GigabitEthernet0/2, RPF nbr 0.0.0.0
  Outgoing interface list:
    GigabitEthernet0/0, Prune/Sparse-Dense, 00:01:11/00:01:48
    GigabitEthernet0/1, Forward/Sparse-Dense, 00:01:11/stopped
```

As expected, R2 forwards the group traffic to R3 via Gi0/1. But it prunes the Gi0/0 interface facing R1, since there are no clients requesting multicast traffic for the group. To get a clearer picture of what's happening, we can use the mtrace command to draw the path from the source (R7) to the destination (R4). We just need to specify the source IP, destination IP, and group address as follows:

```
R3#mtrace 10.0.27.7 10.0.34.4 239.7.7.7
Type escape sequence to abort.
Mtrace from 10.0.27.7 to 10.0.34.4 via group 239.7.7.7
From source (?) to destination (?)
Querying full reverse path...
 0  10.0.34.4
-1  10.0.34.3 ==> 10.0.23.3 PIM  [10.0.0.0/16]
-2  10.0.23.2 ==> 10.0.27.2 PIM_MT  [10.0.27.0/28]
-3  10.0.27.7
```

From R4, the reverse path is R3 to R2 to R7. The collection of routers between the source and destination subnets for a group composes the *shortest-path tree* (SPT) or source tree for the group. To use graph terminology, the source is the root of the tree, the receivers are the leaves, and the intermediate routers are the branches.

You may find it helpful to think about how Prune and Join/Graft operations affect the shape of the tree. In this case, the tree for group 239.7.7.7 has R7 as its root and R4 as its only leaf. Now consider what would happen if R4 were to leave the group. Since R4 is currently the only leaf, the tree would be leafless, and in fact would cease to exist altogether. Without any leaves (receivers), there are no branches (intermediate multicast routers), and thus no SPT. We'd expect, then, that all the intermediate routers would prune traffic for the group 239.7.7.7. Let's remove R4 from the group and see what happens:

```
R4(config)#int gi0/0
R4(config-if)#no ip igmp join-group 239.7.7.7
```

R3 immediately stops forwarding the multicast traffic to R4:

```
R3#show ip mroute 239.7.7.7 10.0.27.7 | b Timers
 Timers: Uptime/Expires
 Interface state: Interface, Next-Hop or VCD, State/Mode
(10.0.27.7, 239.7.7.7), 00:00:30/00:02:29, flags: PT
   Incoming interface: GigabitEthernet0/1, RPF nbr 10.0.23.2
   Outgoing interface list: Null
```

Likewise, R2 stops forwarding the group traffic to R3:

```
R2#show ip mroute 239.7.7.7 10.0.27.7 | b Timers
 Timers: Uptime/Expires
 Interface state: Interface, Next-Hop or VCD, State/Mode
(10.0.27.7, 239.7.7.7), 00:00:26/00:02:33, flags: PT
   Incoming interface: GigabitEthernet0/2, RPF nbr 0.0.0.0
   Outgoing interface list:
     GigabitEthernet0/0, Prune/Sparse-Dense, 00:00:26/00:02:33
     GigabitEthernet0/1, Prune/Sparse-Dense, 00:00:00/00:02:59
```

This makes more efficient use of bandwidth by sending the group traffic only toward the hosts that request it.

IP Multicast and Ethernet

Although it goes without saying that IP multicast depends on Ethernet multicast, the two are different things. At layer 2, Ethernet frames sent to multicast destination addresses (which include broadcasts) are kept within the broadcast domain. The way a switch treats multicasts and unknown unicasts is nearly identical. Hence, Ethernet multicast by itself requires no IP routing or addressing whatsoever. (If that seems strange, just think about why Ethernet unicast doesn't require IP routing or addressing either. Two hosts in the same broadcast domain can exchange Ethernet frames all day long without ever using IP.)

IP multicast, on the other hand, involves IP packets sent to multicast IP addresses. This is where things can get confusing quickly, so to understand IP multicast, let's walk through two simple scenarios loosely based on earlier examples.

Scenario #1: IP Multicast without Routing

A multicast source begins sending IP packets addressed to 239.7.7.7. The source encapsulates each packet in an Ethernet frame addressed to 0100.5e07.0707, with its own unicast MAC address as the source. Recall that a multicast IP address can be converted to a multicast MAC. However, the particular MAC address that results isn't unique. Many multicast IP addresses can map to the same MAC, so there's some ambiguity. The source sends the frame to a switch that floods it to all nodes in the VLAN. Connected to the VLAN is a receiver that's interested in receiving traffic for the 239.7.7.7 group. Based on the destination MAC address, the receiver knows that the frame may be addressed to the multicast IP 239.7.7.7. What the receiver does with the frame isn't particularly important. All that matters is that it receives it.

Scenario #2: IP Multicast with Routing

Now consider that the same multicast source sends IP packets addressed to 239.7.7.7. Again, it encapsulates the packet in an Ethernet frame addressed to 0100.5e07.0707, sourced from its own unicast MAC address, and sends it out onto VLAN 10. This time, however, a multicast router is listening that's connected to VLAN 10 and VLAN 20. In VLAN 20, there's a receiver interested in receiving traffic for 239.7.7.7. The multicast router takes the multicast frame from VLAN 10 and decapsulates the multicast IP packet. It sees that the destination IP address is 239.7.7.7, and it knows that a receiver in VLAN 20 wants this traffic. The router re-encapsulates the packet into an Ethernet frame addressed to the same multicast MAC address (0100.5e07.0707), but this time the router uses its own interface MAC address as the source. The router sends the frame out into VLAN 20, and the receiver, listening intently for traffic for the 239.7.7.7 group, receives the frame.

Notice that because only one router connects the source and receiver, there's no need for PIM, only IGMP. Earlier in the chapter, we covered another possible IP multicast routing scenario wherein sources and receivers are separated by several routers. This approach does require the multicast routers to run PIM with one another so that they can build out a SPT for each active multicast group that has receivers.

Summary

NAT as defined in RFC 1631 was originally designed to conserve public IPv4 addresses. As a technology, however, a NAT router can change the source or destination IP address of any IP packet it receives. When changing the source address, it's called "source NAT" (sometimes abbreviated "SNAT"). When changing the destination address, it's called "destination NAT."

NAT classifies addresses along two axes: local/global and inside/outside. Local addresses are reachable from within the inside network. Global addresses are reachable from both the inside and outside networks. In other words, the scope of local addresses is the inside network, whereas the scope of global addresses is, well, global.

Although we tend to talk of inside and outside networks, when configuring NAT, you're actually specifying an inside and outside interface. The outside versus inside distinction is arbitrary, but customarily the inside interface faces the network that you control, whereas the outside interface points to the network that's outside of your control. If you're working on someone else's configuration, never assume you know what the inside and outside interfaces are. Always check.

To reiterate, NAT always involves translating both source and destination IP addresses, depending on whether the original packet's arriving on the inside or the outside interface. The NAT configuration commands are notoriously confusing, so let's clear things up by seeing how the commands relate to what actually happens during the NAT process.

We began with the set of commands that began with `ip nat inside source`. We used these for static and dynamic NAT and PAT. The `inside source` keywords indicate that a packet hitting the inside interface will have its source IP address changed. When the command is `ip nat inside source`, the translation occurs as follows:

Traffic arrives at interface	Address changed
Inside	Source IP
Outside	Destination IP

The last command we looked at began with `ip nat outside source`. A packet arriving at the outside interface will have its source address changed. When using the command `ip nat outside source`, the packet is translated as follows:

Traffic arrives at interface	Address changed
Inside	Destination IP
Outside	Source IP

By remembering this, you can figure out how to achieve any conceivable NAT configuration. Of course, it takes practice, but understanding comes first. Complete the chapter exercises, and as always, once you've done that, feel free to experiment on your own.

Now let's talk about multicast. Multicast is a one-to-many paradigm that allows a source to send a single packet to multiple receivers. In unicast, on the other hand, a sender can send a packet to only one receiver. If the sender needs to send the same data to multiple receivers, it must send a separate packet addressed to each respective receiver.

Multicast actually comes in two different flavors: Ethernet multicast and IP multicast. They're separate things, but in Ethernet networks, IP multicast depends on Ethernet multicast. In just the same way most applications use unicast IP addresses instead of MAC addresses for communications, so most multicast applications use multicast IP addresses instead of multicast MAC addresses. Therefore, thankfully, your experience with multicast will mostly be confined to IP multicast.

At layer 2, a switch generally floods both multicasts and unknown unicasts. However, a switch that supports IGMP snooping (which Cisco switches do by default) will take note of IGMP Membership Reports and add the appropriate entries to its MAC address table to reduce flooding of multicast traffic. Even without IGMP snooping, Ethernet multicast will work just fine. In fact, multicast traffic sent to certain addresses is always flooded regardless of IGMP snooping.

Exam Essentials

Understand the differences among static NAT, dynamic NAT, and PAT.   Static NAT does a one-to-one translation from inside local to inside global. Dynamic NAT also does a one-to-one translation from local to global, but the allocation happens dynamically, and the global addresses are pulled from a pool. PAT, or NAT overload, does a many-to-one translation, typically translating multiple local IPs to a single global address.

Be able to configure NAT.   You should be able to configure static NAT, dynamic NAT, and most importantly PAT, or NAT overload. Although outside static NAT is not something that you're likely to encounter much on the job, some practice configuring it can help solidify your understanding of NAT.

Know how to use access lists and NAT pools.   NAT configuration on Cisco devices also makes use of ACLs. If you aren't comfortable with ACLs, you're not going to be very comfortable configuring NAT. NAT pools are used for specifying multiple inside global addresses.

Understand the differences between multicast and unicast.   Unicast requires a separate packet for each destination host. This allows independently tracking sessions per host. Multicast requires one packet sent to a multicast address, and the routers on the network take care of distributing it to the hosts that need it. The sender is unaware of which hosts are listening and who has received a packet.

Know the difference between Ethernet multicast and IP multicast.   The biggest difference is that Ethernet multicast frames stay within a broadcast domain, whereas IP multicast can—with some exceptions—be routed. IP multicast packets may or may not stay within a broadcast domain, depending on the multicast group address and TTL. Packets sent to addresses in the local network control block (224.0.0.0/24) aren't routed. This is the case with multicasts generated by IGPs such as EIGRP and OSPF. Also, it's possible for a source to send a multicast IP packet with a TTL of 1, ensuring that it won't leave the broadcast domain.

Exercises

EXERCISE 8.1

Configure R1, R2, and R3 as shown in the layer 3 diagram in Figure 8.3 and the layer 2 diagram in Figure 8.4. Alternatively, if you've completed the labs for Chapter 7, "The Border Gateway Protocol (BGP," you may use your existing configuration and don't need to complete this exercise. As you work through the rest of the exercises, you may encounter some OSPF configuration errors, which you may safely disregard.

EXERCISE 8.2

On R2, create an inside static NAT mapping between R2's 10.0.12.2 and R7's 10.0.27.7 addresses.

EXERCISE 8.3

On R2, create a dynamic mapping using a global pool range of 2.0.0.1 through 2.0.0.3. Translate any source addresses in the 7.0.0.0/24 range.

EXERCISE 8.4

Configure PAT on R2 using R2's outside interface address (10.0.12.2). Translate any source addresses in the 7.0.0.0/24 range.

EXERCISE 8.5

Configure destination address translation between 1.1.1.1 and 10.0.12.1 on R2. Make sure R7 receives a route to the 1.1.1.1/32 prefix. When done, remove all NAT configurations on R2 and R4.

EXERCISE 8.6

Referring to the layer 2 diagram in Figure 8.4 and the layer 3 diagrams in Figures 8.3 and 8.5, configure IP multicast routing and PIM sparse-dense mode on R1, R2, and R3.

EXERCISE 8.7

On R7, send traffic to the multicast address 239.7.7.7. Configure R4 to join the group on its Gi0/0 interface. Verify that the multicast RIB on the intermediate routers (R2 and R3) forwards group traffic from R7 to R4.

Review Questions

You can find the answers in the appendix.

1. Which of the following is a valid use of static NAT?

   A. Conserving IP addresses

   B. Hiding a source IP address

   C. Changing a source port number

   D. Hiding a source IP address

2. On your inside network you have a host with the IP address 10.1.1.1. Its next-hop gateway is an Internet router with an IP of 10.1.1.254. The Internet router's interface connected to the ISP router has the interface IP 192.0.2.2. Which of the following are true of this configuration? (Choose two.)

   A. 10.1.1.1 is an inside local address.

   B. 192.0.2.2 is an outside local address.

   C. 192.0.2.2 is an inside global address.

   D. 10.1.1.1 is an inside global address.

   E. 10.1.1.254 is an inside global address.

3. What happens when a router configured for dynamic NAT exhausts its NAT address pool?

   A. Traffic from inside hosts without a mapping will be dropped.

   B. The oldest translation will be deleted.

   C. The router will use PAT.

   D. All translations will be deleted.

4. On a NAT router, which of the following can be an inside global address? (Choose two.)

   A. A loopback interface address

   B. An outside local address

   C. An inside interface address

   D. An outside interface address

5. Which of the following is true of the command `ip nat inside source list 1 pool globalpool`?

   A. Inside local source IP addresses matching ACL 1 will be translated.

   B. Inside local destination IP addresses matching ACL 1 will be translated.

   C. Inside local source IP addresses matching the pool `globalpool` will be translated.

   D. Outside global source IP addresses matching the pool `globalpool` will be translated.

6. A few hours after enabling dynamic NAT on a router, some inside hosts are unable to access Internet resources. You enable NAT debugging on the router and then see the following message:

    `NAT: translation failed (A), dropping packet s=7.0.0.99 d=10.0.12.1`

    Which of the following steps is most likely to independently and permanently resolve the issue? (Choose two.)

    A. Clear the NAT translation table.

    B. Increase the size of the NAT pool.

    C. Use PAT instead of dynamic NAT.

    D. Use static NAT instead of dynamic NAT.

7. How does PAT conserve IP addresses?

    A. By overloading an inside global address

    B. By using a pool of inside global addresses

    C. By performing one-to-one translation between a local and global address

    D. By overloading port numbers

8. Which of the following commands individually configures PAT? (Choose two.)

    A. `ip nat pool natpool 2.0.0.1 2.0.0.3 netmask 255.255.255.248`

    B. `ip nat inside source list 1 pool natpool overload`

    C. `ip nat inside source list 1 pool natpool`

    D. `ip nat inside source list 1 interface gi0/0 overload`

9. Consider the following NAT translation table output:

    ```
    Pro Inside global     Inside local    Outside local      Outside global
    Pro Inside global     Inside local    Outside local      Outside global
    icmp 2.0.0.2:16       7.0.0.12:16     10.0.12.1:16       10.0.12.1:16
    --- 2.0.0.2           7.0.0.12        ---                --
    ```

    Which of the following configurations could this indicate? (Choose two.)

    A. Static NAT

    B. NAT overload

    C. Outside static NAT

    D. Dynamic NAT

10. Consider the following NAT translation table output:

```
Pro Inside global     Inside local     Outside local     Outside global
--- ---               ---              1.1.1.1           10.0.12.1
```

Which of the following can you infer from this??

A. When a host with the source IP 1.1.1.1 sends a packet, the NAT router will translate the source address to 10.0.12.1.

B. When a host on the inside sends a packet to the destination IP 10.0.12.1, the NAT router will translate the destination to 1.1.1.1.

C. When a host on the inside sends a packet to the destination IP 1.1.1.1, the NAT router will translate the destination to 10.0.12.1.

D. When a host with the source IP 10.0.12.1 sends a packet, the NAT router will translate the source address to 1.1.1.1.

11. Which of the following is *not* a multicast IP address?

A. 224.0.0.0

B. 240.0.0.1

C. 239.255.255.1

D. 224.0.1.0

12. Which of the following best describes IP multicast?

A. One-to-many

B. One-to-one

C. Many-to-one

D. Destination-based routing

13. What distinguishes a multicast MAC from a unicast MAC address?

A. In a multicast address, the second-to-left hexadecimal digit is always odd.

B. In a multicast address, the leftmost hexadecimal digit is always even.

C. In a multicast address, the second-to-last hexadecimal digit is always zero.

D. In a unicast address, the second-to-left hexadecimal digit is always zero.

14. Which of the following are true of an Ethernet frame? (Choose two.)

A. It never contains a multicast source address.

B. It may be flooded to all devices in a subnet.

C. It never contains a multicast destination address.

D. It has a TTL.

15. Which of the following is true of a multicast IP packet? (Choose two.)

   A. It always contains a multicast destination address.

   B. It may contain a multicast source address.

   C. It always uses IP protocol 103.

   D. It may have a TTL of 1.

16. Which of the following protocols does a multicast receiver use to join a group?

   A. IGMP

   B. PIM

   C. OSPF

   D. RP

17. Which of the following do routers use to request multicast traffic for a group? (Choose two).

   A. PIM Prune

   B. IGMP Membership Report

   C. PIM Join

   D. PIM Graft

18. A router running PIM has a single multicast RIB entry marked (*, 239.9.9.9). What does this indicate?

   A. The router has sent an IGMP Query to 239.9.9.9.

   B. A receiver has sent an IGMP Membership Report to 239.9.9.9.

   C. The router has sent a PIM Join/Graft to 239.9.9.9.

   D. A receiver has sent an IGMP Query to 239.9.9.9.

19. What multicast address do routers send PIM Hello messages to?

   A. 224.0.0.13

   B. 224.0.0.1

   C. 239.0.0.13

   D. 239.0.0.1

20. What multicast address are IGMP Queries sent to?

   A. 224.0.0.13

   B. 239.0.0.13

   C. 224.0.0.1

   D. The multicast group address being queried

Chapter

9

Quality of Service

THE CCNP ENCOR EXAM OBJECTIVES COVERED IN THIS CHAPTER INCLUDE THE FOLLOWING:

Domain 1.0 Architecture

✓ **1.6   Describe concepts of wired and wireless QoS**

In this chapter, you'll learn how to configure QoS tools that address the problems of network congestion and latency. We'll begin with a brief introduction to QoS concepts, and then dig into the following:

Classification and marking using class maps—Let you identify what types of traffic should be prioritized over others during times of congestion

Policing—Limits the throughput of traffic to stop congestion before it starts

Queuing—Controls congestion when it occurs and prioritizes traffic according to its class

Shaping—Reduces packet drops, particularly on bandwidth-constrained links

Understanding Quality of Service

Congestion occurs when a router or switch receives packets or frames faster than it can forward them. If a router is receiving 2 Gbps of traffic that it must forward out of a 1 Gbps interface, that router experiences congestion. The two classic signs of congestion are delayed and dropped packets (to make things readable, I'll refer to packets and frames as just packets). Router and switch interfaces have output buffers that line up or queue packets until they're ready to be sent. When ingress traffic can be forwarded at the same rate at which it's coming in, the output queues never fill up. A packet comes in and it's immediately forwarded out.

Buffers have a finite size, and when congestion occurs, the buffers begin to fill and the packets are queued up in the order in which they're received. This is called *first-in, first-out (FIFO) queuing*. Now, rather than being immediately forwarded, a packet has to wait in line to be transmitted. As the phrase "waiting in line" suggests, being in a queue necessarily involves a delay; hence, congestion causes increased latency.

Once a buffer fills up, any more packets that come in to be forwarded are simply dropped. This is called a *tail-drop*, since the packets are dropped from the end or tail of the queue. This is like filling up your shopping cart and then proceeding to the (self-)checkout line, hoping to check out quickly, only to see that the line is too long. You leave your cart, and the items you were hoping to buy never leave the store (at least not with you).

The bottom line is that congestion causes delays and packet loss. The twofold goal of QoS is to avoid congestion if possible and mitigate the effects of delay and packet loss when it occurs. In the end, the performance of the applications that are sending and receiving packets is what counts. Therefore, no one-size-fits-all solution exists. Thankfully, QoS offers multiple tools we can use to avoid and deal with congestion:

- Classification, marking, and queuing—This is usually what you think of when you think of QoS. Essentially, you are prioritizing some packets over others according to how they tolerate latency and loss.

- Policing—One way to avoid queue delays is to preemptively drop packets. That's what policing does.

- Shaping—Shaping intentionally delays packets to avoid dropping them. It's essentially the antithesis of policing.

Classification and Marking

The foundation of QoS rests on the concept of *classification*. Not all traffic is created equal, and some packets need to be treated differently than others. The phrase "bits is bits" may sound nice, but it just isn't true. You classify packets according to how you want routers to treat them during times of congestion. Traffic that's sensitive to delay and packet loss may go into one class, whereas traffic that can tolerate high delays and loss might go into a different class.

Differentiated Services

Differentiated Services (DiffServ) is a QoS architecture that uses the type of service (ToS) byte of the IP field (defined in RFC 791) to classify a packet. DiffServ populates the ToS field with a specific DiffServ Code Point (DSCP) value. DiffServ code points use the leftmost (high-order) 6 bits of the ToS field. DSCPs are organized into three different groups called per-hop behavior (PHB) groups.

Per-Hop Behavior Groups

Naturally, before you understand what a PHB group is, you might assume that you must know what a PHB is. Unfortunately, the term PHB is used inconsistently throughout the networking world. As the DiffServ RFC states:

> A per-hop behavior (PHB) is a description of the externally observable forwarding behavior...PHBs may be specified in terms of their resource (e.g., buffer, bandwidth) priority relative to other PHBs, or in terms of their relative observable traffic characteristics (e.g., delay, loss). These PHBs may be used as building blocks to allocate resources and should be specified as a group (PHB group) for consistency.
>
> *RFC 2475, An Architecture for Differentiated Services (https://tools .ietf.org/rfc/rfc2475.txt)*

In other words, a PHB is *supposed* to describe how a router treats a packet. But *really* a PHB is just an arbitrary way of classifying packets by priority. A PHB group, then, is a set of predefined code points you can choose from. PHB groups are primarily for ease of management so that you don't have to memorize a bunch of binary numbers. As you read through these, keep in mind that PHB groups are not mutually exclusive. You can use code points from different PHB groups, and you don't have to stick with a particular group.

Class Selector

Class Selector (CS) offers eight different classes, ranging from CS0 to CS7, with the latter being the highest priority. Table 9.1 shows the possible code points for the CS PHB group.

TABLE 9.1   Class Selector code points

Class Selector name	DSCP binary value	Example traffic class
CS0	000000	Casual web browsing
LE	000001	Unimportant or undesirable
CS1	001000	Unimportant or undesirable
CS2	010000	IT administrative traffic
CS3	011000	Live streaming video
CS4	100000	Video teleconferencing
CS5	101000	IP telephony signaling
CS6	110000	Routing protocols
CS7	111000	Anything more important than routing protocols

There's an odd quirk with selectors CS0, LE, and CS1. CS0 goes by a few different names, including standard, default, and best effort. CS0 is the default class and is for best-effort traffic. CS1 and LE are intended for "lower effort" traffic. This is bottom-of-the-barrel traffic that you may not even want on your network, such as torrents, gaming, or cat videos. All you need to know is that both LE and CS1 get a lower priority than CS0. If you want to know why, check out RFC 3662.

With the exception of the LE selector, an easy way to identify CS code points is that the three low-order (rightmost) bits are always 0.

Assured Forwarding

Assured forwarding (AF) (RFC 2597) allows you specify not only the priority of a packet, but also the likelihood that it will be dropped while it's waiting in a queue—the drop probability or drop precedence. AF offers a total of 12 different classes: four priority classes and three drop probability classes. AF code points take the format AFxy, where x is the priority (lower is higher priority) and y is the drop probability (higher is a higher drop probability). Table 9.2 shows the possible code points for AF.

TABLE 9.2   Assured forwarding names

Priority	Drop Probability		
	Low	Medium	High
1	AF11	AF12	AF13
2	AF21	AF22	AF23
3	AF31	AF32	AF33
4	AF41	AF42	AF43

To give a quick example, suppose two packets marked AF11 and AF12 are waiting in a full queue. The AF12 packet will be dropped from the queue before the AF11 will because AF12 has a higher drop probability.

You'll typically use AF with TCP-based applications that can tolerate packet loss. On-demand streaming media, web browsing, database-backed applications, and file server traffic are good candidates for the AF PHB group.

For the curious, you can use the formula $8x + 2y$ to find the DSCP value of any AF name. For example, AF11 would have a DSCP value of $(8 \times 1) + (2 \times 1) = 10$, a binary value of 001010.

Expedited Forwarding

The expedited forwarding (EF) PHB group isn't really a group—it's just a single code point with the value 46 (binary 101110). It's intended for high-priority traffic that should also be bandwidth limited. Voice-over-IP phone calls are a good example of this. Voice packets need high priority, but you don't want them to ever crowd out data traffic, so you'll limit the amount of bandwidth they can consume. For this reason, EF is not a good choice for bandwidth-intensive applications such as video.

RFC 4594, "Configuration Guidelines for DiffServ Service Classes" (https://tools.ietf.org/rfc/rfc4594.txt) offers recommendations for choosing a PHB group and code point for your different traffic classes.

Layer 2 Marking

What about Ethernet and WLAN QoS markings? The IEEE 802.1Q standard defines a 3-bit *class of service* (CoS) field that can be used to assign one of eight priority code points (PCPs) for QoS classification. This is sometimes called the 802.1p field or PCP field. CoS values range from 0 to 7. The values don't have any official meaning, but most implementations follow the IEEE's recommendation of treating a value of 7 as the highest priority. The CoS markings have the same peculiarity as DSCP when it comes to the lowest two values. A value of 0 is for the default class and is best effort. A value of 1 is for background or "lower effort" traffic and is treated worse than the default class.

Layer 2 frames stay within a subnet, so the CoS field is only useful for intra-subnet traffic. Furthermore, because the CoS field is stored in the 802.1Q header, it is preserved only on trunk links. Therefore, you lose the marking once a frame egresses an access port. The CoS field has no relationship to DiffServ, and no translation occurs between the two. Many folks, however, do manually map CoS values to DSCPs. In this case, when a router or layer 3 switch receives an IP packet inside a tagged 802.1Q frame with a PCP marking, it applies a DSCP to the IP packet before sending it on.

Class Maps and Policy Maps

You want to mark packets as close to the source as possible. In some cases, you may even allow a host to mark its own packets. For instance, you may let an IP telephony server mark its own voice control packets as CS5. Where you set the markings delineates the QoS *trust boundary*. If you let a host set its own markings and you preserve those markings, then that host is within the trust boundary. Otherwise, the host sits outside the boundary. To classify and mark packets, you use class maps and policy maps, respectively.

It might seem surprising, but you use a class map to classify packets. A *class map* can match packets according to a variety of criteria, such IP address, protocol, port number, source MAC address, packet length, DSCP value, or 802.1Q CoS value. Sometimes you can't classify traffic based on port or protocol alone. Applications that use nonstandard or ephemeral port numbers can be hard to pin down. Next-Generation Network-Based Application Recognition (Next-Generation NBAR or NBAR2) uses deep packet inspection to identify what type of application a packet belongs to. It's especially useful for finding undesirable file sharing application traffic. The default class map *class-default* matches all traffic.

Policy maps have the special distinction of both marking packets and performing policing, shaping, and queuing, all of which we'll cover later. Policy maps are applied to interfaces and apply to either inbound or outbound traffic. To give you a taste of what's to come, take a look at the following sample policy map that marks all traffic with the DSCP value CS2:

```
R5(config)#policy-map mark-all
R5(config-pmap)# class class-default
R5(config-pmap-c)#set dscp cs2
```

Pretty simple, right? The policy map simply marks any packets that belong to the class-default class, which covers all traffic. The following applies this policy map to traffic ingressing the Gi0/0 interface:

```
R5(config-pmap-c)#interface gi0/0
R5(config-if)#service-policy input mark-all
```

The net result is that any packets ingressing Gi0/0 will be marked CS2. Of course, this is a simple example. In the next section we'll look at a different way to use policy maps.

Wireless QoS

Just as wired QoS consists of DSCP-marked IP packets and CoS-marked Ethernet frames, so does wireless have two distinct ways of marking layer 2 and layer 3 traffic.

Layer 3 Wireless QoS

A WLAN controller (WLC) can be configured to preserve DSCP markings from wireless clients—something especially crucial for wireless voice and video. The WLC has four pre-set QoS profiles that define the *maximum* DSCP values for wireless client traffic:

Profile	Purpose	DSCP
Platinum	Voice	EF
Gold	Video	AF41
Silver	Best effort	CS0
Bronze	Background	AF11

You apply a profile on a per-SSID basis. For example, suppose an employee's laptop is connected to an SSID associated with the Silver profile, which has a maximum DSCP of CS0. The employee loads up a SIP phone application, which marks voice packets with DSCP EF. The WLC will not honor the marking and will instead re-mark the voice traffic as DSCP CS0.

Now let's say the user loads up a web browser and begins surfing. The packets from the web browser are unmarked, so the WLC marks them as CS0. Figure 9.1 shows the portion of the WLC web interface where you can select a QoS profile for an SSID.

FIGURE 9.1 Setting a QoS profile

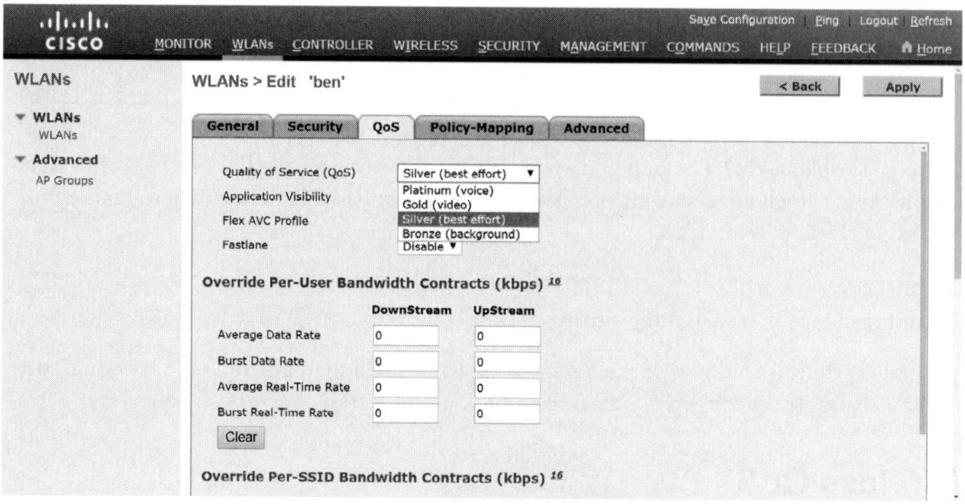

You can edit individual profiles to suit your needs. Figure 9.2 shows the Platinum profile. Note that you can set bandwidth limits on a per-user and per-SSID basis. Also, you can specify a default priority for unmarked traffic.

FIGURE 9.2 The Platinum QoS profile

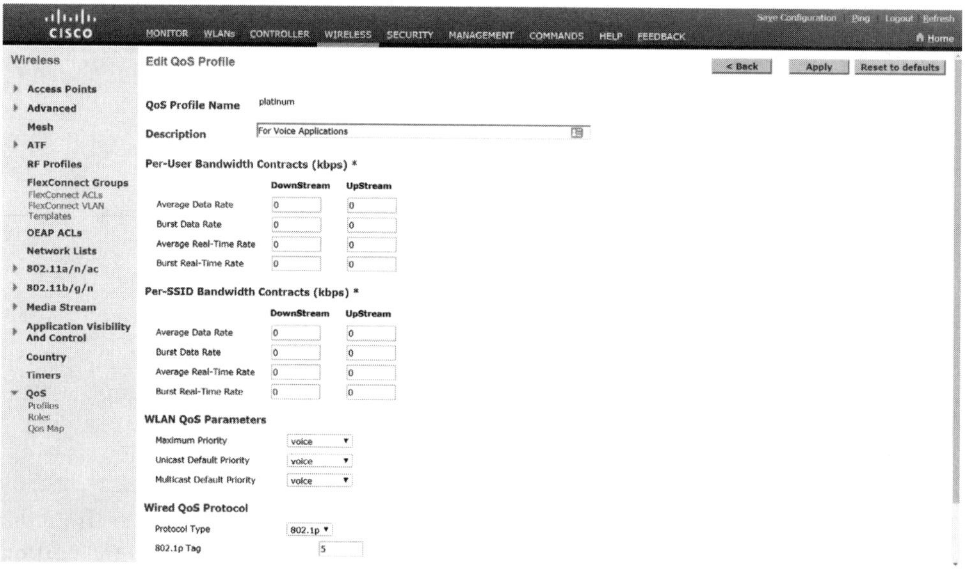

Layer 2 Wireless QoS

Note that the Wired QoS Protocol section includes an 802.1p tag (CoS) value of 5. Things start to get confusing here because 802.11 frames don't include a CoS field. There's a separate standard for layer 2 QoS on 802.11 networks, and it's called 802.11e or Wi-Fi Multimedia (WMM). Clients that support WMM can mark their WLAN frames with one of four WMM values that correspond to an access class. The AP and WLC will translate these WMM values to CoS values as follows:

Access class	WMM (802.11e) value	Translated CoS (802.1p) value
Voice	6	5
Video	5	4
Best effort	0	0
Background	1	1

It's no coincidence that the access class names correspond to the QoS profiles predefined in the WLC. Referring back to Figure 9.2, suppose a wireless client is connected to an SSID with the Voice QoS profile.

1. The client sends an 802.11 frame marked with a WMM value of 5.

2. When the AP receives the frame, it translates the WMM value of 5 to a CoS value of 4. The AP encapsulates the frame in a CAPWAP frame, which it marks with a CoS value of 4.

3. When the WLC receives the frame, it translates the encapsulated 802.11 frame to an 802.3 Ethernet frame with a CoS marking of 4 before sending it out onto the LAN.

Now consider another client connected to the same SSID but that doesn't support WMM. The client sends only unmarked traffic, so before forwarding the client's traffic out onto the LAN, the WLC appends the CoS value configured in the profile, which in this case is 5.

CoS (802.1p) and WMM (802.11e) markings have nothing to do with DSCP values, which are stored in IP headers.

There are a couple of things to keep in mind regarding preserving DSCP markings from wireless clients. When an access point connected to a WLC receives a marked packet from a client, it copies that marking to the CAPWAP-encapsulated packet it sends to the WLC. The original, encapsulated packet retains its marking. It's imperative that the switchports the AP and WLC are connected to don't modify DSCP markings and don't overwrite them.

Policing

Traffic *policing* avoids congestion by rate-limiting (dropping) packets before congestion occurs. But policing is much more nuanced than that. Policing is similar to queuing, with one small difference: rather than classifying each packet according to the packet's properties, as queuing does, policing treats packets differently depending on whether sending or receiving the packet would exceed a certain rate, called the *committed information rate (CIR)*. Any packets that can be sent without exceeding the CIR are said to be conforming, whereas packets that would exceed the CIR are said to be, well, exceeding. Regardless of whether a packet is conforming or exceeding, any packet that a policer processes is said to be a policed packet. You can apply policing to inbound or outbound traffic. Also, you can choose how the policer treats conforming or exceeding packets, but you'll typically pick one of three options:

- Transmit it
- Drop it
- Mark it with a DSCP priority

Let's look at three different ways to configure policing.

Single-Rate, Two-Color Policing

Traffic policing uses colorful terminology, literally. Exceeding traffic is red, and conforming traffic is green. In single-rate, two-color policing, you set one CIR and decide how you want the policer to treat conforming and exceeding traffic. Generally, conforming traffic (green) will be sent untouched, although you may choose to mark it with a particular DSCP value. How you treat exceeding traffic (red) depends on whether you're more interested in congestion avoidance or congestion management. If you are serious about avoiding congestion, you may drop any traffic that exceeds the CIR. Otherwise, you may simply mark exceeding traffic with a low-priority DSCP value.

Token Buckets

The mechanics of policing can get complicated, but it's important to understand them because it's easy to get confused when trying to configure it. Policing works at the packet level using a rather fascinating pay-as-you-go system based on tokens and buckets.

Suppose on an interface you set the CIR for egress traffic to 500,000 bps (equivalent to 500 kbps). A single-rate policer creates a token bucket that can hold up to 500,000 tokens (this is based on the CIR), and it fills up the bucket with these tokens. Now let's say that within the span of one second, the router receives two packets that it must forward: one is 100,000 bits, the other is 450,000 bits. When a router forwards a packet of size x, the policer deducts x tokens from the bucket. Thus, after forwarding the 100,000-bit packet, the policer deducts 100,000 tokens from the bucket, leaving 400,000 left. What about the packet that's 450,000 bits? There are only 400,000 tokens left in the bucket, which isn't enough to cover the 450,000-bit packet. The policer therefore drops the packet. In short, if there are enough tokens to cover a packet, the packet is conforming. Otherwise, the packet is exceeding.

Token Replenishment

The policer replenishes the token bucket with a certain number of tokens based on the time gap between received packets. This is intuitive because if the bucket was continuously being filled completely all the time, no policing would ever occur. To simplify the formula, for every 1/500,000 of a second that there's no traffic, one token is added to the bucket. So, after one second of no traffic, the bucket will be replenished with 500,000 tokens.

Single-Rate, Three-Color Policing

Think of three-color policing as a sort of soft policing where there's a little wiggle room above and beyond the CIR. To use a driving analogy, imagine you're driving to an appointment. If the speed limit is 35 miles per hour (MPH), you might be able to go 40 MPH without getting pulled over, and you'd make it to your appointment on time. But if you go 50 MPH, you're likely to get a ticket—delaying your arrival and possibly making you late. And if you're going 70 MPH, you might not make it to your appointment at all! Three-color policing entails coloring packets one of three colors:

- Green—Packets marked green are conforming and are sent. They may optionally be marked.
- Yellow—These packets are considered exceeding but are still allowed. They're marked with a low-priority DSCP.
- Red—These are considered violating and are dropped.

Single-rate, three-color policing differs from two-color policing in a couple of ways. First, it uses two token buckets instead of one: the *committed burst* bucket (the bc bucket) and the *excess burst* bucket (the be bucket). The principle of operation for the buckets is mostly the same, but neither token bucket's size is constrained by the CIR.

The bc Bucket

Suppose you set a CIR of 500,000 bps but make the bc bucket big enough to hold 750,000 tokens, which corresponds to 750,000 bits. The difference between this value (750,000 bits) and the CIR bit value (500,000) is the committed burst size (CBS or bc). In this case, 750,000 − 500,000 = 250,000, so the bc is 250,000 bits. The operation of the bc bucket is the same as the bucket in a single-rate, two-color policer. But it's more forgiving in that you get extra tokens that allow you to momentarily exceed the CIR. To put a finer point on it, any packets that can be covered using tokens in the bc bucket are conforming.

The be Bucket

The be bucket is another token bucket whose size you define explicitly. If you specify an excess burst size (EBS or be) of 125,000 bits, then the be bucket can hold 125,000 tokens. If you run out of tokens in the bc bucket, packets will dip into the be bucket. Any such packets are colored yellow and are said to be exceeding. Usually, exceeding packets are marked down with a lower DSCP priority. Any packets that aren't covered by tokens in the be bucket are violating and are dropped.

 Because nothing in networking is simple, *bc* and *be* are usually expressed in bytes. I've kept them expressed as bits to keep things understandable.

Filling the Bucket

To understand how tokens are replenished with multiple buckets, another example is in order. This time let's assume empty bc and be buckets. To simplify it a bit, tokens are added to the bc bucket every 1/8 second. After one second of no traffic, the bc bucket will be filled with 500,000 tokens (corresponding to the CIR). After another half-second of no traffic, the bc bucket will be replenished with 250,000 more tokens. At this point, the bc bucket is full. (Remember that the bc bucket can hold 750,000 tokens.) However, the be bucket is still empty. Because the bc bucket is full, any more tokens that would have been given to it spill over into the be bucket. Hence, after another 1/4 of a second of no traffic, the be bucket is replenished with 250,000 tokens.

 If you want more details on single-rate, three-color policing, RFC 2697 (https://tools.ietf.org/rfc/rfc2697.txt) makes for great bedtime reading.

Configuring Policing

The following configuration snippet illustrates how to configure a single-rate, three-color policer for ingress traffic. We'll use a CIR of 500,000 bps, a bc of 31,250 bytes (250,000 bits), and a be of 15,625 bytes (125,000 bits).

```
R6(config)#policy-map ingresspolicy
R6(config-pmap)#class class-default
R6(config-pmap-c)#police cir 500000 bc 31250 be 15625
R6(config-pmap-c-police)#conform-action transmit
R6(config-pmap-c-police)#exceed-action set-dscp-transmit af43
R6(config-pmap-c-police)#violate-action drop
R6(config-pmap-c-police)#int gi0/0
R6(config-if)#service-policy input ingresspolicy
```

Conforming packets are transmitted untouched. Exceeding packets are marked with the DSCP AF43. Violating packets are dropped. You can verify that the policer is working as follows:

```
R6(config-if)#do show policy-map interface gi0/0
 GigabitEthernet0/0

  Service-policy input: ingresspolicy

    Class-map: class-default (match-any)
      3146 packets, 1577372 bytes
      5 minute offered rate 31000 bps, drop rate 2000 bps
      Match: any
      police:
          cir 500000 bps, bc 31250 bytes, be 125000 bytes
        conformed 2585 packets, 740378 bytes; actions:
          transmit
        exceeded 510 packets, 761016 bytes; actions:
          set-dscp-transmit af43
        violated 51 packets, 75978 bytes; actions:
          drop
        conformed 15000 bps, exceeded 16000 bps, violated 2000 bps
```

Two-Rate Policing

If you understand the two preceding policing methods, be thankful. You'll find two-rate policing delightfully easy to grasp. In two-rate policing, you define a CIR and a *peak information rate (PIR)*. The CIR has a corresponding bc bucket, and the PIR has a corresponding be bucket. However, the bc and be buckets are filled simultaneously according to the gap between received packets. Also, they're filled at different rates.

Suppose you have a CIR of 500,000 bps and a PIR of 1,000,000 bps. The bc bucket holds 500,000 tokens, and the be bucket holds 1,000,000 tokens. As usual, tokens are deducted from the bc bucket when a packet is policed, according to the size of the packet. What's different, though, is that the same number of tokens is also deducted from the be bucket. This is to avoid the possibility of combining the tokens in both buckets to achieve an undesirable throughput (1.5 kbps in this case!). The number of tokens in the be bucket will always be equal to or greater than the number of tokens in the bc bucket.

Any packets that can be covered solely by tokens in the bc bucket are said to be conforming. If there aren't enough tokens in the bc bucket to cover a packet, the packet dips into the be bucket. These packets are said to be exceeding. If there aren't enough tokens in the bc and be buckets combined to cover an especially large packet, the packet is violating and is dropped.

Another way two-rate policing differs from the other schemes is in how the buckets are replenished. During one second of no traffic, the bc bucket is refilled with 500,000 tokens, and the be bucket is refilled with 1,000,000 tokens. The buckets are filled at different rates, and there is no spillover.

Because policing uses class maps, you can opt to apply policing to only specific classes of traffic.

Queuing

QoS queuing doesn't kick in until there's congestion. The reason is simple: if there's no congestion, then every packet that enters a queue will immediately leave it. It's true that if you have enough bandwidth, you don't need QoS. But it's also true that QoS is cheaper than making sure you always have more than enough bandwidth.

Queuing entails creating multiple queues, each with a different priority. QoS sorts packets into those queues according to the packet's class. At regular intervals, the router services each queue according to some predictable algorithm—a process called scheduling. This way, packets in higher-priority queues experience less delay than packets in lower-priority queues.

How many queues are created, how big they can get, how they're scheduled, and how packets are treated once in a queue all depend on the queuing algorithm you use. Before looking at specific queuing behaviors, it helps to have a high-level understanding of the possible things that can occur with a given packet:

- Queue the packet and
    - Forward it when possible. This will delay the packet, but it will be sent.
    - Drop it later, perhaps to make room in the queue for higher-priority traffic.
- Drop it immediately. This happens when the queue is full and there's no room for any more packets.

With that understanding, let's look at the only two queuing algorithms that Cisco recommends.

Class-Based Weighted Fair Queuing

Class-based weighted fair queuing (CBWFQ) can create up to 256 queues for 256 different traffic classes. CBWFQ is good for TCP-based applications that adapt to bandwidth constraints and packet drops, but is not good for delay-sensitive traffic such as voice. Each class is assigned to a queue, and each queue has a guaranteed bandwidth. When it comes to the size of the queue, you have two choices: tail-drop and weighted random early detection (WRED).

Tail-Drop

You can explicitly set the size of the queue in packets. If a queue becomes full, excess packets are tail dropped. If you use *tail-drop*, it's important to assign TCP and non-TCP traffic to different queues. The reason is that when TCP encounters packet loss, the sender slows down, whereas with non-TCP traffic (namely UDP) the sender will continue to forward packets because it doesn't know there's packet loss. The result is that UDP traffic will consume all the bandwidth! This phenomenon is called *TCP starvation/UDP dominance*. By moving TCP and non-TCP traffic into separate queues, you ensure that TCP isn't crowded out by UDP traffic.

Weighted Random Early Detection

If you've followed the best practice of placing TCP and non-TCP traffic into separate queues, you still may encounter a problem. Suppose TCP traffic fills a queue and packets begin to drop. When using tail-drop, multiple senders of TCP traffic experience packet drops at roughly the same time. In response, they slow down, allowing the queue to drain. At this point, they'll begin sending again, continually ramping up the rate at which they send until the queue fills again, and the cycle continues. The result is that all TCP senders slow down and speed up in a synchronized fashion—a phenomenon called *TCP global synchronization*. It's a problem because senders are never able to efficiently utilize the bandwidth.

WRED eliminates tail-drops by giving you a practically unlimited queue size, but randomly dropping packets in the queue. As the queue grows, more packets are dropped. This ensures that TCP senders don't all experience packet loss at the same time and avoids the problem of TCP global synchronization. For the assured forwarding (AF) PHB DSCP values, WRED uses the drop probability to determine which packets to drop first. For example, packets marked AF14 will be dropped before packets marked AF11, because AF14 has the higher drop probability.

Configuring Class-Based Weighted Fair Queuing

In this scenario, we'll configure CBWFQ for two different classes of traffic. We'll mark incoming ICMP traffic on R1 Gi0/0 with the DSCP value AF43. We'll mark all other traffic with the value AF11. We'll begin on R1 by creating a class map to match ICMP traffic:

```
R1(config)#class-map icmp
R1(config-cmap)#match protocol icmp
R1(config-cmap)#exit
```

Now we create and verify the policy map:

```
R1(config)#policy-map mark
R1(config-pmap)#class icmp
R1(config-pmap-c)#set dscp af43
```

```
R1(config-pmap-c)#class class-default
R1(config-pmap-c)#set dscp af11
R1(config-pmap-c)#do show policy-map
  Policy Map mark
    Class icmp
      set dscp af43
    Class class-default
      set dscp af11
```

Next, apply the policy map inbound on R1's Gi0/0 interface:

```
R1(config-pmap-c)#int gi0/0
R1(config-if)#service-policy input mark
```

In the background, we generate some UDP and ICMP traffic that traverses R1's Gi0/0 interface. R1 marks the traffic accordingly:

```
R1(config-if)#do show policy-map int gi0/0
 GigabitEthernet0/0

  Service-policy input: mark
! ICMP traffic is marked AF43
    Class-map: icmp (match-all)
      5 packets, 570 bytes
      5 minute offered rate 0000 bps, drop rate 0000 bps
      Match: protocol icmp
      QoS Set
        dscp af43
          Packets marked 5
! The UDP traffic doesn't match a class map, so it falls under the class-default and is
! marked AF11.
    Class-map: class-default (match-any)
      11 packets, 968 bytes
      5 minute offered rate 0000 bps, drop rate 0000 bps
      Match: any
      QoS Set
        dscp af11
          Packets marked 11
```

This is all there is to marking packets! But simply marking them does nothing. We must configure R1 to take some action based on these markings. In this case, we want to create two separate queues for AF43 and AF11. For outbound traffic on Gi0/1, we'll use CBWFQ to guarantee 1 kbps of bandwidth to packets marked AF43. For packets marked AF11, we'll guarantee 2 kbps. To do this, we need to create two more class maps:

```
R1(config)#class-map af43
R1(config-cmap)#match dscp af43
R1(config-cmap)#class-map af11
R1(config-cmap)#match dscp af11
```

We create another policy map that will queue packets according to their markings. Packets marked AF43 will be placed in a queue with a guaranteed bandwidth of 1 kbps. We'll limit the size of the queue to five packets.

```
R1(config-cmap)#policy-map cbwfq
R1(config-pmap)#class af43
```

We'll limit the bandwidth to 1 kbps.

```
R1(config-pmap-c)#bandwidth 1000
```

We'll allow the queue to hold up to five packets. Any packets after this will be tail-dropped.

```
R1(config-pmap-c)#queue-limit 5
```

Now we need to configure queuing for packets marked AF11. We'll guarantee these guys a bandwidth of 2 kbps. Instead of setting a queue length, we'll allow an unlimited queue, but use WRED to randomly drop packets within the queue. This prevents the queue from continuously growing.

```
R1(config-pmap-c)#class af11
R1(config-pmap-c)#bandwidth 2000
! Enable WRED
R1(config-pmap-c)#random-detect
```

Lastly, we'll configure the class-default class to place all other traffic into a dynamic number of queues. This is called *fair queuing*. We'll use WRED for these additional queues.

```
R1(config-pmap-c)#class class-default
! Enable fair queuing to dynamically create queues
R1(config-pmap-c)#fair-queue
! Enable WRED
R1(config-pmap-c)#random-detect
```

You can verify the policy map configuration as follows:

```
R1(config-pmap-c)#do show policy-map cbwfq
  Policy Map cbwfq
    Class af43
      bandwidth 1000 (kbps)
      queue-limit 5 packets
    Class af11
      bandwidth 2000 (kbps)
      wred, exponential weight 9
```

class	min-threshold	max-threshold	mark-probablity
0	-	-	1/10
1	-	-	1/10
2	-	-	1/10
3	-	-	1/10
4	-	-	1/10
5	-	-	1/10
6	-	-	1/10
7	-	-	1/10

```
    Class class-default
      wred, exponential weight 9
```

class	min-threshold	max-threshold	mark-probablity
0	-	-	1/10
1	-	-	1/10
2	-	-	1/10
3	-	-	1/10
4	-	-	1/10
5	-	-	1/10
6	-	-	1/10
7	-	-	1/10

```
    Fair-queue
```

Now let's apply the policy map outbound on the Gi0/1 interface:

```
R1(config-pmap-c)#int gi0/1
R1(config-if)#service-policy output cbwfq
```

In the background, we'll generate some more ICMP and UDP traffic that will ingress R1's `Gi0/0` and egress `Gi0/1`. After that, we'll see how R1 has treated these packets:

```
R1(config-if)#do show policy-map int gi0/1
 GigabitEthernet0/1

  Service-policy output: cbwfq

    Class-map: af43 (match-all)
      17385 packets, 24630530 bytes
      5 minute offered rate 194000 bps, drop rate 0000 bps
      Match:  dscp af43 (38)
      Queueing
      queue limit 5 packets
      (queue depth/total drops/no-buffer drops) 0/0/0
      (pkts output/bytes output) 17385/24630530
      bandwidth 1000 kbps
! Output truncated
```

Notice that the 5-minute offered rate for the AF43 class is well over 1 kbps. This is because R1 isn't experiencing any congestion, so the ICMP traffic, even though it's marked AF43, can use all the available bandwidth. Queuing kicks in only when there's congestion.

Low-Latency Queuing

A *low-latency queue* (LLQ) is a strict priority queue that is always serviced first. When you create an LLQ, you specify a reserved bandwidth in kbps or as a percentage of the interface bandwidth. Where LLQ differs dramatically from CBWFQ is that packets in the LLQ are *limited* to the reserved bandwidth during times of congestion. Packets may be dropped from the LLQ if sending them would exceed the reserved bandwidth. As with CBWFQ, you can choose whether to use tail-drops or WRED to control the drop behavior. LLQ includes bursting, allowing the traffic to momentarily exceed the queue's bandwidth allocation. Bursting works the same way as it does in policing, using a token bucket. By default, the burst size is 20 percent of the reserved bandwidth.

Since much of the configuration is the same as CBWFQ, we won't look at a complete example. You'll use class maps to classify and mark packets in the same way, and you'll reference those class maps in policy maps. But you'll use the `priority` command to place traffic in a LLQ. The following policy map will create an LLQ that reserves 10 percent of the bandwidth for real-time traffic. Remember that this also limits such traffic to 10 percent of the bandwidth during times of congestion.

```
R1(config)#policy-map llq
R1(config-pmap)#class realtime
R1(config-pmap-c)#priority ?
```

```
<1-2000000>  Kilo Bits per second
level        Multi-Level Priority Queue
percent      % of total bandwidth
<cr>
```

Let's set the queue bandwidth to 10 percent of the interface bandwidth. Notice that you may optionally configure a burst size.

```
R1(config-pmap-c)#priority percent 10 ?
  <32-2000000>  Burst in bytes
  <cr>
R1(config-pmap-c)#priority percent 10
R1(config-pmap-c)#int gi0/3
R1(config-if)#service-policy out
R1(config-if)#service-policy output llq
R1(config-if)#do show policy-map interface gi0/3
 GigabitEthernet0/3

  Service-policy output: llq

    queue stats for all priority classes:
    Queueing
    queue limit 64 packets
    (queue depth/total drops/no-buffer drops) 0/0/0
    (pkts output/bytes output) 0/0

   Class-map: realtime (match-all)
     0 packets, 0 bytes
     5 minute offered rate 0000 bps, drop rate 0000 bps
     Match: protocol sip
     Priority: 10% (100000 kbps), burst bytes 2500000, b/w exceed drops: 0


   Class-map: class-default (match-any)
     2 packets, 420 bytes
     5 minute offered rate 0000 bps, drop rate 0000 bps
     Match: any

     queue limit 64 packets
     (queue depth/total drops/no-buffer drops) 0/0/0
     (pkts output/bytes output) 2/420
```

It's possible to configure LLQ for multiple classes, each with a different reserved bandwidth. What happens in that case is that traffic from all classes is placed into a single LLQ but each class is policed at its reserved bandwidth. This approach is useful if you want to place both voice and video into the LLQ but want to ensure that video doesn't hog the entire queue.

You can use both CBWFQ and LLQ in the same policy map.

Explicit Congestion Notification

Recall that WRED randomly drops packets as a way of avoiding TCP global synchronization. The goal of *explicit congestion notification (ECN)* is to provide an alternative to dropping TCP packets while still preventing global synchronization from occurring. ECN is used in conjunction with WRED, and you configure it using the `random-detect ecn` policy map command. When you configure ECN, WRED will not drop any packets.

ECN works by getting a TCP sender to slow down the rate at which it sends by reducing its congestion window. When TCP packets begin to build in a queue, WRED randomly selects some of those packets and sets the Congestion Experienced (CE) bit of the ECN field in those packets. It then forwards them normally. The ECN-compatible receiver, when it sends traffic back to the sender, sets the Explicit Congestion Experienced (ECE) flag in the TCP packet. The receiver notes the flag and halves the congestion window size, causing it to slow down the rate at which it sends traffic. ECN doesn't prevent congestion, but by getting the sender to slow down, it avoids unnecessary packet loss.

The ECN field (defined in RFC 3168) is stored in the rightmost (low-order) 2 bits of the IP ToS field. To put it in context, the ECN field sits just to the right of the DSCP field.

Shaping

Traffic *shaping* is useful at edge routers where you're connecting to a service provider that offers transport at a lower speed than the access rate. For example, you may have a router connected to a Metro Ethernet connection using a 1 Gbps interface speed, but your provider limits your transport to 10 Mbps. You could push 100 Mbps of data through the interface, and your router wouldn't encounter any congestion. However, your service provider may drop those packets within its own network. Traffic shaping allows you to deliberately delay outgoing packets by buffering them, thereby avoiding dropped packets. To sum it up, traffic shaping is useful when the other end is policing.

You configure a shaper with a CIR. Any traffic below the CIR is sent immediately. If traffic exceeds the CIR, the shaper simply buffers the excess traffic, releasing it slowly so as not to forward at a rate greater than the CIR. Shaping queues aren't unlimited and may drop packets if the queue grows too large. Shaping works only with outbound traffic. Shaping may seem the antithesis of congestion avoidance, since queues and congestion are almost synonymous. However, by shaping traffic at one end, you can prevent queuing on the opposite end. Configuring shaping is like configuring policing, but simpler. The following example shows how to limit egress traffic to 500,000 bps using a shaper:

```
R6(config)#policy-map shapeEgress
R6(config-pmap)#class class-default
R6(config-pmap-c)#shape average 500000
```

We'll apply the policy map to the interface and generate some traffic:

```
R6(config-pmap-c)#int gi0/0
R6(config-if)#service-policy output shapeEgress
R6(config-if)#do ping 10.0.56.5 repeat 100 size 18000
Type escape sequence to abort.
Sending 100, 18000-byte ICMP Echos to 10.0.56.5, timeout is 2 seconds:
!!!!!!!!!!!!!!!!!!!!!!!!!!!!!!!!!!!!!!!!!!!!!!!!!!!!!!!!!!!!!!!!!!!!!!!!!!
!!!!!!!!!!!!!!!!!!!!!!!!!!!!!!!!
Success rate is 100 percent (100/100), round-trip min/avg/max = 297/305/317 ms
```

Let's verify the configuration.

```
R6(config-if)#do show policy-map int gi0/0 output
 GigabitEthernet0/0

  Service-policy output: shapeEgress

    Class-map: class-default (match-any)
      2061 packets, 2878056 bytes
      5 minute offered rate 71000 bps, drop rate 0000 bps
      Match: any
      Queueing
      queue limit 64 packets
      (queue depth/total drops/no-buffer drops) 0/0/0
      (pkts output/bytes output) 2061/2878056
      shape (average) cir 500000, bc 2000, be 2000
      target shape rate 500000
```

Shaping operates on the same token bucket system as policing. However, instead of having to decide to send, mark, or drop the packet based on the number of tokens in the bucket, shaping just needs to decide whether to send or hold the packet. Like policing, shaping allows bursting beyond the CIR. Notice in the preceding output that the shaper has calculated a bc size of 2,000 bytes and a be size of 2,000 bytes.

Summary

Not all packets are created equal, and during times of congestion, packets for delay and drop-sensitive applications must be given priority over others. Using class maps and policy maps, you can classify and mark packets according to their tolerance for delays and drops. It's worth noting that once you configure marking, it occurs all the time, even when there's no congestion.

Of course, preventing congestion in the first place is ideal. Policing is a congestion avoidance mechanism that groups packets into colors: green, red, and sometimes yellow. You can configure policing to allow, drop, or re-mark a packet depending on its color. In two-color policing, you'll typically allow green (conforming) traffic and drop red (exceeding) traffic. In three-color policing, you may mark down yellow (exceeding) traffic and drop red (violating) traffic. The specific actions you take are up to you.

The goal of congestion avoidance is to prevent queues from forming in the first place. Outside of policing, the only way to avoid congestion is to add more bandwidth, which is expensive and time-consuming. There's a pervasive logical contradiction in networking literature that says congestion avoidance involves dropping packets from queues. Of course, the very presence of queues indicates congestion is already happening. You can't avoid congestion after it's started. The best you can do is perform congestion management, which involves using scheduling to prioritize some packets over others, and even dropping packets from queues.

Once a packet is marked and congestion begins to occur, queuing will organize packets into separate queues according to their markings. Using CBWFQ, you define multiple queues and assign a guaranteed bandwidth to each. Based on markings, you decide how packets are sorted in those queues. Using LLQ, you have one strict priority queue that's always serviced first, up to its reserved bandwidth. Keep in mind that you can use both CBWFQ and LLQ in the same policy map. To address packets building up in a queue, you can either allow the queue to fill up and tail-drop excess packets, or you can use WRED to randomly drop packets from the queue.

Exam Essentials

Know the reasons for using policing and shaping.   Policing helps prevent congestion by dropping inbound or outbound packets that would cause congestion. Shaping delays outbound packets to avoid packet loss.

Understand how packets are marked.   The usual way of marking packets is using class maps and policy maps. But you can also use policing to mark packets according to color.

Understand how queuing works.   Queuing works like this: Packets are sorted into multiple queues. The queuing algorithm services each queue on a schedule according to its configured bandwidth. LLQs are always serviced first. Within any queue, packets are processed in FIFO order. In other words, once packets are in a queue, they're not rearranged. Some may be dropped, as in the case of WRED, but not shuffled around.

Be able to configure policing, shaping, and queuing.   A little practice goes a long way! Keep it simple but spend some time practicing configuring two- and three-color policing and shaping. Then try your hand at configuring CBWFQ and low-latency queuing.

Exercises

EXERCISE 9.1

On a router and interface of your choice, configure a single-rate, three-color policer with a CIR of 500 kbps, a committed burst size of 250,000 bits, and an exceeding burst size of 125,000 bits. Ensure exceeding traffic is marked AF43 and violating traffic is dropped.

EXERCISE 9.2

On another router, and on an interface of your choice, mark ingress ICMP traffic with the DSCP value AF43 and all other traffic with the value AF11. On a different interface, use CBWFQ with WRED to reserve 1 kbps for packets marked AF43, and 2 kbps for packets marked AF11.

Review Questions

You can find the answers in the appendix.

1. How many classes does the Class Selector PHB group include?

   A. 6

   B. 7

   C. 8

   D. 9

2. Which Class Selector value has the highest priority?

   A. LE

   B. CS0

   C. CS1

   D. CS2

3. Which of the following DSCP PHB groups lets you choose a drop precedence?

   A. CS

   B. AF

   C. EF

   D. CoS

4. AF code points take the format AFxy. What do x and y indicate? (Choose two.)

   A. x is drop priority

   B. x is priority

   C. y is drop precedence

   D. y is priority

5. Which of the following DSCP values is best for TCP-based video teleconferencing traffic?

   A. CS1

   B. EF

   C. CS0

   D. AF41

6. A router receives an IP packet encapsulated in an Ethernet frame tagged with a PCP value of 0. The router isn't configured with any QoS tools. What will happen when the router forwards the IP packet to its next hop over Ethernet?

   A. Convert the PCP to DSCP

   B. Encapsulate the IP packet inside an Ethernet frame with no CoS marking

   C. Preserve the PCP value when forwarding the frame

   D. Drop the frame

7. What is true of traffic policing? (Choose two.)

    A. It can be applied to inbound traffic.

    B. It is always applied to all traffic.

    C. It can be applied to outbound traffic.

    D. Packets that are exceeding are always discarded.

8. In single-rate, two-color policing, given a CIR of 150 kbps, how many tokens can the token bucket hold?

    A. 150

    B. 1,500

    C. 15,000

    D. 150,000

9. In three-color policing, what does red mean?

    A. Packets are violating and will be marked down.

    B. Packets are violating and will be dropped.

    C. Packets are exceeding and will be marked down.

    D. Packets are exceeding and will be dropped.

10. In three-color policing, what does yellow mean?

    A. Packets are violating and will be marked down.

    B. Packets are violating and will be dropped.

    C. Packets are exceeding and will be marked down.

    D. Packets are exceeding and will be dropped.

11. On a router you configure a single-rate, three-color egress policer with a CIR of 1 Mbps, a committed burst size of 64,000 bytes, and an excess burst of 32,000 bytes. In one second, a packet 262,500 bytes in size comes in and must be forwarded. What will the router do with this packet?

    A. Immediately forward it untouched

    B. Drop it

    C. Forward it and mark it down

    D. Queue it

12. A single-rate, three-color egress policer receives a packet. The policer's bc and be buckets are full. To forward the packet would require using all tokens in the bc bucket, without needing to dip into the be bucket. What will happen to the packet?

    A. It will be dropped.

    B. It will be marked down and forwarded.

    C. It will be forwarded as is.

    D. It will be queued.

13. What is true of shaping? (Choose two.)

    A. It works only on outbound traffic.

    B. It works only on inbound traffic.

    C. It may drop packets.

    D. It decreases delay.

14. How does configuring LLQ for voice packets reduce packet delay?

    A. Voice packets are placed at the front of the queue.

    B. The LLQ is emptied before other queues.

    C. The LLQ is given unlimited bandwidth.

    D. TCP packets in the LLQ are dropped.

15. Which queuing algorithm is best for TCP-based applications?

    A. LLQ

    B. CBWFQ

    C. FIFO

    D. WRED

16. With a single, rate, three-color policer, which of the following is true when a packet is violating?

    A. No tokens are removed from any bucket.

    B. Tokens are removed from the bc bucket.

    C. Tokens are removed from the be bucket.

    D. Tokens are removed from both the bc and be buckets.

17. Which of the following can prevent TCP global synchronization?

    A. WRED

    B. Tail-drop

    C. FIFO

    D. Policing

18. What interface configuration command applies the policy map "mark" to ingress traffic?

    A. `policy-map input mark`

    B. `class-map input mark`

    C. `service-policy egress mark`

    D. `service-policy input mark`

19. Which policy map configuration commands enable CBWFQ with WRED? (Choose two.)

- **A.** `priority`
- **B.** `bandwidth`
- **C.** `random-detect`
- **D.** `fair-queue`

20. Which policy map configuration command enables LLQ?

- **A.** `priority`
- **B.** `bandwidth`
- **C.** `random-detect`
- **D.** `fair-queue`

Chapter

10

Network Virtualization

THE CCNP ENCOR EXAM OBJECTIVES COVERED IN THIS CHAPTER INCLUDE THE FOLLOWING:

Domain 2.0 Virtualization

✓ **2.1** Describe device virtualization technologies

✓ **2.2** Configure and verify data path virtualization technologies

✓ **2.3** Describe network virtualization concepts

People love to use the term *virtual*. We have virtual machines, virtual networks, virtual disks, virtual memory, and so on. Unfortunately, the word has been used in so many different products and contexts that we've ended up with a lexicon of similar, even almost identical terms that mean completely different things. In this chapter, we're concerned only with virtualization as it relates to networking. There are four terms that we're especially interested in:

Virtual machine

Virtual networking

Network virtualization

Network functions virtualization

Virtual machine is a term you're probably quite familiar with. But the networking terms are a lot more ambiguous and ill defined. In this chapter, we're going to smoke out the different meanings behind these terms and get some clarity on what "virtual" means. In this chapter, we'll cover the following topics:

Virtual Machines and Server Virtualization

Network Virtualization

Generic Routing Encapsulation (GRE) Tunnels

IPsec

Location/ID Separation Protocol (LISP)

Virtual Extensible LAN (VXLAN)

Virtual Routing and Forwarding (VRF) Tables

Virtual Machines, Hypervisors, and Network Virtualization

In this section, we'll begin by distinguishing between two major types of virtualization:

- Virtual machines and server virtualization
- Network virtualization

You're undoubtedly already aware of many differences between the two. But when you start talking about "virtual networking," "virtual networks," and "network virtualization," things get confusing.

Virtual Machines and Server Virtualization

A *virtual machine (VM)* is an emulated computer running inside a real computer. To be more precise, a real computer running an operating system (OS) runs a VM that runs its own OS. Confusing, right? Simply put, machine virtualization is the act of running one OS inside of another. The outer or parent OS is the host OS, and the virtual OS is called the guest OS. This setup is often called server virtualization, but that term is a bit misleading because server virtualization isn't unique to servers. The term came about because servers were the earliest machines to be virtualized. But any personal computer made within the past 15 years can run a VM.

A VM may be nested inside of another VM. But ultimately, the VM at the top of the stack is running on a real computer.

Hypervisors

The host OS runs natively on x86 hardware, or "bare metal." The host OS contains a software program called a virtual machine monitor (VMM) or *hypervisor* that creates VMs, which are essentially software-emulated computers consisting of CPU, memory, storage, and networking. The guest OS runs inside the VM. Hypervisors are classified into two types: type-1 and type-2. Surprisingly, the terms don't refer to different types of hypervisors, but rather how those hypervisors are implemented and used.

Type-1 Hypervisors—Server Virtualization   Type-1 hypervisors are specially geared toward running VMs on server hardware. Some type-1 hypervisors are VMware ESXi, Microsoft Hyper-V, KVM, and Xen. There's a pervasive myth that type-1 hypervisors run natively on hardware, or "bare metal." But even a type-1 hypervisor is just a program that runs inside an OS. Microsoft Hyper-V, for example, runs on a stripped-down version of Windows Server. What defines a type-1 hypervisor is a customized, stripped-down host OS and lack of a robust GUI interface.

Type-2 Hypervisors—Virtualization for the Masses   Type-2 hypervisors are built for running VMs on a typical personal computer. Some type-2 hypervisors are Oracle VirtualBox, VMware Fusion, VMware Workstation Pro, and Parallels. These are designed to be installed on an existing host OS, so they come with a more robust and (usually) user-friendly interface.

The mythical distinction between type-1 and type-2 hypervisors is so ingrained that you're likely to see a question about it on the ENCOR exam. In that case, it's better to give the answer they're looking for, rather than the correct one. Why the confusion? The type-1 classification conflates the mostly invisible OS with the hypervisor itself. To sum it up, type-1 hypervisors are for server virtualization, and they don't have a lot of bells and whistles. Type-2 hypervisors are made for running VMs on your laptop. The difference between type-1 and type-2 hypervisors comes down to how easy it is to distinguish the hypervisor from the host OS and whether the hypervisor has a robust user interface.

Virtual Machine Networking

Let's bring this around to networking. Hypervisors provide a virtual switch that VMs use to communicate with other VMs on the same host, as well as network devices outside of the VM host. In virtual switching, the hypervisor provides each VM with a virtual NIC (vNIC) that's connected to the virtual switch. Multiple vNICs can connect to a single vSwitch, allowing VMs on a host to communicate with one another at layer 2 without having to go out to a physical switch. Some common virtual switches are as follows:

- **VMware vSwitch**—Comes with VMware ESXi
- **Cisco Application Virtual Switch**—Can be integrated with VMware ESXi
- **Open vSwitch**—Integrates with Xen, KVM, and Oracle VirtualBox

Figure 10.1 shows VM-to-VM layer 2 traffic traversing a virtual switch. Switching is handled by the virtual switch, so the inter-VM traffic never leaves the host.

FIGURE 10.1   L2 VM-to-VM traffic using a virtual switching architecture

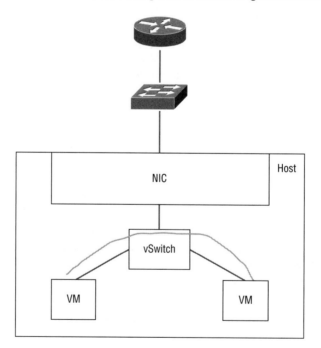

The vSwitch may also be connected to the host's physical NIC to allow VMs to get layer 2 access to the outside world. The light gray line in Figure 10.2 shows the path VM traffic takes through the vSwitch, to the physical NIC, and finally to a physical switch. vSwitches can provide 802.1Q VLAN tagging to separate traffic at layer 2, reducing the need for multiple physical connections to a VM host.

FIGURE 10.2   L2 VM-to-switch traffic using a virtual switching architecture

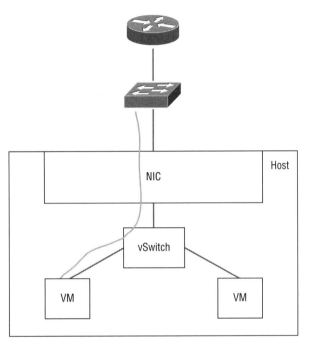

Network Virtualization

We just covered virtual networks, which refer to the virtual network devices provided by a hypervisor, such as virtual NICs and virtual switches. So, what's network virtualization? We should start with a truism: the term *network virtualization* is redundant because all data networks are virtual. Networks are by definition an abstraction of physical connections. Not surprisingly, people use the term network virtualization in completely different and unrelated ways. Network virtualization may refer to

- Network function virtualization (NFV)
- Network overlays

And these aren't the same thing. Let's distinguish the two, starting with the former.

Network Function Virtualization

If you have experience with server virtualization, NFV will be easy to grasp, although the acronyms will get messy. NFV takes the features and functionality of proprietary network equipment and implements them in VMs. These VMs—or virtual appliances—are called *virtual network functions (VNFs)*. For example, the Cisco CSR1000v is a virtual router that runs in a VM, making it a popular choice for deployment both on-premises and in the cloud. You probably don't think of a router as a network function (IP *routing* is a network function, whereas a router is a device). But in the bizarre world of NFV, the entire virtual router is considered a VNF. Using Figure 10.3, let's look at an example of how VMs in different subnets but running on the same host can communicate using a router VNF.

FIGURE 10.3   L3 VM-to-VM traffic using a virtual switch and router VNF

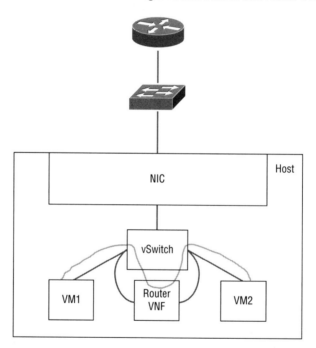

Each VM has a single vNIC connected to the vSwitch. The VNF has two vNICs, also connected to the switch. If VM1 needs to send an IP packet to VM2, the following occurs:

1. VM1 encapsulates the IP packet in an Ethernet frame addressed to the router VNF and forwards it.

2. The vSwitch sends the frame to the router VNF.

3. The router VNF performs IP routing, then reencapsulates the IP packet in an Ethernet frame addressed to VM2 and forwards it.

4. The vSwitch switches the frame to VM2.

The functionality of a VNF isn't limited to routing. Some official VNFs include

- Cisco Integrated Services Virtual Router (ISRv)
- Cisco Firepower Next-Generation Firewall Virtual (NGFWv)
- Cisco Adaptive Security Virtual Appliance (ASAv)

It's important to note that because VNFs are VMs, they can run on any type-1 or type-2 hypervisors. There are also third-party VNFs that provide load balancing and WAN optimization.

Single-Root I/O Virtualization

Server virtualization has been common for well over a decade, but we're only now beginning to see VNFs being widely implemented. One reason for this is that until now, the network performance of VNFs couldn't match that of purpose-built, hardware-based routers and switches.

One of the breakthroughs that improved network performance of VNFs is single-root I/O virtualization (SR-IOV). SR-IOV allows multiple VNFs to share the same physical NIC on a VM host. The way it works is pretty clever: the physical NIC presents itself as multiple separate NICs called virtual functions (VFs). You connect each VM to a different VF, and all VNFs can share the same physical NIC. Note that the hypervisor's virtual switch doesn't make an appearance here. The VM is virtually connected direct to the VF, with no virtual switch in between. How then do VNFs on the same host communicate? The answer is edge virtual bridging.

Edge Virtual Bridging

The term *edge virtual bridging (EVB)* describes using a physical switch to pass layer 2 traffic between VMs running on the same host. But a physical switch isn't necessarily what you think. There are two approaches to implementing EVB:

Internal Edge Virtual Bridging   The physical NIC includes an internal switch that bridges traffic between separate VFs. Essentially, we're moving the hypervisor's virtual switch into the physical NIC! This is called virtual Ethernet bridge (VEB) mode, an odd name considering that the bridge is actually built into the physical NIC. Figure 10.4 illustrates internal edge virtual bridging.

External Edge Virtual Bridging   Traffic from one VNF goes out of the physical NIC to a physical switch, then comes back into the same NIC. This approach is called hairpinning or, as the IEEE 802.1Qbg standard calls it, reflective relay. Figure 10.5 shows an example of external switching using EVB. To use reflective relay, you must configure the NIC to operate in Virtual Ethernet Port Aggregator (VEPA) mode. Also, remember that by default a switch won't forward a frame back out the same interface it was received on. To get around this, you must enable reflective relay on the external switch. To enable reflective relay on a Nexus switch, use the interface configuration command `switchport mode virtual-ethernet-bridge`.

FIGURE 10.4 L2 VM-to-VM traffic switched internally using edge virtual bridging

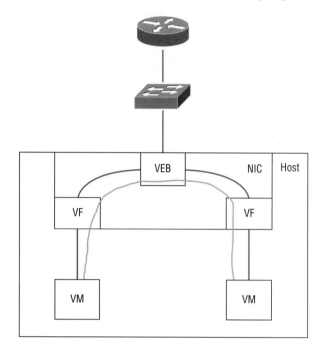

FIGURE 10.5 L2 VM-to-VM traffic switched externally using edge virtual bridging

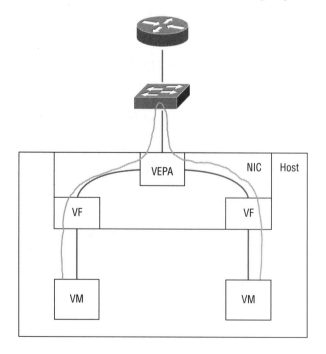

SR-IOV is not a purely software function. The physical NIC must support SR-IOV.

Network Overlays

Most of the time, when people speak of network virtualization, they're talking about overlay networks. A common example of an overlay network is a VPN, which is just a layer 3 network riding on top of (overlaying) another underlying layer 3 network (underlay). Hence, the "real" network is the underlay and the VPN is the overlay. Of course, VPNs aren't the only overlays that exist. Any protocol that uses the word *tunnel* creates an overlay. For example, IPsec tunnels, GRE tunnels, and layer 2 tunnels are all examples of virtual network overlays. Broadly, there are three types of overlays:

Overlay type	Examples
Layer 3 over layer 3	GRE, IPsec tunnels, MPLS L3VPN, LISP
Layer 2 over layer 3	VXLAN, OTV
Layer 2 over layer 2	802.1Q tunneling (Q-in-Q)

You'll notice that layer 3 over layer 2 is absent from the list. IP over Ethernet, for instance, is just a normal network. We don't consider IP riding over Ethernet an overlay network because it's just following the layered approach of the OSI model. But when we start reversing or recursing the layers, then we have a network overlay.

The purpose of overlays is generally to provide something that the underlay can't, such as segmentation, access control, or encryption. Sometimes, people use overlays just because they're convenient. It's much easier to migrate a VM from one data center to another when both data centers share a stretched VLAN. (I hope you never do this outside of a lab environment.) The flexibility of overlay technologies makes it easy to do all sorts of things that you shouldn't, but that doesn't negate the real advantages overlays provide. In the following sections, we're going to cover several overlay technologies, including

- Generic Routing Encapsulation (GRE)
- IP Security (IPsec)
- Location/ID Separation Protocol (LISP)
- Virtual eXtensible Local Area Network (VXLAN)

Generic Routing Encapsulation Tunnels

Generic routing encapsulation (GRE)—defined in RFC 2784—allows you to tunnel almost any layer 3 protocol over another. GRE tunnels are useful when you need to send packets that aren't supported by the underlying network or underlay. The underlay is what we think of as the "physical" network. Some useful tunnel configurations include:

IPv4 over IPv4   Typically used to form a site-to-site VPN tunnel when combined with IPsec. But GRE is also useful for sending multicast traffic over an underlay that supports only unicast traffic.

IPv6 over IPv4   You can't natively route IPv6 packets over routers that only support IPv4. But you can create a GRE tunnel that encapsulates the IPv6 packet inside an IPv4 packet with a GRE header. In GRE-speak, IPv6 is the passenger protocol and IPv4 is the transport protocol. To add some more terminology, the passenger protocol forms the overlay, and the transport protocol forms the underlay.

Configuring a GRE Tunnel to Tunnel IPv4 and IPv6 over IPv4

Let's look at an example of tunneling both IPv4 and IPv6 over IPv4. Consider the topology in Figure 10.6.

FIGURE 10.6   Underlay topology running BGP. R1 (AS 65001) and R2 (AS 65001), each connected to ISP (AS 65555)

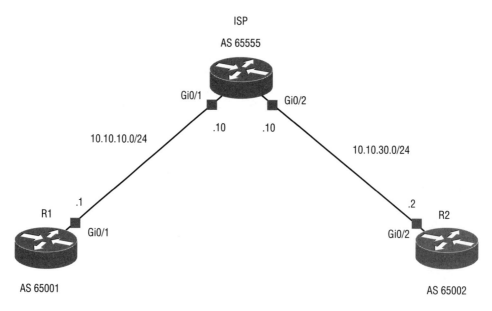

In this diagram, R1 and R2 both have BGP peerings to an ISP router and are advertising their physical interface IP addresses. These IP addresses will serve as the tunnel endpoint addresses, since they demarcate where the tunnel terminates. Figure 10.7 illustrates the concept.

FIGURE 10.7   GRE topology

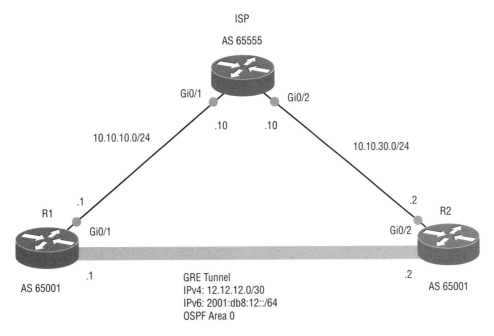

When you configure GRE encapsulation on a router, the router creates a virtual tunnel interface that it treats as a connected interface, so the overlay network appears in the IP routing table as a connected network. You can configure a tunnel interface much like a physical interface. For example, you assign it an IPv4 or IPv6 address, which you can advertise to your favorite IGP. Effectively, it's just another interface, but it's virtual instead of physical. The virtual network formed by the GRE tunnel is called an overlay network, since it runs over the underlying physical network.

 GRE uses IP protocol number 47 for both IPv4 and IPv6 endpoints.

We'll configure a GRE tunnel between R1 and R2. The tunnel interfaces will have both IPv4 and IPv6 addresses. We'll also advertise some IPv4 addresses across the tunnel interface using OSPFv2, and IPv6 addresses using OSPFv3. Note that we will not be establishing any BGP sessions over the tunnel. Let's configure the tunnel interface on R1. We'll start by verifying underlay connectivity:

```
R1#ping 10.10.30.2
Type escape sequence to abort.
Sending 5, 100-byte ICMP Echos to 10.10.30.2, timeout is 2 seconds:
!!!!!
Success rate is 100 percent (5/5), round-trip min/avg/max = 7/8/11 ms
R1#conf t
Enter configuration commands, one per line.  End with CNTL/Z.
```

We need to enable IPv6 unicast routing:

```
R1(config)#ipv6 unicast-routing
```

Next let's create the tunnel interface:

```
R1(config)#int tunnel12
R1(config-if)#
%LINEPROTO-5-UPDOWN: Line protocol on Interface Tunnel12, changed state to down
```

Configure the overlay tunnel IPv4 address:

```
R1(config-if)#ip address 12.12.12.1 255.255.255.252
```

Configure the overlay IPv6 address:

```
R1(config-if)#ipv6 address 2001:db8:12::1/64
```

Specify the underlay tunnel source address (R1's Gi0/1 interface address):

```
R1(config-if)#tunnel source 10.10.10.1
```

Specify the underlay tunnel destination address (R2):

```
R1(config-if)#tunnel destination 10.10.30.2
R1(config-if)#
%LINEPROTO-5-UPDOWN: Line protocol on Interface Tunnel12, changed state to up
```

We'll specify the tunnel encapsulation mode of GRE over IP. This isn't necessary, as the tunnel mode will default to GRE, but it's a good idea to be explicit.

```
R1(config-if)#tunnel mode gre ip
```

Let's confirm that both the IPv4 and IPv6 routes are in the respective RIBs:

```
R1(config-if)#do show ip route | i 12.
      12.0.0.0/8 is variably subnetted, 2 subnets, 2 masks
C        12.12.12.0/30 is directly connected, Tunnel12
L        12.12.12.1/32 is directly connected, Tunnel12
```

```
R1(config-if)#do show ipv6 route | b 2001
C   2001:DB8:12::/64 [0/0]
     via Tunnel12, directly connected
L   2001:DB8:12::1/128 [0/0]
     via Tunnel12, receive
L   FF00::/8 [0/0]
     via Null0, receive
```

Now let's configure the tunnel interface on R2:

```
R2#ping 10.10.30.2
Type escape sequence to abort.
Sending 5, 100-byte ICMP Echos to 10.10.30.2, timeout is 2 seconds:
!!!!!
Success rate is 100 percent (5/5), round-trip min/avg/max = 1/2/4 ms
R2#conf t
Enter configuration commands, one per line.  End with CNTL/Z.
R2(config)#ipv6 unicast-routing
R2(config)#int tun12
R2(config-if)#
%LINEPROTO-5-UPDOWN: Line protocol on Interface Tunnel12, changed state to down
R2(config-if)#ip address 12.12.12.2 255.255.255.252
R2(config-if)#ipv6 address 2001:db8:12::2/64
R2(config-if)#tunnel source 10.10.30.2
R2(config-if)#tunnel destination 10.10.10.1
R2(config-if)#
%LINEPROTO-5-UPDOWN: Line protocol on Interface Tunnel12, changed state to up
R2(config-if)#tunnel mode gre ip
R2(config-if)#^Z
```

Now let's verify IPv4 and IPv6 connectivity over the tunnel:

```
R2#ping 12.12.12.1
Type escape sequence to abort.
Sending 5, 100-byte ICMP Echos to 12.12.12.1, timeout is 2 seconds:
!!!!!
Success rate is 100 percent (5/5), round-trip min/avg/max = 8/8/9 ms
R2#ping 2001:db8:12::1
Type escape sequence to abort.
Sending 5, 100-byte ICMP Echos to 2001:DB8:12::1, timeout is 2 seconds:
!!!!!
Success rate is 100 percent (5/5), round-trip min/avg/max = 8/9/10 ms
```

Advertising IPv4 Routes over a Tunnel Using OSPFv2

Advertising prefixes over a tunnel interface is no different than on a physical interface. We'll enable OSPF on the tunnel interface on R1:

```
R1(config)#router ospf 1
R1(config-router)#network 12.12.12.1 0.0.0.0 area 0
```

And on R2:

```
R2(config-router)#network 12.12.12.2 0.0.0.0 area 0
R2(config-router)#
%OSPF-5-ADJCHG: Process 1, Nbr 12.12.12.1 on Tunnel12 from LOADING to FULL,
Loading Done

R2(config-router)#network 2.2.2.2 0.0.0.0 area 0
```

We'll also create and advertise a loopback:

```
R2(config-router)#int lo20
R2(config-if)#ip address 2.2.2.2 255.255.255.255
```

Back on R1, a view of the IP routing table shows a route to R2's loopback address:

```
R1(config)#do show ip route ospf | b 2.0
      2.0.0.0/32 is subnetted, 1 subnets
O        2.2.2.2 [110/1001] via 12.12.12.2, 00:00:30, Tunnel12
R1(config)#do ping 2.2.2.2 source tun12
Type escape sequence to abort.
Sending 5, 100-byte ICMP Echos to 2.2.2.2, timeout is 2 seconds:
Packet sent with a source address of 12.12.12.1
!!!!!
Success rate is 100 percent (5/5), round-trip min/avg/max = 9/10/11 ms
```

Advertising IPv6 Routes over a Tunnel Using OSPFv3

Next, we'll enable OSPFv3 on the tunnel interfaces. We'll also create an IPv6 loopback on R2 and advertise it. Let's start with R1:

```
R1#conf t
Enter configuration commands, one per line.  End with CNTL/Z.
R1(config)#router ospfv3 1
R1(config-router)#router-id 1.1.1.1
R1(config-router)#int tun12
```

Add the tunnel interface to OSPF area 0:

```
R1(config-if)#ospfv3 1 ipv6 area 0
```

And now we'll enable OSPFv3 on R2's tunnel interface:

```
R2(config)#router ospfv3 1
R2(config-router)#address-family ipv4 unicast
R2(config-router-af)#router-id 2.2.2.2
R2(config-router-af)#int tun12
R2(config-if)#ospfv3 1 ipv6 area 0
R2(config-if)#
%OSPFv3-5-ADJCHG: Process 1, IPv6, Nbr 1.1.1.1 on Tunnel12 from LOADING to FULL,
Loading Done
! The OSPFv3 adjacency with R1 comes up
R2(config-if)#do show ipv6 ospf neighbor

           OSPFv3 Router with ID (2.2.2.2) (Process ID 1)

Neighbor ID    Pri   State         Dead Time   Interface ID    Interface
1.1.1.1          0   FULL/ -       00:00:38    9               Tunnel12
```

Let's create an IPv6 loopback and advertise it:

```
R2(config-if)#int lo20
%LINEPROTO-5-UPDOWN: Line protocol on Interface Loopback20, changed state to up
R2(config-if)#ipv6 address 2001:db8::20/128
! Advertise it via OSPFv3
R2(config-if)#ospfv3 1 ipv6 area 0
```

R1's IPv6 routing table shows R2's IPv6 loopback:

```
R1(config-if)#do show ipv6 route ospf | b 2001
O   2001:DB8::20/128 [110/1000]
     via FE80::E5A:6FF:FE26:2F00, Tunnel12
! Test connectivity
R1#ping 2001:db8::20 source tunnel 12
Type escape sequence to abort.
Sending 5, 100-byte ICMP Echos to 2001:DB8::20, timeout is 2 seconds:
Packet sent with a source address of 2001:DB8:12::1
!!!!!
Success rate is 100 percent (5/5), round-trip min/avg/max = 8/9/11 ms
```

Two separate OSPF processes are running: OSPFv2 carrying the IPv4 routes and OSPFv3 carrying the IPv6 routes.

```
R1(config)#do show ip ospf interface brief
Interface   PID   Area        IP Address/Mask    Cost  State Nbrs F/C
Tu12        1     0           12.12.12.1/30      1000  P2P   1/1
R1(config)#do show ipv6 ospf interface brief
Interface   PID   Area        Intf ID    Cost  State Nbrs F/C
Tu12        1     0           9          1000  P2P   1/1
```

Recursive Routing

Recursive routing occurs when a route to a tunnel endpoint uses the tunnel interface itself as the next hop. This can happen when you use the same routing protocol to advertise tunnel endpoint prefixes over both the tunnel *and* the physical interfaces used for the tunnel endpoints. To illustrate, we'll establish a BGP session over the tunnel between R1 and R2. On R1, we'll redistribute connected routes via BGP. Recall that BGP is already running on the physical interfaces, and it's advertising the tunnel endpoint prefixes.

```
R1(config)#router bgp 65001
R1(config-router)#neighbor 12.12.12.2 remote-as 65001
R1(config-router)#redistribute connected
```

On R2, after completing the peering relationship, the tunnel immediately collapses:

```
R2(config)#router bgp 65001
R2(config-router)#neighbor 12.12.12.1 remote-as 65001
R2(config-router)#
%BGP-5-ADJCHANGE: neighbor 12.12.12.1 Up
%ADJ-5-PARENT: Midchain parent maintenance for IP midchain out of Tunnel12 -
looped chain attempting to stack
R2(config-router)#
%TUN-5-RECURDOWN: Tunnel12 temporarily disabled due to recursive routing
%LINEPROTO-5-UPDOWN: Line protocol on Interface Tunnel12, changed state to down
%OSPFv3-5-ADJCHG: Process 1, IPv6, Nbr 1.1.1.1 on Tunnel12 from FULL to DOWN,
Neighbor Down: Interface down or detached
%OSPF-5-ADJCHG: Process 1, Nbr 12.12.12.1 on Tunnel12 from FULL to DOWN,
Neighbor Down: Interface down or detached
```

Why this happens isn't immediately obvious. But if you enable IP routing debugs, you'll see the problem:

```
R2#debug ip routing
IP routing debugging is on
R2#
RT: updating bgp 10.10.10.0/24 (0x0)  :
    via 12.12.12.1   0 1048577

RT: closer admin distance for 10.10.10.0, flushing 1 routes
RT: add 10.10.10.0/24 via 12.12.12.1, bgp metric [200/0]
RT: updating bgp 12.12.12.0/30 (0x0)  :
    via 12.12.12.1   0 1048577
RT: rib update return code: 17
R2#
%ADJ-5-PARENT: Midchain parent maintenance for IP midchain out of Tunnel12 -
looped chain attempting to stack
R2#
%TUN-5-RECURDOWN: Tunnel12 temporarily disabled due to recursive routing
```

The Tunnel 12 endpoint is `10.10.10.1` (R1), but the route for `10.10.10.0/24` points to the Tunnel 12 interface (`12.12.12.1`).

```
R2#show int tunnel 12 | i destination|GRE
   Tunnel source 10.10.30.2, destination 10.10.10.1
   Tunnel protocol/transport GRE/IP
```

In other words, the best path to the tunnel endpoint is through the tunnel itself! That forms a loop, and the tunnel collapses. (Incidentally, this command also shows you the tunnel encapsulation type.) A good rule of thumb is not to use the same routing protocol to advertise the underlay network into the overlay network, or vice versa. To solve our ugly tunnel problem, we'll simply break the neighborship between R1 and R2:

```
R2(config)#router bgp 65001
R2(config-router)#no neighbor 12.12.12.1 remote-as 65001
R2(config-router)#
%BGP-3-NOTIFICATION: sent to neighbor 12.12.12.1 6/3 (Peer De-configured) 0
bytes
R2(config-router)#
%BGP_SESSION-5-ADJCHANGE: neighbor 12.12.12.1 IPv4 Unicast topology base removed
from session  Neighbor deleted
%BGP-5-ADJCHANGE: neighbor 12.12.12.1 Down Neighbor deleted
```

The tunnel comes back up and this time it stays up:

```
%LINEPROTO-5-UPDOWN: Line protocol on Interface Tunnel12, changed state to up
%OSPF-5-ADJCHG: Process 1, Nbr 12.12.12.1 on Tunnel12 from LOADING to FULL,
Loading Done
R2(config-router)#
%OSPFv3-5-ADJCHG: Process 1, IPv6, Nbr 1.1.1.1 on Tunnel12 from LOADING to FULL,
Loading Done
```

If for some reason you want to advertise the tunnel endpoints over the tunnel, be sure to use a routing protocol with a higher administrative distance than the one you're using to learn the tunnel endpoint prefixes.

IP Security

IP Security (IPsec) is used to encrypt traffic between two endpoints, be they a router and a computer, two computers, or two routers. As network professionals, we're primarily concerned with setting up IPsec tunnels between routers (which includes firewalls). Our goal isn't to force every host to use end-to-end encryption. Rather, our goal is to make sure traffic is encrypted when traversing insecure or public networks. This includes the Internet, of course, but it can also include private carrier networks, such as Multiprotocol Label Switching (MPLS) or Metro Ethernet circuits. Therefore, when discussing IPsec peers or endpoints, understand that I'm referring to routers and not end-user hosts.

In addition to encryption, IPsec offers data integrity to ensure data isn't changed in transit. It also provides authentication using preshared keys or cryptographic certificates. IPsec's features—encryption, integrity, and authentication—come from the combination of two technologies: Internet Key Exchange (IKE) and Encapsulating Security Payload (ESP).

Here's an overview of how IPsec works: Peers that wish to exchange IPsec packets must first authenticate each other and then exchange symmetric encryption keys that they'll use for encrypting network traffic. Once they've done this, they negotiate an IPsec security association (SA), which is just a fancy term for an IPsec tunnel.

Internet Key Exchange

Peers use the *Internet Key Exchange (IKE)* protocol to exchange the encryption keys that they'll use to encrypt IPsec traffic. They use IKE to generate and exchange keys using the Diffie-Hellman (DH) algorithm. The peers authenticate each other using a shared secret or cryptographic certificate. Once peers authenticate each other, they're said to have established an IKE security association (SA), which is essentially a tunnel. It's important to understand that this is not the same as an IPsec tunnel. IKE is used only for exchanging encryption keys. It's not used for network transport. IKE uses UDP port 500, and the current version of IKE is IKEv2 (RFC 7296).

 You'll see the acronym ISAKMP, which stands for Internet Security Association Key Management Protocol. IKE is just an implementation of ISAKMP, so the two are used interchangeably.

Encapsulating Security Payload

IPsec itself normally uses the *Encapsulating Security Payload (ESP)* protocol (IP protocol 50, RFC 4303) to provide encryption and authentication. Once peers establish an IKE SA and exchange keys, they use those keys to establish an IPsec SA. The ESP header contains several important fields, including the following:

- **Security parameters index**—Identifies which IPsec SA a packet belongs to.

- **Sequence number**—Designed to prevent replay attacks. The sequence number increments with each unicast packet.

- **Integrity check value**—ESP calculates a checksum over the unencrypted data and stores the checksum in this field. If the data is changed in transit, the receiver can detect it.

ESP operates in two different modes: transport and tunnel. The impact of these different modes isn't readily obvious and may even seem trivial. But when we get to configuring them, you'll see the differences.

Transport Mode

In transport mode, only the IP payload is encrypted. For example, suppose you send an IP/UDP packet with some data. The UDP packet and its payload will be encrypted, but the

IP header will not be encrypted. Instead, the source address and destination address in the IP header are preserved intact, and the IP protocol number is changed to 50. After the IP header comes the ESP header, followed by the encrypted payload. The resulting IP packet is routed normally.

Tunnel Mode

In tunnel mode, the entire inner IP packet is encrypted. For instance, if you send an IP/UDP packet, ESP encrypts the entire IP packet, including the IP headers that hold the original source and destination addresses. In other words, to an outside observer, the entire IP packet just looks like gibberish. ESP thus appends its own IP header, with the source and destination addresses always those of the IPsec peers. This is the same idea behind GRE, except with an IPsec header instead of a GRE header.

 ESP always inserts the ESP header between the unencrypted IP header and the encrypted payload. The IP protocol number in the IP header is always changed to 50, indicating that the ESP header follows.

Configuring IPsec in Transport Mode with a GRE Tunnel

In this scenario, we'll create a GRE tunnel and encrypt the GRE packets. In a plain GRE tunnel, the payload (IPv4 or IPv6 traffic) traversing the tunnel is unencrypted. By encrypting the GRE packets that encapsulate the payload, we also encrypt the payload itself. Let's start by configuring ISAKMP on R1:

```
R1(config)#crypto isakmp policy 1
```

We'll use a preshared key for authentication:

```
R1(config-isakmp)#authentication pre-share
```

Let's use SHA-256 as the hashing algorithm for key exchange:

```
R1(config-isakmp)#hash sha256
```

And we'll use AES as the encryption algorithm for key exchange:

```
R1(config-isakmp)#encryption aes
```

DH group 14 corresponds to a 2,048-bit key size. Cisco recommends using group 14 or higher:

```
R1(config-isakmp)#group 14
```

R1's shared secret with R2 (10.10.30.2) is mysecret:

```
R1(config-isakmp)#crypto isakmp key mysecret address 10.10.30.2
```

For encrypting the payload, use AES for encryption and a secure hash algorithm–hash-based message authentication code (SHA-HMAC) for authentication:

```
R1(config)#crypto ipsec transform-set mytransformset esp-aes esp-sha-hmac
R1(cfg-crypto-trans)#mode ?
  transport  transport (payload encapsulation) mode
  tunnel     tunnel (datagram encapsulation) mode
```

We'll select transport mode so that only the payload, and not the entire IP packet, is encrypted:

```
R1(cfg-crypto-trans)#mode transport
```

Next let's configure the IPsec profile, which is a convenient way to tie the tunnel interface to the transform set:

```
R1(cfg-crypto-trans)#crypto ipsec profile myprofile
R1(ipsec-profile)#set transform-set mytransformset
```

The GRE tunnel between R1 and R2 is already established. Now we just need to apply the IPsec profile to it. IPsec profiles replace the old crypto maps, which required you to create an ACL to specify traffic to be encrypted and had to be applied to a physical interface. The tunnel protection tunnel interface command causes IOS to automatically encrypt and decrypt the GRE packets using IPsec:

```
R1(ipsec-profile)#int tunnel12
R1(config-if)#tunnel protection ipsec profile myprofile
R1(config-if)#
%CRYPTO-6-ISAKMP_ON_OFF: ISAKMP is ON
R1(config-if)#
%LINEPROTO-5-UPDOWN: Line protocol on Interface Tunnel12, changed state to down
%OSPFv3-5-ADJCHG: Process 1, IPv6, Nbr 2.2.2.2 on Tunnel12 from FULL to DOWN,
Neighbor Down: Interface down or detached
%OSPF-5-ADJCHG: Process 1, Nbr 12.12.12.2 on Tunnel12 from FULL to DOWN,
Neighbor Down: Interface down or detached
R1(config-if)#
%CRYPTO-4-RECVD_PKT_NOT_IPSEC: Rec'd packet not an IPSEC packet. (ip) vrf/dest_
addr= /10.10.10.1, src_addr= 10.10.30.2, prot= 47
```

R1 is now encrypting its GRE packets to R2. R2, however, isn't yet configured to use IPsec, so it continues to send unencrypted GRE packets, and R1 complains. Let's go to R2 and configure it to use IPsec:

```
R2(config)#crypto isakmp policy 1
R2(config-isakmp)#authentication pre-share
R2(config-isakmp)#hash sha256
R2(config-isakmp)#encryption aes
R2(config-isakmp)#group 14
```

Configure the shared secret with R1 (10.10.10.1):

```
R2(config-isakmp)#crypto isakmp key mysecret address 10.10.10.1
R2(config)#crypto ipsec transform-set mytransformset esp-aes esp-sha-hmac
R2(cfg-crypto-trans)#mode transport
R2(cfg-crypto-trans)#crypto ipsec profile myprofile
R2(ipsec-profile)#set transform-set mytransformset
R2(ipsec-profile)#int tunnel12
R2(config-if)#tunnel protection ipsec profile myprofile
R2(config-if)#
%CRYPTO-6-ISAKMP_ON_OFF: ISAKMP is ON
R2(config-if)#
%OSPF-5-ADJCHG: Process 1, Nbr 12.12.12.1 on Tunnel12 from LOADING to FULL,
Loading Done
R2(config-if)#
%OSPFv3-5-ADJCHG: Process 1, IPv6, Nbr 1.1.1.1 on Tunnel12 from LOADING to FULL,
Loading Done
```

The GRE tunnel gloriously reemerges, this time encrypted with IPsec. This is validation enough, but you should know a few troubleshooting commands as well. Let's view the ISAKMP security association with R1:

```
R2#show crypto isakmp sa
IPv4 Crypto ISAKMP SA
dst            src            state        conn-id status
10.10.10.1     10.10.30.2     QM_IDLE         1001 ACTIVE
```

QM_IDLE indicates that R1 and R2 authenticated each other using the shared secret. Now let's view the IPsec SA details:

```
R2#show crypto ipsec sa | i interface|10.10.|Transport|bound esp
interface: Tunnel12
   Crypto map tag: Tunnel12-head-0, local addr 10.10.30.2
  local  ident (addr/mask/prot/port): (10.10.30.2/255.255.255.255/47/0)
  remote ident (addr/mask/prot/port): (10.10.10.1/255.255.255.255/47/0)
  current_peer 10.10.10.1 port 500
   local crypto endpt.: 10.10.30.2, remote crypto endpt.: 10.10.10.1
! We're using IPsec transport mode on both R1 and R2
     inbound esp sas:
        in use settings ={Transport, }
     outbound esp sas:
        in use settings ={Transport, }
```

IPsec is encrypting all traffic between 10.10.30.2 (R2) and 10.10.10.1 (R1), which are the configured GRE tunnel endpoints. Therefore, all tunnel traffic is also encrypted.

But let's check anyway! R2 tells us that some packets have already been encrypted and decrypted:

```
R2#show crypto ipsec sa | i caps
    #pkts encaps: 211, #pkts encrypt: 211, #pkts digest: 211
    #pkts decaps: 235, #pkts decrypt: 235, #pkts verify: 235
```

Let's send a ping over the tunnel:

```
R2#ping 12.12.12.1
Type escape sequence to abort.
Sending 5, 100-byte ICMP Echos to 12.12.12.1, timeout is 2 seconds:
!!!!!
Success rate is 100 percent (5/5), round-trip min/avg/max = 18/20/26 ms
R2#show crypto ipsec sa | i caps
    #pkts encaps: 218, #pkts encrypt: 218, #pkts digest: 218
    #pkts decaps: 242, #pkts decrypt: 242, #pkts verify: 242
```

The number of packets encrypted and decrypted have incremented. What about IPv6 traffic? Pinging R1's IPv6 overlay address shows that IPv6 traffic is also being encrypted:

```
R2#ping 2001:db8:12::1
Type escape sequence to abort.
Sending 5, 100-byte ICMP Echos to 2001:DB8:12::1, timeout is 2 seconds:
!!!!!
Success rate is 100 percent (5/5), round-trip min/avg/max = 14/17/27 ms
R2#show crypto ipsec sa | i caps
    #pkts encaps: 257, #pkts encrypt: 257, #pkts digest: 257
    #pkts decaps: 281, #pkts decrypt: 281, #pkts verify: 281
R2#ping 2001:db8:12::1
Type escape sequence to abort.
Sending 5, 100-byte ICMP Echos to 2001:DB8:12::1, timeout is 2 seconds:
!!!!!
Success rate is 100 percent (5/5), round-trip min/avg/max = 20/24/32 ms
```

 Packets that don't traverse the GRE tunnel are *not* encrypted.

Configuring IPsec in Tunnel Mode

If you've already configured a GRE tunnel and an IPsec profile, switching over to IPsec tunnel mode is easy. You just change the tunnel interface mode to IPsec:

```
R2(config)#int tun12
R2(config-if)#tunnel mode ipsec ipv4
```

```
R2(config-if)#
%LINEPROTO-5-UPDOWN: Line protocol on Interface Tunnel12, changed state to down
%OSPFv3-5-ADJCHG: Process 1, IPv6, Nbr 1.1.1.1 on Tunnel12 from FULL to DOWN,
Neighbor Down: Interface down or detached
%OSPF-5-ADJCHG: Process 1, Nbr 12.12.12.1 on Tunnel12 from FULL to DOWN,
Neighbor Down: Interface down or detached
R2(config-if)#
%CRYPTO-4-RECVD_PKT_INV_SPI: decaps: rec'd IPSEC packet has invalid spi for
destaddr=10.10.30.2, prot=50, spi=0x8AFA02F7(2331640567), srcaddr=10.10.10.1,
input interface=GigabitEthernet0/2
R2(config-if)#
```

Of course, it seems easy because we already did most of the work. To put this simple change in context, let's look at the entire tunnel interface configuration:

```
R2(config-if)#do show run int tun12
Building configuration...

Current configuration : 243 bytes
!
interface Tunnel12
 ip address 12.12.12.2 255.255.255.252
 ipv6 address 2001:DB8:12::2/64
 ospfv3 1 ipv6 area 0
 tunnel source 10.10.30.2
 tunnel mode ipsec ipv4
 tunnel destination 10.10.10.1
 tunnel protection ipsec profile myprofile
end
```

The required elements for IPsec tunnel mode are a tunnel source and destination, tunnel protection profile, and of course, the tunnel mode set to IPsec. Let's make the corresponding change on R1:

```
R1#conf t
Enter configuration commands, one per line.  End with CNTL/Z.
R1(config)#int tun12
R1(config-if)#tunnel mode ipsec ipv4
R1(config-if)#
%LINEPROTO-5-UPDOWN: Line protocol on Interface Tunnel12, changed state to up
%OSPF-5-ADJCHG: Process 1, Nbr 12.12.12.2 on Tunnel12 from LOADING to FULL,
Loading Done
```

The IPsec SA output looks familiar, with a small difference: we're now using tunnel mode.

```
R1(config-if)#do show crypto ipsec sa | i interface|10.10.|Tunnel,|bound esp
interface: Tunnel12
    Crypto map tag: Tunnel12-head-0, local addr 10.10.10.1
  current_peer 10.10.30.2 port 500
    local crypto endpt.: 10.10.10.1, remote crypto endpt.: 10.10.30.2
    inbound esp sas:
      in use settings ={Tunnel, }
    outbound esp sas:
      in use settings ={Tunnel, }
```

 IPsec also supports a protocol called the Authentication Header. It provides authentication and can tell whether a packet has been modified in transit, but it doesn't provide encryption and is thus rarely used.

Location/ID Separation Protocol

The location/ID separation protocol (LISP, RFCs 6830 through 6833) is designed to reduce the growth of the global Internet routing tables. The RFCs that define LISP and its components are hard to follow and obscure how its mechanisms actually achieve its stated goal. Conceptually, LISP has some things in common that you might not think of as being related. It bears striking similarities to BGP and the Domain Name System (DNS). If you're familiar with Dynamic Multipoint Virtual Private Network (DMVPN) with Next Hop Resolution Protocol (NHRP), you'll also notice some similarities. Essentially, LISP does two things:

- Allows a router to discover the IP address of a router that has knowledge of a prefix

- Creates a dynamic tunnel between the routers so that they can exchange traffic to and from that prefix

Consider again the topology in Figure 10.6. There are two sites, each with a BGP peering to an ISP. Imagine that each site is advertising hundreds of different prefixes. Although the diagram shows only one ISP router, in real life these routes would be propagated and aggregated throughout the Internet, adding to the total size of the global Internet routing table.

LISP aims to reduce this growth by avoiding the need of each site to advertise multiple prefixes into BGP. Instead, LISP routers advertise their prefixes—called *endpoint IDs (EIDs)*—to a *map resolver/map server (MR/MS)* that is reachable by both sites—usually over the Internet.

LISP doesn't have widespread adoption. Nevertheless, it exists, and some large organizations use it, so you should at least understand how it works. Let's start by considering the topology in Figure 10.8.

FIGURE 10.8   Using LISP for IP mobility

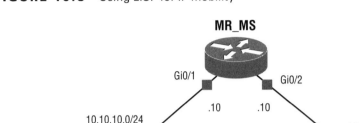

xTR1 has a connected route for 172.16.3.3/32 and an Internet-facing IP address of 10.10.10.1, which is its *routing locator (RLOC)*. xTR1 is configured to use MR_MS as its map server/map resolver. xTR1 creates an EID-to-RLOC mapping that maps the EID 172.16.3.3/32 to its RLOC 10.10.10.1 and registers this mapping with the map server. The terminology may sound strange, but this is somewhat like advertising the 172.16.3.3/32 prefix with a next-hop address of 10.10.10.1.

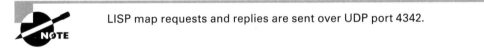

LISP map requests and replies are sent over UDP port 4342.

xTR2, at the other site, has MR_MS configured as its map resolver. When XTR2 needs to send an IP packet to 172.16.3.3/32, it sends a map request to the map resolver. The map resolver then returns a map reply with the EID-to-RLOC mapping, indicating an EID of 172.16.3.3/32 and xTR1's RLOC of 10.10.10.1.

At this point, xTR2 encapsulates the IP packet in an IP/UDP packet addressed to xTR1's RLOC 10.10.10.1, UDP port 4341. xTR1 receives it, decapsulates the outer IP/UDP packet, and sends the inner IP packet to the EID—172.16.3.3/32.

LISP Terminology

The LISP terminology is not what you're used to, and it appears a lot in the configuration, so it helps to explicitly define some terms before starting. A LISP router can be an *ingress tunnel router (ITR)*, *egress tunnel router (ETR)*, or both (xTR). I'll warn you that these definitions are obtuse and won't make much sense at first, but once you see the configuration things will start to come together.

Ingress Tunnel Router (ITR)

An ITR receives a packet from an endpoint, encapsulates it in a LISP packet, and sends it addressed to an ETR's RLOC. An ITR sends EID-to-RLOC map requests to a map resolver and receives replies back.

Egress Tunnel Router (ETR)

An ETR decapsulates LISP packets received from an ITR and sends the inner packet along to the EID. The RLOC is just the IP address of an ETR that's globally reachable. An ETR registers EID-to-RLOC mappings with the map server.

Map Server/Map Resolver

The map server receives and stores mappings from ETRs. An ITR sends a map request for an EID to the map resolver, which responds with the RLOC address of the ETR that has the EID. Map servers and map resolvers perform separate functions, but they're often the same device. Map servers and map resolvers are conceptually like DNS servers and resolvers. A map server/map resolver isn't considered a LISP router.

Essentially, LISP helps an ITR router discover on which ETR an EID is located. It then creates a dynamic tunnel between the ITR and the ETR. It's not much different than creating a GRE tunnel between two routers to create an overlay network. The advantage of the map server/map resolver is IP mobility. An EID can move around to different locations and still be reachable (again, not unlike BGP).

Configuring LISP

In this scenario we'll configure the simple dual-homed LISP topology shown in Figure 10.8. Although you might think of this as consisting of two sites, LISP terminology defines a LISP site as edge routers under a single technical administration—much like a BGP autonomous system. In our case, both xTR1 and xTR2 are part of the same LISP site.

Although not shown, the configuration begins with two BGP sessions established between

▪ xTR1 and MR_MS

▪ xTR2 and MR_MS

For simplicity, MR_MS functions as both the map server/map resolver and core router. But in a real-world implementation they would be different devices.

Configuring the LISP Map Resolver/Map Server

We'll start by configuring the map server and map resolver.

```
MR_MS#conf t
Enter configuration commands, one per line.  End with CNTL/Z.
MR_MS(config)#router lisp
```

Configure the LISP site with the name coastal:

```
MR_MS(config-router-lisp)#site coastal
```

The xTRs will use an authentication key to register EID-to-RLOC mappings with the map server:

```
MR_MS(config-router-lisp-site)#authentication-key mysecret
```

Define the EID prefixes that the map server will accept mappings for. For flexibility, we'll define 172.16.0.0/16 and allow more specific prefixes to be registered.

```
MR_MS(config-router-lisp-site)#eid-prefix 172.16.0.0/16 accept-more-specifics
MR_MS(config-router-lisp-site)#exit
```

Let's enable the map server for IPv4 addresses:

```
MR_MS(config-router-lisp)#ipv4 map-server
```

And enable the map resolver for IPv4 addresses:

```
MR_MS(config-router-lisp)#ipv4 map-resolver
MR_MS(config-router-lisp)#exit
```

Configuring xTR1

Now let's configure xTR1 as a combination ITR and ETR, also known as an xTR:

```
xTR1(config-if)#router lisp
```

We want to periodically probe the other xTR to validate locator reachability:

```
xTR1(config-router-lisp)#loc-reach-algorithm rloc-probing
```

Next, we'll add a database mapping the EID 172.16.3.3/32 to the xTR1's RLOC 10.10.10.1:

```
xTR1(config-router-lisp)#database-mapping 172.16.3.3/32 10.10.10.1 priority 1
weight 1
```

We want to use the map resolver to discover other RLOCs for the EID:

```
xTR1(config-router-lisp)#database-mapping 172.16.3.3/32 auto-discover-rlocs
```

Let's define the map resolver:

```
xTR1(config-router-lisp)#ipv4 itr map-resolver 10.10.10.10
```

We'll make xTR1 an ingress tunnel router:

```
xTR1(config-router-lisp)#ipv4 itr
%LINEPROTO-5-UPDOWN: Line protocol on Interface LISP0, changed state to up
! Notice that the preceding command creates a LISP0 interface.
```

Next, let's define the map server:

```
xTR1(config-router-lisp)#ipv4 etr map-server 10.10.10.10 key mysecret
```

And we'll also make xTR1 an egress tunnel router:

```
xTR1(config-router-lisp)#ipv4 etr
XTR1(config-router-lisp)#exit
```

Next, we'll configure xTR1 with a loopback address of 172.16.3.3/32:

```
xTR1(config)#int lo1
xTR1(config-if)#
%LINK-3-UPDOWN: Interface Loopback1, changed state to up
xTR1(config-if)#
%LINEPROTO-5-UPDOWN: Line protocol on Interface Loopback1, changed state to up
xTR1(config-if)#ip address 172.16.3.3 255.255.255.255
```

We will *not* advertise this prefix into BGP. The only routes in the BGP RIB are those needed to reach xTR1's and xTR2's RLOCs.

```
XTR1(config-if)#do show ip bgp | b Network
     Network          Next Hop          Metric LocPrf Weight Path
  r> 10.10.10.0/24    10.10.10.10            0             0 65555 i
  *> 10.10.30.0/24    10.10.10.10            0             0 65555 i
```

A quick check of the LISP database shows the 172.16.3.3/32 EID is reachable via xTR1:

```
xTR1(config-if)#do show ip lisp database
LISP ETR IPv4 Mapping Database for EID-table default (IID 0), LSBs: 0x1
Entries total 1, no-route 0, inactive 0

172.16.3.3/32, auto-discover-rlocs
  Locator     Pri/Wgt Source    State
  10.10.10.1   1/1    cfg-addr  site-self, reachable
```

Configuring xTR2

Now let's configure xTR2. The commands will be almost identical to xTR1, but we'll register a different EID-to-RLOC mapping:

```
xTR2#conf t
Enter configuration commands, one per line.  End with CNTL/Z.
xTR2(config)#router lisp
xTR2(config-router-lisp)#loc-reach-algorithm rloc-probing
```

Register the EID 172.16.3.3/32 with xTR2's RLOC of 10.10.30.2:

```
xTR2(config-router-lisp)#database-mapping 172.16.3.3/32 10.10.30.2 priority 1 weight 1
xTR2(config-router-lisp)# database-mapping 172.16.3.3/32 auto-discover-rlocs
xTR2(config-router-lisp)# ipv4 itr map-resolver 10.10.30.10
xTR2(config-router-lisp)# ipv4 itr
xTR2(config-router-lisp)# ipv4 etr map-server 55.55.55.55 key mysecret
xTR2(config-router-lisp)# ipv4 etr
xTR2(config-router-lisp)#exit
```

The EID 172.16.3.3/32 is not in xTR2's IP routing table. Therefore, xTR2 registers this EID with the map server as unreachable via its own RLOC. Let's view the LISP database on xTR2.

```
xTR2(config)#do sh ip lisp database
LISP ETR IPv4 Mapping Database for EID-table default (IID 0), LSBs: 0x1
Entries total 1, no-route 1, inactive 0
*** ALL ACTIVE LOCAL EID PREFIXES HAVE NO ROUTE ***
***     REPORTING LOCAL RLOCS AS UNREACHABLE    ***
172.16.3.3/32, auto-discover-rlocs *** NO ROUTE TO EID PREFIX ***
  Locator     Pri/Wgt  Source     State
! XTR1 reports the EID is reachable
  10.10.10.1   1/1     auto-disc  site-other, report-reachable
! XTR2 reports that the EID is not reachable
  10.10.30.2   1/1     cfg-addr   site-self, unreachable
```

The LISP Internet Groper (LIG) shows the current EID-to-RLOC mappings:

```
xTR2(config)#do lig 172.16.3.3
Mapping information for EID 172.16.3.3 from 10.10.10.1 with RTT 17 msecs
172.16.3.3/32, uptime: 00:04:31, expires: 23:59:59, via map-reply, self,
complete
  Locator     Uptime     State      Pri/Wgt
! The active RLOC is 10.10.10.1
  10.10.10.1  00:04:31   up            1/1
  10.10.30.2  00:03:32   admin-down  255/1
```

The output indicates that 172.16.3.3/32 is reachable via 10.10.10.1 (xTR1). The admin-down flag next to 10.10.10.2 (xTR2) indicates that xTR2 has registered a negative map entry for the EID because it doesn't have an IP route to 172.16.3.3/32. Let's try to ping the EID from xTR2:

```
xTR2(config)#do ping 172.16.3.3
Type escape sequence to abort.
Sending 5, 100-byte ICMP Echos to 172.16.3.3, timeout is 2 seconds:
!!!!!
Success rate is 100 percent (5/5), round-trip min/avg/max = 9/14/28 ms
```

Once again, the prefix is not in the IP routing table. However, it is in the CEF FIB:

```
xTR2(config)#do show ip route 172.16.3.3
% Network not in table
xTR2(config)#do show ip cef lisp eid remote
Prefix                  Fwd action  Locator status bits
0.0.0.0/0               signal      0x00000000
  packets/bytes         0/0
172.16.3.3/32           encap       0x00000001
  packets/bytes         10/860
```

Simulating IP Mobility

Now comes the real test. We're going to move 172.16.3.3/32 from xTR1 to xTR2. To do this, we'll remove the loopback interface from xTR1:

```
xTR1(config-if)#no int lo1
xTR1(config)#
%LINK-5-CHANGED: Interface Loopback1, changed state to administratively down
%LINEPROTO-5-UPDOWN: Line protocol on Interface Loopback1, changed state to down
```

This will immediately trigger xTR1 to send a negative mapping entry to the map server. This entry indicates that xTR1 no longer has reachability to the 172.16.3.3/32 EID. At this point, the map server has no mappings for the 172.16.3.3/32 EID:

```
xTR1(config)#do lig 172.16.3.3
Mapping information for EID 172.16.3.3 from 10.10.10.10 with RTT 9 msecs
172.16.3.3/32, uptime: 00:00:33, expires: 00:00:59, via map-reply, self, forward-native
  Negative cache entry, action: forward-native
```

Now we'll create a new loopback interface on xTR2 and add the EID 172.16.3.3/32 to it.:

```
xTR2(config)#int lo1
%LINK-3-UPDOWN: Interface Loopback1, changed state to up
xTR2(config-if)#
%LINEPROTO-5-UPDOWN: Line protocol on Interface Loopback1, changed state to up
xTR2(config-if)#ip address 172.16.3.3 255.255.255.255
```

The LIG output shows that the EID has flip-flopped from xTR1 to xTR2:

```
xTR2(config-if)#do lig self
Mapping information for EID 172.16.3.3 from 10.10.10.1 with RTT 160 msecs
172.16.3.3/32, uptime: 00:00:00, expires: 1d00h, via map-reply, self, complete
  Locator     Uptime    State       Pri/Wgt
! The EID via xTR1 is showing down, because now xTR1 is advertising it as unreachable
  10.10.10.1  00:00:00  admin-down  255/1
```

! **XTR2 has a route to the EID, so it advertises it to the map server as reachable**
  10.10.30.2 00:00:00 up, self   1/1

Now let's go to xTR1 and attempt to ping the EID:

```
xTR1(config)#do ping 172.16.3.3
Type escape sequence to abort.
Sending 5, 100-byte ICMP Echos to 172.16.3.3, timeout is 2 seconds:
!!!!!
Success rate is 100 percent (5/5), round-trip min/avg/max = 8/9/12 ms
```

Let's look at some more detailed CEF output this time:

```
xTR1(config)#do show ip cef lisp eid remote 172.16.3.3
Prefix                Fwd action  Locator status bits
172.16.3.3/32           encap       0x00000002
  packets/bytes      10/860
  path list 10AC962C, 3 locks, per-destination, flags 0x49 [shble, rif, hwcn]
    ifnums:
      LISP0(11): 10.10.30.2
    1 path
      path 10AC9B7C, share 1/1, type attached nexthop, for IPv4
```
! **Notice the next hop is the RLOC of xTR2 (10.10.30.2), forwarded out of the**
! **LISP0 interface**
```
        nexthop 10.10.30.2 LISP0, IP midchain out of LISP0, addr 10.10.30.2 0F6A4028
    1 output chain
      chain[0]: IP midchain out of LISP0, addr 10.10.30.2 0F6A4028
              IP adj out of GigabitEthernet0/1, addr 10.10.10.10 0F6A4158
```

We can see that packets are being switched using LISP by viewing the interface statistics:

```
xTR1#show int lisp 0 switching
LISP0
```

Protocol IP				
Switching path	Pkts In	Chars In	Pkts Out	Chars Out
Process	0	0	9	1224
Cache misses	0	-	-	-
Fast	0	0	0	0
Auton/SSE	0	0	0	0

```
NOTE: all counts are cumulative and reset only after a reload.
```

In this case, packets are processed switched because they're generated by the xTR1 router. When forwarding packets from other hosts, the router would use CEF switching instead.

To illustrate how LISP helps keeps the global routing tables clean, look at the IP routing table on the core MR_MS router. It doesn't have the `172.16.3.3/32` prefix:

```
MR_MS#show ip route | b 10.
      10.0.0.0/8 is variably subnetted, 4 subnets, 2 masks
C        10.10.10.0/24 is directly connected, GigabitEthernet0/1
L        10.10.10.10/32 is directly connected, GigabitEthernet0/1
C        10.10.30.0/24 is directly connected, GigabitEthernet0/2
L        10.10.30.10/32 is directly connected, GigabitEthernet0/2
```

To reiterate, the `172.16.3.3/32` prefix never appears anywhere in a BGP RIB. The MR_MS router, acting as the core, only passes LISP-encapsulated data traffic between xTR1 and xTR2. MR_MS isn't configured as a LISP ITR or ETR, and it doesn't encapsulate or decapsulate any LISP-encapsulated data traffic.

LISP can also be used with IPv6 EIDs and IPv4 RLOCs, allowing you to use it to tunnel IPv6 traffic over IPv4 networks. This isn't the purpose of LISP, but it's a valid use of it. Also, it's worth noting that LISP doesn't extend subnets across layer 3 networks—which is a bad idea anyway. It is, however, sometimes used as a control plane protocol with LAN extensions such as VXLAN, which we'll cover in the next section.

Is LISP a Routing Protocol?

LISP is more like a shared IP routing table. ETRs register their EIDs with a map server. The map server stores these EID-to-RLOC mappings. The EID is just a prefix, and the RLOC looks and acts an awful lot like a next hop—the two very things you'd find in an IP routing table entry—except instead of being stored on a router, the routes are stored on a map server. LISP doesn't perform shortest-path calculations like a routing protocol does.

Virtual Extensible Local Area Network

A VXLAN (RFC 7348) lets you create layer 2 tunnels across layer 3 networks. More specifically, it tunnels Ethernet frames over IP/UDP. This makes it even easier to create large, stretched subnets—something I've been ranting against throughout this book. Although I recommend using routed versus switched connections whenever possible, I must admit that VXLAN is fun to configure and experiment with. Some server virtualization vendors encourage using VXLAN in this way to facilitate moving virtual machines between data centers without having to change their IP addresses. This is a terrible idea, but it's a common practice.

Here's the overview of how VXLAN works: A switch configured as a *VXLAN tunnel endpoint (VTEP)* has a normal switched interface that's typically connected to a host, such as a VM host. If the host sends a frame toward the VTEP, the following occurs:

1. The switched interface on the VTEP receives an Ethernet (MAC) frame from the host.

2. The VTEP prepends a VXLAN header and tucks the entire thing in an IP/UDP packet, addressed to a peer VTEP over UDP port 4789.

3. The VTEP sends the packet to the peer VTEP over a routed network.

4. The peer VTEP decapsulates the MAC frame from the UDP packet.

5. The peer VTEP forwards the frame out based on its destination MAC address.

Of course, configuring VXLAN is a little more complicated than such simplicity suggests. To really understand VXLAN, we need to briefly revisit how Ethernet works.

MAC Address Learning

Ethernet doesn't have a separate control plane protocol for learning the interface location of MAC addresses. Switches learn the location of MAC addresses by sniffing the source MAC address of incoming frames. If a switch receives a frame addressed to an unknown MAC address, it simply floods the frame with the hope that the destination will respond, allowing the switch to learn what interface it's reachable on. This is an example of data plane learning. VXLAN natively performs data plane learning, too, except that it uses IP multicast to implement a similar flood-and-learn approach. Here's how it works:

1. VTEPs all join a shared multicast group.

2. When one VTEP receives an unknown unicast frame or broadcast on its switched interface, it encapsulates the MAC frame in a VXLAN packet and sends it to the multicast group.

3. Other VTEPs in the group receive the packet and make note of the sending VTEP's source IP address and the source MAC address in the encapsulated frame. Each VTEP adds this information to its MAC address table.

In short, VTEPs use multicast to initially flood unknown unicasts and broadcasts. Peers receiving these multicasts learn the source MAC addresses and which VTEP to reach them on.

Forwarding

To reiterate, unknown unicasts are always flooded via multicast. *Known* unicasts, however, are handled differently. When a VTEP needs to send traffic to a MAC address that it knows is reachable via a peer VTEP, it encapsulates the frame and addresses the VXLAN packet to the peer VTEP's *unicast* address. This reduces the amount of multicast traffic and saves other VTEPs from having to receive and process useless traffic.

Configuring VXLAN

We'll illustrate a simple flood-and-learn VXLAN configuration using multicast. In the diagram in Figure 10.9, we have two Nexus virtual switches—SW1 and SW2—connected to each other via a routed link. Note that this link could just as well be any number of routers. The point is that the switches have no layer 2 connectivity and are only connected via IP. R1 is connected to SW1, and R2 is connected to SW2. Notice that both routers reside in VLAN 50 on their respective switches and share a common IP subnet (172.16.1.0/24). To reemphasize, these are two separate layer 2 domains. We're going to use VXLAN to bridge these domains, creating one stretched subnet. When we're done, R1 and R2 will be able to exchange Ethernet frames at layer 2.

FIGURE 10.9   VXLAN flood-and-learn configuration using multicast

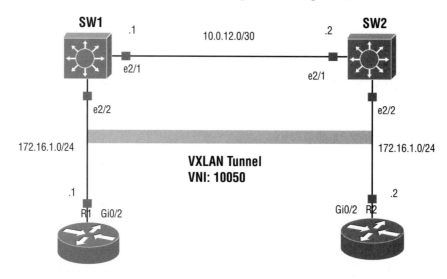

The configuration for SW1 and SW2 is nearly identical. For brevity, I'll show the configuration steps for only SW2, making notes of what is different on SW1. Additionally, the configuration files are available in the online materials for this book.

VXLAN Control Planes

The flood-and-learn behavior is native to VXLAN, but it's not required. If you don't want to use multicast for data plane MAC learning, you can implement a separate control plane protocol to advertise MAC addresses to VTEPs without the need for flooding. Two options for the control plane are LISP and Ethernet VPN (EVPN) with BGP. We won't be configuring these, but just know they're options.

Configuring the Underlay

We'll start by enabling the necessary features for VXLAN and multicast. First, we need to enable OSPF:

```
SW2(config)# feature ospf
```

Next, we'll enable PIM:

```
SW2(config)# feature pim
```

And finally, we'll enable the VXLAN features:

```
SW2(config)# feature vn-segment-vlan-based
SW2(config)# feature nv overlay
```

The flood-and-learn mechanism uses multicast. When a VTEP (SW1 or SW2) receives an unknown unicast from its connected router on VLAN 50, it will encapsulate the frame and send it to the multicast address we'll later configure (230.1.1.1). Although not quite flooding, it's the closest we can get to flooding on an IP underlay.

Because both SW1 and SW2 will be sourcing multicast traffic, they must be able to reach each other's unicast source IP addresses. Recall from Chapter 8, "Network Address Translation and Multicast," that PIM performs an RPF check against a multicast source as a loop-prevention mechanism. Therefore, we need to create a loopback interface and advertise it via OSPF:

```
SW2(config)# interface loopback0
! When configuring on SW1, make sure to make the loopback address different
SW2(config-if)# ip address 10.255.255.2/32
```

Let's enable PIM sparse mode for the loopback:

```
SW2(config-if)# ip pim sparse-mode
Let's advertise the loopback into OSPF.
SW2(config-if)# ip router ospf underlay area 0
```

We need to configure the routed interface to SW1. We'll also enable PIM on this interface and advertise its prefix via OSPF. Let's convert it to a routed interface:

```
SW2(config-if)# int e2/1
SW2(config-if)# no switchport
```

Naturally, the IP address will be different on SW1. Refer to Figure 10.9 if needed.

```
SW2(config-if)# ip address 10.0.12.2/30
SW2(config-if)# ip router ospf underlay area 0
SW2(config-if)# ! Enable PIM sparse mode
SW2(config-if)# ip pim sparse-mode
SW2(config-if)# no shutdown
SW2(config-if)# exit
```

Because we're running PIM in sparse mode, we need to specify at least one rendezvous point (RP). We'll configure both SW1 and SW2 as RPs:

```
SW2(config)# ip pim rp-address 10.255.255.1 group-list 224.0.0.0/4
SW2(config)# ip pim rp-address 10.255.255.2 group-list 224.0.0.0/4
```

To complete the underlay configuration, we need to enable the OSPF process, naming it underlay. (You can name it anything you wish since the process name is only locally significant.)

```
SW2(config)# router ospf underlay
SW2(config-router)# no shut
```

Configuring the Overlay

Now we'll configure VLAN 50, linking it to VXLAN Network Identifier (VNI) 10050. This is similar in concept to VLAN tagging, except in this case, the VNI tag is stored in the VXLAN header, not in an 802.1Q Ethernet header. The VNI number can range from 4096 to 16773119 and doesn't have to bear any relationship to the VLAN ID.

```
SW2(config)# vlan 50
SW2(config-vlan)# vn-segment 10050
```

We happen to be using VLAN 50 on both SW1 and SW2, but there's no requirement that the VLAN IDs match on the VTEPs. Remember, we're not doing any 802.1Q tagging, so the MAC frames carry no VLAN information. The VNI tag is the only value that must match between the VTEPs, since that's how they distinguish different layer 2 domains. Next, we need to create a network virtual edge (NVE) interface. This is what ties together the VNI and multicast group:

```
SW2(config-if)# interface nve1
```

Specify the loopback interface that the multicast traffic will be sourced from:

```
SW2(config-if-nve)# source-interface loopback0
```

Associate VNI 10050 with the NVE and multicast group 230.1.1.1:

```
SW2(config-if-nve)# member vni 10050 mcast-group 230.1.1.1
SW2(config-if-nve)# no shutdown
```

It's time for the moment of truth. If all went well, we should see the VNI in an Up state:

```
SW2(config-if-nve)# do show nve vni
Codes: CP - Control Plane        DP - Data Plane
       UC - Unconfigured         SA - Suppress ARP
       SU - Suppress Unknown Unicast


Interface VNI      Multicast-group   State Mode Type [BD/VRF]      Flags
--------- -------- ----------------- ----- ---- ----------------- -----
nve1      10050    230.1.1.1         Up    DP   L2 [50]
SW2(config-if-nve)# end
```

The multicast routing table for the group's (*,G) entry should show interface E2/1 as the incoming interface and nve1 in the outgoing interface list. Multicast group traffic ingressing E2/1—ostensibly VXLAN packets—will be passed along to the nve1 interface to be decapsulated and forwarded on to VLAN 50.

```
SW2# show ip mroute 230.1.1.1
IP Multicast Routing Table for VRF "default"

(*, 230.1.1.1/32), uptime: 06:57:46, nve ip pim
  Incoming interface: Ethernet2/1, RPF nbr: 10.0.12.1
  Outgoing interface list: (count: 1)
    nve1, uptime: 06:57:46, nve
(10.255.255.2/32, 230.1.1.1/32), uptime: 06:57:46, nve mrib ip pim
  Incoming interface: loopback0, RPF nbr: 10.255.255.2
  Outgoing interface list: (count: 1)
    Ethernet2/1, uptime: 06:39:31, pim
```

To complete the overlay configuration, we need to configure the interface facing R2 as an access port, placing it in VLAN 50:

```
SW2(config)# int e2/2
SW2(config-if)# switchport
SW2(config-if)# switchport mode access
SW2(config-if)# switchport access vlan 50
SW2(config-if)# no shutdown
```

Configuring R1 and R2

R1 and R2 have no configuration beyond what you'd infer from the diagram, so I'm going to leave out the configuration steps, considering they're pretty basic. Neither is running any routing protocol, nor do they have static routes. Each is simply configured with an IP address on its Gi0/2 interface. Because each is connected to a VLAN 50 access port, there are no 802.1Q trunks. To test everything, on R1, we'll ping R2's interface IP (172.16.1.2):

```
R1#ping 172.16.1.2
Type escape sequence to abort.
Sending 5, 100-byte ICMP Echos to 172.16.1.2, timeout is 2 seconds:
!!!!!
Success rate is 100 percent (5/5), round-trip min/avg/max = 10/12/15 ms
```

As far as R1 can tell, 172.16.1.2 is in the same broadcast domain as itself. The ARP cache shows R2's interface MAC address, and the CEF FIB shows an adjacency, proving that no IP routing is occurring in the overlay.

```
R1#show arp 172.16.1.2
Protocol  Address         Age (min)  Hardware Addr   Type   Interface
Internet  172.16.1.2             0   0c32.21d5.6802  ARPA   GigabitEthernet0/2
```

```
R1#show ip cef adjacency gi0/2 172.16.1.2 detail
IPv4 CEF is enabled and running
VRF Default
 13 prefixes (13/0 fwd/non-fwd)
 Table id 0x0
 Database epoch:         0 (13 entries at this epoch)

172.16.1.2/32, epoch 0, flags [attached]
  Adj source: IP adj out of GigabitEthernet0/2, addr 172.16.1.2 0F6A4158
    Dependent covered prefix type adjfib, cover 172.16.1.0/24
  attached to GigabitEthernet0/2
```

Let's look at things from SW1's perspective. The MAC address table shows R2's interface MAC address, with the adjacent interface nve1 and SW2's loopback IP address (which is cut off in the output).

```
SW1# show system internal l2fwder mac
```

Stl	Static	BD	MAC-Address	FTAG.Sid/L2_Intf	GM	Type	Age
0	0	50	0c:32:21:34:c9:02	Eth2/2	0	0	09:36:21*
0	0	50	0c:32:21:d5:68:02	nve1 10.255.25	0	0	00:01:55*

> On a physical switch, you can use the show mac address-table command to view MAC address entries learned via VXLAN.

Virtual Routing and Forwarding

Virtual routing and forwarding (VRF) instances allow a single router to maintain multiple separate virtual IP routing tables. A VRF instance consists of a dedicated IP routing table and CEF FIB. Routing protocols can also maintain a separate RIB for each VRF. The goal of VRFs is to allow a single router to serve different customers without the risk of one customer's routes or traffic leaking into another's. Because the VRFs are separate, the same IP routes can exist in both without conflict. In practice, organizations often use VRFs to separate network management traffic from others.

Configuring a VRF

In Figure 10.10, R1 and R2 represent routers belonging to two different customers. R1 and R2 both use the 192.168.1.0/30 IP subnet. They're also running EIGRP AS 1 and advertising a loopback address.

FIGURE 10.10   VRF topology

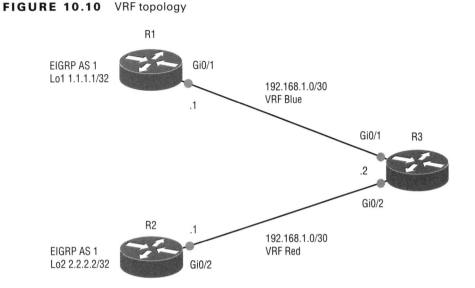

In this scenario, we're going to configure R3 with two VRF instances named Blue and Red. The connection to R1 will be in VRF Blue, and the connection to R2 will be in VRF Red. R3 will also run separate EIGRP processes with R1 and R2. Let's start by configuring VRF Blue for Customer 1:

```
R3(config)#ip vrf Blue
R3(config-vrf)#exit
```

We'll add Gi0/1 (facing R1) to VRF Blue. VRF names are locally significant and don't have to match on different routers. You should do this first, before addressing the interface. If you address the interface first and then add the interface to the VRF, it will remove the IP address.

```
R3(config)#int gi0/1
R3(config-if)#ip vrf forwarding Blue
R3(config-if)#ip address 192.168.1.2 255.255.255.252
R3(config-if)#no shut
```

Now we'll configure VRF Red for Customer 2:

```
R3(config)#ip vrf Red
R3(config-vrf)#exit
R3(config)#int gi0/2
R3(config-if)#ip vrf forwarding Red
R3(config-if)#ip address 192.168.1.2 255.255.255.252
R3(config-if)#no shut
```

Configuring Multi-VRF EIGRP

Next, let's configure EIGRP. Even though R1 and R2 are both using EIGRP AS 1, the AS number we specify doesn't matter here. In a moment we're going to specify the AS independently for each VRF.

```
R3(config-if)#router eigrp 3
```

We'll enter address family configuration mode for VRF Blue. This is where we'll configure the EIGRP process for VRF Blue:

```
R3(config-router)#address-family ipv4 vrf Blue
```

Specify AS 1 to match R1's AS:

```
R3(config-router-af)#autonomous-system 1
```

Enable EIGRP on all interfaces. Because this is isolated to VRF Blue, EIGRP will be enabled only on the interface facing R1:

```
R3(config-router-af)#network 0.0.0.0 0.0.0.0
```

The adjacency with R1 comes up:

```
%DUAL-5-NBRCHANGE: EIGRP-IPv4 1: Neighbor 192.168.1.1 (GigabitEthernet0/1) is
up: new adjacency
R3(config-router-af)#no auto-summary
```

We'll enter EIGRP address family configuration mode for VRF Red:

```
R3(config-router-af)#address-family ipv4 vrf Red
```

R2 is also running EIGRP AS 1. Despite the fact that R1 and R2 have the same AS number, there won't be any conflicts because this is a different VRF.

```
R3(config-router-af)#autonomous-system 1
R3(config-router-af)#network 0.0.0.0 0.0.0.0
R3(config-router-af)#no auto
%DUAL-5-NBRCHANGE: EIGRP-IPv4 1: Neighbor 192.168.1.1 (GigabitEthernet0/2) is
up: new adjacency
```

Now it's time to verify the configuration. Let's start by viewing the IP routing table for VRF Blue:

```
R3#show ip route vrf Blue

Routing Table: Blue
Codes: L - local, C - connected, S - static, R - RIP, M - mobile, B - BGP
       D - EIGRP, EX - EIGRP external, O - OSPF, IA - OSPF inter area
       N1 - OSPF NSSA external type 1, N2 - OSPF NSSA external type 2
       E1 - OSPF external type 1, E2 - OSPF external type 2
```

```
       i - IS-IS, su - IS-IS summary, L1 - IS-IS level-1, L2 - IS-IS level-2
       ia - IS-IS inter area, * - candidate default, U - per-user static route
       o - ODR, P - periodic downloaded static route, H - NHRP, l - LISP
       a - application route
       + - replicated route, % - next hop override, p - overrides from PfR

Gateway of last resort is not set
! Note the EIGRP learned route from R1
      1.0.0.0/32 is subnetted, 1 subnets
D        1.1.1.1 [90/130816] via 192.168.1.1, 00:04:57, GigabitEthernet0/1
      192.168.1.0/24 is variably subnetted, 2 subnets, 2 masks
C        192.168.1.0/30 is directly connected, GigabitEthernet0/1
L        192.168.1.2/32 is directly connected, GigabitEthernet0/1
```

Now let's check the IP routing table for VRF Red:

```
R3#show ip route vrf Red

Routing Table: Red
Codes: L - local, C - connected, S - static, R - RIP, M - mobile, B - BGP
       D - EIGRP, EX - EIGRP external, O - OSPF, IA - OSPF inter area
       N1 - OSPF NSSA external type 1, N2 - OSPF NSSA external type 2
       E1 - OSPF external type 1, E2 - OSPF external type 2
       i - IS-IS, su - IS-IS summary, L1 - IS-IS level-1, L2 - IS-IS level-2
       ia - IS-IS inter area, * - candidate default, U - per-user static route
       o - ODR, P - periodic downloaded static route, H - NHRP, l - LISP
       a - application route
       + - replicated route, % - next hop override, p - overrides from PfR

Gateway of last resort is not set
! Here's the loopback from R2.
      2.0.0.0/32 is subnetted, 1 subnets
D        2.2.2.2 [90/130816] via 192.168.1.1, 00:03:27, GigabitEthernet0/2
      192.168.1.0/24 is variably subnetted, 2 subnets, 2 masks
C        192.168.1.0/30 is directly connected, GigabitEthernet0/2
L        192.168.1.2/32 is directly connected, GigabitEthernet0/2
```

If we look at R3's global IP routing table without specify a VRF, we see it's empty:

```
R3#show ip route
Codes: L - local, C - connected, S - static, R - RIP, M - mobile, B - BGP
       D - EIGRP, EX - EIGRP external, O - OSPF, IA - OSPF inter area
       N1 - OSPF NSSA external type 1, N2 - OSPF NSSA external type 2
       E1 - OSPF external type 1, E2 - OSPF external type 2
```

```
      i - IS-IS, su - IS-IS summary, L1 - IS-IS level-1, L2 - IS-IS level-2
      ia - IS-IS inter area, * - candidate default, U - per-user static route
      o - ODR, P - periodic downloaded static route, H - NHRP, l - LISP
      a - application route
      + - replicated route, % - next hop override, p - overrides from PfR
```

```
Gateway of last resort is not set
Pinging 192.168.1.1 fails because we haven't specified a VRF.
R3#ping 192.168.1.1
Type escape sequence to abort.
Sending 5, 100-byte ICMP Echos to 192.168.1.1, timeout is 2 seconds:
.....
Success rate is 0 percent (0/5)
```

However, if we specify VRF Blue and ping 192.168.1.1, we get a response from R1:

```
R3#ping vrf Blue 192.168.1.1
Type escape sequence to abort.
Sending 5, 100-byte ICMP Echos to 192.168.1.1, timeout is 2 seconds:
!!!!!
Success rate is 100 percent (5/5), round-trip min/avg/max = 4/4/5 ms
```

Likewise, pinging the same IP address in VRF Red, we get a response from R2:

```
R3#ping vrf Red 192.168.1.1
Type escape sequence to abort.
Sending 5, 100-byte ICMP Echos to 192.168.1.1, timeout is 2 seconds:
!!!!!
Success rate is 100 percent (5/5), round-trip min/avg/max = 5/6/8 ms
```

Naturally, each VRF gets not only its own IP routing table, but its own CEF FIB:

```
R3#show ip cef vrf Blue | i Int|Gig
Prefix               Next Hop          Interface
1.1.1.1/32           192.168.1.1       GigabitEthernet0/1
192.168.1.0/30       attached          GigabitEthernet0/1
192.168.1.0/32       receive           GigabitEthernet0/1
192.168.1.1/32       attached          GigabitEthernet0/1
192.168.1.2/32       receive           GigabitEthernet0/1
192.168.1.3/32       receive           GigabitEthernet0/1
R3#show ip cef vrf Red | i Int|Gig
Prefix               Next Hop          Interface
2.2.2.2/32           192.168.1.1       GigabitEthernet0/2
192.168.1.0/30       attached          GigabitEthernet0/2
192.168.1.0/32       receive           GigabitEthernet0/2
```

```
192.168.1.1/32        attached        GigabitEthernet0/2
192.168.1.2/32        receive         GigabitEthernet0/2
192.168.1.3/32        receive         GigabitEthernet0/2
```

This is just one example of how VRFs are typically used in a multi-tenant situation. But you can create separate VRFs and apply them to tunnel interfaces, subinterfaces, and even SVIs.

Summary

Network virtualization is a broad term that covers a variety of technologies and architectures. Because the terms used in this area are so similar, they blend together and aren't very descriptive. Let's revisit how these terms are commonly used and what they really mean.

VM networking relates to the virtual network interfaces and other virtual network infrastructure—such as virtual switches—that VMs use to communicate both intra-host and inter-host. VM networking is often called virtual networking.

Network functions virtualization refers to running network devices that are traditionally purpose-built hardware—routers, switches, load balancers, and firewalls—on VMs that run on commodity x86/64 hardware.

Network virtualization refers to creating overlays, usually for the purpose of abstracting the complexity of underlay. The idea behind network virtualization is to make the network easier to manage. The underlay stays mostly static, whereas the overlay is flexible and can be changed and scaled relatively easily.

Overlays are synonymous with tunnels, and include GRE tunnels, IPsec tunnels, LISP tunnels, and VXLAN tunnels. GRE, IPsec, and LISP tunnels can carry layer 3 protocols over layer 3. VXLAN carries MAC frames over UDP. IPsec stands out as unique among these because it offers encryption, data integrity, and authentication.

Exam Essentials

Know what network functions virtualization means.   Network functions virtualization (NFV) refers to using commodity servers and VM infrastructure to run virtual network appliances such as routers, switches, firewalls, load balancers, and WAN optimizers, or VNFs.

Understand the purpose and operation of LISP.   LISP is designed to reduce the size of the global Internet routing tables by tunneling traffic between endpoints that use IP addresses called endpoint identifiers (EIDs). EIDs are reachable only via egress tunnel routers (ETRs) that have publicly reachable IP addresses called RLOCs. Only the RLOCs are advertised into the global routing tables, and the EIDs are not.

Understand the purpose and operation of VXLAN.   VXLAN is designed to tunnel MAC frames over layer 3 networks. Natively, VXLAN uses multicast to implement a flood-and-learn approach for MAC address learning. But you can use LISP or EVPN with BGP to implement a separate control plane for MAC address learning.

Be able to configure GRE tunnels, IPsec tunnels, and VRFs.   Practice configuring GRE to tunnel IPv4 and IPv6 over IPv4. You should be able to configure a site-to-site VPN using IPsec in transport or tunnel mode. Lastly, be able to configure VRFs to segregate layer 3 traffic on the same router. VRFs are often used with overlays to achieve traffic segregation among different tunnels that terminate on a single router.

Exercises

EXERCISE 10.1

Following the topology in Figure 10.7, configure a GRE tunnel between R1 and R2. Address the tunnel interface using both IPv4 and IPv6 addresses.

EXERCISE 10.2

Using the GRE tunnel that you created in Exercise 10.1, configure tunnel protection mode using IPsec in transport mode.

EXERCISE 10.3

Referring to the topology in Figure 10.10, R1 and R2. On R3, configure VRFs Blue and Red. Using these VRFs on R3, configure EIGRP adjacencies with R1 and R2.

Review Questions

You can find the answers in the appendix.

1. Which two of the following are commonly considered type-1 hypervisors? (Choose two.)
   A. Oracle VirtualBox
   B. VMware ESXi
   C. KVM
   D. VMware Fusion

2. Which of the following best describes a type-1 hypervisor?
   A. Costs money
   B. Runs without an OS
   C. Contains a robust user-friendly interface
   D. Designed to run on server hardware

3. What virtual network device does a hypervisor include to enable VMs to communicate with one another and the outside world?
   A. Network overlay
   B. VNF
   C. Virtual router
   D. Virtual switch

4. Which two of the following features enable an external physical switch to pass traffic between VMs that are running on the same host? (Choose two.)
   A. Reflective relay
   B. Internal EVB
   C. External EVB
   D. VEB

5. What will prevent a GRE tunnel from forming?
   A. The absence of an IPv4 address on the tunnel interface
   B. An access list that blocks IP protocol 47
   C. An access list that blocks UDP
   D. Failing to specify the tunnel mode

6. Which two of the following are valid uses of GRE tunnels? (Choose two.)
   A. VPNs
   B. IPv6 over IPv4
   C. MAC over IPv4
   D. MAC over IPv6
   E. Reducing the size of routing tables

7. You want to create an OSPFv2 adjacency over an existing GRE tunnel. Which of the following must you do?

   A. Disable IPsec

   B. Enable OSPF on the physical interfaces

   C. Enable OSPF on the tunnel interfaces

   D. Set the router IDs

8. Which of the following can cause recursive routing when using GRE?

   A. Advertising the tunnel interface over the physical interface being used as the tunnel endpoint

   B. Advertising tunnel endpoint prefixes over the tunnel

   C. Advertising the tunnel interface over the tunnel

   D. Having a static route to the tunnel endpoint

9. When configuring IPsec, what's the minimum Diffie-Hellman group number you should use for ISAKMP?

   A. 2

   B. 14

   C. 2,048

   D. 19

10. What protocol and port does IKE use?

    A. UDP/50

    B. TCP/50

    C. UDP/500

    D. TCP/500

11. What protocol does ESP use?

    A. IP protocol 50

    B. UDP

    C. TCP

    D. IP protocol 47

12. Which of the following commands will tell you whether an IPsec tunnel under interface Tunnel0 is using tunnel or transport mode?

    A. `show crypto isakmp sa`

    B. `show interface tunnel0`

    C. `show crypto ipsec sa`

    D. `show crypto ipsec profile`

13. What protocol and port does LISP use for tunneling IP packets?

    A. UDP/4341

    B. UDP/4342

    C. UDP/4789

    D. UDP/47

14. Which LISP router configuration command maps the EID 172.16.3.3/32 to the RLOC 10.10.10.1?

    A. `database-mapping 172.16.3.3/32 auto-discover-rlocs`

    B. `rloc-mapping 172.16.3.3/32 10.10.10.1 priority 1 weight 1`

    C. `database-mapping 10.10.10.1 172.16.3.3/32 priority 1 weight 1`

    D. `database-mapping 172.16.3.3/32 10.10.10.1 priority 1 weight 1`

15. Consider the following LIG output:

```
xTR2(config)#do lig 172.16.3.3
Mapping information for EID 172.16.3.3 from 10.10.10.1 with RTT 17 msecs
172.16.3.3/32, uptime: 00:04:31, expires: 23:59:59, via map-reply, self, complete
  Locator     Uptime    State       Pri/Wgt
  10.10.10.1  00:04:31  up          1/1
  10.10.30.2  00:03:32  admin-down  255/1
```

What can you infer from the output? (Choose two.)

    A. 10.10.10.1 is the RLOC for 172.16.3.3/32.

    B. 172.16.3.3/32 isn't reachable via 10.10.10.1.

    C. 172.16.3.3/32 doesn't exist in xTR2's IP routing table.

    D. xTR2 doesn't have an EID-to-RLOC mapping configured.

16. What two techniques does LISP use to reduce the size of IP routing tables? (Choose two.)

    A. BGP summarization

    B. Tunneling

    C. Encapsulation

    D. IP mobility

17. What protocol and port does VXLAN use?

    A. TCP/4789

    B. UDP/4341

    C. UDP/4342

    D. UDP/4789

18. What are two options for MAC address learning in VXLAN? (Choose two.)

    A. Broadcast

    B. Flood-and-learn

    C. OSPF

    D. EVPN

19. Where do you map a VXLAN VNI to a multicast group address?

    A. NVE configuration

    B. Switched interface configuration

    C. VLAN configuration

    D. PIM configuration

20. Which of the following set of commands map VLAN 50 to VNI 10050? (Choose two.)

    A. `vn-segment 10050`

    B. `vlan 50`

    C. `member vni 10050`

    D. `switchport mode access vlan 50`

21. Which of the following is true of VRFs?

    A. A physical interface can be a member of multiple VRFs.

    B. VRFs can have overlapping routes.

    C. You must configure an IP address on an interface before adding it to a VRF.

    D. VRF names must be globally unique.

22. Which interface command adds an interface to VRF Green?

    A. `address-family ipv4 vrf Green`

    B. `ip vrf forwarding Green`

    C. `ip vrf Green`

    D. `ip forwarding Green`

23. Which set of commands enables EIGRP AS 10 for VRF Yellow?

    A. `router eigrp 10`
        `address-family ipv4 vrf Yellow`
        `network 0.0.0.0 0.0.0.0`

    B. `router eigrp 10`
        `address-family ipv4 vrf Yellow`
        `autonomous-system vrf`
        `network 0.0.0.0 0.0.0.0`

C. router eigrp 10
   address-family ipv4 vrf Yellow
   autonomous-system 10
   network 0.0.0.0 0.0.0.0 vrf

D. router eigrp 11
   address-family ipv4 vrf Yellow
   autonomous-system 10
   network 0.0.0.0 0.0.0.0

24. Which command will show the IP routing table for VRF Orange?

A. show ip route vrf Orange

B. show ip vrf

C. show ip route

D. show ip vrf route Orange

Chapter

11

Software-Defined Networking and Network Programmability

THE CCNP ENCOR EXAM OBJECTIVES COVERED IN THIS CHAPTER INCLUDE THE FOLLOWING:

Domain 1 Architecture

✓ **1.3 Differentiate between on-premises and cloud infrastructure deployments**

✓ **1.4 Explain the working principles of the Cisco SD-WAN solution**

✓ **1.5 Explain the working principles of the Cisco SD-Access solution**

Domain 4 Network Assurance

✓ **4.6 Describe Cisco DNA Center workflows to apply network configuration, monitoring, and management**

✓ **4.7 Configure and verify NETCONF and RESTCONF**

Domain 5 Security

✓ **5.3 Describe REST API security**

Domain 6 Automation

✓ **6.1 Interpret basic Python components and scripts**

✓ **6.2 Construct valid JSON encoded file**

✓ **6.3 Describe the high-level principles and benefits of a data modeling language, such as YANG**

✓ 6.4   Describe APIs for Cisco DNA Center and vManage

✓ 6.5   Interpret REST API response codes and results in payload using Cisco DNA Center and RESTCONF

✓ 6.6   Construct EEM applet to automate configuration, troubleshooting, or data collection

✓ 6.7   Compare agent vs. agentless orchestration tools, such as Chef, Puppet, Ansible, and SaltStack

In this chapter, you'll learn about two of Cisco's software-defined networking (SDN) products: Software-Defined Access (SD-Access) and Software-Defined WAN (SD-WAN). We'll then cover how to programmatically interact with your network, through these SDN products, to make configuration changes and pull device details. We'll also take a behind-the-scenes look at *how* these SDN products perform device configuration using the NETCONF protocol. After that, you'll learn how to automate network configuration tasks and diagnostics using Embedded Event Manager. Finally, we'll look at some other configuration automation tools, namely Ansible, Chef, Puppet, and SaltStack.

What Is Software-Defined Networking?

When you hear the term *software-defined networking (SDN)*, network automation may not be the first thing that comes to mind. But that's exactly what SDN is. Specifically, SDN is the marriage of network automation with network virtualization and overlays.

You've probably heard the term *fabric*. A fabric describes a cohesive overlay network that obscures the underlay to the point that it's practically invisible. For example, a switched fabric is multiple connected switches abstracted into a single logical switch. You configure the individual links or worry about the traffic paths between switches. All of that is abstracted away so that you don't even have to think about it.

VXLANs are another example of a fabric. When VMs communicate at layer 2 over a VXLAN tunnel, they know nothing of the underlying layer 3 network that's carrying their traffic. The VXLAN, even though it's actually separate subnets connected via a routed network, forms a layer 2 fabric.

The term fabric suggests piecing together individual components to form something that looks and behaves differently than the components. When you look at an article of clothing, you probably don't notice the individual threads, the different paths that they take, their length and braiding, or how easily they can break. When you configure overlays such as GRE tunnels, IPsec tunnels, or VXLAN tunnels, it's like sewing together a shirt by hand. SDN, on the other hand, is like a fully automated, industrial sewing machine that does all the work for you. Whether you sew it by hand or use a machine, a shirt is a shirt. A shirt made by a machine rips just as easily as one made by hand. And the same is true of networking. Whether you create an overlay fabric by hand or use SDN, a network is a network. And a network fabric created by an SDN solution can be just as brittle and break-able as one you spend hours configuring in front of a glowing screen.

The advantage of SDN is that it automates the creation of not just overlay networks but underlay networks as well. That means you can make configuration changes faster and with fewer errors. Configuring NAT, IP routing, and VPNs are just a few examples of com-mon configuration tasks that networking professionals are accustomed to doing by hand. SDN hides and automates most of the gnarly configuration steps. To be clear, the same steps still occur behind the scenes, but they're hidden from you. All you have to do is fill in the blanks, so to speak.

SDN can also provide automatic remediation and enforce configuration compliance. If something falls out of compliance—for instance, if someone disables OSPF on an interface—the SDN platform can detect it and automatically reenable OSPF. To give another analogy, SDN is like a point-and-click OS GUI, whereas the IOS command line is like an OS's terminal shell. The GUI is easier and sometimes faster. The terminal shell is more complex but more powerful, allowing you to do things that the GUI doesn't. It's not uncommon to hear bombastic talk about how SDN is the future and is going to put "tra-ditional" networking professionals in the unemployment line. But the history of OSs tells us that this isn't an either/or situation of choosing between SDN and the CLI. Rather, each has its own strengths and weaknesses. Therefore, your time is best spent on understanding SDN's advantages and limitations and what SDN products Cisco offers, as opposed to how to configure a particular SDN product. Cisco offers three SDN solutions for different types of networks:

- Campus and branch networks—Software-Defined Access (SD-Access)

- Wide area networks—Software-Defined WAN (SD-WAN)

- Data center networks—Application Centric Infrastructure (ACI)

- Service provider networks—Virtual Topology System (VTS)

Because the ENCOR exam covers campus and WAN networks, in this chapter we're going to cover only the first two.

Software-Defined Access

SD-Access is a turnkey network automation solution designed for campus and branch net-works. Although other SDN products tend to focus on the data center, what sets SD-Access apart is its focus on users and end-user devices. Some tasks SD-Access can automate are

Network Device Configuration   Even though SD-Access mostly saves you from the CLI, you still have to provide the configuration details. You interact with SD-Access using the Cisco DNA Center user interface. Cisco DNA Center is what actually handles the configuration tasks behind the scenes. It also performs sanity checking and validation to ensure that any configuration change you make doesn't cause problems or unintended consequences.

Monitoring and Analytics   SD-Access keeps track of device health and performance, IP reachability, traffic patterns, and other interesting metrics. The marketing term for monitoring is *network assurance.*

Network Segmentation and Access Control   The purpose of segmentation is to isolate one host from another—for example, isolating the guest Wi-Fi from a production network. You can control access to network resources based on user or device identity, IP address, MAC address, or even the type of device connecting.

IP Mobility   Users can move around and connect to the wired or wireless network from any location without any manual provisioning. They can also roam between WAPs seamlessly. Segmentation, access control, and IP mobility are achieved through the use of network overlays.

SD-Access Layers

Conceptually, SD-Access consists of several layers:

- Physical
- Network underlay
- Fabric overlay
- Controller
- Management

It's important to understand that these aren't layers in the same sense as OSI layers, wherein a layer is dependent on the layers below it. Rather, they're simply ways of organizing the different components of SD-Access.

Physical Layer

The physical network consists of the physical gear required for SD-Access. This includes physical routers, switches, and access points. SD-Access works only with fabric-enabled Cisco devices, including

- Cisco Catalyst and Nexus switches
- Cisco ASR, ISR, ISRv, and CSRv routers
- Cisco WLAN controllers and Aironet access points

These devices that are designed to work with SD-Access include protocols and APIs that SD-Access uses to push configurations. You can't just plug in any old switch and expect it to work with SD-Access.

The physical layer also includes two hardware appliances:

- Cisco DNA Center controller—This is the brains of SD-Access. It runs the Cisco DNA Center software that you use to configure and monitor your network.

- Cisco Secure Network Server (SNS) 3500 Series—This runs the Identity Services Engine (ISE), which is the foundation of network access control and micro segmentation. The Cisco ISE may run in a VM instead of on the hardware appliance.

Network Underlay

The best way to understand the network underlay is that it's the network you would build if you weren't using SD-Access at all. The goal of the underlay is to provide reliable, fast transport for the overlay tunnels that SD-Access builds. As such, it should be as simple and resilient as possible. That means building in lots of redundancy: redundant connections, rapidly converging dynamic routing protocols, and FHRP.

Cisco recommends that the network underlay consist of point-to-point layer 3 connections. You already know the reason for this: creating a large layer 2 domain and depending on Spanning Tree is asking for trouble! Having devices connected in a mesh of point-to-point routed links provides stability and resiliency that Spanning Tree can't.

You have two options for the underlay: you can create a custom underlay network manually, or you can have SD-Access automatically create it for you.

Custom Network Underlay

In a custom underlay, you have to configure everything using the CLI or an API, instead of using Cisco DNA Center. It's up to you to configure an IGP and enable full IP connectivity among all the devices in your network. You'll also have to tweak certain parameters such as MTU size to accommodate the overlay tunnels. If you get any of this wrong, the overlay will perform poorly or not at all.

One reason you may consider this option, however, is if you want network devices that are incompatible with SD-Access to be a part of the overlay fabric. Although SD-Access can't manage such devices, as long as the underlay is properly configured on them, SD-Access can utilize them for tunnel transport.

Cisco provides a handy underlay configuration template for switches at

www.cisco.com/c/en/us/solutions/collateral/enterprise-networks/software-defined-access/guide-c07-741859.html#_Toc2934407

Automatic Network Underlay

Cisco DNA Center can orchestrate the configuration of both the underlay and overlay networks. If you decide to have Cisco DNA create the underlay, it configures IP addresses, the IS-IS routing protocol, and implements multicast with PIM sparse mode. You have to provide details unique to your environment, such as public IP addresses. Also, you do have to initially perform some manual configuration. Cisco DNA Center requires you to manually configure a seed device and connect it to the other devices in the underlay. Cisco DNA Center's LAN Automation feature coordinates with the seed device to discover the other devices and adds them to its managed inventory. So, you'll have to do a little bit of work, but not much.

Automatic configuration of the network underlay sounds good, but there are a couple of reasons you might not want to go this route. You give up control and the chance to make any customizations. Also, SD-Access can configure only those devices that are compatible with SD-Access. If you want those devices to be a part of your network, you have to configure them manually.

Fabric Overlay

The fabric overlay provides transport for hosts, such as end-user devices and servers. Unlike the underlay, which can be configured manually or automatically, SD-Access must always configure the fabric overlay automatically. Of course, it's technically possible to build your own tunnels by hand, but doing so defeats the purpose of SD-Access, which is automation.

The fabric overlay is an interesting concoction of nonstandard LISP-based forwarding and nonstandard VXLAN tunnels riding over the underlay. Even if you understand LISP and VXLAN, the way SD-Access implements them in the overlay can be difficult to understand because it's, well, nonstandard. Keep that in mind. SD-Access divides the fabric overlay into three planes of operation, which happen to overlap each other significantly:

- The data plane
- The control plane
- The policy plane

We'll begin with a high-level overview of each, and then we'll dig into the details of how they're implemented in SD-Access.

Data Plane

The data plane uses a proprietary VXLAN encapsulation for transporting data between hosts. The data plane is segmented into virtual networks (VNs), which are isolated layer 3 routing and forwarding domains. A VN will generally mirror the way you'd configure a traditional campus network. For example, assuming that hosts, Internet edge firewalls, and printers all need connectivity to one another, they'd all reside in the same routing domain. Likewise, you'd place all of these devices in the same VN. When it comes to a guest network, you probably want that completely isolated from your production network. In that case, you'd create a separate VN for guests.

SD-Access assigns every host to a VN. To maintain traffic segregation among VNs, each router and switch in the fabric has a separate virtual routing and forwarding (VRF) for each VN. VNs span the entire fabric, so there isn't a need to manually configure a switch to use a VN in the same way that you'd have to configure a VLAN. By default, any two devices in the same VN can communicate. Any communication between devices inter-VN must pass through a router that redistributes routes between the VRFs associated with those VNs.

Of course, you're always going to need some form of access control even within a VN. To provide this, SD-Access uses a modified VXLAN header that supports *scalable group tags (SGTs)*, also known as security tags. SGTs, which we'll discuss in a moment, are used by the policy plane to provide micro segmentation within a VN.

Control Plane

The control plane uses LISP for routing and forwarding in the overlay. LISP enables IP mobility and reduces the load on individual devices in the network, since they don't have to maintain large routing tables or perform shortest-path calculations. Instead, SD-Access creates a LISP MR/MS, which maintains routing and forwarding information for the entire overlay.

Policy Plane

The proprietary VXLAN header includes a scalable group tag that's used to apply security and QoS policies to a virtual network. SGTs are applied at ingress by adding an SGT to the Ethernet header—a process called inline tagging. (Incidentally, this is one of the reasons SD-Access only works with compatible devices.) VTEPs map the SGT into the VXLAN header to preserve it in transport. Access control policies are enforced at the egress point, so a packet denied by policy may traverse the network and make it all the way to its would-be egress point before getting dropped. By the way, the marketing term for using SGTs in this way is Cisco TrustSec.

In SD-Access, SGTs are assigned to scalable groups that typically correspond with an organizational role, such as employees or contractors. Think of a scalable group as a container for hosts. Host assignment to scalable groups can be done by tying a group to a particular switchport, or it can be dynamic and based on how the device (or user) authenticates. For example, the user may enter their Active Directory (AD) credentials and be placed into a particular scalable group based on their account permissions.

NOTE

When a VXLAN header includes an SGT, the tag is called a Group Policy ID and the VXLAN packet is said to use the Virtual Extensible LAN - Group Policy Option (VXLAN-GPO) format.

Fabric Roles

Now you'll learn how SD-Access implements the data, control, and policy planes. Any device that actively participates in both the underlay and overlay networks and is managed by Cisco DNA Center is called a fabric-enabled network device. (These are the same devices mentioned in the discussion on the Physical layer of SD-Access.) A fabric-enabled device can serve one of four functions or roles:

- Control plane node
- Fabric border node
- Fabric edge node
- Fabric WLAN controller

Control Plane Node

The control plane node is a Cisco router or switch that acts as the LISP MR/MS for the overlay. The control plane node functions as a centralized IP routing and MAC address table for the entire overlay. It's also responsible for mapping SGTs between Ethernet and VXLAN headers.

Fabric Edge Node

The fabric edge node is what hosts connect to, and it acts as their point-of-entry into a VN. A fabric edge node is configured as LISP xTR. But it's not quite the same xTR configuration as you saw in Chapter 10, "Network VIrtualization." By default, LISP uses its own LISP header that allows it to create layer 3 tunnels. SD-Access, however, replaces the LISP encapsulation with VXLAN encapsulation. Hence, ITR-ETR traffic is encapsulated in a VXLAN packet instead. This enables SD-Access to dynamically create layer 2 and layer 3 tunnels across the overlay.

Before looking at some examples, you need to understand how SD-Access handles host IP address assignment. As always, a host can have a static IP address—typically the case with servers and printers. SD-Access can also perform address assignment via DHCP, based on the switchport the host is connected to, or based on how the host authenticates. (Recall that the VN a host resides in is determined in much the same way. It can be based on the switchport the host is connected to, or it can be assigned dynamically.) The pairing of a host's IP subnet and its VN is called a host address pool—or just host pool for short. The control plane node is aware of every host address pool in the fabric.

Every fabric edge node is configured with a SVI that shares the same MAC address and IP address for each host address pool. For example, for the subnet `192.168.1.0/24`, all fabric edge nodes may be configured with an SVI IP address of `192.168.1.254`, and the same MAC address. This way, wherever a host moves in the VN, it can continue to use its configured default gateway IP. This configuration is called an *anycast gateway*.

When a host connects to the network, SD-Access registers on the map server two different EID-to-RLOC mappings for the host: an IPv4 mapping and a MAC address mapping.

IPv4 Mapping   Maps host IP addresses to the RLOC (underlay IP address) of the fabric edge node. This is the normal LISP operation that you learned about in Chapter 10. To support IP mobility, EIDs are registered with the map server with /32 host masks, even if the host is configured with a different subnet mask.

MAC Mapping Maps host MAC addresses to the RLOC of the fabric node. This is an example of VXLAN using the LISP control plane for MAC address learning, also mentioned in Chapter 10.

What's amazing about this is that it enables full IP mobility by extending the layer 2 domain wherever it's needed. To give a quick example of how this works: imagine that xTR1 and xTR2 are both fabric edge nodes, and 1.1.1.1/24 is connected to xTR1 and 1.1.1.2/24 is on xTR2. The controller node has host mappings for both IP addresses (1.1.1.1/32 and 1.1.1.2/32), as well their MAC addresses.

1. Suppose now that 1.1.1.1 sends an IP packet to 1.1.1.2.

2. Both hosts are configured with a /24 subnet mask, so 1.1.1.1 sends an ARP request for 1.1.1.2's MAC address.

3. xTR1 sees the ARP request and contacts the LISP map resolver to get 1.1.1.2's MAC address.

4. The map resolver, having what's essentially an ARP entry for 1.1.1.2, replies to xTR1, which in turn sends an ARP reply to 1.1.1.1.

5. 1.1.1.1 encapsulates the IP packet in a Ethernet frame addressed to 1.1.1.2's MAC address and forwards it.

6. xTR1 consults its MAC address table and sees (based on the earlier reply from the map resolver) that 1.1.1.2's MAC address is reachable via xTR1's RLOC.

7. xTR1 encapsulates the Ethernet frame in a VXLAN packet and sends it to xTR2.

8. xTR2 receives the packet, decapsulates the Ethernet frame, and forwards it to 1.1.1.2.

Fabric edge nodes also apply scalable group tags at ingress, authenticate endpoints using 802.1X, and function as the default gateway for connected hosts.

Even though fabric edge nodes use both LISP and VXLAN, the tunnels they form between each other use VXLAN encapsulation and are thus VXLAN tunnels, not LISP tunnels.

Fabric Border Node

The fabric border node is a LISP xTR that provides connectivity to devices outside of the overlay fabric, such as Internet gateways or cloud gateways. It performs route redistribution between IP prefixes that are internal to the fabric and those that are external, such as those in a public cloud environment. For example, if you're running a virtual private cloud (VPC) in Amazon Web Services (AWS), the fabric border node is responsible for advertising the cloud prefixes into the SD-Access campus fabric, and vice versa. Alternatively, the fabric border node can simply advertise a default route into the fabric. When configured in this way, it's called a default border node.

Fabric WLAN Controller Node

Despite the name, the fabric WLAN controller (WLC) node doesn't actually participate in the SD-Access fabric. Instead, it connects to a fabric border node. Access points (APs), however, connect to a fabric edge node. The WLC and access points form a CAPWAP tunnel, as they normally would, but the tunnel is itself encapsulated in a VXLAN tunnel as it traverses the fabric from the fabric edge node to the fabric border node that the WLC connects to.

Here's how this differs from a traditional WLAN deployment: the CAPWAP tunnel between the AP and WLC is only used for control plane traffic, such as AP configuration. For data traffic, the AP and fabric edge form a VXLAN tunnel. This allows the fabric edge node to apply security tags, enforce egress policies, and make forwarding decisions. By removing the WLC from the data path, the fabric can treat wireless clients almost just like wired clients.

Controller Layer

The controller layer consists of three main components that all communicate with one another using *application programming interfaces* (APIs):

Cisco Network Controller Platform (NCP)—Automation The NCP provides automation of the underlay configuration. Rather than sending strings of IOS configuration commands as you'd do on the command line, NCP configures the underlay using the Network Configuration (NETCONF) protocol and the Yet Another Next Generation (YANG) data modeling language to represent the configuration parameters (we'll cover NETCONF and YANG a bit later). This is another reason devices must be SD-Access compatible. The NCP also performs device discovery. It runs on the same physical appliance as Cisco DNA Center and provides two key DNAC services: Cisco DNA Design and Cisco DNA Provision. We'll cover these and other Cisco DNA Center services in a moment.

Cisco Network Data Platform (NDP)—Assurance NDP performs monitoring, which nowadays has been graced with the marketing term *assurance*. NDP collects metrics from fabric devices and performs traffic and health analytics. NDP can collect data from various sources, including Switched Port Analyzer (SPAN) captures, SNMP, and NetFlow. It also runs on the same appliance as Cisco DNA Center and supports the Cisco DNA Assurance service.

Cisco Identity Services Engine (ISE)—Identity and Policy We touched on ISE earlier when discussing the Physical layer. ISE provides network access control (NAC) and policy enforcement for the SD-Access fabric. It supports RADIUS, TACACS+, 802.1X with EAP, and local and centralized WebAuth. ISE also supports MAC authentication bypass (MAB), which permits or denies access to the network based on the host's MAC address. Cisco ISE supports the Cisco DNA Policy service.

Management Layer

Now we get to where the rubber meets the road with SD-Access. Cisco DNA Center provides the user interface to the SD-Access fabric. Cisco DNA Center is divided into four services or workflows that you need to walk through to configure your SD-Access fabric. Cisco DNA Center handles most of the tricky configuration details for you, so you don't need to be an expert on VXLAN, LISP, or ISE. But you should understand the underlying technologies so that you can troubleshoot your network when the times comes (and it will!)

Cisco DNA Policy

This is where you define the virtual networks for your fabric. A default VN (aptly named Default_VN) is included. You can create scalable groups and associate them to a VN. Figure 11.1 shows a list of scalable groups in Cisco DNA Center.

FIGURE 11.1   Scalable groups in Cisco DNA Center

Cisco DNA Center	DESIGN	**POLICY**	PROVISION	ASSURANCE	PLATFORM			

Group-Based Access Control ˅   IP Based Access Control ˅   Application ˅   Traffic Copy ˅   Virtual Network

Scalable Groups (26)   Last updated: 6:04 PM   ↻ Refresh   ⊕ Create Scalable Group

▽ Filter | Actions ˅ Deploy

☐	Name	Tag Value	Description	Deployed	Learned From ˄	Policies	Virtual Networks
☐	Contractors	5/0x5	Contractor Security Group	Yes		1	DEFAULT_VN
☐	Developers	8/0x8	Developer Security Group	Yes		0	DEFAULT_VN
☐	Development_Servers	12/0xc	Development Servers Security Group	Yes		1	DEFAULT_VN
☐	Doctors	18/0x12		Yes		0	DEFAULT_VN
☐	Employees	4/0x4	Employee Security Group	Yes		3	DEFAULT_VN

Show 10 entries   Showing 1 - 10 of 26   [ ] 1 2 3 Next

Note that each group has a numeric tag, shown in both decimal and hexadecimal. This is the SGT mentioned earlier. You can associate one or more policies to a scalable group. Figure 11.2 shows a list of access policies applied to the Employees group.

The access policy prevents any device in the Employees group from reaching any other device in the Employees group or the HVAC group. Devices in the Employees group do, however, have access to the Unknown group, which is indicated by an SGT value of 0.

The Policy workflow is where you can configure QoS settings, set up IP-based access control, and even set up traffic mirroring to an Encapsulated Remote Switched Port Analyzer (ERSPAN) analyzer using the traffic copy feature.

FIGURE 11.2 Group-based access control policies in Cisco DNA Center

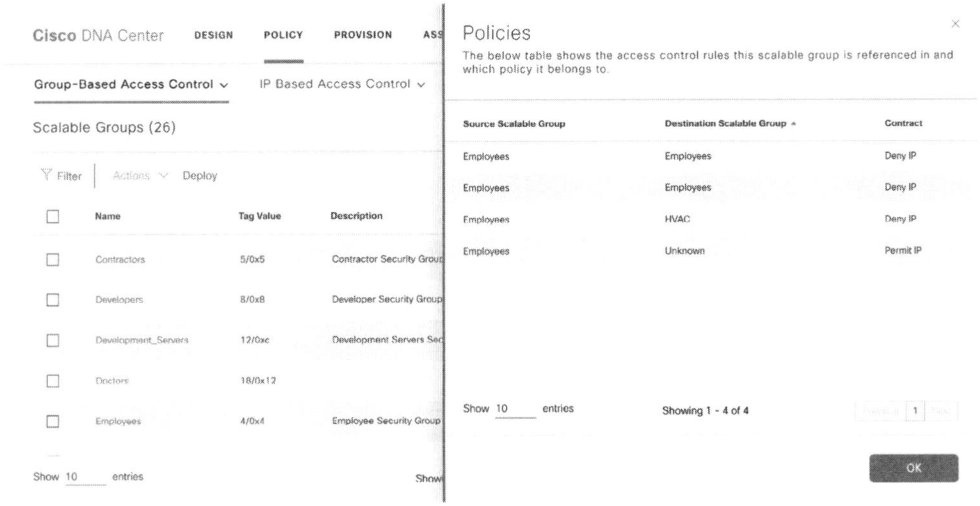

Cisco DNA Design

This is where you specify your network configuration details, such as IP address pools, wireless SSIDs and AP settings, DHCP settings, NTP servers, and so on. You also can view your device's IOS versions and perform upgrades from here. Figure 11.3 shows the Network Settings page, where you can configure DHCP and DNS servers.

FIGURE 11.3 Network Settings page under the Design workflow of Cisco DNA Center

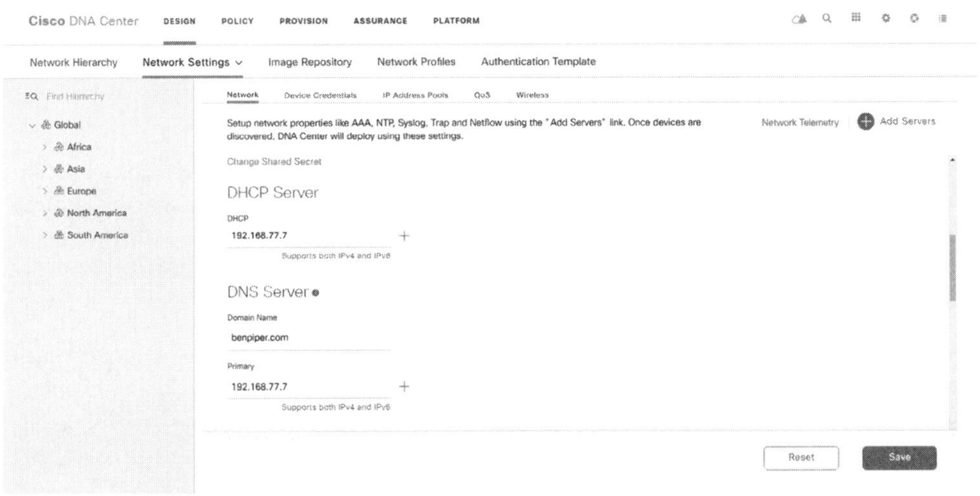

Cisco DNA Provision

This is where the fabric underlay configuration happens. Here you can discover devices, onboard them, and assign them to a fabric device role. You can also configure host authentication settings and host address pools. Figure 11.4 shows a sample inventory of nodes that are a part of the fabric.

FIGURE 11.4   Inventory page under the Provision workflow of Cisco DNA Center

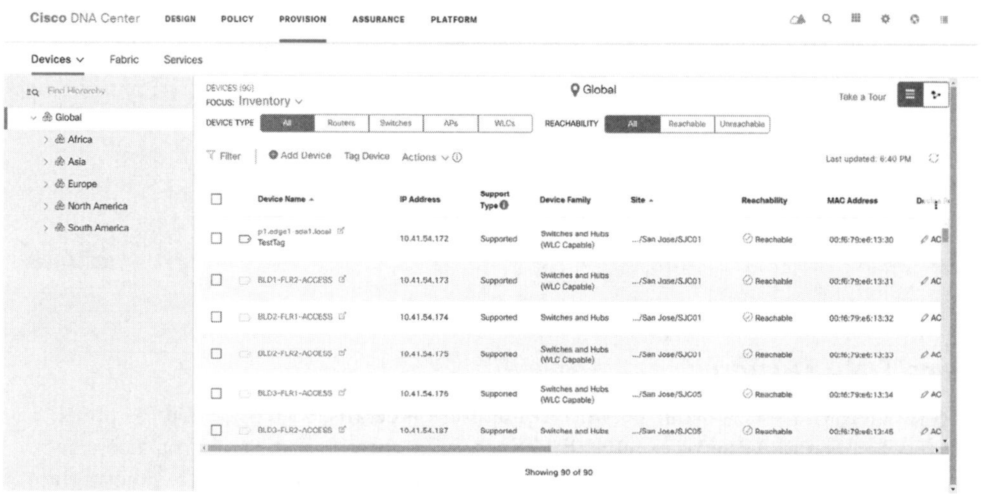

Figure 11.5 shows the configuration of a switch that's configured as both a fabric edge node and an embedded WLAN controller.

FIGURE 11.5   Fabric Infrastructure page under the Provision workflow of Cisco DNA Center

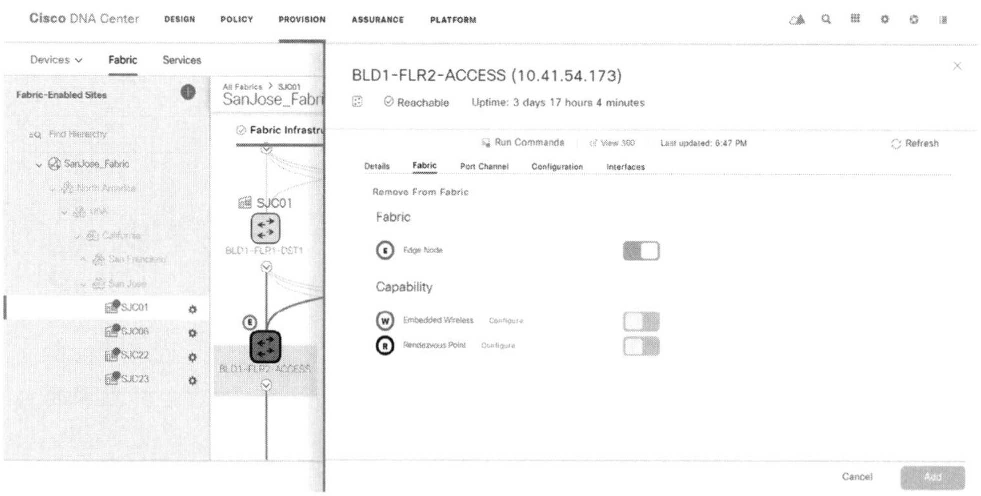

Finally, Figure 11.6 shows the Host Onboarding page, where you can assign virtual networks and host address pools.

FIGURE 11.6   Fabric Host Onboarding page under the Provision workflow of Cisco DNA Center

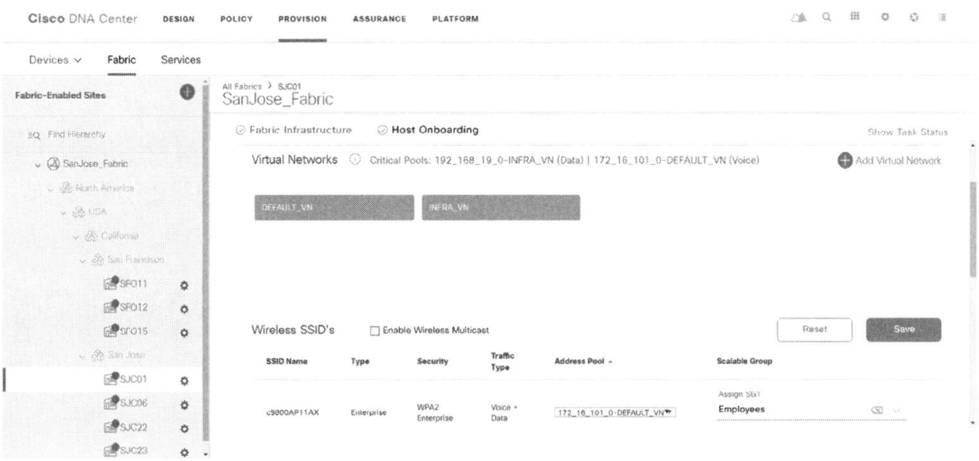

Cisco DNA Assurance

The Assurance workflow provides a plethora of charts, graphs, and analytics to help you monitor the traffic patterns, latency, packet drops, wireless signal strength and performance, and application performance and usage. The workflow provides four different dashboards:

- Overall Health
- Application Health
- Client Health
- Network Health

The Overall Health dashboard, shown in Figure 11.7, can help you spot issues early. It gives you a high-level view of the health of your fabric devices, broken down by role. It also shows a health overview of both wired and wireless clients.

The Application Health dashboard, shown in Figure 11.8, shows you the applications in use on the network, as well as their network performance. This can come in handy when someone complains about an application being slow!

FIGURE 11.7 The Overall Health dashboard in the Assurance workflow of Cisco DNA Center

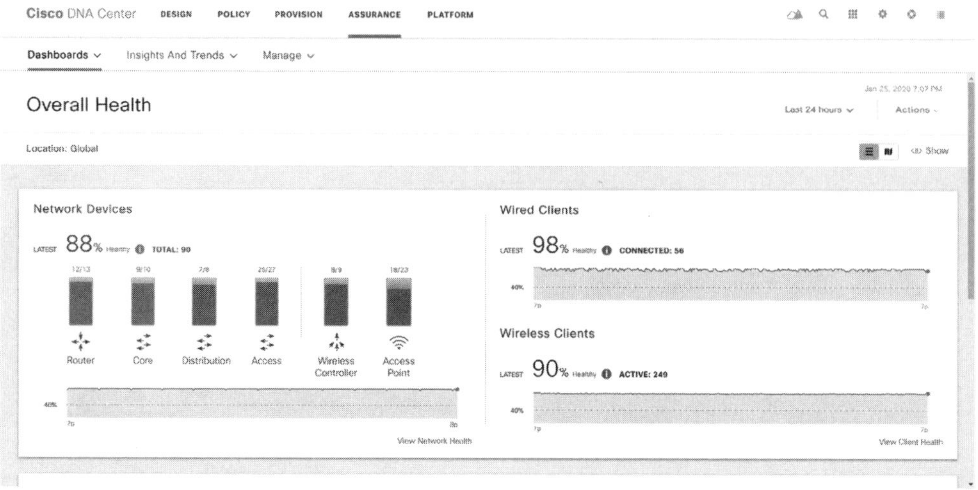

FIGURE 11.8 The Application Health dashboard in the Assurance workflow of Cisco DNA Center

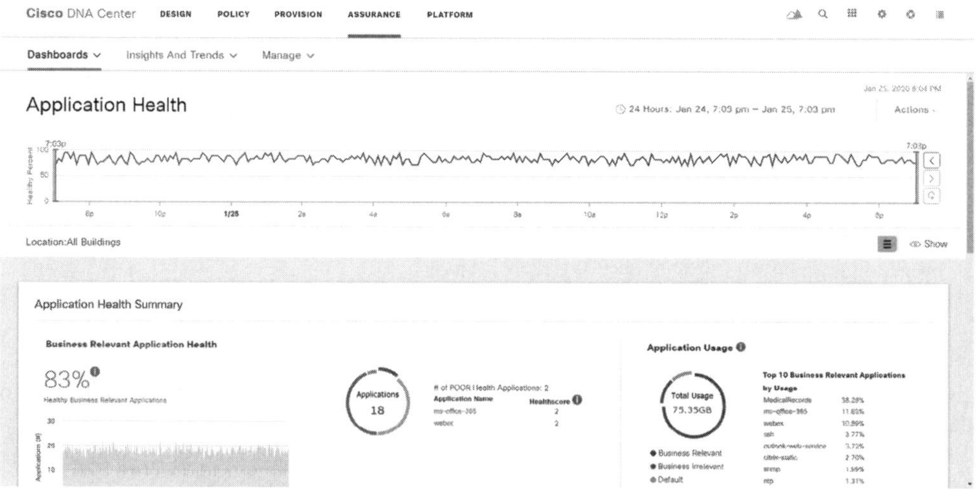

The Client Health dashboard shown in Figure 11.9 gives you a lot of detail about client performance, such as how long it takes to connect to the network, wireless interference, device types, throughput rates, and more.

FIGURE 11.9 The Client Health dashboard in the Assurance workflow of Cisco DNA Center

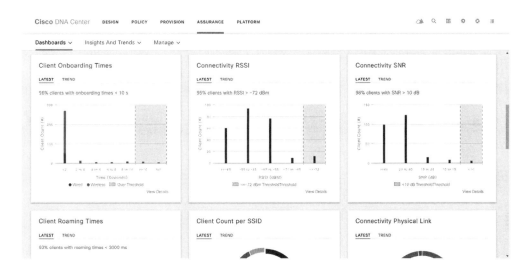

Software-Defined WAN

Cisco's SD-WAN solution was originally developed by a company named Viptela, so you'll sometimes see references to Viptela to distinguish Cisco SD-WAN from its other SD-WAN solution, Meraki SD-WAN, which we're not going to cover here. The giveaway is that many Cisco SD-WAN components begin with the letter *v*, as you're about to see.

The idea behind Cisco SD-WAN is to virtualize the WAN by treating Internet transport and traditional WAN connections (such as MPLS or Metro Ethernet) as the underlay and creating seamless overlay tunnels on top of them and thus forming—you guessed it—a fabric. Combine this with automation to provision and configure WAN edge devices, and you've got something that sounds a lot like SD-Access, only applied to the WAN. The fabric Cisco SD-WAN creates is called a secure extensible network (SEN), and it consists of four components:

- vManage Network Management System (NMS)
- vSmart Controller
- vBond Orchestrator
- vEdge Routers

(There are those *v* components I was telling you about.)

vManage Network Management System

Somewhat analogous to Cisco DNA Center, this is the GUI for managing the SEN fabric. The NMS runs on a server, typically in a data center or other centralized location. It's the central configuration and certificate repository for all the vEdge routers at the edge of each site and provides connectivity to the SEN fabric. Figure 11.10 gives you a glimpse of the vManage NMS.

FIGURE 11.10   The vManage Network Management System web interface

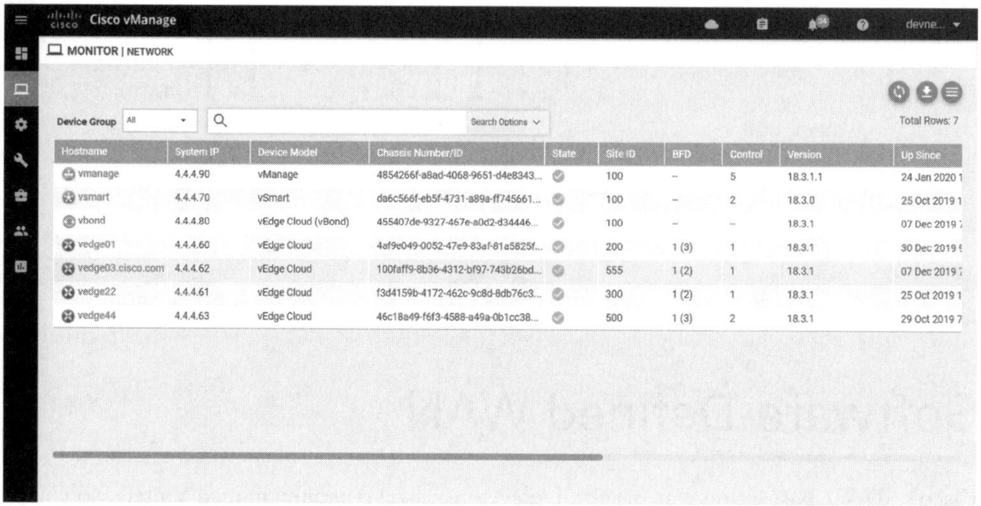

vSmart Controller

The vSmart controller is responsible for authenticating vEdge routers, granting them permission to participate in the SEN fabric. The controller establishes an encrypted Datagram Transport Layer Security (DTLS) tunnel to each vEdge router, over which it sends and receives routing and forwarding information using the Overlay Management Protocol (OMP). The controller maintains a centralized route table (much akin to a LISP map server). It also uses this tunnel to push traffic segmentation, access control, and traffic engineering policies.

The vSmart controller may run on the same hardware as the vManage NMS. Alternatively, it can run as a VM. Other than providing an IP address for the controller and the IP address of the vBond orchestrator, you don't have to configure the vSmart controller manually. The NMS is responsible for provisioning the vSmart controller. For resiliency and load balancing, you can have up to 20 controllers participating in a single SEN fabric.

vBond Orchestrator

The vBond orchestrator plays matchmaker between vSmart controllers and vEdge routers. The vBond orchestrator must have a public IP address so that vEdge routers and vSmart controllers can initially connect to it. This overcomes any NAT traversal issues caused by the vSmart Controller and vEdge routers from being hidden behind NAT routers. Also, the vBond orchestrator authenticates any vEdge routers that try to join the fabric. (This authentication occurs separately from the authentication performed by the vSmart controller.) The vBond orchestrator actually runs on a vEdge router, but because it doesn't actively participate in data transport for the SEN fabric, it's referred to generically as a vEdge device.

vEdge Routers

The vEdge router, as you probably expect, sits at the edge of the WAN connection and serves as the data on-ramp to the SEN fabric. Each pair of vEdge routers builds an IPsec tunnel, creating a fully meshed overlay that composes the data plane of the SEN fabric. Each WAN interface on the router is assigned a color corresponding to the type of WAN transport. If the WAN transport is private (e.g., MPLS or Metro Ethernet), such that it uses private IP addresses, then you can use one of the predefined private colors, such as `mpls` and `metro-ethernet`. In this case, the router will build its tunnels using the private WAN IP addresses.

On the other hand, if the WAN transport uses a public IP address (such as an Internet circuit), there's a good chance one or both routers is behind a NAT router and can't be reached via a public IP address. In that case, the vEdge routers will use NAT traversal (NAT-T) tricks to establish the tunnel. Certain colors are reserved for public WAN transport, including blue, red, green, gold, silver, and of course `internet`, `public-internet`, and `default`.

SD-WAN achieves traffic segmentation using separate VPNs. Think of a VPN as a VRF or VN, except instead of being identified by a text string, each VPN is identified by a unique number. VPN 0 is always the transport VPN, and it's associated with the interfaces that face the WAN circuits. VPN 512 is reserved for the management interface. Any other VPNs you create are called service VPNs, and they contain interfaces that connect to the LAN side of the vEdge router.

The vEdge router offers standard routing protocols such as BGP and OSPF, first-hop redundancy using VRRP, and all the other normal features you'd expect to find on a router, including QoS, ACLs, and 802.1Q VLAN tagging. To make the cloud a part of your SD-WAN, you can deploy a vEdge cloud router, also called a cEdge router, into your cloud environment. The NMS is responsible for provisioning each vEdge router.

Network Programmability and Automation

We've talked at a high level about how Cisco SD-Access and Cisco SD-WAN automate campus and WAN network deployments, changes, and monitoring. Now it's time to discuss how this automation works under the hood. The network automation these SDN solutions provide can be broken down into two categories:

- **Application programming interfaces (APIs)**—Fabric network devices use APIs to communicate with the Cisco DNA Center controller, for example, to send authentication requests on behalf of hosts that connect.

- **Device programmability**—Cisco DNA Center and vManage NMS use the NETCONF protocol and device APIs to push device configurations to fabric devices, such as fabric edge nodes and vEdge routers. You'll also learn about NETCONF's cousin, Representational State Transfer Configuration (RESTCONF).

We're going to look at some straightforward programmatic examples of how to use these various APIs. Don't worry if you don't have programming experience. The ENCOR exam doesn't require you to know how to use them, only that you understand them.

The Cisco DNA Center Intent API

Unless you have a software development background, you probably haven't thought too much about APIs. You use them all the time, but unless you know what to look for, they're almost invisible. When performing workflow tasks using the Cisco DNA Center web interface, behind the scenes, the web interface is communicating with the DNAC network controller platform (NCP) subsystem using what's called the Intent API. The Intent API uses standard HTTPS actions to send commands and receive data from the NCP. APIs that use HTTPS actions—GET, POST, PUT, and DELETE—are said to be using representational state transfer (REST), so they're called REST or RESTful APIs.

So, what's the big deal about the Intent API? Cisco DNAC exposes the Intent API to programs outside of the Cisco DNAC platform. Such APIs are commonly called northbound APIs, in contrast to the southbound APIs that the controller uses to communicate with managed devices. Third-party programs can send API calls to the NCP to do almost anything you can do using the Cisco DNA Center web interface! For example, you could write a script to get detailed device information on a switch. In fact, you're going to learn how to do that right now!

Python

You're going to use the Python programming language interpreter to explore the Intent API. Go to www.python.org/downloads/ to download Python 3 or later. Once you've installed it, be sure to install the required requests and urllib3 libraries using the command pip3 install requests urllib3. They will allow Python to send RESTful API requests.

```
PS C:\Users\ben> pip3 install requests urllib3
Collecting requests
  Downloading
https://files.pythonhosted.org/packages/51/bd/23c926cd341ea6b7dd0b2a00aba99ae0f828
be89d72b2190f27c11d4b7fb
/requests-2.22.0-py2.py3-none-any.whl (57kB)
     61kB 660kB/s
Collecting urllib3
  Downloading
https://files.pythonhosted.org/packages/e8/74/6e4f91745020f967d09332bb2b8b9b
10090957334692eb88ea4afe91b77f
/urllib3-1.25.8-py2.py3-none-any.whl (125kB)
     133kB 1.6MB/s
Collecting idna<2.9,>=2.5 (from requests)
  Downloading
https://files.pythonhosted.org/packages/14/2c/
cd551d81dbe15200be1cf41cd03869a46fe7226e7450af7a6545bfc474c9
/idna-2.8-py2.py3-none-any.whl (58kB)
     61kB 3.8MB/s
Collecting chardet<3.1.0,>=3.0.2 (from requests)
  Downloading
https://files.pythonhosted.org/packages/bc/a9/01ffebfb562e4274b6487b4bb1ddec7ca5
5ec7510b22e4c51f14098443b8
/chardet-3.0.4-py2.py3-none-any.whl (133kB)
     143kB 3.3MB/s
Collecting certifi>=2017.4.17 (from requests)
  Downloading
https://files.pythonhosted.org/packages/b9/63/
df50cac98ea0d5b006c55a399c3bf1db9da7b5a24de7890bc9cfd5dd9e99
/certifi-2019.11.28-py2.py3-none-any.whl (156kB)
     163kB 2.2MB/s
Installing collected packages: urllib3, idna, chardet, certifi, requests
Successfully installed certifi-2019.11.28 chardet-3.0.4 idna-2.8 requests-2.22.0
urllib3-1.25.8
```

Now open your Python interpreter, and let's get started! By the way, if you don't feel like typing a lot, or just want to view the code by itself, it's available for download at https://github.com/benpiper/ccnp-encor.

```
C:\Users\ben>python
Python 3.8.1 (tags/v3.8.1:1b293b6, Dec 18 2019, 23:11:46) [MSC v.1916 64 bit
(AMD64)] on win32
Type "help", "copyright", "credits" or "license" for more information.
```

Import the Python libraries we'll need to use the Intent API:

```
>>> import json
>>> import requests
>>> import urllib3
>>> from requests.auth import HTTPBasicAuth
```

Intent API Authentication

Cisco DevNet (https://developer.cisco.com/site/sandbox) offers free sandbox environments that you can use to practice your skills. We'll be using the free Cisco DNA Center sandbox. Using the username **devnetuser** and the password **Cisco123!**, authenticate to Cisco DNA Center to obtain a token that you'll use in future API requests. This saves you from having to provide a username and password with every API request:

```
>>> response = requests.post("https://sandboxdnac.cisco.com/api/system/v1/auth/
token",
auth=HTTPBasicAuth("devnetuser","Cisco123!"))
```

View the HTTP response code:

```
>>> response
<Response [200]>
>>>
```

The response code is HTTP 200 OK, which means that the request was successful. Let's view the response body in JavaScript Object Notation (JSON) format:

```
>>> response.json()
```
```
{'Token':
'eyJ0eXAiOiJKV1QiLCJhbGciOiJIUzI1NiJ9.eyJzdWIiOiI1ZGM0OWJhZDE0ODVjNTAwNGMwZmJlZmUiLCJh
dXRoU291cmNlIjoiaW50ZXJuYWwiLCJ0ZW5hbnROYW1lIjoiVE5UMCIsInJvbGVzIjpbIjVkYYzQ0NGQ1MTQ4NW
M1MDA0YzBmYjIxMiJdLCJ0ZW5hbnRJZCI6IjVkYYzQ0NGQzMTQ4NWM1MDA0YzBmYjIwYiIsImV4cCI6MTU4MDA4
Mzg4NiwidXNlcm5hbWUiOiJkZXZuZXR1c2VyIn0.bgOGJrW4r6wgXgt7sNzBQEO6Dg1hPvif7bblPkPzPw4'}
```
```
>>>
```

The format of JSON is that of a key and value pair, separated by a colon. Token is the key and the long random string that follows it is the value. Multiple key-value pairs can be stored within a JSON object, the beginning and end of which are marked by curly braces. Next, let's extract the token value and store it in the variable token:

```
>>> token = response.json()["Token"]
```

To authenticate to the API, we need to pass in the token value using the x-auth-token HTTP header. We'll structure the header in JSON format:

```
>>> headers = {
... 'x-auth-token': response.json()["Token"]
... }
>>>
```

Next, we'll use the network-device API to obtain information on all network devices under the control of a Cisco DNA Center controller:

```
>>> url="https://sandboxdnac.cisco.com/dna/intent/api/v1/network-device"
>>>
>>> # Send the GET request
>>> response = requests.get(url, headers=headers)
```

The response body is in JSON and it's long, making it difficult to read. We'll clean it up a bit using the json.dumps function:

```
>>> print(json.dumps(response.json(), indent=2))
{
  "response": [
    {
      "family": "Routers",
      "type": "Cisco ASR 1001-X Router",
      "errorCode": null,
      "location": null,
      "macAddress": "00:c8:8b:80:bb:00",
      "hostname": "asr1001-x.abc.inc",
      "role": "BORDER ROUTER",
      "lastUpdateTime": 1580079254622,
      "serialNumber": "FXS1932Q1SE",
      "softwareVersion": "16.3.2",
      "locationName": null,
      "upTime": "79 days, 22:41:33.38",
      "lastUpdated": "2020-01-26 22:54:14",
      "tagCount": "0",
```

```
        "inventoryStatusDetail": "<status><general code=\"SUCCESS\"/></status>",
        "errorDescription": null,
        "softwareType": "IOS-XE",
        "collectionInterval": "Global Default",
        "roleSource": "AUTO",
        "bootDateTime": "2019-11-08 00:14:32",
        "apManagerInterfaceIp": "",
        "associatedWlcIp": "",
        "collectionStatus": "Managed",
        "interfaceCount": "12",
        "lineCardCount": "9",
        "managementIpAddress": "10.10.22.253",
        "memorySize": "3819298032",
        "platformId": "ASR1001-X",
        "reachabilityFailureReason": "",
        "reachabilityStatus": "Reachable",
        "series": "Cisco ASR 1000 Series Aggregation Services Routers",
        "snmpContact": "",
        "snmpLocation": "",
        "tunnelUdpPort": null,
        "waasDeviceMode": null,
        "instanceTenantId": "5dc444d31485c5004c0fb20b",
        "instanceUuid": "1cfd383a-7265-47fb-96b3-f069191a0ed5",
        "id": "1cfd383a-7265-47fb-96b3-f069191a0ed5"
    },
# Output truncated for brevity
```

We can get detailed information on a device by using a different API call and specify the device's IP address. Let's try `10.10.22.70`:

```
>>> url="https://sandboxdnac.cisco.com/dna/intent/api/v1/network-device/
ip-address/10.10.22.70"
>>> response = requests.get(url, headers=headers)
>>> print(json.dumps(response.json(), indent=2))
{
  "response": {
    "family": "Switches and Hubs",
    "type": "Cisco Catalyst 9300 Switch",
    "errorCode": null,
    "location": null,
```

```
    "macAddress": "f8:7b:20:71:4d:80",
    "hostname": "cat_9k_2.abc.inc",
    "role": "ACCESS",
    "lastUpdateTime": 1580078733427,
    "serialNumber": "FCW2140L039",
    "softwareVersion": "16.6.4a",
    "locationName": null,
    "upTime": "79 days, 22:01:33.99",
    "lastUpdated": "2020-01-26 22:45:33",
    "tagCount": "0",
    "inventoryStatusDetail": "<status><general code=\"SYNC\"/></status>",
    "errorDescription": null,
    "softwareType": "IOS-XE",
    "collectionInterval": "Global Default",
    "roleSource": "AUTO",
    "bootDateTime": "2019-11-08 00:40:00",
    "apManagerInterfaceIp": "",
    "associatedWlcIp": "",
    "collectionStatus": "In Progress",
    "interfaceCount": "41",
    "lineCardCount": "2",
    "lineCardId": "8c81b39d-4003-43f6-a94b-894174a3033e, e4fcc471-4308-4ea7-
b5b2-e4eace5189c9",
    "managementIpAddress": "10.10.22.70",
    "memorySize": "1425966824",
    "platformId": "C9300-24UX",
    "reachabilityFailureReason": "",
    "reachabilityStatus": "Reachable",
    "series": "Cisco Catalyst 9300 Series Switches",
    "snmpContact": "",
    "snmpLocation": "",
    "tunnelUdpPort": null,
    "waasDeviceMode": null,
    "instanceTenantId": "5dc444d31485c5004c0fb20b",
    "instanceUuid": "3e48558a-237a-4bca-8823-0580b88c6acf",
    "id": "3e48558a-237a-4bca-8823-0580b88c6acf"
  },
  "version": "1.0"
}
```

The Intent API makes it easy to create scripts to pull information and push configurations in much the same way server administrators have done for years. If you want to try out some more API calls, official documentation for the Intent API is at `https://developer.cisco.com/docs/dna-center/api/1-3-3-x`.

HTTP Response Codes

An HTTP response code that begins with $2xx$ is what you want, but it's not always what you get. If we had used invalid credentials when authenticating, we would have instead gotten an HTTP 401 Not Authenticated error:

```
>>> response401 =
requests.post("https://sandboxdnac.cisco.com/api/system/v1/auth/token",
auth=HTTPBasicAuth("devnetuser","wrongpassword"))
```

The response text gives us another clue:

```
>>> response401.text
'Authentication has failed. Please provide valid credentials.'
```

You'll also get a 401 response if you try to call the API without specifying a valid token. Notice we're leaving out the headers that contain the authentication token:

```
>>> requests.get(url)
<Response [401]>
```

If you accidentally call a nonexistent API, you'll get an HTTP 404 Not Found error:

```
>>> wrongurl="https://sandboxdnac.cisco.com/api/v1/networkdevices"
>>> requests.get(wrongurl, headers=headers)
<Response [404]>
```

Table 11.1 shows a list of HTTP response codes and their interpretations.

TABLE 11.1   HTTP response codes

HTTP response code	Status	Notes
200	Successful GET or PUT	Used when requesting information or pushing configuration changes.
201	Successful POST	A POST is typically used to create new resources.
202	Success—Accepted	The request will take a while to process. The response body contains an execution ID, which you can use to check on the status of the request.

HTTP response code	Status	Notes
204	Successful DELETE	This is the opposite of POST.
30x	Redirect	Occurs if you use HTTP instead of HTTPS.
400	Failure	Usually means a request was not formatted properly.
401	Not authenticated	Occurs if you don't specify a valid token with your request.
403	Forbidden	Not to be confused with 401, this error means you're not *authorized* to make the request.
404	Not found	You probably mistyped the URL.
405	Method not allowed	You may get this if you use the wrong verb for an API call, e.g., as a POST instead of a GET.
500	Server failure	It's not your fault. An internal server error is to blame.

vManage REST API

If you understand the way the Cisco DNA Center Intent API works, then you'll find the vManage REST API easy to follow. There are some differences in the way we interact with this API regarding authentication. But otherwise, the way you use the API to get data and push configuration changes will look very familiar.

Let's jump back into the Python interpreter and view the OMP routes being advertised to a certain vEdge router. If you want to follow along, the code for this is also available on my GitHub repository at https://github.com/benpiper/ccnp-encor. As before, we'll import the needed libraries:

```
Python 3.8.1 (tags/v3.8.1:1b293b6, Dec 18 2019, 23:11:46) [MSC v.1916 64 bit
(AMD64)] on win32
Type "help", "copyright", "credits" or "license" for more information.
>>> import json
>>> import requests
>>> import urllib3
>>> from requests.auth import HTTPBasicAuth
```

First, we'll authenticate to the vManage controller. It uses cookies for authentication, so we won't have to manually store and pass a token as before.

```
>>> s = requests.Session()
>>> data = {
...             'j_username': "devnetuser",
...             'j_password': "Cisco123!"
...         }
>>> url = "https://sandboxsdwan.cisco.com:8443/j_security_check"
>>> response = s.post(url, data=data, verify=False)
```

Because we're not checking the validity of the TLS certificate (thanks to the verify=False directive), Python complains. For clarity, I've removed the warning from subsequent output.

```
InsecureRequestWarning: Unverified HTTPS request is being made to host
'sandboxsdwan.cisco.com'. Adding certificate verification is strongly advised.
```

Use the vManage API to view the OMP routes being advertised to the vEdge Cloud (cEdge) router with the IP address 4.4.4.60:

```
>>> url = "https://sandboxsdwan.cisco.com:8443/dataservice/device/omp/routes/
received?deviceId=4.4.4.60"
>>> response = s.get(url, data=data, verify=False)
```

The response contains column heading definitions, so to show only the interesting information, we'll restrict the output to the data JSON object, which contains a separate nested object to represent each OMP route.

```
>>> print(json.dumps(response.json()["data"], indent=2))
[
  {
    "overlay-id": "1",
    "color": "default",
    "vdevice-name": "4.4.4.60",
    "prefix": "1.1.1.0/24",
    "ip": "4.4.4.62",
    "from-peer": "4.4.4.70",
    "label": "1003",
    "encap": "ipsec",
    "site-id": "555",
    "originator": "4.4.4.62",
    "vpn-id": "1",
    "vdevice-host-name": "vedge01",
```

```
      "path-id": "116387",
      "protocol": "connected",
      "vdevice-dataKey": "4.4.4.60-ipv4-1",
      "metric": "0",
      "lastupdated": 1580094942989,
      "attribute-type": "installed",
      "address-family": "ipv4",
      "status": "R S"
    },
    {
      "overlay-id": "1",
      "color": "default",
      "vdevice-name": "4.4.4.60",
      "prefix": "1.1.1.0/24",
      "ip": "4.4.4.62",
      "from-peer": "4.4.4.70",
      "label": "1003",
      "encap": "ipsec",
      "site-id": "555",
      "originator": "4.4.4.62",
      "vpn-id": "1",
      "vdevice-host-name": "vedge01",
      "path-id": "116388",
      "protocol": "connected",
      "vdevice-dataKey": "4.4.4.60-ipv4-1",
      "metric": "0",
      "lastupdated": 1580094942989,
      "attribute-type": "installed",
      "address-family": "ipv4",
      "status": "C I R"
    },
    {
      "overlay-id": "1",
      "color": "default",
      "vdevice-name": "4.4.4.60",
      "prefix": "2.2.2.0/24",
      "ip": "4.4.4.60",
      "from-peer": "0.0.0.0",
      "label": "1002",
      "encap": "ipsec",
```

```
      "site-id": "200",
      "originator": "4.4.4.60",
      "vpn-id": "1",
      "vdevice-host-name": "vedge01",
      "path-id": "65",
      "protocol": "connected",
      "vdevice-dataKey": "4.4.4.60-ipv4-1",
      "metric": "0",
      "lastupdated": 1580094942989,
      "attribute-type": "installed",
      "address-family": "ipv4",
      "status": "C Red R"
    },
    {
      "overlay-id": "1",
      "color": "default",
      "vdevice-name": "4.4.4.60",
      "prefix": "4.4.4.0/24",
      "ip": "4.4.4.63",
      "from-peer": "4.4.4.70",
      "label": "1005",
      "encap": "ipsec",
      "site-id": "500",
      "originator": "4.4.4.63",
      "vpn-id": "1",
      "vdevice-host-name": "vedge01",
      "path-id": "116386",
      "protocol": "connected",
      "vdevice-dataKey": "4.4.4.60-ipv4-1",
      "metric": "0",
      "lastupdated": 1580094942989,
      "attribute-type": "installed",
      "address-family": "ipv4",
      "status": "R S"
    },
    {
      "overlay-id": "1",
      "color": "default",
      "vdevice-name": "4.4.4.60",
      "prefix": "4.4.4.0/24",
```

```
        "ip": "4.4.4.63",
        "from-peer": "4.4.4.70",
        "label": "1005",
        "encap": "ipsec",
        "site-id": "500",
        "originator": "4.4.4.63",
        "vpn-id": "1",
        "vdevice-host-name": "vedge01",
        "path-id": "116389",
        "protocol": "connected",
        "vdevice-dataKey": "4.4.4.60-ipv4-1",
        "metric": "0",
        "lastupdated": 1580094942989,
        "attribute-type": "installed",
        "address-family": "ipv4",
        "status": "C I R"
    }
]
>>>
```

NETCONF

Cisco DNA Center and vManage use the NETCONF to configure they devices they manage. NETCONF (RFC 6241) provides a standardized API for configuring and retrieving configuration and state information from network devices. NETCONF listens on TCP port 830 by default. NETCONF differs from a REST API in a couple of ways. First, it's designed for making configuration changes on—and not retrieving information from—a device. Second, NETCONF uses SSH for transport rather than HTTPS.

It's important to understand that NETCONF is not another way of getting to the CLI. Cisco DNA Center doesn't use NETCONF to send a string of configuration commands to each device it configures, as you may do if you're copying a configuration from Notepad into an SSH session. Instead, NETCONF represents configuration directives and data in a hierarchical Extensible Markup Language (XML) format. Consider the following XML snippet that sets the IP address of interface GigabitEthernet1. This is representative of the data that Cisco DNA Center would send to a router via the NETCONF protocol.

```
<rpc message-id="101"
    xmlns="urn:ietf:params:xml:ns:netconf:base:1.0">
    <edit-config>
        <target>
            <running/>
```

```
            </target>
            <config>
                <interfaces xmlns="urn:ietf:params:xml:ns:yang:ietf-interfaces">
                    <interface>
                        <name>GigabitEthernet1</name>
                        <ipv4 xmlns="urn:ietf:params:xml:ns:yang:ietf-ip">
                            <address>
                                <ip>10.97.53.10</ip>
                                <prefix-length>24</prefix-length>
                            </address>
                        </ipv6>
                    </interface>
                </interfaces>
            </config>
        </edit-config>
</rpc>
```

The first thing you should notice is that almost none of that is intuitive. Your eyes probably went right to the IP address. But what about the rest of it? The `<edit-config>` tag describes the operation we want to execute—that is, to edit the configuration. (To just read it, we'd use the `<get-config>` operation.). The `<target>` and `<running/>` tags indicate we're editing the running configuration, as opposed to the startup configuration. The rest of the XML, to some extent, follows the familiar CLI hierarchy. The `<interface>` tag indicates we're configuring an interface, specified by the value beside the `<name>` tag. Under that, we specify an IPv4 address and prefix length.

YANG

The XML structure, required elements, and allowed values are dictated by various YANG data models. YANG is a structured data modeling language designed specifically for NETCONF. Essentially, YANG models set the rules for what constitutes valid configuration parameters. To better understand how this works, look next to the `<ipv4>` tag in the XML where there's a reference to `urn:ietf:params:xml:ns:yang:ietf-ip`. This is an IETF standardized YANG model for assigning IPv4 addresses to interfaces. Following is a YANG snippet from this model:

```
list address {
    key "ip";
    description
    "The list of IPv4 addresses on the interface.";
    leaf ip {
        type inet:ipv4-address-no-zone;
        description
        "The IPv4 address on the interface.";
```

```
    }
    choice subnet {
        mandatory true;
        description
        "The subnet can be specified as a prefix length or,
            if the server supports non-contiguous netmasks, as
            a netmask.";
        leaf prefix-length {
            type uint8 {
                range "0..32";
            }
        description
            "The length of the subnet prefix.";
        }
        leaf netmask {
            if-feature ipv4-non-contiguous-netmasks;
            type yang:dotted-quad;
            description
                "The subnet specified as a netmask.";
        }
    }
}
```

Notice that the subnet is mandatory and that the prefix length must be between 0 and 32 bits. Alternatively, the subnet may be specified as a dotted-decimal netmask. If you're curious, you can find the entire model at `https://github.com/YangModels/yang/blob/master/standard/ietf/RFC/ietf-ip%402018-02-22.yang`.

Both the devices sending and receiving the XML via NETCONF have this (and other) YANG models. That way, the sender (e.g., Cisco DNA Center) knows exactly how to format the XML in such a way that the receiver (e.g., the switch) can understand it. YANG models specific to Cisco devices can be found at `https://github.com/YangModels/yang/tree/master/vendor/cisco`.

RESTCONF

RESTCONF (RFC 8040) is a lot like NETCONF with a RESTful API. It differs from NETCONF in a few significant ways. Because it's RESTful, it uses HTTP instead of SSH. It transfers configuration data using JSON or XML. However, the XML looks different than with NETCONF. For starters, instead of using XML tags to define the operation, such as `<get-config>` or `<edit-config>`, RESTCONF uses HTTP verbs such as `GET` for retrieving information, and `POST`, `PUT`, `PATCH`, or `DELETE` for editing the configuration. RESTCONF moves the YANG model references out of the body (XML or JSON) and into the URL. For example, to set the IP address for GigabitEthernet1 on a device, you'd send a `PUT` request to the device's RESTCONF endpoint URL. Such a URL may look like this:

```
https://ios-xe-mgmt.cisco.com:9443/restconf/data/ietf-interfaces:interfaces/
interface=GigabitEthernet1.
```

The body of the request could be in XML or JSON, and would need to include the interface name, type, IP address, and netmask. For example, the JSON-formatted request body may look like this:

```
{
  "name": "GigabitEthernet1",
  "ipv4": {
    "address": {
      "ip": "10.97.53.10",
      "netmask": "255.255.255.0"
    }
  }
}
```

There are no YANG references in the body because they're in the URL. This makes the code easier both to read and to write. If you were writing a program to configure a device, you might prefer RESTCONF because it offers you the flexibility of choosing between XML or JSON.

Embedded Event Manager

Your network automation options aren't limited to SDN products. Outside of the SDN world, there are several other automation platforms that you can use to automate device configurations and collect device information. One such tool is Cisco's Embedded Event Manager.

Embedded Event Manager (EEM) is an on-device automation tool that uses the Tcl scripting language that you learned about in Chapter 7, "The Border Gateway Protocol (BGP)." The scripts that you write for EEM are called *applets*. An EEM applet can take some action based on a condition or event, such as an interface going down. For instance, if the line protocol (i.e., Ethernet) goes down on the GigabitEthernet1 interface, you can have EEM automatically enter the CLI commands to bounce the interface by shutting it down and bringing it back up. The following code snippet shows how to create the EEM applet to accomplish this:

```
R1(config)#event manager applet WatchGig0/1
R1(config-applet)#event syslog pattern "Line protocol on Interface
GigabitEthernet0/1, changed state to down" period 1
R1(config-applet)#action 1.0 cli command "enable"
R1(config-applet)#action 2.0 cli command "configure terminal"
R1(config-applet)#action 3.0 cli command "interface gi0/1"
R1(config-applet)#action 4.0 cli command "shut"
R1(config-applet)#action 5.0 cli command "no shut"
R1(config-applet)#exit
```

The applet is triggered by the syslog message indicating that the line protocol on Gi0/1 is down. This is the event that triggers the actions that follow. The actions are executed in the order in which you number them. You can number the actions using integers (such as 10, 20, etc.) or by using floating-point values as in the previous snippet. It's a good practice to leave gaps between the numbers so you can go in later and add additional actions before or after, if needed. Once you create this script, EEM immediately begins monitoring for the event. Let's test it out by shutting down the Gi0/1 interface:

```
R1(config)#int gi0/1
R1(config-if)#shut
R1(config-if)#^Z
R1#
%SYS-5-CONFIG_I: Configured from console by console
R1#
! The interface shuts down, bringing the line protocol down with it.
%LINK-5-CHANGED: Interface GigabitEthernet0/1, changed state to administratively down
%LINEPROTO-5-UPDOWN: Line protocol on Interface GigabitEthernet0/1, changed
state to down
R1#
! Immediately, EEM kicks in and executes the actions, bringing the interface
back up.
%LINK-3-UPDOWN: Interface GigabitEthernet0/1, changed state to up
R1#
%LINEPROTO-5-UPDOWN: Line protocol on Interface GigabitEthernet0/1, changed
state to up
```

You can view the history of EEM applet executions by using the show event manager history events command. Another handy thing you can do with EEM is create scripts that you can run manually. The following EEM applet pulls a summary of IP routing and CEF information and writes the information to the syslog:

```
event manager applet routingsummary
 event none
 action 1.0 cli command "enable"
 action 2.0 cli command "show ip route summary"
 action 2.5 syslog msg "$_cli_result"
 action 3.0 cli command "show ip proto summary"
 action 3.5 syslog msg "$_cli_result"
 action 4.0 cli command "show ip cef summary"
 action 4.5 syslog msg "$_cli_result"
```

To run the script, execute the following command:

```
R1#event manager run routingsummary

%HA_EM-6-LOG: routingsummary:
IP routing table name is default (0x0)
IP routing table maximum-paths is 32
Route Source    Networks      Subnets      Replicates  Overhead    Memory (bytes)
connected       0             2            0           136         360
static          0             0            0           0           0
application     0             0            0           0           0
ospf 1          0             0            0           0           0
  Intra-area: 0 Inter-area: 0 External-1: 0 External-2: 0
  NSSA External-1: 0 NSSA External-2: 0
internal        1                                                  440

R1#Total        1             2            0           136         800
R1#
%HA_EM-6-LOG: routingsummary:
Index Process Name
0       connected
1       static
2       application
3       ospf 1
*** IP Routing is NSF aware ***

R1#
%HA_EM-6-LOG: routingsummary:
IPv4 CEF is enabled and running
VRF Default
 13 prefixes (13/0 fwd/non-fwd)
 Table id 0x0
 Database epoch:        0 (13 entries at this epoch)

R1#
```

This can save you a lot of typing, particularly with show commands!

Configuration Management Platforms

Configuration management platforms were originally designed for administering servers using an infrastructure-as-code (IaC) approach. In the IaC approach, you place configuration information in structured files, and the configuration management tool reads the files and applies the configuration to the appropriate servers. This might sound a lot like scripting, and in fact it essentially is. But whereas scripting is concerned with simply running commands, configuration management is all about enforcing a consistent configuration state on a system.

Configuration management tools have been extended to support network devices, including Cisco. Some such tools include Ansible, Chef, Puppet, and SaltStack. These platforms are massive, and many books have been written on them, so we're not going to cover them all in detail here. Instead, we'll look at each one's approach to configuration management and how they differ. There are two main areas where configuration management tools differ.

Agent-Based and Agentless

An automation tool can be agent-based or agentless. An agent-based tool requires a special program called an agent to be installed on the device that you want to configure. An agentless tool uses standard protocols, such as SSH, to push configurations down to a device. Platforms that use agents include Puppet, Chef, and SaltStack.

Sometimes, the decision to use an agentless versus agent-based platform might be made for you. On some devices, it's simply not possible to install an agent. For example, you can't install the Puppet agent on a Catalyst switch. Also, security requirements might forbid installing an agent on a device. In those cases, you'll need an agentless platform that uses SSH, such as Ansible, Puppet Bolt, or SaltStack SSH.

Language

The language you use for defining configuration information also varies by platform, but Ruby and YAML (YAML Ain't Markup Language, originally Yet Another Markup Language) are the two most common. YAML is very similar in form to YANG and is easily readable. Following is an example of a YAML configuration file for Ansible (don't worry about the content—just note the format):

```
---
- name: Enable OSPF
  nclu:
    commands:
    - add ospf router-id {{ rid }}
    - add ospf network {{ prefix }} area {{ area }}
    atomic: true
    description: "Enable OSPF"
```

Ruby bears more of a resemblance to Python. To make the language easier to understand, read, and use for nonprogrammers, the platforms that use Ruby abstract away a lot of the Ruby-specific details, leaving you with a simpler version of the language called a domain-specific language (DSL). The following is an example of Puppet manifest file using the Puppet DSL:

```
class webserver::apache {

  $apache = $operatingsystem ? {
    centos => 'httpd',
    ubuntu => 'apache2',
  }

  package { $apache:
    ensure => 'installed',
  }

  service { "$apache":
    enable => true,
    ensure => running,
  }

}
```

Terminology

Another area of difference among the platforms is, of course, terminology. The device configuration directives are always stored in files and usually in some sort of centralized versioned Git repository. Table 11.2 shows a comparison of the different configuration management platforms, including what they call the device configuration files.

TABLE 11.2 Comparison of configuration management tools

Platform	Mode	Language	Device configurations stored in	TCP port numbers
Puppet	Agent-based	Ruby	Manifests	443, 8140, 8142
Puppet Bolt	Agentless	Ruby	Manifests	22, 5985, 5986
Chef	Agent-based	Ruby	Recipes	80, 443
SaltStack	Agent-based	YAML	Formulas	4505, 4506
SaltStack SSH	Agentless	YAML	Formulas	22
Ansible	Agentless	YAML	Playbooks	22

If you know the naming theme of each platform, it's not too difficult to figure out what platform a particular term goes with. For example, Chef has a tool called "knife." A Puppet server is called a "Puppet master." In SaltStack, device-specific configuration details are called "grains." You get the idea.

Summary

If one thing should be clear, it's that SDN and network automation are more complex and initially require much more work than just using the CLI. Some network professionals fear that automation will put them out of a job or make obsolete the skills they've worked so hard to build. But as you've seen, the opposite is true. Without a solid foundation of networking concepts, one can't make heads or tails of SDN workflows or API calls. Although you will need to become more proficient in programming paradigms, that doesn't mean you have to start calling yourself a programmer.

The programming aspect of network programmability is aimed at automation, which reduces the risk of human error (but doesn't eliminate it) and makes adds and changes faster. In some cases, trending and analytics can help you stop problems before they start. But there is a downside. The additional complexity of automation and the use of tunnels makes troubleshooting harder. There will always be software bugs, physical connectivity problems, and misconfigurations. One good reason to learn SDN and network automation is so that you can be the hero who knows how to troubleshoot the network and get it back up and running when it breaks—and it will!

Exam Essentials

Know the Cisco DNA Center workflows.   The four workflows are Policy workflow, Assurance workflow, etc.

Understand the difference between the underlay and overlay networks in SD-Access.   The underlay network uses the IS-IS routing protocol and PIM sparse mode. The overlay uses LISP with proprietary VXLAN encapsulation.

Be able to write and execute an EEM applet.   EEM applets consists of triggering events and actions, the latter including CLI commands. Know how to create EEM applets, both those that are triggered by events and those that must be run manually.

Know the standard HTTP response codes and what they mean.   Broadly speaking, $2xx$ response codes are good and $4xx$ response codes are bad. In particular, a 401 code indicates that you haven't authenticated to the API endpoint.

Understand the purpose of YANG. YANG models provide a standard way of representing configuration information for devices. YANG was specifically created for use with NETCONF.

Exercises

EXERCISE 11.1

Using the code example in this chapter, create a Python script that interacts with the Cisco DNA Center Intent API.

EXERCISE 11.2

Using the code example in this chapter, create a Python script that interacts with the vManage API.

Review Questions

You can find the answers in the appendix.

1. Which of the following SD-Access fabric node roles can provide connectivity to a public cloud?

    A. Fabric edge node

    B. Fabric border node

    C. Control plane node

    D. Fabric WLAN controller node

2. Your SD-WAN consists of a data center and several branch offices. Which of the following must you do to add a cloud environment to your SD-WAN?

    A. Deploy a vEdge router at a branch office

    B. Deploy a vEdge Cloud router at the data center

    C. Deploy a cEdge router into the cloud

    D. Follow the cloud provider's instructions for creating an IPsec VPN

3. Why does SD-Access use VXLAN encapsulation instead of LISP encapsulation?

    A. SD-Access doesn't use VXLAN encapsulation

    B. To extend subnets

    C. To enable IP mobility

    D. To support IPv6

4. Which of the following is true of the VXLAN header used by SD-Access?

    A. It carries IS-IS traffic.

    B. It contains Group Policy tags.

    C. It's encrypted.

    D. It is a standard VXLAN header.

5. Which of the following was designed for campus networks?

    A. Cisco SD-WAN

    B. Cisco SD-Access

    C. Cisco ACI

    D. Cisco VTS

    E. Cisco SDN Center

6. Which of the following control plane protocols does SD-Access use for route advertisements in the overlay?

A. OMP

B. VXLAN

C. Multicast

D. LISP

E. BGP

7. Which of the following components of the SD-Access controller layer provides authentication services?

A. Network Data Platform

B. Network Controller Platform

C. Identity Services Engine

D. TrustSec

E. Network access control

8. Which of the following are *not* part of Cisco SD-WAN? (Choose all that apply.)

A. BGP

B. vSmart controller

C. vBond orchestrator

D. vManage NMS

E. IPsec

F. LISP

9. Which of the following networks can SD-WAN work with? (Choose all that apply.)

A. MPLS

B. T1

C. Metro Ethernet

D. Dedicated Internet access

10. Which SD-WAN component authenticates both vEdge routers and the vSmart controller?

A. OMP

B. vManage orchestrator

C. vManage NMS

D. vBond orchestrator

11. Which of the following is true of SD-WAN?

A. OMP traffic is tunneled over DTLS.

B. The default color can be used with MPLS.

C. The vManage NMS maintains a centralized routing table.

D. The vSmart controller must be configured manually.

12. Which of the following VPN identifiers is used for SD-WAN router management?

    A. 0

    B. 1

    C. 512

    D. 1024

13. Two vEdge routers are behind NAT firewalls connected to an Internet circuit. Which of the following is required to get them to form a tunnel with each other?

    A. One router must be given a public IP address.

    B. No action is required; the routers will use NAT traversal to establish an IPsec tunnel.

    C. Each router must have a public IP address.

    D. You must configure port forwarding.

14. Which Python function would you use to authenticate to the Cisco DNA Center API?

    A. `requests.put()`

    B. `requests.post()`

    C. `requests.get()`

    D. `requests.patch()`

15. Which of the following is true of JSON?

    A. It uses curly braces to denote an object.

    B. It uses colons to denote an object.

    C. It uses curly braces to denote a key-value pair.

    D. It doesn't use commas.

16. What are the differences between YANG and XML? (Choose all that apply.)

    A. YANG is used for carrying configuration data.

    B. YANG uses tags.

    C. XML is used for carrying configuration data.

    D. YANG is used for modeling configuration parameters.

17. What HTTP response code indicates a successful request that will take some time to process?

    A. 200

    B. 201

    C. 202

    D. 204

18. Which of the following HTTP response codes probably indicates that you mistyped a URL? (Choose all that apply.)

   A. 204

   B. 401

   C. 403

   D. 404

   E. 500

19. What's true of the following EEM applet?

```
event manager applet showrib
event none
action 1.0 cli command "enable"
action 20 cli command "show ip route"
```

   A. It will write the output to the syslog.

   B. It can only be executed manually.

   C. It will display the IP routing table in the terminal console.

   D. It won't run.

20. The following code is an example of what language?

```
---
- hosts: switches
  roles:
  - ospf
```

   A. Python

   B. YAML

   C. Ruby

   D. YANG

   E. XML

Chapter

12

Network Security and Monitoring

THE CCNP ENCOR EXAM OBJECTIVES COVERED IN THIS CHAPTER INCLUDE THE FOLLOWING:

3.0 Infrastructure

✓ **3.4 IP Services**

4.0 Network Assurance

✓ **4.1 Diagnose network problems using tools such as debugs, conditional debugs, trace route, ping, SNMP, and syslog**

✓ **4.2 Configure and verify device monitoring using syslog for remote logging**

✓ **4.3 Configure and verify NetFlow and Flexible NetFlow**

✓ **4.4 Configure and verify SPAN/RSPAN/ERSPAN**

✓ **4.5 Configure and verify IPSLA**

5.0 Security

✓ **5.1 Configure and verify device access control**

✓ **5.2 Configure and verify infrastructure security features**

✓ **5.4 Configure and verify wireless security features**

✓ **5.5 Describe the components of network security design**

Security is integrated into every aspect of networking, so getting a holistic look at security requires covering a lot of ground without glossing over the all-important technical fundamentals. In this chapter, we'll look at security from four perspectives: infrastructure security, security products, wireless security, and monitoring.

We'll start by covering infrastructure security. This includes

Locking down device access

Configuring authentication, authorization, and accounting

Creating ACLs

Implementing control plane policing

After that, we'll investigate some Cisco security products and features for endpoint and network security, including

Malware protection

Firepower next-generation firewall

TrustSec and MACsec

We'll then dive into wireless security—particularly authentication using

802.1X and EAP

MAC authentication bypass

WebAuth

Last but not least, we'll take a look at configuring some tried-and-true monitoring tools:

Debugs

SNMP

Syslog

NetFlow

SPAN

IP SLA

Infrastructure Security

It's difficult to separate infrastructure security from network security in general. When we say *infrastructure security*, we're talking about securing management access to network devices and protecting control plane protocols and traffic. At a bare minimum, the two main ways we do that are using authentication and access lists.

Device Access

Although how we manage network devices is changing with the advent of RESTCONF and NETCONF, the old-school way of using the CLI isn't ever going to go away. After all, you can't troubleshoot those new management tools without CLI access.

Terminal Lines

There are three ways you get into the router:

- Console (con or cty) port—This requires using a serial rollover cable and a terminal.
- Auxiliary (aux) port—Similar to the console port, the aux port is occasionally connected to a dial-up modem for out-of-band management.
- Virtual terminal (vty) lines—Used for SSH and telnet connections.

Let's start by taking a look at the configuration of the console line on R1:

```
R1#show run | s line con 0
line con 0
 exec-timeout 0 0
 privilege level 15
 logging synchronous
```

When a user connects to the console, they're immediately dropped into privileged EXEC mode (aka enable mode) with full (level 15) privileges, enabling them to do anything on the router. The expectation is that anyone who's not authorized to administer the router shouldn't have physical access to it. Of course, we know better. That's why we're going to configure authentication for not just the console line, but for the VTY and AUX lines as well.

 You can completely disable CLI access to a terminal line by issuing the command **no exec** under the line's respective configuration. This doesn't prevent connecting to VTY lines. To disable the VTY lines altogether, use the **transport input none** command.

We have a few options when it comes to authentication:

- **Local password only**—Not a good idea, since it doesn't let us know who's logging in.
- **Server-based authentication**—Usernames and passwords are stored on a server, allowing a single credential to be used to administer multiple devices.
- **Local username and password**—Requires per-device configuration but also doesn't depend on the availability of an authentication server.

The latter two are what we're going to focus on in this chapter.

Configuring Local Authentication

Configuring local login using a username and password doesn't require using a third-party server. All you have to do is create a local user on the device and enable local logins for one or more terminal lines. The following shows how to create the user amber with privileged (level 15) access:

```
R2(config)#username amber privilege 15 secret cisco
```

To allow this user to connect via the console, do the following:

```
R2(config)#line console 0
R2(config-line)#login local
```

Assuming that you're logged into the console and testing this on a device nobody else is using at the moment, it's a good idea to schedule the device for a reload in 5 minutes just in case you misconfigured something. That way, you won't lock yourself out.

```
R2#reload in 5
System configuration has been modified. Save? [yes/no]: no
Reload scheduled in 5 minutes by amber on console
Reload reason: Reload Command
Proceed with reload? [confirm]
R2#
***
*** --- SHUTDOWN in 0:05:00 ---
***
```

Now we'll log out of the console and try to log in as amber:

```
User Access Verification
Username: amber
Password:
Reload scheduled in 4 minutes and 51 seconds by console
Reload reason: Reload Command
R2#
```

The login works, and we can now test the user's privileges by aborting the shutdown:

```
R2#reload cancel
R2#
***
*** --- SHUTDOWN ABORTED ---
***
R2#
```

To use local logins for the VTY lines, we must issue the same login local command under the VTY line configuration, but we also must enable SSH. Telnet is insecure, so we want to enable only SSH for remote administration. We'll start by enabling SSH version 2:

```
R2#conf t
Enter configuration commands, one per line.  End with CNTL/Z.
R2(config)#ip domain-name benpiper.com
```

Next, we'll generate cryptographic RSA keys:

```
R2(config)#crypto key generate rsa
The name for the keys will be: R2.benpiper.com
Choose the size of the key modulus in the range of 360 to 4096 for your
  General Purpose Keys. Choosing a key modulus greater than 512 may take
  a few minutes.

How many bits in the modulus [512]: 2048
% Generating 2048 bit RSA keys, keys will be non-exportable...
[OK] (elapsed time was 3 seconds)

R2(config)#
%SSH-5-ENABLED: SSH 1.99 has been enabled
R2(config)#
```

SSH 1.99 is enabled by default, so we'll enable version 2:

```
R2(config)#ip ssh version 2
```

Let's enable SSH access to the VTY lines:

```
R2(config)#line vty 0 ?
  <1-924>  Last Line number
  <cr>

R2(config)#line vty 0 924
R2(config-line)#transport input ssh
```

For added security, we'll configure the router to log the user out after 5 minutes of inactivity:

```
R2(config-line)#exec-timeout 5 0
```

Next, let's enable logging in using a local username and verify the configuration:

```
R2(config-line)#login local
R2(config-line)#end
R2#show run | s line vty
line vty 0 4
 exec-timeout 5 0
 no login
 transport input ssh
line vty 5 924
 exec-timeout 5 0
 no login
 transport input ssh
```

Using an SSH client, the user amber is able to log in to the router:

```
root@osboxes:/# ssh amber@192.168.2.20
Password:
R2#
```

Authentication, Authorization, and Accounting

Server-based authentication is often lumped into the triad authentication, authorization, and accounting (AAA). *Authentication* is essentially a binary decision: do you have the right credentials or not? Such credentials may be a username and password, a one-time-use token, a fingerprint, or some combination of these. We're not getting fancy, so for our purposes a simple username and password will suffice.

Authorization determines what you're able to do once you authenticate. For example, can you get into privileged EXEC mode? Once you log in, can you reload the device or erase the startup configuration? These are questions of authorization. Many organizations don't bother with authorization, choosing to trust that those with proper credentials know what they're doing and should have access to all available commands.

Accounting is useful for keeping track of what commands users run. This can be especially useful during sudden network outages when people start finger-pointing!

We'll begin with authentication. Cisco supports two types of AAA servers: Terminal Access Controller Access Control System Plus (TACACS+) and Remote Authentication Dial-In User Service (RADIUS).

 Cisco Identity Services Engine (ISE) offers RADIUS and TACACS+ services.

TACACS+

TACACS+ supports authentication, authorization, and accounting. It's developed by Cisco and integrated with ISE, but there are many free TACACS+ server implementations such as tac_plus (www.shrubbery.net/tac_plus). TACACS+ uses TCP port 49, and it encrypts all packets.

Configuring Authentication with TACACS+

We'll configure authentication using an existing TACACS+ server. The server has already been configured with two users: ben and laine. To avoid getting locked out of R1, we'll create a local administrative user. Once we complete the configuration, if the TACACS+ server goes down, we'll still be able to administer the router.

```
R1(config)#username admin privilege 15 secret cisco
Let's enable the AAA feature on the router.
R1(config)#aaa new-model
```

We'll define the TACACS+ server, giving it an arbitrary name of aaaserver1:

```
R1(config)#tacacs server aaaserver1
```

Next, we specify the IP address of the server:

```
R1(config-server-tacacs)#address ipv4 192.168.3.2
```

The server is configured with a secret key, which we must specify here. This is not specific to any user, but it only allows the router to use the server for performing authentication and authorization.

```
R1(config-server-tacacs)#key cisco
```

Next, we'll configure a TACACS+ server group, which we'll name aaaservers:

```
R1(config-server-tacacs)#aaa group server tacacs+ aaaservers
```

The only member of the group will be aaaserver1:

```
R1(config-sg-tacacs+)#server name aaaserver1
```

Finally, we get to the good part. We'll enable login authentication for all lines. When a user tries to log in, their credentials will be checked against the TACACS+ server defined in the aaaservers group.

```
R1(config-sg-tacacs+)#aaa authentication login default group aaaservers local
```

The default keyword applies the configuration to all lines. If the TACACS+ server is down, the router will fall back to local authentication, which is that admin username we configured earlier. Now let's log out of R1 and attempt to log in at the console:

```
R1 con0 is now available
Press RETURN to get started.
User Access Verification
Username: ben
Password:
R1#who
    Line        User        Host(s)           Idle        Location
*   0 con 0     ben         idle              00:00:00

    Interface   User                  Mode        Idle    Peer Address
```

Simply creating a local user doesn't mean they can log in. You must enable local authentication, too!

Authentication against the TACACS+ server is successful. Recall that because the line console is configured with privilege level 15, as soon as we authenticate to the console, it drops us into enable mode. You might be tempted to change this so that it drops the user into the less dangerous user EXEC mode (privilege level 1). But that won't prevent the user from typing enable and getting elevated privileges.

We've tested via the console, so now let's try to log in using the VTY lines. Assuming that we've enabled SSH access using the steps shown earlier, we'll attempt to open an SSH session to the router using the TACACS+ credentials for the user laine.

```
root@osboxes:/# ssh laine@192.168.1.10
Password:
R1>enable
% Error in authentication.
```

Recall that the VTY lines configuration doesn't have the privilege level 15 command, so we don't get the enable prompt. Authentication works, but oddly enough, even after typing enable we get an authentication error. The reason is that we haven't configured an enable secret. From the console of R1, we'll create an enable secret and try again:

```
R1(config)#enable secret cisco
! Trying again, we see that it works now.
root@osboxes:/# ssh laine@192.168.1.10
Password:
R1>en
Password:
R1#
```

Configuring Authorization with TACACS+

Once a user is authenticated, you may want to control what specific commands they're allowed to run. For example, you may want someone to be able to run only show commands. Or you may want to prevent them from deleting the startup configuration. On the TACACS+ server, you can define what specific services a user can use and what commands they can run. Although we're discussing AAA in the context of device administration, TACACS+ can also be used to authenticate users for other things such as Point-to-Point Protocol (PPP) sessions. This is outside the scope of the ENCOR exam, but knowing this will help you understand some of the configuration we're about to complete.

When a user authenticates, the first thing that occurs is that they're given an EXEC shell—in other words, the CLI. If you're using TACACS+ for things other than just defining Cisco device administrators, you want to ensure that those non-admins can't get to the CLI. To do that, you enable authorization for the EXEC shell using the following command:

```
R1(config)#aaa authorization exec default group aaaservers if-authenticated
```

This causes the router to check that the user is authorized to use the CLI. But what if the TACACS+ server is down? That's where if-authenticated comes in. As long as we can authenticate—in this case, using the local username we created earlier—the router will authorize us to use the CLI. To enable authorization checks for user and privileged commands (command authorization), issue the following commands:

```
R1(config)#aaa authorization commands 1 default group aaaservers if-authenticated
R1(config)#aaa authorization commands 15 default group aaaservers if-authenticated
```

If the TACACS+ server goes down, the if-authenticated parameter will automatically permit the user to execute the command. Before testing it out, let's enable authorization debugs on R1's console:

```
R1#debug aaa authorization
```

The user laine is configured on the server with permission to run only show commands. We'll open an SSH session to R1 as laine and attempt to do some mischief:

```
root@osboxes:/# ssh laine@192.168.1.10
Password:
R1>en
Password:
! Try to get into global configuration mode
R1#conf t
Command authorization failed.
! Try to delete the startup configuration
R1#delete nvram:startup-config
Command authorization failed.

R1#show run | count interface
Number of lines which match regexp = 5
```

Attempts to get into global configuration mode and delete the startup configuration fail. But showing the running configuration works just fine. Moving back to the R1 console, the debug shows the failure:

```
AAA/AUTHOR/TAC+: (133110557): send AV cmd=delete
AAA/AUTHOR/TAC+: (133110557): send AV cmd-arg=nvram:startup-config
AAA/AUTHOR/TAC+: (133110557): send AV cmd-arg=nvram:startup-config
AAA/AUTHOR/TAC+: (133110557): send AV cmd-arg=<cr>
AAA/AUTHOR (133110557): Post authorization status = FAIL
```

However, let's try something different. After turning off debugs, let's attempt to log into the console as laine:

```
R1 con0 is now available
Press RETURN to get started.
User Access Verification
Username: laine
```

```
Password:
R1#conf t
Enter configuration commands, one per line.  End with CNTL/Z.
R1(config)#no int lo22
R1(config)#
%LINK-5-CHANGED: Interface Loopback22, changed state to administratively down
%LINEPROTO-5-UPDOWN: Line protocol on Interface Loopback22, changed state to down
```

By default, authorization doesn't apply to the console line! If someone can log in via the console and get into enable mode, they have free reign. For a bit of extra security, we can enforce console-line authorization with the following command:

```
R1(config)#aaa authorization console
```

This is all well and good for a read-only user. But what if you want to restrict access to specific configuration commands for users who have access to global configuration mode? That's easy. Just issue the following command:

```
R1(config)# aaa authorization config-commands
```

Any configuration commands the user enters will be sent to the server for authorization.

Configuring Accounting with TACACS+

Configuring accounting is very similar to configuring authorization. Assuming we want to enable accounting for all commands that we have authorization enabled for, just use the following:

```
R1(config)#aaa accounting exec default start-stop group aaaservers
R1(config)#aaa accounting commands 1 default start-stop group aaaservers
R1(config)#aaa accounting commands 15 default start-stop group aaaservers
```

For the first command, the start-stop keyword causes an accounting entry to be sent when the exec process starts and when it stops—in other words, when the user logs in and logs out of the CLI. For the latter two commands, the start-stop doesn't make much sense. Consider it a quirk of the CLI.

RADIUS

RADIUS (RFCs 2865 and 2866) doesn't separate the processes of authentication and authorization. When a user authenticates to a RADIUS server, the server responds with a list of authorizations, such as privilege level and whether the user can begin a CLI session, access the CLI, and execute commands. Cisco devices can't use RADIUS to authorize individual CLI commands the way TACACS+ does. Likewise, when it comes to RADIUS, Cisco doesn't support accounting of individual commands that are entered in the CLI. The only accounting that actually occurs is logon and logoff. But if all you need is authentication, RADIUS is a good choice, and there are several free RADIUS servers available, such as FreeRADIUS (https://freeradius.org).

The port numbers that RADIUS uses are confusing. Traditionally, RADIUS has used UDP 1645 for authentication and UDP 1646 for accounting. Officially, however, UDP 1812 is for authentication and UDP 1813 is for accounting. RADIUS encrypts only the password. The rest of the packet is sent in the clear.

Access Control Lists

You're undoubtedly familiar with the basics of ACLs. They are processed in top-down order and always contain an implicit deny at the end. They're used in a variety of contexts, from route filtering, to NAT, to traffic classification, to conditional debugs. In this chapter, we're chiefly interested in ACLs for security. It's easy to think of ACLs as being boring things that you set and forget about. But remember that almost every feature you configure on a switch or router depends on having proper layer 2 or layer 3 connectivity to work. A single misconfigured ACL can take a perfectly functional network and wreak havoc. Your primary concern when configuring ACLs for security should be security, of course. But you should be cognizant of what other things your ACLs might break, and most importantly, how to troubleshoot them when they do. This is why I've saved this discussion for the last chapter. It's easy to create a highly secure network that doesn't function. But knowing how to create a highly secure network that functions well is much harder. To begin, let's get a lay of the land of ACLs. ACLs are divided into two groups:

- **IP ACLs**—Match packets based on IP source or destination address
    - **Standard**—Match packets based only on source address
    - **Extended**—Can match packets based on source or destination address, IP protocol, port number, or ToS value
- **MAC ACLs**—Match frames based on source or destination MAC address, Ethertype, VLAN, or CoS value. We're not going to cover these because they're rarely used.

We'll begin with troubleshooting IP access lists, throwing in some conditional debugs along the way.

IP Extended Access Lists

Imagine that a server on your network is establishing a rogue OSPF adjacency with router R2. Your apprentice, whom you've tasked with preventing the adjacency, has created the following configuration:

```
R2#show ip int | i is up|list
GigabitEthernet0/2 is up, line protocol is up
  Outgoing access list is not set
  Inbound  access list is NoOSPF
```

The IP named access list NoOSPF is assigned as an inbound ACL for Gi0/2. Let's take a look at the ACL:

```
R2#show access-list
Extended IP access list NoOSPF
    10 deny ospf any host 224.0.0.5 log (10 matches)
    20 permit ip any any (4032 matches)
```

Line 10 of the ACL denies OSPF (IP protocol 89) traffic from any host to the destination address 224.0.0.5, which you'll recognize at the OSPF AllRouters multicast address. The log keyword triggers a log entry whenever the ACL has a match. This keyword causes matching packets to be process switched, increasing CPU utilization. You can view the number of packets being process switched using the following command:

```
R2#show int gi0/2 switching | s IP
    Protocol  IP
           Switching path   Pkts In   Chars In   Pkts Out   Chars Out
                 Process       4566     509088       4599      515282
            Cache misses          0          -          -           -
                    Fast       6265    4668412       6265     4670872
               Auton/SSE          0          0          0           0
```

Let's view the ACL in the running configuration:

```
R2#show run | s access-list
ip access-list extended NoOSPF
 deny    ospf any host 224.0.0.5 log
 permit ip any any
```

Incidentally, the correct way to block a rogue OSPF neighbor isn't to use an ACL, but to use OSPF interface authentication. Removing the ACL from the Gi0/2 interface is easy:

```
R2(config)#int gi0/2
R2(config-if)#no ip access-group in
R2#show ip int gi0/2 | i list
  Outgoing access list is not set
  Inbound  access list is not set
```

Whenever tasked with blocking traffic for a specific purpose, consider alternatives to using an ACL. And if you do use an ACL, be as specific as possible. Let's look at another example. Consider the diagram in Figure 12.1.

Suppose you want to block traffic from the 192.168.1.0/24 subnet to 192.168.3.2 on TCP port 49. Let's start by creating an access list on SW1:

```
SW1(config)#ip access-list extended notac
SW1(config-ext-nacl)#deny tcp 192.168.1.0 0.0.0.255 host 192.168.3.2 eq 49
SW1(config-ext-nacl)#permit ip any any
```

FIGURE 12.1 Example network topology

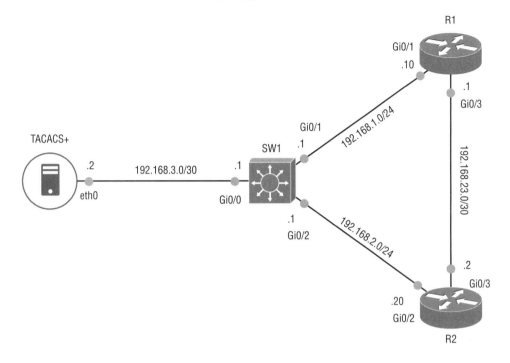

IP ACLs can be applied to switched, routed, or switched virtual interfaces. It's a good practice to apply the ACL inbound on the interface closest to the source. That would seem to be SW1's Gi0/1 interface. But there is another possibility.

```
SW1#show ip int brief | i 192.168.1
Vlan10                192.168.1.1    YES manual up                    up
```

SW1 has an SVI in the 192.168.1.0/24 subnet. The presence of the SVI means that in the future, packets sourced from the 192.168.1.0/24 subnet could ingress an interface other than Gi0/1. To ensure coverage, we need to apply the ACL inbound to the SVI.

```
SW1(config)#int vlan10
SW1(config-if)#ip access-group notac in
```

After generating some matching traffic from R1, we can see that the ACL is effective:

```
SW1(config-if)#do show ip access-l
Extended IP access list notac
    10 deny tcp 192.168.1.0 0.0.0.255 host 192.168.3.2 eq tacacs (4 matches)
    20 permit ip any any (556 matches)
```

You can apply only one inbound and one outbound ACL per interface.

Standard Access Lists

Standard ACLs don't get a lot of love, but they're useful when the destination address doesn't matter. For instance, if you want to restrict the source IP addresses that can open a SSH session to a router, the destination IP address doesn't make a difference. You just want to restrict access based on the source. The following example shows how to allow inbound SSH access only from IP addresses in the 192.168.3.0/30 subnet:

```
R1(config)#access-list 2 permit 192.168.3.0 0.0.0.3
R1(config)#line vty 0 924
R1(config-line)#access-class 2 in
```

Note the wildcard mask 0.0.0.3. To calculate the wildcard mask, just start with 255.255.255.255 and subtract the subnet mask from each octet. In this case, the subnet mask for /30 is 255.255.255.252. Let's attempt to open an SSH session from 192.168.3.2:

```
root@osboxes:/# ssh ben@192.168.1.10
Password:
R1#who
    Line        User      Host(s)          Idle         Location
  0 con 0       ben       idle             00:01:48
*578 vty 0      ben       idle             00:00:00 192.168.3.2
```

Now let's try from R2, sourcing traffic from its interface IP address 192.168.2.20 (Gi0/2):

```
R2(config)#ip ssh source-interface gi0/2
R2(config)#^Z
R2#ssh -l ben 192.168.1.10
% Connection refused by remote host
```

By the way, you can use access-class with the out keyword to restrict outbound SSH access from a console or SSH session:

```
R1(config)#access-list 3 deny any
R1(config)#line vty 0 924
R1(config-line)#access-class 3 out
```

If you have a VTY session with R1, you won't be able to open an SSH session outbound to any other device. To set the same restriction for when you're on the console, use the following:

```
R1(config)#line con 0
R1(config-line)#access-class 3 out
R1(config-line)#^Z
R1#ssh -l admin 192.168.2.20
% Connections to that host not permitted from this terminal
```

In this case, we're logged in via the console and the attempt to open an SSH session to R2 from here fails.

VLAN Access Maps

When you apply an ACL to a switchport, it's called a *port ACL*. A port ACL can be an IP ACL or a MAC ACL. Port ACLs come with some restrictions. You can't apply them to outbound traffic, only inbound. You also can't use them to filter certain control plane protocols such as ARP, CDP, or STP. If you want to block specific traffic within a VLAN on a switch, applying port ACLs to every member port in the VLAN is cumbersome. Instead, you can use a *VLAN access map*—sometimes called a VLAN ACL.

In the following example, we'll configure a VLAN access map to block ICMP traffic in VLAN 20 but allow everything else. VLAN access maps work a lot like route maps. They're sequenced, contain match clauses, and use access lists to match traffic. The first step is to create an IP access list to permit (match) ICMP traffic:

```
SW1(config)#ip access-list extended ping
SW1(config-ext-nacl)#permit icmp any any
SW1(config-ext-nacl)#exit
```

Next, we'll create another list to match all IP traffic:

```
SW1(config)#ip access-list extended everything
SW1(config-ext-nacl)#permit ip any any
SW1(config-ext-nacl)#exit
```

Next, we'll create a VLAN access map. In it we'll match the IP access list named ping. The VACL will drop any matching traffic.

```
SW1(config)#vlan access-map VACL20
SW1(config-access-map)#match ip address ping
SW1(config-access-map)#action drop
SW1(config-access-map)#exit
```

In the next sequence, we'll match the IP ACL named everything. The action for this will be to forward matching traffic.

```
SW1(config)#vlan access-map VACL20
SW1(config-access-map)#match ip address everything
SW1(config-access-map)#action forward
SW1(config-access-map)#exit
```

Recall that route maps exhibit similar behavior. Any traffic that doesn't match a sequence in the VACL is dropped because of the implicit deny at the end. Finally, we'll associate the access map to VLAN 20:

```
SW1(config)#vlan filter VACL20 vlan-list 20
```

R2 has an interface in VLAN 20, so let's attempt to ping SW1's VLAN 20 SVI:

```
R2#ping 192.168.2.1
Type escape sequence to abort.
Sending 5, 100-byte ICMP Echos to 192.168.2.1, timeout is 2 seconds:
.....
Success rate is 0 percent (0/5)
R2#ssh -l admin 192.168.1.10
% Connection refused by remote host
```

The ping fails as expected. The attempt to SSH to 192.168.1.10 (R1) succeeds, as shown by the fact that it actively refused the connection. To remove the VLAN filter for VLAN 20, just issue the following command:

```
SW1(config)#no vlan filter VACL20 vlan-list 20
```

 If you have concurrent port ACLs and VLAN ACLs, the port ACLs are always processed first.

Control Plane Policing

Control plane policing (CoPP) is a mechanism to rate-limit control plane traffic ingressing or egressing a router or switch. Control plane traffic refers to traffic either generated or terminated by the device itself, as opposed to data plane traffic that flows through it. Control plane traffic is always process switched, so too much of it can overwhelm a device's CPU. Some examples of control plane traffic are

- Routing protocols
- ICMP
- SSH
- IPsec
- PIM
- DHCP

In this section we'll configure CoPP for ICMP traffic. The process will look familiar, as it's nearly identical to the way you configured QoS queuing in Chapter 9, "Quality of Service." The first step is to create an access list to match all ICMP packets:

```
R2(config)#ip access-list extended all-icmp
R2(config-ext-nacl)#permit icmp any any
```

Next, we'll create the class map to classify the matching ICMP traffic:

```
R2(config-ext-nacl)#class-map match-all all-icmp
R2(config-cmap)#match access-group name all-icmp
```

Let's create the policy map to implement a single-rate, two-color policer:

```
R2(config-cmap)#policy-map CoPP
R2(config-pmap)#class all-icmp
R2(config-pmap-c)#police 8000 conform-action transmit exceed-action drop
R2(config-pmap-c-police)#exit
```

Lastly, we'll apply the policy to the control plane as follows:

```
R2(config-pmap-c)#control-plane
R2(config-cp)#service-policy input CoPP
```

Behind the scenes, we'll start a continuous ping to R1. Verification using the show policy-map command is similar to regular QoS, except that we don't have to specify an interface:

```
R2(config-cp)#do show policy-map control-plane
 Control Plane

  Service-policy input: CoPP

    Class-map: all-icmp (match-all)
      139 packets, 136446 bytes
      5 minute offered rate 8000 bps, drop rate 4000 bps
      Match: access-group name all-icmp
      police:
          cir 8000 bps, bc 1500 bytes
        conformed 72 packets, 68508 bytes; actions:
          transmit
        exceeded 67 packets, 67938 bytes; actions:
          drop
        conformed 4000 bps, exceeded 4000 bps

    Class-map: class-default (match-any)
      39 packets, 5484 bytes
      5 minute offered rate 0000 bps, drop rate 0000 bps
      Match: any
```

 CoPP for layer 2 control traffic such as Spanning Tree and CDP is possible, but policing for these protocols is disabled by default because it's generally not needed.

Cisco Security Products

Cisco offers an array of security products and features. If you've achieved a Cisco certification in the past, you know how important it is to have some familiarity with Cisco product names and their uses. In this section, we'll cover several key security products that Cisco offers for endpoint and network security.

AnyConnect Secure Mobility Client

The Cisco AnyConnect Secure Mobility Client enables user-friendly VPN access using a variety of tunneling protocols, including IPsec, DTLS, and TLS. AnyConnect can scan the endpoint for security compliance prior to connecting, reducing the risk that an infected endpoint will introduce malware into the network. For example, you may want to require the client endpoint to have the latest operating system security patches and antivirus definitions installed. If an endpoint is out of compliance, AnyConnect can take automatic actions to remedy the issue. Using the Network Visibility module, you can even have AnyConnect spy on and report what programs an endpoint is running and what sort of traffic those programs are sending and receiving.

Umbrella

Cisco Umbrella is a DNS service that protects endpoints by failing to resolve the domain names of known malicious sites. Evil hackers are continually buying new domain names and setting up new sites designed for phishing and spreading malware, so Umbrella continuously monitors incoming DNS requests to identify new potential threats. Because Umbrella is DNS based, using it requires that endpoints use the Umbrella DNS servers. There are two ways to do this:

- Configure the endpoints to use Umbrella's anycast IP addresses as their DNS servers.

- If the endpoints are using a privately hosted DNS server, configure the DNS server to use Umbrella's servers as forwarders.

Umbrella's enterprise features include logging, analytics, and advanced malware protection. But they also offer free protection against malware and phishing sites. Just use the DNS servers 208.67.222.123 and 208.67.220.123.

Advanced Malware Protection ThreatGrid

Advanced Malware Protection ThreatGrid performs analysis of files to determine whether they contain malware. By running malware in a VM and analyzing its behavior, it determines what the malware is doing and the potential threat it poses. ThreatGrid gets real-time feeds from Talos, Cisco's group that monitors cyber threats, so it can identify the latest malware. Talos aggregates and provides intelligence feeds from various public and private sources. You can deploy ThreatGrid on an appliance or use Cisco's hosted solution in the cloud.

Advanced Malware Protection for Endpoints

Advanced Malware Protection (AMP) for Endpoints is Cisco's antivirus engine. It scans files on endpoints to determine whether they're infected with known malware. If it's uncertain whether a file is clean or malicious, the file can be sent to ThreatGrid for analysis, or to Cisco's AMP cloud service. AMP can integrate with AnyConnect to determine based on its security posture whether an endpoint should be allowed to connect.

Firepower Next-Generation Firewall

Firewalls perform stateful inspection of network traffic and allow or deny the traffic based on a set of rules. It's a bit of an oversimplification, but a firewall is a device built for the primary purpose of implementing access lists. Traditional firewalls are based on address, protocol, port, or signature matching.

Cisco's Firepower Next-Generation Firewall (NGFW) is based on the old Adaptive Security Appliance (ASA). Firepower NGFW comes on specialized Firepower appliances, or it can be added as a feature on the ASA 5500-X series. You can also install Firepower services on certain Cisco ISR models. Naturally, there's a virtual Firepower NGFW (NGFWv) you can run on-premises or in the cloud. The following five features that the Firepower ecosystem provides compose what's called Firepower Threat Defense.

Firepower Intrusion Prevention   An Intrusion Prevention System (IPS) analyzes traffic looking for patterns that could indicate someone attempting to attack or invade your network. What differentiates an IPS from regular firewall functionality is that it analyzes broad traffic patterns and not just packets or flows. Firepower IPS uses real-time statistical and protocol analysis to identify anomalies that could indicate a threat. It also looks for known attack signatures provided by the Talos intelligence feed.

Advanced Malware Protection ThreatGrid   Certain Firepower NGFW appliances can include ThreatGrid to analyze potential malware.

Application Visibility and Control   Application Visibility and Control (AVC) lets you see the applications in use on your network. You can restrict or enforce QoS for broad categories of applications such as social media, streaming, torrents, and games.

Reputation-Based URL Filtering   Reputation-based URL filtering blocks dangerous or unacceptable domain names. It achieves a similar function as Umbrella but blocking is performed by the firewall itself, unlike Umbrella, which refuses to resolve DNS queries for blocked domains.

Firepower Management Center   Sometimes called Firesight, the Firepower Management Center gives you full visibility into everything happening on your network. You can identify threats, applications, servers, operating systems, mobile devices, VoIP phones, and more. It can also recommend or automatically take security actions in response to new discoveries. The Firepower Management Center runs on a physical or virtual server, and not on the firewall itself.

TrustSec

We covered TrustSec a bit back in Chapter 11, "Software-Defined Networking and Network Programmability." As noted there, TrustSec is the term Cisco uses for placing SGTs in an Ethernet frame and using the tags for outbound enforcement of access control policies. SGTs are defined and stored in the ISE as numeric values, but for clarity they're given user-friendly names. For example, you might have tags named Employee_Laptop and Employee_BYOD, allowing you to create different access policies for each. An SGT tag has a three-stage lifecycle.

Ingress—Classification

As noted earlier, the SGT can be assigned dynamically based on the authentication context of the user or device. Some authentication options for accessing the network include WebAuth, MAC authentication bypass, and 802.1X. 802.1X can play a key role in dynamic SGT assignment. For instance, suppose an employee brings their personal laptop and authenticates using their company credentials. Because their credentials, but not their machine, are authenticated, they get assigned the SGT Employee_BYOD.

Now let's consider what might happen differently if that employee was logging in on their company laptop. Cisco has a proprietary authentication mode called EAP Flexible Authentication via Secure Tunneling (EAP-FAST). EAP-FAST supports *EAP chaining*, which allows simultaneous authentication of both the user and the machine. Once ISE simultaneously authenticates the user and their machine, it assigns the user the tag Employee_Laptop.

If 802.1X authentication fails, MAC can be used to authenticate the endpoint, but not the user. MAB uses the MAC address of the endpoint as its identity. The switch sends the MAC address to the RADIUS server, and if the server accepts it, the switch will authenticate the endpoint. Endpoints that authenticate with MAB should get restricted access because it's trivial to fake a MAC address.

If 802.1X or MAB fails, or if it's just not configured, then you can use WebAuth to authenticate users, but not endpoints. WebAuth is a web portal that prompts the user for credentials, which can be checked against a local database or an ISE server. Note that if 802.1X isn't available, you can combine MAB and WebAuth to authenticate both the endpoint and user, respectively and individually. Alternatively, SGTs can be assigned statically based on things like IP address, VLAN, or physical or virtual interface.

Forwarding—Tagging

Regardless of the method, the SGT is inserted into an Ethernet frame by the first-hop or edge device, typically a switch or WLC. As long as all devices in the network are

TrustSec-compatible, the tag is preserved even across subnets. However, if there are any intermediate devices that don't support SGTs, then your only option is to use the *Security Group Exchange Protocol* (SXP). Here's an example of how it works:

1. Two TrustSec-compatible switches, SW1 and SW2, separated by intermediate devices that don't support SGTs, set up an SXP peering.

2. When SW1 receives an Ethernet frame with an SGT tag, it creates a mapping that ties the source IP address to the tag. It sends that IP-to-SGT mapping to its SXP peer, SW2.

3. SW1 then forwards the frame across the network through intermediate devices that don't preserve the SGT.

4. The frame moves through the network until it reaches SW2.

5. SW2 sees that the frame contains an IP packet that matches the IP-SGT mapping. It applies the SGT to the Ethernet frame containing the IP packet and forwards it.

 ISE can also speak SXP and send IP-to-SGT mappings to switches. SXP uses TCP port 64999.

Egress—Enforcement

The final step of the SGT journey is enforcement of policies at the egress point. Just as extended IP access lists are based on source and destination IP addresses, so security group ACLs are based on source and destination SGTs. For example, the `Employee_Laptop` SGT may be permitted to access the `Print_Servers` SGT, whereas the `Employee_BYOD` SGT is denied. Custom actions may also be specified, such as permitting access only on certain ports, as Table 12.1 illustrates.

TABLE 12.1   Group-based access control

Source SGT	Destination SGT	Action
Employee_Laptop	Print_Servers	Permit any
Employee_Laptop	Internet	Permit any
Employee_Laptop	Database_Servers	Permit TCP/1433
Employee_BYOD	Print_Servers	Deny
Employee_BYOD	Internet	Permit TCP/443
Employee_BYOD	Database_Servers	Deny

MAC Security

MAC Security (MACsec) is a layer 2 authentication and encryption scheme defined by the IEEE 802.1AE standards family. What makes MACsec peculiar is that it encrypts Ethernet frames between two devices connected directly at the link layer. MACsec works by encrypting the entire Ethernet frame and encapsulating it in another Ethernet frame with an EtherType of 0x88e5. Each device that receives a MACsec-encrypted frame must decrypt it, read the original encapsulated frame to figure out what to do with it, and then if it needs to forward the frame, it must reencrypt it.

MACsec between switches can use the proprietary *Security Association Protocol* (SAP) or the *MACsec Key Agreement* (MKA) protocol to negotiate encryption between switches. Keep in mind that a non-Cisco switch may support MACsec, but because SAP is proprietary, you'll have to use MKA with non-Cisco switches. Between switches, MACsec can use either 802.1X or manual authentication. MACsec between a switch and an endpoint always uses the MKA protocol. You can also use 802.1X for authentication, but it's not required to use MACsec encryption.

As you can imagine, this process could slow down the network quite miserably, so MACsec is implemented in specialized application-specific integrated circuits (ASICs) that can perform the encryption and decryption fast enough not to impede throughput. Of course, that also means MACsec requires compatible devices that are more expensive. MACsec does not provide end-to-end encryption, and it's not intended to. Its main purpose is to protect SGTs from unauthorized modification.

Wireless Security

In Chapter 4, "Wireless LAN (WLAN)," you learned the operating principles behind wireless networks, including encryption using WPA and WPA2. In this section, we'll look at configuring authentication on a WLC using WebAuth, 802.1X, and preshared keys. You don't need a WLC to follow along, but refer to the figures throughout to make sure you understand all the steps.

WebAuth

We'll begin by going over the steps to configure WebAuth:

1. On the top menu bar of the WLC web interface, click Security.

2. On the left-side menu bar, expand WebAuth and click Web Login Page.

3. Under Web Authentication Type, select Internal (Default) from the drop-down menu. Refer to Figure 12.2.

FIGURE 12.2   WebAuth login page configuration

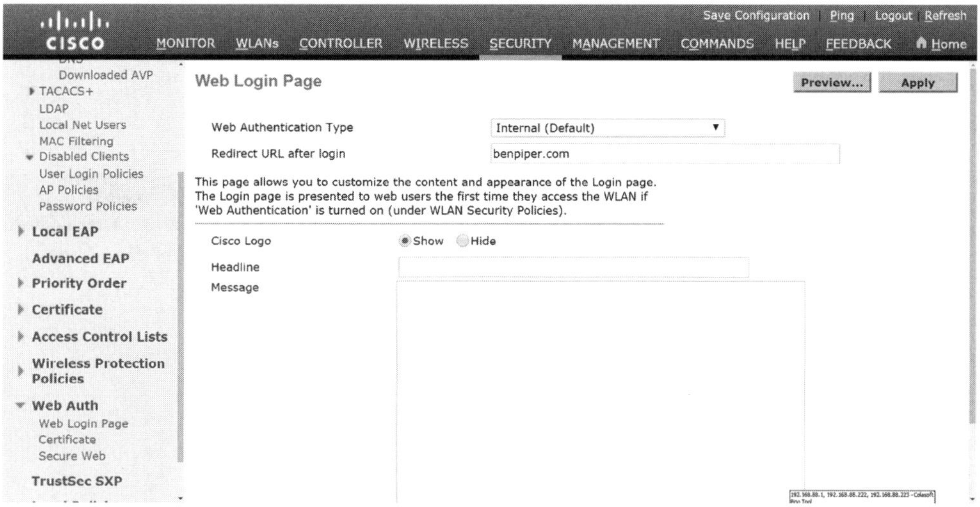

4. In the Redirect URL After Login field, enter a URL to redirect users to after they authenticate.

5. Click the Apply button.

6. On the top menu bar, click WLANs.

7. Click the number of the WLAN ID you wish to enable WebAuth for. Refer to Figure 12.3.

FIGURE 12.3   WLAN list

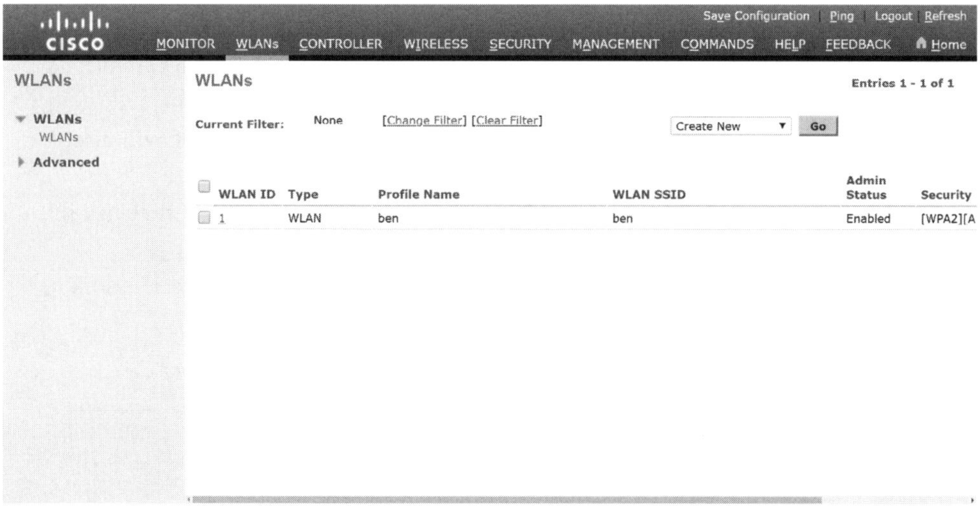

8. Click the Security tab (just to the right of the General tab).

9. Underneath that, click the Layer 2 tab.

10. In the Layer 2 Security drop-down, select None. WebAuth can't be used with WPA or 802.1X. Refer to Figure 12.4.

FIGURE 12.4   WLAN layer 2 configuration

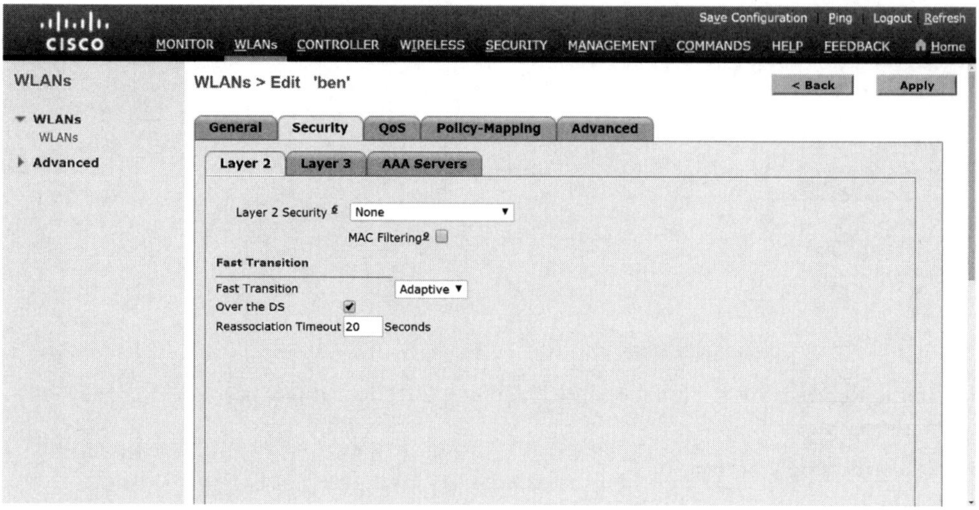

11. Click the Layer 3 tab.

12. In the Layer 3 Security drop-down, click Web Policy. Your browser will pop up an alert indicating that the WLC will forward DNS traffic from users before they authenticate unless you explicitly deny it using a preauthentication ACL. Dismiss the alert dialog box by clicking OK.

13. Make sure the Authentication radio button is selected. (Optionally, you can select a preauthentication ACL if you have one created.)

14. Click Apply. You'll get another dialog box warning you that proceeding will disconnect WLAN users. Click OK to continue.

15. Now we'll configure a RADIUS server to authenticate users via WebAuth. Click the Security option in the top menu bar.

16. On the left-side menu, expand AAA, expand RADIUS, and click Authentication.

17. Click the New button.

18. Enter the RADIUS server IP address in the Server IP Address field. Refer to Figure 12.5.

FIGURE 12.5   RADIUS server configuration

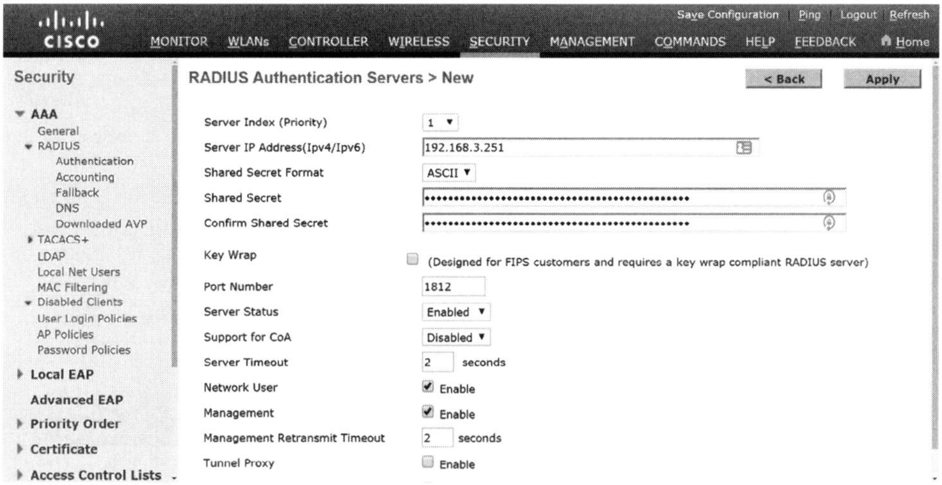

19. Enter the shared secret for the RADIUS server in the Shared Secret and Confirm Shared Secret fields.
20. Check that the default port number (1812) is correct. Ensure that Server Status is Enabled, and that the Network User check box is selected. Click Apply.
21. In the top menu, click WLANs again.
22. Click the WLAN ID you enabled WebAuth for earlier.
23. Click the Security tab, and then click the AAA Servers tab.
24. Under the drop-down for Server1, select the RADIUS server you added a moment ago. Refer to Figure 12.6.

FIGURE 12.6   AAA server configuration

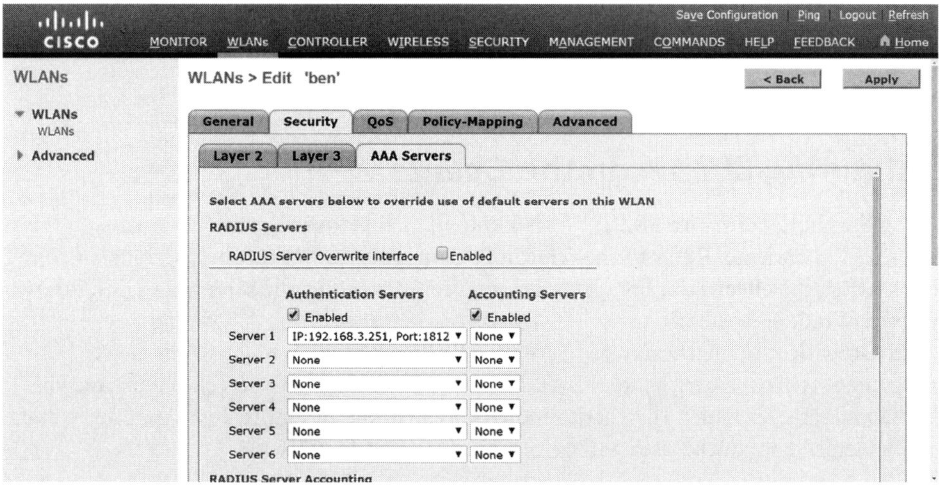

25. Click Apply. You'll be presented with another warning about disconnecting WLAN users. Click OK to proceed.

Configuring WPA2 with 802.1X

Next, we'll use WPA2 with 802.1X to enable layer 2 authentication. When a user connects, they must authenticate to a RADIUS server with their user credentials.

1. Edit the wireless network you configured RADIUS on.

2. Click the Security tab, followed by the Layer 2 tab.

3. Under Layer 2 Security, select WPA+WPA2. Refer to Figure 12.7.

FIGURE 12.7 WLAN WPA2 and 802.1X configuration

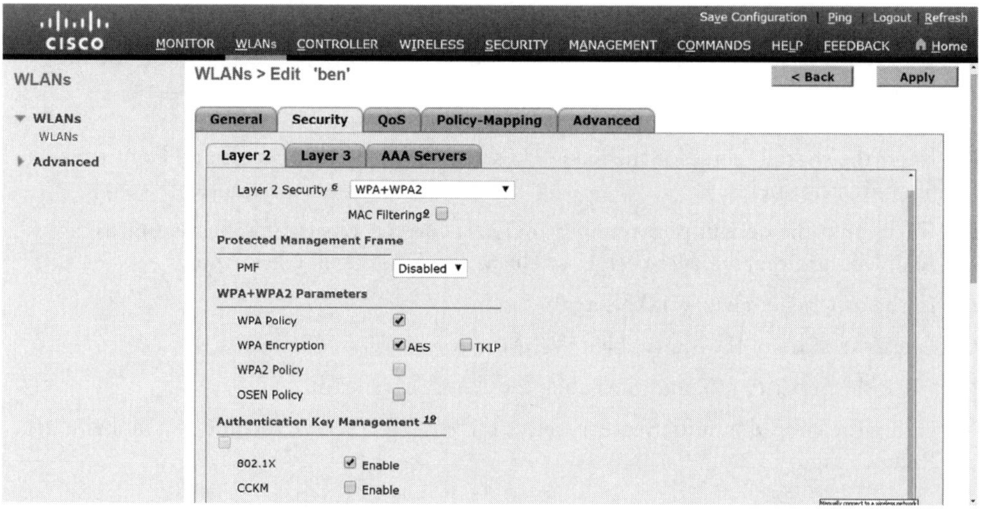

4. Under WPA+WPA2 Parameters, select the WPA Policy and WPA2 Policy check boxes.

5. Scroll down to Authentication Key Management and click the Enable check box next to 802.1X.

Configuring 802.1X on the Client

Users will need to configure 802.1X—also known as EAP over LANs (EAPoL)—on their devices to authenticate. Refer to the relevant OS documentation for instructions on configuring EAP on the client side. For guidance, Figure 12.8 shows the screen for configuring EAP on a Windows system.

The authentication method is *protected EAP (PEAP)*, which requires the server but not the client to have a certificate. PEAP forms a TLS tunnel between the client and the RADIUS server over which the client sends its credentials. In Figure 12.9, user authentication is specified so that the user will be prompted for credentials.

FIGURE 12.8   Specifying security and encryption authentication method

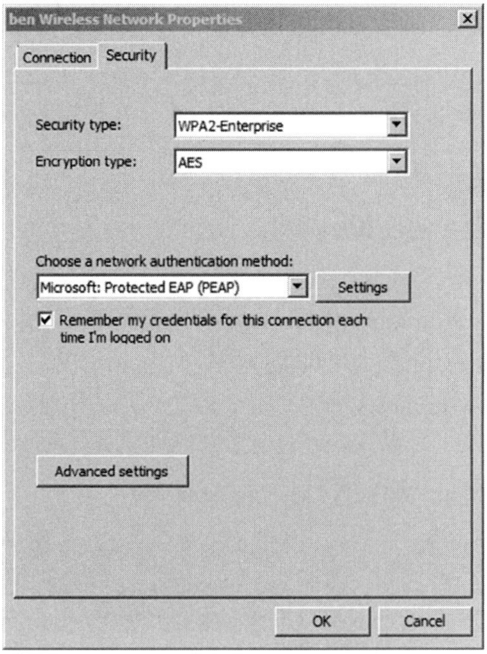

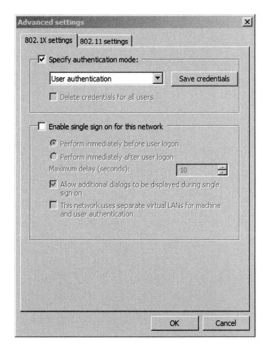

FIGURE 12.9   Specifying user authentication mode

The reason PEAP requires a server certificate is to prevent clients from connecting to rogue servers that may attempt to steal user credentials. Thus, using PEAP requires installing the server's certificate on the client.

 TACACS+ isn't compatible with EAP.

Configure Preshared Keys

Finally, you'll learn how to configure preshared key authentication for WPA and WPA2.

1. Edit the WLAN you want to enable preshared key authentication for.
2. Under Layer 2 Security, select WPA+WPA2.
3. Under WPA+WPA2 Parameters, click the WPA Policy and WPA2 Policy check boxes. Ensure the AES boxes are all checked. Refer to Figure 12.10.

FIGURE 12.10 Setting a WPA/WPA2 preshared key

cisco	Save Configuration Ping Logout Refresh

MONITOR WLANs CONTROLLER WIRELESS SECURITY MANAGEMENT COMMANDS HELP FEEDBACK 🏠 Home

WLANs

▼ **WLANs**
  WLANs
▶ **Advanced**

General | **Security** | QoS | Policy-Mapping | Advanced

Layer 2 | Layer 3 | AAA Servers

WPA+WPA2 Parameters

WPA Policy	☑
WPA Encryption	☑ AES ☐ TKIP
WPA2 Policy	☑
WPA2 Encryption	☑ AES ☐ TKIP ☐ CCMP256 ☐ GCMP128 ☐ GCMP256
OSEN Policy	☐

Authentication Key Management [19]

802.1X	☐ Enable
CCKM	☐ Enable
PSK	☑ Enable
FT 802.1X	☐ Enable
FT PSK	☐ Enable
PSK Format	ASCII ▼
	••
SUITEB-1X	☐ Enable

4. Under Authentication Key Management, click Enable next to PSK.
5. Enter the preshared key in the field next to PSK Format.
6. Click Apply, then click OK.

Monitoring

Throughout the book, you've learned how to use network diagnostic tools such as ping, traceroute, and debugs. In this section, we'll look at more advanced diagnostic and trouble-shooting tools, including

- Conditional debugs
- SNMP
- Syslog
- NetFlow
- SPAN/RSPAN/ERSPAN
- IPSLA

Conditional Debugs

Conditional debugs are useful for capturing specific IP source or destination addresses when doing IP packet debugs. Configuring a conditional debug is easy and requires little more than configuring an access list. In this example, we want to view only IP packets with a destination address of `192.168.3.2`:

```
R1(config)#access-list 101 permit ip any host 192.168.3.2
```

All you have to do now is enable IP packet debugs, specifying the ACL number as a parameter:

```
R1#debug ip packet 101
IP packet debugging is on for access list 101
R1#
```

Only the matching packets are displayed:

```
IP: s=192.168.1.10 (local), d=192.168.3.2 (GigabitEthernet0/1), len 40, sending
IP: s=192.168.1.10 (local), d=192.168.3.2 (GigabitEthernet0/1), len 40, sending
full packet
R1#undebug all
All possible debugging has been turned off
```

Simple Network Management Protocol (SNMP)

For decades, the *Simple Network Management Protocol (SNMP)* has been a staple of network monitoring. In response to events, SNMP sends traps containing event or device information, such as routing protocol changes, link failures, device access, and reboots. In addition to traps, SNMP supports polling, allowing a monitoring host to request specific device information. For example, a NMS may periodically poll for the number of bytes that have ingressed an interface. This allows the NMS to calculate and track bandwidth utilization over time. The security of SNMP depends on the version. SNMP comes in three versions:

- SNMPv1 and SNMPv2c—Offer no encryption, and authentication consists of a plaintext community string

- SNMPv3—Offers AES encryption and can use HMAC-SHA for secure authentication

To see how it works, let's enable SNMP traps for CPU, OSPF, and configuration-related events:

```
R1(config)#snmp-server enable traps cpu
R1(config)#snmp-server enable traps ospf
R1(config)#snmp-server enable traps config
```

We'll send traps to the NMS server at 192.168.3.2, using the community string mycommunitystring for authentication:

```
R1(config)#snmp-server host 192.168.3.2 traps mycommunitystring
```

That's all there is to it! Configuring the NMS is beyond the scope of this book, but if you want to try out a free one, check out OpenNMS (www.opennms.com).

Syslog

Syslog (RFC 5424) is a way to decouple the logs that a device generates from the device itself. By providing a standard way of categorizing and recording log events, Syslog makes it possible to consolidate logs from multiple devices by funneling them into a single server for storage and analysis. The Syslog message format requires certain elements to be present in each log event message:

- Timestamp
- Host name
- Process identifier
- Message text
- Facility
- Severity

With the exception of the last two, these are pretty self-explanatory. Facility and severity are easy to confuse, but they refer to completely different things. Facility indicates the type of program that generated the message. Since we're dealing with networking devices, the facility number doesn't matter. What we really care about is the severity level, which indicates the level of adverse impact of the event being logged. There are eight severity levels, as shown in Table 12.2.

TABLE 12.2   Syslog severity levels

Value	Severity	Example
0	Emergency	%LINK-0-UNAVAILABLE
1	Alert	%LICENSE-1-UNAVAILABLE
2	Critical	%LINK-2-INTVULN
3	Error	%HARDWARE-3-ASICNUM_ERROR
4	Warning	%CVAC-4-WRITE_FAIL
5	Notice	%LINEPROTO-5-UPDOWN
6	Informational	%MCAST-6-IGMP_BADPKT
7	Debug	%MPLS_VPN_HA-7-LABELFREE

Notice that each example has a number corresponding to the severity level. When looking through a log, it's easy to see an event's severity level just by looking at the number. You'll also notice that most of the event messages you'll see are severity level 5.

You can control which severity levels are logged for the logging buffer, console, and terminal monitor. The logging buffer is what you see when you type show logging. Console logging events are sent to the console port. Monitor logging events are sent to whatever VTY you're logged into.

```
R2#sh logging | i level
    Console logging: level debugging, 31 messages logged, xml disabled,
    Monitor logging: level debugging, 0 messages logged, xml disabled,
    Buffer logging:  level debugging, 31 messages logged, xml disabled,
```

The severity level is set to debugging (level 7) for all three. The specified severity level includes all lower levels, so setting the severity level to debugging will capture debug messages and everything else. If you're doing a lot of debugs but don't want to fill up the logging buffer, you may choose to set a lower severity level, like so:

```
R2(config)#logging buffered informational
%SYS-5-LOG_CONFIG_CHANGE: Buffer logging: level informational, xml disabled,
filtering disabled, size (8192)
R2(config)#do show logging | i Buffer
    Buffer logging:  level informational, 32 messages logged, xml disabled,
Log Buffer (8192 bytes):
%SYS-5-LOG_CONFIG_CHANGE: Buffer logging: level informational, xml disabled,
filtering disabled, size (8192)
```

If you want debugging messages to be written to the logging buffered instead of being displayed in the terminal monitor, you can prevent debugging messages from being written to the terminal monitor using the `logging monitor informational` or `no logging monitor` commands. The latter will completely disable logging to the terminal monitor. The `logging buffered debugging` command ensures debugging messages get written to the logging buffer, which is the default behavior. If you want to send Syslogs to an NMS, you can do that. It's called trap logging, and it's easy to set up:

```
R2(config)#logging host 192.168.3.2
R2(config)#
%SYS-6-LOGGINGHOST_STARTSTOP: Logging to host 192.168.3.2 port 514 started - CLI
initiated
```

Syslog uses UDP port 514. To configure the severity level for trap logging, use the following:

```
R2(config)#logging trap informational
R2(config)#do show logging | i Trap
    Trap logging: level informational, 41 message lines logged
R2(config)#do show logging | s Trap
    Trap logging: level informational, 41 message lines logged
        Logging to 192.168.3.2  (udp port 514, audit disabled,
            link up),
        4 message lines logged,
        0 message lines rate-limited,
        0 message lines dropped-by-MD,
        xml disabled, sequence number disabled
        filtering disabled
    Logging Source-Interface:      VRF Name:
```

Network Time Protocol

Network Time Protocol (NTP) is an important component of logging. If a device is set to the wrong time, the timestamps in the event records will be wrong. The solution is to configure NTP to automatically set the correct time. NTP uses UDP protocol 123. In this example, 192.168.3.2 is configured as an NTP server. We'll configure R1 to pull its time from there:

```
R1(config)#ntp server 192.168.3.2
```

R1 has an association with the NTP server, with a slight offset. The offset, measured in milliseconds, is the estimated time difference between R1 and the NTP server:

```
R1#show ntp associations
    address         ref clock      st   when   poll reach  delay  offset   disp
```

```
*~192.168.3.2      199.102.46.76    2      0      64      1 15.343  60.802 437.58
 * sys.peer, # selected, + candidate, - outlyer, x falseticker, ~ configured
```

The st column is short for stratum. A stratum 1 server is an authoritative reference clock, whereas higher numbered strata are increasingly further away from the reference clock and hence less accurate. The configured NTP server is one hop away from an authoritative NTP time source, so the NTP server is actually stratum 2. R1 is thus a stratum 3 client, as shown:

```
R1#show ntp status
Clock is synchronized, stratum 3, reference is 192.168.3.2
nominal freq is 1000.0003 Hz, actual freq is 999.5003 Hz, precision is 2**14
ntp uptime is 149300 (1/100 of seconds), resolution is 1001
reference time is E1DF2215.F633CB9C (22:00:53.961 UTC Fri Jan 31 2020)
clock offset is 58.0951 msec, root delay is 89.05 msec
root dispersion is 895.80 msec, peer dispersion is 190.00 msec
loopfilter state is 'CTRL' (Normal Controlled Loop), drift is 0.000499999 s/s
system poll interval is 64, last update was 61 sec ago.
```

Even though R1 is an NTP client, we can configure it to act as an NTP server for other devices in the network:

```
R1(config)#ntp master
```

Now let's configure R2 to use R1 as its NTP server:

```
R2(config)#ntp server 1.1.1.1
R2(config)#^Z
R2#show ntp associations
  address          ref clock      st   when   poll reach  delay  offset   disp
 ~1.1.1.1          192.168.3.2     3     16     64     0  0.000   0.000 15937.
 * sys.peer, # selected, + candidate, - outlyer, x falseticker, ~ configured
```

NetFlow and Flexible NetFlow

NetFlow collects IP flow information and captures the packet or byte count associated with each flow. A flow is a collection of packets that share the following values:

- Source IP address
- Destination IP address
- IP protocol
- Source port (0 if not applicable)
- Destination port, ICMP type and code, or 0 if not applicable
- IP ToS

NetFlow is useful for figuring out what sort of applications are in use on the network, who the top talkers are, and how much bandwidth a particular host consumes. Flows are stored in flow records, which can then be exported to a NetFlow collector. In this example we'll configure NetFlow on R1 to collect ingress and egress flow information from Gi0/3 and export the flow records to 192.168.3.2 on UDP port 9995. NetFlow doesn't have to use any specific port, but 9995 is a commonly used one.

```
R2(config)#ip flow-export version 9
R2(config)#ip flow-export destination 192.168.3.2 9995
R2(config)#int gi0/3
R2(config-if)#ip flow egress
R2(config-if)#ip flow ingress
```

You can view the flow cache to see what NetFlow is capturing:

```
R2#show ip cache flow
IP packet size distribution (159 total packets):
   1-32   64   96  128  160  192  224  256  288  320  352  384  416  448  480
   .000 .100 .207 .691 .000 .000 .000 .000 .000 .000 .000 .000 .000 .000 .000

   512  544  576 1024 1536 2048 2560 3072 3584 4096 4608
   .000 .000 .000 .000 .000 .000 .000 .000 .000 .000 .000

IP Flow Switching Cache, 278544 bytes
  1 active, 4095 inactive, 8 added
  420 ager polls, 0 flow alloc failures
  Active flows timeout in 30 minutes
  Inactive flows timeout in 15 seconds
IP Sub Flow Cache, 34056 bytes
  1 active, 1023 inactive, 8 added, 8 added to flow
  0 alloc failures, 0 force free
  1 chunk, 1 chunk added
  last clearing of statistics never
```

Protocol	Total Flows	Flows /Sec	Packets /Flow	Bytes /Pkt	Packets /Sec	Active(Sec) /Flow	Idle(Sec) /Flow
TCP-Telnet	1	0.0	12	42	0.0	2.3	1.8
TCP-other	4	0.0	1	44	0.0	0.0	15.7
ICMP	2	0.0	55	100	0.0	2.7	15.5
Total:	7	0.0	18	92	0.0	1.1	13.7

SrcIf	SrcIPaddress	DstIf	DstIPaddress	Pr	SrcP	DstP	Pkts
Gi0/3	192.168.23.1	Null	224.0.0.5	59	0000	0000	33

Top Talkers

If you want to know which devices are consuming the most bandwidth, turn on the NetFlow Top Talkers feature. You can track up to 200 top talkers, but in this example, we'll stick to 10:

```
R2(config)#ip flow-top-talkers
R2(config-flow-top-talkers)#top 10
R2(config-flow-top-talkers)#sort-by bytes
R2(config-flow-top-talkers)#end
To view the results, issue the following command:
R2#show ip flow top-talkers

SrcIf        SrcIPaddress    DstIf       DstIPaddress    Pr SrcP DstP Bytes
Gi0/3        192.168.1.10    Gi0/2       192.168.2.1     01 0000 0800    41K
Gi0/3        192.168.23.1    Null        224.0.0.5       59 0000 0000   9572
Gi0/3        192.168.3.2     Local       192.168.23.2    01 0000 0800   8484
3 of 10 top talkers shown. 3 flows processed.
```

Flexible NetFlow

Flexible NetFlow provides a different way to configure NetFlow. It uses a modular approach much like the modular QoS CLI. The configuration is broken down into four steps:

- Configure a flow record configuration that identifies the flows you want to record
- Configure an exporter configuration that defines the server and port to export flow records to
- Configure a flow monitor to set cache sizes and timeouts, such as how frequently to export flows
- Apply the flow monitor to an interface

First, we'll configure a flow record to number of bytes for each IP address:

```
R1(config)#flow record all-ip
R1(config-flow-record)#match ipv4 destination address
R1(config-flow-record)#collect counter bytes
```

Next, we'll configure the exporter to use the latest version of NetFlow (version 9), sending the flow records to 192.168.3.2 on UDP port 9995:

```
R1(config)#flow exporter myexporter
R1(config-flow-exporter)#destination 192.168.3.2
R1(config-flow-exporter)#transport udp 9995
R1(config-flow-exporter)#export-protocol netflow-v9
R1(config-flow-exporter)#exit
```

Now we'll configure a flow monitor to match the flow record. We won't set any custom cache or timeout settings here.

```
R1(config)#flow monitor myflowmonitor
R1(config-flow-monitor)#record all-ip
R1(config-flow-monitor)#end
R1#show flow monitor
Flow Monitor myflowmonitor:
  Description:        User defined
  Flow Record:       all-ip
  Cache:
    Type:                normal
    Status:              not allocated
    Size:                4096 entries / 0 bytes
    Inactive Timeout:    15 secs
    Active Timeout:      1800 secs
```

Notice the default cache size and timeout settings. The `Active Timeout` line determines how frequently NetFlow sends records to the collector. In this case, it's every 30 minutes. The active and inactive timeouts you should use depend on the collector you're using. The cache size is 4,096 entries, but you may want to raise or lower this depending on the device's available memory and the number of flows you expect to collect. The last step is to apply the flow monitor to some interfaces to monitor ingress and egress traffic.

```
R1(config)#int range gi0/1,gi0/3
R1(config-if-range)#ip flow monitor myflowmonitor input
R1(config-if-range)#ip flow monitor myflowmonitor output
```

Switched Port Analyzer

Switched Port Analyzer (SPAN) allows switches to copy traffic from one port or VLAN and mirror it to a different port. Some call recording products use SPAN to capture voice traffic from IP phones. It's also useful for network monitoring and of course troubleshooting. SPAN comes in three flavors:

- **SPAN**—This is the traditional SPAN that captures traffic on a local switch and mirrors it out of a port on the same switch.

- **Remote SPAN**—Captured traffic can be sent over a dedicated RSPAN VLAN and mirrored out a port on a different switch.

- **Encapsulated RSPAN**—Captured traffic is IP-encapsulated and routed to another switch that decapsulates the traffic and mirrors it out of a local port.

If you're practicing with virtual switches (and you probably are), the SPAN configuration commands are unlikely to work.

Configuring SPAN

To take ingress and egress traffic traversing `Gi0/2` and mirror it out of `Gi0/0`, use the following:

```
SW1(config)#monitor session 1 source interface gi0/2
SW1(config)#monitor session 1 destination interface gi0/0
```

If you're mirroring a trunk port, you can optionally limit captures to specific VLANs on the trunk. For instance, to monitor only VLAN 2 traffic, use the command `monitor session 1 filter vlan 2`. If you want to monitor an entire VLAN rather than just individual interfaces, use the following command:

```
SW1(config)#monitor session 1 source vlan 20 rx
```

The `rx` causes SPAN to mirror only traffic received by VLAN 20. The reason is that if you monitor both directions (the default behavior), then you'll get duplicate frames: once when traffic ingresses a port in the VLAN, and another when it egresses a port in the VLAN.

Configuring RSPAN

Configuring RSPAN requires a few more steps. You have to configure a dedicated RSPAN VLAN on both the source and destination switches, like so:

```
vlan 3333
name RSPAN
remote-span
```

On the source switch, configure the source interface as before, but set the destination as the RSPAN VLAN:

```
SW1(config)#monitor session 1 source interface Gi0/2
SW1(config)#monitor session 1 destination remote vlan 3333
```

The configuration is essentially the reverse on the destination switch, with the source being the RSPAN VLAN:

```
SW2(config)# monitor session 1 source remote vlan 3333
SW2(config)# monitor session 1 destination interface Gi3/2
```

If your RSPAN VLAN is on a trunk with other traffic, it could saturate your interswitch links. It's a good idea, if possible, to place your RSPAN VLAN traffic on dedicated links. Refer to Chapter 2, "Spanning Tree Protocols," for a refresher on how to do that.

Configuring ERSPAN

Last up in the SPAN lineup is ERSPAN. The concept is similar to RSPAN, except because we're encapsulating frames in IP, we need to specify IP addresses and uniquely identify each monitoring session. In this instance, we'll configure SW1 to monitor VLAN 20 traffic and send it to a remote switch (SW2) with the IP address 192.168.4.1. The following shows the configuration on SW1:

```
SW1(config)# monitor session 1 type erspan-source
SW1(config-mon-erspan-src)#source vlan 20 rx
SW1(config-mon-erspan-src)#destination
SW1(config-mon-erspan-src-dst)#erspan-id 20
SW1(config-mon-erspan-src-dst)#ip address 192.168.4.1
SW1(config-mon-erspan-src-dst)#origin ip address 192.168.2.1
On the destination switch, we'll configure the following:
SW2(config)#monitor session 1 type erspan-destination
SW2(config-mon-erspan-dst)#destination interface Gi3/1
SW2(config-mon-erspan-dst)#source
SW2(config-mon-erspan-dst-src)#erspan-id 20
SW2(config-mon-erspan-dst-src)#ip address 192.168.4.1
```

If you want to set a ToS value for QoS, you can optionally use the erspan tos tos-value global configuration command. This can be helpful to ensure that ERSPAN traffic doesn't overwhelm the network. There are a few restrictions to keep in mind with all versions of SPAN. You can't mix and match versions for the same traffic. That means you can't mirror the same VLAN using both SPAN and RSPAN.

IP Service Level Agreement

IP Service Level Agreement (IP SLA) allows you to monitor network performance and reachability and take some action based on the results. You configure an IP SLA monitor or probe to monitor different aspects of the network, such as reachability, latency, and jitter. Consider a situation where you have a router with a default route to an Internet gateway. If the Internet gateway's IP address becomes unreachable, you may want to fail over to a backup default static route (called a floating static route). In this example, we'll configure an IP SLA tracker to do just that. The first step is to create an IP SLA probe:

```
R1(config)#ip sla 1
```

We'll configure it to send a ping to 192.168.1.1, our next-hop router. The ping will occur every 5 seconds, and time out after 5 seconds:

```
R1(config-ip-sla)#icmp-echo 192.168.1.1
R1(config-ip-sla-echo)#timeout 5000
R1(config-ip-sla-echo)#frequency 5
```

We'll configure this probe to begin monitoring immediately:

```
R1(config-ip-sla-echo)#ip sla schedule 1 life forever start-time now
```

The next step is to create an object tracker that will monitor the state of the IP SLA probe. Specifically, we want to monitor the reachability of the next hop address—whether it's up or down:

```
R1(config)#track 1 ip sla 1 reachability
```

Next, we'll create two default static routes. The existence of the primary default static route will depend on the IP SLA object tracker being up. If the tracker returns a down status, the static route will disappear from the routing table.

```
R1(config)#ip route 0.0.0.0 0.0.0.0 192.168.1.1 track 1
```

When the primary default static route disappears, we want a backup or floating static route to take its place. We'll accomplish that by creating another one with an administrative distance of 254:

```
R1(config)#ip route 0.0.0.0 0.0.0.0 192.168.23.2 254
```

The highest possible administrative distance is 255. A route with this distance is unreachable and won't be installed in the IP routing table.

The tracker shows that the address 192.168.1.1 is responding to pings and is up. Therefore, the static default route remains in place.

```
R1(config)#do show track
Track 1
  IP SLA 1 reachability
  Reachability is Up
    1 change, last change 00:01:24
  Latest operation return code: OK
  Latest RTT (millisecs) 14
  Tracked by:
    Static IP Routing 0
R1(config)#do show ip route static | i 0
Gateway of last resort is 192.168.1.1 to network 0.0.0.0
S*    0.0.0.0/0 [1/0] via 192.168.1.1
```

To simulate a behind-the-scenes failure, we'll shut down the device with the 192.168.1.1 address:

```
R1#show ip route static | i 0
Gateway of last resort is 192.168.1.1 to network 0.0.0.0
S*    0.0.0.0/0 [1/0] via 192.168.1.1
R1#
%TRACK-6-STATE: 1 ip sla 1 reachability Up -> Down
```

```
R1#show ip route static | i 0
Gateway of last resort is 192.168.23.2 to network 0.0.0.0
S*    0.0.0.0/0 [254/0] via 192.168.23.2
```

Once the tracker goes into a down state, it removes the primary static route, making room for the floating static route to kick in. Once the 192.168.1.1 gateway comes back up, the primary static route will be reinstalled.

```
%TRACK-6-STATE: 1 ip sla 1 reachability Down -> Up
R1#show ip route static | i 0
Gateway of last resort is 192.168.1.1 to network 0.0.0.0
S*    0.0.0.0/0 [1/0] via 192.168.1.1
```

Summary

Network security encompasses device security, network access, monitoring, and logging. If you've used Cisco gear for a while, you know that the tools we use to administer, secure, and monitor our networks haven't changed much over the years. We still log into devices using the console or SSH. We still use access lists to filter traffic. Even TACACS+ and RADIUS are old hat. And monitoring tools such as SNMP, Syslog, and IP SLA? They've been around for a long time, too. They're tried and tested, which means they're almost ubiquitous, so be sure to review and master them.

Although we often think of security as preventing and responding to threats, it's just as much about compliance with regulations—checking the right boxes, if you will. It's important to understand not just how to secure a network in a sensible way, but in various unusual and perhaps even nonsensical ways to comply with whatever regulations may apply to the environment you're working in. Sometimes security is just as much about show as it is about security. Understanding the sometimes confusing acronyms can help you to talk the talk, as well as solidify your understanding of the all-important fundamentals that lie beneath them.

Security is a game of cat-and-mouse. Something you may have noticed is that the newer security products we covered could more accurately be called security services. With some exceptions, most of them aren't just products you buy and configure. They're services that require an ongoing subscription. AnyConnect, ThreatGrid, AMP for Endpoints, and Firepower NGFW all integrate with Talos intelligence feeds or Umbrella. Short of locking down your network to the point of uselessness, having real-time intelligence is the only way to defend against emerging threats.

The addition of new products that automatically create network overlays and other abstractions will likely pose a significant troubleshooting and design challenge well into the future. Mastering networking fundamentals is more important now than it ever has been because the fundamentals are no longer staring you in the face all the time. They're often hidden behind a colorful user interface or slick marketing language.

Before taking the ENCOR exam, there are a few things to keep in mind. One of the neglected skills required on any Cisco exam is speed. Being able to troubleshoot a 10-router OSPF topology is good. Taking 15 minutes to do it is not so good. I can't stress enough the importance of spending quality time with the CLI. At least 50 percent of your study time should be spent on configuring and troubleshooting a variety of topologies and technologies. Keep a running list of questions you're not sure about. Chances are if you find something confusing, a lot of other people did too, and that makes it good fodder for the exam. Finally, recognize that no single resource can cover everything that may possibly show up on the exam. Don't assume that just because a topic isn't on the exam blueprint it won't be on the exam. Even though the CCNA certification isn't required to take the ENCOR exam, it's reasonable to expect you to have CCNA-level skills. Until next time, be sure to visit `https://benpiper.com/encor` for book resources, updates, and errata.

Exam Essentials

Be able to configure SSH and console device access using local and AAA authentication. This includes knowing how to disable telnet and how to use ACLs to restrict management traffic to VTY lines.

Know the difference between authentication, authorization, and accounting. In short, authentication is a go/no-go decision as to whether a user is permitted to log in. Authorization determines what the user can do after they've logged in. Accounting logs what the user did and when.

Understand the different use cases for TACACS+ and RADIUS. Use TACACS+ for device access if you also need authorization and accounting of CLI commands. Use RADIUS if you need 802.1X authentication.

Be able to configure and apply IP access lists and VLAN access maps. IP access lists you should already be familiar with. But note that IP ACLs applied to switchports can't be used to filter control plane traffic. VLAN access maps (or VACLs) let you control what traffic can ingress or egress a VLAN. IP ACLs and VACLs have one thing in common: an implicit deny at the end of the list.

Know the differences among Cisco's security products. Specifically, know the key features of Cisco AnyConnect, Umbrella, ThreatGrid, AMP, Firepower NGFW, TrustSec, and MACsec.

Understand the differences among 802.1X, MAB, and WebAuth. All three are used for authentication. 802.1X can be used to authenticate a user and an endpoint. MAB can be used only to authenticate an endpoint. WebAuth can only authenticate a user. Hence, the latter two are often used together when 802.1X isn't available.

Be able to configure network monitoring features. This includes debugs, SNMP, Syslog, NetFlow, SPAN, and IP SLA.

Exercises

EXERCISE 12.1

Configure TACACS+ authentication with local fallback. You won't have a TACACS+ server to test with, so verify your configuration by ensuring that local authentication works.

EXERCISE 12.2

On a router or switch of your choice, enable SSH version 2. Allow logins only from private IP addresses. Disable telnet logins.

EXERCISE 12.3

Configure an ACL to deny traffic with a source prefix of 192.168.10.8/30, a destination prefix of 6.0.0.0/8, and a destination TCP port 443.

EXERCISE 12.4

Configure CoPP for ICMP traffic. Set the conforming rate to 10 kbps and drop exceeding traffic.

Review Questions

You can find the answers in the appendix.

1. Which command prevents insecure telnet connections to a router?

   A. `no exec`

   B. `transport input ssh`

   C. `telnet input none`

   D. `exec-timeout 0 0`

2. Which command enables authentication using local usernames?

   A. `privilege level 15`

   B. `transport input ssh`

   C. `login local`

   D. `login`

3. What protocol and port does TACACS+ use? (Choose two.)

   A. TCP

   B. UDP

   C. 49

   D. 1812

   E. 1813

4. What official protocol and port does RADIUS use? (Choose two.)

   A. 1645

   B. UDP

   C. 1812

   D. TCP

   E. 49

5. You've configured TACACS+ authentication with local fallback. You've also configured authorization using the following command:

   `aaa authorization exec default group aaaservers`

   What will be true when all the servers in the group aaaservers fail? (Choose two.)

   A. Local users won't be able to access the CLI upon logging in.

   B. TACACS+ users will be able to authenticate.

   C. Users already in the CLI will be able to run commands.

   D. Local users won't be able to authenticate.

6. Which of the following configurations represents a port ACL?

A. `SW1(config-if)# switchport`
`SW1(config-if)# ip access-group myacl in`

B. `SW1(config-if)# no switchport`
`SW1(config-if)# mac access-group myacl in`

C. `SW1(config-if)# no switchport`
`SW1(config-if)# ip access-group myacl in`

D. `SW1(config-if)# switchport`
`SW1(config-if)# vlan filter VACL20 vlan-list 20`

7. Which of the following runs malware in a virtual sandbox to analyze its behavior?

A. Firepower NGFW

B. AMP for Endpoints

C. Umbrella

D. AMP ThreatGrid

8. Which of the following operates at layer 3?

A. EAP

B. 802.1X

C. RADIUS

D. WPA2

9. Which of the following is not compatible with 802.1X?

A. 802.3

B. TACACS+

C. PEAP

D. RADIUS

10. Which proprietary feature allows simultaneous authentication of a user and endpoint?

A. WebAuth

B. EAPoL

C. EAP-FAST

D. MAB

11. Which of the following will configure an exporter to export NetFlow using the latest version? (Choose two.)

A. `ip flow-export version 9`

B. `transport udp 9`

C. `export-protocol netflow-v9`

D. `flow record all-ip netflow-v8`

12. What's one difference between NetFlow and Flexible NetFlow?

- **A.** NetFlow doesn't have a Top Talkers feature.
- **B.** Flexible NetFlow requires fewer commands.
- **C.** Flexible NetFlow is like the modular QoS CLI.
- **D.** NetFlow must use UDP port 9995.

13. Which version of SPAN requires the most bandwidth?

- **A.** ERSPAN
- **B.** SPAN
- **C.** RSPAN
- **D.** CSPAN

14. Which of the following versions of SPAN can send traffic to a destination VLAN?

- **A.** RSPAN
- **B.** ERSPAN
- **C.** SPAN
- **D.** All of these

15. After configuring SPAN to mirror VLAN 20 traffic to a port connected to a packet analyzer, your packet analyzer shows duplicates of every frame. Which of the following configuration commands could be the culprit?

- **A.** `monitor session 1 source vlan 20 tx`
- **B.** `monitor session 1 source vlan 20 rx`
- **C.** `monitor session 1 source vlan 20 both`
- **D.** `monitor session 1 source interface gi0/2-3`

16. You want to use a conditional IP packet debug to view packets with a destination address of 192.168.33.3. Which of the following access lists should you create?

- **A.** `access-list 101 permit ip host 192.168.33.3 any`
- **B.** `access-list 101 permit ip any host 192.168.33.3`
- **C.** `access-list 11 permit ip any host 192.168.33.3`
- **D.** `access-list 101 permit ip any 192.168.33.3`

17. Which Syslog severity level is used for informational messages?

- **A.** 1
- **B.** 4
- **C.** 5
- **D.** 6

18. You want to use IP SLA to remove a static default route when the next hop (`192.168.1.1`) goes down. You also want to create a floating static default route with a next hop of `192.168.23.2`. Which of the following commands will you need to use? (Choose two.)

A. `ip route 0.0.0.0 0.0.0.0 192.168.1.1 254 track 1`

B. `ip route 0.0.0.0 0.0.0.0 192.168.1.1 track 1`

C. `ip route 0.0.0.0 0.0.0.0 192.168.23.2`

D. `ip route 0.0.0.0 0.0.0.0 192.168.23.2 254`

E. `ip route 0.0.0.0 0.0.0.0 192.168.23.2 track 1`

19. Which of the following is true of NTP? (Choose all that apply.)

A. An authoritative clock has a stratum of 1.

B. An authoritative clock has a stratum of 0.

C. It uses UDP port 123.

D. It uses UDP port 321.

E. It requires an atomic reference clock.

20. When logged into a router using SSH, you want to prevent debug messages from being displayed. You only want them written to the logging buffer. Which of the following commands will accomplish this? (Choose three.)

A. `logging monitor informational`

B. `logging console informational`

C. `logging buffered informational`

D. `logging buffered debugging`

E. `no logging monitor`

Appendix

Answers to Review Questions

Chapter 1: Networking Fundamentals

1. B. IEEE 802.3 Ethernet operates at both the Physical and Data Link layers. PPP and HDLC are Data Link layer protocols. Twisted pair is a type of cable; physical media isn't part of the Physical layer.

2. C. PPP is a Data Link layer protocol. IPv4 and OSPF are Network layer protocols. UDP is a Transport layer protocol.

3. A. You'll hear disagreement as to whether ARP is a layer 2 or layer 3 protocol. Some even go so far as to call it a layer 2.5 protocol! ARP packets fit the definition of what the OSI model calls protocol control information. In addition to just providing a mapping between MAC and IP addresses, the fact that a node sends ARP packets indicates its willingness to use IP. In that respect, ARP is decidedly a layer 2 protocol.

4. B. Data Link layer protocols such as Ethernet and PPP provide for node-to-node data transfer over a shared medium.

5. B, D. Wireless and a single pair of wires for sending and receiving each represent a single collision domain. The other two allow for full-duplex communication.

6. C. You can achieve full-duplex communication by separating the transmitting and receiving functions. This can be done by using either separate media or separate frequencies. There's no need to use fiber-optic cables, TCP, or a speed greater than 10 Mbps.

7. C. VLAN 10 is one broadcast domain, and VLAN 20 is another.

8. A. A collision domain is where two nodes transmitting simultaneously will interfere with each other. In full-duplex communication, both nodes can transmit simultaneously.

9. B. The default aging timeout is 300 seconds (5 minutes). It can be disabled or set as high as 1,000,000 seconds, although neither of those extremes are recommended, because the size of the MAC address table is limited based on the amount of memory available in the CAM table.

10. C. Once the MAC address table is full, the switch will flood traffic to every destination MAC not in the table. The oldest entries are not necessarily aged out, since the aging time is based on when the switch last saw traffic from the MAC address. It's not based on when the entry was created.

11. D. The interface MTU is the maximum size of the Data field in an Ethernet frame, measured in bytes.

12. A. Bridges—usually called switches—perform a crude form of routing using the MAC address table. This reduces the need for flooding but doesn't reduce the size of the broadcast domain. Bridges don't perform IP-based routing and don't connect VLANs together.

13. B, D. The MAC address table stores a source MAC address and the VLAN and interface where it was last seen. The MAC address table doesn't store IP addresses or ARP entries.

14. C. ARP maps IP addresses to MAC addresses by broadcasting an ARP request with the IP address to resolve. The node that has that IP address sends a unicast ARP reply that contains its MAC address.

15. B, C. Client A and Server A are in separate VLANs, but because both share the same IP subnet (172.16.3.0/24), Client A assumes Server A is in the same broadcast domain. Client A therefore sends an ARP request. Server A doesn't receive the request because it's in a different broadcast domain. Without getting an ARP reply, Client A can't even send the ping.

16. B. ARP requests are sent to the broadcast MAC address. They are not sent using IP.

17. D. ARP replies are unicast—that is, they're sent to the MAC address that sourced the request. ARP doesn't use IP.

18. C. The default timeout is 4 hours, and you can modify it on a per-interface basis.

19. B. The purpose of TCP connection establishment is to synchronize sequence numbers.

20. B. The IP protocol number for TCP is 6. The protocol number for ICMP is 1. For UDP, it's 17. For OSPF, it's 89.

Chapter 2: Spanning Tree Protocols

1. A, C. You can reduce the size of a broadcast domain in two ways. First, if you're running a trunk between switches, you can prune a VLAN from the trunk to prevent traffic for that VLAN from traversing the trunk. Second, instead of running a trunk between switches, you can use routed links.

2. A. SW1 has the lowest base MAC address, so it will be the root.

3. C. Setting the priority to 61440 would make it the highest priority, and thus the least preferred; 0 would make it best; 32768 would make it even, and it's the default. Just plugging SW4 in would make it root since it has the lowest burned-in address.

4. B. To determine the cost to the root, a switch looks at the interface cost listed in the BPDU it receives and adds its own port cost. Only if it has multiple equal-cost paths does it consider port priority or bridge priority. A switch never adds its own bridge priority or port priority to that which it receives in a BPDU.

5. B. To determine the cost to the root, a switch looks at the interface cost listed in the BPDU it receives and adds its own port cost. Only if the it has multiple equal-cost paths does it consider port priority or bridge priority. A switch never adds its own bridge priority or port priority to that which it receives in a BPDU.

6. C. The command to enable RPVST+ is `spanning-tree mode rapid-pvst`. The Spanning Tree mode is enabled per switch, not per VLAN.

7. B. Every 2 seconds, a switch sends a configuration/Hello BPDU out of every nonblocking port.

8. A, C. The transmitting bridge ID simply identifies the switch that sent the BPDU. The root bridge ID contains the base MAC address of the root bridge. Because each switch initially assumes it's the root, the transmitting bridge ID and root bridge ID can refer to the same switch. The base MAC address isn't based on an interface MAC.

9. B, C. Bridge priorities must be configured in increments of 4,096. The reason is that the VLAN ID is appended onto the configured priority. Hence, you can calculate that SW1 has a configured priority of 32768 and is in VLAN 20. SW3 has a configured priority of 36864 and is also in VLAN 20. SW1, having the lowest priority, is root. SW2 has a bridge priority of 32770, so it must have a configured priority of 32768 and be in VLAN 2.

10. A. SW1 will become the root since its priority is the same as SW2 and it has the lower base MAC address.

11. A. All VLANs map to MST0 by default, so VLAN 2 would be included. Hence, all that's needed is to make SW2 the root for MST0. Mapping VLAN 2 to MST1 would preclude making SW2 the root, since it's also mapped to VLAN 1, for which SW1 is already the root. Making SW1 the root for MST1 would cause SW1 to become the root for VLAN 1.

12. B, D. Region name, revision number, and a list of VLAN-to-instance mappings must be the same on all switches.

13. B. The MST configuration command used to map VLANs 100, 400, and 900 to MST3 is instance 3 vlan 100,400,900.

14. B, C. When you map only one VLAN to an instance, that VLAN must exist in the switch's local VLAN database. In order to save your changes, you must type exit in MST configuration mode. There's no need to save the running configuration, although it's a good idea. The show command given in the question is correct.

15. A, B. When a switch running MST is connected to a switch running RPVST+, the MST simulates PVST with the connected switch. The MST switch advertises itself as the root for all VLANs. If the other switch advertises itself as the root, the MST switch will block its ports to that switch, placing them in a PVST Simulation Inconsistent state. Since SW1's ports are forwarding in all VLANs, it's clear that SW1 is the root for all VLANs.

16. D. Root Guard prevents another switch from becoming root. Use the interface command `spanning-tree guard root` on any ports that you do not want to become root ports.

17. C. BPDU Guard error-disables a port if it receives a BPDU. BPDU Filter prevents a switch from sending or processing received BPDUs. Loop Guard places a port into a loop-inconsistent state if it fails to receive BPDUs. Root Guard prevents another switch from becoming root.

18. D. You can issue the global command `spanning-tree portfast edge bpduguard default` to automatically enable BPDU Guard for any interface that has PortFast enabled, which you should do on all interfaces connected to end-user devices.

19. A, C. In normal mode, UDLD will only detect a unidirectional link but won't disable the port. To enable normal mode, use the interface command `udld port`.

20. A, C, D. Loop Guard places a port in an error-disabled state on a per-VLAN basis if it doesn't receive BPDUs for that VLAN. UDLD can be configured to detect a loop and then either take no action or disable the interface, stopping all traffic on it.

21. B, D. `switchport mode dynamic desirable`, if configured on both ends, will result in a trunk. Specifying the encapsulation type as dot1q using the command `switchport trunk encapsulation dot1q` will ensure that it's an 802.1Q trunk. Setting both sides to negotiate the encapsulation will result in an ISL trunk. Auto/auto won't form a trunk, since neither side will attempt to initiate negotiation. The command to create an unconditional trunk is `switchport mode trunk`.

22. A, D. Enabling native VLAN tagging will allow you to prune VLAN 1 from all trunks. You can't remove VLAN 1 or shut it down.

Chapter 3: Enterprise Network Design

1. B. East-West traffic typically describes server-to-server traffic.

2. A. North-South traffic generally describes client-server traffic flows.

3. C. The three-tier architecture is the most scalable because it's modular, but this also makes it costly. The three-tier collapsed core combines the Access and Distribution/Aggregation layers into one layer, allowing you to get by with fewer switches. Leaf-and-spine architecture is a good choice for networks with predominantly East-West traffic patterns such as data center networks. Routed is not a physical architecture, but rather a layer 2 architecture.

4. D. Configuration in the Core layer should be as simple as possible, so all connections within the core should always be routed. Routing may be a good choice for the Access and Distribution/Aggregation layers, but there are times when it may be more convenient to use switching in these layers.

5. A, C. Hosts that have a similar function should be placed in the same distribution block. This provides isolation and scalability. For example, a web server and a web application load balancer would belong in the same distribution block. An IP phone would likely be in a separate block along with other campus devices such as printers and workstations. An Internet router may be in a block along with other WAN edge devices such as firewalls.

6. D. A routed interface can have a primary and a secondary IP address. You can't assign an IP address directly to a switched interface. However, you can assign a primary and a secondary IP address to an SVI.

7. A, C. Looped, loop-free invert-U, and VSS topologies allow you to span a VLAN across more than two access switches.

8. B. Stateful switchover (SSO) with non-stop forwarding (NSF) lets you configure the virtual switch IP as a default gateway for hosts. If one switch fails, the other will take over. There's no need to use an FHRP. You should still run Spanning Tree with VSS to block any accidental redundant links that fall outside of an EtherChannel. Only the active switch does IP routing.

9. B. The looped square will consume fewer ports on the distribution switches. A loop-free U topology can support VLANs that span up to two access switches. The routed topology supports only one access switch per VLAN.

10. B, D. The underlying physical topology of VSS can have loops, but the VSS is logically loop-free because the member switches behave as a single switch and the access switches use multichassis EtherChannel. VSS thus doesn't require Spanning Tree to block any links. The looped triangle depends on Spanning Tree to prevent bridging loops. Any topology can use EtherChannels.

11. B. The command configured on Switch A creates a static port channel. Hence, in order to get a working EtherChannel link, the other side must also be configured to create a static port channel. The channel group numbers don't have to match on both ends.

12. A. If one end is Active, the other end must be Active or Passive to form an EtherChannel.

13. C. You can have up to eight active links in a port channel.

14. C. You can have up to eight backup ports in a port channel.

15. D. Valid PAgP modes are Auto and Desirable.

16. D. If a router's interface IP is the same as the VRRP group's virtual IP, then the router is the IP address owner and automatically takes on a priority of 255. The default priority is 100.

17. B. The default priority for HSRP is 100. If the priority is equal on all routers in the group, the one with the highest IP address becomes the active router.

18. A. HSRP version 1 uses the "all routers" multicast address 224.0.0.2. HSRP uses 224.0.0.18. GLBP and HSRP version 2 use 224.0.0.102.

19. A. The virtual MAC address format for VRRP is 0000.5e00.01xx, with xx being the group number in hexadecimal.

20. B, C. An AVG can be an AVF. GLBP achieves load balancing by having multiple AVFs active at a time. There can't be multiple AVGs active at a time. You configure the load-balancing method on the AVG.

21. B, D. LACP modes are Active and Passive.

Chapter 4: Wireless LAN (WLAN)

1. B. The law of 3s states that a 3 dB difference indicates a twofold difference in the measured signals.

2. A. The law of 3s states that every 3 dB indicates a twofold change. Hence, 6 dB would indicate a fourfold change.

3. B. When a signal decreases in comparison to the reference, it's a negative dB. Hence, the answer is –10 dB. If the signal had increased by 10×, then it would be +10 dB.

4. C. A 10 dB indicates a 10× increase, and 3dB indicates a 2× increase. Combining them, you get 100 mW * 10 * 2 = 2000 mW.

5. D. The EIRP is calculated by taking the transmit power, subtracting the cable loss, and adding the antenna gain. Hence, 40 dBm – 4 dB + 12 dBi = 48 dBm.

6. D. The 802.11ac standard supports data rates up to 3.464 Gbps.

7. B. As the quality of a signal degrades, the AP will reduce data throughput by using a different modulation scheme.

8. C. The MIMO notation is written as T×R, where T is the number of transmitting antennas and R is the number of receiving antennas.

9. D. Open Authentication can be used with WebAuth. The client associates with an AP, and then goes to a captive portal page to authenticate to gain access to network resources.

10. B, D. WPA2 Enterprise mode uses 802.1X with EAP. WPA personal mode uses a preshared key.

11. B. In autonomous mode, the traffic will flow only through the AP and won't touch the switch.

12. B. An AP forms a single CAPWAP tunnel with a WLC.

13. B, C. In addition to preconfigured WLC addresses and a subnet broadcast on UDP port 5246, an AP can use DHCP option 43 or a DNS query to discover a WLC.

14. B. Configuring the WLC as the primary WLC is the only way to ensure that the AP always uses it. The other methods aren't as foolproof.

15. C. An AP builds only one CAPWAP tunnel with a single WLC. Because the AP discovered both WLCs through a broadcast (as opposed to having them preconfigured), it will choose the least-loaded WLC.

16. B. A client disassociates from an AP and associates with another AP providing the same SSID. A client won't necessarily change VLANs. In autonomous mode, an AP doesn't use a WLC.

17. A, D. This is an intercontroller roam since the client is moving from one WLC to another. VLANs don't extend between WLCs, so the foreign controller forms a CAPWAP tunnel with the anchor controller, allowing the client to keep its IP address. This is a layer 3 roam.

18. A. Location Services uses the station's RSSI as measured from at least three APs to determine its location.

19. C. CAPWAP tunnels are used between an AP and a WLC in any lightweight deployment. Autonomous mode doesn't use WLCs and doesn't require a CAPWAP tunnel.

20. D. Auto-anchor mobility can route all traffic through a particular WLC.

Chapter 5: Open Shortest Path First (OSPF)

1. D. During a DR election, the router with the highest interface priority will be elected.

2. C. Setting the interface priority to 0 will prevent a router from becoming a DR or BDR on that segment.

3. C. All OSPF routes have a default AD of 110.

4. D. OSPF uses 224.0.0.5 over IP protocol 89 to send Hello packets.

5. B. The MTU must match. The network statements and OSPF process numbers don't have to, but they can. Router IDs must not match on different OSPF routers.

6. A. The type 5 External LSA is advertised to all normal areas. The others remain within an area.

7. B. The router can have another interface in Area 0 (also known as Area 0.0.0.0), making it an ABR. It can also have another interface in Area 51. But it can't have an interface in another nonzero area unless it's bordering Area 0.

8. D. On a broadcast segment, one router is elected as the DR. Only the DR receives type 1 LSAs from other OSPF routers on the segment and uses these to generate and send a type 2 Network LSA that describes all the routers on the segment.

9. D. Type 2 Network LSAs are generated by a designated router. DRs only exist on broadcast or transit network types, but not point-to-point network types. The presence of a backup designated router implies the presence of a designated router.

10. B. A type 3 Summary LSA is generated by an ABR and summarizes the information in type 1 and type 2 LSAs from one area. It doesn't necessarily include an IP network summary.

11. A, D. An OSPF router bordering two areas is an ABR, whereas one that redistributes routes into OSPF is an ASBR. A single router can be both.

12. B. No two OSPF routers in a topology should have the same RID. A RID must be between 0.0.0.1 and 255.255.255.255.

13. C. The area number is the only thing that must match. The subnet type doesn't have to match on a point-to-point interface. The network types don't have to match to form an adjacency, only to exchange routes. Each router must have a unique RID.

14. A. It's a good idea to sketch a diagram of this topology, as shown. R2 and R3 can't have interfaces in the same area for two reasons. First, R2 and R3 can't be connected via Area 0 because R1 already has an interface in Area 0, and doing so would split Area 0, which isn't allowed. R2 and R3 can't be connected via a nonzero area because nonzero areas must be connected to Area 0. It's perfectly allowable for R1 to have another interface in Area 7 or Area 12, since it's an ABR.

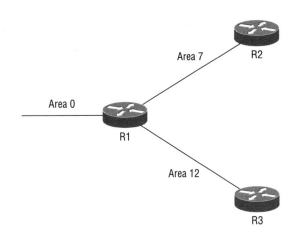

15. C. In a broadcast network, non-(B)DR neighbors remain in the two-way state.

16. D. Routers initially exchange full link-state information in the Loading stage. In the Exchange stage, they only exchange LSA headers.

17. A. OSPF cryptographic authentication uses the MD5 hashing algorithm.

18. C. The command area 2 authentication message-digest enables MD5 authentication for all interfaces in Area 2. Failing to specify the message-digest keyword will enable clear-text authentication.

19. B. There isn't a "secret" authentication type.

20. A, C. Passive interfaces are configured under the OSPF router configuration, not the interface configuration.

Chapter 6: Enhanced Interior Gateway Routing Protocol (EIGRP)

1. C. EIGRP sends Hello packets to 224.0.0.10.

2. B. EIGRP uses IP protocol 88.

3. D. The default AD for an external EIGRP route is 170.

4. B. The default AD for an internal EIGRP route is 90.

5. B. The default CEF load-sharing algorithm is based on a hash of the source and destination IP addresses.

6. **D.** A variance of 1 means that EIGRP will perform only equal-cost multipathing. 10.0.45.4 is the successor because it has the lowest feasible distance. 10.0.56.6 is a feasible successor because its advertised distance is less than 10.0.45.4's feasible distance.

7. **C.** The feasibility condition precludes the possibility of feasible successors that may create a routing loop. The purpose of using feasible successors is to enable rapid convergence. The DUAL algorithm attempts to find the shortest loop-free path. The feasibility condition has nothing to do with route filtering.

8. **B, C, D.** When there's no feasible successor, the router places the route in the active state, starts the active timer, advertises the route with an infinite metric, and sends queries to its neighbors. The route isn't stuck in active until the active timer expires.

9. **A.** When the active timer expires, the router resets its adjacency with its neighbor. The other steps occur prior to the active timer expiring.

10. **A, B.** K1 and K2 are associated with bandwidth. Keep in mind that the default values are K1 = 1 and K2 = 0.

11. **C.** K3 is associated with delay, and its default value is 1.

12. **B.** Assuming the default K values of K1 = 1, K2 = 0, K3 = 1, K4 = 0, and K5 = 0, the weighted metric formula can be boiled down to 256 × (bandwidth + delay).

13. **D.** The ratio of the routes is about 10.7, so increasing the variance multiplier to 11 will enable unequal cost multipathing. The default maximum paths is 4, so there's no need to change it to 2. Making both routes equal will enable equal cost multipathing. Disabling CEF won't make any difference.

14. **C.** The default SIA timer is 3 minutes.

15. **D.** EIGRP inverts the actual constrained bandwidth so that the higher the bandwidth, the smaller the metric.

16. **B.** The constrained bandwidth is the minimum bandwidth along a path, so it would be 1 Gbps.

17. **D.** EIGRP uses the cumulative delay along a path, which would be 130 μsec.

18. **B.** The traffic share count is based on the ratio of the distances. To calculate this manually, add the distances for R1 and R2 (3,328 + 5,632 = 8,960). Then divide R1's distance by the total to get the traffic share percentage (3,328 ÷ 8,960 ≈ .37).

19. **D.** MTU isn't used in metric calculations, even though it is advertised in route updates.

20. **C.** A cut fiber can lead to packet loss, which can result in a route getting SIA. A routing loop wouldn't cause SIA because EIGRP neighbors communicate using a link-local multicast address. An MTU mismatch may cause an adjacency not to form but wouldn't cause SIA.

Chapter 7: The Border Gateway Protocol (BGP)

1. C. BGP is a path vector protocol that uses the AS path count rather than the hop count in calculating the best path to a prefix.

2. B. On Cisco routers, BGP uses weight and local preference, followed by AS path, in that order.

3. D. BGP can consider IGP metrics in best path decisions.

4. A. AS numbers that can be used on the Internet range from 1 to 64,495 and from 131,072 to 4,199,999,999.

5. C. BGP uses the AS path for loop prevention. Upon receiving a route with its own AS in the AS path, an eBGP router will discard the route, meaning it won't install it in its BGP RIB or IP routing table, nor will it advertise the route.

6. A. BGP peers use TCP port 179.

7. B. BGP peers send keepalive messages every 60 seconds.

8. D. The default BGP hold timer is 180 seconds (3 minutes).

9. D. In the Established state, BGP peers exchange routes. The Active state is when the active router—the one with the highest IP address—initiates a new TCP connection with its neighbor.

10. B, C. You specify the AS of a router in the router configuration command. You specify the AS of the neighbor using the remote-as keyword.

11. D. The command `show ip bgp neighbors` will give you details on the BGP session state. `show ip route` can show you installed routes, but it's possible that due to BGP's slow reconvergence times a BGP route may linger in the IP routing table even if the BGP session it came from is down. For the same reason, `show bgp` and `show ip bgp` are wrong, and neither includes information on the session state.

12. C. To advertise 10.0.24.0/24, you need to specify both the subnet and the subnet mask. If you don't specify the subnet mask, BGP will assume the classful mask (255.0.0.0). Redistributing connected routes won't work because the route is an OSPF-learned route.

13. C. The router would determine the best path by analyzing weight, local preference, and shortest AS path. Since the AS path length is equal, the next attribute it would consider would be the origin type.

14. B. IGP origin types are preferred over incomplete. EGP is a defunct origin type whose namesake is the defunct precursor to BGP—the Exterior Gateway Protocol. Oldest isn't an origin type.

15. B. 10.9.0.0/24 doesn't exist in R1's routing table, so the network command will have no effect. Instead, the `redistribute eigrp 50` command will redistribute the 10.9.0.0/16 prefix into BGP with an incomplete origin type.

16. B. Local preference is advertised only within an AS, between iBGP peers. AS path, MED, and origin type are advertised between eBGP peers.

17. B, D. Modifying the AS path can create a routing loop, and it can also be used to prefer one route over another. It will not make two routes equally preferred, since if the AS path length is equal between two routes, BGP will consider other attributes. Modifying the AS path for a route will not change the origin type.

18. D. The network statement will advertise a prefix as an IGP origin type. Redistributing a prefix will always advertise it as an incomplete origin type.

19. C. `clear ip bgp * soft` will cause BGP to perform a soft reconfiguration. Using the network command with the shutdown keyword will simply shut down the BGP session with 1.3.3.7. The other commands aren't valid.

20. A. This is a complex configuration and might require some scratch paper. The prefix list matches any prefix with a subnet falling into the 10.0.0.0/8 range with a prefix length from 8 to 32. This includes 10.0.0.0/8 and 10.0.0.0/16. The first sequence in the route map is a deny sequence that matches the IP prefix list. Hence, these prefixes will match the sequence and will be denied. When applied as an inbound route map, any incoming routes for 10.0.0.0/8 or 10.0.0.0/16 won't be installed in R1's IP routing table. The second sequence in the route map is a permit sequence that matches all other prefixes by default, so R1 may still install other routes learned from the neighbor 1.3.3.7. Nothing in this configuration, however, will stop R1 from advertising these prefixes (for instance, if it learns them from elsewhere, such as another neighbor).

Chapter 8: Network Address Translation and Multicast

1. B. Static NAT hides the inside local address by changing the inside source IP of a packet to an outside address before sending it out the outside interface. This is the antithesis of address conservation. Static NAT doesn't change any port numbers.

2. A, C. The address 10.1.1.1 is accessible from the inside network, making it an inside local address. 192.0.2.2 is a globally reachable address, but it's assigned to an interface on the Internet router on the inside network, so it's an inside global address.

3. A. When the global address pool is exhausted, the NAT router will drop packets from subsequent hosts that send traffic to the outside network.

4. A, D. An inside global address can be one assigned to an outside interface (an inside global address) or a loopback interface. Any interface marked as an inside interface can't be used as the source for an inside global address. An outside local address is a local address in an outside network, so it obviously couldn't be used as an inside global address.

5. A. Any inside local source IP addresses matching ACL 1 will be translated to one of the inside global addresses listed in the NAT pool named globalpool.

6. B, C. It appears that the NAT router is running out of inside global addresses in the NAT pool. Thus, increasing the size of the NAT pool will probably resolve the issue. Alternatively, using PAT instead of dynamic NAT will let all inside hosts share a single inside global IP address. Clearing the NAT translation table might provide only a temporary fix.

7. A. With PAT, multiple inside source addresses can be translated to the same inside global address—a process called NAT overloading.

8. B, D. Port address translation—also known as NAT overload—translates multiple inside local source addresses to a single global address. The global address can come from an outside interface or from a pool.

9. A, D. The output indicates a one-to-one mapping between an inside local and an inside global address, so it must be static or dynamic NAT.

10. C. It's crucial to carefully read the output of the translation table. The outside local address is 1.1.1.1 and the outside global address is 10.0.12.1, whereas the inside local and inside global addresses are blank. This indicates an outside static NAT configuration. Recalling that only inside hosts can resolve local addresses, we can infer that the inside host sends traffic to the destination IP 1.1.1.1, and the NAT router translates the destination to the global address 10.0.12.1.

11. B. Multicast IP addresses range from 224.0.0.0 to 239.255.255.255 inclusive.

12. A. Multicast distributes a single frame or packet to multiple receivers. Unicast, on the other hand, involves sending a packet to one and only one receiver. Destination-based routing refers to routing a packet according to its destination IP address and is what unicast routing is usually based on. In contrast, multicast routing is based on the location of the group members or receivers.

13. A. The second-to-left hexadecimal digit of a multicast address is always odd, whereas the same digit of a unicast address is always either even or zero.

14. A, B. An Ethernet frame can't contain a multicast source address and doesn't have a TTL. It may contain a multicast destination address, and it may be flooded to all devices in a subnet (e.g., a broadcast frame).

15. A, D. A multicast IP packet always has a multicast destination address (that's what makes it a multicast packet), and it may have a TTL of 1. It will never contain a multicast source address.

16. A. Multicast receivers send IGMP Membership Report messages to join a group.

17. C, D. PIM routers running in sparse mode use PIM Joins to request traffic for a group, whereas those running in dense mode use Grafts. PIM Prunes indicate that a router doesn't want to receive traffic for a group. Routers do not request traffic using IGMP.

18. B. When a receiver joins a multicast group, it sends an IGMP Membership Report to the group address. Receivers don't send IGMP Queries. Routers don't send IGMP Queries or PIM messages to group addresses.

19. A. PIM Hello messages are sent to 224.0.0.13.

20. C. Routers send IGMP Queries to 224.0.0.1. Receivers send IGMP Membership Reports to the multicast group address they want to receive traffic for.

Chapter 9: Quality of Service

1. D. There are nine possible values: CS0 through CS7, and LE.

2. D. LE and CS1 are for "lower effort" traffic and are sometimes referred to as scavenger classes. CS0 is the default class and is for best-effort traffic. CS2 has the highest DSCP value and thus the highest priority.

3. B. Only the assured forwarding (AF) PHB values include drop precedence. CoS is an Ethernet field used for QoS, but it's not part of the DSCP specification.

4. B, C. x is the priority; y is the drop precedence or drop priority.

5. D. What constitutes the best DSCP value for an application can be subjective. A video teleconferencing application will have tight delay requirements, so CS0 and CS1 are not candidates because they're for best-effort and lower-effort traffic, respectively. EF is designed for voice and is usually bandwidth constrained. AF41 offers a reasonably high priority, and the assured forwarding group is meant for applications that can tolerate some packet loss.

6. B. When a router routes an IP packet, it decapsulates the packet and discards the frame. It encapsulates the packet in a new frame before forwarding. CoS values are included in 802.1Q frames, and the router isn't configured to do any marking. Hence, the new frame will have no CoS marking.

7. A, C. Policing can be applied to inbound or outbound traffic. You can choose the traffic you want to police and what action to take for traffic that exceeds the CIR.

8. D. The bucket size is one token for every bit of the CIR. A CIR of 150,000 bps would create a bucket that can hold 150,000 tokens.

9. B. Red means packets are violating—exceeding the number of tokens in both the bc and be buckets—and will be dropped.

10. C. Yellow means packets are exceeding only the number of tokens in the bc bucket but not the number of tokens in the bc and be buckets combined. Yellow packets are forwarded after being marked down.

11. B. The policer can burst up to about 1.77 Mbps, but the packet is 2,100,000 bits in size. The router will therefore drop it.

12. C. If a packet can be forwarded using only the tokens in the bc bucket, it's said to be conforming and will be forwarded as is.

13. A, C. Shapers increase delay by queuing packets. Shapers work only on outbound traffic and may drop packets if the shaping queue grows too large.

14. B. The LLQ is serviced before any other queues, so packets in the LLQ won't wait any longer than necessary. Within the LLQ, the queuing algorithm is FIFO. The LLQ has a limited bandwidth.

15. B. CBWFQ lets you allocate a set bandwidth to each queue. If there's extra bandwidth available, the queue can exceed it. TCP applications tolerate delay and loss, and adapt to use all available bandwidth, so CBWFQ is the best choice. FIFO (which is the same as no QoS) is not a good choice because of TCP global synchronization. WRED is not a queuing algorithm.

16. A. When a packet is violating, it's dropped, and no tokens are removed from any bucket.

17. A. TCP global synchronization occurs when multiple TCP flows back off, then ramp up simultaneously. This can happen when a queue fills and excess packets are tail-dropped. WRED is an alternative to tail-drop that randomly drops packets as the queue fills.

18. D. The command service-policy input mark applies the policy map "mark" to inbound traffic.

19. B, C. The bandwidth command enables CBWFQ. The random-detect command enables WRED.

20. A. The priority command enables LLQ.

Chapter 10: Network Virtualization

1. B, C. Some type-1 hypervisors are VMware ESXi, Microsoft Hyper-V, KVM, and Xen.

2. D. Type-1 hypervisors are specially geared toward running VMs on server hardware. Type-1 hypervisors are for server virtualization and don't have a lot of bells and whistles.

3. D. Hypervisors provide a virtual switch that VMs use to communicate with other VMs on the same host, as well as network devices outside of the VM host.

4. A, C. The term edge virtual bridging (EVB) describes using a physical switch to pass layer 2 traffic between VMs running on the same host. In external edge virtual bridging, traffic from one VNF goes out of the physical NIC to a physical switch and then comes back into the same NIC. The IEEE 802.1Qbg standard calls this reflective relay.

5. B. Anything that blocks IP protocol 47 is going to block a GRE tunnel from forming.

6. A, B. GRE allows you to tunnel almost any layer 3 protocol over another. GRE is typically used to form a site-to-site VPN tunnel when combined with IPsec.

7. C. You just need to enable OSPF on the tunnel interfaces. There's no requirement to explicitly set router IDs in OSPFv2, although it's a good idea. There's no need to enable OSPF on the physical interface to enable it over the tunnel, nor is there any need to disable IPsec.

8. B. Recursive routing occurs when a route to tunnel endpoint uses the tunnel interface itself as the next hop. This can happen when you use the same routing protocol to advertise tunnel endpoint prefixes over both the tunnel and the physical interfaces used for the tunnel endpoints.

9. B. The minimum acceptable DH group number is 14, which provides a 2,048-bit key size.

10. A. ESP uses IP protocol 47.

11. A. ESP uses IP protocol 47.

12. C. show crypto ipsec sa will show the IPsec ESP security associations details, including whether tunnel or transport mode is being used.

13. A. LISP uses UDP/4341 for tunneling packets.

14. D. The command database-mapping 172.16.3.3/32 10.10.10.1 priority 1 weight 1 will map the EID 172.16.3.3/32 to the RLOC 10.10.10.1.

15. A, C. The output indicates that 172.16.3.3/32 is reachable via 10.10.10.1 (xTR1). The admin-down flag next to 10.10.10.2 (xTR2) indicates that xTR2 has registered a negative map entry for the EID because it doesn't have an IP route to 172.16.3.3/32.

16. B, C. LISP encapsulates IP packets (with source and destination EIDs) to create a tunnel between ITRs and ETRs. Because the EIDs are encapsulated, intermediate routers don't need to maintain routes for them.

17. D. VXLAN uses UDP/4789.

18. B, D. Flood-and-learn with multicast, EVPN with BGP, and LISP are options for MAC address learning with VXLAN.

19. A. You map the VNI to a multicast group under the NVE configuration. For example, to map VNI 10050 to 230.1.1.1, you'd use the command member vni 10050 mcast-group 230.1.1.1.

20. A, B. To map VLAN 50 to VNI 10050, for example, you'd use the following set of commands:

```
Nexus(config)# vlan 50
Nexus(config-vlan)# vn-segment 10050
```

21. B. The advantage of VRFs is that you have completely separate and independent IP routing tables and FIBs, so having overlapping routes is permitted.

22. B. The command to add an interface to VRF Green is `ip vrf forwarding Green`.

23. D. You must specify the AS number under the address family configuration. The AS number in the `router eigrp` command doesn't specify the AS number used in the VRF.

24. A. `show ip route vrf Orange` will show the IP routing table for VRF Orange.

Chapter 11: Software-Defined Networking and Network Programmability

1. B. The fabric border node performs route redistribution between IP prefixes that are internal to the fabric and those that are external, such as those in a public cloud environment.

2. C. To make the cloud a part of your SD-WAN, you can deploy a vEdge cloud router, also called a cEdge router, into your cloud environment.

3. C. SD-Access uses VXLAN encapsulation because it can carry Ethernet frames, whereas LISP encapsulation can't.

4. B. SD-Access uses a proprietary VXLAN header that contains scalable group tags, also known as Group Policy tags. The standard VXLAN header doesn't.

5. B. SD-Access was designed for campus networks. ACI was designed for the data center. VTS is for service providers.

6. D. SD-Access uses LISP to store IP routes for the overlay.

7. C. The Identity Services Engine (ISE) provides network access control, which encompasses authentication and policy enforcement.

8. A, F. SD-WAN doesn't use LISP or BGP. SD-WAN uses OMP, which is a lot like BGP, which is somewhat like LISP. But OMP is not BGP.

9. A, B, C, D. SD-WAN vEdge routers have Ethernet WAN interfaces, so they can work with all of these.

10. D. The vBond orchestrator authenticates the vEdge routers and the vSmart controller using a DTLS connection.

11. A. OMP traffic is tunneled over DTLS.

12. C. VPN 512 is reserved for the management interface.

13. B. vEdge routers use NAT traversal techniques to establish an IPsec tunnel through a NAT firewall.

14. A. The requests.put() function is used to send your credentials to the API to obtain a token.

15. A. JSON uses curly braces to denote an object. To separate key-value pairs, it uses a comma. Key names and values are separated by a colon.

16. C, D. NETCONF uses XML for carrying configuration data. YANG is a data modeling language that represents the structure and constraints of configuration data.

17. C. 202 indicates the request has been accepted but will take time to process.

18. C, D. 403 Forbidden could indicate that you called an API you're not authorized to access, perhaps by mistyping the URL. 404 Not found means the URL isn't valid.

19. B. The applet doesn't specify a triggering event, so it can only be run manually. The script won't display any output or write data to the syslog simply because there's no action to instruct it to do so.

20. B. The code is an example of YAML. One clue is the use of three dashes (---) on the first line.

Chapter 12: Network Security and Monitoring

1. B. Unless you explicitly enable telnet, it's going to be disabled.

2. C. The login local command requires authenticating using a local username. The login command by itself requires a password to be set on the line itself.

3. A, C. TACACS+ uses TCP port 49.

4. B, C. RADIUS officially uses UDP port 1812 for authentication.

5. A, C. Local users, even if they authenticate, won't be authorized to obtain a CLI shell because the if-authenticated keyword is missing. Users who are already in the CLI will be able to run commands because command authorization is not configured.

6. A. A port ACL is an ACL applied to a switchport.

7. D. AMP ThreatGrid runs suspicious executables in a virtual environment to analyze its behavior to determine whether it's malware.

8. C. RADIUS uses IP, so it operates at layer 3. 802.1X and WPA2 operate at layer 2. EAP is an application protocol.

9. B. TACACS+ can't be used for EAP authentication, implying it can't be used with 802.1X. 802.1X can use RADIUS, PEAP, and obviously 802.3.

10. C. EAP-FAST is a proprietary protocol that supports EAP chaining, which allows simultaneous authentication of both the user and the machine.

11. A, C. The latest version of NetFlow is 9. `ip flow-export version 9` configures a flow exporter using NetFlow, whereas `export-protocol netflow-v9` configures a flow exporter using Flexible NetFlow.

12. C. Configuring Flexible NetFlow is much like configuring QoS using the modular QoS CLI.

13. A. ERSPAN encapsulates MAC frames in IP, increasing the amount of bandwidth required.

14. A. Only RSPAN can send traffic to a destination VLAN (the RSPAN VLAN). All versions can capture traffic from a VLAN.

15. C. If you monitor both directions (the default behavior), then you'll get duplicate frames: once when traffic ingresses a port in the VLAN, and another when it egresses a port in the VLAN.

16. B. Because you're specifying a destination, you'll need to use an IP extended access list. The correct command is `access-list 101 permit ip any host 192.168.33.3`.

17. D. Severity level 6 is used for informational messages.

18. B, D. You need to associate the object tracker with the primary static route, which should have a default administrative distance of 1 (which it does by default). The floating static route should have a higher administrative distance (254 in this case) and should not be associated with an object tracker.

19. A, C. NTP uses UDP port 123. The reference clock has a stratum of 1. An atomic clock isn't required.

20. A, D, E. You can prevent debugging messages from being written to the terminal monitor using the `logging monitor informational` or `no logging monitor` commands. The `logging buffered debugging` command ensures debugging messages get written to the logging buffer.

Index

Note to the Reader: Throughout this index **boldfaced** page numbers indicate primary discussions of a topic. *Italicized* page numbers indicate illustrations.

A

AAA (authentication, authorization, and accounting)
  RADIUS, **406–407**
  server configuration, 421–422, *421*
  TACACS+, **402–406**
ABRs (area border routers), **139–140**
access, device, **399–402**
access-class command, 410
access control lists (ACLs)
  BGP, 222
  extended, **407–409**, *409*
  overview, **407**
  standard, **410–411**
  VLAN access maps, **411–412**
access-distribution blocks in three-tier architecture, **71–72**, *72*
access layer in three-tier architecture, 73
access-list deny command, 410
access-list permit command, 243, 410
access maps in VLANs, **411–412**
access point (AP) modes
  autonomous, **124**
  lightweight, **124–125**
  WLC selection, **125–126**
access point (AP) power levels, 110
accounting
  description, 402
  TACACS+, 406
Acknowledgment (ACK) packets in EIGRP, 173
acknowledgments in 802.11 standards, 122
ACLs. *See* access control lists (ACLs)
Active mode for LACP, 90
active-passive configuration in HSRP, 92
Active state in BGP, 201
active timers in EIGRP, 175
active virtual forwarders (AVFs) in GLBP, **95–96**
active virtual gateways (AVGs) in GLBP, 95–96
active VLANs, **36–38**
address-family ipv4 command, 317, 342
Address Resolution Protocol (ARP)
  fabric edge node, 362
  GLBP, 96
  overview, **16–17**
  request forwarding, 14–15
  unicasts, 254–255
  VXLAN, 339
adjacencies
  EIGRP, 180, **186–187**
  OSPF, **141–144**
  PIM, 258
administratively scoped blocks in multicast, 253

Advanced Malware Protection (AMP)
  AMP for Endpoints, **415**
  ThreatGrid, **414–415**
advertised distance in EIGRP, 175
advertising
  BGP, 200
    prefixes, **204–205**
    summary routes, **220–222**
  IPv4 routes using OSPFv2, **316**
  IPv6 routes using OSPFv3, **316–317**
  RIDs, 136
AES encryption, **321–322**
AF (assured forwarding) in Differentiated Services, **279**
agent-based tools, 389
agentless tools, 389
aggregation, route, **220–222**
aggregation layer in three-tier architecture, **72–73**
aggressive mode in UDLD, 58
aging times in MAC address tables, 11
allowed VLANs, **36–38**
alternate port roles in RPVST+, 49
AM (amplitude modulation), 110
AMP (Advanced Malware Protection)
  AMP for Endpoints, **415**
  ThreatGrid, **414–415**
amplitude, RF, **107–109**, *107*
amplitude modulation (AM), 110
analytics in SD-Access, 357
anchor controllers, 127
antenna types, **112–113**
anycast gateways, 361
AnyConnect Secure Mobility Client, 414
AP (access point) modes
  autonomous, **124**
  lightweight, **124–125**
  WLC selection, **125–126**
applets, EEM, **386–387**
Application Health dashboard, 367, *368*
application programming interfaces (APIs)
  network programmability, 372
  SD-Access, 363
Application Visibility and Control (AVC), 415
Area 0 in OSPF, 157
  authentication, 154, **156–157**
  configuring, **142–145**
  inter-area summarization, 161
  LSAs, **146–148**, 152
  overview, 137, *140*
  route filtering, 162
Area 23 configuration on point-to-point networks, **149–152**
area border routers (ABRs), **139–140**
ARP. *See* Address Resolution Protocol (ARP)

ASBR (autonomous system boundary router) LSAs, 140
ASs (autonomous systems)
  BGP, **198–201**, *200–201*
  EIGRP, 342
associations in 802.11 standards, **120–121**
assurance, NCP, 363
Assurance workflow in DNA Center, **367–368**, *368–369*
assured forwarding (AF) in Differentiated Services, **279**
authentication
  802.11 standards, 120
  description, 402
  device access, **399–400**
  Intent API, **374–378**
  IPsec configuration, **321–322**
  LISP, 329
  OSPF, **154–155**
    area, **156–157**
    default routes, **159–160**
    distribute lists, **162–163**
    inter-area summarization, 161
    interface, **155–156**
    passive interfaces, **158–159**
    route filtering, 162
    types, 155
  preshared keys, **321–322**
  TACACS+, **402–404**
  wireless security, **418–422**, *419–421*
  WPA2, **422–424**, *423*
authentication, authorization, and accounting (AAA)
  RADIUS, **406–407**
  server configuration, 421–422, *421*
  TACACS+, **402–406**
Authentication Header protocol, 326
authorization
  description, 402
  TACACS+, **404–406**
auto-anchor mobility, **127–128**
auto-discover-rlocs command, **330–331**
Auto mode
  DTP, 34
  PAgP, **88–89**
automatic network underlays in SD-Access, **358–359**
automation
  NCP, 363
  network programmability. *See* network programmability
autonomous APs
  description, 124
  roaming between, **126–127**
autonomous system boundary router (ASBR) LSAs, 140

autonomous systems (ASs)
BGP, **198–201**, *200–201*
EIGRP, 342
auxiliary (aux) ports for device access, 399
AVC (Application Visibility and Control),
415
AVFs (active virtual forwarders) in GLBP,
95–96
AVGs (active virtual gateways) in GLBP, 95–96

B

backup designated routers (BDRs), 143–146
backup port roles in RPVST+, 49
bandwidth
CBWFQ, 288–289, 291
channels, 116–119
EIGRP, **176–177**, 182–183
EtherChannels, 82–83
expedited forwarding, 279
LLQ, 293–295
physical design, 68–69
spanning tree protocols, 42
Top Talkers, 431
wireless QoS, 282
WRED, 291–292
bc (committed burst) buckets, **285**
BDRs (backup designated routers), 143–146
be (excess burst) buckets, **285–286**
BIAs (burned-in addresses) for root bridge
elections, 38
blocked ports, calculating, **48–49**
Border Gateway Protocol (BGP), **198**
AS numbers, **199–201**, *200–201*
configuring, 202–203, *202*
advertising prefixes, **204–205**
advertising summary routes,
220–222
IP reachability tests, 214–215
path selection, **205–210**
route filtering, 222–225
route redistribution, 210–213
troubleshooting, 215–218
weight, **218–220**
exam essentials, 226
exercises, 226–227
fundamentals, 198–199
LSAs, **140**
review questions, 228–231
session states, 201–202
summary, 225–226
Bridge Protocol Data Units (BPDUs)
blocked ports, 49
BPDU Filter, 57
BPDU Guard, 57
root bridge elections, 38–39
spanning tree protocols, 55–57
bridging loops, 33
broadcast addresses, 11
ARP, 16
EIGRP, 173

multicasts, 253–255
OSPF, 138–139, **142–143**
broadcast networks for LSAs, **139**
broadcast storms
spanning tree protocols, 8, 31
switched topologies, 76
buffers in QoS, 276
burned-in addresses (BIAs) for root bridge
elections, 38
burst size in LLQ, **294**

C

CAM (content-addressable memory) tables
IGMP snooping, 256
MAC addresses, 10–11
multicast, 254
campus networks, 69
CAPWAP (Control and Provisioning of
Wireless Access Points) tunnels
fabric overlays, 363
WLCs, **125–127**
carrier frequency in RF, **109–110**
CBWFQ (class-based weighted fair
queuing), **288–293**
CCMP encryption, 121
CEF (Cisco Express Forwarding)
EIGRP, 181–182, **185–187**
subnets, 15
VSS, 81
channel groups in EtherChannels,
84–85
channels in 802.11 standards, **115–119**
CIDR in Network layer, 13–14
CIR (committed information rate)
QoS, 284, 287
traffic shaping, 296–297
Cisco Express Forwarding (CEF)
EIGRP, 181–182, **185–187**
subnets, 15
VSS, 81
class-based weighted fair queuing
(CBWFQ), **288–293**
class-default maps, 280–281, 286–287
class maps
CBWFQ, 289–291
CoPP, 412
QoS, 280–281, 286–287
class of service (CoS) field in QoS, 280
Class Selector (CS) in Differentiated
Services, **278**
classification in TrustSec, **416**
clear ip bgp command, 224
clear ip nat translation command, 246
clear ip ospf process command, 145
clear text authentication in OSPF, 155
Client Health dashboard, 368, *369*
committed burst (bc) buckets, **285**
committed information rate (CIR)
QoS, 284, 287
traffic shaping, 296–297

conditional debugging
overview, 425
static NAT, **240–241**
congestion avoidance in TCP, **20**
Connect state in BGP, 201
connections in TCP, **19–20**
console ports for device access, 399–400
content-addressable memory (CAM) tables
IGMP snooping, 256
MAC addresses, 10–11
multicast, 254
Control and Provisioning of Wireless Access
Points (CAPWAP) tunnels
fabric overlays, 363
WLCs, **125–127**
control plane node for fabric overlays, 361
control plane policing (CoPP), **412–413**
control planes
SD-Access, 360
VXLAN, **336**
controller layer in SD-Access, 363
converting multicast MAC addresses and IP
addresses, **254–255**
CoPP (control plane policing), **412–413**
core layer in three-tier architecture, **71**
CoS (class of service) field in QoS, **280**
cps (cycles-per-second) in RF, 108
CRC (cyclic redundancy check), 9
cryptographic authentication. *See also*
encryption
IPsec, 321–323
OSPF, 155
CS (Class Selector) in Differentiated
Services, **278**
custom network underlays in SD-Access,
358
cycles-per-second (cps) in RF, 108
cyclic redundancy check (CRC), 9

D

data center networks, **69–70**, *70*
Data Link layer (layer 2)
802.11 standards, **119–123**
design, 74, *74*
routed access topology, **81–82**
switched and routed interfaces,
75–76
switched topologies, 76–81, *77–80*
Ethernet history, **8–10**, *9*
MAC address tables, **10–11**, *12*
MTUs, **12**
QoS marking, 280
roaming, 127
subnet limits, **12**
wireless QoS, **283**
data planes in SD-Access, 359–360
database mapping, 329–331
Datagram Transport Layer Security (DTLS)
tunnels, 370
datagrams in UDP, 19

DBm (decibel-milliwatts), **112**
dBs (decibels), **111–112**
DCF (distributed coordination function), 120
debugging
    conditional, **425**
    EIGRP packets, 184
    IP packets, 240, 425
    IP routing, 318
    NAT
        source address lists, 244
        static, **240–241**
    OSPF, 142
    TACACS+, 405
decapsulation in TCP, **21–22**, *21*
decibel-milliwatts (DBm), **112**
decibels (dBs), **111–112**
default-information originate command, 160
default routes in OSPF, **159–160**
delay in EIGRP, 177, 183
dense mode PIM, 257
design
    DNA Center, **365**, *365*
    enterprise networks. *See* enterprise
        network design
designated routers (DRs)
    elections, **144–146**
    link-state advertisements, 138–139
Desirable mode
    DTP, 34–35
    PAgP, 88–89
destination IP load-balancing mode, 84
devices
    access, **399–402**
    configuration files, 390
    programmability, 372
DevNet, 374
Differentiated Services (DiffServ), **277–280**
Diffie-Hellman (DH) algorithm, 320
diffusing update algorithm (DUAL),
    173–176, *174*
Dijkstra, Edsger, 173
directional antennas, 113
discarding port states in RPVST+, 49
discovery in WLCs, **125–126**
distribute lists in OSPF, **162–163**
distributed coordination function (DCF), 120
distribution layer in three-tier architecture,
    72–73
diversity in MIMO, 123
DIX (Ethernet II) specification, 9
DNA Center
    assurance, **367–368**, *368–369*
    design, **365**, *365*
    Intent API, **372–378**
    policy, 364, *364–365*
    provision, **366–367**, *366–367*
    SD-Access, 358
domain-specific languages (DSLs), 390
down state in OSPF adjacencies, 141
DRs (designated routers)
    elections, **144–146**
    link-state advertisements, 138–139

DSLs (domain-specific languages), 390
DTLS (Datagram Transport Layer Security)
    tunnels, 370
DTP (Dynamic Trunking Protocol), **34–35**
DUAL (diffusing update algorithm),
    173–176, *174*
dynamic NAT
    configuring, **242**
    loopback interfaces, **242–243**
    overview, **241–242**
Dynamic Trunking Protocol (DTP), **34–35**

E

EAP (Extensible Authentication Protocol)
    802.11 standards, 120
    EAP chaining, 416
    EAPoL, 422
EAP Flexible Authentication via Secure
    Tunneling (EAP-FAST), 416
EAP over LANs (EAPoL), 422
East-West traffic, 69, *70*
eBGP (external BGP), 201, 207
ECMP (equal cost multipath)
    data center networks, 69
    EIGRP, **181–182**
ECN (explicit congestion notification), 295
edge virtual bridging (EVB), 309, *310*
EEM (Embedded Event Manager), **386–388**
EF (expedited forwarding) in Differentiated
    Services, 279
effective isotropic radiated power (EIRP), 113
EGP (Exterior Gateway Protocol), 198
egress security in TrustSec, 417
egress tunnel routers (ETRs), 328
EIDs (endpoint IDs) in LISP, 326, *327*, 329
802.11 standards, 115
    layer 2, **119–123**
    physical layer, **115–119**
    WPA2 configuration, **422–424**
EIGRP. *See* Enhanced Interior Gateway
    Routing Protocol (EIGRP)
EIRP (effective isotropic radiated power),
    113
elections
    designated routers, **144–146**
    root bridge, **38–41**, *41*
electromagnetic RF energy, 107
Embedded Event Manager (EEM), **386–388**
Embedded Wireless Controller (WEC), 125
enable secrets, 404
Encapsulated Remote Switched Port
    Analyzer (ERSPAN) analyzer, 364,
    432–434
Encapsulating Security Payload (ESP)
    protocol, **320–321**
encapsulation
    GRE. *See* Generic routing
        encapsulation (GRE) tunnels
    PDUs, 6
    switches, **34–37**

    TCP, **21–22**, *21*
    VXLAN, 359, 361–362
encryption
    802.11 standards, 121
    authentication, 120
    device access, 401
    IPsec, **319–320**
        ESP, **320–321**
        IKE, 320
        transport mode, **321–324**
        tunnel mode, **324–326**
    MAC security, **418**
endpoint IDs (EIDs) in LISP, 326, *327*, 329
enforcement in TrustSec security, **417**
Enhanced Interior Gateway Routing
    Protocol (EIGRP)
    configuring
        ECMP, **181–182**
        metrics, **182–185**
        overview, **178–181**, *178*
        switching types, **185–187**
        unequal cost multipathing,
            187–190
    DUAL, **173–176**, *174*
    exam essentials, 190
    exercises, **191**, *191*
    LSAs, 140
    multi-VRF, **342–345**
    packet types, **172–173**
    review questions, **192–195**
    route redistribution, **211–213**
    summary, 190
    weighted metrics, **176–178**, *176*
enterprise network design, 68
    EtherChannels, **82–91**, *83*
    exam essentials, **98–99**
    first-hop redundancy protocols,
        91–97
    layer 2 design, **74–82**, *77–80*, *82*
    physical network architectures, **68–74**,
        70–73
    review questions, **100–103**
    summary, **97–98**
equal cost multipath (ECMP)
    data center networks, 69
    EIGRP, **181–182**
error control
    802.11 standards, 122
    TCP, 20
error-enabled interfaces, **57–58**
ERSPAN (Encapsulated Remote Switched
    Port Analyzer) analyzer, 364,
    432–434
erspan tos tos-value command, 434
ESP (Encapsulating Security Payload)
    protocol, **320–321**
Established state in BGP, 202
EtherChannels
    LACP, **90–91**
    load-balancing methods, **83–84**
    overview, **82–83**, *83*
    PAgP, **88–90**
    static, **84–88**

Ethernet
history, 8–10, *9*
and multicast, 264–265
Ethernet II (DIX) specification, 9
Ethernet VPN (EVPN), 336
ETRs (egress tunnel routers), 328
EVB (edge virtual bridging), 309, *310*
event manager run routingsummary
command, 388
EVPN (Ethernet VPN), 336
excess burst (be) buckets, 285–286
exchange state in OSPF adjacencies, 142
eXclusive OR (XOR) methods load-
balancing mode, 84
exec-timeout command, 401
expedited forwarding (EF) in Differentiated
Services, 279
explicit congestion notification (ECN), 295
exstart state in OSPF adjacencies, 141
extended ACLs, 407–409, *409*
Extensible Authentication Protocol (EAP)
802.11 standards, 120
EAP chaining, 416
EAPoL, 422
Extensible Markup Language (XML)
format, 383–384
extensions in spanning tree protocols,
55–58
Exterior Gateway Protocol (EGP), 198
external BGP (eBGP), 201, 207
external edge virtual bridging, 309, *310*

F

fabrics
description, 355–356
overlays
fabric border node, 362
fabric edge node, 361–362
SD-Access, 359–363
fair queuing, 291
FCS (frame check sequence)
802.11 standards, **122**
Ethernet, 9
feasibility conditions in EIGRP, 175
feasible distance (FD) in EIGRP, 174
feasible successors in EIGRP, 174–175
FHRP. *See* first-hop redundancy protocols
(FHRP)
FIB (Forwarding Information Base)
EIGRP, 181–182, 185
subnets, 15
VSS, 81
filtering routes
BGP, 222–225
OSPF, 162
Firepower Management Center, 415–416
Firepower Threat Defense, 415
firewalls, NGFW, 415–416
first-hop redundancy protocols (FHRP)
GLBP, 95–97

HSRP, 92–94
overview, 91–92
VRRP, 94–95
first-in, first-out (FIFO) buffer queuing,
276
5 GHz band, 118
Flexible NetFlow, 431–432
flow control
802.11 standards, **122**
Flexible NetFlow, 431–432
TCP, 20
FM (frequency modulation), **109**
foreign controllers, 127
forwarding
vs. routing, 18
RSTP ports, 49
in subnets, 14–16, *15*
TrustSec, 416–417
VXLAN, 335
Forwarding Information Base (FIB)
EIGRP, 181–182, 185
subnets, 15
VSS, 81
forwarding port states in RPVST+, 49
fragmentation in Network layer, 17–18
frame check sequence (FCS)
802.11 standards, **122**
Ethernet, 9
free space path loss, 113–114
frequency
802.11 standards, 115–119
RF, **107–109**, *107*
frequency modulation (FM), **109**
frequency-shift keying (FSK), 109
full-duplex communication, 8
full state in OSPF adjacencies, 142

G

Gateway Load Balancing Protocol (GLBP),
95–97
Generic routing encapsulation (GRE)
tunnels
IPsec configuration, 321–324
IPv4 and IPv6 over IPv4, 312–315,
312–313
IPv4 using OSPFv2, 316
overview, 312
recursive routing, 318–319
GLBP (Gateway Load Balancing Protocol),
95–97
global IP addresses
description, 235, *235*
dynamic NAT pools, 243
PAT, 247–249
GRE. *See* Generic routing encapsulation
(GRE) tunnels
group numbers in VRRP, 94
Group Policy ID in VXLAN, 360
guest tunneling, 127

H

half-duplex communication, 8
hashing algorithms, 321–322
Hello packets in EIGRP, **173**
Hello timer in OSPF, 141
Hertz (Hz) in RF, 108
host-dependent load-balancing methods in
GLBP, 96
Hot Standby Router Protocol (HSRP),
92–94
HTTP (Hypertext Transfer Protocol), 4
HTTP response codes in Intent API,
378–379
HTTPS (Hypertext Transfer Protocol
Secure), 4
hypervisors, 305–306
Hz (Hertz) in RF, 108

I

IaC (infrastructure-as-code) approach,
388–389
IANA (Internet Assigned Numbers
Authority), 199
iBGP (internal BGP), 201, 207
Identity Services Engine (ISE), **363**
Idle state in BGP, 201
IGMP (Internet Group Management
Protocol), 256, 262
IGPs (interior gateway protocols), 199,
206–207
IKE (Internet Key Exchange) protocol, **320**
indirectly connected switches in root port
calculations, 44–46
infrastructure-as-code (IaC) approach,
388–389
infrastructure security, 398
AAA
RADIUS, 406–407
TACACS+, 402–406
access control lists, 407–412, *409*
control plane policing, 412–413
device access, 399–402
ingress security in TrustSec, 416
Ingress Tunnel Router - Egress Tunnel
Router (ITR-ETR), 361
ingress tunnel routers (ITRs), 328
init state in OSPF adjacencies, 141
inside IP addresses, 234–236, *235*
Integrity check value field in ESP headers,
320
Intent API
authentication, 374–378
HTTP response codes, 378–379
overview, 372
Python programming language,
372–374
inter-area summarization in OSPF, **161**
intercontroller roams, 127

interface authentication
configuring, 155–156
OSPF, 154
interior gateway protocols (IGPs), 199, 206–207
internal BGP (iBGP), 201, 207
internal edge virtual bridging, 309
Internal Spanning Tree (IST), 51, 53–54
International Organization for Standardization (ISO), 2
Internet Assigned Numbers Authority (IANA), 199
Internet Group Management Protocol (IGMP), 256, 262
Internet Key Exchange (IKE) protocol, 320
Internet Protocol (IP), 5, *5*
Internet Security Association Key Management Protocol (ISAKMP), 320
internetwork control blocks in multicast, 253
intracontroller roams, 127
Intrusion Prevention System (IPS), 415
ip access-group notac command, 409
ip access-list extended command, 408, 411
ip address command, 75
IP addresses
access control lists, 407–412, *409*
ARP, 16
fabric overlays, 361–362
HSRP, 92–93
layer 2 design, 75
MAC address conversions, 254–255
multicast. *See* multicast
NAT. *See* network address translation (NAT)
reachability tests, 214–215
types, 234–236, *235*
VRRP, 94
ip flow command, 430–432
ip flow-export command, 430
ip flow-top-talkers command, 431
ip igmp join-group command, 264
IP (Internet Protocol), 5, *5*
IP load-balancing mode in EtherChannels, 84
IP mobility
fabric edge node, 361–362
LISP, 327–328, *327*
SD-Access, 357
simulating, 332–334
IP multicast packets, 253
ip multicast-routing command, 259
ip nat inside command, 239, 244, 247
ip nat outside command, 239, 250–251
ip nat pool command, 243
ip ospf authentication-key command, 156
ip ospf authentication message-digest command, 155
ip ospf message-digest-key interface command, 156
ip ospf message-digest-key md5 oursecret command, 157
ip ospf network command, 149
ip pim rp-address command, 338

ip pim sparse-dense-mode command, 259
ip pim sparse-mode command, 337
ip prefix-list command, 163, 222
ip router ospf underlay area command, 337
IP routing tables for multicast, 260–261
IP Security (IPsec)
configuring
transport mode, **321–324**
tunnel mode, **324–326**
EPS, 320–321
IKE, 320
overview, **319–320**
transport mode, 320–321
IP Service Level Agreement (IP SLA), 434–436
ip ssh source-interface command, 410
ip ssh version command, 401
ip vrf command, 341
IPS (Intrusion Prevention System), 415
IPv4
GRE tunnels, 316
mapping fabric overlays, 361–362
IPv4 and IPv6 over IPv4 in GRE tunnels, 312–315, *312–313*
ipv4 etr map-server command, 330–331
ipv4 itr command, 330–331
ipv4 map-resolver command, 329
ipv4 map-server command, 329
ipv6 address command, 314–315
IPv6 for GRE tunnels, 316–317
ipv6 unicast-routing command, 314
ISAKMP (Internet Security Association Key Management Protocol), 320
ISE (Identity Services Engine), 363
ISO (International Organization for Standardization), 2
isotropic antennas, 112–113
IST (Internal Spanning Tree), 51, 53–54
ITR-ETR (Ingress Tunnel Router - Egress Tunnel Router), 361
ITRs (ingress tunnel routers), 328

J

JavaScript Object Notation (JSON) format, 374–378
join requests in WLCs, **125**
json.dumps function, 375–376

K

kluges in link-state advertisements, 139

L

LACP (Link Aggregation Control Protocol), **90–91**

LAN multicast, **253–256**
languages for network programmability, 389–390
law of 3s, 111–112
law of 10s, 111
law of zeros, 112
Layer 1 (Physical layer), 7–8
802.11 standards, **115–119**
SD-Access, 357–358
Layer 2. *See* Data Link layer (layer 2)
Layer 3. *See* Network layer (layer 3)
Layer 4 (Transport layer)
overview, **18–19**
TCP, 19–20
leaf-and-spine architecture, 69, *70*
learning port states in RPVST+, 49
LIG (LISP Internet Groper), 331–332
lightweight APs
overview, **124–125**
roaming between, 127
line console command, 400
line vty command, 401
Link Aggregation Control Protocol (LACP), 90–91
link-state advertisements (LSAs)
areas, 137
overview, 136–137
types, 137–140, *140*
viewing, 146–147
link-state database (LSDB), 137
link state IDs for LSAs, 136
link types in RPVST+, 49–50
LISP. *See* location/ID separation protocol (LISP)
LISP Internet Groper (LIG), 331–332
LLC (logical link control), 123
LLQ (low-latency queue), **293–295**
load-balancing methods
EtherChannels, 83–84
GLBP, 96–97
load in EIGRP, **177**
loading state in OSPF adjacencies, 142
loc-reach-algorithm command, 329–330
local authentication for device access, 399–400
local IP addresses, 235, *235*
local network control blocks in multicast, 253
local passwords for device access, 399
local preference in BGP path selection, 206
location/ID separation protocol (LISP)
configuring, 328–332
description, **334**
IP mobility simulation, 332–334
overview, 326–327, *327*
terminology, 328
Location Services feature, **128**
logging buffered debugging command, 428
logging monitor informational command, 428
logging trap informational command, 428
logical link control (LLC), **123**
login local command, 400

logins for device access, 400–402
logs, Syslog, 426–428
loop-free topologies, 78–79, *78–80*
Loop Guard, 58
loopback interfaces in dynamic NAT, 242–243
loopback networks in link-state advertisements, 139
looped topologies, 77, *77–78*
loops
    BGP, 200–201
    spanning tree protocols, 31, *31*
low-latency queue (LLQ), 293–295
LSAs. *See* link-state advertisements (LSAs)

M

mac address-table aging-time command, 11
MAC addresses. *See* Media Access Control (MAC) addresses
MAC authentication bypass (MAB), 416
MAC load-balancing mode in EtherChannels, 84
MAC (Media Access Control) layer, **119–123**
MAC Security (MACsec), 418
MACsec Key Agreement (MKA) protocol, 418
management layer in SD-Access, 364–368, *364–369*
map resolver/map server (MR/MS), 326–329, *327*
maps
    QoS, 280–281
    route, 222–225
    VLAN access, 411–412
match access-group command, 412
match ip address prefix-list command, 223
match protocol icmp command, 289
maximum-paths command, 182
maximum transmission units (MTUs), 12
MD5 authentication, 92
MECs (multichassis EtherChannels), 81
MED (multi-exit discriminator), 206
Media Access Control (MAC) addresses, 9
    address tables, 10–11, *12*
    ARP, 16
    fabric overlays, 361–362
    GLBP, 96
    HSRP, 92
    layer 2 design, 75
    learning in VXLAN, 335
    MAB, 416
    mapping in fabric overlays, 362
    multicast, 254–255, 265
    root bridge elections, 38, 40–41
    VRRP, 94
Media Access Control (MAC) layer, **119–123**
member ports in EtherChannels, 84
Membership Report in IGMP, *256–257*

message-digest authentication in OSPF, 155
metrics in EIGRP, 176–178, *176*, 182–185
MIMO (multiple-input and multiple-output), 123
MKA (MACsec Key Agreement) protocol, 418
monitor session command, 433–434
monitoring
    conditional debugs, 425
    exam essentials, 437
    exercises, 438
    Flexible NetFlow, 431–432
    IP SLA, 434–436
    NetFlow, 429–431
    NTP, 428–429
    review questions, 439–442
    SD-Access, 357
    SNMP, 425–426
    SPAN, 432–434
    summary, 436–437
    Syslog, 426–428
MR/MS (map resolver/map server), 326–329, *327*
MST. *See* Multiple Spanning Tree (MST)
mtrace command, 262–263
MTUs (maximum transmission units), 12
multi-exit discriminator (MED), 206
multi-VRF EIGRP, 342–345
multicast
    and Ethernet, 264–265
    exam essentials, 267
    exercises, 268–269
    IP, 253
    LAN, 253–256
    overview, 252
    receiver configuration, 262–264
    review questions, 270–273
    routing, 257–262
    summary, 265–267
    VXLAN, 336, *336*
multichassis EtherChannels (MECs), 81
multiple-input and multiple-output (MIMO), 123
Multiple Spanning Tree (MST)
    description, 33–34
    internal spanning tree, 53–54
    native VLAN, 54–55
    overview, **51–52**
    root bridges and port priority, 52–53, *52*
    topology change detection, 55
multiplexing in TCP, 21

N

NAT. *See* network address translation (NAT)
NAT traversal (NAT-T), 371
native VLAN, 54–55
NCP (Network Controller Platform), 363
neighbors

    BGP, 200–203, *201*, 218–219
    EIGRP, 173–176, 180
    OSPF
        adjacencies, 143–146
        operations, **141–142**
    PIM, 258–259
    reverse routing, 318–319
    UDLD, 58
NetFlow, 429–431
network address translation (NAT)
    address types, 234–236, *235*
    dynamic, 241–246
    exam essentials, 267
    exercises, 268–269
    overload, 247–249
    overview, 234
    removing configurations, 251–252
    review questions, 270–273
    static, 236–241, *237–239*, 250–251
    summary, 265–267
network assurance in SD-Access, 357
network command, 179, 208
Network Configuration (NETCONF) protocol, 363, 383–384
Network Controller Platform (NCP), 363
network device configuration for SD-Access, 356–357
network function virtualization (NFV), 308–309
Network layer (layer 3), 13–14, *13*
    ARP, 16–17
    fragmentation, 17–18
    roaming, 127
    routing vs. forwarding, 18
    subnets, 14–16, *15*
    wireless QoS, 281–282, *282*
Network LSAs
    overview, 138–139
    viewing, 148–149
network programmability
    configuration management platforms, 388–391
    Embedded Event Manager, 386–388
    exam essentials, 391–392
    exercises, 392
    Intent API, 372–378
    NETCONF, 383–384
    overview, 372
    RESTCONF, 385–386
    review questions, 393–396
    summary, 391
    vManage REST API, 379–383
    YANG, 384–385
network segmentation and access control, 357
Network Time Protocol (NTP), **428–429**
network underlay layer in SD-Access, 358–359
network virtual edge (NVE) interface, 338
network virtualization
    EVB, 309, *310*
    exam essentials, 345–346
    exercises, **346**

GRE tunnels, 312–319, *312–313*
IPsec, 319–326
LISP, 326–334
network function virtualization,
    308–309
overlays, 311
overview, 304
review questions, 347–351
SR-IOV, 309
summary, 345
virtual machines and server
    virtualization, 305–307,
    306–307
VRF, 340–345, *341*
VXLAN, 334–340, *336*
networking fundamentals. *See* Open
    Systems Interconnection (OSI)
    reference model
Next-Generation Firewall (NGFW),
    415–416
next hops in BGP, 204, 207
NFV (network function virtualization),
    308–309
no exec command, 399
no ip cef command, 187
no ip route-cache command, 187
no vlan filter command, 412
noise and noise flow in RF, 115
non-stop forwarding (NSF), 81
normal mode in UDLD, 58
North-South traffic, 69
northbound APIs, 372
NSF (non-stop forwarding), 81
ntp master command, 429
NTP (Network Time Protocol), 428–429
ntp server command, 429
null authentication in OSPF, 155
NVE (network virtual edge) interface, 338

O

oldest routes in BGP path selection, 207
omnidirectional antennas, 113
OMP (Overlay Management Protocol), 370
Open Shortest Path First (OSPF), 136
    areas, 137
    configuring
        Area 0 on broadcast networks,
            142–143
        Area 23 on point-to-point
            networks, 149–152
        authentication, 154–157
        designated router election,
            144–146
        LSAs, 146–147
        neighbor adjacencies, 143–144
        Network LSAs, 148–149
        Router LSAs, 147–148
        Summary LSAs, 152–154
    exam essentials, 164
    exercises, 164–165, *165*

LSAs, 136–140, *140*
neighbor operations, 141–142
review questions, 166–169
route redistribution, 210–211
summary, 163–164
open systems in 802.11 standards, 120
Open Systems Interconnection (OSI)
    reference model
    Data Link layer, 8–12, *9*, *12*
    exam essentials, 22–23
    intention, 4–6, *5–6*
    layers overview, 2–3
    lower layers overview, 6–7
    Network layer, 13–18
    Physical layer, 7–8
    review questions, 24–27
    Transport layer, 18–22
    upper layers, 4
OpenConfirm state in BGP, 202
OpenSent state in BGP, 202
Origin type in BGP path selection, 206
OSPF. *See* Open Shortest Path First (OSPF)
OSPFv2 for GRE tunnels, 316
OSPFv3 for GRE tunnels, 316–317
outside IP addresses, 234–236, *235*
outside static NAT, 250–251
Overall Health dashboard, 367, *368*
Overlay Management Protocol (OMP), 370
overlays
    fabrics
        fabric border node, **362**
        fabric edge node, 361–362
        SD-Access, 359–363
    network, 311
    VXLAN, 338–339

P

P2P edge links in RPVST+, 50
P2P (Point-to-Point) links in RPVST+, 50
packet types in EIGRP, 172–173
PAgP (Port Aggregation Control Protocol),
    88–90
panning-tree command, 57
parabolic dish antennas, 113
passive interfaces
    EIGRP, 179
    OSPF, 158–159
Passive mode in LACP, 90
passwords for device access, 399
PAT (port address translation), 247–249
path lengths for AS numbers, 199–200, *200*
path selection in BGP, 205–210
PDUs (protocol data units), 5–6, *6*
peak information rate (PIR), 287
PEAP (protected EAP), 422–424, *423*
peering sessions in BGP, 201–202
per-destination sharing option in EIGRP,
    181–182
per-hop behavior (PHB) groups, 277–278
Per-VLAN Spanning Tree (PVST), 53

Per-VLAN Spanning Tree+ (PVST+), 33
permit icmp command, 411
phase-shift keying (PSK), 109
PHB (per-hop behavior) groups, 277–278
Physical layer (layer 1), 7–8
    802.11 standards, 115–119
    SD-Access, 357–358
physical loops in STP, 31, *31*
physical network architectures
    campus networks, 69
    data center networks, 69–70, *70*
    overview, 68
    three-tier architecture, 70–72, *71–72*
    two-tier collapsed core, 73–74, *73*
PIM. *See* Protocol-Independent Multicast
    (PIM)
pip3 install command, 373
PIR (peak information rate), 287
point-to-point networks, **139**
Point-to-Point (P2P) links in RPVST+, 50
policing in QoS, 284–287
policy, DNA Center, 364, *364–365*
policy maps
    CoPP, 413
    QoS, 280–281
        CBWFQ, 289–291
        ingress traffic, 286
        LLQ, 293
        traffic shaping, 296
policy planes in SD-Access, 360
pooled NAT, 241
port address translation (PAT), 247–249
Port Aggregation Control Protocol (PAgP),
    88–90
port channels in EtherChannels, 83–84
port priority in MST, 52–53, *52*
ports
    RPVST+, 49
    spanning tree protocols, 31–33, *32*
power law distribution, 111
power levels
    antenna types, 112–113
    decibels, 111–112
    EIRP, 113
    free space path loss and wavelength,
        113–114
    overview, 110–111, *111*
    RSSI, 114–115
    SNR, 115
pre-key authentication, 120
prefix lists in route filtering, 222–225
preshared keys, 424, *424*
priority
    LLQ, 293–294
    MST bridges, 52–53, *52*
    root bridge elections, 38–39
    root ports, 47–48, *48*
priority command, 293
privilege level command, 404
process switching in EIGRP, 187
profiles for wireless QoS, 281–282, *282*
programmability, network. *See* network
    programmability

protected EAP (PEAP), 422–424, *423*
protocol data units (PDUs), 5–6, *6*
Protocol-Independent Multicast (PIM)
 configuring
  IP routing table viewing, 260–261
  overview, 258–259, *258*
  reverse path forwarding checks,
   261–262
  sources, 260
 overview, 257–258
Provision workflow in DNA Center, 366–
 367, *366–367*
PSK (phase-shift keying), 109
Puppet DSL, 390
PVST (Per-VLAN Spanning Tree), 53
PVST+ (Per-VLAN Spanning Tree+), 33
Python programming language, 372–374

Q

quadrature amplitude modulation (QAM),
 110
quadrature PSK (QPSK), 109
Quality of Service (QoS)
 classification and marking
  class maps and policy maps,
   280–281
  Differentiated Services, 277–280
  Layer 2 marking, 280
  wireless, 281–283, *282*
 exam essentials, 297–298
 exercises, 298
 overview, 276–277
 policing, 284–287
 queuing, 276
  CBWFQ, 288–293
  ECN, 295
  LLQ, 293–295
  overview, 288
 review questions, 299–302
 shaping, 295–297
 summary, 297
queries in EIGRP, 175–176

R

radio frequency (RF) fundamentals
 carrier frequency, 109–110
 frequency and amplitude, 107–109, *107*
 overview, 106–107
 power levels, 110–115, *111*
RADIUS (Remote Authentication Dial-In
 User Service), 402
 configuring, 420–421, *421*
 overview, 406–407
random-detect ecn policy map command,
 295

Rapid Per-VLAN Spanning Tree (RPVST+)
 link types, 49–50
 port roles, 49
 port states, 49
 root bridge elections, 38–41, *41*
 root port calculations, 41–49, *42*
reachability tests, 214–215
received signal strength indicator (RSSI),
 114–115
receiver configuration for multicast,
 262–264
recursive routing, 318–319
redistribute connected command, 208
redistribution, route
 between BGP and EIGRP, 211–213
 between BGP and OSPF, 210–211
 origin types, 250
 recursive routing, 318
 troubleshooting, 216–217
reliability in EIGRP, 178
Reliable Transport Protocol (RTP), 173
Remote Authentication Dial-In User Service
 (RADIUS), 402
 configuring, 420–421, *421*
 overview, 406–407
Remote SPAN (RSPAN), 432–433
rendezvous points (RPs)
 PIM, 258
 VXLAN, 338
replies in EIGRP, 175–176
reported distance in EIGRP, 175
representational state transfer (REST)
 APIs, 372
reputation-based URL filtering, 415
request-to-send/clear-to-send (RTS/CTS),
 122–123
resets for TCP connections, 20
REST (representational state transfer)
 APIs, 372
RESTCONF, 385–386
reverse path forwarding (RPF) checks,
 261–262
RF. *See* radio frequency (RF) fundamentals
RIDs (router IDs)
 BGP path selection, 207–210
 LSAs, 136
RLOC (routing locator), 328, 331
roaming
 between autonomous APs, 126–127
 between lightweight APs, 127
 overview, 126
root bridge elections in RPVST+, 38–41,
 41
root bridges in MST, 52–53, *52*
Root Guard, 55–57
root port calculations, 41–44, *42*
 blocked ports, 48–49
 cost modification, 46–47
 indirectly connected switches, 44–46
 priority modification, 47–48, *48*
round-robin load-balancing methods,
 96–97
route aggregation, 220–222

route filtering
 BGP, 222–225
 OSPF, 162
route maps, 222–225
route redistribution
 between BGP and EIGRP, 211–213
 between BGP and OSPF, 210–211
 origin types, 250
 recursive routing, 318
 troubleshooting, 216–217
routed access topology, 81–82
routed interfaces in layer 2 design, 75–76
router IDs (RIDs)
 BGP path selection, 207–210
 LSAs, 136
Router LSAs
 overview, 138
 viewing, 147–148
routers
 subnet forwarding, 14–16, *15*
 vEdge, 371
routing
 vs. forwarding, 18
 multicast, 257–262
 recursive, 318–319
routing locator (RLOC), 328, 331
routingsummary command, 388
RPF (reverse path forwarding) checks,
 261–262
RPs (rendezvous points)
 PIM, 258
 VXLAN, 338
RPVST+. *See* Rapid Per-VLAN Spanning
 Tree (RPVST+)
RSA encryption for device access, 401
RSPAN (Remote SPAN), 432–433
RSSI (received signal strength indicator),
 114–115
RST flag for TCP connections, 20
RTP (Reliable Transport Protocol), 173
RTS/CTS (request-to-send/clear-to-send),
 122–123
Ruby language, 389–390

S

sandbox environments, 374
SAP (Security Association Protocol), 418
scalable group tags (SGTs)
 DNA Center, 364
 SD-Access, 360–361
 TrustSec, 416–417
scalable groups in DNA Center, 364, *364*
SD-Access. *See* Software-Defined Access
 (SD-Access)
SD-WAN. *See* Software-Defined WAN
 (SD-WAN)
secondary root bridges, 41
secure hash algorithm-hash-based message
 authentication code (SHA-HMAC),
 322

Secure Network Server (SNS), 358
Secure Shell (SSH) for device access, 401–402
security
    authentication. *See* authentication
    encryption. *See* encryption
    exam essentials, **437**
    exercises, **438**
    infrastructure. *See* infrastructure
      security
    IPsec, **319–326**
    overview, **398**
    products, **414–418**
    review questions, **439–442**
    summary, **436–437**
    wireless, **418–424**, *419–424*
Security Association Protocol (SAP), 418
Security Group Exchange Protocol (SXP), 417
Security parameters index field in ESP headers, 320
security tags for SD-Access, 361
segments in TCP, 19
Sequence number field in ESP headers, 320
server-based authentication for device access, 399
server virtualization, **305–307**
service level agreements, **434–436**
service-policy input command, 281, 290, 413
service-policy output command, 292, 296
service set identifiers (SSIDs)
    associations, **120–121**
    WLC profiles, 281–283
session states in BGP, **201–202**
severity levels in Syslog, **426–427**
SGTs (scalable group tags)
    DNA Center, 364
    SD-Access, 360–361
    TrustSec, **416–417**
SHA-HMAC (secure hash algorithm-hash-based message authentication code), 322
shaping, traffic, **295–297**
shared-key authentication, 120
shared links in RPVST+, 50
Shared Spanning Tree Protocol (SSTP), 33
shortest AS path in BGP path selection, 206
shortest-path trees (SPTs), 263–264
show access-list command, 408
show adjacency detail command, 186
show arp command, 339
show arp dynamic command, 16–17
show crypto ipsec sa command, 326
show event manager history events command, 387
show int tunnel command, 319
show interfaces command, 36
show interfaces gigabitEthernet command, 35, 75, 177
show ip bgp command, 205, 208–209, 212
show ip bgp summary command, 203
show ip cache flow command, 430
show ip cef command, 186, 221

show ip cef adjacency command, 340
show ip cef lisp eid command, 332–333
show ip cef vrf command, 344
show ip eigrp neighbors command, 180
show ip eigrp topology command, 180, 185, 187, 216
show ip lisp database command, 330–331
show ip mroute command, 260–261, 263–264, 339
show ip nat statistics command, 249
show ip nat translation command, 239–240, 244–246, 248–249, 251
show ip ospf command, 157
show ip ospf database command, 146, 161, 210
show ip ospf database external command, 160, 163
show ip ospf database network command, 148
show ip ospf database router command, 147, 158
show ip ospf database summary command, 152–154, 162
show ip ospf interface command, 145, 317
show ip ospf neighbor command, 143, 146, 150
show ip protocols command, 179
show ip route command, 159, 204–205
show ip route bgp command, 213, 215
show ip route connected command, 207
show ip route eigrp command, 181
show ip route ospf command, 153, 160–162, 316
show ip route vrf command, 342–343
show ipv6 ospf neighbor command, 317
show ipv6 route command, 315
show logging command, 428
show mac address-table aging-time command, 11
show mac address-table dynamic command, 10
show ntp associations command, 428–429
show ntp status command, 429
show nve vni command, 338
show policy-map command, 290, 292–293, 296
show policy-map control-plane command, 413
show policy-map interface command, 287
show spanning-tree inconsistentports command, 57
show spanning-tree interface gigabitEthernet command, 43–45
show spanning-tree vlan command, 40, 43
show track command, 435
SIA (stuck-in-active) routes in EIGRP, 175, 180
signal degradation, **118–119**
signal-to-noise ratio (SNR), **115**
Simple Network Management Protocol (SNMP), **425–426**
single-rate, three-color policing in QoS, **285–287**

single-rate, two-color policing in QoS, **284–285**
single-root I/O virtualization (SR-IOV), 309, 311
SNMP (Simple Network Management Protocol), **425–426**
snooping in IGMP, 256
SNR (signal-to-noise ratio), 115
SNS (Secure Network Server), 358
Software-Defined Access (SD-Access)
    layers
        controller, 363
        fabric overlays, 359–363
        management, 364–368, *364–369*
        network underlay, 358–359
        overview, 357
        physical, 357–358
    overview, 356–357
software-defined networking (SDN)
    exam essentials, **391–392**
    exercises, 392
    overview, 355–356
    review questions, 393–396
    SD-Access. *See* Software-Defined Access (SD-Access)
    summary, 391
Software-Defined WAN (SD-WAN)
    overview, **369**
    vBond orchestrator, **371**
    vEdge routers, **371**
    vManage Network Management System, 370, *370*
    vSmart controller, **370–371**
source filtering in IGMP, 256
source IP load-balancing mode, 84
source NAT access lists, 243
southbound APIs, 372
SPAN (Switched Port Analyzer), **432–434**
spanning-tree bpduguard enable command, 57
spanning-tree guard loop command, 58
spanning-tree guard root command, 55
spanning-tree link-type point-to-point command, 50
spanning-tree mode rapid-pvst command, 38
spanning-tree portfast edge bpdufilter default command, 57
spanning-tree portfast edge bpduguard default command, 57
spanning-tree portfast edge interface command, 50
spanning-tree portfast edge trunk interface command., 50
spanning tree protocols
    exam essentials, **59**
    exercises, **60–61**, *60*
    extensions, 55–58
    MST, **51–55**, *52*
    need for, **31–32**, *31–32*
    overview, **30**
    port priority, 47, 54
    review questions, **62–66**

RPVST+. *See* Rapid Per-VLAN
    Spanning Tree (RPVST+)
summary, 58–59
VLANs and trunking, 32–34, *33*
    active and allowed VLANs, 35–36
    dynamic trunking, 34–35
    unconditional trunking, 35–36
sparse mode in PIM, 257
sparse-dense mode in PIM, 259
spatial multiplexing in MIMO, 123
speed command in EIGRP, 183
split-MAC architecture, 124
splitting process in TCP, 22
spread spectrum channels, 116
SPTs (shortest-path trees), 263–264
SR-IOV (single-root I/O virtualization),
    309, 311
SSH (Secure Shell) for device access,
    401–402
SSIDs (service set identifiers)
    associations, 120–121
    WLC profiles, 281–283
SSTP (Shared Spanning Tree Protocol), 33
standard ACLs, 407, 410–411
stateful switchover, 81
static EtherChannels, 84–88
static NAT
    conditional debugging, 240–241
    configuring, 238–240, *238–239*
    outside, 250–251
    overview, 236–238, *237*
stub networks
    LSAs, 139
    OSPF, 151
stuck-in-active (SIA) routes in EIGRP, 175, 180
subnets
    BGP, 204–205, 215–217
    Data Link layer limits, **12**
    forwarding in, **14–16**, *15*
    HSRP, 92
    layer 3, **13**
    NAT, 254, 256–258
    OSPF, 142–144, 151–154, 158–159
Summary LSAs
    overview, 139–140, *140*
    viewing, **152–154**
summary routes, advertising, 220–222
SVI (switched virtual interface)
    fabric overlays, 361
    layer 2 design, 75
switched interfaces in layer 2 design, 75–76
Switched Port Analyzer (SPAN), **432–434**
switched topologies, 76–77
    loop-free, 78–79, *78–80*
    looped, 77, *77–78*
    VSS, 80–81, *80*
switched virtual interface (SVI)
    fabric overlays, 361
    layer 2 design, 75
switches
    Data Link layer, 9–11, *12*
    root port calculations, 44–46
    virtual, 306–307, *306–307*

switching types in EIGRP, 185–187
switchport access vlan interface command,
    34
switchport mode dynamic interface
    command, 34
switchport mode virtual-ethernet-bridge
    command, 309
switchport trunk allowed command,
    38
switchports
    dynamic trunking, 34
    EtherChannels, 85
    EVB, 309
    layer 2 design, **75–76**
    unconditional trunking, 35–36
    VLANs, 37–38
    VXLAN, 339
SXP (Security Group Exchange Protocol),
    417
Syslog, **426–428**

T

TACACS+ (Terminal Access Controller
    Access Control System Plus)
    accounting, **406**
    authentication, 402–404
    authorization, 404–406
tags
    DNA Center, 364
    SD-Access, 360–361
    TrustSec, **416–417**
tail drop
    buffers, 276
    CBWFQ, **289**
Tcl (Tool Command Language) scripts for
    IP reachability tests, 214–215
TCP. *See* Transmission Control Protocol
    (TCP)
TCP global synchronization in CBWFQ,
    289
TCP starvation/UDP dominance in
    CBWFQ, 289
temporal key integrity protocol (TKIP),
    121
Terminal Access Controller Access Control
    System Plus (TACACS+)
    accounting, **406**
    authentication, 402–404
    authorization, 404–406
terminal lines for device access, **399**
termination for TCP connections, 20
testing IP reachability, 214–215
ThreatGrid, **414–415**
three-tier architecture, 70
    access-distribution blocks, 71–72, *72*
    access layer, **73**
    core layer, **71**
    distribution layer, 72–73
throughput for channels, 116
timers in EIGRP, 175

TKIP (temporal key integrity protocol),
    121
TLS (Transport Layer Security) in OSI
    model, 4
token buckets in QoS, **284–286**
Tool Command Language (Tcl) scripts for
    IP reachability tests, **214–215**
Top Talkers feature, **431**
topology change detection in MST, 55
traceroute command
    EIGRP, 182
    PAT, 248–249
    Summary LSAs, 153–154
traffic shaping, **295–297**
traffic share count setting, 189–190
Transmission Control Protocol (TCP)
    connections, **19–20**
    encapsulation and decapsulation,
        21–22, *21*
    features, **19**
    OSI model, 5, *5*
transmit networks, **139**
transmitting bridge identifiers in root
    bridge elections, 38–39
transport input none command, 399
transport input ssh command, 401
Transport layer (layer 4)
    overview, **18–19**
    TCP, **19–20**
Transport Layer Security (TLS) in OSI
    model, 4
transport mode in IPsec, **320–324**
traps
    SNMP, 426
    Syslog, 428
troubleshooting
    BGP, 215–218
    IP access lists, 407–409, *409*
    spanning tree protocols, 32, 59
trunking
    dynamic, 34–35
    unconditional, **35–36**
    VLANs, 32–34, *33*
trust boundaries in QoS, 280
TrustSec, 360, **416–417**
tunnel destination command,
    314–315
tunnel mode
    ESP, **321**
    GRE, 314–315
    IPsec, **324–326**
tunnel protection command, 322
Tunnel Router (xTR), 361
tunnels
    GRE, **312–319**, *312–313*
    VPN, 311
2.4 GHz band, **117–118**
two-rate policing in QoS, **287–288**
two-tier collapsed core in physical network
    architectures, 73–74, *73*
two-way state in OSPF adjacencies, 141
Type-1 and Type-2 hypervisors,
    305–306

U

U-topologies, loop-free, **79**, *79–80*
udld aggressive command, *58*
udld enable command, *58*
udld port command, *58*
UDLD (Unidirectional Link Detection)
protocol, *58*
Umbrella service, **414**
unconditional trunking, **35–36**
underlays
SD-Access, **358–359**
VXLAN, **337–338**
unequal cost multipathing in EIGRP,
187–190
unicasts
acknowledgments, *122*
GRE, *314*
IGMP snooping, *256*
MAC address tables, *11*
vs. multicasts, **253–254**, *257*
VTEPs, *335*
WLC discovery, *125*
Unidirectional Link Detection (UDLD)
protocol, *58*
update packets in EIGRP, *173*
usernames, **399–403**

V

vBond orchestrator, **371**
VEB (virtual Ethernet bridge) mode,
309
vEdge routers, **371**
VEPA (Virtual Ethernet Port Aggregator)
mode, *309*
VFs (virtual functions), *309*
virtual Ethernet bridge (VEB) mode, *309*
Virtual Ethernet Port Aggregator (VEPA)
mode, *309*
virtual extensible local area network
(VXLAN), *16*
configuring
overlays, **338–339**
overview, **336**, *336*
routers, **339–340**
underlays, **337–338**
control planes, *336*
data planes, *359*
fabric, *355*
forwarding, *335*
MAC address learning, *335*
overview, **334–335**
policy planes, *360*
VXLAN-GPO format, *360*
virtual functions (VFs), *309*
virtual link networks, *139*
virtual machine monitors (VMMs),
305–306

virtual machines (VMs), **305–307**, *306–307*
virtual network functions (VNFs), **308–309**
virtual NICs (vNICs), *306*
virtual private networks (VPNs), *311*
Virtual Router Redundancy Protocol
(VRRP), **94–95**
virtual routing and forwarding (VRF),
340–345, *341*
virtual switch links (VSLs), *81*
virtual switching system (VSS), **80–81**, *80*
virtual terminal (vty) lines for device access,
399, **404**
virtualization, network. *See* network
virtualization
vlan dot1q tag native command, *54*
VLANs
access maps, **411–412**
active and allowed, **36–38**
native, **54–55**
trunking, **32–34**, *33*
vManage Network Management System,
370, *370*
vManage REST API, **379–383**
VMMs (virtual machine monitors),
305–306
VMs (virtual machines), **305–307**,
306–307
VNFs (virtual network functions),
308–309
vNICs (virtual NICs), *306*
VPNs (virtual private networks), *311*
VRF (virtual routing and forwarding),
340–345, *341*
VRRP (Virtual Router Redundancy
Protocol), **94–95**
VSLs (virtual switch links), *81*
vSmart controller, **370–371**
VSS (virtual switching system), **80–81**, *80*
vSwitches, **306–307**, *306–307*
VTEPs (VXLAN tunnel endpoints), *335*
vty (virtual terminal) lines for device access,
399, **404**
VXLAN. *See* virtual extensible local area
network (VXLAN)
VXLAN-GPO format, *360*
VXLAN tunnel endpoints (VTEPs), *335*

W

wavelength and free space path loss,
113–114
WebAuth authentication
802.11 standards, *120*
configuring, **418–422**, *419–421*
WEC (Embedded Wireless Controller),
125
weight in BGP
modifying, **218–220**
path selection, *206*
weighted load-balancing methods, *96*

weighted metrics in EIGRP, **176–178**, *176*
weighted random early detection (WRED),
289
WEP (wired equivalent privacy), *121*
whip antennas, *113*
Wi-Fi Multimedia (WMM), *283*
wi-fi protected access (WPA), *121*
wired equivalent privacy (WEP), *121*
wireless LAN controllers (WLCs),
124–125
discovery, **125–126**
security, **416–417**
selection, **125–126**
wireless QoS, *281*, *283*
wireless LANs (WLANs), **106**
802.11 standards. *See* 802.11
standards
access point modes, **124–126**
exam essentials, *129*
review questions, **130–133**
RF fundamentals. *See* radio frequency
(RF) fundamentals
roaming and location services,
126–128
summary, **128**
wireless QoS, **281–283**, *282*
wireless security, **418–422**, *419–421*
WLAN controller (WLC) node for fabric
overlays, *363*
WLANs. *See* wireless LANs (WLANs)
WLCs. *See* wireless LAN controllers
(WLCs)
WMM (Wi-Fi Multimedia), *283*
WPA enterprise mode, *121*
WPA personal mode, *121*
WPA (wi-fi protected access), *121*
WPA2
configuring, **422–424**, *423*
description, *121*
WPA3, *121*
WRED (weighted random early detection),
289

X

XML (Extensible Markup Language)
format, **383–384**
XOR (eXclusive OR) methods load-
balancing mode, *84*
xTR (Tunnel Router), *361*

Y

Yagi antennas, *113*
YAML (YAML Ain't Markup Language),
389
Yet Another Next Generation (YANG) data
modeling language, *363*, **384–385**

Online Test Bank

Register to gain one year of FREE access to the online interactive test bank to help you study for your CCNP Enterprise certification exam—included with your purchase of this book! All of the chapter review questions and the practice tests in this book are included in the online test bank so you can practice in a timed and graded setting.

Register and Access the Online Test Bank

To register your book and get access to the online test bank, follow these steps:

1. Go to bit.ly/SybexTest (this address is case sensitive)!
2. Select your book from the list.
3. Complete the required registration information, including answering the security verification to prove book ownership. You will be emailed a pin code.
4. Follow the directions in the email or go to www.wiley.com/go/sybextestprep.
5. Find your book on that page and click the "Register or Login" link with it. Then enter the pin code you received and click the "Activate PIN" button.
6. On the Create an Account or Login page, enter your username and password, and click Login or, if you don't have an account already, create a new account.
7. At this point, you should be in the test bank site with your new test bank listed at the top of the page. If you do not see it there, please refresh the page or log out and log back in.